FOUNDATIONAL FACTS, RELATIVE TRUTHS

EUROPEAN FAMILY LAW SERIES

FOUNDATIONAL FACTS, RELATIVE TRUTHS

A comparative law study on children's right to know their genetic origins

RICHARD J. BLAUWHOFF

intersentia

Antwerp – Oxford – Portland

Distribution for the UK:
Hart Publishing Ltd.
16C Worcester Place
Oxford OX1 2JW
UK
Tel: + 44 1865 51 75 30
Fax: + 44 1865 51 07 10

Distribution for the USA and Canada:
International Specialized Book
Services
920 NE 58th Ave Suite 300
Portland, OR 97213
USA
Tel.: +1 800 944 6190 (toll free)
Tel.: +1 503 287 3093
Fax: +1 503 280 8832
Email: info@isbs.com

Distribution for Switzerland and Germany:
Stämpfli Verlag AG
Wölflistrasse 1
CH-3001 Bern
Switzerland
Tel: + 41 (0)31 300 63 18
Fax: + 41 (0)31 300 66 88

Distribution for other countries:
Intersentia Publishers
Groenstraat 31
BE-2640 Mortsel
Belgium
Tel: + 32 3 680 15 50
Fax: + 32 3 658 71 21

This volume is based on the dissertation defended by the author at Utrecht University on 15 May 2009.

Typesetting: G.J. Wiarda Institute for Legal Research, Boothstraat 6, 3512 BW Utrecht.

Richard J. Blauwhoff
Foundational facts, relative truths. A comparative law study on children's right to know their genetic origins

ISBN 978-90-5095-913-1
D/2009/7849/29
NUR 822

ACKNOWLEDGEMENTS

Looking back on the past four years, I can affirm, like so many researchers before me, that the writing of a dissertation can be a formative experience, not just academically but also personally. When I applied for a position as a Ph.D researcher at the Molengraaff Institute for Private Law in December 2004, I was lured by the comparative and human rights aspects of the research proposal because of my background in international and European public law. The subject matter, which the 'right to know one's origins', also had a definite romantic sound to it. At the same time, the research topic still seemed very elusive and unfathomable. As far as I could tell, the research topic had to do with an individual search for one's distant past and introspection. I also knew that once I would set myself such a task I would really want to finish it. This sense of commitment proved important for writing this book. But I questioned how one would be able to discuss such personal issues from a legal perspective.

Thus, back in 2004, I felt some apprehension at first. Indeed, 'at root', I wondered whether I would be able to combine academic distance with a personal interest in the topic. Soon after I started to immerse myself in the research topic, this initial apprehension and discomfort waned. I took an active interest in family law and I discovered that I could develop my own ideas about this research topic.

Four years later, I can still not claim this book to be fully my own. By this I mean that I will remain deeply indebted to a number of persons. First of all, I would like to thank my supervisor Katharina Boele-Woelki who, right from the very beginning, expressed her confidence in my ability to bring this research to a successful end. Your strong ideas about what comparative law should entail, provide but one example of how you manage to keep a broad horizon and an open mind while also insisting upon high standards for comparative law research. Moreover, your ability to combine a firm commitment to your own ambitions with an honest interest in all of your individual Ph.D candidates inspires admiration.

I would further like to thank all of my direct colleagues Bente, Christina, Christine, Ellen, Ian, Merel, Nora, Pia and Vesna for having contributed so much to creating a stimulating and friendly working environment. Among my direct colleagues, I would like to thank Wendy Schrama above all for her numerous invaluable comments and suggestions. Furthermore, a special thanks goes to Machteld Vonk for sharing her insights into parentage law and her legal expertise in the area of donor insemination and surrogacy. I also want to thank Peter Morris for editing my English and Titia Kloos and Willemien Vreekamp for making my manuscript camera-ready with such efficiency.

As I spent a considerable amount of time abroad over the past four years, I would also like to thank professor Frédérique Ferrand of the Université Jean Moulin Lyon III for her comments on French law. In addition, I would like to thank Professor Tobias Helms of the Philipps-Universität Marburg took much time to discuss developments in German law and gave me such a cordial welcome during my stay in Marburg and also commented on my manuscript. In addition, I would like to thank professor Guilherme de Oliveira of the Universidade de Coimbra for his time during my research period in Portugal. In Coimbra, I would also like to thank doctor Rafael Vale e Reis and his wife Carla Barbosa for their valuable comments and Portuguese hospitality. Moreover, I would like to thank doctor Willem Breemhaar, judge at the Leeuwarden Court of Appeal and professor Gerard René de Groot of Maastricht University and professors Jenny Goldschmidt and Jaap Sijmons of Utrecht University for their comments on my manuscript.

I would further like to thank my friends, both here in the Netherlands and abroad, for their enduring friendship which adds colour to my life. Without them this would surely have been a much more solitary enterprise. In particular, I would also like to thank my 'paranymphs' Christoph Jeloschek and Eline Veltkamp for their long-standing loyal friendship and kindness.

Last but very from least, I am fortunate to have found 'true' parents in Martin and Daphne and to have a sister like Fiona. Now closing a long chapter, 'in a sense even before the book unfolds itself', I am glad to be able to cherish fond memories and to be able to rely on strong and solid bonds.

TABLE OF CONTENTS

LIST OF ABBREVIATIONS

AdvermG	Adoptionvermittlungsgesetz (German Mediation in Adoption Act)
Appl. No.	Application Number
AG	Amtsgericht (German local district court)
ART	Artificial reproductive technologies
art./arts.	Article, articles
BDSG	Bundesdatenschutzgesetz (Federal German Data Protection Act)
BGB	Bundesgesetzbuch (German Civil Code)
BGH	Bundesgerichtshof (Federal Appeal Court)
BT-Drucks.	Bundestag Drucksachen (publications of the Federal German Parliament)
BVerfGE	Bundesverfassungsgericht (Federal German Constitutional Court)
CA	Cour d'Appel (French Appeal Court)
Cass.	Cour de Cassation (French Cassation Court)
CDU/CSU	Christlich Demokratische Union (Christian Democratic Union)
CJFA	Centre Juridique Franco-Allemand
CNAOP	Conseil National pour l'Accès aux Origines Personnelles (French National Council for Access to Personal Origins)
DCC	Dutch Civil Code (Burgerlijk Wetboek)
DI	Donor insemination
DIY	Do it yourself
DNA	Desoxyribo Nucleic Acid
EC	European Communities
ed/eds	editor/editors
e.g.	for example
ECHR	European Convention on Human Rights
ECtHR	European Court of Human Rights
EschG	Embryoschutzgesetz (German Embryo Protection Act)
EU	European Union
FamRZ	Zeitschrift für das Gesamte Familienrecht

FIOM	Federatie van Instellingen voor Ongehuwde Moeders (Dutch federation of institutions for unmarried mothers)
FPR	Familie, Partnerschaft und Recht
GG	Grundgesetz (German Basic Law or German Federal Constitution)
HR	Hoge Raad (Dutch Supreme Court)
ICCPR	International Convention on Civil and Political Rights
ICSI	intracytoplasmic sperm injection
i.e.	that is; in other words
IVF	In vitro fertilisation
IRCO	Immigrant and Refugee Community Organisation
LG	Landsgericht (German regional court)
LJN	Landelijk jurisprudentienummer (Dutch national case-law reference number_
LPMA	Lei da Procriação Medicamente Assistida (Portuguese Medically Assisted Conception Act)
NCJM-Bulletin	Nederlands Juristen Comité voor de Mensenrechten-Bulletin
NGO	Non-governmental organisation
NJ	Nederlandse Jurisprudentie
NJB	Nederlands Juristenblad
No	Number
NJW	Neue Juristische Wochenschrift
NVOG	Nederlandse Vereniging voor Obstetrie en Gynaecologie (Dutch association for obstetry and gynecology)
OLG	Oberlandesgericht (German regional court of appeal)
Para.	Paragraph
PCC	Portuguese Civil Code (Código Civil Português)
PS	Partido Socialista (Socialist Party) (Portugal)
PstG	Personenstandsgesetz (German Civil Registration Act)
Rb	Rechtbank (Dutch first instance court)
Rdnr.	Randnummer (margin note number)
RG	Reichsgericht (Court of the German Empire)
RoP	Rules of Procedure
SchKG	Schwangerschaftskonfliktsgesetz (German Pregnancy Conflict Act)
SPD	Sozialdemokratische Partei Deutschlands (Social-Democratic Party of Germany)
Stb.	Staatsblad (Dutch official journal)
StGB	Strafgesetzbuch (German Criminal Code)
TGI	Tribunal de Grande Instance (French Court of First Instance)

UN	United Nations
UNCRC	United Nations Convention on the Rights of the Child
ZPO	Zivilprozessordnung (German Civil Procedural Code)

PART I
UNKNOWN ORIGINS

CHAPTER I
UNKNOWN ORIGINS AND THE BIOLOGICAL TRUTH

1. UNTOLD TRUTHS

1.1. TRUTH, TRUTHFULNESS AND LEGAL EMPOWERMENT

No man can know where he is going unless he knows exactly where he has been and exactly how he arrived at his present place.
Maya Angelou, New York Times, 16 December 1972

And you shall know the truth, and the truth shall make you free.
John 8:32

Most people know who their birthparents are. Most people also desire to make sense of their own past in order to understand their present. This requires some prior knowledge about such basic facts. Those who do not know about these basic facts may therefore have difficulty in making sense of their past. We do not need to be historians to *know* that there are certain historical truths about our own personal lives that may matter to us. We may remember a few prosaic 'truths' about what we did yesterday and we know, or we may recall a few more poetic versions of the truth about a more distant past. As far as major events can go in life, however, we are unable to tap into our own memory when it comes to knowing the circumstances surrounding our own conception and birth.

In making sense of one's own personal past, it is required to have been put in a position to interpret facts. Nonetheless, in modern culture, it is also questioned whether the truth about the historical past is accessible and therefore also whether it lends itself to a reasonably objective interpretation.

As far as our biological origins are concerned, most of us rest satisfied with their beliefs rather than with any objective scientific truth. People know who their 'true parents' are, in one or various meanings of that adjective. In ordinary language, truth is associated with trust and trustworthiness in speech. As children grow up, most children find good reason to assume that their parents are their biological parents. If a father says he is the father, his word will be taken for what it is. It will be believed. In fact, biology may seem to matter little as long as there are sufficient connections in one's personal narrative that allow the person to makes sense of this story. Therefore, as long as the personal narrative appears truthful, which does not necessarily involve having scientifically accurate DNA evidence regarding one's genetic descent, one may, in fact, not feel induced to submit one's own beliefs to a more critical inquiry. True enough, perhaps we may also have an interest in not dispelling certain important myths about the past either. Accordingly, in interpreting our historical past, it would appear that it is truthfulness and trust rather than truth that truly matters.[1] But, of course, for those who 'know', this is a facile assumption. How does one face the truth if one has been deceived or has otherwise found sufficient reason to question one's beliefs, to trust those closest to us?

The desire to establish the 'truth' about one's past is hardly new. In fact, Aristotle already claimed that 'all men by their nature want to know' and this desire for information is what distinguishes humans from animals.[2] Articulated as a legal interest, the wish to identify one's birthparents can to a significant extent, however, be traced back to bio-medical developments that took place in the 1980s. Although in the 1920s it was already possible to rule out genetic connections as a result of the invention of blood testing by the **Austrian** Landsteiner, the development of DNA testing marked a turning point in parentage testing.[3] Until the late 19th Century, however, both in science and culture, the 'truth' about paternity and biological heredity were couched in profound mystery, 'irritating for being both incomprehensible and banal, prodigious and unexceptional, (thereby) making them excellent material for constructions of ideology'.[4]

Notwithstanding the greater certainty in our DNA age, ideological and cultural conceptualisations of blood-ties have remained important. As Western societies and legal systems first became acquainted with DNA testing from the 1980s, a reinterpretation of the legal significance of biological truth has become necessary. In law, apart from offering scope for forensic research in criminal procee-

1 WILLIAMS (2002), p. 257-258.

2 ARISTOTLE, *Metaphysics*.

3 ALBRECHT & SCHULTHEISS (2004), p. 31-37; GESERICK (2002), p. 380-383; ANDERLIK (2003), p. 291-314.

4 ANDRÉOLI (1998), p. 15.

dings, DNA testing has primarily been important for people in establishing verifiable facts about their biological parentage.[5]

1.2. ORIGINS OF A RIGHT TO KNOW ONE'S ORIGINS?

In tracing this recent historical development of a *right* to know one's biological parentage, the individual accounts of adoptees during the 1950s and 60s fulfilled an important role as well.[6] In a way, individual accounts and social science studies exposed the relativity of the 'otherness' of the experience of adoptees. In particular, such accounts and experiences of adopted children also gave rise to the question whether donor-conceived children also had an emotional need or ideological interest in knowing the biological truth. By December 1984, **Sweden** decided to confer on donor-conceived persons a right to know the identity of the donor.[7]

Ever since the mid-80s DNA testing exposed myths about biological fatherhood in courts throughout Western jurisdictions. As a result, regional and international law have been induced to rethink the significance of the genetic link in the establishment of parentage.[8] As a landmark in the articulation of this interest in one's genetic descent, the United Children's Rights Convention in 1989 affirmed that children have a 'right, as far as possible, to know and be cared for by their parents'.[9] This reflected the empowering idea that pervades the Convention that children are legal subjects and should therefore be put in a decisional position on important issues, including the identification of their parents. In Europe, in that same year, **Germany** pioneered when the Federal Constitutional Court recognised the right to know one's origins on the basis of its Basic Law.[10] As shall emerge, this development has in turn influenced constitutional developments in other parts of Europe.[11]

In redefining their legal relationship to the biological truth on the basis of greater equality, DNA has also been regarded as an empowering device by fathers. Accordingly, in the **United States** in the 1990s DNA testing already

---

5 A probability of 99.9% can be achieved. ANDERLIK (2003), p. 291-314; ROTHSTEIN (2005), p. 229.

6 SANTS (1964), p. 133-140; TRISELIOTIS (1973), p. 109-123.

7 *Svensk förtfattningssamling* (SFS), **Swedish** Code of Statutes, SFS 1984:1140.

8 This development shall be dealt with extensively in Chapters II, III and IV.

9 Art. 7-1 UN Children's Rights Convention.

10 BVerfGE, 18 January 1988, *FamRZ* 1989, p. 147. See further Chapter IV.

11 See in particular Chapter IV.

created widespread resentment among men who wondered whether the children they were required to support were actually biologically related to them. Since then, from this male perspective, both the media and publicity ads of commercial laboratories have further bolstered the popular belief that the newly found scientific truth about their genetic link will help relieve many of them from a state of financial and emotional victimization.[12] Infidelity is depicted as a rampant problem with the issue of 'paternity fraud' assuming the dimensions of a national 'epidemic.'[13]

What is more, other attempts to make sense of the past have also been based on the advances made in DNA technology. Thus, the African-American Roots Project of the University of Massachusetts seeks to help student and teachers 'participate in a research effort to bridge the four-century old chasm between African-Americans and their ancestral origins in West Africa.'[14] The scientific goal of this project is to match Y chromosome and mitochondria DNA lineages of African-Americans and Caribbean people of African ancestry to those found in West African tribes. Thanks to this DNA technology, it is possible for some African-Americans to trace back their ancestral roots in Africa that were broken through the colonial slave trade.

Even so, bio-medical developments are not seen exclusively in terms of a quick route to legal empowerment within the family. The desire to establish the biological truth at all costs is at once also seen as a morally defective symptom of our own times. In that regard, we may think of the often sensationalist media depictions that capitalize enthusiastically on the entertainment value of stories about pitiful 'duped dads' and programmes in which blood-relations find each other after many years of separation. All too often some of these media stories also foster the belief that achieving a sense of emotional wholeness is a normal expectation for people, who may have never met after birth, to have if only they had access to DNA certainty.[15]

Thus, both the searchers and 'duped dads' are represented accordingly, as the helpless victims of the DNA age. Typically, both may be depicted as having grandiose expectations about the significance that the discovery of the objective truth about their genetic descent will have for them. Caricatured as maladjusted persons, these persons are found to make fantastic claims such as: 'We need the

---

12 Nelkin (2005), p. 11.
13 Nelkin (2005), p. 12.
14 Http://www.uml.edu/roots/Mission.html.
15 Nelkin (2005), p. 12.

roadmap to our genetic blueprint', or as one donor conceived person: 'I was conceived like pigs are, with no rights to know my genetic heritage.'[16]

Small wonder, then, that the charge is also heard that the search for origins is symptomatic of an excessive preoccupation with biological truth and associable with a quest to recapture an authenticity that seems to have been lost in a complex modern world. From a critical viewpoint, both the genetic essentialism and conservatism believed to be implicit in the right to know one's origins are targeted for reinforcing not only cultural stereotypes, but also conveying a reductionist idea about human identity. In Europe, such critical views have been expressed notably by **French** scholars. Labrusse-Riou has suggested, for example, that the recognition of such a constitutional right to information in **Germany** originates in a racist and eugenic concept of identity.[17] In addition, the philosopher Legendre has gone as far as likening the resurgence of interest in biological ties with a 'butcher's concept of humanity'.[18]

All the same, such radically critical appraisals of the worth of genetic information also beg further questions. Putting such 'extremist' viewpoints aside, it is wondered: 'could "the truth" not lie somewhere in the middle?' After all, who may those sceptics – who, indeed, for all we know, may very well be have known and been brought up by their biological parents – be to call into question the genuineness of individual informational needs that some persons may experience in a profound way?

Rather than making one's own assessment of the importance of biological information, in this book the author shall attempt to make some *legal* sense of the current interest in the biological truth without caricaturizing the motives, whether shallow or profound, that searchers may have. It is the author's belief that better protection of the right is required, even if the motives behind individual searches are at least in part culturally constructed. In attempting to arrive at new, better 'legal truths' surrounding the issue, other normative assumptions will also be necessary as long as they can be justified. For now, however, it will

16 NELKIN (2005), p. 12.

17 LABRUSSE-RIOU & GUIDEC (1996), p. 89. '*La jurisprudence allemande ressuscite ainsi, au nom des droits de l'homme, une vision purement biologique des origines qui avait pourtant donné lieu aux pires errements politiques et sociaux quelques années auparavant. La modification du fondement juridique, les lois raciales et eugéniques ayant fait place au droit subjectif de l'individu à son épanouissement, ne modifie pas pour autant les moyens de droit ni peut-être leur veritable signification.*' Also quoted by: HELMS (1999), p. 226.

18 Pierre Legendre, as quoted by LEFAUCHEUR (2004), p. 333.

be sufficient to assume that, with this objective in mind, some *legal truths* will require reinterpretation.

2. DISPARITIES BETWEEN PARENTAL STATUS AND THE BIOLOGICAL TRUTH

The lawyer's truth is not Truth, but consistency or consistent expediency[19]
Henry David Thoreau

At present, the informational need of *adopted* children to find out who their birthparents are is no longer seriously called into question by social scientists and lawyers alike.[20] Organisations that give assistance to adopted children who search are well established in **North America** and parts of **Europe**.[21] Considerable evidence has been gathered in the social sciences over the past decades, too, that adopted children are more likely than other children to experience identity problems.[22] In particular, in inter-country adoption, the physical dissimilarities will indicate the existence of an underlying disparity.

There is only little empirical evidence considering the total number of children born to parents who are not their biological parents, but the evidence that there is suggests appreciable numbers.[23] The scarcity of reliable empirical research can be accounted for by the fact that many persons will be unaware of any such disparity. For those who have not been adopted from abroad, the disparity between their legal and biological parentage will, after all, often not be apparent. Disparities between legal and biological parentage may, however, arise in a wide range of other situations:

- legal attribution of paternity to a man who bears no genetic link to the child;
- assisted donor conception by an egg or sperm donor;
- some forms of surrogate motherhood;
- a mother's decision to give birth anonymously or discreetly.

---

19 THOREAU, *On the Duty of Civil Obedience* (1848).
20 TRISELIOTIS (1973), p. 154-163; BRODZINSKY (1992).
21 See for example; www.adoption.com.
22 SANTS (1964), p. 133-140; TRISELIOTIS (1973); SCHECHTER & BERTOCCI (1990); BONNET (1990); BRODZINSKY (1992); HOKSBERGE & WALENKAMP (1983).
23 HAAS & WALDENMAIER (2004), believe that ten per cent of children have another legal than a biological father , p. 21. In an earlier **British** study, the number of children was even as high as 20%, BAKER & BELLIS (1993), p. 218.

It should be underlined that the aforementioned list of factual situations is not exhaustive. The factual diversity in which the issue may arise is greater still. As such, separation from one's biological parents is also capable of occurring under very diverse factual circumstances at different stages of a person's life. Other factual scenarios could include, for example, a biological parent's disappearance in circumstances of war or a premature death of a parent whose status has not been documented. Because these situations will in reality be quite rare, they will not be discussed *ab extenso* in this book, however.

Other factual situations may nowadays be more common, however: in contemporary patchwork families, a biological parent may disappear from a young child's life subsequent to divorce, for example. This may provoke the question whether the right to know one's origins, as a legal concept, could have implications for such situations. Thus, children of divorced parents may in such a situation, perhaps already at an early age, experience a need to maintain contact with that parent. While establishing regular contact with a parent could very well often be the ulterior aim of some children in identifying a parent, it is suggested that it is already quite substantial that such a child knows the parent's name and will generally be able to attach a face to that person.[24]

3. A LEGAL RIGHT WITH ETHICAL IMPLICATIONS, A MORAL RIGHT WITH LEGAL IMPLICATIONS

Typically, a 'constitutional right' is framed in a very broad statement that guarantees each individual an equal status.[25] Accordingly, the right to information also leaves considerable scope for legislative and judicial interpretation. In fact, it can even be appreciated already on the basis of a black-letter analysis of Article 7-1 UNCRC that the right has *not* been lent an *absolute* character, since the child's right must be ensured only 'as far as possible'.[26]

It follows that scope is offered for both rather extensive and less extensive interpretations of a state's legal obligations towards children in this respect. As will emerge in this book, there are situations in which states interpret the right

[24] WILSON (1997), p. 270-297. Still for adoptees, the disclosure of the legal identity of their parents is often sufficient. There is evidence that one face-to-face encounter is sufficient for many adoptees.

[25] For a contemporary account of the definitional debate on the concept of constitutional or 'fundamental legal rights', see: ZUCCA (2007), p. 27-48.

[26] This provision shall be discussed in much greater detail in Chapter II.

so restrictively that it could seriously be questioned if the 'inner core' of the right is not so undermined that the right is rendered meaningless.[27] Even so, two decades on, at least the *justifications* of the right's constitutional status have become less questioned.[28] In part this may be the outcome of constitutionalisation: once a human rights' norm has become enshrined in legal instruments and case law, it will become more difficult to reverse such a trend.[29]

In spite of this progressively greater constitutional recognition from around 1990, however, manifold legal and ethical questions remain unanswered. These legal issues involve the interpretation of the conceptual and procedural boundaries of the right to know one's origins. For this reason, one of the primary aims of this book is to contribute to a more precise delineation of the right's scope and to devise and define legal principles that could be of guidance in this discussion.

4. JUSTIFICATIONS OF A RIGHT TO KNOW ONE'S ORIGINS

In this section, a discussion shall be undertaken of the moral and legal reasons that have been adduced in justifying a right to know one's origins. In this discussion, insights from various disciplines shall be gathered, with a focus on social science, (legal) philosophy and legal history. This general overview shall serve as a contextualization of the analysis of relevant constitutional law in the following Chapters. It must be underlined, however, that a discussion of the justifications of the elevation of the interest or need to know to the status of a 'right' is not the main aim of this legal study.

As MacCormick holds, there are common features shared by all that we call 'rights'. Normative orders can afford to individuals security in the enjoyment of what are normally goods for individuals; that someone has a right implies (a) that x or freedom or discretion in relation to x is a good, and (b) is true if in one mode or another the individual fulfils the conditions for having some appropriate form of normative security over x or freedom or discretion in relation to x.[30] At the basis of rights ultimately lie interests and not only choices, even though will-

---

27 BESSON (2007), p. 148.
28 See for example, BESSON (2007), p. 138-140; FREEMAN (1996), p. 273-297; WILSON (1997).
29 As far as our discussion goes, see Chapters II, III, IV. Also see BLAUWHOFF (2008).
30 MACCORMICK (1982), p. 337, 346. See also: FREEMAN (1996), p. 275.

based theories of rights may also be relevant for our discussion.[31] Nonetheless, at this point of this introductory chapter, it seems more appropriate to focus on the interests that have been acknowledged as justifications of a right to know one's origins rather than on a notion of autonomy, will or decisional privacy.[32]

In that connection, a general overview of recurrent multidisciplinary aspects is presented that draws on the social science literature discussed in the leading accounts in contemporary legal discourse regarding the subject-matter in this section.[33] In addition, on the basis of the author's own research, contemporary philosophers and social scientists whose writings have a clear connection to the subject-matter shall also be discussed.

4.1. MARRIAGE AND BIOLOGY AS LEGAL DETERMINANTS OF PARENTAGE

For centuries, the existence of a legal relationship between parents and children was determined by marriage. Most children were born within marriage and the mother's husband was also presumed to be the biological father. If a child happened to be born outside marriage, the mother's declaration that he was the child's father could sometimes mean that the mother and the child had certain rights in respect of the father. While natural science had not unravelled the mystery of conception, a father's genetic link to a child literally often had to be taken at face value.[34] A major breakthrough came with the discoveries of the sperm cell by Antoni van Leeuwenhoek and the publication of that scientific discovery by Johan van Ham. Even so, in the absence of scientific evidence, non-marital paternity was often determined on the basis of a mother's declaration or a child's resemblance to his father. It was not until the late 19th Century that the function of eggs (ooycytes) in human reproduction came to be understood. In the 1930s, the use of blood tests in paternity proceedings allowed for the exclusion, but not a conclusive establishment, of the biological link between fathers and children. By the mid-1980s, these tests became obsolete through the use of DNA-based parentage tests.

---

31 Likewise, FREEMAN (1996), p. 276.

32 On the importance of decisional privacy and will see further Chapters V and XI.

33 Notably O'DONOVAN (1988), BUEREN (1995), FREEMAN (1996), WILSON (1997); HELMS (1999); JACKSON (2001), CALLUS (2004), ROTHSTEIN, MURRAY, KAEBNICK & M. MAJUMDER (2005); EEKELAAR (2006); BESSON (2007), VAN RAAK-KUIPER (2007), STOLL (2008).

34 ALBRECHT & SCHULTHEISS (2004), p. 33.

Broadly speaking, both bio-medical developments and the diminished importance of (heterosexual) marriage in assigning parental status may therefore be considered to have prompted the contemporary debate on the normative weight that biology should have in the legal relationship between children and parents. Throughout Europe the number of children born outside marriage has increased sharply over the past decades.[35] This phenomenon therefore also prompts questions about how parent relationships should be rendered visible and, in that connection, what consequences should be attached to such a relationship.[36] Furthermore, there is also an increased societal acceptance of donor insemination[37] as well as broad sympathy for those afflicted by involuntary childlessness. In addition, there is an increased societal acceptance in some countries of same-sex marriage and of same-sex families. Against the background of these broad societal trends, the significance of the genetic connections between parents and children has been undergoing legal reinterpretation for a number of decades.

In particular, the immediate preponderance that an adult's genetic link to the child may assume in the attribution of parental rights has received criticism from some legal scholars.[38] As such, in the establishment of paternity, the allegedly increased focus on biology would reinforce the ancient Roman idea of *patria potestas* which asserted a broad right over persons and property, including children, held by the eldest male in the family.[39] From that viewpoint, the apparent upsurge of legal interest in biology would be difficult to reconcile with the contemporary consensus that children have a moral and legal status of their own. In this light, the biologism of parentage law is readily associated with widely discredited patriarchal ideas that children had better be kept in the dependent, non-decisional situation that they had in the past.

Such sceptical views raise questions about the immediacy of biology. In particular, the cultural bias for biological parenthood would carry within it considerable risks in many individual cases. Given the profound impact of the legal consequences of the attribution of parental status on the child's development, biology would, according to critics, all too often be a deficient criterion to base legal parentage upon in the concrete, individual case. In particular, in case of conflict between both genetic parents, the law's abstract adherence to biology would be

35 Www.eurostat.com 2005.

36 Dewar (2000), p. 66; Vonk (2007), p. 6.

37 Takes (2006), p. 25-50.

38 See for example Lawrence Hill (1991), pp.353-420; Murray (2005), p. 18-34; Dwyer (2006), p. 26-40.

39 Grossberg (1985); Murray (2005), p. 34-35.

an overtly dogmatic legal criterion when it comes to the individual child. Maternity rules, in particular, in assigning parental rights by virtue of birth would often give the mother an 'imperfectly tailored right' because the fact that a mother has given birth would in some cases not even ensure minimally adequate caring.[40]

In that same vein, it has been suggested by Dwyer that many paternity suits in the **United States** are, in fact, motivated primarily by a sense of vindictiveness, by irresponsible or immature biological fathers wishing to establish a tie against the mother's wishes.[41] In that view, 'biology' would in other cases also hardly be in the child's interests, especially in proceedings in which paternity is denied because both the emotional and economic impact on a child's development could be devastating. For some children it may have lasting formative implications to lose a parent, irrespective of whether this person is a genetic or a social parent. For such reasons, there would be no *a priori* reason to consider socially constructed forms of legal parentage deserving less legal protection than those vested in a genetic link between two generations.

Nonetheless, some attempts have also been made in various disciplines to justify the immediacy of biology in assigning parental rights. From evolutionary psychology and sociobiology a case for the precedence of biology over social notions has, for example, been made. Here, a variation exists regarding the concept of the so-called 'selfish gene': the idea that an upbringing by one's biological parents is an expression of a pervasive and powerful natural force that may be highly advantageous to the child. This advantage would derive from the fact that a child is raised by adults with a strong disposition to care for the child that stems from natural selection because the parents have a direct interest in seeing the survival of their own genes and being passed on to the next generation.[42] In connection with that controversial idea, it has, for example, been theorized by a **Dutch** pedagogical scholar that males will disfavour children who have been conceived by other males with the same female, because it is firmly ingrained in the male brain that one's own offspring should survive and reproduce.[43]

---

40 DWYER (2006), p. 27. Even so, Dwyer detracts from this controversial idea in admitting that this is 'not the whole story' about maternity rules, since in many jurisdictions the child can soon after birth be adopted and a mother's parental authority may be removed upon the child's birth.

41 DWYER (2006), p. 34.

42 MURRAY (2005), p. 25, gives an explanation of this theory.

43 CROMBRUGGE (1991), p. 302-316.

Furthermore, a case for giving biology precedence in assigning parental responsibilities has been made on the basis of the controversial 'invisible loyalties' theory espoused by the **Hungarian** psychiatrist Böszörmenyi-Nagy.[44] His theory, still popular among critics of adoption for obvious reasons, draws on the basic assumption that strong bonds between children and their biological parents are something innate, rather than being largely socially constructed or ascribable to the influence of 'nurture'.

On that assumption, it would only be 'natural' that adopted children should experience a conflict of loyalties towards their birthparents and legal parents. Since loyalty is represented in this theory as a function of nature rather than nurture, it would be understandable why so many adopted children seem to experience identity problems, because loyalty towards the socio-legal parents would almost irretrievably entail a form of disloyalty towards the birthparents.

In addition, biology as an immediate, logical criterion in attributing legal parentage has also been justified openly by reason of gender politics.[45] Greater emphasis on biology is believed in this view to help restore a balance in parentage law, which for too long had discounted the interests of 'duped dads' that allows women 'to get away with' infidelity. In this heavily genderised view, referred to above, DNA testing is represented as a liberating force, a means capable of promoting a male cause. Accordingly, 'duped dads' may find that DNA tests available on the Internet offer an expedient legal avenue conducive to freeing them from child support obligations.[46] Conversely, DNA evidence is also given empowering qualities in view of its capacity to bolster paternity claims with a claim to scientific truth in case a mother or her new partner opposes parental claims. Instrumentalising DNA as a way to back up parental claims, however, clearly ignores the fact that biology may not only favour men, but also deprive them of parental status against their own will. Moreover, it ignores the fact that birthmothers acquire the legal status of parent by the fact of birth. This, in turn, may be viewed as both a factor capable of limiting and empowering women's decisional power in respect of children.

---

44 BOSZORMENYI-NAGY (1984).

45 NELKIN (2005), p. 10.

46 See Chapter VIII for a discussion of Internet-based paternity tests.

4.2. THE UTILITY OF PARENT-IDENTIFYING INFORMATION

Before delving into autonomy-based justifications of the child's right to information, it will be appropriate to expand upon the reasons that centre on the beneficence or utility of the provision of parent identifying information. In the following sub-sections we shall first examine the utility-oriented justifications (4.3.) before turning to autonomy-based arguments and justifications (4.4). As shall emerge, the distinction between both sets of justifications is not sharp, since it may be said that autonomy should be regarded in the 'final analysis' also a utility-oriented notion, because it helps to protect certain interests, in particular the psychological integrity of the person.

4.3. JUSTIFICATIONS FOR A RIGHT TO INFORMATION AND ITS SOCIAL EFFICACIOUSNESS

Within the broad field of legal philosophy, legal positivistic strands of thought challenge the viewpoint that law and ethics are two interconnected domains of normative thinking. Since the Second World War, this view has come under increased criticism. In non-positivistic legal literature, the recognition of constitutional rights is said to be contingent upon the constitutional norm's social efficaciousness and certain ethical standards. Both positivists and non-positivists agree that law must be issued by a competent legal authority. In contrast to positivistic legal philosophers, however, non-positivists hold that a minimal ethical content is also an essential prerequisite in order to speak of 'law' and 'rights', especially in the domain of human rights. At the same time, the moral or ethical content of a right in itself will also not be a sufficient condition to define a constitutional or fundamental right. It has been emphasised by the **German** legal philosopher Robert Alexy, for example, that the existence of a fundamental right also requires a right to be minimally socially efficacious.[47]

It is considered that the aforementioned definitional criteria of 'law' will help to understand the justification of the right to know one's origins. Even so, it must be said that it will be problematic to state that the right to information exists because it reflects a socially efficacious norm. Thus, even though people whose legal status does not accord with their biological parentage are the exception in society, this may not mean that this in itself is indicative of a societal consensus that everyone should be able to establish the truth about their genetic descent. In fact, it may be so that on legal issues with ethical implications, such as the

---

47 ALEXY (2002b), p. 89-95.

right to information, a social consensus may not be expected.[48] In the absence of any empirical evidence to the contrary, a majority of people in a given society could hold the view that constitutional recognition is unnecessary or not particularly important, even if legal scholars may find otherwise.[49] Presumably, most people will either be indifferent or sympathetic but generally not opposed to the wide recognition that the right to know one's origins has gained in a number of jurisdictions, as long as not overtly intrusive public measures are taken to help implement the right.

Presumably, too, if empiricist studies focusing on public opinion about the right's social utility were conducted, they could therefore reveal a conditioned and context-specific approval of the recognition of people's right to information about their genetic descent. Allowing adoptive children to access their original birth records would by many, for example, be considered not to be a particularly socially taxing measure and, as such, could be considered to correspond with a 'socially efficacious' norm. In contrast, public opinion regarding a duty to openness among mothers about the conception of children outside their relationship with the legal father would probably not be able to rely on a comparable level of sympathy or approval, not least because it may target a greater number of individuals. However, the potential burden on society in itself does not mean that their right to information would not be justifiable.

Given this ambiguity and given the fact that the right may only really matter to a minority of the population, the requirement of social efficaciousness will therefore not be an effective legal criterion in determining to which extent the attribution of constitutional status is justified. It is considered that the underlying justifications of a constitutional right to know one's biological parents should accordingly be sought foremost in ethics, rather than empiricist studies that measure public opinion. First, we shall examine the interest-oriented arguments ('utility') and then choice-oriented arguments ('autonomy').

---

48 PENNINGS (2000), p. 1-15.

49 See above.

4.3.1. The psychological rationale for providing parent-identifying information

Marceline: *There is your father!*
Figaro: *Ooh. Ah me!*
Marceline: *Has nature not told you so a thousand times?*
Figaro: *Never.*[50]

The psychological rationale for providing parent-identifying information as a key to self-understanding has ancient origins. Thus, accounts of unknown parental origins have been a great source of literary inspiration.[51] Not knowing who one's biological parents are may have disastrous consequences. In the well-known Greek myth of Oedipus, Jocasta went against Apollo's oracle that had told her not to have a child, because he would kill his father. Nonetheless, the King of Laios one day drank too much and conceived Oedipus. Left to die of exposure as a foundling, Oedipus was saved by a herdsman. Nonetheless, as a foundling he was insulted for not being the 'true' child of his ostensible parents.[52] Years later Oedipus himself sought counsel at the oracle of Delphi who predicted that he would not only kill his own father, but would marry and impregnate his own mother Jocasta. The oracle was fulfilled as Jocasta bore him two sons and two daughters. But the legacy of Oedipus was calamitous: the plague broke out, his sons feuded and war broke out. With their identities unknown to one another, Oedipus and his father had their fatal encounter at the crossroads near the city of Thebes.[53] In Sophocles' play, Oedipus subsequently blinds himself because he cannot bear to kill himself as this would confront him with both of his parents in the Underworld.

It is remarkable that in some other ancient accounts, foundlings also 'find themselves,' rising to the occasion of fulfilling a central role as leaders in spite of their humble origins. In the book of Exodus, as a baby, Moses was set adrift in a basket of reeds to escape the slaying of all firstborn males and is picked up by the family of the Pharaoh. Moses eventually became the leader of the Hebrew people. Likewise, Romulus and Remus, too, having been brought up by a wolf in the wilderness become founding fathers of Rome. Yet unknown origins do not always indicate an augurous destiny. In the quoted example, however, because

---

50 HONORÉ DE BALZAC, *Le mariage de Figaro.*

51 MOSSMAN (1998), p. 40-61.

52 BUXTON (2004), p. 164-166.

53 As is well known, this myth prompted Sigmund Freud to refer to the Oedipus complex, referring to a male child's unconscious desire for the exclusive love of his mother.

Figaro is also a foundling of unknown origin, this means that he can foster a dream that he could, in fact, 'be anyone at all'. His unknown origins lead him to fantasize about having aristocratic origins, a popular literary theme in the 18th Century. In contrast to Moses and Romulus and Remus, he suffers from an unstable self-image as a result.

As just a few literary examples of the problem of unknown origins, they attest to the fact that the Western cultural fascination with origins is not merely the outcome of recent bio-medical developments. At the same time, it has been established earlier on in this Chapter that there can be little doubt that the discovery of DNA and scientific advances in parentage testing has imposed a need for social scientists and lawyers to rethink the significance of biological parentage, in particular paternity.

Before DNA testing became common, however, the term 'genealogical bewilderment' already came to be used in the adoption context in the 1960s. This term came to denote a profound sense of loss or abandonment and of having been cut off from a fundamental aspect of their lives that some adoptees reported. An important early social science study in this field was John Triseliotis' *In search of origins*, which studied the reasons behind individual searches of adoptees in **Scotland**.[54]

Since Sants and Triseliotis, a great number of social studies have been undertaken that demonstrate that many adopted children experience a need to establish the identity of their birthparents during adolescence.[55] The greater the dissatisfaction with their home life, the greater, too, the possibility that the adoptees would be searching for their original parents.[56] During adolescence, as a child further develops her or his personality and own points of view on a wide range of issues, a child may otherwise be prone to idealization of the unknown biological parent.[57] There is research that supports the theory that this risk of idealization may be greater when a person has little or no information at her or his disposal.[58] Because this positive image cannot be challenged, this myth cannot be dispelled and as a result the development of the child's own sense of identity could be affected in a negative way. Furthermore, it is known that many adopted children can experience a profound sense of abandonment and want to establish

54 TRISELIOTIS (1973), p. 79-91.
55 See for example ERIKSON (1975); SCHECHTER & BERTOCCI (1990); BRODZINSKY (1992).
56 TRISELIOTIS (1973), p. 77.
57 ERIKSON (1975).
58 KAMPEN (1990); MEERUM TERWOGT (1989), p. 209-216.

the reasons why their birthparents were unable or did not want to take care of them.[59] For such reasons, it is generally accepted that adoptees would benefit from being able to identify their birthparents and accessing their adoption files.

A further reason for promoting openness has been found in the risk of a child's accidental discovery or a third party disclosure.[60] This reason involves a 'deeper moral right,' This involves an idea of harm that may result from a conspiracy of silence.[61] Following this argument, the effects of such an accidental discovery could be disastrous, since they would erode trust among family members. If a person does not learn to trust people within the family, it would be much more difficult for this person to establish fulfilling friendships and relationships.

Though research on the informational needs of donor-conceived persons is more limited than in adoption because secrecy has surrounded the practice of donation, there is some evidence to suggest that donor offspring also experience a need to know the parent.[62] It has also been revealed that donor-conceived persons often reported an environment of mistrust within their family and had difficulties in finding someone who could relate to their situation.[63]

4.3.2. Various concepts of personal identity

The right to know one's origins has also been defined as a dimension of the broader right to ascertain and preserve one's identity.[64] Identity may in this sense be understood as a means to establish psychological connections between one's past and present.[65] As such, this justification of the right to information connects with the psychological benefits of openness that have been discussed in the preceding sub-section. Nonetheless, personal identity also involves a very com-

---

59 BRODZINSKY (1992).

60 PASQUALE, MASTROIANNI & MASTROIANNI (2001), p. 2038; MCGEE, VAUGHAN-BRAKMAN, GURMANKIN (1993), p. 2033; FREEMAN (1996), p. 290.

61 O'DONOVAN (1988), p. 37-38.

62 SCHEIB (2005), p. 239. The results of this **American** study revealed that 82.6% among a group of 29 adolescent donor offspring were at least 'moderately interested' in identifying the donor in the future. In another study, it was revealed that 15 of the 16 participants aged between 26 years and 55 years and located in **Australia**, the **United Kingdom**, the **United States** and **Canada** had expressed a wish to identify the donor: TURNER & COYLE (2000), p. 243.

63 TURNER & COYLE (2000), p. 246-247.

64 BESSON (2007), p. 141.

65 FREEMAN (1996). p. 290.

plex culturally and ethically charged concept. Being so very multidimensional, it comes as no surprise that identity has so far not been given a legal definition.[66]

Personal identity may be understood as a fluid concept that is strongly connected to time and a person's social environment and personal experiences. As a dynamic rather than a static concept, the concept of personal identity has been considered to cover a wide range of memberships including not only biological membership, but also familial, social, cultural and political memberships.[67] On that view, Freeman considers 'identity to be what we know and what we feel. It is an organising framework for holding together our past and our present and it provides some anticipated shape to future life'.[68]

There are, however, other ways of approaching the concept. As an ethical concept, a distinction has been made between *numerical* and *narrative* identities.[69] Numerical identity relates to our capacity to persist as human animals while we exist. It is therefore connected to our biological survival. It also transmits the idea that an immanent first-person view of the self continues to exist over the course of time. In contrast, narrative identity may be understood as the sense of human identity that concerns people in everyday life, when someone wonders what sort of person he or she is, what is most important, and with what or whom she identifies in securing a sense of self. Narrative identity is therefore closely connected to the idea of continuity of psychological connections between a person's past and present. However, this does not mean that narrative identity, being the more dynamic and socially important notion, denies the importance of numerical identity. Rather, numerical identity serves a precondition for a person being able to develop a narrative identity.[70]

Narrative identity is, however, the more important notion of identity for our discussion. To be able to shape an idea of who one is at present requires an interpretation of a person's past. In order to be able to create a narrative identity of one's own, it will, however, often be necessary to tap into the memory that other people may have of ourselves. A narrative identity therefore bridges the historical past to the present and the future. In that sense, Haimes and Timms

66 Likewise, BESSON (2006), p. 141.
67 STEWART (1992), p. 226-227.
68 FREEMAN (1996), p. 290.
69 FREEMAN (2005), p. 114.
70 FREEMAN (2005), p. 114.

have concluded that some adopted people want a narrative 'in order to place themselves in a continuum of their past'.[71]

Furthermore, the idea of a *narrative* identity may also be seen, to some extent, as being opposed to a *fixed* identity.[72] This latter concept evokes a more stable notion of identity and is therefore more directly associable with the idea of biological immanence. Wilson holds that, rather than on the basis of narrative identity, disclosure may sometimes be 'more easily, perhaps only, justifiable under a notion of "fixed identity".'[73] In particular, the provision of information could therefore be difficult to defend in relation to donors and other biological parents with whom little if any social contact existed. Especially if there has been little in terms of a past shared with one's biological parents, it could be particularly difficult to justify disclosure under this notion of identity.

Even so, the concept of 'narrative identity', being the more dynamic notion of identity, is reconcilable with the idea that the need to have information about one's parents is a largely socially constructed need. Thus, the concept of 'narrative identity' allows a person to re-evaluate and reinterpret who he or she is, based on whatever information and experiences that one receives.[74] Given this more fluid quality of this concept of identity, the concept has the advantage of being able to accommodate the idea that blood ties could be crucial to a person's identity, but it does not dismiss the importance of having a social family either.

Thus, the concept of narrative identity goes some way in explaining why it may be important to have information about one's parents in many situations, especially if the biological parents have been part of the child's early childhood and the parents have had a joint history together. On the other hand, it is sufficiently flexible to accommodate the idea that the informational need may be largely socially constructed and dependent on dominant Western ideas about biology. In that regard, it seems appropriate to cite O'Donovan: 'the notion of need is socially constructed, (this) does not represent a denial that it may be experienced in a profound sense by adopted and other persons. But it does arise partially from the cultural significance attached to the blood tie.'[75]

---

71 HAIMES & TIMMS (1985), p. 3.
72 WILSON (1997), p. 282.
73 WILSON (1997), p. 282.
74 WILSON (1997), p. 281.
75 O'DONOVAN (1989), p. 111.

4.3.3. Medical rationale

Apart from the psychological and identity-related interest in knowing who one's biological parents are, an interest in knowing one's origins has also been justified on the basis of medical reasons. If a blood-relation has been exposed to hereditary conditions, for example, cardiovascular diseases or forms of cancer, this could help prevent the onset of diseases or conditions which pose a threat to the person's health. Clearly, some people will not wish to be informed to which extent they have a greater hereditary risk of developing certain ailments or conditions.[76] Nevertheless, prospective gamete donors will in most countries be routinely screened and questioned on their medical history, personal motives and family diseases. This can acquiesce the possibly lingering fears of the recipient couple that certain hereditary conditions be excluded.[77] In spite of such precautionary measures, however, the onset of certain diseases cannot always be prevented. If the child has not been informed about donor conception, it is conceivable that this could present a moral dilemma to the medical professional whether she or he should be the first to inform the child or the parents.

A reproductive choice of a couple may be partly contingent upon their prior awareness of serious hereditary medical conditions within one of their families. This could prompt them to seek alternatives to fulfil their child wish. In particular, uteral problems may provide a reason to look for a surrogate mother to carry a pregnancy to term.[78] Outside the assisted conception and surrogacy contexts, there may also be valid medical reasons to seek the identification of one's biological parent.

4.3.4. The prevention of persons entering into the prohibited degrees of consanguinity

In the aforementioned saga of Oedipus, the inadvertent incest between a mother and son is a source of mythology. Animal and human studies show that individuals choose mates partly on the basis of similarity, a tendency referred to as homogamy. Since it is a cross-cultural phenomenon, evolutionary explanations have been sought. Thus, it has been demonstrated that homogamy is attained partly by sexual imprinting on the opposite sex during early childhood. Persons are able to identify the odour of first-degree relatives but have been found

---

76 On the medical right not to know, see in particular: ANDORNO (2006), p. 435-440.

77 WERT & EVERS (1993), p. 2155-2158.

78 NVOG Richtlijn 1999.

unable to recognise the odour of their step-siblings. Nowadays, the prevention of prohibited degrees of relationship is still an area of family law which does not only reflect a widely held social taboo, but may also be said to serve the aim of minimizing hereditary medical risks and promoting greater openness about genetic descent.[79]

4.4. ETHICAL JUSTIFICATIONS BASED ON THE NOTION OF AUTONOMY

4.4.1. Autonomy as a value protecting a right to informational self-determination or decisional privacy

Deceiving others, that is what the world calls a romance.
Oscar Wilde

So far we have examined benefits associated with the disclosure of information regarding biological parentage. The aforementioned psychological, cultural, identity-related and medical reasons as well as the prevention of consanguinity are associable with a principle of beneficence. When such benefits are spurious or uncertain, which may often very well be the case, it could be argued that disclosure should be withheld because the benefits will at best only be speculative. On the other hand, it could also be argued that a desire to know truth 'for the sake of knowing the truth' could also be a legitimate reason, in principle *quite irrespective* of the expected psychological or medical benefits of disclosure. Conceivably, a person may already have a solid self-image but still be very interested in finding out who her or his biological parents are. It is quite conceivable, too, that a confrontation with the truth may sometimes have an adverse impact on a person's identity.

If emphasis is put on an autonomous person's right to informational self-determination, this interest could be more easily justifiable. It will then be closely linked to the Kantian idea that autonomous persons should never be used as a means to an end and, ultimately, as autonomous beings all have an interest in not being deceived and not deceiving one another. On that ethical premise, what makes something good, should not, or at least not exclusively, be assessed in terms of its beneficence. If a child's informational interests were interpreted primarily on the basis of external factors, such as the overall stability of family life, or even other persons' views of what is in that particular child's interests,

79 See section 5.3.1.

whatever beneficence a disclosure of a biological parent's identity may have, could end up being subjugated to the interests of others, notably parents.

These are ideas closely linked to Kantian philosophy. Interpreted rigorously, a well-intentioned refusal to disclose the truth will never be justifiable. Thus, for Kant, lying and deception are wrong because the other 'cannot assent to my mode of acting against him' and is 'unable to contain the end of this action in himself'.[80] Whatever the benefits or discomfort a disclosure entails, that person 'doesn't know what the real end of the action is, and is therefore not in a position to make it his own – to choose, freely, to contribute to its realisation.'[81] On that strict Kantian view, if a parent withholds available information about another biological parent, this will therefore be morally wrong, in principle quite regardless of the question whether a person is psychologically burdened by not knowing.

Modern Kantian philosophers have more regard for circumstance and the contingency of ethics. Thus, Tamar Schapiro holds, for example, that actions construed as right and wrong may be properly picked out 'by fine-grained, context-sensitive descriptions rather than general descriptions like 'deception'.[82] In defence of Kant, she distinguishes between the general claim that deception is wrong in itself – which, it is recalled, may be called the 'classic' or 'standard Kantian argument' – and a theoretically more flexible claim, namely that 'deception is in itself morally indeterminate until further specified'.[83] While reaffirming that it is the manipulative character what makes deception such a fundamental form of wrongdoing, she suggests that exceptions may be possible, especially in relation to children and other not fully autonomous individuals.[84]

4.4.2. Informational self-determination and children

Autonomy is indeed not an unproblematic concept in relation to children. On the concept of autonomy, Rawls already assumed that the very first principle of government would be a guarantee of basic liberties for all, since personal liberties are fundamental prerequisites for developing and exercising autonomy, for

80 KANT, 'Groundwork of the Metaphysics of Morals' in: *Practical Philosophy*, Cambridge Edition of the Works of Immanuel Kant in Translation, 1997, p. 80.
81 KORSGAARD (1988), p. 347.
82 SCHAPIRO (2006), p. 37.
83 SCHAPIRO (2006), p. 37.
84 SCHAPIRO (2006), p. 37-38.

pursuing one's own conception of the good.[85] In this way, Rawls suggested that the potentiality of autonomy is what matters more than its realisation, thereby affirming that children also have basic rights.[86] All the same, commentators have criticized Rawls for largely ignoring political and legal issues in family relationships in his discussion of distributive goods.[87] Accordingly, Rawls did not expand on children's potentiality for autonomy and the significance of that claim.

The Rawlsian concept of autonomy in respect of the relationship rights of both adults and children has, however, been taken further by Dwyer.[88] In Dwyer's view, for adults, 'an autonomy-based outlook more straightforwardly insists that autonomous persons be treated as sovereign over their own lives, including their participation in relationship with others'.[89] For adults, this means that they are generally entitled to choose with whom they wish to have relationships. For children, this position will not always be tenable to the same extent, especially in relation to their parents. All the same, Dwyer concludes that both welfarist and autonomy-based analyses must generate the conclusion that children are at least morally entitled to interest-protecting legal rights and choice-protecting rights.[90]

Following that viewpoint, the age at which minors will become the best judges of their own welfare will depend in large measure on the nature of the issue. As far as the identification of a biological parent is concerned, it will be clear that this potentially has significant implications for the child's welfare. It has been suggested above that the denial of paternity could, for example, entail more negative than positive consequences, especially, for example, in case there is no second legal parent. At this point it may therefore be assumed that the legal parents may be in the best position to oversee the consequences of a minor's wish to identify a birthparent. Having said that, the assumption must however also be made that their interpretation of the child's welfare should also take into account the child's autonomy inasmuch as it can be considered to be present. Presumably, if the child's potential for autonomy were seen as a legal benchmark, then the risk of paternalistic justifications of non-disclosure would be lessened considerably. For this reason alone, it should be held that an autonomy-

---

85 RAWLS (1971), p. 42.
86 RAWLS (1971), p. 509.
87 OKIN (1989); DWYER (2006).
88 DWYER (2006), p. 115-122.
89 DWYER (2006), p. 121.
90 DWYER (2006), p. 160-169.

based approach to the informational interests of minors will generally be preferable to one that only takes a speculative beneficence of disclosure into account.

4.5. THE DISTINCTION BETWEEN SINCERITY AND ACCURACY

There are no facts, only interpretations.[91]

4.5.1. Sincerity and accuracy

To finish off the multidisciplinary discussion undertaken in this Chapter, it seems appropriate to examine the understanding of the notion of 'truth' in philosophy more closely. As has been suggested at the beginning of this Chapter, in Western culture there is a strong commitment against deceptiveness and a readiness not to be fooled. This is also verifiable in the media, parliamentary democracy and the social and natural sciences. The value attached to truth in a free press helps to ensure, for example, that politicians cannot deceive their voters at will for too long, whatever cynics may say. At the same time, though, there is also a suspicion that 'truth', should it exist in a relevant way at all, must generally be either very relative or subjective. On the one side, there is a strand of thought that denies that truth, assuming that it even can be said to exist, should ever be the object of critical inquiry at all. Against this charge, others may reply that they know perfectly well, for example, that some facts are simply true, that today it is 15 May 2009, that Utrecht is located in **the Netherlands** and, less objectively, that the *Academiegebouw* is both a daunting and beautiful edifice.[92] In this way, it may be said that there are many truths. However, the notion of truth that is relevant for our discussion is clearly a different one. As has been suggested, it also engages the idea of being able to provide a truthful (rather than strictly true) account of one's own past.

The account *Truth and Truthfulness* by the **British** philosopher Bernard Williams is to the author's knowledge the best acclaimed contemporary reply to those who deny the value of truth. Williams distinguishes two virtues of truthfulness: *Sincerity* and *Accuracy*. Both of these concepts are connected to the idea of truth. Sincerity is not just a disposition to make sure that any (linguistic) assertion one makes expresses a genuine belief or an avoidance of lying. It

---

91 Attributed to Nietzsche.

92 WILLIAMS (2002), p. 1-5.

also involves trustworthiness in speech.[93] Accordingly, sometimes an assertion may be sincere when a person who does not have all relevant information available to him expresses a belief that he or she believes to be true. Unlike Sincerity, the other value of truthfulness, *Accuracy,* does not only aim at the truth, but importantly, also requires a form of investigative investment. As Williams puts it, the value of Accuracy implies care, reliability, and so on, in discovering and coming to believe a truth.[94] In particular, Accuracy may also be understood as a value in holding on to the notion of reality when one wishes a reality to be otherwise.[95]

Williams illustrates that these values have for long been applied in *legal* contexts. In contract law, the virtues of Sincerity and Accuracy are therefore helpful, for example, for persons in constructing the beliefs that each party to a contract may have.[96] If a party sincerely promises to another party that he will pay a certain amount for the delivery of a good, that assertion will be valued on the basis of its truthfulness. Accuracy, rather than Sincerity, will gain in importance if those conditions are not met. For our purposes, in family law, too, there will usually be the reliable expectation that the husband of the mother is, in fact, the child's biological father. The child and the father may believe that this information is accurate. Furthermore, the mother will in most cases also be sincere if she makes an assertion to that end.

For our purposes, in cases in which legal and biological parentage are congruent with each other, a father will also be fostering a sincere belief that he is the father, regardless of his genetic link. The Accuracy of his claim may not be directly questionable because his trustworthiness is not at issue either. Regardless of his status, the nature of his behaviour or speech ('I am your father') will generally instill normal expectations that he is indeed what he sincerely asserts to be. Indeed, most biological fathers and adolescents in traditional families may believe this without even contemplating the use of a DNA test. The human need for truthfulness, however, makes it understandable why some children will eventually make demands for Accuracy rather than Sincerity. If this is the case, it is quite conceivable that a greater demand for accurate information may be required, for example, by conceiving of a child that insists upon DNA evidence. In particular, it would seem that this moral demand for Accuracy will become more urgent when the value of Sincerity has for one reason or another become

---

93 Williams (2002), p. 97.
94 Williams (2002), p. 127.
95 Williams (2002), p. 140.
96 Williams (2002), p. 82.

open to question to a greater extent than before. Typically, this may especially be the case if the child believes that he or she has been deceived. Unlike the value of Sincerity, which will generally have to be taken on face value, the value of Accuracy involves a commitment to establish the objective truth. As such, it also involves a measure of initiative on the part of the person who seeks truth. That person must make and be able to make an investigative investment. For minors, this is problematic, since they may not be able to make such an investigative investment. For adults, however, the case would appear to be different: as long as they do not find reason to call the truth into question, a sincere speech act may be sufficient in order to enable them to have an interpretation of the past that is truthful *to them.*

4.5.2. The requirement of an investigative investment in respect of autonomous individuals

For the parents this distinction between the two values of truth could be relevant. Thus, it may not only be assumed, for example, that a mother may not only be required to be sincere in her relations with a child. Presumably, the value of Accuracy could also put greater demands on her when it is considered that she may have to go to greater lengths to verify whether a particular man is indeed the father if more than one man were indicated. If she fails to make such an investigative investment, it will also be difficult for her to be sincere in her relations with the child if her information is deficient. As a result, it could also be said that she will undermine the child's possibilities to establish a truthful account of her or his past. This child will only be able to make a demand for accurate information upon becoming capable of making an investigative investment.

If there are no grounds to call into question a parent's truthfulness, the likelihood that an adult will actually make such an investigative investment is, of course, limited. In fact, a person may not have a reason to call into question the biological truth unless the person suspects that he or she already has been deceived. Thus, a minimal awareness of the possibility of an underlying disparity must be present and a willingness to enquire further. In order to ensure that the person can make an autonomous choice to access information, a further investigative investment will however be necessary. How otherwise is one to ensure an autonomous adult's right to obtain accurate information and that person's right *not* to know?[97] This issue will be taken further in the concluding Chapter.

---

97 On a (medical) right *not* to know see in particular: ANDORNO (2006); LAURIE (2006).

In the light of the aforementioned examples, it may be assumed that an awareness of the distinction between these two values of truthfulness, Sincerity and Accuracy, helps us to understand the need for an investigative investment in ensuring autonomous choice for persons considering whether to access the 'biological truth'.

Thus, it may be said that although the truth will mean different things to different people, it will be a value that is important for almost everyone. However, the moral demand for accurate information will only become relevant for some, in particular for those who have found reason to rephrase their moral interest in establishing the truth as a legal right to information, information which presumably has to be able to lay claim to a greater level of objective accuracy. As such, the pursuit of truth may sometimes induce persons to require DNA evidence. Bearing this in mind, it will be sufficient to consider that in family relations:

1. Sincerity incorporates the trustworthiness of acts of speech and as such will also govern most child-parent relations;
2. Accuracy requires, albeit to different degrees, an investigative investment not only on the part of parents, but also in respect of children capable of making such an enquiry; and
3. Accuracy will, in respect of parents, to a large extent be contingent upon the parent's own responsibility in contributing to a situation in which the child is more likely to be exposed to a situation in which the parent cannot be sincere about his genetic link to the child.

5. METHODOLOGY AND STRUCTURE

5.1. RESEARCH QUESTIONS

As a primary aim, this book proposes an examination of the relevant regulatory legal framework from a comparative law perspective to English-speaking readers. To the author's knowledge, a recent in-depth comparative law discussion of continental European jurisdictions concerning the right to information, in which all the aforementioned situations are analysed, has not been undertaken. As shall be explored in sub-section 5.3, the choice of jurisdictions has been guided by the comparability of these continental European systems.

In pursuing this comparative analysis, the aim is to determine whether the current legal structures should be considered to be capable of effectively meeting the informational needs children may have in establishing the identity of their biological parents. With regard to this latter aim, the question is raised to which extent national legal interpretations of the scope of the right to know one's biological parents differ from or accord with international and regional constitutional legal norms.

Thus, in presenting an essentially legal analysis, a further aim is to provide a comprehensive overview of the relevant law across the various factual contexts in which the identification of biological parents could become legally relevant. On the basis of the analysis of the constitutional legal framework, principles shall be deduced that will serve as the main analytical backdrop to the relevant national law. Accordingly, these principles are formulated with a view to guiding the assessment of the scope of the right. In examining ways in which the right may be implemented, a further aim is also to examine both legal avenues and non-legal avenues through which access to information could be realised. In connection with that aim, an attempt shall be made at circumscribing the boundaries between the state's and the parents' legal obligations in facilitating disclosure. Finally, the author wishes to express the hope that this discussion will be of some interest to legal scholars and legislative jurists alike.

5.2. COMPARATIVE METHOD

Within the legal discipline of comparative law, the *functional* (problem-solving) method has been used in this book.[98] This approach has been chosen because it allows for a comparison at a detailed level in respect of the most prevalent situations in which information concerning a biological parent could become relevant. The comparison is *successive* as far as the international, European and national constitutional law is concerned so as to provide a general overview of the recurrent legal issues in these constitutional discourses (Chapters II, III, IV and V). Once the main ramifications of this overarching legal framework have been carved out, the comparison will, by and large, become *simultaneous* (Chapters VI, VII, VIII and IX).[99]

The general aim of studying this subject-matter in a comparative way is to unravel and to analyse the differences and similarities and to assess the strengths and weaknesses of the approaches taken in different continental European jurisdictions in implementing a right to know one's origins and defining its

98 SCHWENZER (2003), p. 143-158; ODERKERK (1999), p. 67-68.
99 KOKKINI-IATRIDOU (1988), p. 187-190.

conceptual boundaries. The ulterior aim in conducting a comparison in this way is not only to broaden and to deepen the understanding of the legal concept of the right to know. Furthermore, the book aims to provide a useful analytical backdrop for legislative jurists and judges who are confronted with claims in which the identification of a biological parent is directly or indirectly at issue.

In making a comparison, the researcher must be ensured that the objects that he wishes to compare are sufficiently similar. The objects of comparison are, in the first place, the most common situations surrounding conception and birth or the period thereafter, the factually most prevalent situations objectively capable of giving rise to a perceived informational need on the part of the individual. At the same time, the legal institutions governing these situations are often framed within the context of parentage law. This is the body of law governing the modalities according to which the legal child-parent relationship is established. It follows that this area of law is a key target of the comparison.

A primary objective is therefore to compare the body of parentage law of the selected jurisdictions. The approach is from a constitutional rights perspective that it focuses on ensuring the child's possible informational needs, rather than from a *parentage law perspective*. In other words, the question is rather: to what extent do national parentage law systems facilitate or form an obstacle to children who attempt to access identifying information regarding their biological parents? Approaching the subject-matter in this way, a further question is raised. This goes to the issue whether parentage law actually provides an appropriate legal avenue for ensuring a satisfactory level of the child's informational interests. If the answer is in the negative, an enquiry into alternate legal (but, quite possibly, also non-legal) mechanisms will have to be considered in order to promote the right's effectiveness.

The comparative method proposed by the author includes a description, comparison and explanation,[100] but also includes what Örücü has labelled as 'conceptualisation' and 'evaluation'.[101] Örücü distinguishes five stages of comparative research, which have generally been applied throughout this book.[102]

100 KOKKINI-IATRIDOU (1988), p. 187-190.
101 ÖRÜCÜ (2004), p. 52-58.
102 ÖRÜCÜ (2007), p. 37-40.

The structure of comparative analysis serves to illustrate the five research stages that Örücü describes as:

1. conceptualisation;
2. description;
3. identification of the similarities and differences ;
4. analysis and explanation;
5. evaluation.

5.3. THE CHOICE OF JURISDICTIONS

Leaving aside the analysis of relevant international and European law, the choice of jurisdictions has been restricted to four jurisdictions. As a common feature, these national jurisdictions are all civil law jurisdictions that incorporate Roman notions of parentage law. Thus, **France**, **Germany**, **the Netherlands** and **Portugal** all belong to the general Western legal culture, even if they are also rooted to varying extents in Protestant, northern and Catholic, southern cultural traditions.[103] Notwithstanding this broad division, they have all been said to form part of a larger, Romanistic-Germanic civil code family.[104] All of these countries are all parties to the same international and regional conventions which constitute to a great extent the subject-matter of this book.[105] Such shared features will contribute to the analytical value of comparative observations.

Although this choice has been determined partly by the author's linguistic skills, some well-pondered legal reasons may also be put forward in motivating the author's choice. Thus, in **France**, in July 2005 an extensive parentage law reform took place, of which one of the main aims consisted of further aligning status with biological truth. As a salient feature of **French** law, the long-standing historical tradition in permitting and regulating anonymous and discreet birth especially deserves mention. In 2003, the ECtHR decided a landmark case on the admissibility of this historical tradition in a claim which engaged an adult child's right to identify her birthmother.[106] It was considered that anonymous birth fell within the margin of appreciation accorded to **France**.

Germany, in contrast to **France**, has been at the forefront in the recognition of a right to know one's origins. Accordingly, the subject-matter is even known as

---

103 HUSA (2004), p. 11-38.

104 ZWEIGERT & KÖTZ (1995), p. 74-84, 101-102 and 108.

105 Thus, the European Convention on Human Rights (ECHR) and the UN Convention on the Rights of the Child (CRC) apply in each jurisdiction.

106 ECtHR *Odièvre v. France*, Appl. No. 42326/98, 13 February 2003.

a *Topos* of modern **German** legal discourse.[107] In 1989 the Bundesverfassungsgericht attributed a constitutional character to a child's right to know on the basis of its personality right doctrine. Ever since, a number of interesting legal developments have ensued which resulted last year in the enactment of a new law, which seeks to promote the enforcement of the constitutional right at the procedural level.[108]

In **the Netherlands**, the right to know has also been recognised on the basis of a personality right doctrine, a development that has been ascribed to the influence of **German** constitutional law. Moreover, in 1998 **Dutch** parentage law was reformed to a great extent, thereby further bringing it into conformity with the biological truth. For our discussion, perhaps the most significant development in the last few years, however, has been the entry into force of the Donor Information Act following lengthy parliamentary and scholarly debates. This law foresees a waiver of an absolute guarantee on donor anonymity and a regime of gradual disclosure of information.

Finally, as an under-researched jurisdiction which so far has seldom been the object of comparative law research, in the **Portuguese** legal system the right to know has also gained progressive recognition. Interestingly, this has also been the result to some extent of the influence of **German** constitutional legal doctrine. Moreover, as shall be established, its parentage law system, last reformed in 1977, has traditionally borne a strong biologistic imprint. In particular, the biological father without status has since 1966 had a right to challenge the husband's paternity. Furthermore, in 2007, the **Portuguese** Assisted Conception Law entered into force. Although this new law does not waive donor anonymity, if the donor-conceived child is capable of substantiating weighty reasons a disclosure may become possible.[109]

All jurisdictions shall be discussed in the alphabetical order of their names in the English language, unless there are compelling reasons to justify another order. As an example of a thematic legal comparison, in the next sub-section the legal problem concerning the prohibited degrees of consanguinity shall be analysed. Since the evaluative criteria are only presented in Chapter V, no evaluation of the criteria is presented.

---

107 HELMS (1999), p. 49.

108 See Chapter VIII.

109 See Chapter X.

5.3.1. *Example of a comparison: the prohibited degrees of consanguinity*

In **France**, marriage is prohibited between all ascendants and descendants and the relatives by marriage in the same lineage.[110] The reasons behind this prohibition derive from reasons of morality and the minimisation of physiological and eugenic risks for offspring. Marriage within the adoptive family is in principle also prohibited, although a dispensation may be given to adopted children of the same individual and between the adoptee and the adopter's children by the Presidency.[111]

In **the Netherlands**, in civil law, there is a bar against marriage and registered partnerships between siblings and the non-recognition of children from incestuous relationships.[112] As in **France**, for persons who have become siblings through adoption this prohibition may be lifted, albeit by the Minister of Justice.[113] In **Portugal**, consanguinity between parents and children and siblings is also an impediment to marriage, but in the case of adoption the Public Prosecutor may lift the bar to marriage.[114]

In **France, the Netherlands** and **Portugal** incest as such is not liable to criminal prosecution. Incest is, however, a criminal offence in **Germany**.[115] In February 2008, a case arose involving a brother and sister who had grown up separately, only to meet as adults years later and to fall in love.[116] They subsequently had four children, two of whom were handicapped and three in care. They sought to challenge the law against incest so that they could continue their relationship without the threat of imprisonment. The Court held that because it criminalises sexual intercourse between siblings the criminal law statute does not mean that the law seriously restrains a right to sexual self-determination. Allegedly, moreover, a reason behind the criminal law provision was the fostering of lawful marriages and normal family relationships apart from minimising health risks to incestuous offspring. For such reasons, the measure was considered to meet the

---

110 Art. 161 **French** Code Civil. For 'registered partnerships' (PACS), Art. 515-2 **French** Code Civil. See further: CURRY-SUMNER (2005), p. 84-85 and TERRÉ & FENOUILLET (2006), p. 347.

111 Art. 366 **French** Code Civil. TERRÉ & FENOUILLET (2006), p. 349.

112 Art. 1:80a(1) in conjunction with 1:41 and 1:204 (1) under (a) DCC. See further: CURRY-SUMNER (2005), p. 124-125.

113 Art. 1:41 (2) DCC.

114 Art. 1602 (a) and (b) in conjunction with Art. 1609 PCC.

115 § 173 (2) II Strafgesetzbuch (StGB) = **German** Criminal Code.

116 BVerfG, 2 BvR 392/07 of the 26th of February 2008. See also: http://www.guardian.co.uk/world/2007/feb/27/germany.kateconnolly.

requirements of proportionality. The decision provoked a renewed scientific and media interest in the phenomenon of genetic sexual attraction.

6. TERMINOLOGY

A few definitional issues will require clarification in view of the fact that there is no specific terminology regarding the subject-matter that is generally accepted. Especially given the wide range of families today, the term 'parent' may elude easy definition.[117] Although the legal definition of the term parent involves a central question of parentage law, it may be emphasized that this study does not aim to devise a more functional parentage law system. Rather, the focus of our concern shall be on the identification of biological parents in accordance with the law.

Accordingly, the terms 'parent', '(biological) father' and 'mother' will be used as a generic term, which refers to biological parentage unless specified otherwise.[118] An exception is made with regard to donors because of the moral bias for biology that the word 'father' or 'mother' could otherwise suggest. When legal parentage is at issue, the term 'parent' shall be used to include all adults who are either part of the child's resident family or have some kind of parental relationship outside the resident family; this may be a genetic link or a social link based on parental responsibility.[119]

It is worth observing too that the term 'biological' parent, 'biological father' and 'biological mother' shall be used instead of the term 'genetic parent', 'genetic father' and 'genetic mother'. Only in the surrogacy context is the use of the term 'genetic mother' used because both the genetic mother and the gestational mother could be said to fulfil a biological role and are therefore 'biological parents.' While only the genetic mother will provide her DNA to the child, the

117 LAWRENCE HILL (1991), p. 360-362.

118 On the figurative and genderised use of the terms père/paternité and mère/maternité in French, see: BOLUSSET (1998), p. 73-82. He notes that the use of *père* is generally more positive than the use of mère: *Le temps est père de la vérité* (time is the father of truth) *le travail est père des bonnes mœurs* (work is the father of good manners) and *l'indécision est la mère de l'échec* (indecision is the mother of all failure) and *l'ignorance est la mère de tous les crimes* (ignorance is the mother of all crimes).

119 Likewise, VONK (2007), p. 16.

gestational mother cannot be said not to fulfil a biological role because she carries the pregnancy to term.[120]

Furthermore, in distinguishing between legal and biological forms of parenthood, the term 'paternity' shall be used exclusively to refer to the legal concept, while 'fatherhood' shall be used in respect of the biological concept, thereby potentially including sperm donors. The term 'maternity' shall be used in a legal way, too, whereas the term 'motherhood' shall refer to the various biological concepts, thereby extending to egg donors, genetic mothers and gestational mothers.

The words 'child' and 'children' will also be used in a generic way, in denoting a person's relationship to her or his parents irrespective of that person's age. If the child is an adult, the term 'adult child' shall be used, for want of a better term. The plural term ('children') will generally be used in order to avoid the use of genderised or neutral possessive pronouns in the English language. As such, the use of the plural form 'children' does not only avoid objectifying the child, but it also avoids the impression of a gender bias that could result when possessive pronouns such as 'her', 'his' are used or the depersonalized feature associated with the possessive pronoun 'its' when used in relation to the singular form 'child.'

If the legal context is only relevant for children under adult age, the term 'minor(s)' shall be used Similarly, the apparently self-contradictory words 'adult child' and 'adult children' will be used to clarify that a situation is specifically relevant for people above adult age in relation to their biological parents.

For reasons of both style and brevity, the 'right to know one's origins' may be used interchangeably with the terms 'right to know' and 'informational right' and 'right to information.' Whenever a specific terminological use is appropriate for defining the right as a legal concept, this will be specified.

7. LIMITATIONS

This book contains an analysis of the law which regulates access to information in the international and **European** legal order, as well as in **the Netherlands**, **France, Germany** and **Portugal**. It follows that this book does not incorporate

---

120 VONK (2008), p. 120.

any comprehensive legal analysis of comparable laws that may be found in other jurisdictions, however interesting their solutions may be. In attempting to mitigate some of the limitations that such a selection implies – indeed, an issue with which the comparative lawyer inevitably grapples – it was considered methodologically justifiable to occasionally refer to original legal solutions from other jurisdictions. As shall emerge, these alternate solutions are found primarily in common law jurisdictions such as **England & Wales** and **Australia** as well as a number of **Nordic** jurisdictions. Given the limited time available for the research, it was considered appropriate to only expand exceptionally upon solutions found in common law systems, all the more so since the book aims to provide an insight into legal developments in continental legal systems which are broadly comparable (see section 5.3). As far as the Nordic jurisdictions are concerned, the author had too little time at his disposal to learn Scandinavian languages with a view to conducting an in-depth comparative law research.

While the primary focus shall be on a children's right to information, some attention shall also be devoted to the informational interests of parents. In view of the juncture that the child-parent relationship represents, a rigorous distinction between perspectives on parental and children's interests will be untenable. When a father's paternity is established before the courts, this will often mean that the informational interests of both generations shall be met. However, this is not necessarily the case. As shall emerge, the informational interests of both generations may not conflate and the argument cannot be sustained that they can claim to have an equally strong ideological basis. All the same, in **Germany**, a legal father's right to know his progeny also received constitutional recognition on the basis of the personality right by the Bundesverfassungsgericht in 2007.[121]

Even though some attention shall therefore be devoted to the (perceived) informational needs of parents, this study shall not enter into a detailed discussion of the legal interest that other relatives might have in establishing details concerning their genetic link. Quite simply, these interests have so far received too limited constitutional recognition to warrant a separate discussion, whereas the child's right to information is in itself already an encompassing and multifaceted subject-matter. Nonetheless, the author does acknowledge that some legal recognition of the informational interests of siblings and other blood-relations could be justified, but this may not mean that they are worthy of constitutional rights protection. In that connection, it is worth pointing out that such rights and obligations between such blood-relations have, from a historical

121 BVerfGE, 13 February 2007, *FamRZ* 2007, p. 441.

perspective, been less developed with the possible exception of inheritance law and some alimentary rights, certainly in comparison to the legal child-parent relationship.

Given this background the constitutional recognition of rights of other blood-relations may be considered to be too under-developed at present to command a comprehensive, comparative analysis. Furthermore, it may be a pertinent factor that relations between siblings and other blood-relations, including grandparents and children, may be considered to be too far removed from the principle of procreational responsibility between two generations.[122]

Moreover, it is a safe assertion that legal certainty requires that certain legal limits be set to the exercising of rights. Although a moral right for one donor-conceived child to know another donor-conceived sister may exist, it can be doubted whether the legislature should recognize such a right.[123] To summarise, then, it seemed more appropriate in this study to focus on the rights of 'children', whether minors or adults, in identifying their biological parents as their right to information has undergone more legal development than those of other possible rights holders.

8. STRUCTURE OF THE BOOK

This book is divided into Chapters. Chapters are further divided into sections and sub-sections. In Chapter II, a critical overview shall be given of the relevant international legal norms. These derive primarily, though not exclusively, from the United Nations Children's Rights Convention (UNCRC). In particular, attention shall be given to the drafting history and interpretation of Articles 7 and 8 of the UNCRC which contain the most important provisions at the international level. In Chapter III, a legal analysis of the regional legal structure will be undertaken. This incorporates a critical overview of the interpretation of the

122 See Chapter V for a discussion of this principle.

123 Www.ukdonorlink.org.uk In the **United Kingdom**, a voluntary register, subsidised with public funds, does enable siblings conceived by one donor to establish contact with one another on the basis of a system of voluntary registry. Through another **American** website, www.donorsiblingregistry.com, it has been claimed that some 5,961 donor-conceived (half) siblings have managed to trace each other. In one case the parents of two four-year-old boys living in **Finland** and **Britain** were able to establish that they were conceived by the same **Danish** donor through this website. The families are considering meeting up when the boys are eight. *Sunday Times*, 5 October 2008, p. 10.

body of relevant case law that has developed ever since the 1989 *Gaskin* decision, for all intents and purposes a veritable 'landmark case' in which the applicant relied on the notion of the right to private life and family life, as protected under Article 8 of the European Convention on Human Rights, in order to access information concerning his early childhood to overcome the psychological problems he was facing as an adult.[124] Although the bulk of relevant regional law is found in this case law, some attention shall be devoted to data and privacy protection law emanating from the legal order of the European Union as well.

In Chapter IV, our discussion turns to constitutional legal norms and case law at the regional level. It shall become clear that in **Germany**, but also in **the Netherlands** and in **Portugal,** the right to know one's origins has gained progressive recognition over the past decades, primarily on the basis of a 'personality right'. As will be demonstrated, **France** constitutes a notable exception in a number of respects as regards this constitutional recognition of a legal interest in the biological truth.

As the patient reader has worked her or his way through a top-down analysis of the constitutional legal order, from the overarching international and regional norms down to the national legal order, it will be appropriate to take time for a moment of critical reflection. At that point, some recurrent aspects will be summarized first. Furthermore, legal principles shall be formulated on the basis of the previous analysis. The aim of this Chapter V shall be to provide an analytical backdrop for the comparative analysis to be undertaken thereafter.

Chapters VI, VII, VIII and IX incorporate a context-specific comparative legal analysis. These Chapters shall accordingly propose a more detailed, thematic comparison of non-constitutional, statutory law. A broad thematic sub-division is made in that respect. Chapters VI and VII shall first discuss disparities between biological and legal parentage which arise in natural reproduction, in respect of maternity and paternity. In Chapter VIII, procedural aspects such as the issue of compulsory DNA testing shall be addressed. Subsequently, the Chapters IX and X shall incorporate an analysis of relevant situations outside natural reproduction. As such, the right's scope in adoption and artificial reproductive technologies in which the state has assumed a more prominent role in regulating informational rights shall be discussed.

---

124 ECtHR *Gaskin v. United Kingdom*, Appl. No. 10454/83, 7 July 1989.

Finally, Chapter XI attempts to formulate evaluative answers to the basic research questions, against the analytical backdrop and normative criteria that Chapter V provides. In that connection, a more modest aim will involve answering the question whether developments in the four jurisdictions may be considered consistent with current interpretations in the overarching constitutional legal order.

PART II
THE CONSTITUTIONAL LEGAL FRAMEWORK

CHAPTER II
THE INTERNATIONAL PROTECTION OF CHILDREN'S RIGHT TO KNOW THEIR ORIGINS

1. OUTLINE

The bulk of this Chapter consists of a legal interpretation of the substantive provisions of the United Nations Convention on the Rights of the Child (UNCRC) that bear relevance to the subject -matter. It is beyond dispute that the UNCRC, adopted by the General Assembly of the United Nations on 20 November 1989, marked a watershed in the global recognition of children's rights. Substantively, it is relevant for our discussion that much of the innovativeness of the UNCRC may be ascribed to its focus on identity-related rights. On the other hand, the implementation of the rights which the UNCRC incorporates is largely contingent upon the interpretation of these substantive provisions within different national legal cultures.[1] Two decades ago, Article 7 of the UNCRC, now acknowledged as a primary legal source of the right to know one's origins, was still principally associated with the right for adopted children to trace their biological parents.[2] As will become clear, however, the Committee on the Rights of the Child has extended the provision's application to other situations in which the knowledge of one's genetic origins may be of importance to the child. This broader interpretation is also verifiable in some of the jurisdictions which shall be studied in greater depth in this book.

---

1 O'Donovan (2000), p. 73.
2 Detrick (1999), p. 153-154.

2. THE UNITED NATIONS CONVENTION ON THE RIGHTS OF THE CHILD

2.1. HISTORICAL NOTE

If evaluated solely on the basis of its ratification history, the UNCRC still stands out as the most successful international human rights' standard-setting document ever, with only **Somalia** and the **United States** hitherto not having become parties.[3] Accordingly, the claim that it has an almost universal application and binding character does not seem excessive, even if it must be conceded that its provisions have not always been incorporated directly into the national law of each of the States Parties.[4] The UNCRC is the fruit of negotiations that lasted over a decade, following a proposal by **Poland** to draft a charter of children's rights back in 1978.[5] It was not until September 1990, however, that the UNCRC entered into force. This long time-span can be accounted for by the drafting process as this relied exclusively on the basis of a principle of consensus, thereby delaying the drafting process significantly. This commitment to achieving consensus meant that a programmatic wording often had to be chosen. States have been incited, above all, to 'undertake' certain measures, or to pledge that they 'shall ensure' the substantive rights contained in the UNCRC.[6]

In spite of these features, the ratification success of the UNCRC remains remarkable, if considered in the wider historical context of the international tradition in the protection of children's rights. Thus, as referred to in the UNCRC's Preamble, the League of Nations Geneva Declaration of the Rights of the Child (1924) alongside the Declaration of the Rights of the Child (1959), adopted by the United Nations' General Assembly precisely thirty years before are considered the earliest enumerations of international children's rights. These latter two documents were, however, drafted in a more hortatory, programmatic fashion and lack commensurate enforcement mechanisms such as periodic country reports that are required under the UNCRC.[7]

---

3 Source: http://www.ohchr.org/english/bodies/UNUNCRC/index.htm.
4 FOTTRELL (2000), p. 13.
5 UN Doc. E/CN.4/L.1366.
6 See *inter alia* Arts. 2 (2), 3(2), p. 20.
7 Art. 44 (1) UNCRC.

2.2. ADDRESSEES

The addressees of the Convention are not only states, but also children and, to a rather indefinite extent, parents. Article 2 UNCRC contains an equality principle, requiring that the States Parties 'respect and ensure' that the rights listed are extended to all children 'without discrimination of any kind, irrespective of the child's or his or her parents' or legal guardian's race, colour, sex, language, religion, political or other opinion, national, ethnic or social origin, property, disability, birth or other status'. This, in itself, arguably indicates that the right to information, as contained in Article 7 UNCRC, potentially extends to all children, irrespective of the particular circumstances surrounding their conception or birth.

A culturally sensitive question involves the definition of the term 'child.' At an initial stage of the drafting process, it was proposed that children should be defined as persons who have not yet reached 'majority', or rather, the age when full legal capacity is acquired.[8] Still, the current definition of Article 1 which provides for an upper age-limit of eighteen years ultimately proved acceptable. Although age-related criteria restrict the scope of the Convention to a more or less circumscribed group of persons, its potential implications for transforming the interpretation of human rights associated with adult age have not gone unnoticed in legal scholarship. Thus, in discussing the legal significance of the UNCRC, John Eekelaar points out, for example, that 'to recognise people as having rights from the moment of their birth continuously into adulthood could turn out, politically, to be the most radical step of all. If all young people are secured all the physical, social and economic rights proclaimed in the Convention, the lives of millions of adults of the next generation would be transformed. It would be a grievous mistake to see the Convention applying to childhood alone. Childhood is not an end in itself, but part of the process of forming the adults of the next generation. The Convention is for all people.'[9]

2.3. RELEVANT LEGAL PRINCIPLES

The regard for the child as an autonomous bearer of rights that permeates the provisions of the UNCRC also sets it off against some of its precursors, such as the 1924 Geneva Declaration. As such, the UNCRC, attests to a marked shift in

---

8 DETRICK (1999), p. 59.

9 See also BESSON (2007), p. 139, who seems to take the view that the rights of adults to know their genetic parentage were already recognised before the ratification of the UNCRC only to be extended expressly to children thereafter.

both legal and pedagogical views of the child's needs that occurred in the late twentieth Century. Reflecting such broad societal developments, it does not only include provisions aiming at the child's protection by the State Parties, but also participatory rights regarding the receiving and imparting of information[10] and participation in cultural life and the arts.[11]

A fundamental principle which underlies all substantive provisions is found in Article 3 (1)which affirms that 'in all actions concerning children, whether undertaken by public or private social welfare institutions, courts of law, administrative authorities or legislative bodies, the best interests of the child shall be a primary consideration'. If not necessarily paramount, then the UNCRC requires that the child's best interests be regarded a primary consideration in legal issues concerning children. Though prone to criticism for its open-endedness and ambiguity, it may be said that the more precise wording of the substantive rights contained in the UNCRC adds flesh to the contents of the 'best interests' formulation. This child-centred perspective and emphasis on children's autonomy that Article 3 conveys, has not received general approval. Thus, a more traditional legal concept of children's rights resounds, for example, in the argument that 'children are inherently dependent persons – a concept less of law than of nature.'[12] Therefore, the UNCRC and Article 3 in particular, have received criticism for implying a break with legal tradition, by conferring primary responsibility on states at the expense of 'pluralist democratic tradition' that looked at 'parents and families and not the state' for promoting the interests of the child.[13] Yet this criticism of state intervention in the family sphere seems to overlook the fact that to be effective, the UNCRC requires a sustained and active involvement of the parents in implementing the child's rights.

The conceptualisation of the child as a bearer of rights is expressed, too, in Article 5 UNCRC which conveys the basic idea that children should be regarded as an autonomous human being, requiring less and less direction as they mature. Even so, the legitimate interests of parents and, if applicable, legal guardians in children's upbringing have certainly not come to be regarded as irrelevant. Thus, States parties are required to respect the responsibilities, rights and duties of parents to provide 'appropriate direction and guidance', in a manner consistent with the 'evolving capacities of the child.'

---

10 Art. 13 UNCRC.
11 Art. 31 UNCRC.
12 HAFEN & HAFEN (1996), p. 484.
13 HAFEN & HAFEN (1996), p. 484.

This responsibility of parents in implementing children's rights also resurfaces in Article 14, for example, with regard to a child's freedom of religion, where States Parties are required to 'respect the rights and duties of parents and, when applicable, legal guardians to provide direction to the child in the exercise of his or her right in a manner consistent with the evolving capacities of the child.' Clearly an otherwise inherently problematic aspect, the division between parents and the state in implementing the UNCRC, subject as it may be to divergent cultural interpretations, has been said to engage a presumption of competency rather than a presumption of a lack thereof in respect of parents.[14] It follows that the burden of proof would be on the state to prove that parents are not complying with their responsibilities in meeting the requirements of the UNCRC.[15]

For our discussion, this may indicate that an important legal responsibility is vested in parents in making the identity of genetic parents known to the child, but that access and disclosure certainly also engages the public authorities. For now, it may be assumed that this state responsibility will become especially relevant so if there are grounds to believe that the parents are not committed to promoting the child's rights.

2.4. IDENTITY RIGHTS PROTECTED UNDER THE UNITED NATIONS CONVENTION ON THE RIGHTS OF THE CHILD

2.4.1. The legal background of Article 7(1) UNCRC

> *1. The child shall be registered immediately after birth and shall have the right from birth to a name, the right to acquire a nationality and, as far as possible, the right to know and be cared for by his or her parents.*
> *2. States Parties shall ensure the implementation of these rights in accordance with their national law and their obligations under the relevant international instruments in this field, in particular, where the child would otherwise be stateless.*

The *travaux préparatoires* of the UNCRC draw attention to the fact that Article 24(2)) of the International Convention on Civil and Political Rights provides the legal basis for the child's right to be registered immediately after birth.[16] Accor-

14 BUEREN (1995), p. 51.
15 BUEREN (1995), p. 51.
16 See e.g. UN Docs. E/CN.4/L.1542, para. 37 (1980); E/CN.4/1989/WG.1/CRP.1/Add.1, p. 4; E/CN.4/1989/48, para. 106.

dingly, this general human rights provision has been interpreted as containing a right to know one's origins as well.[17]

In its General Comment on Article 24 ICCPR, the UN Human Rights Committee reveals that the main rationale behind the inclusion of the child's right to have a name is to reduce the danger of the abduction of children as well as other types of treatment in relation to the rights that the ICCPR contains. This document affirms that this right to have a name and to be registered after birth may in some countries be especially important for children born out of wedlock. From a global perspective this is hardly surprising, because on an annual basis some fifty million newborn babies are estimated not to be registered officially, i.e. a full thirty percent of all births.[18]

It has also been argued that the right to a name can be based on the right to privacy as contained in Article 17 ICCPR[19] As an aspect of a person's private life, the right to a name from birth covers not only the family name from birth but also a first name identifying the child. In addition, States Parties are required to indicate the specific measures taken or envisaged to ensure that every child is registered immediately after birth.[20] Furthermore, steps taken to remove certain social or cultural obstacles with regard to displaced persons, asylum-seeking and refugee children in particular should be reported.[21] An obligation to sensitize and mobilize public opinion on the importance of birth registration of children and to provide adequate training to registry personnel is also incumbent on the States Parties. Moreover, the elements of the child's identity included in the birth registration and the measures adopted to prevent any stigmatisation or discrimination of the child should be reported.

---

17 Art. 24 ICCPR:
2. Every child shall be registered immediately after birth and have a name. Interpreting Articles 17 and 24 ICCPR as containing a right to know, DETRICK (1999), p. 145; BESSON (2007), p. 141 and STOLL (2008), p. 29.

18 Http://www.unicef.org/protection/index_birthregistration.html.

19 NOWAK (2005), p. 432. Art. 17 ICCPR:
1. No one shall be subjected to arbitrary interference with his privacy, family, home or correspondence, nor to unlawful attacks on his honour and reputation.
2. Everyone has the right to the protection of the law against such interference or attacks.

20 UN Doc. UNCRC/C/58, p. 13, para. 49 (1996).

21 UN Doc. UNCRC/C/58, p. 13, para. 49 (1996).

The right to freedom of opinion and the right to impart information have also been brought into connection with the right to know.[22] Van Bueren has pointed out that the right to know was already protected on the basis of Article 19(2) ICCPR prior to the approval of the final draft of Article 7(1) UNCRC.[23] While the link with a general right to petition information seems clear, it would appear, however, that such an interpretation is rather extensive.

Less contestable is that the right to a nationality has been ingrained in general human rights documents for a considerable time. Thus, over the past century the determination of nationality is no longer exclusively the realm of states. As early as 1930 the League of Nations adopted the 1930 Hague Convention on Certain Questions relating to the Conflict of Nationality Laws which entered into force in 1937. With regard to the acquisition of nationality by children, a number of principles were posited, including the *ius soli* principle of Article 14 with regard to foundlings and those children whose parents are unknown. In the *Nottebohm* case, the International Court of Justice posited the principle that, according to state practice, nationality was 'a legal bond having as its basis a social fact of attachment, a genuine connection of existence, interests and sentiments, together with the existence of reciprocal rights and duties.'[24] Where other states become involved, a 'genuine link' must exist between the rules and circumstances under which states grant nationality. Although this criterion only applies to international cases,[25] the wide discretion accorded to states has been curtailed by a number of conventions concerning nationality which have centred on the reduction of statelessness and the avoidance of dual nationality.

In the aftermath of the Second World War, the mass denationalisation of ethnic minorities provided an incentive for the international community to counter statelessness through a concerted legal effort. In that light, Article 15 of the Universal Declaration of Human Rights also recognised everyone's right to a nationality. As early as 1948 the UN Secretary-General formulated two basic principles in that regard: 1) every child should receive a nationality at birth; and

---

22 Art. 19 ICCPR:
1. Everyone shall have the right to hold opinions without public interference.
2. Everyone shall have the right to freedom of expression; this right shall include freedom to seek, receive and impart information and ideas of all kinds, regardless of frontiers, either orally in writing or in print, in the form of art, or through any other media of his choice.
Note that Article 13(1) UNCRC also protects children's right to have the freedom to seek and receive information 'of all kinds.'

23 BUEREN (1995), p. 123.

24 *ICJ Reports* (1955), p. 23.

25 GROOT & TRATNIK (2002), p. 24.

2) no person should lose his or her nationality until he or she has acquired a new one. In 1961 the moderately successful Convention on the Reduction of Statelessness was adopted which entered into force in 1975. In Article 8(1) of this Convention it is held that a person shall not be deprived by a state of nationality if this would bring about statelessness. Furthermore, subject to a few conditions the Contracting States agreed to grant their nationality to persons born on their territory if that person would otherwise be stateless.

During the *travaux préparatoires* of the UNCRC, the conditions under which nationality may be granted or lost were discussed. In the *General Guidelines* for periodic reports the States parties are requested to provide information in their reports on the measures adopted to ensure that the right to a nationality is implemented, especially in those situations where the child would otherwise be likely to become stateless. The domestic criteria applied for the acquisition of nationality, such as those derived from parentage, and specific information with regard to children born out of wedlock, asylum-seeking and refugee children are requested.[26] In what follows, the right to a nationality and a name shall not be further discussed as they are beyond the thematic scope of the book, even though they may be considered to contain important aspects of an encompassing 'right to a legal identity', as it is understood in the framework of the UNCRC.

2.4.2. Article 7(1) UNCRC: 'the right to know and be cared for by one's parents as far as possible'

The role of Muslim countries has been important in the adoption of the child's right to know one's origins at the international level. Pursuant to a joint proposal by the delegations of **Algeria, Egypt, Iraq, Jordan, Kuwait, Libyan Arab Jamahiriya, Morocco, Oman, Pakistan** and **Tunisia**, a 'right to know and be cared for by one's parents' was not introduced until at a relatively late stage of the drafting process. The original proposal of these Muslim countries took the view that the right to know one's parents is so fundamental for children's psychological stability and well-being that it should be accorded equal weight as other, connected identity rights such as the right to a name and to acquire a nationality subsequent to birth. The delegate of **Egypt** observed that the right to know one's parents was 'quite essential to the child and equal to his right to a name or a nationality, which were only important for him at a certain age.'[27] By implica-

[26] UN Doc. UNCRC/C/58, 13-14, paras. 48 and 53 (1996).

[27] UN Doc. E/Cn.4/1989/48, p. 18-22.

tion, children's informational needs were therefore regarded as something not connected or restricted to any particular age.

The *travaux préparatoires* of the UNCRC do not fail to reveal that even a watered down version of the original proposal was still capable of giving rise to a heated debate. Thus, **Canada** observed that a further recognition of a right to be cared for by one's parents was uncalled for, having been already covered by Article 9, which establishes that the child shall not be separated involuntarily from her or his parents. Furthermore, **Germany** and the **United States** observed that the recognition of this right to know would be difficult to reconcile with their condoning of the practice of secret adoption. In the end, these governments insisted that the words 'as far as possible' should be included, even though the **United States** did not become a party to the UNCRC. Only this version proved acceptable on the basis of consensus voting.[28] How contentious it might have been to accept a more absolute wording may be appreciated when it is considered that express reservations were made by a few countries. Thus, the **Czech Republic** objected to disclosure in case of artificial fertilisation and adoption. Furthermore, **Poland** also insisted that reservations on secret adoption should be made, whereas **Luxembourg** underscored the fact that an exception was necessary in view of its sanctioning of a mother's right to give birth anonymously.[29]

In brief, then, the clause 'as far as possible' was introduced to conciliate some divergent views surrounding the right's scope that had been voiced by a number of delegations. In that regard, Hodgkin and Newell have distinguished three situations.[30] Thus, a parent may (factually) not be identifiable or a mother may refuse to make the identity of the genetic father known to the child. Finally, a State may decide that it is better that a parent should not be identified. The obligations under Article 7(1) UNCRC may not be affected to a comparable extent in the former two situations as they are in the latter. If the state withholds information whenever it is available, it would breach its obligations under the Convention. For Stoll, apart from adoption this should include at least the situation in which gamete donors have been registered.[31]

28 UN Doc. E/CN.4.1989/48, 18-22/ These included *inter alia* the **New Zealand** proposal '*subject to the provisions of this Convention*' and the **United States** proposal '*in the best interests of the child*'.

29 UN Doc. E/CN.4.1989/48, p. 18-22.

30 HODGKIN & NEWELL (2002), p. 117-119.

31 STOLL (2008), p. 32.

While the General Guidelines require States Parties to list the measures they have taken to enable the child to know her or his parents, they do not specify what these measures might entail. Still, as a minimum requirement, States Parties should provide relevant information concerning the minimum legal age from which consent may be given to a change of legal identity, which incorporates the child's name, the modification of family relations and guardianship. By virtue of Article 1 UNCRC, some information should also be provided concerning access to information regarding biological parentage.

In that connection, it is worth observing that a child's right to access birth records has not been covered by the UNCRC.[32] Even so, this may be relevant in particular in the adoption context, However, Article 30 of the Hague Convention on the Protection of Children and Co-operation in respect of Inter-country Adoption 1993 does require states to preserve available information concerning the child's origins such as the identity of the birth parents and medical data. Still, this state obligation is attenuated somewhat through the insertion of Article 11 which also entitles the state of origin to withhold information identifying the birth parents from the receiving state. As a consequence, as Van Bueren suggests, the Hague Convention still leaves considerable room for ranking the privacy of birthparents higher than the child's right to information. This she considers understandable, since in some states of origin of adoption the preservation of confidentiality in respect of a parent having handed over a child for adoption would be a matter of life and death.[33]

2.4.3. Article 8: a broad conceptualisation of a child's identity

> *1. States Parties undertake to respect the right of the child to preserve his or her identity, including nationality, name and family relations as recognised by law without unlawful interference.*
> *2. Where a child is illegally deprived of some or all of the elements of his or her identity, States Parties shall provide appropriate assistance and protection, with a view to speedily re-establishing his or her identity.*

Article 8 UNCRC supplements the legal basis of the right to know as covered by Article 7(1) UNCRC. Article 8 is known as the 'Argentine' article. Thus, in **Argentina**, during the Videla dictatorship, between 1975 and 1983, 145 to 170 children 'disappeared' because they were either kidnapped with their parents by

32 BUEREN (1995), p. 122.
33 BUEREN (1995), p. 122.

the authorities or were born in captivity to imprisoned women and then separated from their mothers.[34] Following an arduous search led by the group called the Mothers of the Plaza de Mayo,[35] only 41 of these children were traced back and reunited with their parents.

In seeking to prevent such gross violations of identity rights, **Argentina** submitted a proposal which sought to establish a child's 'inalienable right to retain his true and genuine personal, legal and family identity.'[36] The representatives of **the Netherlands** and **Norway** expressed their apprehension over the need to include such a separate article in the UNCRC, notably because Article 7 on name and nationality, Article 9 on separation from parents and Article 18 on parental responsibilities would already embody the legal identity of the child.[37] The Argentine delegation contended, nonetheless, that a more bracing view of 'identity' was indicated.

Detrick has also drawn attention to the fact that the innovativeness of Article 8 UNCRC in relation to the other provisions concerning the child's identity is implicit in the word 'including', which allows for a broad conceptualisation of a child's identity.[38] In that connection, Hodgson has advocated the view that a minor's evolving 'sexual, linguistic and religious identity could conceivably be comprehended'.[39]

Further, from the *travaux préparatoires* it emerges that the words 'as recognised by law' did not initially refer to the child's 'identity' as such, but were adopted after **the Netherlands** had insisted that the significance of the words 'family relations' and 'family identity' required further specification. On the basis of the present Article 8 UNCRC, it cannot be established if the genetic link between a parent and a child is considered to constitute an integrative part of 'family identity'. This interpretation could be too extensive since no more is required than that States Parties act 'as recognised by law.'

On the other hand, some authoritative commentators have voiced a remarkably extensive interpretation of the child's identity as a legal concept envisaged in the UNCRC. Accordingly, Hodgkin and Newell maintain that a child's right to know

---

34 DETRICK (1999), p. 160.
35 Asociación Madres Plaza de Mayo.
36 DETRICK (1999), p. 160.
37 DETRICK (1999), p. 160.
38 DETRICK (1999), p. 161.
39 HODGSON (1993), p. 255-270, at p. 265. Handbook for the Convention.

encompasses three forms of parenthood. A child would have the right to know not only the genetic parents, but also the birth parents (in surrogacy) and her or his psychological parents.[40] With regard to **Norway**, the Committee on the Rights of the Child has remarked upon the contradiction between 'the child's right to know his or her genetic origins' and the (now abandoned) **Norwegian** policy 'in relation to artificial insemination, namely in keeping the identity of donors secret'.[41] Likewise, **Denmark** has, for example, been criticised for its policy on anonymous donor insemination.[42] In addition, as regards the **French** practice of permitting mothers to give birth anonymously, the Committee has been moderately critical, considering that this 'might not fully reflect the provisions of the Convention, particularly its general principals'.[43] From such comments it may be inferred that the right contained in both Articles 7 and 8 at least covers knowledge of genetic parentage and that this extends to any situation in which the state may influence the availability of information. It follows that the words 'as far as possible' contained in Article 7, far from simply offering a malleable formula or an escape clause, require an appreciable effort on behalf of the States Parties to enable children to access such identifying information.

3. THE UNIVERSAL DECLARATION OF THE HUMAN GENOME AND HUMAN RIGHTS

In discussing the protection of an individual's genetic identity, mention should be made of the Universal Declaration of the Human Genome and Human Rights. This 'soft law' document was adopted unanimously and by acclamation by the General Conference of UNESCO at its 29th Session on 11 November 1997. In a general way, it prohibits cloning and discrimination on the basis of genetically determined characteristics. The underlying rationale for its drafting lies in its attempt to strike a balance between safeguarding respect for human rights and fundamental freedoms and the need to ensure freedom of research. In particular, mention is made of the right of each individual to decide in respect of information concerning the results of genetic examination and the consequences of such an examination contained in Article 5(c). When the person is not in a position to provide consent, in the case of a minor, for example, 'consent or authorization

---

40 HODGKIN & NEWELL (2002), p. 105.
41 HODGKIN & NEWELL (2002), p. 107.
42 Denmark IRCO, Add.33, para. 11, in HODGKIN & NEWELL (2002), p. 119.
43 France IRCO, Add. 20, para. 14 ; Luxembourg IRCO, Add.92, paras. 11 and 29, in HODGKIN & NEWELL (2002), p. 117.

shall be obtained in the manner prescribed by law, guided by the person's best interest', pursuant to Article 5(b). Debatably, then, this provision contains within it an indication that, whenever genetic testing must be conducted – in particular, paternity testing in parentage proceedings – individual autonomy (in the meaning of decisional privacy) should be respected.

4. INTERNATIONAL IMPLEMENTATION MECHANISMS

4.1. ENFORCEMENT OF THE UNCRC

Although the UNCRC undeniably was a huge ratification success, the enforcement of its provisions still depends in large measure on the willingness of the States Parties to implement the rights it contains. In this respect, it is symptomatic that not only has no individual petition right been envisaged for children, but the creation of any procedural mechanism for inter-State challenges is also lacking. The monitoring of the UNCRC has been entrusted to an international Committee of Experts that calls on the States Parties to provide detailed periodical reports on the enforcement mechanisms they have adopted to abide by the Convention's requirements. As from 1 February 2003, the Committee consists of eighteen experts. In accordance with Article 43 UNCRC, these experts have to be chosen on the basis of their high moral standing and competence in the field covered by this Convention. The members of the Committee are elected by States Parties from among their own nationals and serve in their personal capacity, consideration being given to an equitable geographical distribution, as well as to a fair representation of the various legal systems of the world.

By putting particular issues high on the international agenda and sustaining a consistent dialogue with the States Parties, the Committee seeks to enquire about the role played by NGOs in implementing the UNCRC's provisions. The General Guidelines regarding the form and content of initial reports to be submitted by States parties under Article 44, 1(a) and under Article 44, 1(b) draw particular attention to the *de facto* situation rather than the legal situation. Initial reports should be submitted two years after the coming into effect of the UNCRC, whereas periodic reports should be submitted every five years. The Concluding Observations are made public and published in the sessional report and as a separate UN document. In the event of unsatisfactory reporting, the Committee has the right to request additional information. Given the continuous backlog in reporting and the ongoing time constraints which the Committee faces, it has assumed a discretion to choose to present no more than its final concluding observations, while retaining a right to request additional information. If States Parties are overdue in reporting, the Secretariat sends reminders. These reminders may result in a warning that the situation will be examined by experts if no report is presented.

In discussing enforcement mechanisms, as a strength of the UNCRC should also be considered its use as an interpretive tool by courts in both municipal law and regional, especially European, law. As such, it has been said that domestic courts, albeit especially in Europe, have drawn increasingly on the detailed and specific nature of the convention's provisions while referring in some jurisdictions to its international recognition and binding character.[44]

4.2. OTHER INTERNATIONAL IMPLEMENTATION MECHANISMS

Although it goes beyond the scope of this book to describe and assess all alternative remedies and enforcement mechanisms based upon international general human rights treaties, because of their relevance to identity rights they should at least be mentioned. Thus, the UNCRC Committee stated in 1997 that in the absence of a specific mandate, individual communications can only be considered in the light of a spirit of dialogue and as part of the reporting procedure.[45] By contrast, individual communications may be brought to the attention of other human rights treaty bodies.[46]

The United Nations Human Rights Committee may consider individual complaints relating to States Parties to the First Protocol of the ICCPR. Whenever a large number of individual complaints demonstrate 'a consistent pattern of gross and reliably attested violations of human rights', the so-called 1503 procedure, established by the Economic and Social Council in 1970, may be lodged against a State. For our purposes, it is ventured that it may not be entirely inconceivable that this procedure could be lodged, if there has been a gross violation of children's identity rights, for example, to the extent that such violations occurred during the **Argentine** dictatorship.

---

44 KILKELLY (2000), p. 326.

45 VANDENHOLE (2004), p. 283.

46 VANDENHOLE (2004), p. 283.

In principle, the individual complaints procedure before the Human Rights Committee bears a confidential nature, but significant exceptions may be made. Thus, the name of the author may be disclosed, unless the Committee decides otherwise.[47] The rules applicable to the confidentiality regime are contained in Rule 96 of the Committee's Rules of Procedure. Solely written applications are admitted in accordance with Rule 97. Perhaps most significant among the admissibility requirements is the requirement of the exhaustion of domestic remedies, since this is considered by some to be the main reason for refuting a claim. The burden of proof lies with the State to prove that remedies are available and effective. If the allegations are sufficiently well documented by the author, the burden of proof reverts, at least in part, to the State. The State will subsequently have to contribute to the clarification of the matter.[48]

If the Committee concludes that a violation has occurred, a Separate Conclusion is submitted indicating the need for individual reparation and preventive measures.[49] In a case of custody and children's rights, for example, the Committee requested that **Australia** make amends in order to make regular contact by children with their parents and siblings possible.[50] Thus, **Australia** has been requested to refrain from separating a minor from her parents on the basis of the ICCPR.[51]

5. CONCLUDING REMARKS

As has been established, the child's right to know her or his parentage has gained broad recognition internationally, primarily on the basis of Article 7(1) UNCRC. Although the right has not been conceived of as an absolute right, so much is clear that it potentially extends to any situation in which a genetic parent is not known. International protection may become relevant especially if the state has a more or less direct role in influencing the availability of such information. Accordingly, the situations of donor insemination and adoption must at least be covered, but its applicability in socio-legally constructed paternity can, for example, should not a priori be excluded.

47 Rule 96 RoP; UN Doc. A/52/40 (Part I), para. 454.
48 VANDENHOLE (2004), p. 198.
49 UN Doc. A/48/40 (Part I).
50 VANDENHOLE (2004), p. 234; Communication No. 514/1992, *Sandra Frei v. Colombia*, UN Doc. CCPR/C/53/D/514/1992, para. 10.
51 VANDENHOLE (2004), p. 234; Communication No. 930/2000, *Winata v. Australia*, UN Doc. CCPR/C/72/D/930/2000, para. 9.

Although the addressees of the relevant substantive norms are first and foremost children, the recognition of a right to know on the basis of Article 7(1) UNCRC should be regarded as a significant step in the recognition of individual identity rights in general, thereby including adult offspring.

Both parents and the state have a role to fulfil in the implementation of the right to know one's origins, as protected by the UNCRC. Furthermore, doctrinal commentaries add force to the assumption that the right to know one's parents does not lose significance after the child reaches the age of eighteen or ceases to be a minor. There must be something to say for this in view of the formative implications of this right for the construction and evolvement of the child's identity. In protecting a wider, but ill-defined concept of identity, Article 8 UNCRC may also cover the genetic link that children share with their 'parents'. However, it has been observed, too, that Article 8 UNCRC is also sufficiently open-ended, so as to accommodate interpretations which include a child's socio-legal parentage, religious and cultural identity. Furthermore, substantive provisions of the UNCRC and other general human rights documents in the United Nations framework fulfil a complementary character. In terms of enforceability, periodic reports help to ensure a level of protection of the right to information at the international level. Nonetheless, the bottom-line must be that the true effectiveness and reception of international provisions relevant for our discussion is better assessed in an analysis of the national jurisdictions.

CHAPTER III
THE PROTECTION OF CHILDREN'S RIGHT TO KNOW THEIR ORIGINS AT THE REGIONAL LEVEL

1. OUTLINE

This Chapter provides a legal analysis of the scope of the right to know in the regional, European legal framework. The case law on the basis of the notion of the right to private life, as protected under Article 8 ECHR, provides the most significant regional source of law. Some attention will, however, also be devoted to substantive legal provisions. Thus, the data protection instruments of the European Union shall *inter alia* be discussed. The case law shall, in principle, be presented in a chronological order. Nonetheless, a thematic approach has been chosen whenever the factual or legal background of the cases indicates otherwise.

2. SUBSTANTIVE LAW

2.1. THE COUNCIL OF EUROPE

Even though the current body of case law dealing with a right to know one's origins has drawn mostly on the notion of 'private life' as protected under Article 8 ECHR, other regional substantive provisions also bear legal relevance. As far as the ECHR is concerned, it may, for example, be possible that proceedings specifically geared towards obtaining knowledge of one's genetic parentage will be successfully lodged on the basis of Article 10 ECHR, which protects a general right to impart and receive information.[1]

As regards genetic testing, the *Convention on Human Rights and Biomedicine* of 1997 contains as a general rule that consent must be obtained for all medical

1 GRUNDERBEECK (2003), p. 345.

and health interventions.[2] This provision may be relevant for genetic parentage tests if someone wishes to have certainty about hereditary medical conditions. A person's medical right to know in this context will encompass all information collected about his or her health, whether it be diagnosis, prognosis or any other relevant fact.[3] Such a right to obtain genetic information on medical grounds also covers a 'right *not* to know', which is contained in the second paragraph.

Furthermore, during the *XXVIIth Colloquy on European Law on 'Legal problems relating to Parentage'*[4] which took place in Valletta in **Malta** in September 1997, the Council of Europe's Committee of Experts on Family Law (CJ-FA) instructed a Working Party to draw up a comprehensive report containing principles relating to the establishment and legal consequence of parentage. Their efforts resulted in a *White Paper on principles concerning the establishment and legal consequences of parentage* which was adopted in January 2002.[5] Although its twenty-nine Principles lack a legally binding status, it can be contended that, as guidelines to States parties for drafting new legislation concerning the establishment of parentage, they hold some normative authority.

Even though these principles deal primarily with the establishment of legal parentage, they may be relevant for persons who seek to establish details about their genetic parentage.[6] It is specified that the Principles 'are intended to reflect a balance 'between the biological truth', reflecting primarily biological and genetic parentage, and the 'social parenthood', reflecting the fact with whom the child is living and who is taking care of him or her'. This is exemplified by Principle 7 of the 'White Paper.'[7] Principle 7 draws on Article 4 of the 1975

---

2 Art. 10(1) European Convention on Human Rights and Biomedicine.

3 Explanatory Report to the Convention on Biomedicine No. 164, www.coe.int; HERINGA (2005), p. 38.

4 *Legal problems relating to parentage: proceedings. XXVIIth Colloquy on European Law, Foundation for International Studies*, Valletta 1997.

5 [CJFA/docs2001/cj-fa (2001) 16 Rev] PDF.Doc. These principles have also served as a legal source for the Principles Concerning the Establishment and Legal Consequences of Parentage of the 15 January 2002. See: www.coe.int.

6 [CJFA/docs2001/cj-fa (2001) 16 Rev] PDF.Doc.

7 Principle 7:
1. If paternal affiliation is not established by presumptions, the law shall provide for the possibility to establish paternal affiliation by voluntary recognition.
2. States may decide to make such establishment conditional on one or both of the following:
a) the consent of the child, but if the child is not considered by the internal law as having sufficient understanding, the consent of the child's representative;
b) the consent of his or her mother.
3. States can also make the establishment of paternal affiliation by voluntary recognition

European Convention on the legal status of children born out of wedlock in stating that the voluntary recognition of a child may not be opposed or contested in so far as the internal law provides for these procedures, unless the person seeking to recognise the child is not the biological father. An exception to this rule is made in the Principles in relation to medically assisted procreation where it is recommended that paternity should not be based on any biological criterion but on the consent of the mother's life-companion to the fertility treatment. Furthermore, Principle 14 of the *White Paper* calls on the States parties to make available new medical and genetic techniques as well as the use of information concerning the establishment and contestation of parentage.[8]

For our discussion, Principle 28 of the White Paper, because it refers to a 'right' of the child to know his or her origins, retains more immediate relevance.[9] The Commentary[10] on this Principle attests to the Working Group's awareness of the 'controversial nature of this subject' in drafting this provision. In their view this is 'particularly due to the inexistence of a uniform interpretation of Article 7 of the United Nations Convention on the rights of the child'.[11]

In the Commentary it is added that no absolute right should be envisaged. In that connection, some of the already debatable normative content of the word 'right' may have been detracted further in the Working Group's reference thereafter to a children's 'legitimate interest' – as opposed to a 'right' – in respect of knowing their origins.'[12] It is added that in 'certain situations the best interests of the child may justify withholding from the child such information or parts of it.' A passage is also included which refers to the child's 'vital interest' in establishing the truth, on the basis of the *Mikulić* case, which was pending before the ECtHR at the time of the drafting of the White Paper.[13]

---

conditional on the consent or confirmation of a competent authority, when the purpose of this is to ensure that the person having recognised the child meets the requirements prescribed by law.

8 Principle 14:
States shall take steps in order to promote the availability, in proceedings concerning the establishment and contestation of parentage, of new medical and genetic techniques and allow the use of information resulting from such techniques as evidence.

9 Principle 28:
The interest of a child as regards information on his or her biological origin should be duly taken into account in law.

10 [CJFA/docs2001/cj-fa (2001) 16 Rev] PDF.Doc.

11 [CJFA/docs2001/cj-fa (2001) 16 Rev] PDF.Doc.

12 [CJFA/docs2001/cj-fa (2001) 16 Rev] PDF.Doc.

13 ECtHR *Mikulić v. Croatia*, Appl. No. 53176/99, 7 February 2002, para. 59.

Furthermore, in the specific context of ART, mention should be made of the Principles set forth in the *Report on Human Artificial Procreation of the Ad Hoc Committee of Experts on Progress in the Biomedical Sciences* (CAHBI), which were intended as authoritative guidelines for States parties legislating in this field.[14] Remarkably enough, Principle 13 of this report affirms, as a basic rule, that donor anonymity should be maintained.[15] At the same time, however, the Principle does not defend an absolute right to donor anonymity. Rather, the child's health is specifically mentioned as a concern which could indicate a waiver of donor anonymity. It cannot be established on the basis of the Paper's text, however, who in view of such overriding medical concerns should disclose the identifying information to the child.

Even though the lawfulness of a choice for donor anonymity does not appear to have been called into question, states also appear to have considerable leeway in deciding whether they wish to restrict the anonymity of the donor. The possibility is not excluded that a restriction may 'even' culminate in the 'identification' of the donor. Although it has not been specified what 'identification' entails, the wording of this paragraph suggests that it goes beyond the disclosure of the method through which the person had been conceived.

In addition, with regard to adoption, some provisions have also been enacted. These provisions deal with the disclosure of information identifying the birth parents to the adoptee and her or his adoptive family. Accordingly, the European Convention on the Adoption of Children, adopted as early as 24 April 1967, acknowledges the adoptee's right to know, albeit in rather restrictive terms.[16]

---

14 Principles set out in the report of the Ad Hoc Committee of Experts on Progress in the Biomedical Sciences (CAHBI), 1989.

15 Principle 13:
1. The physician and the staff of the establishment using the techniques of artificial procreation shall maintain the anonymity of the donor and, subject to the requirements of the national law in legal proceedings, shall keep secret the identity of the members of the couple as well as the fact of artificial procreation. Where it is necessary in the interests of the child's health or for the purpose of genetic counselling, information on the genetic characteristics of the donor can be given.
2. However, national law may provide that the child, at an appropriate age, may have access to information relating to the manner of his or her conception or even to the identity of the donor.

16 Art. 20 of the European Convention on the Adoption of Children:
1. Provision shall be made to enable an adoption to be completed without disclosing to the child's family the identity of the adopter.
2. Provision shall be made to require or permit adoption proceedings to take place in camera.
3. The adopter and the adopted person shall be able to obtain a document which contains

States parties are only required to provide children with access to extracts from public records mentioning no more than the fact, date and place of birth of the adoptee.

2.2. EUROPEAN UNION DATA PROTECTION LAW

Not only the Council of Europe, but also the European Union has in recent years developed a human rights' framework which may not just become relevant for the protection of the children's right to information but could also be important in safeguarding countervailing rights of parents. As such, Article 3(1) of the *EU Charter of Fundamental Rights* protects the physical and mental integrity of persons. Article 3(2) of the EU Charter specifies *inter alia* that in the field of medicine and biology the free and informed consent of the person must be obtained. This could arguably be read as an indication against compulsory parentage testing without having obtained such consent from the persons concerned.

At the same time, however, Article 7 protects a right to private and family life. More specifically, Article 8(2) of the Fundamental Charter may become relevant for those searching for their genetic origins. This latter provision ensures a right of access to data which have been collected concerning him or her, and the right to have such data rectified.

The central piece of data protection in the European Union consists of the privacy *Directive 95/46/EC* ('the data protection directive'). Each member state provides for at least one public authority which monitors the application within its territory of the provisions that they adopt pursuant to the data protection directive.[17] In addition, the so-called Article 29 Working Group gives independent advice on a wide range of data protection issues. If the Working Group finds that divergences among the Member States may affect the equivalence of the level of protection, it must inform the European Commission.[18]

---

extracts from the public records attesting the fact, date and place of birth of the adopted person, but not expressly revealing the fact of adoption or the identity of his former parents. 4. Public records shall be kept and, in any event, their contents reproduced in such a way as to prevent persons who do not have a legitimate interest from learning the fact that a person has been adopted or, if that is disclosed, the identity of his former parents.

17 Art. 28 EC Directive 95/46/EC.

18 Art. 29(2) EC Directive 95/46/EC.

In the data protection directive, personal data have been defined as 'any information relating to an identified or identifiable natural person ('data subject'); an identifiable person is one who can be identified, directly or indirectly, in particular by reference to an identification number or to one or more factors specific to his physical, mental, economic, cultural or social identity'.[19] Given the broad definition of data that fall under the data protection directive, there is no reason to see why it could not extend to such personal data as information concerning one's birth registration or the processing of genetic data.

That said, the data protection directive does list important exemptions that could also be brought into connection with issues concerning genetic parent-identifying information. Thus, in Article 3(2) of the data protection directive it is made clear that its scope does not extend to 'natural persons in the course of a purely personal' activity. Conceivably, this could include searching for a genetic parent without establishing any contact with him. Furthermore, the processing of such personal data by public authorities may be permitted if processing is 'necessary in order to protect the vital interests of the data subject'.[20] Moreover, states have been accorded a measure of freedom in restricting the protection of personal data if the rights and freedoms of others and the protection of another data subject are at issue.[21]

While awaiting an *ad hoc* advice or recommendation from the Article 29 Working Group, the tentative conclusion may be drawn that the data protection directive leaves room for divergent interpretations in this area. They may favour both the 'vital interests' of the child or the parent who withholds identifying information.

3. THE CASE LAW OF THE EUROPEAN COURT OF HUMAN RIGHTS

3.1. GASKIN: ACCESS TO AN 'INDEPENDENT AUTHORITY'

In tracing the origins of the increased acknowledgement of a right to information concerning one's genetic origins at the regional level, there can be little

[19] Art. 2(1) EC Directive 95/46/EC.
[20] Art. 7(d) EC Directive 95/46/EC.
[21] Art. 13(1) under (g) EC Directive 95/46/EC.

doubt that the ECtHR's judgment in *Gaskin v. the United Kingdom*[22] signified a watershed. For one thing, it is remarkable that this decision followed shortly after the **German** Bundesverfassungsgericht had passed its landmark judgment in that year.[23] What's more, the UNCRC was also adopted by the General Assembly in that same year.

Nonetheless, *Gaskin* can only with some effort be analogized with the issue of access to one's genetic parentage. Thus, the basic question raised in *Gaskin* under Article 8 concerned the extent to which individuals should be entitled to access files compiled on them by public authorities. Indeed, the ECtHR was also careful to add its usual caveat that it was 'not called upon to decide in *abstracto* on questions of general principle.'[24]

The facts concerned a **British** citizen, Mr Gaskin, who, following the death of his mother less than a year after his birth, had been taken into prolonged periods of care by the Liverpool City Council. The applicant claimed that, during his upbringing, he had suffered severe psychological abuse in care during his childhood. In order to overcome the psychological problems he had been facing, he considered it essential to learn as much as he could about his early past. As a result, Mr Gaskin's claim became readily associable with individual interests in the (re)construction of a narrative identity on the basis of one's childhood and remote past, even though he knew the identity of his genetic parents.

Having single-handedly removed a part of the personal records without obtaining the prior consent of Liverpool City Council to which limited access had been granted by the Social Services Department, Mr Gaskin had subsequently made a formal application to access all of his case records. Several years after the High Court had ruled against such disclosure on the ground that this would be in contravention of the public interest, Mr Gaskin applied to the then still active Commission of the ECtHR. The Commission affirmed that a lack of access to information concerning the applicant's childhood, development and history raised issues under Article 8 ECHR, under the notion of both private and family life.

The ECtHR also conceded that the petitioned files concerned Mr Gaskin's 'private and family life' and that the issue fell within the ambit of Article 8

22 ECtHR *Gaskin v. United Kingdom*, Appl. No. 10454/ 7 July 1989.
23 BVerfG, 31 January 1989, *FamRZ* 1989, p. 255. See Chapter IV.
24 ECtHR *Gaskin v. United Kingdom*, Appl. No. 10545/83, 7 July 1989, para. 37.

ECHR.[25] Still, it emphasised the confidentiality of public records. In that connection, the ECtHR added that this confidential nature may also be necessary for the protection of third persons.[26] A system like the **British** one, which had made access to records dependent on the consent of the contributor, could in the Court's view in principle be considered to be reconcilable with the obligations under Article 8 ECHR, while taking into account the State's 'margin of appreciation'. Nonetheless, under such a system the interests of the individual seeking access to records relating to his private and family life would have to be secured when the contributor to the records had either not been available or improperly had refused consent.

Therefore, the ECtHR drew particular attention to the requirement of having an 'independent authority.' It specified that a system like the **British** one would only have been reconcilable with the principle of proportionality if such an 'independent authority' had been able to decide *in concreto* on granting access in cases where a contributor fails to answer or withholds consent. Crucially, though, no such procedure had been made available to Mr Gaskin. Consequently, there had been a failure on the part of the English Courts to secure respect for the applicant's private and family life.[27]

Even so, Mr Gaskin's complaint under Article 10 ECHR proved unsuccessful. In this connection, the ECtHR observed, in accordance with its earlier *Leander v. Sweden*[28] judgment, that the right to freedom to receive information basically prohibits a government from restricting a person from receiving information that others wish or may be willing to impart. It was therefore evident that the information gathered by the public authorities in that earlier case which allegedly related to the applicant's affiliation to a communist party was essentially different from the kind of personal records at stake in *Gaskin*. Notwithstanding such differences, though, the ECtHR held that Article 10 ECHR did not embody any obligation on the State concerned to impart the information.[29] Clearly enough, then, the argument cannot be sustained on the basis of *Gaskin* that a claim under Article 10 ECHR would have been conceded had the applicant been a minor.[30]

---

25 ECtHR *Gaskin v. United Kingdom*, Appl. No. 10454/83, 7 July 1989, para. 37.
26 ECtHR *Gaskin v. United Kingdom*, Appl. No. 10454/83, 7 July 1989, para. 49.
27 ECtHR *Gaskin v. United Kingdom*, Appl. No. 10454/83, 7 July 1989, para. 49.
28 ECtHR *Leander v. Sweden*, Appl. No. 9248/81, 26 March 1987, para. 74.
29 ECtHR *Gaskin v. United Kingdom*, Appl. No. 10454/83, 7 July 1989, para. 51.
30 BUEREN (1995), p. 45.

The bottom-line must be that the factual background in the *Gaskin* case was such that the genetic parents had not been unknown to the applicant and that the decision is therefore only indirectly relevant for claims under Article 8 ECHR to access origins. Even so, the decision retains relevance in view of its insistence on an independent authority to assess claims of a personal nature that affect a person's 'basic identity', which must surely encompass parent-identifying information.

3.2. THE STATE'S 'MARGIN OF APPRECIATION' IN PATERNITY PROCEEDINGS

In the case of *M.B. v. UK*[31] the putative father had wrongly believed that the mother would separate from her husband and come to live with him. She refused to enter into a parental responsibility agreement with the applicant and denied that he was the father. Following a directions hearing before the magistrates' court, the magistrate transferred the applications to the High Court. The High Court decided that no order for tests determining paternity should be made because the applicant had never seen the child. Moreover, the parties had agreed that the relationship between the applicant and the mother had broken down since he had discovered that she had been pregnant. Given this factual background, the High Court considered it unfair to expose the child to the risk of losing the presumption of legitimacy that she had hitherto enjoyed. In addition, it stated that a paternity test should not be carried out against the will of the parent who had sole parental responsibility 'at the behest of a stranger to the marriage' in order to satisfy that 'stranger's own desire to know the truth.'

The Court of Appeal reached a similar conclusion in drawing attention to the fact that the child's welfare depended for the foreseeable future (primarily) on her relationship with her mother, considering the continuity of a stable family environment for the child more important than the presumptive biological father's interests. Having exhausted domestic remedies, the applicant submitted that he had been deprived of a fair hearing contrary to Article 6 ECHR since the **English** courts had refused to order paternity tests. Furthermore, he alleged that his rights under Article 8 ECHR had been breached. Thus, he claimed that the authorities had 'prevented the truth about an aspect of personal identity being discovered.' He added, too, that the courts had deprived the child of knowledge which would enable her to avoid marrying within the prohibited degrees of relationship and that could be relevant to her health. Finally, the applicant

[31] ECtHR *M.B. v. United Kingdom,* Appl. No. 22920/93, 6 April 1994.

submitted that Article 14 ECHR had been infringed in view of the fact that no legal obstacles existed for mothers to see their legal relationship with the child recognised, whereas unmarried fathers were dependent on the co-operation of the mother.

In relation to the applicant's claim under Article 6 ECHR, the Commission concluded that the refusal to give orders for testing had been fully reasoned. The Commission considered that the applicant could not – as a third party – argue that his own rights mirrored the child's 'right to the truth'. Key considerations in that respect were the fact that the applicant had not cohabited with the mother and that the relationship had only lasted six to seven months. As such, the mother's assertion that her husband was the child's biological father was not called into question. Rather, the Commission drew attention to requirements of legal certainty and the security of family relationships. These would allow States to prescribe a general presumption according to which a married man would be regarded as the father of his wife's children while insisting upon 'good cause' in relation to third parties (or 'strangers') such as an (unmarried, putative) biological father. Thus, in this case the fact that the pregnancy had not been planned and that the putative biological father had never seen the child, much less been able to form any emotional bond with the child, appeared to have been decisive in not allowing 'biology' to prevail.

By contrast, in *Keegan,* the ECtHR affirmed that a bond amounting to family life between the child and both parents may exist irrespective of the fact that at the time of the child's birth the parents are no longer cohabiting and their relationship had terminated prior to the child's birth.[32] In that regard, the Court considered that the child's conception had been the result of a deliberate, joint decision, and that the couple had planned to marry. Furthermore, the biological father in *Keegan* had objected to the fact that, following the breakdown of the relationship, the mother had given the child up for adoption. Because such factors would distinguish the case from *M.B. v. UK,* Forder has insisted that 'the crucial thing is the presence or absence of a mutual and discussed intention to conceive a baby and thus to share, not necessarily at all equally, the responsibility for that baby.'[33] Thus, the biological link of the father did not create rights with regard to the establishment of his paternity in either case. Rather, it was this fact in combination with the consensual nature of the procreative choice – their shared intention- at the time of conception which allegedly were decisive

32 ECtHR *Keegan v. Ireland,* Appl. No. 16969/90, 26 May 1994.
33 FORDER (1997), p. 133-134.

in the recognition that in *Keegan* the father's rights under Article 8 ECHR had been breached, whereas in *M.B. v. UK* they had not.

3.3. A FATHER'S RIGHTS TO KNOW THE 'TRUTH'?

In *Kroon and Others v. The Netherlands*[34] the ECtHR faced a claim involving the impossibility of the **Dutch** mother, Catharina Kroon, under the **Dutch** law as it stood, to challenge the paternity of her **Moroccan** husband, Omar M'Hallem Driss, whose whereabouts had become unknown. Ms Kroon did not cohabit with the biological father, Ali Zerrouk. Nonetheless, they had a long stable relationship from which a child, Samir, was born. Under Section 1:198 of the **Dutch** Civil Code the possibility for the mother of a 'legitimate' child to deny the paternity of her husband was only open in respect of a child born within 306 days of the dissolution of the marriage.

The applicants complained that under Articles 8 and 14 ECHR it was not possible for Ms Kroon to have entered in the **Dutch** register of births any statement that Mr M'Halem-Driss was not Samir's father, resulting effectively in an impossibility for Mr Zerrouk to recognise 'his' genetic child. Since the applicants did not wish to marry or to opt for step-parent adoption, suggested by the **Dutch** government as viable alternatives available to them under **Dutch** law, the marital presumption rule retained full force under **Dutch** law as it stood.

The fact that four children had been born from the relationship between Ms Kroon and Mr Zerrouk, formed an important factor in assuming family life notwithstanding the fact that both parents had lived apart.[35] Accordingly, Samir could *ipso iure* be regarded as forming part of the family unit from his birth and by the very fact thereof.[36] Quite regardless of Mr Zerrouk's modest contribution to Samir's upbringing, then, 'family life' between the parties and their son was assumed.[37] The ECtHR could therefore confront the question whether the impossibility to challenge the marital presumption of paternity interfered with the exercise of the parents' family life under Article 8 ECHR. With regard to that question, the court formulated a three-layered rule which holds that 'respect for family life under that provision requires that biological and social reality prevail over a legal presumption which flies in the face of both established fact (1) and

---

34 ECtHR *Kroon and Others v. The Netherlands*, Appl. No. 18535/91, 27 October 1994.

35 ECtHR *Kroon and Others v. The Netherlands*, Appl. No. 18535/91, 27 October 1994, para. 30.

36 ECtHR *Keegan v. Ireland*, Appl. No. 16969/90, 26 May 1994, para. 44.

37 ECtHR *Kroon and Others v. The Netherlands*, Appl. No. 18535/91, 27 October 1994, para. 30.

the wishes of those concerned (2) without actually benefiting anyone (3)'.[38] Consequently, **the Netherlands** had breached its obligations under the Convention.

In *Ibrahim Yildirim v. Austria*[39] the ECtHR decided that the impossibility for the applicant, a **Turkish** immigrant, to rebut a marital presumption rule of paternity under **Austrian** law fell short of the three requirements of the aforementioned *Kroon* formula. Thus, under **Austrian** law, the applicant could not challenge his marriage-based paternity outside the statutory time-limit of one year. Following the expiry of this time-limit, it was up to the Public Prosecutor to file for a rebuttal of the presumption, but the state had waived this competency on the basis of the child's interests. Therefore, the Public Prosecutor attached greater weight to the risk that the child could otherwise lose a maintenance claim against the applicant, even though the applicant had contested that he was the child's father.

In contrast to *Kroon*, in *Ibrahim Yildirim* it was the biological – rather than the legal – father who had become traceless. As such, the ECtHR was careful to distinguish the circumstances of both cases. In fact, in *Ibrahim Yildirim* it could not reasonably be defended either that the marital presumption 'benefited no one', or even that it 'flew in the face of biological and social reality' , because the child had been receiving maintenance from the applicant and would otherwise be deprived of a father, even though by all appearances he shared no genetic link with him. Consequently, 'biology' did not prevail.

In *Jörgen Nylund v. Finland*, a mother had refused the applicant's offer to pay for a voluntary DNA test.[40] Both had disagreed whether it would be at all possible to start legal proceedings concerning only the determination of the biological fact. The father claimed not to be interested in establishing a legal father-child relationship. Moreover, as in *M.B. v. UK*, the applicant sought to 'usurp' the child's fundamental right to know her origins, which the mother allegedly had failed to recognise. The mother was therefore accused by the father of 'judicially kidnapping the child on the formal ground that she had married someone else.'

---

38 ECtHR *Kroon and Others v. The Netherlands*, Appl. No. 18535/91, 27 October 1994, para. 40.
39 ECtHR *Ibrahim Yildirim v. Austria*, Appl. No. 34308/96, 19 October 1999.
40 ECtHR *Nylund v. Finland*, Appl. No. 27110/95, 29 June 1999.

The Court of Appeal rejected the applicant's claims because biological fatherhood in itself would not create any rights or obligations in respect of either the child or the man. Moreover, doubts were cast as to the genuineness of the applicant's concern over the perceived informational needs of the child, since in reality this would be tantamount to a request for the annulment of the husband's presumption of the mother's legal paternity. As the right to information was apparently being used as a cloak, the applicant would therefore not have any legal interest in establishing the truth.

In this case, the ECtHR reiterated the *Kroon* formula, stating that it had been the wish of the mother and her husband not to have their family relationships disturbed by a paternity test. It considered it justifiable for the **Finnish** courts to have given greater weight to the interests of the child and the family than to the interest of the applicant in establishing the biological truth, which, he had claimed, would also have served the child's interests. In that respect, the ECtHR suggested that the child could, at the age of fifteen, decide for herself whether or not she wished to institute paternity proceedings.

This *Nylund* case is highly interesting for our discussion. Firstly, it illustrates the fact that the ECtHR interprets that the child's interests may be better served with requirements of legal certainty and the continuity of a stable family life. In that connection, it shows a certain scepticism towards the interest in establishing the biological fact 'for the sake of truth'. Firstly, this was because the child was still at a tender age and, secondly, because the quest for truth emanated entirely from a third, adult party.

Since *Nylund* a presumptive genetic father has not claimed an identity-related right to know the truth under Article 8. Still, such a man may find himself barred from establishing paternity even if the mother is not married to the legal father. Thus, in the *Różański* case, the applicant also found himself deprived of any possibility of creating legal ties between himself and his child because the child's paternity had been established by the mother's new, unmarried partner, to whom she had given her consent to make a recognition of paternity.[41]The ECtHR considered that 'it was obviously reasonable to take into consideration the fact that the legal paternity of the child had already been established'. However, it held that the **Polish** authorities should have taken steps to establish 'the actual circumstances' of the case.[42] Interestingly, the ECtHR also suggested

41 ECtHR *Różański v. Poland,* Appl. No. 55339/00, 18 May 2006, para. 77.
42 ECtHR *Różański v. Poland,* Appl. No. 55339/00, 18 May 2006, para. 77.

that an interview with the putative father could, for example, have been conducted in order to have his parental skills assessed by the authorities.[43]

3.4. THE INFORMATIONAL INTEREST OF A BIRTHPARENT IN ADOPTION

In *Tiziana Pipoli v. Italy* the ECtHR faced a claim by a birthmother, Ms Pipoli, under Articles 8, 13 and 20 ECHR in relation to the imminent adoption of her children. Her husband had subsequently abandoned both her and the children. Three of the mother's children had been taken into public care. Ms Pipoli, her husband and her father were summoned to appear before the Genoa Youth Court, while facing a warning that if they failed to appear, the children would automatically be declared available for adoption. Because she had not paid heed to this warning, an adoption order by the Genoa Youth Court followed.

The children's grandfather – Ms Pipoli's own father – protested against the adoption order which was then suspended for a period of six months. Subsequently, a psychological report on Ms Pipoli and her husband was drafted which concluded that she was unfit to assume parental responsibility, even to the extent that she represented an obstacle to the children's future emotional development.

The court therefore insisted that the children be placed for adoption. Ms Pipoli invoked Article 8 ECHR and Article 20 of the European Convention on Adoption, pointing out that she did not wish to be given the address of her children, but that her children be enabled to contact her by providing them with her address while also leaving behind some personal information concerning her life.

On the basis of Article 20 and Article 8 ECHR, Ms Pipoli insisted that it was essential for her children's education and emotional development to be informed about their mother, particularly when they would reach majority. Furthermore, Ms Pipoli maintained that her children had the right to grow up together and to keep in touch with each other. On the basis of Article 8 ECHR she claimed a right, as a parent, to control whether this right of her children to 'not be erased from their memory' had been respected. Finally, under Article 13 ECHR she also complained that she had no domestic remedy against the above alleged violations.

---

[43] ECtHR *Różański v. Poland,* Appl. No. 55339/00, 18 May 2006, para. 77.

Still, the ECtHR considered that **Italy** was under no obligation to restore family life after Ms Pipoli's actions. As a consequence, her complaint was even considered to be 'manifestly ill-founded'. In addition, the ECtHR concluded that the **Italian** authorities had not been under any obligation to inform a birthmother whether 'her' three adopted children had been adopted by the same family. Furthermore, the mother would not have a right either under Article 8 ECHR to know whether her children were still in touch with each other. Rather, in the court's eyes it could be considered necessary to limit a parent's freedom in a democratic society to protect the health and interests of the children. As far as the children's right to know was concerned, the ECtHR submitted that there was nothing which suggested that their emotional development had been or would be adversely influenced by not being able to find out about her.

As such, as had occurred previously in the *Nylund* case, the ECtHR showed strong reservations against a parent instrumentalising, or even 'hijacking,' a child's right to know even if the parent had no ulterior motive in reviewing or maintaining a family law relationship with the child. The question whether the children might have been able to benefit from obtaining such information was, however, disregarded by the ECtHR.

3.5. A STATE'S MARGIN OF APPRECIATION 'IN RELATION TO DONOR ANONYMITY'

The case of *X, Y and Z v. the United Kingdom*[44] concerned a couple, X and Y, composed of a post-operative female-to-male transsexual (X) and a woman (Y) who had produced a child, Z, as a result of artificial insemination by anonymous donor. This was not the first case in which the ECtHR had to decide on issues involving the legal concept of family life in the context of artificial insemination. Thus, in an earlier case, the ECtHR had already observed that the situation in which a person donated sperm with a view to enabling a woman to become pregnant did not give a known donor a right to respect for family life with the child.[45]

Yet in *X, Y and Z*, the ECtHR was faced with a rather different claim. It involved a social 'father', whose uncertainty over the legal consequences as a result of gender reassignment constituted a complicating factor, which, however, is not immediately relevant for our discussion. The **British** Government had not

44 ECtHR *X, Y and Z v. the United Kingdom*, Appl. No. 21830/93, 22 April 1997.
45 ECtHR *J.R.M. v. the Netherlands*, Appl. No. 16944/90, 8 February 1993.

accepted the complaint of the applicants that the concept of 'family life' extended to their relationship and had refused to register X as the father of Z. According to the applicant, this amounted to a violation of Article 8 ECHR in conjunction with Article 14.

In the ECtHR's submission, the **United Kingdom** had to be accorded a wide 'margin of appreciation' in meeting its obligations under Article 8 ECHR.[46] It considered that the **United Kingdom** had been justifiably cautious in reviewing the law in view of undesirable or unforeseen consequences for children in Z's position.[47] In foreseeing profound legal consequences if the law had to be amended, the ECtHR did not regard the impossibility for Z to inherit from X as an obstacle.[48] The legal problem concerning intestate succession could be solved by X if the applicant made a will.

The applicants had expressed concern that Z's sense of personal identity and security within her family might become affected as a result of X's impossibility to be registered as the father of Z.[49] While dispensing with any attempt to delve into the deeper ethical issues at hand, the ECtHR stated that, unless X and Y were to choose to disclose anything, neither the child nor any third party would have to find out that X, as Z's social father, had in fact been born female. Thus, in the ECtHR's view the situation of the applicants could be analogised with that of any other family in which, for whatever reason, a person taking on the role of the child's 'father' is not registered as such. Moreover, the stigma attached to children or families in such circumstances would have diminished.[50] In addition, the Court recalled that a birth certificate in the **United Kingdom** was not commonly used for administrative or identification purposes, with occasions when it is necessary to produce a full length certificate being few.[51] Furthermore, nothing prevented X from giving 'his' surname to Z.[52]In that light, the Court concluded that Article 8 ECHR could not be taken to imply an obligation for the respondent State formally to recognise as the father of a child 'a person who is not the biological father'.[53]

---

46 ECtHR *X, Y and Z v. the United Kingdom*, Appl. No. 21830/93, 22 April 1997, para. 44.
47 ECtHR *X, Y and Z v. the United Kingdom*, Appl. No. 21830/93, 22 April 1997, para. 47.
48 ECtHR *X, Y and Z v. the United Kingdom*, Appl. No. 21830/93, 22 April 1997, para. 48.
49 ECtHR *X, Y and Z v. the United Kingdom*, Appl. No. 21830/93, 22 April 1997, para. 50.
50 ECtHR *X, Y and Z v. the United Kingdom*, Appl. No. 21830/93, 22 April 1997, para. 49.
51 ECtHR *X, Y and Z v. the United Kingdom*, Appl. No. 21830/93, 22 April 1997, para. 49.
52 ECtHR *X, Y and Z v. the United Kingdom*, Appl. No. 21830/93, 22 April 1997, para. 50.
53 ECtHR *X, Y and Z v. the United Kingdom*, Appl. No. 21830/93, 22 April 1997, para. 52.

For our discussion, it was especially interesting that in a Concurring Opinion Judge Pettiti referred to the issue of a child's right to know.[54] In his view, the Court should have given more thought to the child's needs in that respect. As such, Z would sooner or later come to consider that her own interest lies in finding out who her biological father was.[55] From that viewpoint, it would have been better if the case had been framed into such a prospective mould, which would thereby also have to take into consideration Article 7-1 of the UNCRC. As such, the case may indeed have been a missed opportunity to draw attention to the child's (prospective) informational legal interest under Article 8 ECHR.

3.6. MIKULIĆ: A 'VITAL INTEREST' IN RECEIVING INFORMATION

It was not until the case of *Mikulić*[56] came before the ECtHR that a 'right' to know unequivocally achieved some recognition under the notion of the right to private life. The case was important in at least two respects. Firstly, the ECtHR referred more expressly to the determination of parentage as an issue relevant for the development of individual identity and therefore worth legal protection under Article 8 ECHR. Secondly, more strict procedural and time-related safeguards, providing a check on a state's discretion in deciding on paternity proceedings, were built into the court's line of argumentation.

The applicant was a child born out of wedlock aged two months at the time when her mother filed a suit against the Zagreb Municipal Court in order to establish her putative father's paternity. Before the domestic **Croatian** courts, the putative father had refused on no fewer than six occasions to undergo testing relying instead on the '*exceptio plurium concubentium*', thereby suggesting that the mother had had sexual relations with other men at the time of the applicant's conception. As a result, the appellate court found that the First Instance Court had failed to establish all the relevant evidence, while adding that paternity could not just be established on a putative father's refusal to undergo a DNA test. In the ensuing proceedings, the First Instance Court concluded the case and passed its judgment, which nonetheless established the defendant's paternity and granted the applicant full child maintenance. At this point, it was found that the

[54] Concurring Opinion of Judge Pettiti, ECtHR *X, Y and Z v. the United Kingdom*, Appl. No. 21830/93, 22 April 1997, para. 49.

[55] Concurring Opinion of Judge Pettiti, ECtHR *X, Y and Z v. the United Kingdom*, Appl. No. 21830/93, 22 April 1997, para. 49.

[56] ECtHR *Mikulić v. Croatia*, Appl. No. 53176/99, 7 February 2002.

persistent refusal to co-operate with testing only served to corroborate the mother's testimony that he was, in actual fact, the applicant's begetter.

Before the ECtHR the applicant complained that **Croatia** had failed to conduct the paternity proceedings within a reasonable time-limit, as required by Article 6(1) of the Convention. While conceding that special urgency could be required in family proceedings, **Croatia** submitted that the mother had contributed to the delay in the proceedings because she had not petitioned for an order for DNA testing until a relatively late stage in the proceedings.

The ECtHR objected, pointing out that particular diligence is required in cases concerning civil status and capacity.[57] In this regard, it stressed that the minor's right to have her paternity established or refuted and to have her uncertainty as to the identity of her natural father eliminated, fell within the ambit of Article 6(1) ECHR. Accordingly, **Croatia** had been under a duty to observe particular diligence in ensuring the progress of the proceedings.[58]

The ECtHR emphasised that the proceedings had been pending for over four years during which it had been impossible to adjourn even a single hearing on account of the applicant's conduct. The government's contention that this was partly attributable to the persistent refusal of the putative father to undergo testing did not prevent the Court from finding that Article 6(1) ECHR had been violated by the public authorities.

But the applicant's claim went beyond that issue. She had also submitted that the resultant state of prolonged uncertainty as to her personal identity on account of the inefficiency of the domestic courts had resulted in a violation of Article 8 ECHR. The ECtHR was therefore required to determine whether the right invoked by the applicant fell within the scope of the concept of 'respect for private and family life' laid down in Article 8 ECHR.

In examining whether the claim could be brought under the notion of 'family life' under Article 8 ECHR, the ECtHR first observed that paternity proceedings fall under that provision's scope. In contradistinction to its earlier case law, it added, however, that no family tie had ever been able to develop between the applicant and the putative father. However, under the notion of private life, it proved less difficult to bring this claim under the scope of Article 8 ECHR. Since

---

57 ECtHR *Bock v. Germany,* judgment of 29 March 1989, Series A No. 150, p. 23, para. 49.
58 ECtHR *Mikulić v. Croatia,* Appl. No. 53176/99, 7 February 2002, para. 44.

Rasmussen, 'private life' had been assumed to have been affected with regard to proceedings in which paternity had been challenged.[59] In the instant case, however, it had proved impossible to establish family ties between the putative father and the child in the first place.

Even so, the right to 'private life', in the ECtHR's view, also covered a person's physical and psychological integrity and could sometimes embrace aspects of an individual's physical and social identity. Conceptualised in this way, respect for 'private life' would also comprise, to a certain degree, a right to establish relationships with other human beings.[60] As a result, there was no reason of principle why the notion of 'private life' would exclude the determination of a legal relationship between a child born out of wedlock and her natural father.[61] In brief, then, the complaint fell under the notion of 'private life'.

In unravelling its 'classical' line of argumentation in Article 8 cases, the ECtHR affirmed that respect for 'family life' and 'private life' require a State to take on 'positive obligations'; it added that distinctions between 'positive' and 'negative obligations' do not lend themselves to a precise definition. In order to assess whether such a positive obligation exists, regard would have to be had to the fair balance which must be struck between the general interests vis-à-vis those pertaining to the individual. As established time and again in its case law, the State would also enjoy a 'margin of appreciation' in striking such a 'fair balance' in paternity proceedings.

In particular, the ECtHR went on to make a statement, hitherto unheard, with potentially profound implications for the scope of the right to know one's origins. Thus, it stated that persons in the applicant's situation had a 'vital interest, protected by the Convention, in receiving the information necessary to uncover the truth about an important aspect of their personal identity'. These words, in which the earlier case of *Gaskin* resounded, were cast into a slightly different mould. Debatably, this was the Court's first tentative avowal that a minor child had a constitutional right to access information concerning her or his genetic parentage under Article 8. At the very least, it affirmed that the

---

59 ECtHR *Judmaier v. Austria*, Appl. No. 24659/94, 28 June 1995; ECtHR *Manfred Burger v. Austria*, Appl. No. 26100/95, 16 October 1996; ECtHR *Ibrahim Yildirim v. Austria*, Appl. No. 34308/96, 19 October 1999.

60 ECtHR *Mikulić v. Croatia*, Appl. No. 53176/99, 7 February 2002, para. 53; see also: ECtHR *Niemitz v. Germany*, Appl. No. 13710/88, 16 December 1992, para. 29.

61 ECtHR *Mikulić v. Croatia*, Appl. No. 53176/99, 7 February 2002, para. 53.

disclosure of information concerning one's genetic parentage could have potentially strong formative implications in relation to an individual's sense of identity.

Furthermore, in the requirement pertaining to the availability of alternative means enabling an 'independent authority' to determine a paternity claim speedily, the earlier case of *Gaskin* also resounded. Yet given the factual background to this case, it addressed the establishment of paternity.[62]

On this issue, the ECtHR stated that 'it must be borne in mind that the protection of third persons may preclude their being compelled to make themselves available for medical testing of any kind, including DNA testing.'[63] In this regard, the ECtHR took note of the variety of solutions that the States parties to the Convention displayed in addressing legal problems that arise when a putative father refuses to comply with court orders to submit to the tests which are necessary to establish the facts.[64]

The lack of means for compelling the putative father to comply with a court order for DNA tests to be carried out in **Croatia** could, accordingly, in principle be considered to be compatible with the obligations deriving from Article 8 ECHR, while taking into account the State's 'margin of appreciation'.[65] The ECtHR considered that in a system lacking any compulsory physical examination to undergo paternity testing, as the **Croatian** one, the interests of the individual seeking the establishment of paternity would still have to be secured by alternative means. Therefore, the lack of any procedural measure at all under **Croatian** law to compel the putative father to comply with the court order failed to meet the requirements of the principle of proportionality which meant that an independent authority could not determine the paternity claim speedily.

Not long after *Mikulić*, in *Szarapo v. Poland*[66] the ECtHR was faced with another complaint concerning a persistent refusal on the part of the putative biological father to undergo DNA testing. Here it had taken the **Polish** judicial authorities a staggering fifteen years to decide on a single paternity claim. In drawing attention to the absurd length of the proceedings, the ECtHR observed that particular diligence was required in cases concerning civil status and capacity. In that light, it was concluded that very grave judicial errors had been

---

62 ECtHR *Mikulić v. Croatia,* Appl. No. 53176/99, 7 February 2002, para. 64.

63 ECtHR *Mikulić v. Croatia,* Appl. No. 53176/99, 7 February 2002, para. 64.

64 ECtHR *Mikulić v. Croatia,* Appl. No. 53176/99, 7 February 2002, para. 64

65 ECtHR *Mikulić v. Croatia,* Appl. No. 53176/99, 7 February 2002, para. 64.

66 ECtHR *Szarapo v. Poland,* Appl. No. 40835/98, 23 May 2002.

made by the **Polish** authorities. This was considered to be especially pertinent given the fact that the **Polish** courts at an early stage of the proceedings had already had voluminous evidence at their disposal, including, *inter alia*, the testimony of witnesses, several expert opinions as well as two conclusive sets of biological tests.[67] Taken together, this in the ECtHR's view provided a sufficiently strong basis for a decision establishing the paternity of the defendant. Accordingly, the length of the proceedings had manifestly transgressed the requirements incumbent on **Poland** pursuant to Article 6 ECHR on a reasonable procedural length and effectiveness.[68]

3.7. HAAS: THE RELEVANCE OF AN IDEOLOGICAL MOTIVE

In *Haas v. the Netherlands*[69] the applicant stated that he had been born from a relationship between his mother and a civil law notary[70] named Mr P., who had never married the mother or recognised paternity. Even so, he had made regular payments towards the applicant's upbringing and care and had regular contact with him throughout his childhood.

Remarkably enough for someone who had been a civil law notary during his working life, the putative father had passed away without leaving any will. In accordance with the **Dutch** law of intestate succession, his nephew was then identified as the sole heir. His 'son', the applicant objected, had brought proceedings which were geared towards claiming his share of the inheritance back from the nephew. The Arnhem Regional Court dismissed his claim on grounds of legal certainty, which would be such that they required that only persons with a demonstrable legal family connection with the deceased would be able to inherit.

In the absence of proof of a genetic link between him and the deceased, the applicant's mother affirmed that she had not had sexual relations with any other man until nine years after the applicant's birth. Furthermore, none of the four witnesses who appeared before the Arnhem Court of Appeal denied that the civil law notary called into question that the deceased had been the applicant's genetic father. Still, the Arnhem Court of Appeal rejected the applicant's inhe-

67 ECtHR *Szarapo v. Poland,* Appl. No. 40835/98, 23 May 2002, para. 43.

68 The length of paternity proceedings also violated Art. 6 ECHR in an earlier, similar case concerning a putative father's persistent refusal to undergo testing. See: ECtHR *Bánošová v. Slovakia,* Appl. No. 38798/97, 19 April 2001.

69 ECtHR *Haas v. the Netherlands*, Appl. No. 36983/97, 13 January 2004.

70 *Notaris.*

ritance claim in the absence of any family law relationship. An appeal on points of law before the Supreme Court also failed for largely similar reasons.[71]

Having exhausted all the domestic judicial remedies, the applicant brought his claim under Article 8 ECHR in conjunction with Article 14 ECHR before the ECtHR. Thus, the applicant claimed to have been made a victim of a difference in treatment between 'illegitimate' offspring who had had the 'fortune' of having been recognised by their father, whereas other 'illegitimate' offspring could not claim any inheritance.[72] For its part, the **Dutch** Government insisted that no 'family life' had ever existed between the applicant and the deceased, while adding that DNA testing could in principle have been used to demonstrate the existence of the genetic link between Mr P. and the applicant. But because the body of the deceased had already been cremated and he had left no other children with whom his genetic material could be compared, no reliable test could be taken. The fact that the putative father had never made the effort to recognise his paternity was considered important in the **Dutch** government's view. Moreover, it made no difference, in the Government's submission, that legislation had been enacted to the effect of allowing a *post mortem* judicial determination of paternity because this would have no bearing on the applicant's case.[73]

In determining whether the prerequisite 'family life' had ever existed between the applicant and the civil law notary, the ECtHR drew a distinction with its earlier case of *Camp and Bourimi v. the Netherlands.*[74] In that case, which had also concerned an intestate succession of a child who had never been recognised by his father, it had not been called into question that Mr Bourimi had wished to establish a legal child-father relationship. Here letters of legitimation had provided sufficient proof of family-law relationships. For that reason, *Camp and Bourimi* would be distinguishable from *Haas* because the putative father had clearly not wished, during his lifetime, to become the applicant's legal father. It followed that in *Haas* the applicant had to rely on informal tokens of supposedly fatherly feelings, such as family photos and letters, to challenge such assertions.

In effect, then, in the *Haas* case, the ECtHR denied that the applicant had any identity-related legal interest in establishing his father's paternity posthumously. Rather, the ECtHR paraphrased the applicant's claim as being essentially a

---

71 Hoge Raad 17 January 1997, *NJ* 1997, p. 483.

72 ECtHR *Haas v. the Netherlands*, Appl. No. 36983/97, 13 January 2004, para. 33.

73 ECtHR *Haas v. the Netherlands*, Appl. No. 36983/97, 13 January 2004, para. 39.

74 ECtHR *Camp and Bourimi v. The Netherlands,* Appl. No. 28369/95, 3 October 2000.

complaint about the refusal of the courts to examine and recognise his claim to the estate of Mr P. over that of his nephew.[75] Plainly, it was not about a deeper question involving his personal identity but about the division of an inheritance. If he had really been so concerned about finding out the truth, then, sure enough, he would not have been 'convinced in his own mind that he is the unrecognised illegitimate son of Mr P'? In the court's eyes, then, the claim was 'not aimed at imbuing him with any emotional security of knowing that he is part of a family, even less so to enable him to create ties with Mr P.'s surviving family – he is convinced in his own mind that he is the unrecognised illegitimate son of Mr P.'[76] In this way, the ECtHR not only insinuated that the applicant's wish to establish paternity with the clear, ulterior aim of claiming an inheritance was not worthy of protection under Article 8 ECHR. It also affirmed that the genuineness of the applicant's motive in establishing the biological truth in relation to his own identity may apparently be scrutinised by the courts.

3.8. ODIÈVRE: ANONYMOUS AND DISCREET BIRTH

In *Odièvre v. France*,[77] the ECtHR was faced with a claim which went to some core issues affecting the scope of the right to know one's genetic origins. The **French** government claimed a set of public interests in defence of the right of women to give birth anonymously. Although it has been suggested that the value of the judgment is limited because of its highly specific context, some apparent argumentative flaws and the lack of consensus between the judges, the case stands out as a landmark case in assessing the scope of the right to know under the ECHR.[78]

The applicant, Pascale Odièvre, had been born in March 1965. Her birthmother requested that her birth be kept secret and handed her over to the public authorities for adoption. A full adoption order took effect in February 1969, in favour of Mr and Mrs Odièvre, whose surname the applicant replaced for that appearing on her original birth certificate. She maintained that her request for information about strictly personal aspects of her history and childhood fell within the ambit of Article 8 ECHR, not only as part of her 'private life', but also under the notion of 'family life' with her natural family, with whom she hoped to establish emotional ties.

---

75 ECtHR *Haas v. Netherlands*, Appl. No. 36983/97, 13 January 2004, para. 43.

76 ECtHR *Haas v. the Netherlands*, Appl. No. 36983/97, 13 January 2004, para. 42.

77 ECtHR *Odièvre v. France*, Appl. No. 42326/98, 13 February 2003.

78 Kilkelly (2004), p. 9.

In presenting herself to the **French** media as a champion of children's rights,[79] the applicant maintained that she had been prevented from establishing such ties with her genetic parents. A long-standing historical legal tradition, popularly and internationally known as the '*accouchement sous X*', gave mothers a right to give birth anonymously and thereby to withhold identifying information from the child.[80]

The ECtHR's assessment of the applicant's claims under the notions of private life and family life under Article 8 ECHR were preceded by a historical and comparative overview. This served as an explanatory note, or one daresay, an attempt to find some 'redeeming features' in the **French** system to account for its anomalous position in the wider European context. Notwithstanding some attempts by the **French** government to strike a balance between the competing interests of the state, the mother and the child, the applicant criticised **French** law's 'blind preference for the mother's alleged interests, in manifest contempt of the rights of the child.'[81]

The applicant's claim under the notion of family life in Article 8 ECHR was denied since the applicant's family life would only affect her legal, adoptive family.[82] Still, the impact of **French** law on her right to private life was admitted, since the applicant had a 'vital interest protected by the Convention in obtaining information necessary to discover the truth concerning important aspects of one's personal identity, such as the identity of one's parents'.[83] Accordingly, the ECtHR conceded that the circumstances in which a child is born form part of a child's, and subsequently an adult's, 'private life.'[84]

The ECtHR went on to affirm *expressis verbis* that 'people have a right to know their origins, that right being derived from a wide interpretation of the scope of the notion of private life'. The court had not yet expressly acknowledged such a right. Even so, the ECtHR immediately detracted from the obviously potentially far-reaching implications of its words, in also acknowledging 'a woman's interest in remaining anonymous in order to protect her health by giving birth in appropriate medical conditions.' Showing little empathy for the applicant or understanding why she would go to such lengths to identify her mother, the

---

79 ECtHR *Odièvre v. France*, Appl. No. 42326/98, 13 February 2003, para. 31.
80 See Chapter VI.
81 ECtHR *Odièvre v. France*, Appl. No. 42326/98, 13 February 2003, para. 33.
82 ECtHR *Odièvre v. France*, Appl. No. 42326/98, 13 February 2003, para. 28.
83 ECtHR *Mikulić v. Croatia*, Appl. No. 53176/99, paras. 54 and 64.
84 ECtHR *Odièvre v. France*, Appl. No. 42326/98, 13 February 2003, para. 28.

ECtHR found that her birthmother had in fact shown a 'total indifference' towards her.[85]

Moreover, the ECtHR attached weight to the fact that both applicants were adults at the time of the proceedings. As a consequence, the interest of two adults in both enjoying a right to private (or family life) would in principle have to be weighed on a 'footing of equality.' Furthermore, the interests of third parties would have to be taken into consideration.[86]In drawing attention to the fact that the applicant had already been adopted at the age of four, the ECtHR stressed that any non-consensual disclosure would entail substantial 'risks.' Such risks would not only undermine the privacy interests of the birthmother, but also those of her adoptive family, who had brought her up, and, lest it be forgotten, also those of her 'natural father and siblings, each of whom also had a right to respect for his or her privacy and family life.'[87]

This high regard for the interests of the adoptive family was remarkable since it cannot be inferred from the decision that they had in fact opposed the applicant's claim. Moreover, the elevation of the interests of third parties appeared to contradict the ECtHR's earlier observation that the applicant's family life had not been affected. If her own 'family life' was not affected, then, it would appear all the less credible to state that the family life of siblings or family life in general *had* been jeopardised.[88]

Having explored the conflict of rights at the horizontal level, the ECtHR then went on to consider the public interests which opposed disclosure. In that connection, the right to respect for life, as a 'higher-ranking value of the Convention',[89] was identified as a core principle of the **French** system. As a consequence, due regard would have to be paid to such supervening public interests. In that respect, **France** was given a broad 'margin of appreciation', notwithstanding the clearly anomalous position of **French** law *vis-à-vis* the vast majority of European states.

Rather than calling into question the isolated position of **France**, Judge Ress concurred that **France** should enjoy a broad 'margin of appreciation' in view of

85 ECtHR *Odièvre v. France*, Appl. No. 42326/98, 13 February 2003, para. 44.
86 ECtHR *Odièvre v. France*, Appl. No. 42326/98, 13 February 2003, para. 44.
87 ECtHR *Odièvre v. France*, Appl. No. 42326/98, 13 February 2003, para. 44.
88 Callus (2004), p. 665.
89 ECtHR *Odièvre v. France*, Appl. No. 42326/98, 13 February 2003, para. 45.

the legitimate aims which '*accouchement sous X*' pursued.[90] Judge Ress also contended that the State party is entitled in situations of distress for the mother to give precedence to her interests over the child's right to know. An outright disdain for the applicant's wish to know her genetic descent was, in fact, barely masked in Judge Ress' assertion, who suggested that 'persons who seek disclosure at any price, even against the express will of their natural mother, must ask themselves whether they would have been born had it not been for the right to give birth anonymously.' Still, this remarkable Concurring Opinion raised the question whether the **French** system of anonymous births had actually succeeded in reducing the number of abortions. The alternative of automatic adoption, while guaranteeing the essence of the right to know, would entail a risk factor in that regard.

The question whether the measures of the **French** system were proportionate to the public aims pursued was not further explored. With its implicit recognition that these measures were proportional, the ECtHR probably did not mean to say that a protection of the right to life would be at peril in the overwhelming majority of European countries, where a higher incidences of clandestine abortions or neo-naticide has not been attested.[91]

Finally, the ECtHR affirmed that a sufficiently broad 'margin of appreciation' must be accorded to the state in view of the 'complex and sensitive nature of the issue of access to information about one's origins'. In that connection, it set forth four relevant factors. Thus, in balancing the right to know, it was important, too, to consider the 'choices of the natural parents, the existing family ties and the adoptive parents'.[92] Furthermore, attention would, as a rule, have to be drawn to the fact that the applicant had been given access to non-identifying information about her mother and natural family. As a consequence, some of her informational needs would have been met. In particular, a waiver of the confidentiality of the information, something which had technically become a possibility in **France** since 2002, was significant. In addition, the creation of an independent authority dealing with questions of access to parent-identifying information and equipped with 'professional people with good practical knowledge of the issues' was considered to be a relevant factor in assuming that the new **French** legislation had sought to strike a fair balance and to ensure sufficient protection between the competing interests.

---

90 Concurring Opinion of Judge Ress joined by Judge Kūris, ECtHR *Odièvre v. France*, Appl. No. 42326/98, 13 February 2003, para. 3.

91 CALLUS (2004), p. 664; MALLET-CRIOUT (2003), p. 1243.

92 ECtHR *Odièvre v. France*, Appl. No. 42326/98, 13 February 2003, para. 49.

As far as the applicant's claim under Article 14 ECHR was concerned, the ECtHR argued that her claim derived essentially from a desire to find out her genetic origins. In that respect, the ECtHR distinguished the facts of the case from *Haas*, in which the applicant had made no secret of his motives to claim an inheritance. In *Odièvre*, however, the applicant already had parental ties with her adoptive family from whom she could inherit.[93] It followed that her situation with regard to her natural mother should not be compared with that of other children who have parental ties with their own natural mother.[94]

In 2008, the ECtHR came to decide upon another case on *accouchement sous X*, in which an **Irish** woman had gone to **France** to give birth anonymously in 2002 to a daughter conceived in an extramarital relationship.[95] The conditions and effects of an anonymous registration of a birth had been explained to her during two interviews, particularly the two-month period within which, after handing the child over to the **French** public authorities, the mother could still request the child's return. Since the mother could not speak or understand French, the applicant was assisted by a nurse and doctor who spoke English and acted as interpreters. Having regretted her decision, the applicant complained of the shortness of this two-month period and argued that she had not been provided with adequate linguistic assistance. The ECtHR considered, however, that the time-limit given to the birthmother for review should be considered sufficient and that she had been informed as thoroughly as possible in English of the consequences of her choice. As such, the ECtHR in this latest case seems to have reaffirmed that anonymous birth in **France** is in principle compatible with the state's margin of appreciation under Article 8 ECHR.

3.9. EVANS: WITHDRAWAL OF CONSENT TO IVF TREATMENT AND THE 'RIGHT TO A GENETICALLY-RELATED CHILD'

In *Evans*, the ECtHR was confronted with a case concerning the withdrawal of consent by an unmarried man to the IVF treatment that a woman, Ms Evans, suffering from ovarian cancer, had sought.[96] Ms Evans brought a claim under both Article 2 ECHR and Article 8 ECHR in conjunction with Article 14 ECHR. Since her ovaries had been removed but she still wished to have a genetically-related child, embryos were created with her eggs and her former partner's

---

93 ECtHR *Odièvre v. France*, Appl. No. 42326/98, 13 February 2003, para. 56.

94 ECtHR *Odièvre v. France*, Appl. No. 42326/98, 13 February 2003, para. 56.

95 ECtHR *Kearns v. France*, Appl. No. 35991/04, 10 January 2008.

96 ECtHR *Evans v. the United Kingdom*, Appl. No. 6339/05, 7 March 2006; KÜTHE & TURVEY (2007), p. 872-876.

sperm. Taking the view that the **British** government should not have allowed her former partner to resile from his assurances with impunity, Ms Evans held that her ex-partner had compromised his own freedom by having previously agreed to have her last eggs fertilised.[97]

The **English** Court of Appeal considered that the case was essentially about a woman seeking IVF treatment whose partner had withdrawn his consent. On the other hand, it contended that the real comparators should be fertile versus infertile women, since the genetic father could always withdraw his consent to a procreative choice at a later stage unlike in ordinary sexual intercourse. Moreover, IVF treatment entailed a much heavier burden on the female than the male party, both physically and psychologically. Even so, the parties had not called into question before the domestic courts that the so-called 'bright-line' rule implied in Schedule 3 of the Human Fertilisation and Embryology Act 1990 applied, which permitted a withdrawal of consent no later than the implantation of the embryo. Furthermore, both parties had not previously disputed that the male party had withdrawn consent in 'good faith'. In that connection, the Court of Appeal recalled that a primary policy objective had been the promotion of the welfare of the child born as a result of the IVF treatment. As a further policy objective, the continued bilateral consent throughout the process up to the implantation of embryos was to be ensured through the 'bright-line' legislation, which meant that parenthood would not be thrust upon either party.

For its part, the ECtHR recalled that the in the absence of consensus in European jurisdictions on the scientific and legal definition of the beginning of life, the issue if and when the right to life, as protected by Article 2 ECHR, fell within the margin of appreciation of the States Parties.[98] Accordingly, it would not be irreconcilable with the protection of the right to life protected under Article 2 ECHR for the **United Kingdom** to maintain that an embryo does not have independent rights or interests under **English** law.[99] Nonetheless, the ECtHR acknowledged that IVF treatment gave rise to sensitive moral and ethical issues while the case touched upon areas where no clear common ground could yet be discerned amongst the Member States. As such, it was submitted that a State party would require a wide margin of appreciation.

---

97 ECtHR *Evans v. the United Kingdom,* Appl. No. 6339/05, 7 March 2006, para. 49.

98 ECtHR *Evans v. the United Kingdom,* Appl. No. 6339/05, 7 March 2006, para. 46; ECtHR *Vo v. France*, 8 July 2004, Appl. No. 53924/00, para. 82.

99 ECtHR *Evans v. the United Kingdom,* Appl. No. 6339/05, 7 March 2006, para. 46.

The ECtHR distinguished the case from both *Pretty v. the United Kingdom,*[100] which had concerned assisted suicide, as well as the *Odièvre* case. Both of these ECtHR cases had been invoked by the **British** government as precedents to the extent that they would attest to the legitimacy of so-called 'bright-line' rules in ethical areas where private interests could clash. According to the **British** government, a 'bright-line' rule could be required in the law, even in a highly sensitive, ethical area in order to provide legal certainty and to maintain public confidence in the law.[101] The ECHR conceded that making the withdrawal of the male donor's consent relevant but not conclusive or granting decisional power to individual clinics would have occasioned further problems affecting the appropriate weight to be attached to the respective individual rights.[102] In particular, a change in circumstances subsequent to the beginning of IVF treatment could provoke 'new and even more intractable difficulties of arbitrariness and inconsistency' being created.[103]

The ECtHR did not follow the applicant's argument that the situation of the male and female could not be equated because the female invariably carries a heavier physical and psychological burden in IVF treatment[104] Thus, Ms Evans had claimed that, generally, a fair balance could only be preserved by holding the male donor to his word and not to enable him to withdraw consent. Following the High Court's opinion, the ECtHR observed, though, that Schedule 3 applied equally to all patients undergoing IVF treatment, irrespective of their sex. The ECtHR also replicated the High Court's observation that it would not be difficult to conceive of an infertile man facing a dilemma similar to that of Ms Evans in a case of egg donation. For such reasons, the ECtHR concluded that in having adopted a clear and principled rule, which had been clearly set out in the forms which both parties had signed, the **United Kingdom** had not overstepped its margin of appreciation.

As a subsidiary claim, Ms Evans held that her rights under Article 8 in conjunction with Article 14 ECHR had also been breached since she – unlike fertile women – had been unable to conceive without assistance and public control and interference over how fertilised eggs developed, having been left at the whim of a sperm donor. The state would have condoned a situation in which a man had

100 ECtHR *Pretty v. the United Kingdom,* Appl. No. 2346/02, 29 April 2002. See further Chapter V.
101 ECtHR *Evans v. the United Kingdom,* Appl. No. 6339/05, 7 March 2006, para. 65.
102 ECtHR *Evans v. the United Kingdom,* Appl. No. 6339/05, 7 March 2006, para. 65.
103 ECtHR *Evans v. the United Kingdom,* Appl. No. 6339/05, 7 March 2006, paras. 19, 20 and 65.
104 ECtHR *Evans v. the United Kingdom,* Appl. No. 6339/05, 7 March 2006, para. 66.

absolute power under the 1990 Act to prevent her from giving birth to a genetically-related child.

On this point, the ECtHR, although sympathetic to women in Ms Evans' medical situation, added that the real question was not whether an alternative legislative solution could have been found, but whether the **United Kingdom** had exceeded its margin of appreciation. Having paraphrased the legal question in those terms, the ECtHR insisted that the **United Kingdom** had not adopted an anomalous legislative choice in drafting a 'bright-line' rule.

Even so, Judges Traja and Mijović submitted that the 'bright-line' rule amounted to a violation of Article 8 ECHR.[105] Thus, in *Evans* the case would have involved a 'right to procreate' under the notion of the right to private life. Moreover, the judges took the view that the relevant law had been applied too rigidly. Furthermore, these judges found that the conflict had been more about individual interests than between the private and public interest, although they admitted that both sets of interests could be intertwined. As such, the ECtHR would not sufficiently have taken into consideration the fact that one party effectively would have absolute power over the other, which would be contrary to the public interest in facilitating conception by couples who cannot easily or at all conceive in the natural way.[106] Furthermore, they attached great weight to the lack of any alternative means for the woman to reproduce, noting that in an Israeli precedent, the *Nachmani v. Nachmani* case, this had been a crucial argument for the court to decide in the woman's favour.[107]

The dissenting judges also refuted the argument that the man had acted in 'good faith', because this argument, deriving from considerations of contract law, would be misguided. Thus, they suggested that the ECtHR could have made an exception to the strict adherence to the 'bright-line rule' if the man had withdrawn his consent in 'bad faith'. Indeed, this seems a valid point, because if strict adherence to legal rules is always appropriate in a bio-ethical situation, then whether the person withdrawing consent acts in 'good' or 'bad faith' may not matter. In addition, they drew attention to the fact that the 1990 Act did not

105 Joint Dissenting Opinion of Judges Traja and Mijović in ECtHR *Evans v. the United Kingdom*, Appl. No. 6339/05, 7 March 2006.

106 Joint Dissenting Opinion of Judges Traja and Mijović in ECtHR *Evans v. the United Kingdom*, Appl. No. 6339/05, 7 March 2006, paras. 2 and 4.

107 Joint Dissenting Opinion of Judges Traja and Mijović in ECtHR *Evans v. the United Kingdom*, Appl. No. 6339/05, 7 March 2006, para. 6; ECtHR *Odièvre v. France*, Appl. No. 42326/98, 13 February 2003, para. 44.

consider the situation in which a couple become 'estranged' during IVF treatment or even divorce.[108] In such a situation, it would not be appropriate to just apply bright-line legislation either. For such reasons, the Dissenting Opinion argued that adherence to strict 'bright-line' legislation should have been more strictly scrutinised.[109]

As such, for the dissenting judges, the specific circumstances of the case would have warranted a balancing of the interests of private parties.[110] Thus, the interests of the party who withdraws consent and wants to see the embryos destroyed would in principle prevail (if domestic law so provides), unless the other party (a) has no other means to have a genetically-related child; (b) has no children at all; and (c) does not intend to have recourse to a surrogate mother in the process of implantation. In their submission, this context-specific formula would strike a fair balance between public and private interests, as well as between conflicting individual rights themselves. Moreover, this test would have the advantage of being completely gender neutral, being equally applicable to both female and male parties.

The *Evans* case, though not directly relevant to the scope of the right to know one's origins, touches upon related issues concerning procreative freedom and the role of the legislator in a sensitive bio-ethical area. In addition, the *Evans* case engaged issues which affect the role of the state in restricting individual decisional privacy in a horizontal conflict. While the majority suggested that clear legislative rules create public advantages of legal certainty, the minority insisted upon the necessity of balancing private interests in the concrete case. At the same time, the minority also suggested that such balancing should be guided by more or less concrete rules. In casting the legal problems into a public vs. private interests mould, while largely ignoring the conflict between the couple, the ECtHR can hardly be blamed for having shied away from the moral and legal issues at hand and sheltering behind its view that the state should have a broad margin of appreciation. After all, the ECtHR decides in a vertical conflict between individuals and the state.

---

108 Joint Dissenting Opinion of Judges Traja and Mijović in ECtHR *Evans v. the United Kingdom*, Appl. No. 6339/05, 7 March 2006, para.7; ECtHR *Silver and Others v. the United Kingdom*. 24 October 1983, paras. 86-88.

109 Joint Dissenting Opinion of Judges Traja and Mijović in ECtHR *Evans v. the United Kingdom*, Appl. No. 6339/05, 7 March 2006, para. 9.

110 Joint Dissenting Opinion of Judges Traja and Mijović in ECtHR *Evans v. the United Kingdom*, Appl. No. 6339/05, 7 March 2006, para. 9.

Having said that, it may have been better if the majority decision would have taken the view that the period over which consent can be withdrawn should be shortened. Such a rule would be more reconcilable with Article 8 ECHR. This rule, while still sufficiently rigid, could take into account the more taxing consequences of IVF treatment on women than men. On the other hand, creating a specific formula in a similar way as the dissenting judges had done, however, could have risked tendentious interpretations to the effect that an active state role in enforcing a rather speculative 'right to procreate' or a 'right to genetically-related children' would be protected under Article 8 ECHR.

In 2006 in the *Dickson v. the United Kingdom case*, the applicants complained that the refusal by the British Secretary of State to allow a prisoner convicted of murder and sentenced to life and his partner access to artificial insemination and his constituted a violation of that applicant's rights, both under Article 8 and Article 12 ECHR, which protects the right to marry and found a family.[111] The applicant had met his wife, who had also been in prison, through a prison penpal network. Reference was given to the gravity of the applicant's crime and the welfare of the child who might be conceived. The Grand Chamber held, however, that there had been a violation of Article 8 ECHR, but found it unnecessary to look into Article 12.[112]

Notably, the Grand Chamber observed that 'where a particularly important facet of an individual's existence or identity is at stake, such as the choice (emphasis added) to become a genetic parent, the margin of appreciation accorded to a State will in general be restricted. Regardless of the capacities of the applicant's abilities to become good parents, the court found that the threshold had been set to high for the applicants to have access to treatment. In this way, the court seemed to follow the argument of the applicants that prisoners have a right to procreate unless there were compelling reasons against to restrict this freedom. The policy was so restrictive, however, that it amounted to a ban with regard to prisoners. Accordingly, it fell out of the margin of appreciation accorded to the United Kingdom. It follows that the *Dickson* will stand out as an important indication that at present very few restrictions regarding reproductive freedom under Article 8 ECHR are permissible, An important reason for this seems to be that important aspects of the identity of (prospective) parents are involved.

---

111 ECtHR *Dickson v. the United Kingdom*, Appl. No. 44362/04, 18 April 2006.

112 ECtHR *Dickson v. the United Kingdom*, Appl. No. 44362/04, 4 December 2007.

3.10. JÄGGI: THE POST MORTEM IDENTIFICATION OF BIOLOGICAL FATHERS BY AN ADULT SEARCHER

In two decisions from 2006, *Ebrü* [113] and *Jäggi*,[114] the ECtHR adopted a more bracing view of the right to know, which has been explained to some extent as a response to criticism of the *Odièvre* case.[115] Nonetheless, these two decisions were factually rather distinct from *Odièvre*. Still, in the *Jäggi* case the applicant searcher was also primarily emotionally and ideologically driven in his quest for certainty, rather than being concerned with a modification of legal status. The applicant, Andreas Jäggi, had been born in Geneva in July 1939. A person known as A.H. had been mentioned as the father by his mother before the civil status registrar. In old **Swiss** law, the putative father (A.H.) had been in a position to lawfully obstruct the paternity suits that had been lodged against him in January 1948 by claiming that other men might have also fathered the child. This procedural mechanism – the *exceptio plurium concubentium* – had been preserved in **Swiss** law until 1976, which, incidentally, also happened to be the year that A.H. had passed away. Following the initial 1948 proceedings, Mr Jäggi was placed in a foster family. Mr Jäggi stressed that the putative father had sought regular contact with him during his childhood apart from providing him with modest financial contributions towards his upbringing. Shortly after his death, Mr Jäggi provided a private laboratory with blood samples of himself and A.H. As the lease on the grave of A.H. began to come to an end, Jäggi successfully filed for the acquisition and prolongation of the rights on the tombstone in 1997. As a significant step, the ECtHR referred in this case to the applicant's 'right to know his genetic descent' as part of an encompassing 'right to identity' also protected under Article 8.[116] Moreover, in performing its proportionality test between the various rights it reached a rather different result in comparison to *Odièvre*. As such, in the aftermath of *Odièvre*, the ECtHR pointed out in *Jäggi* that the 'interest an individual may have in knowing her or his (genetic) descent does not decrease as one ages, but rather on the contrary'.[117]

---

113 ECtHR *Ebrü v. Turkey*, Appl. No. 60176/00, 30 May 2006. This case will not be dealt with because the legal issues differed little from the *Mikulić* case. In the *Ebrü* case, in accordance with Arts. 6 and 8 of the Convention, the ECtHR concluded that the inability of the Turkish courts to settle the paternity issue in a timely manner had left the applicants in a prolonged state of uncertainty as to the child's individual identity.

114 ECtHR *Jäggi v. Switzerland*, Appl. No. 58757/00, 13 July 2006.

115 Besson (2007), p. 151.

116 ECtHR *Jäggi v. Switzerland*, Appl. No. 58757/00, 13 July 2006, para. 25.

117 ECtHR *Jäggi v. Switzerland*, Appl. No. 58757/00, 13 July 2006, para. 40.

Conscious of the emotionally and culturally charged dimensions involved in a *post mortem* judicial determination of paternity, the ECtHR framed the case in the context of a conflict between the 'right to know' and the 'right to respect for the dead'. Even so, the ECtHR chose not delve into the ethical implications of the latter right, apart from remarking, in a rather laconic way, that even this legal interest has but a 'temporary nature'.[118] While understandably cautious in defining its ethical position in respect of the rights of the dead, the ECtHR cast aside the deeper legal and moral issues under a mere reference to the expiry date of the lease on the tomb by 2016, apparently as a sufficient legal indication that **Swiss** law could deny the dead a perpetual right to rest in peace.[119]

Remarkably enough for a secular court, the ECtHR relied on the prior **Swiss** proceedings in drawing attention to the lack of any objections of a religious or philosophical kind by surviving family members. In connection with such ethical objections, one judge, Judge Hedigan, justifiably pointed out that the majority decision had overlooked the fact that the exhumation of a corpse may very well also displease, not to say appall, surviving close relatives, quite regardless of their moral or religious convictions.[120] As such, the specific regard for religious objections would have been misguided.

Nonetheless, in *Jäggi*, the ECtHR recognised that an exhumation could tarnish the living memory that close relatives may have of a deceased parent, if only because it could strike them as something particularly morbid. As in *Odièvre,* the ECtHR accordingly recognised the possible interests of third parties, notably close relatives, in opposing a claim, while dispensing with any further elaboration of the nature of third party interests.

Still, if third party interests required such consideration, it was somewhat infelicitous for the ECtHR to claim then that, at least in this case, testing was 'not particularly intrusive' anyway.[121] Whether the ECtHR intended to say that DNA paternity testing would be even less intrusive for a living putative father, appears circumspect; had this been so, the remark would have been quite understandable for this involves a less contentious and emotionally-charged situation than the exhumation of a corpse. In *Mikulić,* however, as we have seen, the ECtHR had insisted that the use of physical compulsion in parentage testing,

---

118 ECtHR *Jäggi v. Switzerland*, Appl. No. 58757/00, 13 July 2006, para. 41.
119 ECtHR *Jäggi v. Switzerland*, Appl. No. 58757/00, 13 July 2006, para. 41.
120 See the Dissenting Opinion of Judge Hedigan, to which Judge Gyulumyan also subscribed, ECtHR *Jäggi v. Switzerland*, Appl. No. 58757/00, 13 July 2006.
121 ECtHR *Jäggi v. Switzerland*, Appl. No. 58757/00, 13 July 2006, para. 41.

while infringing upon a person's physical integrity, requires commensurate justification.[122] That said, neither a clarification of the applicant's legal status nor an inheritance claim had been at stake in *Jäggi*. The court's remark may therefore essentially have been a statement about the *effects* of testing. Because they were concerned with an individual interest in the biological truth rather than status, they were indeed less 'intrusive.'

In other words, the relatively straightforward recognition by the ECtHR of the applicant's right to information in the *Jäggi* case would at least in part appear ascribable to the fact that the case was of little consequence for the establishment of his legal parentage.[123]

This approach could also be verified in some other recent cases. In *Paulik v. Slovakia*, a man who had been the legal father since 1970 but had only, thanks to improved testing methods, discovered through a DNA test in 2004 that he did not share a genetic link with his daughter. Meanwhile, he had become unable to deny paternity following the expiry of statutory time-limits.[124] From the moment of birth the applicant had had little contact with this daughter. In this case the ECtHR was again prepared to accept that the lack of a legal mechanism to enable the applicant to protect his right to respect for his private life could generally be explained by the 'legitimate interest' in ensuring legal certainty and security of family relationships and by the need to protect the interests of children. As to the general interest, the court observed that the applicant's putative daughter was almost 40 years old, had her own family and is not dependent on the applicant for maintenance (contrasted with *Yildirim*, cited above). The general interest in protecting her rights at this stage would therefore have lost much of its importance compared to when she was a child. Furthermore, the daughter had initiated the DNA test and said that she had no objection to the applicant's disclaiming paternity. In citing the *Kroon* formula, the court contended that the lack of a procedure for aligning the legal position with the biological reality flew in the face of the wishes of those concerned and did not

---

122 That states have been offered such relative leeway may also be inferred from the case ECtHR *Szarapó vs. Poland*, Appl. No. 40835/98, 23rd of May 2002, para. 42. Thus, presumably, for states to comply with the requirements of *Mikulić* and *Szarapó*, adverse inferences could in a paternity case also be drawn against the putative father to the effect that his paternity could be established upon a (persistent) refusal to undergo testing. This solution is chosen in countries such as the **UK**, **France**, **Italy** and **the Netherlands**. See *inter alia* the various country reports in Spickhoff, Schwab, Henrich, Gottwald (2007).

123 Compare, *mutatis mutandis*, ECtHR *Haas v. the Netherlands*, Appl. No. 36983/97, 13 January 2004, *supra*.

124 ECtHR *Paulik v. Slovakia*, Appl. No. 10699/05, 10 October 2006.

in fact benefit anyone. For this reason, the court accepted that there had been a violation of Article 8 ECHR. Furthermore, it also recognised that Article 14 ECHR had been violated, because there had been an unjustifiable treatment – in the light of the circumstances of the case – in the treatment of persons with an interest in disclaiming paternity according to whether paternity had been merely presumed or whether paternity had been determined in a (judicial) decision that had already become final. In this case the applicant did not have any domestic procedural remedy anymore by which he could challenge the declaration of his paternity, while other parties in an analogous situation did. The domestic courts in the eyes of the ECtHR had failed to appreciate the specific circumstances of the applicant's case, such as, for example, the (adult) age, personal situation and the attitude of the daughter and of the other parties concerned, who had supported the applicant's proceedings. Accordingly, the court encouraged Slovakia to review the rigorous application of procedural time-limits in paternity proceedings, where this was against the wishes of all parties and did not benefit anyone.

In the *Phinikaridou v. Cyprus* case, the applicant was also well into adulthood and had enjoyed a legal relationship with a socio-legal father for a prolonged period. Having denied her legal father's paternity but having had a firm belief as to who her biological father was, she was also faced with a procedural time-limit in establishing the latter man's paternity. The ECtHR established that 'a distinction must be made between cases in which an applicant has no opportunity to obtain knowledge of the facts and cases where an applicant knows with certainty or has grounds for assuming who his or her father is but for reasons unconnected with the law takes no steps to institute proceedings within the statutory time-limit'.[125] In this latter case, the ECtHR therefore drew attention to the fact that 'it had not been shown how the general interest in protecting legal certainty of family relationships or the interest of the presumed father and his family outweighed the applicant's right to have at least one opportunity to seek judicial determination of paternity'.[126] As the bare minimum, then, Article 8 ECHR would require 'one real opportunity' to establish paternity in accordance with the biological truth in a comparable situation.

By implication, the ECtHR suggested that in a situation wherein an adult child shows procedural inertia, having more than an inkling of who his actual biological father really is, but failing to undertake any procedural action, such an adult child should not be brought into a position to postpone paternity proceedings

125 ECtHR *Phinikaridou v. Cyprus*, Appl. No. 23890/02, 20 December 2007, para. 63.
126 ECtHR *Phinikaridou v. Cyprus*, Appl. No. 23890/02, 20 December 2007, para. 58.

until whenever she deems opportune, for example, once an inheritance can be claimed. Conversely, a claim will be 'meritorious' under the adult child's right to private life if the expiry of a procedural time-limit to establish paternity is attributable to objective factors beyond the searcher's subjective control. It follows that the States Parties may under certain circumstances also need to interpret procedural time-limits for reviewing parental status in a flexible way, since the child should at least have 'one real opportunity'.[127]

In respect of that argument, the *Phinikaridou* case stands out as an interesting case in having recognised what may be coined a genetic parent's 'procreational privacy', a legal interest that would gain force with the passage of time. Thus, under certain circumstances, a child's claim could, as it were, become 'estopped' and a parent could claim a right to be 'left alone.'[128] Accordingly, the ECtHR specified further 'a presumed father's interest in being protected from stale claims concerning facts that go back many years and cannot be denied' under Article 8 ECHR, since this would be necessary in the prevention of 'possible injustice if courts were required to make findings of fact that went back many years.'[129]

4. CONCLUDING REMARKS

Given the sheer variety of factual and legal situations in which a right to know can manifest itself as a legal issue in the regional legal order, it seems appropriate to summarise some salient and recurrent points. These points may serve as a starting point for the discussion of legal principles in Chapter V which will serve as an analytical backdrop to the thematic comparative analysis that follows thereafter.

On the basis of the analysis of the substantive provisions and the case law presented above, it may be safely concluded that the right to know one's genetic parentage has only fairly recently been acknowledged. Apart from the ECHR

127 For the requirement of an effective remedy to deny (marital) paternity by the legal father under Art. 8 in conjunction with Art. 6 of the ECHR, see also: ECtHR *Mizzi v. Malta*, Appl. No. 26111/02, 12 January 2006, para. 134.

128 Contrast this with the mother's right to give birth anonymously in **France** which was considered reconcilable with the margin of appreciation accorded to the **French** state under Art. 8 of the Convention in *Odièvre v. France*, Appl. No. 42326/98, 13 February 2003.

129 ECtHR *Phinikaridou v. Cyprus*, Appl. No. 23890/02, 20 December 2007, para. 51 and 53. These interests were also acknowledged in: ECtHR *Mizzi v. Malta*, Appl. No. 26111/02, 12 January 2006, para. 83 and ECtHR, *Shofman v. Russia*, Appl. No. 74826/01, para. 39.

and a number of other Council of Europe conventions, the relevance of the European Union's data protection law cannot be ruled out, especially in respect of parental privacy. Still, the regional legal basis of the right to know one's origins essentially derives primarily on a gradually expanding docket of case law of the ECtHR on Article 8 ECHR under the notion of the right to 'private life'. Since claims under the notion of 'family life' of Article 8 ECHR and Article 10 ECHR have so far not gained recognition, their legal basis remains, at best, debatable.

Furthermore, the case law of the ECtHR reveals a far from linear recognition of a right to know one's genetic origins over the past two decades. In *Gaskin* a right of a person to construe a personal narrative identity of one's own on the basis of personal documents not hindered by public interference may have been the underlying ethical issue. An *expressis verbis* acknowledgement of the existence of a 'right to know' under Article 8 ECHR did not occur until much later, with *Odièvre* and *Jäggi*. Interestingly, in *Odièvre*, the ECtHR referred to an otherwise underexplored 'right to one's personal history', which conveys a potentially far more encompassing legal concept than the 'right to know one's genetic origins' and evokes concern over a person's need for a narrative identity, which, arguably, had already been recognised in *Gaskin*.[130]

The *Gaskin* case was interpreted throughout Europe as relevant for the issue of knowing one's genetic parentage notwithstanding the facts of the case, forestalling legal developments in Strasbourg.[131] As a consequence, the ECtHR has relied on its judicial policy of according states a wide 'margin of appreciation' in deciding on issues affecting persons' access to a their 'basic identity.'[132] In cases in which the public authorities withhold consent to such information, at a minimum it is required of states that they set up an 'independent authority' to decide whether access should be granted.

Already on the basis of this wide public discretion, it becomes apparent that such an informational right has so far not been imbued with any absolute character by the ECtHR. An assumption that the ECtHR is in principle always prepared to come down in favour of an applicant seeking information about genetic origins would be tantamount to assuming that the court would fail to acknowledge competing interests, something which is quite unthinkable for a court that

130 ECtHR *Odièvre v. France*, Appl. No. 42326/98, 13 February 2003, para. 49.
131 FORDER (1998), p. 88.
132 ECtHR *Gaskin v. United Kingdom*, Appl. No. 10454/83, 7 July 1989, para. 39.

adheres to a 'margin of appreciation' doctrine.[133]As such, the approach that the ECtHR has adopted recognises that the right to know be weighed in concrete cases against other countervailing (public) interests.

On that premise, the ECtHR has suggested that the countervailing private interests of the birthparent as well as overriding concerns deriving from public interests and higher ranking rights or moral values, in particular the right to life, may prevail over the right to know.[134] As far as the interests of the birthparent are concerned, these have been interpreted to include not only a mother's decision to give birth anonymously, but also a right of a (presumptive) genetic parent to be able to rely on the fact that he will not be faced with a 'stale claim' after a certain period has elapsed and the child is an adult who had previously benefited from a legal child-father relationship.[135] In the eyes of the ECtHR, the recognition of the right to know therefore leaves some scope for a measure of '*procreational privacy*', which may gain importance as the child matures and the moment of conception accordingly lies in a more distant past. Nonetheless, such a principle of procreational privacy is clearly far from absolute and apparently contingent to a great extent upon the child's age and the moment that paternity is established. Thus, recently, in *Remmerswaal v. The Netherlands* the ECtHR found that the mere declaration of a man's paternity and affirmed that the 'imposition' of a new family member – still a minor – could not be regarded as an unjustified interference prohibited by Article 8.[136]

The discussion has not been framed exclusively as being essentially a conflict between the informational interests of the child versus the privacy interests of the parent. After all, private parties usually lodge proceedings against the state. Moreover, however, 'third' party interests have also been recognised covering at least the interests of another birthparent[137] as well as the interests of adoptive parents.[138] Even the privacy interests of siblings in non-disclosure may apparently require legal protection,[139] alongside those of the family of the putative father.[140] Unfortunately, though, the scope of these interests has hitherto not

133 Stoll (2008), p. 40.
134 ECtHR *Odièvre v. France*, Appl. No. 42326/98, 13 February 2003, para. 45.
135 ECtHR *Phinikaridou v. Cyprus*, Appl. No. 23890/02, 20 December 2007, paras. 51 and 53.
136 ECtHR *Remmerswaal and others v. the Netherl*ands, Appl. No. 34441/05, 9 September 2008.
137 ECtHR *Mikulić v. Croatia*, Appl. No. 53176/99, 7 February 2002, para. 64; ECtHR *Odièvre v. France*, Appl. No. 42326/98, 13 February 2003, para. 44; ECtHR *Jäggi v. Switzerland*, 13 July 2006, para. 39.
138 ECtHR *Odièvre v. France*, Appl. No. 42326/98, 13 February 2003, para. 44.
139 ECtHR *Odièvre v. France*, Appl. No. 42326/98, 13 February 2003, para. 44.
140 ECtHR *Phinikaridou v. Cyprus*, Appl. No. 23890/02, 20 December 2007, para. 53.

been explored. It can only be established on the basis of the current docket of case law that they may require some legal consideration.

Furthermore, the establishment of legal parentage has been recognised to constitute an issue essentially distinct from issues concerning access to identifying information of one's genetic parentage.[141] Still, a state may not be required to protect a child's legal interest in establishing the biological fact *per se* under Article 8 ECHR, or at least if it is the genetic parent who says that 'the child must know'.[142] In that connection, a biological father who claims that his interest in knowing an important aspect of his identity squares well with an informational interest of the child in knowing him has not met with judicial approval.[143] As a further analogy, a birthmother was unsuccessful in her claim on behalf of children adopted by different families when she had insisted that, as siblings, they had an interest in growing up together and to establish details about their mother's life.[144] In brief, then, the court does not seem really prepared to recognise a 'right of the putative biological parent to know her or his offspring.'

Having said that, though, the (unmarried) biological father has conditioned rights to establish paternity as long as he has had a relatively long relationship with the mother and their procreational choice followed a consensual decision.[145] Thus, if the biological father had been unable to obtain consent from the mother to establish such a legal relationship, and had not been able to avail himself of a 'legal avenue' to have his paternity established, in view of the fact that the mother had meanwhile given her consent to a man other than the father, the state may be in breach of the latter's right to private life under Article 8 ECHR.[146]

The ECHR has so far not taken any firm position on DNA testing in establishing genetic relations, but has considered testing relatively unintrusive, quite remarkably so in a *post mortem* case (*Jäggi*). Essentially, there is an obligation incum-

---

141 ECtHR *Mikulić v. Croatia*, Appl. No. 53176/99, 7 February 2002, para. 59; ECtHR *Jäggi v. Switzerland*, Appl. No. 58757/00, 13 July 2006, para. 25.

142 ECtHR *Nylund v. Finland*, Appl. No. 27110/95, 29 June 1999.

143 ECtHR *M.B. v. United Kingdom*, Appl. No. 22920/93, 6 April 1994.

144 ECtHR *Tiziana Pipoli v. Italy*, Appl. No. 27145/95, 30 March 1999.

145 ECtHR *Keegan v. Ireland*, Appl. No. 16969/90, 26 May 1994; ECtHR *Kroon and Others v. the Netherlands*, Appl. No. 18535/91, 27 October 1994; ECtHR *Różanski v. Poland*, Appl. No. 55339/00, 10 March 2005. *Mutatis mutandis:* ECtHR *M.B. v. United Kingdom*, Appl. No. 22920/93, 6 April 1994.

146 ECtHR *Różanski v. Poland*, Appl. No. 55339/00, 10 March 2005.

bent on States to also establish parentage in an expedient and effective way.[147] This allows for the use of DNA testing, but it may not be necessary.

A right to physical integrity of the putative parent has also been acknowledged by way of principle. On the other hand, where the parent's identification is of little legal consequence, even if that genetic parent has died, the national public authorities may also find that testing is 'not very intrusive'.[148] Furthermore, it is worth recalling that, as a further minimum requirement, a presumption of paternity should not 'fly into the face of biological and social reality' and contradict the wishes of all parties concerned.[149]

As a further salient characteristic of the examined case law, the applicant's age while enforcing the right to know appears to represent a very relevant factor in the eyes of the ECtHR. While the case law remains insufficient to fully assess the legal significance of an applicant's age or emotional maturity, so much is clear that knowing the truth has also been considered important for young children. Thus, a minor aged five apparently already had a 'vital interest' in establishing an 'important aspect of her identity'.[150] Paradoxically, though, in *Odièvre* the applicant's adult age detracted from the force of her right to know, since it had to be seen on 'a footing of equality' with countervailing interests.[151] Nonetheless, a few years later in *Jäggi* old age in itself came to be regarded as a legal factor pleading in favour of the applicant's right, with the ECtHR even going as far as to suggest that a person's interest in knowing the truth does not decrease, but rather increases in old age.[152]

As a final point to keep in mind, Article 8 ECHR offers States a 'margin of appreciation' to make a review of parental status contingent upon time-limits in the interests of legal certainty.[153] At the very least, the child should have at least 'one opportunity' to have paternity established and the child may become estopped from exercising a right to access the truth if it had previously been in a situation

147 ECtHR *Mikulić v. Croatia,* Appl. No. 53176/99, 7 February 2002, para. 64. Yet in this case the 'vital interest' that this minor may have had in knowing her true genetic descent, may in the eyes of the court have been more directly related to her interest in establishing a legal child-father relationship.

148 ECtHR *Jäggi v. Switzerland,* Appl. No. 58757/00, 13 July 2006, para. 41.

149 ECtHR *Kroon and Others v. the Netherlands,* Appl. No. 18535/91, 27 October 1994, para. 40.

150 ECtHR *Mikulić v. Croatia,* Appl. No. 53176/99, 7 February 2002, para. 64.

151 ECtHR *Odièvre v. France,* Appl. No. 42326/98, 13 February 2003, para. 44

152 ECtHR *Jäggi v. Switzerland* Appl. No. 58757/00, 13 July 2006, para. 40.

153 For example: ECtHR *Rasmussen v. Denmark,* Appl. No. 8777/79, 28 November 1984, para. 33; ECtHR *Phinikaridou v. Cyprus,* Appl. No. 23890/02, 20 December 2007.

to lodge proceedings, but has failed to do so.[154] Not only may DNA scientific certainty be dispensed with in enforcing a person's right to know under Article 8 ECHR, in the court's interpretation a person's 'knowledge' may sometimes be considered to have been already enforced to a satisfactory extent. This may be the case if the person has for a prolonged period of time had an inkling as to the identity of the genetic parent.[155] An (adult) person may, after all, also be 'convinced in his own mind' who his genetic father is.[156] Under the Convention, such a diminished level of certainty could be sufficient if an ulterior, inheritance-related aim on the part of the applicant is present.[157]

---

154 ECtHR *Phinikaridou v. Cyprus*, Appl. No. 23890/02, 20 December 2007.

155 ECtHR *Haas v. the Netherlands*, Appl. No. 36983/97, 13 January 2004; ECtHR *Phinikaridou v. Cyprus*, Appl. No. 23890/02, 20 December 2007.

156 ECtHR *Haas v. the Netherlands*, Appl. No. 36983/97, 13 January 2004, para. 42.

157 Conversely, it may well be so that, under the Convention, a higher level of certainty may be required if such an ulterior legal interest is absent. Compare: ECtHR *Jäggi v. Switzerland* Appl. No. 58757/00, 13 July 2006, paras. 40 and 41.

CHAPTER IV
THE PROTECTION OF THE RIGHT TO KNOW ONE'S ORIGINS IN NATIONAL CONSTITUTIONAL LAW

1. OUTLINE

Having examined the international and regional legal framework, in this Chapter attention shall be drawn to the national constitutional legal order of the selected jurisdictions. In addition, a general overview of the historical evolvement of parentage law in these four jurisdictions shall be provided. This historical contextualisation is required as background information for the thematic comparative discussion.

As a more general aim, a legal analysis of the main cases in which the right to know gained constitutional recognition at the national level is provided. Accordingly, this Chapter aims to provide the reader with a general overview of the legal discussion in each jurisdiction.

Since **Germany** has, without doubt, been at the forefront in recognising a constitutional right to know one's origins, the historical development of parentage law in that jurisdiction shall be dealt with first. Otherwise, the alphabetical order of the names of the countries in English is followed. As such, this Chapter goes on to discuss the legal history and constitutional legal development in **France**, before turning to **the Netherlands** and **Portugal**.

2. GERMANY

2.1. EARLY MODERN HISTORY

In some of the first codifications of civil law and customary law which were drafted in the various **German** principalities in the early nineteenth Century, the influences of the Napoleonic Code Civil were considerable. As a result, some

'**French**' legal institutions were introduced, but they came under the critical scrutiny of **German** legal scholars because of diverging local notions of public morality as well as pragmatic considerations.[1] When the first **German** Civil Code was drafted the recognition of maternity by the unmarried mother was, for example, left out.[2] Other legal issues, in particular the conditions under which paternity could be challenged, also proved contentious.[3] The judicial determination of paternity was only admitted if it was part of a wider child maintenance claim. Apart from being perceived as threats to public morality and the overall stability of family life, the difficulty in obtaining scientifically sound evidence also meant that parentage proceedings were sometimes declared inadmissible. Adoption and subsequent legitimisation were regarded as the only appropriate means to smooth out the rough edges in respect of the weak legal status of children who had been born out of wedlock in inheritance and child maintenance law. All the same, it was at least in theory possible for children born out of wedlock to institute proceedings involving a maintenance claim against the begetter.

The mother's husband could challenge the falsity of marriage-based paternity because a public interest in the prevention of false registrations of birth had been recognised.[4] Considering the consequences of a loss of legitimacy for the child, the courts refrained from using their broad discretion to allow husbands to deny their paternity to the detriment of the child. Therefore, the determination of the identity of the child's biological father was typically subsumed in civil procedure into the wider legal issues associated with child maintenance in the late nineteenth and early twentieth Century.

During the Weimar Republic the determination of the genetic tie had already come to serve as the decisive factor in maintenance claims by children born out of wedlock, perhaps as a result of scientific developments in blood testing. In the legal literature of the Weimar Republic the view was still advanced, however, that the factual existence of a biological link between the child and the parent as such could not represent a legal relationship.[5] After the National Socialists assumed power, however, the evidence of familial blood ties gained an importance until then unattested in **German** parentage law. Accordingly, parentage law underwent a paradigm shift during the Nazi regime because the determina-

1 HELMS (1999), p. 32-35.
2 SCHUBERT (1977), p. 472-473; HELMS (1999), p. 32-35.
3 HELMS (1999), p. 32-35.
4 HELMS (1999), p. 34.
5 ROQUETTE (1935), p. 2476; FISCHER (1936), p. 237-238.

tion of the biological truth came to represent a value worth legal protection in itself. Sure enough, the totalitarian regime's interest in the determination of the biological truth had little to do with concern over the individual's narrative identity. Rather, a general public interest in the truth reflected the racial segregationist and eugenic public policy objectives.

This paradigm shift was visible in the case law. Following a decision of October 1937, the Supreme Court of the **German** Reich[6] for the first time admitted a claim involving a determination of paternity in which no child maintenance or ancillary financial issue was in dispute.[7] Furthermore, in a decision of 15 June 1939 the court affirmed that there was a public interest in status determination in establishing the biological truth, in view of the **German** people's interest in maintaining racial purity.[8]

As a result, a new provision, §256 ZPO, was used to allow for a solely informational determination of the child's illegitimate status. A father of racially pure descent could thereby 'free himself' of child maintenance obligations in respect of a non-Aryan child[9] or a child could lodge paternity proceedings to lose the socio-legal stigma attached to the label 'Jewish mixture'.[10] As the Nazi regime was alarmed by the fact that non-Aryan genetic descent could also pass on to children born within marriage, a new law was enacted which gave the Public Ministry a competence to determine the genetic and racial status of children within marriage too.[11] In this way the Public Ministry was given a right to interfere in the family sphere whenever this was deemed advantageous for the public interest in the purity of race.

At the procedural level, this marked public interest in the 'biological truth' found expression in the **German** Civil Procedural Code,[12] through the insertion of a compulsory legal obligation which became incumbent on all respondents to undergo scientific testing. Given their collective, public nature, these interests inherently prevailed over the child's individual interests, whose resultant loss of legitimate status in comparison presented a negligible legal interest. If a person

6 *Reichsgericht* (RG).
7 RG, 14 October 1937, *JW* 1938, p. 245-246.
8 RG, 15 June 1939, *RGZ* 160, p. 293-296.
9 HELMS (1999), p. 37.
10 OLG Celle, *JW* 1939, p. 967-968.
11 RGZ 160, 293-296, 24 May 1941.
12 **German** Civil Procedure Act, abbreviated as ZPO in this book.

refused to co-operate with the bio-medical test being conducted, the public authorities were required to use their competence to exert physical compulsion.

As may be expected, these strong biologistic overtones came under the critical scrutiny of post-war legislative reform. Even so, however, a considerable part of the relevant legal provisions was left virtually intact by reform. Thus, the mere fact that much of the legislation had originated in a murky past was not in itself considered a sufficient reason to justify their deletion.

Rather, another paradigm shift occurred in the post-war period: the necessity to cast the existent legislation into a radically different ideological mould which would be directed primarily towards the individual's identity rather than racist conceptions of national identity. In this new conception of the meaning of blood, some parts of parentage law could escape legal reform.

Indicative of this change are the words of one post-war **German** legal scholar: '(...) Whoever has no father, or has more than one father, cannot be considered a human being in any full sense. Every person irrespective of his birth has a naturally ordained right to have established who his father is before and against anyone. Whoever claims to value an individual's personality, shall not deny him such a right'.[13]

Following the entry into force of the **German** Basic Law, the Grundgesetz (GG), on 25 May 1949, the relevance of two constitutional grounds was acknowledged in respect of a newly discovered human rights basis in the interest of biological truth. Firstly, there was the so-called 'general personality right' and, secondly, the principled equality of children born outside marriage and those born within marriage. This 'general personality right' derived from a joint reading of two constitutional provisions.

Firstly, Article 1 I GG, affirming the inviolability of human dignity, creates a state obligation to respect and protect it. Secondly, Article 2 I GG states that 'everyone has the right to the free development of his personality insofar as he does not violate the rights of others or offend against the constitutional order or the moral code'. Remarkably enough, some early comments on the Basic Law already conveyed the idea that this general personality right incorporated a right to know one's genetic origins.[14] All the same, in the aftermath of the war, no

13 GUGGUMOS (1947/48), p. 59-60.

14 ENNECCERUS & NIPPERDEY (1959); NEUMANN-DUESBERG (1950), p. 14.

attempt was made to delineate the conceptual and procedural implications of the recognition of such a 'right'. For some courts, such early doctrinal views were nonetheless considered authoritative, especially in cases in which children born out of wedlock sought a judicial establishment of paternity.[15]

Alongside this personality right, and as a further constitutional legal basis, it was suggested that concern for the equality of children born outside marriage, enshrined in Article 6 V GG, should be considered. The Federal Court of Justice, the Bundesgerichtshof (BGH),[16] accordingly acknowledged a legal interest of children born out of wedlock in the determination of parentage as an issue essentially distinct from their interest in receiving child maintenance.[17]

Provisions which had permitted the Public Prosecutor to interfere in the determination of the status of children born within marriage at any time, a legislative legacy of the national socialists, were deleted altogether in a 1961 general family law reform.[18] But where the rights of the state in challenging paternity were lost, the rights of the child, the legal parents and even the parents of the husband to challenge marriage-based paternity were reinforced, pursuant to §1596 and §1598 BGB.

2.2. TOWARDS RECOGNITION OF A CONSTITUTIONAL RIGIIT TO KNOW ONE'S ORIGINS AND A MOTHER'S DUTY TO TELL

The public policy of achieving greater equality between those born within marriage and outside marriage inspired further reforms in 1969.[19] All children could from that year inherit from their biological father irrespective of their status. As a further novelty, the possibility for legally fatherless, non-marital children to lodge paternity proceedings against the presumptive biological father was introduced. The memorandum made it clear that the legislator did not only have in mind the idea of promoting greater status equality, but also forestalled a child's right to know her or his genetic descent.[20] Some scope for cynics about the public interest in individual identity rights was, however, offered by the

15 OLG Stuttgart, 11 May 1956, *MDR* 1956, p. 621.

16 'Federal Court of Justice', the country's highest court of appeal, abbreviated as BGH in this book.

17 BGH 28 April 1952, p. 385-397.

18 *BT-Drucks.* III/530, 7 August 1958, p. 2 and p. 14.

19 *BT-Drucks.* V/2370 , 7 December 1967, p. 37.

20 *BT-Drucks.* V/2370, 7 December 1967, p. 37.

open admission that a swift determination of the parentage of all children born out of wedlock was 'further' justified by the financial relief it meant for the state in view of potentially high public costs in respect of single mothers.[21]

In the mid-1970s much of the legal debate centred on the extensive competences of child welfare guardians, appointed by the state, in matters concerning the determination of a child's parentage. Thus, pursuant to §1706 BGB (*old*) the Child Welfare Authorities[22] could represent the child in lieu of the unmarried mother in case of a possible conflict of interests. The mother could, however, deny that there was any such conflict of interests and avoid the child's representation by the Child Welfare Authorities.[23] Under this legal regime, unmarried mothers were requested by the guardian to disclose the name of the child's father in view of the public aims mentioned above. Views were divided over the issue whether automatic guardianship would have to be continued until the unmarried mother was prepared to disclose the father's name.[24]

In 1981, the BGH went as far as to hold that automatic guardianship by the Child Welfare Authorities would have to continue unless the unmarried mother disclosed the father's name.[25] In that connection, the BGH drew particular emphasis to children's interest in knowing who their father is. This interest would derive, in the court's eyes, primarily from the implications for the children's personal development if they were kept in the dark about their father's identity. This legal regime continued until 1998 when automatic guardianship by the Child Welfare Authorities was finally repealed. The end of automatic guardianship has been ascribed to a significant extent to the unfamiliarity of Germans in the former **German Democratic Republic** with this peculiar legal institution.[26]

By the mid-80s, however, the question whether non-marital children had a right to compel the mother to disclose the name of the biological father reached the forefront of developments in **German** family law.[27] In fact, it had already been hypothesised during the codification of the first BGB in 1900 that such a right

---

21 *BT-Drucks.* V/2370, 7 December 1937, 26. See also HELMS (1999), p. 44.

22 *Jugendamt.*

23 §1706 BGB. *Amtspflegschaft.*

24 For: SIMITIS (1970), Against: BGH, 8 October 1981, BGHZ 82, 173=*NJW* 1982, p. 381.

25 BGH, 11 November 1981, *FamRZ* 1982, p. 159-160.

26 *BT-Drucks.* 13/892.

27 BGH, 20 October 1958, *FamRZ* 1959, p. 16 -17; LG Köln, 30 October 1962, *FamRZ* 1963, p. 55; BayOLG, 6 June 1972, *FamRZ* 1972, p. 521-522; BGH, 11 November *FamRZ* 1982, p. 159-160.

could exist.[28] In his 1976 dissertation Kleineke had also suggested that a child had this right, while acknowledging, too, that the mother could exceptionally have a right to remain silent when enquired by the father about the identity of the father.[29]

A mother's duty was read into §1618a BGB by two Bavarian courts.[30] This civil law provision affirmed that children and parents 'owe each other support and consideration.' Taken together with the constitutional equality clause contained in Article 6 V GG, this civil law provision came to provide the legal basis for the (unmarried) mother's duty to tell. Nonetheless, it was commented that this duty could be difficult to reconcile with the fact that the mother also had a right to withhold testimony in civil proceedings.[31] On that view, Coester-Waltjen held that if the mother did not hold parental authority – notably when the child had become an adult – the duty to disclose the father's name would have come to an end.[32] As a further basis, it has been held that the unwritten civil law norm of 'good faith'[33] as contained in §242 BGB provides a legal basis for this duty.[34] Even so, it remained unclear how this duty would have to be enforced or which sanctions are permissible in case of a violation. At the governmental level, this duty of mutual care has at least been considered a 'guideline' for conduct in the child-parent relationship.[35] In 2008, the Federal Court of Justice concurred with the decisions of the lower courts that the mother could lawfully be compelled, subject to cumulating fines, to disclose the biological father's name to the legal father. In that respect, it added, though, that the mother in principle by virtue of her personality right could decide to some extent to whom she wanted to disclose details about her personal life. Nonetheless, it was considered that there was an overriding public interest in the prevention of men in the position of the father to disprove paternity and claim child maintenance back from the biological father.[36]

The Federal Constitutional Court clarified that this duty of the (unmarried) mother to disclose the father's name fell within the ambit of the constitutional

28 MUSCHELER & BLOCH (2002), p. 346.
29 KLEINEKE (1976), p. 136-147.
30 AG Passau, 15 July 1987, *FamRZ* 1987, p. 1309; LG Passau, 26 November 1987, *NJW* 1988, p. 144.
31 §383 I(3) ZPO. See: COESTER-WALTJEN/GERNHUBER (2006), p. 586.
32 COESTER-WALTJEN (2006), p. 587.
33 *Treu und Glaube.*
34 MUSCHELER & BLOCH (2002), p. 347.
35 *BT-Drucks.* 8/2788, p. 36-43.
36 BGH, 3 July 2008, *FamRZ* 2008, p. 1751.

equality principle of Article 6 V GG.[37] Interpreted on the basis of this principle, the referred civil law provision of 'mutual care' were taken as requiring that the mother disclose information concerning the plaintiff's natural father to her daughter.

Furthermore, in 1990 the Münster Regional Court also centred its argumentation on the civil law obligation enshrined in §1618a BGB. In that remarkable case a daughter had lodged proceedings involving both personal and inheritance-related interests. The Münster court insisted that the mother disclose all the names of the four men with whom she had allegedly had sexual relations during the period of the conception to the (adult) applicant, who had spent most of her childhood in foster families.[38] The mother refused to tell, submitting that not only her privacy right but also the rights of the four men she had slept with at the time would have to be taken into consideration, all the more so because these men had in the meantime established families of their own. Far from willing to delve further into these 'third party' interests, the court insisted that the mother had an enduring 'lifelong responsibility' towards the applicant for having given birth to her.

Less extensive judicial interpretations of the mother's duty to tell could nonetheless also be found in the early 1990s. In a case before the Regional Court of Appeal of Hamm, the Jugendamt had lodged proceedings under §1618a BGB against a mother, a social worker in a psychiatric hospital, in order to compel her to disclose the identity of a child's father.[39] Here the court considered that disclosure would be more appropriate at a later stage when the child would have reached a certain emotional maturity, especially because it was found that the mother had good reason for professional reasons to withhold the information because the presumed father was a psychiatric patient in her care.

In 1997, the aformentioned 'Münster' case came before the Federal Constitutional Court, in which the mother complained that her personality right had been breached. The daughter had, however, compelled her to disclose her father's name under reference to her personality right as well as the equality principle.[40]

---

37 LG Münster, 21 January 1990, *FamRZ* 1990, p. 1031; COESTER-WALTJEN/GERNHUBER (2006), p. 586.

38 LG Münster, 21 January 1990, *FamRZ* 1990, p. 1031.

39 OLG Hamm, 22 March 1991, *FamRZ* 1991, p. 229.

40 BVerfGE, 6 May 1997, *FamRZ* 1997, p. 869. The applicant invoked Arts. 2(1) and 1(1) of the Federal Constitution (the general personality right) and, subsidiarily, Art. 6 V (equality of status for children born within and outside marriage).

This time around the Federal Constitutional Court quashed the decision that had been taken on appeal. Even though it concurred with them that the child's right should in principle have prevailed over that of the mother, it held that a unilateral prioritization of the child's right should not have been made. Moreover, the Federal Constitutional Court found that the lower courts had elevated the conflict to the constitutional level all too readily, without having made any real attempt to derive the mother's duty to tell from the referred civil law obligation of 'mutual care between parents and children'.[41]

The court further specified that the child's constitutional right to information only protected a right 'not to be withheld the requested information by public authorities'.[42] The Federal Constitutional Court suggested that the Münster court had not taken the mother's specific position sufficiently into account. Furthermore, it criticized the reasoning of the lower court for having suggested that it was the mother's own responsibility that the child had been born outside marriage, because this denoted an idea of blameworthiness. Rather, the mother's duty to tell would not derive from the fact that she had given birth outside marriage, but because the child was not responsible for her own creation.[43]

Since then, the unmarried mother's duty to tell has been at issue on a number of other occasions. It has been considered justifiable not to extend this duty to married mothers because to require otherwise would mean that the legislator effectively denied the validity of the marital presumption rule, which holds that the mother's husband is the child's father, from the outset.[44] Because the duty is untenable (*nicht vetretbare Handlung*), it is in principle possible to claim civil damages from the mother who refuses to disclose the father's name.[45] A (temporary) divestment of parental authority is also possible.[46] The mother cannot claim that she has simply forgotten or that she is unsure because she had sexual relations with more than one man during the conception period.[47] However, because the obligation in principle only applies in the mother's private and not her public relations, it has been suggested that the mother cannot be charged with a falsification of the child's personal status.[48] In her relations, towards the

41 §1618a BGB.
42 BVerfGE, 6 May 1997, *FamRZ* 1997, p. 869.
43 The so-called '*Veranlasserprinzip*'.
44 EIDENMÜLLER (1998), p. 789.
45 §888 I and III ZPO.
46 §1666 BGB.
47 MUSCHELER & BLOCH (2002), p. 13-14.
48 §169 StGB = German Criminal Code. Falsification of personal status = *Personenstandsunterdrückung*.

public authorities she will have a right to remain silent about the father's identity.[49]

2.3. RECOGNITION OF THE RIGHT TO KNOW ON THE BASIS OF THE PERSONALITY RIGHT

In a case before the Federal Constitutional Court from 1988, a thirty-year old woman sought certainty as to her father's name in the pursuance of property rights.[50] The lower courts had already decided that children born out of wedlock enjoyed a right to find out their father's name through their mother, who had nonetheless argued that imposing a duty to disclose would be in breach of her personality rights. The Federal Constitutional Court concurred with the (adult) child's claim, while affirming that such a duty existed. The decision that was to follow the year after gained greater recognition and provoked more debates because of the emphatically more generalistic character that the right acquired in that decision.

Thus, it was not until 1989 that the Federal Constitutional Court in acknowledging the right to know one's genetic parentage as an aspect of the personality right, seemingly irrespective of a person's status or the circumstances at birth, fulfilled its globally pioneering role.[51] This has contributed to the right to know having become a veritable *Topos* of contemporary **German** constitutional legal culture.[52]

Accordingly, the line of argumentation differed fundamentally from the court's decision the year before. The 1988 decision had concerned a non-marital child, which left scope for interpretations that brought it into connection with the status equality between children born within and outside marriage, an implicit consideration of Article 6 V of the Federal Constitution. By contrast, the 1989 decision, while also involving an 'adult' daughter, concerned a denial of the husband of her mother. Even though this daughter had for a long time been fully aware of her genetic father's identity, she had not challenged paternity. It is not without irony, therefore, that a constitutional recognition of the right to *know who* was framed in this context of denial proceedings. But because the daughter's

---

49 §383 I ZPO. MUSCHELER & BLOCH (2002), p. 14.

50 BVerfGE, 18 January 1988, *FamRZ* 1989, p. 147.

51 BVerfGE 79, 256 = *FamRZ* 1989, p. 255, on reference from the Amtsgericht Hamburg, 3 March 1987.

52 HELMS (1999), p. 49.

parents had been married, however, the equality principle could not provide a viable constitutional basis.

The Federal Constitutional Court, while conceding that the child's right to know her or his father was 'not without limits', considered that information relevant to the identity of one's father should not be withheld if available. The court saw such a possible restriction in the interest of salvaging the mother's marriage. However, in the instant case, the effect of §1596(1) (*old*) would be such that it vitiated the whole meaning of the child's personality right. German parentage law, as it stood, meant that the paternity of the mother's husband could effectively only be challenged in case the mother would divorce or separate from her husband. This being so, the court recurred to an alternate constitutional basis, affirming that the general personality right protected a general right to know one's genetic origins. This was tantamount to a break with tradition which had relied on the equality notion implicit in Article 6 V of the Constitution.

In that light, it is appropriate to quote the crucial part of the argumentation:

'Knowledge of one's parentage is one of the elements which has a decisive significance for the development of the personality. The connection to one's ancestors can provide a vital key to the individual's self-awareness and position in society. The knowledge of one's origins can provide an important point of reference for comprehension of family links and for the development of one's personality. The inability to discover one's parentage can constitute a serious burden to the individual and cause profound uncertainty. For these reasons the general right of personality encompasses the right to know one's parentage'.[53]

Why was this decision a watershed? First, the Federal Constitutional Court had relied on an implicit personality right, rather than Article 6 V GG. As such, a child's individual interest in the biological truth was distinguished from the child's interest in status determination. By implication, reliance on the personality right meant that the protection of marriage and family life could lend themselves to interpretations in which they could become subordinate to this 'new' right. As a matter of fact, the right in principle henceforth came to extend 'to each and every person', regardless of their parents being married or not.[54] Finally, the personality right may have reinforced the idea, already implicit in

53 As translated by FORDER (1995), p. 100.
54 HELMS (1999), p. 49.

the 1988 decision, that a person's interest in clarifying her or his genetic descent should not be made contingent upon that person's adult age.

The decision provoked an impassioned doctrinal debate. While authors welcomed the decision,[55] others barely masked their scepticism or even disdain. A particularly dismissive reaction suggested that the right to know one's genetic origins was a 'miscarriage characteristic of the contemporary tendency to elevate ordinary legal problems to the constitutional level'.[56] Furthermore, Koch saw in it a dangerous relapse into 'unenlightened ideology' that had just decades before glorified the significance of the blood tie, while being oblivious to the legitimacy of contemporary legal institutions such as adoption and the transfer of parental authority to a step-parent after divorce.[57]

Both Koch and Ramm suggested, moreover, that there was no unequivocal evidence in the social sciences which actually confirmed that knowledge of one's genetic origins would indeed be so fundamental for building a solid sense of personal identity as was popularly believed.[58] What the Federal Constitutional Court had misguidedly taken for a constitutional right could 'at its roots' be a 'pathological' form of curiosity.[59] What is more, one author even likened the right to know to a blessing in disguise, as it would actually be a stumbling-block for the 'ongoing spiritual and psychological process' of construing a personal identity.

In particular, the constitutional argument would be misguided to the extent that it assumed that indissoluble, affective bonds would necessarily exist between genetic parents and their children whereas in fact this would all too often rely on 'wishful thinking' on the part of the child.[60] Furthermore, the question was raised as to what – if anything – could still restrict the right's scope, if it derived from a notion of 'human dignity'. Accordingly, the 'magnanimous and abstract wording' of the decision was targeted because it would convey a sense of absoluteness in dispensing with any reference to potential restrictions other than the mother's marriage (which amounted to little in practice).[61] Following that line

---

55 STARCK (1989), p. 338

56 DEICHFUß (1989), p. 116.

57 KOCH (1990), p. 573.

58 RAMM (1989), p. 1594-1596; KOCH (1990), p. 573.

59 RAMM (1989), p. 1594-1596.

60 HASSENSTEIN (1988), p. 122-123.

61 BVerfGE 79, 256 , 31 January 1989, *FamRZ* 1989, 255. There does seem to be tension between the repeated use of the verb 'to be able to', suggesting a hypothetical and subjective need, and words which suggest absoluteness in the decision: ***can*** *provide a vital key...* ***can*** *provide an*

of argumentation, as a 'newborn' constitutional right, the right to know would be a constitutional 'non-starter', especially in view of the fact that, as a right ultimately based upon human dignity, it would inherently not be 'negotiable' in the sense of lending itself to balanced interpretations.[62]

2.4. EARLY DOCTRINAL DEBATES ON THE FEASIBILITY OF THE CREATION OF AN 'ISOLATED' PROCEDURE

Even though strong words as to the constitutionality of a right to know are easy to find in such early reactions, soon thereafter debates abated on its constitutional justification. Rather, the nature of the debate shifted towards its procedural implications, in exploring the idea whether it would be feasible to create a procedure in which 'solely' the factual existence of genetic ties (known as a so-called '*isolierte Abstammungsfeststellungsklage*') between children and parents would be established.

In part this debate drew on the 1989 decision itself because the Federal Constitutional Court had been called upon to create conditions for the procedural enforcement of the child's right to know. Furthermore, in a case which followed soon afterwards, the applicant sought the identification of his genetic father without seeking a review of the legal relationship with his legal father.[63] The applicant alleged, rather, that his interest derived from a deeply-felt wish to fill up some narrative gaps in his personal history. While the regional court refrained from stating that a legal avenue for the verification of biological facts should be made available, it dismissed the claim with reference to the expiry of statutory time-limits for status procedures.

Still, a debate ensued as to the desirability of such an exclusively informational procedure. Such a procedure would be concerned exclusively with the clarification of the factual existence of the biological fact. A small number of authors enthusiastically warmed to this idea.[64] As a basic advantage, the informational needs of the child would be satisfied without requiring the applicant to sacrifice existing family law relationships. Moreover, in the field of adoption such a right to access without reviewing the applicant's legal relationship with his socio-legal

*important point of reference for comprehension of family links and for the development of one's personality... **can** constitute a serious burden to the individual and cause profound uncertainty.*

62 DEICHFUß (1989), p. 115.

63 OLG Oldenburg, 17 July 1990, *FamRZ* 1991, p. 351-352.

64 MUTSCHLER (1994) p. 65-70; more sceptical: GERNHUBER/COESTER-WALTJEN (2006), p. 587-588.

parents was already believed to exist, without this seemingly provoking any insurmountable problems.[65] Still, this analogy was dismissed as the nature of adoption would *ab initio* be different in many respects from other forms of socio-legally constructed parenthood.[66] Thus, whereas adoption would be geared 'openly' towards the creation of a legal relationship with parents other than the genetic parents, in traditional families the legal interest in privacy would be fundamentally different.

In the early parliamentary debates, the creation of such a procedure was also dismissed.[67] In connection with problems resulting from interference by a 'third parent', the procedure would only undermine the child's integration within the socio-legal family and well-being. Meanwhile, having established the identity of the genetic father, maintenance or inheritance interests could be maintained by the child in respect of the socio-legal father. As a result, the latter's form of paternity would have become 'downgraded' to a '*Zahlvaterschaft*', effectively little more than a pitiable form of second-rate parenthood only connected with financial duties.

2.5. THE 1996 PARENTAGE LAW REFORM ACT

In 1994 the procedural time-limits in denying paternity came under constitutional scrutiny.[68] The Federal Constitutional Court considered that it was irreconcilable with the personality right if a child, unaware of his legal father not being his genetic father, were unable to challenge paternity upon having become an adult. This decision accordingly also went in the direction of affirming that a child's right to know does not end as one matures.

Meanwhile, the federal government had introduced a draft law on March 22, 1996 for a major reform of parentage law.[69] The main aim of this reform was to end the difference in legal treatment between legitimate and illegitimate children. The act was promulgated on December 19, 1997 and it entered into force on July 1, 1998.[70] It was part of a wider legislative plan to improve children's rights, extending to areas such as visitation rights, guardianship, inheritance and

---

65 COESTER-WALTJEN *FamRZ* 1992, p. 369.

66 RAUSCHER/STAUDINGER (2004), BGB, §1592, No. 4, 227-228.

67 Gesetz zur Reform des Kindschaftsrechts (KindRG), BGBl, I 1997, No. 84, 19 December 1997; *BT-Drucks.* 13/4899, p. 56.

68 BVerfGE, 26 April 1994, *FamRZ* 1994, p. 881.

69 *BT-Drucks.* 180/96, 22 March 1996.

70 *BT-Drucks.* 13/4183, p. 6.

child maintenance.[71] As far as the establishment of parentage was concerned, the reform first defined the mother of the child as the woman who gave birth to that child.[72] Legitimacy and illegitimacy have since then no longer been in use as legal terminology.

2.6. EXTRA-JUDICIAL PATERNITY TESTS AND RECOGNITION OF THE FATHER'S CONSTITUTIONAL RIGHT TO KNOW HIS PROGENY

From the year 2000 a number of revolving baby 'hatches or slots' called *Babyklappen* (incubator-like containers usually built into a hospital wall) spread across **Germany**, allowing mothers to give birth discreetly. Although sharply criticised and considered unconstitutional, these have been able to continue to operate in a legal grey-zone. Around the year 2000, access to parentage tests without the prior consent of a court or a family member reached the forefront of broad media and political attention, too. The issue also received broad legal attention.[73] As an outcome of this legal debate, which shall be further explored in Chapter VII, it has in recent years emerged that a constitutional right to know one's genetic descent may also be successfully claimed by persons other than the child, notably the legal father.[74] Nonetheless, as shall become clear, this 'right to know one's progeny' is still very recent and its further constitutional development must be awaited at the time of writing. Suffice it to mention here that the Federal Court of Justice does not consider this right to be hierarchically subordinate to the child's right.[75]

2.7. VERIFICATION OF THE (NON-)EXISTENCE OF BIOLOGICAL TIES WITHIN THE LEGAL FAMILY BEFORE GERMAN COURTS

As the most recent important legal development, after a decision of the Federal Constitutional Court in 2007, the debate on the desirability of an exclusively informational procedure revived in earnest in the Bundestag.[76] In this decision,

---

71 See further: EDENFELD (1996), p. 190-196; FRANK (1997), p. 167-182; MUSCHELER & BEISENHERTZ (1999), p. 356-361.

72 §1591 BGB. See Chapters VI and X.

73 See Chapter VII.

74 BVerfGE 816, 9 April 2004 , *FamRZ* 2003, p. 816; COESTER-WALTJEN (2006), p. 787.

75 BGH 12 January 2005, XII ZR 227/03 (OLG Celle), *NJW* 2005, 497; BGH 12 January 2005, XII ZR 60/03 (OLG Jena).

76 BVerfGE, 13 February 2007, *FamRZ* 2007, p. 441.

the court called upon the federal legislature to foresee in the creation of a legal procedure by the end of March 2008 for the enforcement of the father's constitutional right to know his progeny.[77] However, it was agreed that the procedural effectiveness of the child's and the mother's rights would also have to be enhanced. Thus, in October 2007, the Federal **German** Government came up with a law proposal regarding 'the ascertaining of paternity independent from proceedings involving a denial of paternity'.[78] This new procedure entered into force in April 2008 and will be discussed in Chapter VII.

In October 2008, the Federal Constitutional Court again considered that a denial of the right of a (presumptive) biological father to challenge an established socio-legal paternity may be reconcilable with Article 6(2) of the Basic Law, which protects the right and duty of parents to take care of children.[79] In this case the socio-legal relationship between the child and the socio-legal father was considered to represent a higher-ranking constitutional value. More remarkably in the light of the recent legislation, the Federal Constitutional Court considered that the biological father was not entitled to an informational procedure on the basis of his right to know his progeny, a derivative of his personality right.[80] Although this right of the father covered both a right of the biological father to request information as to whether a child is his, as well as the right to dispel doubts as to the genetic link when the man is in fact the child's legal father. This right was not taken as an absolute right, however, because the child also has a right to a stable legal and socio-familiar relationship with the (legal) father; both the mother and child had in the court's eyes, moreover, an interest in not disclosing personal information to the father. An interest in having biological fatherhood confirmed in the existence of a legal paternity would therefore not be protected by the personality right.

---

[77] Art. 2 1 in conjunction with Art. 1 1 Federal Constitution = Grundgesetz (GG). *Recht des rechtlichen Vaters auf Kenntnis seiner Nachkommenschaft (Nachwuchses).*

[78] Entwurf eines Gesetzes zur Klärung der Vaterschaft unabhänging vom Anfechtungsverfahren, 4 October 2007, *BT-Drucks.* 16/6561.

[79] BVerfGE, 1 BvR 1548/03, 13 October 2008.

[80] Art. 2 I in conjunction with Art. 1 I GG. See above.

3. FRANCE

3.1. EARLY MODERN HISTORY

Before the **French** Revolution, family law generally permitted child maintenance claims by children born out of wedlock in respect of the begetter.[81] Children born out of wedlock could be legitimized and obtain inheritance rights by the father's subsequent marriage to the mother or by royal decree. The Catholic Church urged both mothers and fathers of illegitimate children to pay child maintenance in accordance with the maxim *'qui a fait l'enfant, doit le nourrir'*.[82] But in the aftermath of the **French** Revolution, the Republican government decreed the *Loi du 12 brumaire an II* which established the formal equality of non-marital children with those born within marriage.[83] Child maintenance rights and inheritance rights were made subject to a formal recognition.[84] However, if the child had a *possession d'état* (civil status relationship) with regard to the (unmarried) father, evidence thereof could substantiate a child maintenance claim.[85] The biological link in itself was regarded as insufficient in that respect.

The revolutionaries banned determinations of paternity before the courts. Allegedly, the evidential problems in determining paternity played a crucial role in this radical decision, but the undesirability of defamatory proceedings, coupled with a public interest in the stability of family life, were also considered relevant factors.[86] Moreover, the husband remained entitled to deny paternity. Accordingly, it may have been expected that there would be no need for a judicial determination of paternity since it came to be regarded as something predicated upon a man's will, rather than being a reflection of biological truth.[87] Thus, this different conceptualization of fatherhood can be appreciated with reference to a new paradigm: '*L'homme libre ... n'est père que par effet de sa volonté*'.[88]

81 RENAUT (2003), p. 50-51.
82 SZRAMKIEWICZ (1995), p. 56. 'Whoever creates the child, must feed him'.
83 SCHMIDT-HIDDING (1967), p. 367.
84 GARAUD & SZRAMKIEWICZ (1978), p. 117.
85 GARAUD & SZRAMKIEWICZ (1978), p. 118; HELMS (1999), p. 17. See Chapter VII for a further description of civil status or *possession d'etat.*
86 SCHMIDT-HIDDING (1967), p. 27.
87 SZRAMKIEWICZ (1995), p. 87.
88 MULLIEZ (1989), p. 419.

As such, the marital presumption of paternity also came under a different light: if it was determined on the assumption of biological truth and the expectation that the mother would generally be faithful to her husband, it came to express the idea that the husband assumed responsibility towards all children born within marriage.[89] Only in the case of a physical impossibility would the husband be able to 'disacknowledge' – rather than 'deny' – paternity.[90] Apart from permitting divorce, as a token of the liberal imprint of the revolutionary family law reforms, adoption was also admitted, after having been virtually unknown since Roman times in Western Europe,

The first **French** Code Civil, the Code Napoléon, drew on this new conceptualization of parenthood as rooted primarily in free will. However, in Article 340 the words '*la recherche de paternité est interdite*' not only echoed the erstwhile ban on the judicial determination of paternity, but became a more general prohibition on paternity proceedings.[91] This prohibition was associated with the Emperor's personal fear of unwanted heirs as well as public reasons for the protection of a stable family life and sexual morality.[92]As the *travaux préparatoires* demonstrate, such collective interests were openly considered to represent higher-ranking societal values than individual and children's rights.[93] Among illegitimate children, a distinction was made between incestuous, adulterine and *enfants naturels simples* born out of wedlock.[94] Only the last-mentioned group were entitled to benefit from a recognition, even if they still could not inherit like legitimate children to the same extent. As far as the establishment of maternity was concerned, court proceedings were allowed, but were few, notably because the practice of *accouchement sous X* was also sanctioned by law.[95]

Nonetheless, the **French** courts began to attenuate the rougher edges of the prohibitive regime on paternity proceedings by awarding damages consisting of child maintenance to the mother if the father refused to make a recognition.[96] Formally, these damages relied on the illegal character of seducing a woman rather than on the establishment of paternity before the court. Still, it was not until November 1912 that the prohibition was lifted and a conditioned possibil-

---

89 SCHMIDT-HIDDING (1967), p. 29; HELMS (1999), p. 19.
90 MULLIEZ (1989), p. 377.
91 The determination of paternity is forbidden.
92 SCHMIDT-HIDDING (1967). p. 30.
93 SCHMIDT-HIDDING (1967), p. 32.
94 SZRAMKIEWICZ (1995), p. 104.
95 See Chapter VI.
96 MOLENGRAAFF (1896), p. 9; SZRAMKIEWICZ (1995), p. 137; HELMS (1999), p. 22.

ity to lodge paternity proceedings was readmitted, albeit still only in respect of *enfants naturels simples*. As such, in situations which involved rape, or in which a written document in which the man's paternity was suggested, or evidence of a seduction existed with a promise of marriage or a period of co-habitation with the mother or even a modest financial contribution by the man to the child's education and upbringing, the mother would have standing.[97] Even so, sometimes men could rely on an *exceptio plurium*, if the mother had a dubious moral reputation, suggesting that she had had sexual relations with more than one man during the conception period. This possibility was retained until 1972.

In July 1955, for the first time, adulterine and incestuous children could claim child maintenance in respect of the begetter.[98] This *action alimentaire* involved a separate maintenance claim that could be lodged independently from paternity proceedings. Ironically, as a result, the *enfants naturels simples* found themselves in a worse position than incestuous or adulterine children since a general right to claim child maintenance for illegitimate children was not recognised until 1969.[99]

This case law was reflected in the parentage law reform of 3 January 1972, which established formal equality between legitimate and illegitimate children, except in inheritance law.[100] The *action alimentaire* introduced in 1955 was replaced by an *action à fins de subsides* which could also be instituted by adulterine and incestuous children against the man who had had sexual relations with the mother during the conception period. If a child's legitimate status was corroborated by her or his civil status, it further became possible for another man to claim paternity by making a recognition.[101]

In 1976, the Cassation Court determined that, in the absence of a civil status relationship in respect of the father, any person with a sufficient interest would be able, within a thirty-year period, to lodge paternity proceedings.[102] As such, the child was given a right to challenge paternity for the first time. In contrast to this leeway offered if social family ties were non-existent, the right of the legal father to deny paternity in the absence of the biological link had only been

97 Schmidt-Hidding (1967), p. 85.
98 Madlener (1969), p. 210.
99 Cass., 20 May 1969, D.1969, 429.
100 Massip (2006), p. 7.
101 Art. 334-9 **French** Code Civil (*old*).
102 Cass., 9 June 1976, D.1976, 593.

extended from one month after the birth to six months.[103] In accordance with the 1972 reform, the mother had also been accorded a right to deny her husband's paternity, but only under the condition that she would remarry the biological father, who was required to produce letters of legitimation.[104] Scepticism was also expressed with regard to the question whether it would really be in the child's interests to have a legal father who assumed parental responsibilities not out of free choice, but because a court had imposed it.[105] In that connection, too, a very specific case law developed on the basis of the 1972 reform in which the judicial determination of paternity became subject to serious, preliminary indications of non-paternity known as *indices graves*.[106] Judicial insistence on such preliminary indications was not lifted until the latest 2005 reform.

3.2. THE CREATION OF A NATIONAL COUNCIL FOR ACCESS TO PERSONAL ORIGINS (CNAOP)

Article 326 of the **French** Code Civil allows mothers to give birth without disclosing details about their identity in **France**.[107] It thereby enshrines the '**French**' legal tradition permitting anonymous births.[108] In January 2002, partly in response to criticisms voiced by the UN Children's Rights Committeee, the **French** legislator introduced new provisions into the Family and Social Action Code to help enforce the child's right to know. Although the right to information did not gain recognition under the Constitution, it was considered that the mother who intends to give birth anonymously must be informed about its importance for the child to find out.[109] The mother is therefore expressly 'invited' to leave behind details about not only her own identity, but also that of the father, her medical information and the personal circumstances surrounding the birth. This information is now registered centrally by a special National Council for Access to Personal Origins (*Conseil National d'Accès aux Origines Personnelles*). The mother can choose to have this information sealed in an envelope, while retaining a right to revoke the secrecy surrounding her identity at any time. If the mother has died without leaving behind any written objection

---

103 Art. 316(1) **French** Code Civil (*old*).

104 Art. 318(1) **French** Code Civil (*old*).

105 VIDAL (1978), p. 1130 ; RUBELLIN-DEVICHI (1995), p. 329.

106 RUBELLIN-DEVICHI (1993), p. 3659.

107 *Lors de l'acchouchement, la mere peut demander que le secret de son admission et de son identité soit préservé.*

108 See the discussion of the ECtHR *Odièvre* case, in Chapter III, and Chapter VI for a more detailed discussion.

109 Art. L 147-6 Code de l'action sociale et de la famille.

to the disclosure of her identity, her information will be disclosed to children upon their request.

3.3. THE 2005 REFORM OF PARENTAGE LAW

On the 4 July 2005, a comprehensive legislative reform was passed, which provided for a profound revision of Title VII on parentage ('*de la filiation*').[110] The new **French** parentage law entered into force on 1 July 2006.[111] As a general aim, the reform has sought to achieve greater equality between marital and non-marital children. Furthermore, it seeks to reduce and simplify the number of procedures. It was considered that the biological truth should play a more important role whenever parentage relations are contested, but that the child's interests in growing up in a stable family environment and parental privacy require that a review of legal parent-child relationships should, upon the expiry of certain time-limits, no longer be possible. As such, the 'sociological truth' continues to play a key role in **French** parentage law.[112]

4. THE NETHERLANDS

4.1. EARLY MODERN LEGISLATIVE HISTORY

Old **Dutch** law distinguished between legitimate and illegitimate children. The latter group was sub-divided into natural, incestuous and adulterine children. The begetter only owed illegitimate children maintenance. Legitimisation was made contingent upon a subsequent marriage or could be granted by governmental decree. Paternity suits were generally admitted on the basis of a mother's declaration.[113]

The Napoleonic Code for the Kingdom of Holland, ruled by Napoleon's brother Louis, distinguished between legitimate and illegitimate children in a way broadly similar to old **Dutch** law.[114] The **Dutch** Civil Code of 1838 by and large incorporated such **French** influences. Accordingly, the prohibition on paternity

110 *Ordonnance* No. 2005-759 of 4 July 2005, Journal Officiel of 6 July 2005, p. 11159.

111 Décret No. 2006-640 of 1 June 2006, Journal Officiel of 2 June 2006, p. 8332; Circulaire CIV/13/06 de presentation de l'ordonnance n. 759-2005 du 4 juillet 2005 portant réforme de la filiation.

112 FERRAND (2007), p. 95.

113 ASSER-DE BOER (2006), No. 689, p. 549-550.

114 ASSER-DE BOER (2006), No. 689, p. 550-551.

suits also made its way into **Dutch** law in 1811.[115] As in France, the courts sought to circumvent the prohibition by awarding damages to mothers on the grounds of seduction. The prohibition occupied centre stage of scholarly and public debates towards the end of the nineteenth Century, rallying support for a burgeoning feminist movement.[116]

In particular, an article by the legal scholar Molengraaff published in a socio-cultural journal in 1896 proved important in exerting pressure on the legislature. As such, Molengraaff went as far as to consider the judicial determination of paternity to be an ethical command of all civilized nations, suggesting that an unmarried father had both a moral and legal duty to remove the stigma attached to illegitimacy. In that connection, it remains an interesting fact that he denied that evidential problems would present a legal problem, as paternity could still be determined in most cases. Furthermore, Molengraaff exposed the popular myth that if a judicial determination of paternity were to be reintroduced, reputable men would otherwise be left at the whim of the slightest procedural opportunity.[117] Though far ahead of his time, then, Molengraaff considered that although child maintenance should be admitted in respect of illegitimate children, they should not be able to inherit to the same extent in order to protect and promote marriage.

It was not until almost a decade after this key publication that some of Molengraaff's proposals were reflected in a legislative reform of 1909.[118] Subsequent to this reform, it became possible for the mother to claim child maintenance from the man who had fathered the child during the child's minority. In the absence of recognition by the unmarried man, no legal child-father relationship was created. However, even the procedural effectiveness of the maintenance claim was limited in view of the fact that it was only possible to institute proceedings during the first five years after birth primarily in order to protect the man's privacy.[119] Furthermore, the man could sometimes claim that the mother had had other sexual relations during the period of conception.

---

115 Art. 342 **Dutch** Civil Code (*old*).

116 BOELE-WOELKI & DE HONDT (1998), p. 28-30.

117 MOLENGRAAFF (1896), p. 15.

118 Act of 16 November 1909, *Staatsblad* 363.

119 Art. 1:394 DCC. The time-limit was abandoned after the 1998 reform following a proposal by de Boer. See: DE BOER (1998), p. 1075.

4.2. THE 1998 REFORM OF DUTCH PARENTAGE LAW

1 April 1998 heralded major changes in **Dutch** family law resulting from the entry into force of a new code of parentage law.[120] The sheer length of parliamentary deliberations, prior to the reform, attests to a particularly toilsome legislative process. As such, genuine efforts at reform had already begun when the Minister of Justice drafted a preliminary proposal in 1981. This proposal resulted in law proposal 20 626, which was repealed in 1993. The second proposal, which also included adoption law, was more short-lived and halted following a negative appraisal by the Council of State. The final, successful proposal was not presented until March 1996.

As a general aim, the reform was geared towards bringing 'classical' parentage law in accordance with 'requirements of the contemporary age'.[121] This contemporary vision of parentage relations was deemed to boil down to the furthering of especially two main objectives. First, it was considered expedient to achieve greater equality between children born within and out of marriage. Whereas most discriminatory substantive provisions had already been eliminated prior to the reform, it was considered necessary to delete the terms 'legitimate' and 'illegitimate'. Furthermore, the term 'family law relationship'[122] replaced the obsolete 'civil law relationship'. Second, it was considered that legal parentage should reflect natural descent to a greater extent. This was one of the reasons behind the (re)introduction of the judicial determination of paternity more than a century after Molengraaff's publication.

Nonetheless, the possibility to access information concerning one's genetic parentage, 'which must be presumed not to concern registers of the civil status registry or those protected by the councils for the protection of minors,' was regarded by the legislature as an issue which was 'far removed' from the purposes of the legislative proposal.[123] As a consequence, it was submitted that covering both issues in a single legislative proposal would 'not be prudent.'[124]

---

120 Law of 24 December 1997, *Staatsblad* 772 (*Kamerstukken* 24 649). Enacted on 21 February 1998, *Staatsblad* 126.

121 *Kamerstukken II* 1996/97, 24 649, No. 6, p. 2.

122 Thus, the term 'familierechtelijke betrekking' replaced 'burgerrechtelijke betrekking'.

123 *Kamerstukken II* 1996/97, 24 649, B, p. 2.

124 *Kamerstukken II* 1996/97, 24 649, B, p. 2.

Still, in view of some case law[125] and the wording of the provision,[126] Article 7(1) UNCRC is believed to be potentially directly applicable in the Netherlands, which, as a fundamentally monistic legal system, considers international (and European) legal norms to apply directly. Accordingly, Article 7(1) UNCRC has been invoked before courts. In one such case, a 27-year-old woman, who suspected that her socio-legal parents were not her genetic parents, applied for a court-ordered DNA test since they had been unwilling to undergo testing.[127] The applicant contended that she had been suffering from psychological problems which she ascribed to some extent to her uncertainty as to her genetic origins. As she had refused to undergo psychological counselling, however, the court submitted that no link could be established between the gap in her knowledge about her past and her current problems.

Still, the applicant also suggested that she was exposed to a hereditary blood disease. Furthermore, she suggested that the court should take note of the physical dissimilarities between her and her legal parents. In that connection, the regional court took the view that Article 7 UNCRC should be interpreted not only as a right to know who one's genetic parents are, but also to verify whether one's legal parents are *not* one's genetic parents. Even so, the legal parents would have a constitutional right to corporal (physical) integrity, guaranteed under Article 11 of the Dutch Constitution. It was emphasized that the child's right under the UNCRC is not absolute. Ultimately, the court denied the applicant's claim in the absence of medical and psychological evidence of harm and found physical dissimilarities as such insufficient grounds to order testing.

In another case, a minor sought to establish contact with his presumptive genetic father, also with direct reference to Article 7(1) UNCRC.[128] This case antedated the reform, which meant that his desire for certainty could not be framed as a judicial determination of paternity under Article 1:207 of the Dutch Civil Code. Still, the Dutch Supreme Court took the view that the applicant's right protected under Article 7 UNCRC involved more than a disclosure of the parent's name.

At the same time, though, it was argued that it could not be presumed that the States Parties had envisaged a right that permitted a child, who the father had not recognised and with whom the man desired not to have any contact, could be compelled to maintain such contact. The decision met with strong reactions

---

125 Ruitenberg (2003), p. 92-99 and p. 193.

126 Meuwese, Morelli & Wolthuis (2000), p. 193.

127 Rechtbank 's-Hertogenbosch, 27 March 1997, *KG* 1997, No. 147.

128 Hoge Raad, 22 December 1995, *NJ* 1996, p. 419; *NJCM* 1996 21-3, p. 426-427.

from a number of annotators.[129] As such, von Brucken Fock pointed out that the most natural way to know one's parents would necessitate regular contact.[130]

Nonetheless, it was also considered that a right to contact would require a far more extensive right than requiring a genetic parent to be identifiable under **Dutch** law.[131] At the very least, in the view of the **Dutch** Supreme Court, as a legal concept, the 'right to know' under Article 7-1 UNCRC involved information on a parent's name.

4.3. THE *VALKENHORST I* CASE

For the constitutionalisation of access to genetic origins under **Dutch** law, the proceedings instituted by a woman against the charitable foundation called *Valkenhorst*, in Breda, where she spent most of her childhood, have remained benchmarks. Although these cases antedated the ratification by the **Dutch** government of the UNCRC, the court already referred to the relevance of Article 7 UNCRC. The charitable foundation's predecessor, *Moederheil*, was a Catholic birth clinic for unmarried mothers. In the 1920s and 1930s a large number of children were born in *Moederheil*. By the end of the 1980s, their 'children' wished to obtain access to their files which had been sealed by the institution in the performance of its public health obligations. One claim, known as *Valkenhorst I*, originated in June 1989[132] and was not subject to an appeal in cassation. Her other claim, known as *Valkenhorst II*, was first lodged in March 1991[133] and was subjected to an appeal in cassation in June 1994.

Valkenhorst II was the first case to reach the **Dutch** Supreme Court in which the applicant's desire to access information concerning her genetic parentage was not framed into a legal status procedure. In the absence of any clear legislative norms, the Supreme Court derived such a 'right to know one's origins' from a 'personality right', an unwritten legal concept which was inferred from the **Dutch** Constitution. This was remarkable, since in contrast to **German** constitutional law, the personality right doctrine was – and has remained – very much

129 BRUCKEN FOCK, *FJR* 1996, p. 62-65.
130 BRUCKEN FOCK, *FJR* 1996, p. 64.
131 LEENEN, *FJR* 1999, p. 60. Referred case law: HR, 8 February 1991, *NJ* 1992, p. 21 and HR, 8 February 1991, *NJ* 1992, 22.
132 Rechtbank Breda 20 June 1989, 726; Appeal: Hof 's-Hertogenbosch, 18 September, *NJ* 1991, 796, *NJCM-Bulletin* 17-2 (1992), p. 150.
133 Rechtbank Breda, 5 March 1991, *NJ* 1991, 370; Appeal: Hof 's-Hertogenbosch, 25 November 1992, *NJ* 1993, 211; Supreme Court: HR, 15 April 1994, *NCJM-Bulletin* 19-6 (1994), p. 652.

an underdeveloped legal concept in **Dutch** constitutional law. Instead, it has been said that the Supreme Court could also simply have chosen to rely on the direct effect of the right to private life under Article 8 ECHR in the **Dutch** legal order.[134]

Yet in considering an alternative, new constitutional basis, the **Dutch** Supreme Court created opportunities for its further development. As such, in his comparative law dissertation on the personality right in **Germany** and t**he Netherlands**, Nehmelman also welcomed this incorporation of the **German** personality right doctrine into **Dutch** law in view of its complementary value in claims that involve a fundamental (personality) interest, but for which no clear legal basis could be found in private law.[135] According to Nehmelman, the *Valkenhorst (II)* case constituted an example of such an interpretation.[136] If the cumbersome legislative process of constitutional amendments were bypassed outside private law, more caution would, however, be warranted.[137]

For our discussion, it was especially significant that the **Dutch** Supreme Court expressly denied that the right to know one's genetic parentage had an 'absolute scope', even if it did not say what this meant. Furthermore, it is noteworthy that the *Valkenhorst* cases were also referred to *inter alia* by the ECtHR's mention in the *Odièvre* case.

The applicant in *Valkenhorst I* wished to obtain access to a file that the charitable institution had kept on her since 1927. She argued that she had grounds to believe that the foundation must have continued to keep the file not merely in the exercise of its professional functioning but also with a view to a disclosure of its contents to her in the future. Furthermore, the applicant called upon her 'subjective right to know her origins'. In her submission, that right prevailed over the obligation of non-disclosure incumbent on the foundation. A failure on the part of the foundation to disclose the desired information to her would be tantamount to a violation of unwritten private law norms.

For its part, the foundation relied on its professional obligation not to disclose the information, because it would otherwise become liable to criminal persecu-

---

134 MICHIELS & OVERKLEEFT-VERBURG (2000), p. 270.
135 NEHMELMAN (2002), p. 117.
136 Another case in which a personality right was recognised involved that of Hoge Raad, 22 December 1995, *NJ* 1996, p. 467 ('*Parool*').
137 NEHMELMAN (2002), p. 112.

tion.[138] On the basis of submissions made by both parties, the Breda Court concluded that the information was not generally or publicly known and, as a result, would fall within the ambit of criminally liable professional secrecy.

The applicant denied the confidential nature of the contents of the file kept on her, as the information would only have been lent a confidential character in view of the religious ideology of the foundation. The first instance court insisted that, whether such religious persuasion had been relevant or not, in having given their personal information to the foundation, the mothers had acknowledged that it bore a confidential character.

Nonetheless, the applicant suggested that the file, dating from 1927, would have lost its confidential character in the course of time. The first instance court agreed that time might have an 'eroding impact' on the obligation of non-disclosure, with interests in secrecy and in data protection gradually diluting. In respect of that argument, the first instance court took the view that the identifying information concerning the claimant's begetter could be regarded as such a deep secret that the confidential nature of this information could not be regarded to have lost its significance over the course of time.

The applicant further alleged that her birthmother had wished to inform her of her genetic parentage as she had gathered that she had left behind a sealed envelope with details concerning her identity. Even so, the court denied the existence of any legal obligation to disclose information concerning one's genetic parentage under Dutch law, suggesting that such an 'extra-legal obligation could not be considered to have already become entrenched in a common legal awareness'. In that respect, the court drew attention to the fact that the policy of secrecy served a relationship of confidentiality between mothers, who had to give birth in a situation of distress, and the foundation. For this reason alone, the foundation considered that it could not be forced to disclose information about the mother's identity.

Still, the district court acknowledged that Dutch law could require disclosure in the – unlikely event – that persons, who intended to marry each other, were within prohibited degrees of consanguinity or in case of a heightened risk of exposure to a hereditary disease.[139] Barring such situations, the court insisted that

[138] Art. 272 Dutch Criminal Law Code.
[139] Art. 1:41(1) DCC.

access to identifying information need not be provided in case of a public duty of non-disclosure under **Dutch** law.

On appeal, however, the 's-Hertogenbosch Court of Appeal departed from the basic premise that three conflicting interests were discernible. Thus, it was readily acknowledged, without much further ado, that the applicant indeed had an interest in knowing the identity of her genetic parents and that she could only access this information by obtaining access to the file kept by the institution. As such, the 's-Hertogenbosch Court of Appeal had taken into account the ECtHR's case law, in particular in the *Gaskin* decision. Equipped with a better understanding of international and European law, it also referred to Article 17 ICCPR and Articles 7 and 8 UNCRC in substantiating the applicant's 'interest'.

At the same time, though, the appeal court also took into consideration the public interest of healthcare institutions such as Valkenhorst. In that respect, mention was also made of case law concerning procedural excusal which had detracted from the individual interest in being able to seek support and advice from healthcare professionals.

In the third place, the interest of the registered parent(s) in the protection of their privacy was acknowledged. As such, this interest was deemed to fall within the ambit of both the right to private life, as protected under Article 8 ECHR, as well as Article 17 ICCPR. The information desired by the applicant was considered to be supremely relevant for the 'private and family life' of both the deceased birthmother and that of the putative begetter.

The court considered that none of the enunciated interests carried such moral or legal weight that either would under all circumstances have to give way to the other. In particular, it was suggested that any 'absolutist viewpoint' on access to information concerning genetic parentage would occasion far-reaching and extensive consequences. Thus, it was ventured that extremist interpretations could even incite some mothers to abandon their children (or, perhaps, to give birth anonymously). In view of such dangers, it was deemed more prudent to examine each case affecting access to origins on its individual merits.

Still, the 's-Hertogenbosch Court of Appeal conceived of the applicant as essentially not being more than a third party in relation to the file kept on her, since this formally only established a legal relationship between the birth mother and Valkenhorst. Yet, concededly, the applicant would have to be considered an interested party. This qualification, though, in itself did not give her a right to access the requested information. Rather, the court of appeal presumed that the files had been preserved for so long primarily for medical reasons and possibly to help enforce the birth mother's child maintenance claims in respect of the man who had fathered her.

Even so, the court of appeal considered that the fact that the mother had lived in the clinic for six years gave rise to a relationship governed by unwritten legal norms.[140] Assuming that this relationship existed, account would also have to be taken of the 'justifiable interests of the claimant'. In determining the nature of these requirements regard should be had to general legal principles, prevalent doctrinal views in **the Netherlands** as well as societal and personal interests.[141]

The appeal court also submitted that there were no or insufficient grounds to believe that the birthmother had voluntarily provided information concerning the putative begetter to Valkenhorst. It was rather supposed that it had been the foundation itself that had requested this information to further a claim for financial support in the child's upbringing. It was also argued that the begetter, assuming he was found to be still alive, would, in any event, have to be very old. As a corollary, his privacy interest would have diluted inasmuch as Valkenhorst could no longer claim that a public obligation did not permit the disclosure of his identity. The basis of the privacy interests of the begetter's relatives would accordingly be rendered even more tenuous and hypothetical. It comes as no surprise, therefore, that their interests were not considered sufficiently relevant.

On appeal the argument was replicated that the privacy interest of the birth mother did not necessarily come to an end at the moment of her death. However, it was submitted that this interest might have altered considerably. These alterations related to contemporary societal perceptions of motherhood outside marriage. Furthermore, the court was quick to brush aside the argument that her memory might still be affected by a disclosure. The foundation's argument that disclosure might result in psychological harm for the claimant and that the petitioned information, if provided, might not even prove reliable, was also deemed irrelevant. This was justifiable since the foundation was not called upon to make any such assessment of the moral basis of the request for information in the first place.

140 *Redelijkheid en billijkheid* (civil law norm of 'reasonableness and fairness').
141 Art. 3:12 DCC.

4.4. THE *VALKENHORST II* CASE

In the second action the applicants objected that the policy changes made by the foundation resulting from the decision in *Valkenhorst I* had failed to go quite far enough. All of the applicants in *Valkenhorst II* had been born between 1935 and 1944 in *Moederheil.* One of them, Ms de R., appealed and thereafter requested an appeal in cassation before the **Dutch** Supreme Court. Subsequent to the earlier judgment a few amendments had been made in the policy of the foundation.

The amended policy of the foundation may be summarised as follows. Identifying information concerning the mother would in principle always be disclosed. Other types of information would be subject to a set of rules. A distinction was made as to whether the mother was still alive or not. During the mother's lifetime her consent would be required. By contrast, after the mother's death details about parentage and upbringing would be provided unless the mother had expressly stated that she did not wish the information to be communicated to her child. If the mother could not be traced or was incapable of giving consent, the same regime would apply. If the birthmother had refused to give her consent to the disclosure of her identity, the foundation would neither disclose it during her lifetime nor after her death.

The applicants sought access to all the files and logbooks which in their view concerned them more than anyone else. The Breda Court insisted that the duty of confidentiality which had existed at the time of their birth had not come to an end as a result of the mere passage of time. It was emphasised, moreover, that the petitioned information related to the private life of the mothers. As a consequence, the petitioned information related to the duty of confidentiality that the foundation had taken upon itself. The Court was satisfied that the dependence of the applicants on the collaboration of the foundation for the effectuation of their claim constituted a sufficient interest.

In contradistinction to its ruling in *Valkenhorst I,* the Breda Court took into consideration the provision of the **Dutch** Civil Code which was applicable at the time of the applicants' births and which established an obligation for unmarried mothers to declare births.[142] The existence of this provision was seen as a sufficient indication that an exception had, although perhaps unwittingly, been admitted by the legislator to the basic rule of strict confidentiality incumbent on obstetricians and other medical professionals involved at birth. As a conse-

142 Art. 1:30 DCC (*old*); see above.

quence, information identifying the (unmarried) mothers may have to be provided.

The Breda Court also took the ECtHR's decision in *Gaskin* into consideration. An analogy was drawn between both cases. From *Gaskin* it was deduced that no absolute right to know one's genetic parentage existed on the basis of that decision. This was based on the misguided interpretation that the files the applicant had requested may not have been accessible either.

The claim that the Valkenhorst institution was criminally liable under Article 236 **Dutch** Criminal Code for false registration of births also found no support in the eyes of the Breda Court. This does not come as a surprise if it is considered that a person's *staat* (personal status) does not presuppose a genetic tie between parent and child. In discarding that claim the Breda Court added that no statutory obligation exists under **Dutch** law for anyone to state the identity of the genetic father on the child's birth record. This position could be defended in the absence of the judicial determination of paternity in **Dutch** law as it stood.

The Breda Court paraphrased the basic question as one involving a right to excusal deriving from the duty of confidentiality. The court reiterated that the children's direct connection to the files did not entail a right for them to accede to those files. It was also concluded that the mothers, in any event, had not expressed a wish to absolve the foundation of the confidentiality they had accorded to it. Rather, it was considered that they had expressly wished the identity of the father to remain secret.

On appeal, the applicant Ms de R. called into question that the Valkenhorst institution could rely on the mother's refusal to consent to deny access to the files relating to her. She corroborated her claim further by postulating a '*right*' rather than an '*interest*' in obtaining information concerning her genetic parentage. In that connection, the 's-Hertogenbosch Court of Appeal added that even if such a 'right' were acknowledged, its character would not be absolute in the meaning of a capacity to override the rights and interests of others. Somewhat far-fetched and legalistic was the argument that the applicant was essentially no more than a third party in the relationship between the information provider (the mother) and the information keeper (Valkenhorst). In that connection, the 's-Hertogenbosch Court of Appeal underlined the existence of the duty of confidentiality. The court conceded, however, that the services of the foundation may very well not have exclusively been geared solely towards the protection of birthmothers, but also towards the interests of the resultant children.

The decision of the 's-Hertogenbosch Court of Appeal in its earlier ruling in *Valkenhorst I* resounded because it also distinguished the same three interests. Thus, it was re-established that the applicant had 'an interest' in knowing the identity of her biological father, which could be considered to be fundamental. Fundamental interests in the court's view were, however, also the general public interest in allowing anyone to have free access – i.e. without fear of disclosure – to a service provider like Valkenhorst as well as the right of both the mother and the registered begetter of the applicant to the protection of such sensitive private information. A novel point made by the Court was that the interest of the begetter was nothing more than a subordinate interest in Valkenhorst's policy. As a consequence, in the procedure no preponderant weight could be accorded to that interest either in the court's view. As a **Dutch** judge may discern other interests that have not been adduced by the parties, it is unclear, however, why this interest would apparently have to be deemed to necessarily have been less relevant.

In contrast to Valkenhorst the 's-Hertogenbosch Court of Appeal insisted that the interests at hand require an abstract assessment. This assessment led the court of appeal to conclude that the mother's interest in combination with the aforementioned public interest, in the anticipation of relevant legislation, outweighed that of the applicant. In that connection, it argued that the public interest also required that any anticipatory denial of the mother's interest might, out of fear of absolute claims to information, result in greater harm for children than their dispensing with information on their genetic origins.

The **Dutch** Supreme Court quashed the earlier decisions. The most radically innovative point it made consisted of the recognition of a *right* to know one's origins, a right that was protected under **Dutch** constitutional law. The basis of this new constitutional right was found in a more general underlying freedom of personality. The **Dutch** Supreme Court ruled that basic rights such as respect for private life (Article 8 ECHR), freedom of thought and conscience, freedom of religion and freedom of expression all form aspects of this unwritten personality right. In that regard, it is considered beyond dispute that the **Dutch** Supreme Court relied heavily on **German** constitutional law. In marked contradistinction to **German** federal constitutional law, the personality right doctrine had been (and still remains) underdeveloped in **Dutch** law. Thus, Forder has pointed out the 'striking' likeness between the phrasing of the **Dutch** Supreme Court and the Federal Constitutional Court. The **Dutch** Supreme Court therefore very much 'unearthed' a right.[143] The **German** imprint of the judgment which in a sense led to the importation of a legal transplant into **Dutch** law, for its part, was very much attributable to the counsel provided by Advocate-General Koopmans.

He alleged that the 'societal ostracism' to which extramarital relationships had been exposed had been relegated to the past to a large extent. This he ascribed to three main factors: a combination of greater openness, an altered significance attributed to the institution of marriage, greater promiscuity and an improvement in anti-conception techniques. Koopmans affirmed that **Dutch** statutory law did not acknowledge a *right* to accede to information concerning genetic parentage, but mentioned the (deleted) provision of Article 1:225(2) under (a) BW as an indication of an acknowledgement of an interest. A case of the **Dutch** Supreme Court involving a denial of paternity in the face of exceeded procedural time-limits was also taken as an example in case law that indicated the existence of such an interest.[144] This interest had gained significance as academic literature demonstrated that persons unaware of their origins had gone on searching for their 'roots'. However, he added that 'an interest, however great, cannot inherently be considered to be a right, though'.[145]

Koopmans also took into account the parliamentary debates concerning the reform of parentage law and the waiver of donor anonymity. It was established that no consensus had been reached on the latter issue. However, it was submitted that those who opposed a recognition of the 'right to know' founded their basic argument on an idea exclusively relevant for the debate on donor anonymity, namely that of the feared decrease of available donors. By contrast, in the analogous situation of adoption, more practical experience had been gathered, and recognition of the right accordingly did not meet with similar opposition. In the apparent absence of any definite answers to be derived from **Dutch** law, Koopmans referred to the pioneering landmark case of the **German** Federal Constitutional Court.[146] He therefore admitted to concurring with that judgment that the right to have one's own (individual) identity forms an integrative part of the personality right and that knowledge of one's genetic parentage is 'indispensable' for knowing that identity. Koopmans accordingly very much paved the way for the recognition of the right to know as a constitutional right in **Dutch** law, even if he was quick to add that this *right* would have to be weighed against

143 FORDER (1995), p. 126.
144 Hoge Raad, 17 September 1993, *NJ* 1994 272, p. 1745.
145 Conlusion of Advocate-General Koopmans, HR, 15 April 1994, 608, under 6.
146 Bundesverfassungsgericht, 31 January 1989, *NJW* 1989, p. 891.

the right of the parents or one of them or their constitutionally protected private sphere.

In the concrete terms of the case, this weighing process would prescribe a recognition therein of the mother's wish. This would have the advantage of allowing for a circumvention of cumbersome and possibly ultimately unanswerable questions concerning the moral or legal merits. As the claims in this case originated in a remote past, Koopmans contended that two dimensions of time were relevant. First, it was recognised that for parents generally in the 1930s the interest in hushing up an extramarital relationship was far greater than at present. Far more interesting from a more general point of view, the second dimension of time in the Advocate-General's submission prescribed that, as a rule, the interest of the mother in not disclosing the identity of the father would weigh less heavily as time marches on. Thus, also in a legal sense time was deemed to have a certain healing power. To put it simply, time progressively favours the child's right, as it dilutes a parent's privacy interest.

Rather than expanding on the discussion revolving around the ontological basis of the 'right to know', including the question whether it is a 'right' at all rather than an 'interest', the Court contented itself with Article 7 UNCRC as a basis in positive law. The Court took the narrow interpretation of that international treaty provision, alleging that it (merely) served as a legal basis for a person in the situation of the applicant to petition for identifying data. The **Dutch** Supreme Court did not elaborate on the fact that Article 7 UNCRC delineates the scope of the right by only making it enforceable 'as far as possible'. Nonetheless, the Court concurred that 'the right to know one's genetic parents is not absolute'.

The **Dutch** Supreme Court followed the earlier judgment in acknowledging the relevance of various countervailing interests, which warranted a balancing test. Unlike the 's-Hertogenbosch Appeal Court, however, the **Dutch** Supreme Court refuted the claim that the foundation could invoke other societal interests outside its duty to protect the mother's privacy. In asserting that the hierarchy between the remaining countervailing interests, or rather 'rights', favoured that of the applicants, the **Dutch** Supreme Court submitted a novel criterion. Thus, it alleged that the prevalence of the 'right to know' in the instant case was legitimised not only by the vital interest of the child in knowing, but also by the 'responsibility that the natural mother, as a rule, also carries for the child's existence'. Thereafter, it was expressly – and rather laconically – added that the case did not concern the issue of donor anonymity: clearly, the forestalment of any legislative reform must, in view of the divergent parliamentary and societal views, have appeared a tad too progressive at the time. From the Supreme Court's observation, it may also be inferred that the 'responsibility' argument would hold true for all situations other than AID, in which context the criterion might have been considered ill-founded on account of other reasons as well, such as its associations with a form of supreme altruism. Whatever might have been in the minds of the judges, Forder[147] and Holtrust[148] objected to it since it was not known under what miserable circumstances the children who were born in Valkenhorst were conceived. The mothers could not reasonably be considered to have been 'responsible' for the upbringing of their children, especially in view of the pervasive stigma attached to births outside marriage. In that connection, Forder drew an analogy with a case of IVF treatment in which the 'responsibility' argument was also inept.[149] In this case the person who had carried out the treatment had neglected to wash out the pipette in between treating a couple, of whom the husband was **Aruban,** and a **Dutch** couple.[150] The sperm from the **Aruban** father was introduced into the **Dutch** mother's uterus, thereby raising serious questions about the validity of the 'responsibility' argument. This was presumably a singular case, but certainly provides a telling example of how inept the 'responsibility' argument may be in some circumstances.

Unlike Advocate-General Koopmans, the **Dutch** Supreme Court did not elaborate much on the significance of the two dimensions of time that he had discerned. It cited and paraphrased the argument of the 's-Hertogenbosch Court in *Valkenhorst I* in pointg out that, except for a negligible number of women, in this day and age it could no longer be presumed that many women would be prevented from seeking access to such a charitable institution. Neither could it be said that they would not feel secure in disclosing the identity of the begetter in the same way as they may have felt in the past. This was because societal developments had changed dramatically since the 1930s. The other dimension of time, which concerned the 'redemptive power' of the progression of time ('time healing all wounds'), was regrettably not further looked into by the **Dutch** Supreme Court.

In commenting upon the case, Advocate-General Koopmans nonetheless hypothesised that the parent might have such a privacy interest, but that it would dilute in the course of time. Conversely, the child's right to know would progres-

147 FORDER (1995), p. 132.
148 HOLTRUST (1994), *Nemesis* 1994-95 No. 430 p. 20-21 (para. 9).
149 FORDER (1995), p. 131.
150 *NRC Handelsblad*, Saturday 17 June 1995, p. 1.

sively become more important as time marched on. Although not further elaborated upon in the case law, a similar strand of thought also seems to have been influential the Artificial Insemination (Donor Anonymity) Act. This Act, of course, meant a principled shift after *Valkenhorst* and the Dutch Supreme Court had been careful to distinguish this situation from the one it had been faced with, presumably because it did not want to engage in the legislative process.[151]

5. PORTUGAL

5.1. EARLY MODERN HISTORY

Historically, **Portuguese** parentage law has reflected local and foreign Romanistic influences. Yet over the past decades it has been influenced by **German** and Nordic influences introduced during the last major legislative reforms of 1966 and 1977. The local influences can be traced back to medieval **Portuguese** law. Influences from other kingdoms of the Iberian peninsula were also relevant to the extent that some **Castilian** legal institutions were introduced by the 15th Century *Ordenações Afonsinas*, a compilation of a wide variety of laws and customs which were found to be applicable throughout the kingdom.[152] As in other Romanistic systems, from the Middle Ages up to the 18th Century the legal determination of parentage received scant attention from **Portuguese** jurists. It is believed that the possibilities to rebut paternity were generally restricted to cases of physical and 'moral' impossibility of access during the conception period.

In 1793 the *Lei Brumário* put an end to such uncertainty inasmuch as it clarified that a judicial determination of paternity could only be admitted if the child's civil status, the so-called *posse de estado,* did not correspond with legal paternity. A denial of paternity could only be made by the man. A few years after the enactment of this law the grounds to rebut paternity were further restricted to cases of rape. Several factors have been advanced to explain this restrictive regime. Prevalent social taboos regarding adultery, the protection of the interests of the family, alongside practical impossibilities in proving the existence of the genetic tie appear to have been influential. Such social taboos concerning illegitimate births nonetheless appear to have been considerably less prevalent than in **France**, as the *Ordenações Afonsinas* already allowed for children born

---

151 See Chapter X.

152 OLIVEIRA (2003), p. 52.

out of wedlock to inherit *ab intestato*. Amongst Romanistic regimes this is considered to be remarkable and it has been ascribed to Arab influences on the development of **Portuguese** customary law.

Portuguese parentage law following the Napoleonic invasion also proposed a voluntarist conceptualization of legal parentage. Thus, recognition by unmarried men and marital presumptions of paternity formed the main legal avenues to establish paternity. Once established, paternity could not be easily challenged and was largely dependent on the husband's own procedural initiatives.[153]

The nuptial character of paternity was reflected, for example, in Article 130.° of the *Código de Seabra* as well, although the possibilities were opened for the mother and child to challenge paternity in three situations. Thus, in case the mother had been raped, or in case children's *posse de estado* did not accord with their legal status, or whenever a written document was present on the basis of which it could be concluded that the person involved might not be the genetic father, paternity could be challenged before the courts.

The regime of the *Código de Seabra* was maintained until 1910, when the monarchy was overthrown and legislative reforms were introduced. An additional set of legal criteria were admitted as grounds for rebutting paternity. As such grounds the following were admitted: seduction of a woman in the abuse of power, abuse of trust by a man with false promises of marriage and cohabitation with the mother.

While the ultra-right Salazar regime was still in power, **Portuguese** parentage law came to attach greater weight to biological truth following the 1966 reforms. The legislative changes foresaw in the creation of a number of remarkable legal institutions and a pivotal role for the state. Furthermore, adoption, in both its plenary and restricted form, was introduced in **Portugal** in that year as well.

In the aftermath of the Carnation Revolution of 25 April 1974 led by a group of rebellious officers which led to the downfall of the fascist dictatorship and the installation of a democratic government, a number of legislative changes were made. Thus, as from 1977, the procedural position of both the mother and to a lesser extent that of the child were reinforced. As will become apparent in the next sections, there were key principles underlying these last reforms purporting to achieve greater equality between children born within marriage and outside

153 Oliveira (2003), p. 62.

wedlock as well as a greater concern for the correspondence of biological 'truth' with the establishment of legal parentage in general.

5.2. CONSTITUTIONAL LEGAL RECOGNITION OF A RIGHT TO KNOW ONE'S ORIGINS

The text of the present **Portuguese** Constitution was adopted by the **Portuguese** Parliament on 2 April 1976. Title II is divided into two chapters and contains a set of civil and political rights. As such, Article 25.° guarantees the right to personal integrity (*direito à integridade pessoal*), which is understood to contain both moral-psychological and physical components. In line with **German** constitutional legal doctrine, a personality right has been derived from Article 25.° in conjunction with Article 26.° of the Constitution. These constitutional provisions provide the basis for recognising the right to know one's origins in **Portugal**.[154] Furthermore, it is worth noting that also Article 26.-3° of the **Portuguese** Constitution states that the national law 'shall guarantee personal dignity and the genetic identity of the human being, especially with regard to the creation, development and utilization of technologies and scientific experimentation'. This may also provide an additional constitutional basis for this right. Canotilho and Moreira, in their leading commentary on the **Portuguese** Constitution, refer to a 'right to know one's personal history' (*direito à historicidade pessoal*) instead of a right to know one's origins and it is this latter term that now also seems to have been embraced by the Constitutional Court.[155]

The Constitutional Court has since the turn of the last decade developed case law on the issue. Initially, the Court took a restrictive approach, but in line with **Portuguese** legal literature now conceives of the right in potentially more encompassing terms. Thus, the Court initially made mention of a 'fundamental right of knowledge (and acknowledgement) of one's paternity' (*direito fundamental ao conhecimento (e reconhecimento) da paternidade*). In these early decisions at issue were essentially notions of perceived inequality between children born within and out of wedlock. These resulted primarily from the non-applicability of legal presumptions in relation to 'unrecognised' children

---

[154] Canotilho & Moreira (2007), p. 462; Vale e Reis (2008), p. 65-66. Vale e Reis (2008), p. 58, also connects the right with the constitutional principle of human dignity (*dignidade da pessoa humana*) protected under Art. 1 of the **Portuguese** Constitution.

[155] Tribunal Constitucional, Acórdão N.° 456/2003, 14 October 2003.

born out of wedlock,[156] notwithstanding the recognition of the equality of children born within and out of wedlock in accordance with the Constitution.[157]

Constitutional case law has so far centred on the constitutionality of procedural time-limits in parentage proceedings. Initially, it was argued that strict time-limits to rebut paternity such as those mentioned in the relevant civil law provisions were constitutional in view of concerns of legal certainty, the reduced reliability of scientific evidence (not yet an obsolete argument when the provisions were drafted in 1977) and to prevent claims motivated entirely by inheritance-related concerns. Exceptionally, claims were admitted further into the adulthood of the child who had enjoyed a civil status relationship with the putative father or if there was written evidence of the putative father's paternity.

In 2003 the Constitutional Court again ruled on the 'right to know' in a claim that involved a judicial determination of paternity. As such, the time-limits imposed by Article 1817.° in conjunction with Article 1873 PCC came under constitutional scrutiny. This time, however, the Court decided that these civil law provisions were unconstitutional because the aforementioned reasons had lost their validity. In that connection, it was considered that DNA evidence could be used at any time and that the financial wealth of both the (adult) child and a presumptive father would usually be comparable, rendering the argument that claims would often be motivated by 'greed' much less likely.[158]

In the concrete case, the 31-year-old claimant was too old to establish paternity as he was beyond the statutory time-limit of twenty years of age. Nonetheless, the Court attached preponderant weight to the fact that it could not be expected from the unknowing claimant to have undertaken judicial action earlier. The court therefore suggested that another *dies a quo* time-limit would have been more appropriate. As the child had not been in the position to uncover the truth before, however, the Court concluded that the essence of the child's constitutional right was rendered meaningless. The imposition of this *dies a quo* time-limit has been disputed by Vale e Reis, who argues that the right should in principle not be restrained by a procedural time-limit. However, judges should be able to decide on a case-to-case basis in that author's view to deny a claim if

[156] Tribunal Constitucional, Acórdão N.° 99/88, 22 August 1988; Tribunal Constitucional 213/89, 31 May 1989; Tribunal Constitucional, 218/89, 21 June 1989; Tribunal Constitucional, Acórdão N.°371/92, 25 September 1991; Tribunal Constitucional, Acórdão N.° 96/96, 5 December 1995.

[157] Art. 36.°-4 **Portuguese** Constitution.

[158] Oliveira (2004), p. 11.

the claimant fails to undertake procedural action after having known about the existence of the biological father and appears to be motivated by financial gain.[159]

Since more than one decision affirming unconstitutionality is required to induce the legislator to review the legislation,[160] it has remained in principle only possible for children to have paternity determined during their minority and within two years after having become an adult or two years after the child gains legal capacity.[161] In 2004, the Constitutional Court[162] ruled that the time-limit was unconstitutional by violating an equality principle[163] in respect of children born out of wedlock and the personality right.[164] In 2006, the unconstitutionality of the procedural time-limits for children to have their paternity judicially determined was reaffirmed.[165]

In 2007 and 2008, the constitutionality of another time-limit in parentage proceedings was successfully disputed with reference to children's right to know their origins.[166] This time-limit concerns the denial of the husband's paternity by marital children which is only permitted up to one year after having become an adult.[167] In affirming that the contested civil law norm had to be considered unconstitutional, the court took note of the opinion of the country's leading family law professor, Guilherme de Oliveira, who had observed that the appeal of the imposition of such time-limits had decreased, especially when they do not protect a form of social parentage.[168] On the basis of a comparative analysis in respect of jurisdictions such as **Brazil**, **France, Germany, Spain** and **Switzerland,**[169] the **Portuguese** Constitutional Court also concluded that a trend has emerged that interprets such time-limits in parentage proceedings more flexibly. This trend would have been occasioned to a great extent by bio-medical and social developments that have underscored the child's right to information. Conversely, a so-called 'freedom not to be considered the father' (*liberdade-de-*

---

159 Vale e Reis (2008), p. 211-212.

160 Art. 18 in conjunction with Art. 282 **Portuguese** Constitution.

161 Art. 1817 in conjunction with Art. 1873 PCC.

162 Tribunal Constitucional n. 486/2004, 7 July 2005.

163 Art. 36-4 **Portuguese** Constitution.

164 Arts. 25-1 and 26-1 **Portuguese** Constitution.

165 Tribunal Constitucional n. 23/2006/ 10 January 2006.

166 Tribunal Constitucional n. 609/2007, 11 December 2007; Tribunal Constitucional n. 279/2008, 14 May 2008.

167 Art. 1842-1 PCC.

168 Coelho & Oliveira (2006), p. 137.

169 In **Switzerland**, paternity may exceptionally be denied outside the statutory time-limits if, in the light of the circumstances of the case, it would be unreasonable to restrict the child's right (Art. 256c **Swiss** Civil Code).

não-ser-considerado-pai) as a mere result of the passage of time since the child's conception and a right to evade 'legal responsibility' (*responsabilidade juridical*) was also not considered worthy of legal protection to the extent that the child has a right to have a family law relationship with the biological father.

6. COMPARISON AND EVALUATION

The child's right to know one's origins first gained recognition on the basis of the *personality right* doctrine in **Germany**. It has been found that the **German** personality right doctrine has been inspirational for the recognition of the child's right to information in both **the Netherlands** and **Portugal**. Whereas in **Germany** and **Portugal** there is an express constitutional basis for the right to information on the basis of a personality right, in **the Netherlands** it is more apparent that the **German** constitutional discourse has exerted an influence in the absence of a clear constitutional basis in the **Dutch** constitution, Having said that, however, **the Netherlands** is arguably also the jurisdiction with the most monist character of the four selected systems, at least on this issue. This means that Article 8 ECHR and other relevant provisions emanating from the international and European legal order may in principle be relied upon before the **Dutch** courts. In **the Netherlands**, international treaties of a generally binding nature in principle have a self-executing character after they have been published, as long as they confer rights on the citizen and impose duties on the government.[170] However, it has been found that the relevant provisions of the UNCRC will at best provide a supplementary legal basis before the **Dutch** courts in which the right to information is at issue. In the remaining jurisdictions, the UNCRC is presumably also not of a sufficiently generally binding nature that it could be relied upon directly before the courts.

In addition to the personality right, it has also been established that in both **Germany** and **Portugal** the *equality* principle provides an additional constitutional basis. Probably because **the Netherlands** lacks a constitutional court, the direct relevance of the equality principle is less apparent in the **Dutch** constitutional legal order. Among the four jurisdictions, it may be said that **France** takes an anomalous position because it has so far not recognised the child's right to know on the basis of its national constitution even though **France** does have a largely monist constitutional legal order. Nonetheless, it has been verified that

170 Arts. 93 and 94 of the **Dutch** Constitution.

the **French** legislation has since 2002 been reviewed in order to meet the **French** state's obligations under both the ECHR and the UNCRC.

PART III
TOWARDS A LEGAL FRAMEWORK FOR A COMPARATIVE ANALYSIS OF THE RIGHT TO KNOW

CHAPTER V
A SEARCH FOR GUIDING PRINCIPLES

1. OUTLINE

In the preceding three Chapters, the scope of the right to know one's biological parentage in the constitutional legal order has been analyzed on the basis of the available sources of positive law. In the present Chapter, this analysis shall be taken further with a view to establishing the recurrent principles and dominant legal values in the overall constitutional legal order. This will go some way in providing an interpretive content to the 'inner core' of the legal concept of the right to know one's origins. Accordingly, this Chapter also aims to provide a basic analytical backdrop to the thematic comparative analysis that will be undertaken in Chapters VI, VII, VIII and IX.

In that respect, it is hoped that the comparative analysis will 'add flesh' to these principles. Thus, given the openness of constitutional norms, a precise delineation of what the legal protection of the right could require is not to be expected at the international or regional constitutional level. Thus, at the international level, the UN Children's Rights Committee restricts itself to giving recommendations. At the regional level, there is a form of judicial interpretation. Nonetheless, the ECtHR in principle only decides on a case-to-case basis.[1]

Furthermore, this court will not derogate from its 'margin of appreciation doctrine' on this issue. As we have seen, at the national constitutional level, in **Germany** in particular, the **German** Federal Constitutional Court has decided on numerous occasions on the issue and defined the concept further. As far as an (adult) child's right to know her or his parents goes, there are indications that **German** law has influenced developments in **the Netherlands** and **Portugal**, too. However, in **France**, there has not yet been any express recognition of a right to know on the basis of the national constitutional law.

---

[1] Art. 34 ECHR.

Bearing such features of the constitutional discourse in mind, it is considered that the constitutional legal order remains sufficiently well developed to deepen one's understanding of the recurring legal values or 'principles' already at this stage. When defined, these values may operate as normative criteria or 'constitutional side-constraints' in understanding the scope of the right to know in the various relevant contexts.

In order to do so, it is necessary, however, to gain a very basic understanding of the way constitutional principles operate in constitutional legal philosophy. The aim of such a basic outline is dual: firstly, to examine the possible extent of positive and negative obligations of the state in enforcing the right to know and, secondly, to help delineate the right's 'inner core'. It is presumed that this 'inner core' will come to the fore whenever the right runs into conflict with other legal interests and constitutional rights.

In the second part of this Chapter (section V.III), the author will then be in a position to formulate a set of legal principles. In interpreting the relevance of these principles, the doctrinal views of a number of scholars who have written on the right to know one's origins shall also be examined and, whenever deemed necessary, reanalyzed and supplemented by the author's own interpretation. Thereafter, some of the recurrent conflicts between the right to know and countervailing legal interests at the constitutional level shall be discussed. This discussion will accordingly also contribute to a better understanding of the outer limits of the right's scope.

2. CONSTITUTIONAL RIGHTS THEORY

2.1. PERSPECTIVES ON THE BALANCING OF CONSTITUTIONAL RIGHTS

The dispute over the structure of constitutional rights is said to have begun with the publication of two leading books on rights: Dworkin's *Taking Rights Seriously* and Alexy's *Theory of Constitutional Rights.*[2] Both books provide critiques of the legal positivism of Hart's and Hans Kelsen's legal theories, whose primary concern was to systematize the study of the concept of law by presenting legal

[2] According to ZUCCA (2007), p. 7. DWORKIN (1977, 1991 reprint) and ALEXY (**German** edition 1985, **English** translation 2002).

rules as a system of rules.[3] Both Alexy and Dworkin attacked legal positivism due to its disregard for the role of morality in interpreting norms with an open-ended texture, such as constitutional rights. Even so, their views concur with positivists in the sense that in their definition of law and rights, they do take into account such requirements as 'issuance' by a competent authority and 'social efficacy'.[4]

There are, however, important differences between both non-positivistic strands of thought. Thus, Dworkin defended the idea that there is a right answer to be discovered for every single conceivable legal case.[5] In defending this seemingly 'grandiose' claim, Dworkin distinguishes between rules and principles. Rules are norms that prescribe a definitive command, that forbid or permit something or definitively confer power to some end or another. Rules bear an all or nothing character in the sense that in case of conflict, one retains validity and the other does not. This test can be done on the basis of a positivistic analysis. The strength of principles, however, must be measured by their capability to withstand competition with policies in hard cases.[6] Dworkin's thesis assumes that whenever a principle has to compete with a rule, the principle, by virtue of its protection of an individual right, should prevail over the rule.

According to Dworkin, for a right, which can be derived from a principle, it must in the case of conflict be able to trump over utilitarian concerns. Thus, assuming that Dworkin would conceive of a right to know one's origins as a genuine, fundamental right, then it must in case of conflict be able to 'trump' utilitarian concerns. Presumably, this would mean in the context of donor anonymity that enforcing a donor-conceived child's right to know should not be made contingent upon public concerns, in particular the predicted effect of a drop in the number of available donors in case a waiver of anonymity would not outweigh the child's right to know. Of course the question unanswered by Dworkin remains, however, whether the right to know bears such weight and how this weight could then be measured or assessed.

Moreover, Dworkin's theory provides few clues as to how such a competition of values would operate. Even so, the sovereign virtue, or supreme principle, in Dworkin's legal theory is believed to be equality, which is understood as 'equal

3 See HART (1994) and KELSEN (1991).
4 ALEXY (2002), p. 3-4.
5 DWORKIN (1977), p. 58-84.
6 DWORKIN (1977), p. 92.

concern for the fate of all citizens'.[7] In that sense, Dworkin's theory has been labeled as 'value monist', a notion which transmits the idea that in each conceivable case a superior value can be discerned. A conflict of fundamental rights is to be understood by courts primarily as a clash between concerns over liberty and equality. Furthermore, conflicts between rights can also arise when two mutually exclusive liberties arise. Dworkin suggests, however, that in case of a genuine conflict between liberty and equality, liberty stands to lose out against concerns over equality.[8] For our discussion, it is hypothesized that this could mean that the 'liberty' to identify a biological parent may be compromised by the privacy or the 'right to be left alone' of the biological parent. If both rights are based on equality, for example because they are both adults, it is not clear which right should prevail.[9]

In contrast, Alexy holds that whenever fundamental rights stand in competition, the task for constitutional courts is to examine a maximizing outcome in respect of each right, given both factual and legal possibilities. For Alexy, fundamental or constitutional rights must therefore be considered essentially as nothing more and nothing less than 'optimisation requirements'. In his *Theory of Constitutional Rights*, Alexy summarised his central thesis as such: 'The central thesis of this book is that regardless of their more or less precise formulation, constitutional rights are principles and that principles are optimisation requirements'.[10] What optimization actually requires in the concrete sense will depend on the meaning of the principles. As a circular reasoning, this point of Alexy's theory has been criticised.[11] In addition, the conceptualization of rights as optimization requirements would undermine the firmness of constitutional rights and therefore their 'inner core' (*Kerngehalt*).[12]

In Alexy's theory, it is held, rather, that principles should be balanced against one another inasmuch as this is factually and legally possible.[13] Principles are essentially optimization requirements. Since legal sources are considered to be dependent on moral evaluation, in the face of a competition of principles and values courts will decide on the basis of a moral evaluation.[14]

---

7 DWORKIN (2001), p. 130.
8 DWORKIN (2001), p. 130.
9 Compare: ECtHR *Odièvre v. France*, Appl. No. 42326/98, 13 February 2003, para. 44.
10 ALEXY (2002), p. 388.
11 ZUCCA (2007), p. 21.
12 HABERMAS (1996), p. 254.
13 ALEXY (2002), p. 70.
14 ALEXY (2003a), p. 449.

Instead of establishing a preferred set of moral values to guide the solution of potential conflicts of fundamental rights, like Dworkin does, Alexy proposes a stage theory.[15] Firstly, judges are required to measure and clarify the extent of non-satisfaction of the first principle. In the second phase, the importance of satisfying the second, countervailing principle must be determined and clarified. This may be done through a process of 'ranking', either by attributing a number to one value (ordinal ranking) or through an examination of the specific relationships between two values in order to identify a preference for one over another.

It follows that Alexy acknowledges that the 'tyranny of constitutional values' will be possible in some cases as long as their 'ranking' is higher. If this is the case, then this moral preference should be identified as precisely as possible and circumscribed to the greatest extent. Thus, the freedom of speech, as a central value in Western democracies, would in a very general way prevail over privacy rights, for example.

Finally, recently the **Italian** legal scholar Lorenzo Zucca has provided a critical account of Dworkin's and Alexy's theory.[16] It would, in Zucca's view, be preferable if constitutional (fundamental) rights were conceived inasmuch as possible as hard rules since this will allow us to better understand the nature of their propensity to conflict with each other.[17] In this view, horizontal conflicts between private individuals may often, though not always, be solved by establishing a set of rebuttable legal presumptions. Zucca suggests, for example, that the contest between free speech and privacy is already routinely being decided in an *a priori* way. In an ideal world, courts would therefore 'come clean' and admit to the fact that what they are already engaged in is actually a contextualized ranking of rights.

2.2. BALANCING THE RIGHT TO INFORMATION IN THE NATIONAL CONSTITUTIONAL ORDER

The three, broad perspectives on conflicts of fundamental rights discussed above offer different ways of approaching conflicts between the right to know one's biological parentage and conflicting rights. It appears that the court's approach resembles Alexy's more than Dworkin's in its sustained efforts to 'strike a fair

15 ALEXY (2003b), p. 131-140.
16 ZUCCA (2007).
17 ZUCCA (2007), p. 6.

balance' between competing rights. A more absolutist approach that conceives of the right to information as a possible 'trump' in individual cases can only be discerned to a limited extent. Thus, countervailing public interests have in some instances been given a more absolute interpretation. As has been established, in the *Odièvre* case this meant that the applicant's right to know was almost bereft of meaning beyond the court's nominal recognition that such a right existed.[18] In contrast, in *Jäggi*, it was the applicant's informational right that superseded other rights even though some of these rights were considered to be relevant to the case.[19]

In **Germany**, the right to know one's origins is not lent an absolute character by the Federal Constitutional Court. Nonetheless, it is hard to escape the conclusion that the right does often trump other rights, notably a mother's privacy interest The father's recently constitutional right to know, in contrast, is considered to be subordinated to the child's right in a more abstract sense. In the **Dutch** *Valkenhorst II* case and in recent cases in **Portugal**, the constitutional courts have also favoured the applicant's informational right. In *Valkenhorst II*, although the **Dutch** Supreme Court emphasized that the right was not absolute, it insisted that disclosure was necessary at the expense of the mother's privacy interest. Although the mother's privacy interest was acknowledged, the informational right did, in fact, trump the (speculative) privacy interest altogether.

This raises the question to what extent the mother's right could have been 'optimised,' assuming that her right required legal protection. Thus, in *Valkenhorst II*, the **Dutch** Supreme Court could have chosen a different route. It could, for example, have held that the 'inner core' of the informational right had already been met, because the mother, in opposing any further disclosure, had already stated the (horrendous) circumstances that had surrounded the child's conception. The mother's privacy interest would then also have been protected to a greater extent.

---

18 See Chapter III.
19 See Chapter III.

3. STATE OBLIGATIONS

3.1. THE BOUNDARIES BETWEEN POSITIVE AND NEGATIVE OBLIGATIONS OF THE STATE

Constitutional rights often create a sphere of inviolability for individuals. They therefore require both positive and negative obligations on the part of the state. A negative obligation amounts to an omission to undertake action. In contrast, a positive obligation requires the state to take measures, such as legislative action. In view of the wide range of conceivable measures of state action, however, the boundaries between both sets of obligations will often be blurred and an ongoing constitutional legal discourse.[20] With the possible exception of the protection of free speech, it may be difficult to define a negative state obligation merely as a duty of refraining to interfere with the object of a right. This raises the question whether the distinction between the positive/negative obligations makes sense, in particular for our discussion.

Accordingly, in all of the examined decisions of the ECtHR on *inter alia* Article 8 ECHR, it has referred to this distinction between state obligations but it has consistently added that the boundaries between both types of obligations do not lend themselves to any precise definition. Rather, a 'fair balance' has to be struck between the interest of the applicant, other parties and the state. In that regard, it is recalled, states are accorded a broad margin of appreciation. It will therefore be interesting in the comparative analysis to verify how such state obligations are operationalised.

3.2. THE DISTINCTION BETWEEN POSITIVE AND NEGATIVE STATE OBLIGATIONS

For the moment, it is assumed that the boundaries between a state's obligations in enforcing the right to know one's origins will differ from context to context. At the constitutional level, however, there is a lack of precedent for this claim. Thus, there is no case as yet, for example, on donor-conceived children who have brought forward a claim under Article 8 ECHR to the effect that their informational rights under that provision have been breached. All the same, the fact that the state has already admitted informational claims in a wide range of situations, such as *Odièvre* and *Mikulić*, provides a strong indication that the court is willing to bring the legal right to know one's biological parents within

20 For a recent discussion, see in particular Holmes & Sunstein (2000).

the sphere of the right to private life, in principle irrespective of the situation and requiring a degree of active state protection.[21] Furthermore, the recognition in the **German**, **Dutch** and **Portuguese** constitutional orders of such a right *expressis verbis* also gives a strong indication that the existence of a general right to know should be considered.

Even so, the author's assumption will be that the level of state intervention will be contingent to a significant extent upon the circumstances under which the informational need arises. Thus, historically, the state has a more active role in regulating adoption and in assisted conception through the screening of parents. In contrast, the state's role in case of a 'misattributed paternity', for example, when the mother's husband is not the biological father, will be largely confined to its legislative role in parentage law. It is therefore quite conceivable that this could mean that the extent of the state's duty in promoting the child's right to know *as such* may have a more limited scope.

4. PRINCIPLES

4.1. DECISIONAL PRIVACY AS AN ASPECT OF AUTONOMY

As has been established, the primary basis of the right to know one's origins in the regional constitutional order is the right to private life in Article 8 ECHR. In the *Pretty v. United Kingdom* case, the right to private life under that provision was interpreted in the widest meaning so far given to that right, namely that of a 'right to make important decisions defining their own lives for themselves'.[22] The case revolved around the request of a terminally ill woman to end her life with the assistance of her husband. Although the court did not conclude that her right to private life had been breached by the **United Kingdom**, the court conceded that such ethical issues pertain to a person's private life and therefore fall under Article 8 ECHR.

In the *Pretty* case, the right to private life accordingly incorporated a notion of autonomy in the meaning of decisional privacy. It is a fairly safe analogy to hold that the right to know one's origins will also be associable with this notion of

---

21 ECtHR *Odièvre v. France*, Appl. No. 42326/98, 13 February 2003; ECtHR *Mikulić v. Croatia*, Appl. No. 53176/99, 7 February 2002. See Chapter III.

22 ECtHR *Pretty v. United Kingdom*, Appl. No. 2346/02, 29 April 2002, para. 61.

decisional privacy in the regional legal order, now that the right has already been raised repeatedly in connection with Article 8 ECHR.

In **Germany**, **the Netherlands** and **Portugal**, this connectivity with a principle of decisional privacy may be even more apparent. As a dimension of the personality right, a person's decisional privacy in these jurisdictions is viewed as a dimension of a right to *informational self-determination*, a broader right which applies in respect of the state and other individuals. In denoting a measure of choice and a sphere of personal inviolability, the principle also accommodates the notion of a right *not* to know one's biological parentage.[23]

The recognition of this right *not* to know appears to set a number of conceptual problems. Since no child 'chooses' her or his own biological parents, the connection with a right to informational self-determination could be perceived as fancy and construed. The fact that most children are born in traditional families and grow up with their biological parents raises the (bizarre) question whether the rest of us 'who know' could also have an interest in *not* knowing or not having known our biological parents. Assuming that constitutional recognition of such a right would be at all conceivable, it may be an unanswerable question how such a right of the majority could become practicable.

For one thing, the ECtHR seems to take a different view on the scope of the right to informational self-determination of 'those who think they know': in *Haas*, the applicant, being 'convinced in his own mind' who his father was, was effectively denied a right to seek more accurate information through DNA testing, especially, it seemed, because of his informational interest. One of the main reasons for that denial was the applicant's inheritance-related intentions. His decisional privacy was therefore not seen in isolation from another interest.[24] In *Jäggi*, the fact that the applicant had not suffered psychological problems because of the hiatus in his knowledge was also mentioned as a relevant factor.[25] Conversely, it might have been more interesting to find out whether the Court's reasoning would have been influenced had Mr Jäggi suffered from such problems. Conceivably, this could have made his decision to access information even stronger.

It follows from such examples that decisional privacy in itself is not a factor which is seen in isolation from other interests by the ECtHR. This is understand-

---

23 Bundesverfassungsgericht (BVerfGE), 13 February 2007, *FamRZ* 2007, p. 441. See Chapter IV and Chapter VII.

24 ECtHR *Haas v. the Netherlands*, Appl. No. 36983/97, 13 January 2004. See Chapter III.

25 ECtHR *Jäggi v. Switzerland*, Appl. No. 58757/00, 13 July 2006. See Chapter III.

able, because the principle itself is largely devoid of meaning. The freedom to choose to pursue a right, after all, does not in itself create a legal interest. It is therefore an interesting question how far the court should go in determining the validity of interests. Will the applicant's interests be contingent upon prior psychological problems or the possibility that identification offers to alleviate such problems? Alternatively, such reasons could be foregone in a more deontological line of argumentation that reasons primarily on the basis of the person's decisional privacy to choose (or not to choose) to exercise one's right. In that latter way, the right could be conceived of rather as a 'right for the sake of truth'.

The examples show, however, that this latter course has not really been taken yet. The notion of decisional privacy can accordingly not be viewed in isolation from the specific utility or interest of the information for each particular individual. It follows that in the concrete case equal access may not be possible. As persons who are 'convinced in our own minds' who our biological parents are, we may (or may not) have a right which is worthy of as much legal protection as, say, an adoptee or a donor-conceived person. To this point we shall return in the comparative analysis and in the concluding Chapter.

4.2. RESPONSIBILITY

4.2.1. Procreational responsibility

A degree of responsibility is also implicit in the notion that a parent has a correlative moral duty to disclose her or his own identity of the other parent to the child if the child seeks to identify a parent. Both in the **Dutch** and **German** constitutional tradition this word has been used to justify the child's right to know her or his origins. Thus, in the *Valkenhorst II* case, the **Dutch** Supreme Court even went as far as to consider that a (mother's) responsibility, next to the child's 'vital interest', is a sufficient moral justification for deriving the right to know from the personality right.[26]

In her comparative law dissertation on the legal position of children in respect of their parents in **England & Wales** and **the Netherlands**, Vonk has defined the concept of *procreational responsibility*. As both a moral and legal principle, procreational responsibility in Vonk's thesis operates at two significant levels for our discussion. After conception, procreational responsibility is more closely linked with what I shall refer to as a 'parentage law perspective' on the need for

[26] Hoge Raad 17 January 1997, *NJ* 1997, p. 483. See Chapter IV.

information on one's biological parents. This means that 'the child must be able to depend on the fact that this responsibility may become operational in practice. This means that it must be possible to establish a legal relationship between the child and the parent on the basis of the parent's responsibility by giving this parent the status of a legal parent'.[27]

Procreational responsibility *before conception* is the most directly relevant notion for a discussion which centres on a protection of the child's (prospective) informational needs as such from that moment. Thus, it is concerned with preserving the personal integrity of the child to be conceived.

'This entails ensuring that the child's biological/biological history is available for the child at a later date, and being aware of the fact that the story surrounding his or her conception and birth must be accessible and acceptable to the child. Furthermore, this responsibility before the child's conception involves considering who will have what position in the child's life when a known donor is used. Not everything can be foreseen, but these things need to be thought through beforehand'.[28]

It is worth observing that this definition is to some extent analogous with the term 'honesty 'in spirit', posited by Schapiro in the field of ethics.[29] As a concept and principle, responsibility is sufficiently flexible to leave room for exceptions. In drawing on such a modern account of Kantianism, responsibility for disclosure could involve a respect for reciprocity in communication, which takes into account the child's current level of autonomy and potential to develop autonomy.[30] Just as any principle, it seems, it should be viewed primarily as a point of departure in legal reasoning rather than a hard rule. For minors, in disclosure this reciprocity and empathy may be especially important. What this (moral) requirement of reciprocity could mean for law-makers, will be an issue worth exploring further in the thematic comparative analysis.

When viewed as a dogmatic and abstract criterion, it is conceivable that the principle provokes criticism. Indeed, the express reference to a notion of the responsibility of the biological parent in disclosing identity in the *Valkenhorst II* case prompted Forder to suggest that 'it is possible that the **Dutch** Supreme

27 VONK (2007), p. 270.
28 VONK (2007). p. 270.
29 See Chapter I.
30 In the meaning of decisional privacy described above.

Court is holier than the Pope'.[31] In discussing that case, Forder questioned the principle's legal pertinence since in her view it 'adds nothing to the already entirely convincing argument that the child's need to know his origins is impelling when compared to the parents' interests'.[32]

In suggesting that a notion of responsibility is an inept legal criterion for our discussion, Forder referred to the most exceptional of situations. Thus, she refers to a case in which a person who carried out an IVF treatment had neglected to wash out the pipette in treating a couple of mixed race. Here a couple could not reasonably be held responsible for the existence of the child that was born as the result of a 'technical mistake' but the child would be in need of an explanation 'as great as can be'.[33] Even so, such exceptions may not detract from the fact that a court's emphasizing a parent's responsibility may generally be appropriate in underlining a parent's responsibility with regard to disclosure. After all, the fact that a person has a convincing moral interest in knowing and has a sufficiently well-developed decisional privacy to decide whether access to identifying information does not in itself give rise to any duty to inform. But if the right is to be effective in any legally relevant way, it must be assumed that *some* duty to disclose exists and that this duty must also be incumbent on the candidates that may be held 'responsible' for disclosure: the 'parents' or the state.

Even on the normative assumption that the principle generally holds true, in the light of the factual circumstances of the *Valkenhorst II* case the (express) reference to a notion of procreational responsibility may be considered misguided. Thus, the court failed to take into account the fact that mothers were forced by their socio-familial environment to give up children who had been born out of wedlock at the time.[34] As the dogmatic 'Dutch uncle', the **Dutch** Supreme Court, in other words, had not done its legal history lessons very well.

---

31 FORDER (1995), p. 132. Although it may be defensible to argue that an ideology which focuses on the 'ongoing' moral responsibility of birthparents is more directly associable with a Calvinist individual, 'freedom of conscience' oriented religious morality than with the 'good works' theology implicit in Catholicism. In that regard, the prevalence of anonymous birth as a charitable Catholic institution in Southern Europe may be telling.

32 FORDER (1995), p. 131.

33 FORDER (1995), p. 131. *NRC Handelsblad,* Saturday 17 June 1995, p. 1.

34 FORDER (1995), p. 132.

4.2.2. Procreational responsibility and reproductive freedom

The **Dutch** Supreme Court's insistence on responsibility for disclosure in the *Valkenhorst II* case exposed the dangers that may arise when the principle is seen in a way that is detached from the socio-historical or personal context that surrounded the parent's consensual reproductive choice. In fact, sometimes there may clearly not have been a moral choice at all, in the case of a mother's rape or an incestuous conception, for example. Barring such extreme and horrendous circumstances, however, in contemporary Western societies it could be argued that the validity of the responsibility argument has been reinforced. Thus, in view of greater access to birth control, there could be little reason for the law to take seriously the objection of a father that he had not intended to conceive a child, even in those rare cases in which birth control may subsequently be proved to have been ineffective.[35] Likewise, the mother will for the same reasons generally have a greater responsibility in respect of informing the child of the identity of the biological father.

At this point, it is, however, conceivable that in some cases it may remain problematic to consider either the biological or the legal parent 'responsible' for disclosure. In particular, this could arguably be the case for anonymous donors. How the principle of procreational responsibility may apply in the case of assisted conception with a donor, shall therefore be discussed in Chapter X. In addition, in the other contexts of the comparative analysis the principle shall also be operationalised.

4.2.3. State responsibility, subsidiarity and proportionality

Apart from the legal parents and/or the biological parents, the state is considered to be a likely candidate to be held accountable in facilitating children's access to their biological origins.[36] On the issue of donor anonymity, the **French** legal scholar Thérèse Callus even considers that the question whether there can be 'a duty on the parents or on the state may in, real terms, be the most important element' of the legal debate.[37]

There can be little doubt that some form of state responsibility for disclosure is already assumed at the constitutional level. The **Dutch** government has set up a

35 See Chapter VII on the judicial determination of paternity.

36 O'DONOVAN (1988), p. 39.

37 CALLUS (2004), p. 668.

public foundation that controls access to donor identifying information. Moreover, the recognition of a right to know at the constitutional level in **Germany**, **the Netherlands** and **Portugal** illustrates that the state considers that it has a role to play in facilitating its nationals' access. In that connection, it is significant, too, that virtually all of the world's states are parties to the UNCRC. Moreover, the state also has an international obligation to register births.[38]

The question is, of course, how far this state responsibility should go. As has been suggested above, this is essentially a question of the boundaries between positive and negative obligations of the state. In particular, it may be wondered how far the state should go in ensuring children's privacy while promoting parental awareness of children's informational needs under the principle of procreational responsibility. At this point, it will be sufficient to suppose that this level of state regulation will vary depending on the particular context surrounding the circumstances of birth. Furthermore, courts and other public institutions will have to decide on the informational needs of individual children.

Assuming that a differentiated interpretation with regard to the circumstances of a child's conception is justifiable, it may in particular be wondered how *intrusive* state measures may be in cases of socio-legally constructed paternity. If the state forces all children and parents, for example, to undergo DNA testing upon the child's birth, this may be seen as a disproportionate measure because it would be too intrusive.[39] In view of the intrusiveness of that measure, the state could also promote the idea that it should in principle be up to the legal parents to disclose the information. The state should, in that view, play a subsidiary role in disclosing the information when the parents have not fulfilled their own responsibility with respect to the child.

On the issue concerning the boundaries between positive and negative state obligations, it is ventured that a distinction between contexts could also be relevant. As has already been suggested, the role of the state is more apparent in the case of adoption and assisted conception given the public regulation of those areas. In comparison, in a case of 'misattributed paternity' it will be more appropriate for the public authorities to keep a low profile.'[40] Even so, the state does have its international obligations under the UNCRC in respect of all chil-

[38] See Chapter II.

[39] Leaving aside the argument that it may still not be a cost-efficient solution.

[40] Jackson (2001), p. 214 claims, however, that 'infidelity' may be 'a statistically greater threat to accurate knowledge of our biological origins than the relatively small number of DI births.

dren. In this light, the difficult question should be raised what sort of state responsibility is required when parents do not take responsibility for informing children of their origins. It is hoped that the comparative analysis will shed some light on the relationship between state responsibility and the (sub-) principles of proportionality and subsidiarity that will influence the interpretation of the appropriate scope of such state responsibility.

4.3. EQUALITY

Vis tu cogitare istum quem servum tuum vocas ex isdem seminibus ortum eodem frui caelo, aeque spirare, aeque vivere, aeque mori!
Epistulae morales 47, Seneca[41]

4.3.1. Equality in general

The constitutional character that the right to know one's origins has been lent in itself evokes the idea that each person has such a right given relevant legal and factual restraints. Crucially, however, it has by now already become quite clear that such legal and factual restraints will differ, regardless of the fact that such a right may have a moral force of more general applicability. On the principle of equality, Westen held that its discussion only acquires real meaning if a concrete comparison is made.[42] For this reason, the principle itself need not detain our attention for long. In the next sub-sections, legal questions regarding some of the most important dimensions of this principle will therefore be raised.

At this point, it is important, rather, to hold that the principle of equality always bears an accessory character. Thus, equality may indeed only become a legal concern to the extent that situations can be reasonably considered to be comparable. Furthermore, the principle of equality will also be at issue in the case of unequal treatment, i.e. whenever an applicant has been disadvantaged as compared to another person or group of persons. From that perspective, it is important to establish which forms of unequal treatment may be justifiable and which forms are not.

The **Dutch** legal scholar Janneke Gerards has further theorised upon both of these basic equality tests. She holds that the 'disadvantageous treatment' test is

41 *Consider that he whom you wish to call a slave was conceived in heaven out of the same semen, is breathing the same air and is destined to live and die the same way like you.*

42 Westen (1982), p. 537.

generally to be preferred over the 'comparability' test because considerations of a subjective nature are likely to slip more easily into the latter form of reasoning.[43] In a 'disadvantageous treatment' test the court will ascertain whether a group of persons have factually been disadvantaged as compared to another group of other persons. The applicant's interests must then be objectifiable and the applicant must have a sufficiently important, legally relevant interest.[44] In trying to avoid the problems that characterise equality cases, courts are therefore required to select and define the specific factors that determine the scrutiny and intensity of judicial review.[45]

At the regional level, the accessory character is evinced by Article 14 ECHR. In *Odièvre*, for example, the applicant claimed equal access to inheritance rights solely because of the nature of the parental tie, considering that there had been discrimination on the ground of birth. The court did not delve into that argument.[46] The **French** Government held that there had been no difference in treatment in the instant case because the situation of a child that had been abandoned by the mother was not comparable to that of other children whose parents had assumed responsibility for them. Criticism would only be warranted if there was a difference in treatment between children born under X.[47]

Accordingly, a claim that discrimination on the ground of a person's 'birth' is expressly prohibited under this provision was unsuccessful. It may seriously be questioned, however, whether such a ground will ever be considered sufficiently objectifiable in the context of accessing one's origins.

Assuming that this could be the case, this equality ground could be invoked by someone, for example, whenever the state plays an active role in making the enforcement of the right to know one's origins impossible. Conceivably, such an argument could be mounted in case the state rigidly insists upon ensuring lifelong anonymity for the donor. Assuming that the ECtHR would consider this

---

43 Gerards (2002), p. 726,

44 Gerards (2002), p. 726.

45 Gerards (2002), p. 724.

46 ECtHR *Odièvre v. France*, 13 May 2003, Appl. No. 42326/98, paras. 51 and 52. See Chapter III.

47 Compare *Jäggi*, where relying on Art. 14 of the Convention in conjunction with Art. 8, the applicant complained that he had been subjected to discrimination that had not been based on objective grounds in that the Federal Court had taken into account his state of health and advanced age as reasons for justifying the refusal to perform a DNA test. ECtHR *Jäggi v. Switzerland*, Appl. No. 58757/00, paras. 48-50. The court did not go into this discrimination on the basis of age, considering this claim to be connected with the claim under Art. 8 ECHR. See further Chapter III.

treatment to be a violation of the principle simply because 'all are born equal', the level of judicial scrutiny would have to be particularly high.

The alternate view would be to take a 'disadvantageous treatment' test in respect of those persons who do not know their origins. From that viewpoint, the court could, for example, require that the applicant demonstrate that he has been afflicted by psychological problems that he would otherwise not have experienced had he been in a position to know his biological parents. Conceivably, this would, generally, however, also place a heavier evidential burden on the searching applicant. Thus, this approach could raise evidential problems of causality, for it may be difficult under certain circumstances to prove that the person would not have been afflicted by such specific problems had he known the identity of the biological parent. Quite conceivably, it would also become an insurmountable obstacle if the applicant were required to demonstrate that comparable identity problems are generally absent amongst those who have grown up with their own biological parents.

4.3.2. Equality and the circumstances upon conception and birth

A distinct approach to the access rights of adoptees and donor-conceived children has been defended in view of differences that are considered to be sufficiently important to justify different treatment. Although the contexts will be discussed in greater detail in the next Chapters, some such possibly relevant differences may be mentioned here. Thus, with donor gametes, the child will in many cases be the biological child of one of the parents who is to raise the child, the child does not have to overcome a sense of abandonment by its biological parents, and therefore has no need to come to terms or confront feelings of rejection by her or his birthparents,[48] The need for adoptees to search for their birthparents has been perceived sometimes as a response to negative parenting experiences by the adoptive parents.[49] The more harmonious their adoptive parenting had been experienced, the less likely that the adoptees would search for their birthparents some studies suggest.[50]

As a further distinction considered by some to be relevant the mother of the donor-conceived child experiences a full pregnancy, which among other things for some authors means that friends, family and colleagues are not likely to 'see'

48 GLENN MCGEE, VAUGHAN-BRAKMAN & GURMANKIN (2001) p. 2033.
49 SOULÉ & NOEL (1986), p. 55-56; GIBSON (1992) p. 16.
50 DANIELS & TAYLOR (1993), p. 160; SCHECHTER & BERTOCCI (1990) p. 68.

any physical evidence of the use of donor gametes.[51] It follows that this could reduce the number of others who know about the conception method, thereby minimizing the perceived danger of the child finding out through others than those who may reasonably be held 'responsible' for such disclosure. In other words, the child would be spared a potentially painful experience of disclosure.

It has also been voiced that a distinction between assisted conception and adoption is necessary since secrecy is much more entrenched in the whole process of AI than in adoption. This would also reinforce the case for secrecy in donor insemination.[52] In contrast to inter-country adoptees, donor-conceived children will, for example, typically physically resemble one of their biological parents because from conception they share a biological link to one legal parent.[53] This would make a concerted effort by the parties involved to keep donation a secret more straightforward on the assumption that ignorance may sometimes be bliss. All the same, such a conspiracy of silence, whatever its moral merits, will not take away the risk of an accidental disclosure by a third party, which, it is assumed, may be more discomforting than disclosure by parents or the state.

4.3.3. Equality and age

It is the case law under the ECHR that has created a right for adult offspring to know their origins on the basis of Article 8 of the Convention. In most of the constitutional cases discussed so far the applicant had been an adult. In a sense, this is to be expected since adults may generally be better equipped to articulate their own particular interest in accessing parent-identifying information.

Still, if Articles 7 and 8 of the UNCRC are taken as the right's primary basis, this is a remarkable development, however. In that connection, Ursula Kilkelly also points out that precisely because the ECHR is to some extent enforceable, it can compensate for the poorer enforcement mechanisms of the CRC.[54] Where the case law on the ECHR has so far mostly been concerned with the claims of adults, rights holders under the UNCRC are minors. In spite of this, it is difficult to disagree, however, with John Eekelaar that it would be a 'grievous mistake' to interpret the UNCRC only in respect of minor children, for childhood is not an end in itself but is part of the process of forming the adults of the next genera-

---

51 GLENN MCGEE, VAUGHAN-BRAKMAN & GURMANKIN (2001), p. 2033.
52 GIBSON (1992), p. 4.
53 GIBSON (1992), p. 4.
54 KILKELLY (2001), p. 311, 325-326.

tion.[55] Thus, it has emerged that the UNCRC has been instrumental in the increased recognition of adult children's right to know on the basis of the ECtHR.[56]

Nonetheless, age does seem to matter for the ECtHR. In that respect, it is recalled that in the *Jäggi* case, the ECtHR suggested that the interest in knowing does not decrease but rather increases with age in the court's view.[57] A few years before, it suggested that when the interests of two adults conflict on the issue, the informational interest which a child has must be viewed on an equal footing with that of others.[58] In the *Phinikaridou* case the ECtHR restricted the freedom to impose time-limits following the view that (adult) children must have at least one 'real' opportunity to have their paternity established.[59] It follows from the latter case, too, that someone may effectively become 'estopped' from exercising a right to have her or his (legal) paternity established after a certain period has expired upon becoming aware of the presumptive father's identity.[60] In the recent **Portuguese** constitutional cases, too, the right to know has been interpreted in such a way that the procedural time-limits in denying paternity beyond early adulthood are considered to be unconstitutional.[61]

While there seems to be growing evidence under the ECtHR therefore that adults in principle have a constitutional right to know their biological parents, for children the situation is less clear-cut. Back in 1995, Geraldine Van Bueren even went as far as to state that the only real point at issue in accessing origins 'ought to be whether the child is sufficiently mature to be able to benefit from access to such records'.[62] Although it has become clear that this view would detract from other relevant legal problems, it has also become apparent that the 'age factor' will be an important issue that will require further attention in the thematic comparative analysis. The question whether children have an equally enforceable right, or a right that is at least comparable to that of adults, across various contexts shall therefore be dealt with in more detail in the next Chapters.

---

55 Eekelaar & Šarčević (1993), p. 234.
56 See Chapters II and III, in particular the discussion of the *Jäggi, Ebru* and *Phinikaridou* cases.
57 ECtHR *Jäggi v. Switzerland*, Appl. No. 58757/00, 13 July 2006, para. 44.
58 ECtHR *Odièvre v. France*, Appl. No. 42326/98, 13 February 2003, para. 44. Note that this suggests that the ECtHR disacknowledged that a principle of procreational responsibility applied in the relationship between parents and children.
59 ECtHR *Phinikaridou v. Cyprus*, Appl. No. 23890/02, 20 December 2007, para. 58.
60 ECtHR *Phinikaridou v. Cyprus*. 23890/02, 20 December 2007, para. 58.
61 See Chapter IV.
62 Van Bueren (1995), p. 46.

4.3.4. Equality and gender

As has already become clear from the foregone Chapters, the different roles in human reproduction are reflected in a different legal treatment in the parentage law of mothers and fathers. This fact raises the question whether the child's informational needs, while challenging the legal status of parents, could also create tension with parental rights. Assuming that this might be the case, a further question must then be whether this tension is indissoluble or that the law may create conditions for a child to identify a parent without this resulting in unjustifiable gender discrimination in parentage law.

It may be said that the *Evans* case in particular exposed the tension that may arise with the rights of men and women in reproductive decisions. In tolerating the **British** bright-line legislation, the ECtHR suggested that men and women had equivalent rights in that respect.[63] Just as the man could not force Ms Evans to undergo nine months of unwanted pregnancy and the risks of childbirth, so Ms Evans could not compel her former partner to undergo treatment. In this way, Ms Evans' ex-partner had already made it clear that he did not wish to have a child unless he could be actively involved in parenting, thereby rejecting the idea of fatherhood as merely a legal status with financial obligations.[64] Accordingly, the ECtHR indirectly also acknowledged the importance that biology could have in the child-parent relationship, in particular for fathers, although it effectively denied Ms Evans a right to a genetically-related child under Article 8 ECHR.

As another gender-sensitive case, but more directly concerned with the right to information than reproductive freedom, the *Odièvre* case laid bare the tension that could arise between an (adult) child's interests in identifying her birth-mother and that mother's interest in the non-disclosure of her identity. It demonstrated that the applicant's informational right was capable of creating tension with women's rights and interests, even though this applicant was also female. At the same time, it is conceivable that the mother's privacy interest could also undermine a potential interest of the biological father in making his identity known and establishing a family law relationship with the applicant. In the thematic comparative analysis of anonymous birth, we shall discuss this impact on mothers and fathers'' rights further.[65]

---

63 See also COLLIER & SHELDON (2008), p. 96.

64 COLLIER & SHELDON (2008), p. 97.

65 See Chapter VI.

4.3.4.1. Utility and rights in gender thinking

Even though the subject-matter will essentially be approached from a child's perspective, the rights of mothers and fathers will also be discussed. To some extent, this gender-sensitive dimension of our discussion has already received attention from scholars. In tracing the emergence of 'rights' thinking, Stephen Parker gave a historical account of family law developments in common law systems in **England** and **Australia**.[66] In a nutshell, Parker's account draws on a broad theme in legal philosophy, the conflict between rights and utility. Parker holds that the ideological drift away from the law's promotion of community and family interests from fathers to women and then to children marks a paradigm shift from such utility-oriented rights thinking. The idea that rights have a strong *prima facie* legitimacy is a recent phenomenon according to Parker. This modern ethic, inspired by a Kantian notion of autonomy, is taken to contrast with the erstwhile, utilitarian view that the family as a whole requires protection.

What is important for our discussion is that in providing an example of this paradigm shift, Julie Wallbank has discussed the effect of the children's right to know their origins on mothers rights on the basis of Parker's theory. In connection 'with the child's right, Wallbank makes the bold claim that the current emphasis on the provision of information on the biological link in a familial dispute has provoked a conjunction of children's and fathers' rights. This focus on the rights of children and fathers is used, in her view, to women's detriment while diluting the gains women have made in relation to family life.[67] At the same time, the use of 'rights language' in relation to the child's autonomy, exemplified by the UNCRC, would also lead to a reinforcement of the putative father's position. Thus, at least as far as her analysis of **English** law is concerned, it is suggested that rights-thinking is to be blamed for the fact that women who refuse to consent to a paternity will be 'likely to be viewed as acting against the child's interests in all but the most horrendous situations'.[68]

---

66 PARKER (1992), p. 320.

67 WALLBANK (2004), p. 246; concurring opinion: BRINK (2006), p. 105-106. The latter author also sees a gender bias in the emphasis which the UN Children's Rights Committee puts on the abolition of anonymous birth which would contrast with much more cautious efforts by states to promote fathers to assume their parental responsibilities. The insistence upon *mater semper certa* would therefore be taken to extremes, whereas not everything is undertaken to thrust paternity upon genetic fathers.

68 WALLBANK (2004), p. 251.

In that connection, Wallbank suggests, however, that this power shift within the family to the detriment of women could be avoided. Thus, she acknowledges that a rights approach as well as the ideology behind the right is not inherently 'unsympathetic' to women's rights. Suffice it to quote: 'If the right were firmly entrenched throughout family law, then all private familial disputes would be resolved without the need to castigate women as carers. It would also transmit the message to prospective parents that they have obligations to tell their children of their biological origins'.[69]

In solving such conflicts, Wallbank suggests that it may be better for the law to distinguish between the child's right to know and ancillary issues of contact, parental responsibility and residence. Clearly, it will be worth examining to which extent this idea can be taken further in the comparative analysis because if such a regime were conceivable, then informational needs will be less likely to cause friction between a mother's and father's parental rights.

5. CONFLICT

5.1. PUBLIC INTERESTS

On the basis of the analysis of relevant regional law in Chapter III, it has emerged that the state has a broad margin of appreciation which allows states to sometimes restrict a person's right to know their origins in the pursuance of governmental tasks. If a state imposes procedural time-limits in the public interest because of legal certainty, it is foreseeable that such a requirement could become an obstacle to persons accessing parent-identifying information lawfully.[70] So far the ECtHR has not found the imposition of such time-limits irreconcilable with a state's duties under Article 8 ECHR as long as the state also ensures 'one real opportunity' for a person to align her or his legal parentage with the biological truth.

Another public interest, in the case of a *post mortem* judicial determination of parentage, involves the protection by the state of the right to rest in peace of the deceased parent and in preventing the desecration of graves. Furthermore, as we have seen, in the context of anonymous or discreet birth, the interest in preventing clandestine abortions and neo-naticide and the relief of pregnant women in

69 WALLBANK (2004), p. 246.

70 See Chapter VIII for a discussion of the issue of covert parentage tests on the Internet.

distress have also been recognised.[71] Similarly, if a state's demographic policy is very pro-natalist, then anonymous birth may be perceived as a way to ensure such public policy aims. Moreover, it shall emerge in the next Chapters that a state may also have some interest in ensuring a number of adoptable children and in ensuring that the number of donors will be able to meet demands from recipient coupes.[72]

5.2. PRIVATE INTERESTS: THE PRIVACY OF THE PARENT

The most obvious private interest that can go against a children's right to know their origins involves the privacy interest of parents. This right has been acknowledged in a number of regional cases. Furthermore, this interest has been acknowledged in the national constitutional order.

In none of the examined cases has it so far been defined what the scope of this privacy interest involves beyond the acknowledgement that such a right exists, for example in *Valkenhorst II*. In the *Phinikaridou* case, the strength of the child's right to know was made contingent upon the applicant's age and the fact that considerable time had passed until the (adult) child decided to undertake procedural action. Accordingly, the ECtHR posited the idea that the 'child' had already achieved considerable certainty as to the identity of her biological father. In that light, the ECtHR specified that a paternity claim under Article 8 ECHR is capable of becoming a 'stale' claim as a result of the passage of time.[73]

Otherwise, on the basis of the examined **German** constitutional case law, it has been observed that the (unmarried) mother's privacy interest will generally be restricted by her duty to disclose the father's name to the child.[74] This will mean that her privacy right is generally quite restricted.

In **Portuguese** law, the privacy right of the presumptive father has also eroded to some extent. In that regard, a change in the doctrinal views of De Oliveira has been quoted in recent constitutional case law. It follows that, contrary to what the ECtHR suggests, in **Portuguese** law the father's privacy interest does not become stronger, but may dilute in the course of time.

---

71 ECtHR *Odièvre v. France*, Appl. No. 42326/98, 13 February 2003, para. 44.
72 See in particular Chapter VI.
73 See Chapter III.
74 See Chapter IV.

5.3. PRIVATE INTERESTS: A PARENT'S RIGHT TO CORPORAL INTEGRITY

Strictly speaking, DNA testing does not require interference with the person's right to corporal integrity at all in case human tissue is used that has been separated from that person's body. Under such circumstances, however, it may be difficult to bring the DNA in connection with a biological parent in case that parent refuses to consent to testing. An interference with the parent's physical integrity will therefore generally be required. The ECtHR has, albeit in somewhat implicit terms, considered such forms of testing to be a permissible means to establish parentage.

As far as the national legal systems are concerned, the scope of a parent's right to corporal integrity shall be discussed in further detail in Chapter VIII.

5.4. THIRD PARTY INTERESTS

As has been established in Chapter III, it has been acknowledged by the ECtHR that some third party interests will also require attention. In particular, the interests of a deceased father's other children and close relatives were recognised *inter alia* in the *Jäggi* case. Furthermore, it is recalled that in *Odièvre* the interests of the biological father and the adoptive parents were also acknowledged. In all of these cases, however, the interest that these third parties had was not delineated. In addition, in the national constitutional case law such third party interests have so far not received attention. In the next Chapters, therefore, third party interests will only be discussed to a limited extent in the absence of clear constitutional principles.

5.5. CONCURRENCE OF A PARENT'S AND CHILD'S INFORMATIONAL NEEDS

The ECtHR has so far resisted giving precedence to the right of the (presumptive) biological father to have certainty as regards his genetic link to a child over a state's interest in securing that children have a stable family life with their legal parents. Even if he does not seek to establish legal ties with the child but claims to have such a legal interest in knowing the truth on ideological grounds, availing himself of the argument that the child's informational interests coincide with his own. The Strasbourg court was therefore not entirely sympathetic to the putative biological father's informational interests in the *Nylund* case.[75] For the Strasbourg court the domestic **Finnish** courts had justifiably accorded greater weight to the interests of the child and the family in which the child lived than to the interest of the father, all the more so because the child could, when reaching the age of fifteen years, decide herself whether it was in her interest to institute paternity proceedings. In that way, the court therefore re-emphasised its adherence to the principle of decisional privacy in matters of access to biological parentage in respect of minors. As has been verified, adherence to this principle also requires some respect for the child's right *not* to know.

This position was also corroborated, or so it seems, by the *Tiziana Pipoli* case, in which the interests of young adopted children in a stable family life under Article 8 ECHR were also considered to outweigh the interest in establishing contact and 'knowing' their biological mother that this mother had herself claimed on behalf of those children.[76]

When the informational needs of the father and the child concur or coalesce, the **German** Bundesverfassungsgericht has acknowledged the constitutional character of a father's right to know his progeny, even if it has also suggested that such a parental right to know must be ranked at a level inferior to a child's right to know in order to ensure the latter's right not to know.[77] To this point we shall return in Chapter VII.

6. SELECTION OF EVALUATIVE CRITERIA

It has been established in this Chapter that a number of principles underlie the recognition of the right to know one's origins. These are the principle of procreational responsibility and the principle of autonomy, or rather 'decisional privacy', as well as the equality principle. As has been made clear, these principles do not lend themselves to any absolutist interpretations of the right to know.

Given their broad applicability, it hardly comes as a surprise that these principles have so far not been interpreted in all constitutional orders in a uniform way. It

---

75 ECtHR *Nylund v. Finland*, Appl. No. 27110/95, 29 June 1999. See Chapter III.

76 ECtHR *Tiziana Pipoli v. Italy*, Appl. No. 27145/95, 30 March 1999. See Chapter III.

77 Federal Constitutional Court = Bundesverfassungsgericht (BVerfGE), 13 February 2007, *FamRZ* 2007, p. 441. Art. 2 1 in conjunction with Art. 1 1 Federal Constitution = Grundgesetz (GG). *Recht des rechtlichen Vaters auf Kenntnis seiner Nachkommenschaft (Nachwuchses).*

has been assumed that the force of the principle of procreational responsibility will, for example, vary from context to context. In delineating the boundaries between state and private obligations, the legal principles of subsidiarity and proportionality may apply. If the enforcement of the child's right to know can be realized without taking very intrusive measures on the part of the state, this route will accordingly be preferred. It is presumed that if parents do not assume their responsibility, the state will play a more important role in facilitating information and more intrusive measures could be indicated. To such issues regarding the right's enforcement we shall turn in the next Chapters.

For the moment, it seems safe to conclude that across the examined legal systems, with the debatable exception of **France,** these principles are central to the debate on the right's scope and that they generally provide a strong indication that the right to know one's origins at present demands considerable legal protection even though the right is rarely viewed as an interest which is capable of trumping other rights.

These principles will therefore provide the main normative criteria against that will guide the thematic comparative analysis that shall be undertaken in the following Chapters. In the last Chapter, some evaluative remarks shall be made on their interpretation in the national jurisdictions.

PART IV
THEMATIC COMPARISON

CHAPTER VI
THE IDENTIFICATION OF THE BIRTHMOTHER

1. OUTLINE

The fact that pregnancy and birth are visually perceptible means that the legal identification of the child's genetic mother is relatively straightforward. All the same, there are situations in which the birthmother will not be immediately identifiable or may not be the child's genetic mother. Thus, the mother may have carried the pregnancy to term but be unwilling or unable to take care of the child after having given birth. Furthermore, the birthmother may have only fulfilled a gestational role for commissioning parents and bear no genetic link to the child. This latter situation, involving a high technological form of surrogate motherhood, shall be dealt with in Chapter IX.

Furthermore, the legal modalities which govern birth registration in each jurisdiction shall first be the subject of attention in this Chapter. Thereafter, attention shall be given to the parentage law modalities governing the establishment of legal motherhood (maternity) as well as the law that applies with regard to foundlings. Before entering into a comparative law discussion of anonymous and discreet birth, relevant historical and social science background information in respect of this phenomenon shall be provided.

2. BIRTH REGISTRATION

2.1. REQUIREMENTS

Birth registration is geared towards the integration of children into their family as soon as possible after birth. Legislation on birth registration should therefore meet the requirements of efficiency and expediency. Given its central role in accessing information concerning status, the issue warrants a brief discussion.

Furthermore, the issue has received broad international recognition as a human right in accordance with Article 24 of the ICCPR and Article 7(1) UNCRC.

In **France**, all births must be declared within three days of the delivery before the civil status registrar.[1] For births during sea voyages and international and domestic flights, specific rules apply.[2] The birth is in principle declared by the father, or, in his absence, by the doctors of medicine or surgery, midwives, health officials or other persons present at the delivery.[3] Where the mother has given birth outside her domicile, the person at whose place she has given birth can alternatively make the declaration.

Article 57 of the **French** Code Civil incorporates a volitional element, by respecting a parent's eventual wish not to be identifiable in respect of the child. A record of birth in principle makes mention of the day, the time and the place of birth, the sex of the child, the first names given to him, the family name, and the first names, the family names, ages, occupations and domiciles of the father and mother and those of the applicant. The wording of the provision expressly leaves room, however, for the father and mother to omit to mention their names.[4]

In **Germany**, the birth should be declared before the civil status registrar of the district[5] where the child was born within a week.[6] The Federal Civil Status Act lists the persons who should declare the birth in alternating order. The father charged with parental authority, rather than the mother, is the primary person indicated. Even so, the midwife, the medical professional, or 'any' person present at the birth or having knowledgeable of the birth, and in the last place, the (physically) 'capable' mother are been mentioned. Registration is conceived to be a public duty which only arises whenever another person mentioned before in this alternating order has not declared the child's birth. If the child is born within a public health clinic or a similar public institution or a prison, however, only that institution's manager will be required to declare the birth.[7] This competence may be given by proxy to an obstetrician or a midwife who witnessed the birth. The civil status registrar is required to verify the truthfulness

1 Art. 55 PCC.
2 Art. 59 F.C.C.
3 Art. 56 F.C.C.
4 See below in further detail on anonymous birth in France.
5 *Bezirk.*
6 §16 Personenstandsgesetz (PstG) = (Federal) Civil Status Act. If the child was born dead, the civil status registrar should be notified within a week.
7 §18(1) and (2) PstG.

of the declaration of birth. But whether this entails an obligation to establish the biological truth is unlikely, because the declaration relates to the fact of birth rather than to the existence of a genetic link between mother and child.[8]

The 'birth act' lists the name of the parents, their profession and domicile.[9] It further lists the nationality of the parents if one of them is not **German** and, subject to their consent, also their religious denomination as well as the place, day and hour of birth, sex, name and family name and the identity of the persons who have declared the birth, including their profession and domicile.[10] Failure to comply with the duty to register constitutes a public offence which will in principle be liable to a fine.[11] However, it may arguably also fall within the definition of the criminal offence of falsification of personal status by means of suppression which is liable to two years' imprisonment.[12]

In **the Netherlands**, the birth act is drawn up by the civil status registrar of the municipality where the child is born.[13] Special rules apply when the child is born during a domestic or international flight or during a voyage at sea.[14] The birth act contains the date of the declaration, the time of birth and the names of the child and those of the persons declaring the birth, as well as the child's sex, if the latter can be determined.[15] The mother is regarded as the primary person who is competent to declare the birth.[16] Yet the father has a duty to declare the birth. Even so, any person who was present at the child's birth may also make the declaration. Furthermore, a dweller at the house where the birth took place or, where this took place in a nursing or care institution, in a prison or a similar institution, the head of such an institution, or a subordinate who the head has especially designated by private instrument, may also declare the birth.[17] In the absence of, or in the case of an omission by the aforementioned persons in

---

8 §20 PstG.
9 'Birth certificate' = Geburtenbuch.
10 §21 PstG.
11 §68 PstG.
12 §169 StGB (Personenstandsfälschung in der Form der Personenstandsunterdrückung).
13 Art. 1:19 DCC.
14 Art. 1:19a(2) DCC.
15 Art. 1:19d DCC. The child's sex will again be determined by a medical examination three months after the birth in a new birth act. If this is not possible within this period, the new birth act determines that the child's sex could not be established.
16 Art. 1:19e(1) DCC.
17 Art. 1:19e(3) under (b) DCC.

making a declaration, the mayor of the municipality where the birth certificate must be drawn up will declare the birth.[18]

If the birth has not been declared within three days, the Public Ministry must be informed.[19] The civil status registrar will determine the identity of the person by making a declaration in accordance with the Compulsory Identification Act.[20] A declaration by the obstetrician or medical professional stating that that particular woman has given birth to the child may also suffice.[21]

In **Portugal**, the Civil Registration Code requires the person who makes the declaration of birth to establish, 'as far as possible', the mother's identity.'[22] Specific legislation applies in respect of births during voyages at sea and journeys within the national territory.[23] In the birth act the names of the parents and the birthplace are listed.[24] The parents, close family members whe were present at the birth and medical professionals may notify the civil status registrar.[25] The declaration should be made orally within thirty days before the civil status registrar.[26] Upon the expiry of this period, the civil status registrar and the administrative authorities will have to notify the Public Ministry, which will lodge proceedings against those under a duty to declare the birth.[27] The addressees of this duty have nonetheless not been specified. The civil status registrar is under no obligation to assess the veracity of the declaration, which, if 'false', is challengeable in a maternity procedure.[28]

2.2. COMPARISON AND EVALUATION

By and large, the four jurisdictions display similar modalities regarding birth registration. The birth certificate is drawn up by civil status registrars who in principle list the names of the legal parents, but not necessarily the genetic parents. Only in **France** may the birth certificate be left blank in respect of the parents.

---

18 Art. 1:19e(5) DCC.
19 Art. 1:19e(6) DCC.
20 Art. 1:19e(7) DCC. Wet op de identificatieplicht.
21 Hoge Raad, 1 December 2001, *NJ* 2001, p. 317.
22 Art. 112(1) Código do Registo Civil.
23 Arts 109, 110 and 111 and 128 Código do Registo Civil.
24 Art. 69 Código do Registo Civil.
25 Art. 97 Código do Registo Civil.
26 Art. 117 Código do Registo Civil.
27 Art. 119 Código do Registo Civil.
28 Art. 1807 PCC. See above.

In view of the function of birth registration, it may not come as a surprise that the rules are broadly very similar. The father is the primary person indicated to notify the state of the birth, but, alternatively, the co-operation of the medical professional, the mother or close family members or other persons present at the birth may be required. It is both a public and private interest that registration takes place as quickly as possible after every birth.

3. MATER SEMPER CERTA

3.1 ROMAN LEGAL LOGIC AND BIOLOGICAL FACT

It has been shown that maternity is established in the majority of jurisdictions on the basis of the principle *mater semper certa est*.[29] Originally an adage of Roman law, this principle encapsulates the idea that maternity is both factually and legally best determined on the basis of the perceptibility of the fact of birth.

Some jurisdictions have chosen to codify the *mater semper certa* rule, such as **the Netherlands** and **Germany**. Other jurisdictions, including **Portugal**, while incorporating this legal principle, also foresee challengeable presumptions of maternity.[30] Finally, in a very small number of countries, such as **France**, it is not the fact of birth per se, but the will of the woman to become the child's legal mother which is decisive. Thus, in **France**, this importance attached to the birthmother's will to become the child's legal mother can be implied on the basis of a principle of voluntary designation of her name in the birth act.[31]

3.2. THE ESTABLISHMENT OF MATERNITY

Since the latest parentage law reform, maternity in **France** is established on the basis of a designation in the birth act of the name of the woman who has given birth.[32] Previously, in line with Napoleonic legal tradition, unmarried women were required to make a formal recognition of maternity. Fearing a sharp decline

---

29 SCHWENZER (2007), p. 3. References to national reports of **Austria, Belgium, Canada, China/Macau, Croatia, Denmark, England & Wales, Germany, Japan, the Netherlands.**

30 SCHWENZER (2007), p. 3. **Switzerland, Serbia.**

31 **Luxembourg** also assures a right to anonymous birth, while the **Italian Civil Code** leaves room for a mother to refrain from recognising the child. The child can nonetheless in principle lodge proceedings involving a judicial declaration of motherhood (Art. 260 *Codice Civile Italiano*). In **Spain**, anonymous birth was not abolished until 1999.

32 Art. 311-25 **French** Code Civil; NEYRINCK (2006), p. 9-11.

in the number of adoptable children, adoptive parents' organisations had urged the **French** government not to sign the 1962 CIEC Brussels Treaty, which insisted upon mentioning the mother's name in the birth act.[33]

An aim of the January 1972 reform was to restrict the number of 'motherless' children who had not been recognised. For that reason, Article 337 of the **French** Code Civil was amended to the extent that maternal recognition only became necessary if maternity had not been corroborated by a corresponding civil status relationship. Even so, the concerns over equality between marital and non-marital children since the ECtHR *Marckx* decision were interpreted as requiring a deletion of the requirement of recognition by unmarried mothers. Furthermore, it was acknowledged that it could be physically taxing for unmarried mothers to have to make a recognition before a civil status registrar, 'while the happily married could rest in bed after having given birth'.[34] Since the latest reform, automatic designation of maternity is the basic rule, although this will only take effect if the mother has not chosen to avail herself of the right to give birth anonymously. The mother therefore retains her historic right to keep her identity secret, a right formally enshrined in the Code Civil since 1993.

In contrast, the Civil Codes of **Germany**, **the Netherlands** and **Portugal** all adhere to the *mater semper certa* rule.[35] Codification of this ancient rule is relatively recent in all of these jurisdictions. Thus, up to the 1996 reform of parentage law, in **Germany** legislating upon the legal establishment of maternity was considered unnecessary. It has been associated with **German** legal culture to the extent that the *mater semper certa* rule[36] has been called 'something deeply entrenched in the **German** legal conscience'.[37] Nonetheless, some have suggested that legal presumptions of maternity may be indicated in those cases in which the birth-mother's identity would be unknown.[38]

Even so, **German** legal doctrine recognises that a few conceivable scenarios of uncertain maternity remain. As such, it has been ventured that the basic principle may not be desirable in case of baby swaps in birth clinics and separation between mother and child during circumstances of war. The general view holds,

---

33 Convention relative à l'établissement de la filiation maternelle des enfants naturels, conclue à Bruxelles le 12 septembre 1962.
34 Massip (2006), p. 16.
35 These legal systems shall therefore be dealt with in alphabetical order in the English language.
36 §1591 BGB.
37 Frank & Helms (2001), p. 1341.
38 Gaul (1997), p. 1463.

however, that status, as registered in the birth certificate, would not become challengeable in those exceptional situations.[39]

The **Dutch** Civil Code also provides that the mother of a child is 'the woman who gives birth to the child or who has adopted the child'.[40] The resultant impossibility to challenge maternity before the courts has received some criticism in feminist legal literature for its supposed gender bias.[41] Furthermore, the sheer impossibility for a 'social' mother to recognise a child has also been considered by some to be difficult to reconcile with notions of gender equality, since paternity is historically based to a lesser extent on biological truth.[42]

As a legal problem, maternity historically received scant attention in **Dutch** legal doctrine. In old **Dutch** law, the mother had a legal family relationship with her children irrespective of her marital status.[43] Following the **French** example of the 1804 Code Civil, the 1838 Civil Code also required unmarried mothers to make a formal recognition. A mother's omission to make a recognition could have led to more grievous injustices than in **France**, as adoption was not introduced until 1956. In theory, the child could lodge maternity proceedings against the unmarried birthmother, but this was rare, if only because she could often not be found. Since guardianship over children could be established in a straightforward way, it comes as no surprise that guardianship associations were the main proponents of this system in which maternity had to be recognised by the unmarried.[44]

It was not disputed that married women enjoyed an ipso facto 'civil law relationship' with the newborn from the moment of birth.[45] Above all, this recognition of a legal relationship between mother and a child reflected custom, however, since **Dutch** law still lacked any written legal definition of maternity.[46]

In 1947 the requirement that unmarried mothers had to recognise the child was finally lifted in respect of 'natural children'. Nonetheless, for other non-marital children, adulterine and incestuous, it remained impossible to establish a legal

---

39 EDENFELD (1996), p. 190; GERNHUBER/COESTER-WALTJEN (2006), p. 625; LÖHNIG (2001), p. 47; SCHWAB (2005), p. 240; WANITZEK (2002), p. 211; PALANDT/DIEDERICHSEN (2006), BGB, §1591, No. 20, 1849.

40 Art. 1:198 DCC.

41 VERLOO (1997), p. 166-171.

42 SMITS (1997), p. 27.

43 ASSER-DE BOER (2006), No. 689, p. 549-550.

44 HOLTRUST (1994), p. 48.

45 ASSER-DE BOER (2006), No. 689a, p. 551.

46 HOLTRUST (1994), p. 48.

relationship with the birthmother. This problem was not 'solved' until the *mater semper certa* principle was finally codified in 1998.[47] This also meant, however, that there was no room anymore for any derogation from this basic rule.

In **Portugal**, the Civil Code has since 1977 provided that maternity derives from 'the fact of birth'.[48] Prior to the reform, drawing on a **French** Napoleonic legal tradition, the unmarried mother was required to make a formal recognition.[49] Although *mater semper certa* has been codified, specific legislation on maternity has been drafted in respect of some exceptional situations in which the mother's genetic link to the child is less certain. Part of this legislative concern stems from the historical fact that mothers sometimes sought to elude the attribution of a 'false' paternity if the marital presumption rule were applied.[50] Thus, it was not unheard of that the genetic father instead of the mother's husband recognised a child before the mother's identity had been established. In this scenario a clash between the unmarried man's recognition and the marital presumption of paternity could ensue. In order to solve this conflict of paternity, **Portuguese** law has a single procedure before the civil status registrar in which both maternity and paternity may be established at the same time.[51]

The mere appearance of the mother before the civil status registrar will be sufficient in that situation for the attribution of maternity. Even if no written evidence can be put forward in her absence, maternity will also be considered to have been established if a declaration is made to that effect within a year after the child's birth.[52] If this time-limit has expired, the civil status registrar will have to notify the Public Prosecutor who will then start an investigation to establish the mother's identity.[53]

If the birth act mentioning the mother's name was drawn up by the civil status registrar within a year after birth, maternity is established. But if the birth act had been drawn up over a year after the birth, the presumptive mother may object within a period of fifteen days if she had not been the person who had registered the birth or if she had not been represented.[54] Moreover, if the

47 HOLTRUST (1994), p. 49.
48 Art. 1796 PCC.
49 Art. 1841 PCC (*old*).
50 OLIVEIRA (1979), p. 31-32.
51 Art. 1817 PCC.
52 Art. 1804 PCC; Art. 141 Código do Registo Civil.
53 Art. 1804 PCC; Art. 141 Código do Registo Civil.
54 Art. 1805 PCC in conjunction with Art. 114(1) and (2) Código do Registo Civil.

presumptive mother and the father who had recognised the child are within the prohibited degrees of consanguinity, the civil status registrar will not make any mention of the child's mother.[55]

If the identity of the child's mother could not be established, the child may lodge proceedings involving a judicial determination of maternity.[56] If the mother is known, the father will then act as the minor's legal representative.[57] If the child is also legally fatherless, the minor may have a legal representative appointed by the court.[58] If the minor only claims to have been treated as the putative mother's child or enjoys a public reputation as being the mother's child, this will be taken as sufficient evidence by the court to establish maternity. Even mere proof on the basis of a small written statement will suffice.

If a child has remained legally motherless, he or she may also lodge maternity proceedings at any time against the putative mother.[59] If the putative mother has died, it is conceivable that proceedings involving a post mortem declaration of maternity will be able to be lodged.[60] If the putative mother's husband is still alive, he will be the respondent in this procedure.[61] If he has also died, the deceased putative mother's descendants, parents or siblings may act as respondents. If also these potential respondents prove to be traceless or have also died in the meantime, a special legal representative will be appointed by the court to verify the matter.

Portuguese law also makes amends for proceedings in which a 'false' maternity can still be denied.[62] De Oliveira suggests that the genetic link (rather than a gestational link) must then have been absent.[63] Thus, a procedure may also be instituted by the woman who had herself 'falsely' registered (for example, the gestational mother), but by anyone with a sufficient interest' as well as the

---

55 Art. 1809 PCC and Art. 115(2) Código do Registo Civil.

56 Art. 1814 PCC.

57 Arts. 1910 and 1981 PCC in conjunction with Art. 10 **Portuguese** Code of Civil Procedure.

58 Art. 124 Código do Registo Civil in conjunction with Art. 1935PCC; Art. 10 **Portuguese** Code of Civil Procedure.

59 Art. 1817 PCC. The (married) partner of the 'child' and, alternatively, her or his own direct descendants may then pursue the motherhood procedure.

60 Art. 1819 PCC.

61 Tribunal da Relação do Porto, Acórdão 9720462, 13 May 1997.

62 Art. 1807 PCC.

63 OLIVEIRA (1979), p. 29.

Public Prosecutor.[64] To the author no case law regarding maternity procedures is known, however.

3.3. COMPARISON AND EVALUATION

It makes legal sense to establish maternity in accordance with the *mater semper certa* rule. From a parentage law perspective, legal certainty requires that maternity be established expediently upon birth for the greatest number of children. From a truth-oriented perspective, it is remarkable that **Portuguese** law is so firmly committed to the verification of the identity of the genetic mother, something which becomes apparent in considering the availability of meticulous procedural rules. Given the exceptionality of incongruence between the biological and legal truth here, it may not be demanding for the legal system to create such a procedure to promote the enforcement of the child's right to know. Yet the apparent absence of case law suggests that legislation may be superfluous and unnecessarily complicated. Moreover, adherence to the *mater semper certa* rule may in the vast majority of situations form a truth-oriented perspective.

4. FOUNDLINGS

4.1. SPECIFIC LEGISLATION CONCERNING FOUNDLINGS

In **France**, a person who finds an abandoned newborn child is required to make a declaration to the officer of civil status of the place of discovery. Where he does not consent to take charge of the child, that person must hand over the child to the officer of civil status. A detailed memorandum is drawn up which states the date, time, place and circumstances of the discovery, the apparent age and the child's sex as well as any peculiarities which may contribute to his identification as well as the authority or person to whom he is entrusted.[65] The person who discovered the foundling is required to make a declaration to the officer of civil status of the place of discovery. A detailed memorandum is subsequently drawn up stating the date, time, place and circumstances of the discovery, the apparent age and the sex of the child, any peculiarities which may contribute to his identification as well as the authority or person to whom he is entrusted.

---

64 The standing of the Public Prosecutor has also been specifically mentioned.

65 Art. 34 **French** Code Civil.

In **Germany**, the Civil Status Act deals with the issue of child abandonment.[66] Whoever finds an abandoned newborn child should report to the police within a day after the discovery and they will make an effort to trace the birthparents. After hearing the public health service the competent public authorities, presumably the civil status service, determine the supposed place and time of birth and determine the child's first name and family name. These may be altered if the parents are traced subsequently. If the birth has not been declared within three months, they may have to incur the costs of registration subject to the applicability of the aforementioned order of persons.

In **the Netherlands**, if the place or date of birth of the child is unknown or the surname, including the forenames, of the mother is unknown, the birth certificate with regard to these matters is drawn up pursuant to instructions and in accordance with the directions of the Public Prosecution Service.[67] The Public Prosecution Service, for its part, informs the mayor of the municipality where the child was found. The mayor then has the birth registered before the civil status registrar if the persons who are required to declare the birth have omitted to do so or are absent.[68] Thereafter, the Child Protection Board can petition for a provisional parental responsibilities order. If the parents remain traceless over a protracted period, the court can issue a parental responsibilities order. Typically, parental authority will then be vested in a foster family. If the birthparents remain traceless, however, adoption will not become a possibility for the foster parents as **Dutch** adoption law prescribes the written consent of the birthparents.

In **Portugal**, child abandonment constitutes a crime if the child's life is put at risk.[69] The birth of a foundling will have to be registered in as much detail as possible by whoever finds the child.[70] A copy of the incomplete birth certificate is then handed over to a family court. This court has competence to pass an adoption order 'if the affective bonds between the child and the natural parents have been compromised'. Further adoption criteria include abandonment by unknown legal parents and an unknown parentage in this situation.[71]

---

66 §§25-28 PstG.
67 Art. 1:19b DCC.
68 Art. 1:19e(5) DCC.
69 Art. 138 PCC.
70 Art. 116.° Código de Registo Civil. See, generally, on this point: VALE E REIS (2007), p. 209-210.
71 Art. 1978.° 1(a) and (c) PCC.

4.2 COMPARISON AND EVALUATION

When a newborn is found in a public place, birth registration is no longer the relatively straightforward formality that it usually is. It becomes vital, above all, that the public authorities respond quickly and effectively. Given the immediacy of the problem, swift integration into a stable family environment will be a more pressing concern than establishing parentage in accordance with the biological truth. It becomes only a secondary legislative choice therefore to set rules that help determine the identity of the child's parents.

Otherwise, if at all feasible, a legislative choice may be made to reintegrate the child in the family of the birthparents. If the birthparents cannot be traced or cannot reasonably be deemed fit to take on parental responsibilities, then fostering and a straightforward adoption procedure, as is possible in **Portugal**, may offer an alternative.

It may be inferred from the above that the public policy choices in the four respective countries are all geared towards achieving expediency. They aim to achieve this aim in broadly very similar ways. Yet overtly active state intervention may serve as a deterrent, because the birthparents may wish to avoid the establishment of legal parentage if they do not receive guidance from their social environment or public authorities in assuming their responsibilities.

5. ANONYMOUS AND DISCREET BIRTH

5.1. DEFINITIONAL ISSUES

The term 'abandonment of children' carries within it a strong emotional resonance. It may stir up mediatised images of children languishing in foundling institutions, sleeping rough on the streets of overcrowded, polluted Third World cities, or even of unaccompanied refugee children.

To quote cultural anthropologist Panter-Brick, in contemporary Western discourse, child abandonment is a '(social) construct guided by a highly prescriptive and normative ideology, namely, the vision of what a proper childhood should be. Popular notions of 'nobody's children' therefore spring from a specific discourse about the life course. Children who are not nurtured by responsible adults, who are separated from home, are portrayed as disconnected from family and society; their existence cannot be safe and happy, and therefore they must be rescued or 'saved'.'[72] This victimisation would not always be appropriate. Thus, 'far from being passive and dependent, they (abandoned children) seek to promote their survival, forge an identity and negotiate a place for themselves in society. These children should be viewed as resilient rather than helpless in the face of their adversity'.[73] Panter-Brick therefore suggests that abandonment should be seen 'in terms of a rupture of vital relationships between child, parent and the collectivity, involving a breach of responsibility and displacement'.[74]

Without demeaning the often profound motivations underlying the decisions of the birthparents, the term 'child abandonment' shall nonetheless still be used. It shall be used exclusively, moreover, with reference to the rupture of vital relationships from a historical perspective. It must be conceded, though, that even if used exclusively as a historical term, it may be unavoidable that the use of the term appears derogatory and biased.

Thus, for those favouring the possibility of anonymous birth, an equation with 'abandonment' may be considered a disingenuous term. For them the term shows blatant disregard to real psychological difficulties that have influenced women's decision both in the past and at present. In that same vein, the **French** psychiatrist Bonnet also raised the question: 'Why is the same word, abandonment, used to describe both a choice recognised by law and an act of criminal negligence? Why does this confusion still exist 25 years after the legalisation of abortion?'[75]

5.2. THE DISTINCTION BETWEEN 'ANONYMOUS', 'SECRET' AND 'DISCREET BIRTH'

Not unlike 'child abandonment', the term 'anonymous birth' is also habitually used indiscriminately to cover a wide range of situations in which the mother's identity may be withheld from the child. For our purposes, the term 'anonymous birth' shall also be used to refer to all such situations. Admittedly, however, for two reasons drawing a distinction between anonymous, on the one hand, and secret and discreet birth, on the other, may have analytical value. Firstly, documentation is a distinguishing feature. When the birthmother is documented somewhere, it could be more appropriate to speak of a 'secret' or 'discreet' rather than an 'anonymous' birth. Secondly, the dimensions of time are different. In sharp contrast to anonymity, the terms 'secret' and 'discreet' birth transmit an

72 PANTER-BRICK & SMITH (2000), p. 9.
73 PANTER-BRICK & SMITH (2000), p. 20.
74 PANTER-BRICK & SMITH (2000), p. 12-13.
75 BONNET (1993), p. 503-504.

idea of greater reversibility. By contrast, anonymous birth *strictu sensu* would suggest that the mother's identity has not only never been disclosed, but also that it can, as a matter of fact, not be disclosed either, unless if it were completely perchance. Thus, anonymous birth can also be understood in the terms of an irreversible secrecy sanctioned under the law. As we shall see, the current **French** legal system would position itself between secrecy and anonymity if this definition were adhered to. For that reason, the term 'anonymous birth' is simply used.

5.3. BROAD REGIONAL PATTERNS

In Antiquity and in the early Middle Ages, neo-naticide and child abandonment were particularly common occurrences. In both ancient Rome and in Germanic cultures, the father had the right to grant life or death to his children. The law that allowed fathers to kill their children was only repealed by imperial decree in 374 A.D.

It has been estimated that in urban Rome during the first three centuries of the Christian era no fewer than twenty to forty percent of newborn babies were abandoned.[76] Boswell assumes that most of these children were girls and that poverty was often, but not always, an important reason for abandonment. In the absence of contraception as a means of birth control, Roman moralists did not condemn child exposure as a wicked act. Rather, it was a life-saving institution.[77] Nonetheless, the Roman Empire never developed institutions to care for abandoned children. Instead, children were effectively left at the mercy of the 'kindness of strangers', of which adoption was a token. An adopted child could sometimes return to the birth parents at a later stage when family circumstances could have become less adverse.

From the Middle Ages onwards the church started to organise and regulate child abandonment in foundling homes to some extent. Furthermore, in marked contrast to the Roman Empire, in early Christian Europe there was a general pretence that all children were born into their biological families. Thus, the common idea in Ancient Rome that adoptive parent-child relations were not only as good as, but in some ways superior to their biological counterparts as in Roman adoption, came to lose much of its force by the close of the Middle Ages.[78]

---

76 BOSWELL (1988), p. 135.
77 BOSWELL (1988), p. 135.
78 BOSWELL (1988), p. 431.

The Catholic Church gradually came to play a preponderant role in undertaking charitable initiatives to take care of abandoned children. If this meant that children were less dependent on the 'kindness of strangers', the role of the church was ambiguous. Thus, Boswell suggests that the Church may well have in some areas increased the rate of abandonment by insisting on the absolute necessity of procreative purpose in all human sexual acts. Illegitimacy, also for children of rich parents, therefore became a pervasive social stigma. Nonetheless, the Church also offered regular and relatively humane modes of abandoning infants.[79] Christianity often slowly permeated local custom. As such, while in doctrinal views it was regarded a mortal sin, neo-naticide was often passed off as 'accidents'.

In Europe, from the thirteenth Century onwards, abandoned children were cared for by hospitals and confraternities set up by local ruling powers and the Church. The earliest forms of institutionalised child abandonment were found in **Italy**. Whereas Boswell affirms that by the fourteenth Century large **German**, **French** and **Italian** cities had established foundling hospitals, more recent studies contradict this claim and suggest that it may have taken generations, if not centuries, before this practice had spread to countries other than **Italy**.[80] Overcrowding and a lack of hygiene meant that the vast majority of children died within a few years of admission in most areas of Europe from the time of the emergence of foundling homes until the eighteenth Century.[81]

5.4. THE SOUTHERN EUROPEAN ORIGINS OF THE BABYKLAPPE (BABY-HATCH)

As a common device for securing the anonymity of parents, in Southern Europe the development of the baby-wheel baby-hatch was closely associated with child abandonment. The precise origins of the baby-hatch are unknown but were most probably also found in **Italy**. In 1198 Pope Innocentius III had the first documented version built, a so-called *ruota*, in Rome in the Ospedale di Santo Spirito in Rome. The *ruota* was typically placed in a niche in the wall of the hospital which allowed the mother to deposit the child safely without being observed; thereafter, the bells of the convent or hospital would ring to alert the staff of the new delivery. As such, 'abandonment' and anonymity often lacked a definite character. Foundling hospitals could, for example, sometimes encourage the

---

79 BOSWELL (1988), p. 430.

80 VIAZZO, BORTOLOTTO & ZANOTTO (2000).

81 BOSWELL (1988), p. 432.

child's restitution to the birth parents, especially for economic reasons as a result of overcrowding. Moreover, in some Southern European foundling institutions children were habitually tagged with signs which enabled both staff and birth-parents to trace their origins and maintain regular contact.[82]

Broadly speaking, there were marked regional and religious differences between the Protestant traditions of Northern Europe and the Catholic South in institutionalising child abandonment. For one thing, child abandonment seems to have always been more common in Southern Europe. Thus, the **Portuguese** historian Fonte refers to his research object 'as a universal phenomenon with its epicentre in Catholic Southern Europe'.[83] In Northern Europe, by contrast, anonymity seems to have been much less ingrained in culture and religious practice, even in the Catholic regions. In London, popular opposition against anonymous birth was documented in the fifteenth Century.[84] In the protestant states of Northern **Germany**, in the seventeenth and eighteenth Century anonymous birth did not take hold either. In the north and east of **Germany**, Protestant churches openly denounced the baby-wheel while in the Rhineland and in the Catholic southern regions the practice was almost unknown.[85] Rather, neo-naticide became punishable by particularly high sentences and premarital and extramarital sex was actively discouraged by rigorous criminal laws.[86]

By and large, then, it seems safe to conclude that child abandonment was traditionally more prevalent and socially accepted in the 'Catholic' South than in the 'Protestant' North. It was also in Southern Europe that institutionalised forms of child abandonment developed earlier on.

5.5. EARLY HISTORY OF ANONYMOUS BIRTH IN FRANCE AND PORTUGAL

In **France**, the origins of anonymous birth are usually traced to the foundation of the foundling hospital *Hôtel Dieu* in Paris in the sixteenth Century, when its practise was first registered.[87] In 1556 King Henry II issued an edict which

---

82 GUIMARÃES SÁ (2000), p. 30.
83 FONTE (2005), p. 22.
84 TAYLOR (1978-79), 'Philanthropy and empire: Jonas Hanway and the infant poor of London', *Eighteenth Century Studies* 12, p. 292-293.
85 FRANK (2003), p. 39. During some years in the 18th Century a baby-hatch was nonetheless operative in Hamburg.
86 NEUMANN, (1995), p. 110-117.
87 AZOUX BACRIE (2003), p. 95.

required women to declare their pregnancy to a magistrate subject to allegations of infanticide in cases of stillbirth. This edict was not abolished until the **French** Revolution.

From the first half of the eighteenth Century children, it is documented, were abandoned in baby-hatches in **France**, known as tours in **French**. Lamartine praised the tours for their life-saving capacities, '*une ingénieuse invention de la charité chrétienne, ayant des mains pour recevoir, mais pas d'yeux pour voir, ni de bouche pour parler*'.[88] It is estimated that a full third of all births took place in these institutions at the dawn of the Revolution.[89]

From the eighteenth Century, the state also began to take an active interest in the widespread problem of child abandonment in **Portugal**.[90] The state's openly pro-natalist policy which was prompted by concerns over a far-flung and understaffed colonial empire was backed by the Biblical admonition 'to go and multiply yourselves like the locust.'[91] In sharp contrast to infanticide and abortion, abandonment was therefore perceived as a patriotic act. To foment demographic growth, child abandonment at hospitals was decriminalised in 1783 by a royal decree which encharged important municipalities with setting up public hospitals for abandoned children.[92] Baby-hatches, known as rodas de expostos or rodas de enjeitados, had been known from the late seventeenth Century. They were set up at hospitals run by municipalities, on both the mainland, but also in the Azores and in **Brazil**. In 1803 a decree summed up the demographic advantages of the institution: 'a multitude of children's lives will be saved, the number of abortions and infanticides will drop, useful manpower for the fatherland will be ensured, while women will not be disgraced for their weakness, as they will be all the more cautious not to stray again'.[93]

Even so, traditional justifications were also reversed and used as arguments by the system's opponents. Thus, towards the mid-nineteenth Century the *roda* was perceived increasingly by the Church and politicians alike as a threat to traditional family values and an open invitation to sexual promiscuity without the

88 DUBOSC & VERDIER (2000), p. 53.

89 DUBOSC & VERDIER (2000), p. 53.

90 Unlike in neighbouring **Spain**, where the care for abandoned children remained closely associated with the charitable initiatives of the church and the mothers' anonymity was ensured more through exposure at church porches rather than through the baby-hatch.

91 NAHUM 3:15; FONTE (2005), p. 142-143.

92 FONTE (2005), p. 142-143.

93 FONTE (2005), p. 188 under 296, quoting José Caetano Pereira e Sousa.

societal risk of defamation.[94] Although historical research is still 'literally' in its infancy, the incidence of child abandonment appears to have been relatively high in **Portugal** in the mid-nineteenth Century.[95]

Nonetheless, the history of anonymous birth formally ended with the prohibition of the *roda* in 1866. Thereafter, the most impoverished mothers became entitled to receive small state pensions during the child's first four years while child abandonment was criminalised in the Criminal Code. In 1867 the Civil Code established automatic parental authority for both parents, which therefore in principle extended also to abandoned children.

Whereas in **Portugal** anonymous birth came to an end in the nineteenth Century, in **France** it underwent further institutionalisation. In 1793 a new **French** bill had been promulgated which further institutionalised anonymous birth. As in **Portugal**, little secret was made in **France** of underlying macro-economic and demographical concerns. The new bill prescribed in Article 3 that in each administrative district facilities would be created in which pregnant women, whether married or not, could give birth anonymously, although such a maternity home was, in fact, only set up in Paris.[96] Women who had provoked a termination of pregnancy could be sentenced to death whereas mothers who exposed or abandoned children, habitually in church porches, risked high fines.

Children entrusted to a so-called *maison maternelle* would already become eligible for adoption within weeks after birth. The **French** state took on the responsibility for carrying out the adoption procedure. In the absence of an officially known mother it was the state, too, that authorised the adoption. In view of the preponderant role assigned to the state, the adopted children born under X became known as *pupilles de l'Etat.*

As the number of children born in the *maisons maternelles* soared towards the end of the nineteenth Century, a competence was asserted by medical professionals to scrutinise the specific motives of the mothers whenever the birth had taken place longer than seven months previosly.[97] In the 1830s some *départe-*

---

94 FONTE (2005), p. 468.

95 FONTE (2005), p. 138. Fonte refers to a study conducted under the auspices of the government which found that in 1863, 36,753 children were abandoned on the mainland, the **Azores** and **Madeira** while in metropolitan **France** the number allegedly totalled 76,520 in 1860, though the population of **France** was nine times that of **Portugal**.

96 LEFAUCHEUR (2004), p. 320.

97 DUBOSC & VERDIER (2000), p. 55.

ments had already replaced the tours with a system of financial aid for unmarried mothers who wished to keep their children, but in most areas the tour system had spread rapidly across the country during the first half of the nineteenth Century. By 1860 the last tour closed down. The formal prohibition of the tour system in 1904 did not, however, mean that the number of anonymous births dwindled. The death toll during the Franco-Prussian War, the Industrial Revolution and greater access to anti-conception provided new demographic incentives for pressure groups composed of obstetricians and paediatricians to call on the government to preserve anonymous birth.[98]

5.6. ANONYMOUS BIRTH IN TWENTIETH CENTURY FRANCE

Pro-natalist public policy concerns lay at the heart of the new system which came to be known as *abandon à bureau ouvert.* This system foresaw in the creation of special offices in foundling hospitals which left their doors open for mothers in distress during day and night. From 1904 the only person other than the birth mother who would know the mother's identity became the midwife or obstetrician. Some financial assistance was offered to (single) mothers willing to take care of their child, but lifelong assurances of secrecy could also be offered.

In 1941 the leader of Vichy-France, Marshall Pétain, decreed that all expenses incurred in abandoning children in the maisons maternelles would be covered by the social childcare service of each département. Only the financial aspects were dealt with in this decree; the continued legitimacy of the legal institution in itself was not called into question. In 1942 the number of children 'of unknown descent' registered as children in public care peaked at 1,656, the highest number ever registered in **France.**[99] Still, in 1943 the rigours of lifelong secrecy were attenuated somewhat through the introduction of a period of reflection of one month for the mother to revoke her decision.

In 1956 the Code of the Family and Social Aid reaffirmed free admission to the *bureaux ouverts*, while in 1964 health and social departments were created in all **French** *départements*, known as the DDASS (*direction départementale de l'action sanitaire et sociale*), which are charged with social aid to children and *pupilles de l'État*. In 1966 it was determined that the *pupilles de l'État* would only be eligible for plenary adoption, thereby entrenching secrecy further in the law as any information concerning the birth parents was now to be deleted from

98 LEFAUCHEUR (2004), p. 321.
99 LEFAUCHEUR (2004), p. 322.

the original birth record. However, the period of reflection for the birth mother was also lengthened to three months in 1966.

The number of *pupilles* continued to decrease towards the end of the 1970s. Some highly significant social and legal changes can be adduced to account for this sharp decline. Doubtless, the legalisation of abortion (*interruption volontaire de grossesse*, IVG) in 1975 following a long campaign by the feminist movement was a key event in that respect. The use of contraception soared following the 1967 *Loi Neuwirth* which legalised publicity for birth control. Furthermore, the socio-religious stigma of illegitimacy had become less and less influential. Towards the end of the 1970s a public debate emerged, moreover, which was increasingly critical of the 'culture of secrecy' while *pupilles* also became increasingly vocal in the national media in asserting a (perceived) right to accede to their birth records.

This debate became exacerbated as a result of the enactment of a 1978 law which, subject to overriding public concerns, made it possible for all citizens to accede to public records concerning them, including birth records. If consultation is refused, individuals can seise the *Commission d'accès aux documents administratifs* (CADA), which has an advisory function, or resort to an administrative court. However, persons born under X were completely barred until 1992 from acceding to their, often blank, birth records.

The debate acquired a novel dimension following a publication by psychiatrist Cathérine Bonnet in 1990, which was often cited in the ensuing parliamentary debates. In *Geste d'amour* she advocated the creation of an institutional platform for birth parents and those born under X who requested information concerning their origins.[100] Bonnet sought to justify the tradition not only with reference to the 'classical' public policy arguments, but also by insisting on hitherto ill-defined psychological grounds. Drawing on her professional experience as a therapist, she claimed that anonymous birth should not be misrepresented as a callous act, but rather as a supreme, final act of motherly love bestowed on a child to whom she had given life but could not take care of. Moreover, many of these mothers, she suggested by presenting some 'random' case-studies, were themselves acting out their own painful feelings of neglect and abandonment experienced during their own childhood.

---

[100] BONNET (1990).

Notwithstanding the drop in anonymous births, the tradition of *accouchement sous X* became further entrenched in **French** law through its insertion into the Code Civil in 1993. The Senate prohibited maternity suits for children born under X in accordance with Article 341-1 Code Civil. In 1994 the psychologist Verdier and the psychiatrist Delaisi de Parseval published *Enfant de Personne.*[101] If the authors themselves acknoweldged that this publication resulted in something of a go-between as a scientific study and an impassioned political pamphlet, it did not fail to raise awareness among the general public. The book drew attention to the legal isolationism of **France** in respect of other countries while underlining the 'false' public interests protected by institutionalised secrecy, both in the contexts of anonymous birth and sperm donor anonymity. In denouncing Bonnet's findings, they sustained that secrecy of descent serves neither the interests of the biological mothers nor their children because it would repress an unavoidable process of mourning and leave-taking for both mother and child.[102]

In view of the increased societal exposure to the issue, the Health Minister Mattéi, a Professor of paediatrics and medical genetics, commissioned a report entitled *Enfant d'ici, enfant d'ailleurs: l'adoption sans frontières.*[103] This report made the (otherwise unsubstantiated) claim that non-identifying data would generally suffice to meet the individual's informational need. At the same time, it reaffirmed the mother's absolute right to discretion and an 'alternative to abortion'. Even so, the report did call into question the necessity of irreversible secrecy. As such, it suggested that the mother should be permitted, but only on the basis of her informed consent, to retract her initial decision whenever she wished. This proposal was ultimately revoked, however, as it was considered that requiring the mother to live with an imminent, eventual disclosure of identity would, not without sense of personal drama, put her under an 'unbearable sword of Damocles.'

The *Mattéi report* also suggested that there was a hierarchy of rights. While regarding the right to know one's origins 'in principle equivalent' to the mother's right, it submitted that the mother's right should be able to trump the child's right. In the final analysis, the child 'would in any event not have existed without the mother'. In other words, the report made a direct appeal to 'gratitude' and complacency on the part of those 'fortunate' enough to have been born.

---

101 Delaisi de Parseval & Verdier (1994).

102 As paraphrased by Willenbacher (2004), p. 349.

103 *La Documentation Française*, 1995.

Drawing on this report, the *Loi Mattéi* created the possibility for the mother to put forward non-identifying data or to disclose her identity.[104] The enactment of this bill did not put an end to all parliamentary debates on anonymous birth, however.

Thus, a new report by Lille family lawyer Dekeuwer-Défossez, commissioned by the government, called for a comprehensive reform of **French** family law and criticised the tradition's entrenchment in the Code Civil. This would have led to a further polarisation between advocates and opponents.[105] Nonetheless, the Dekeuwer-Défossez report did not call into question the legitimacy of the legal institution as such.[106] In attempting to break the legislative stalemate, the Youth and Family Policy Minister Ms Ségolène Royal took on the issue once again in January 2001 with a new proposal.

5.7. THE LOI ROYAL AND THE FOUNDATION OF THE CNAOP[107]

Before the foundation of CNAOP, a *pupille de l'Etat* had to go to great lengths to trace her or his birthmother. An application would have to be sent to the *Service de l'Aide Sociale à l'Enfance* of the *département* of birth. Alternatively, the adoption agency could sometimes provide clues as to the birthparents' identity. One of the primary reasons for centralising the information was accordingly found in solving the attested problem of regional and organisational divergence in the handling of applications. In some départements mothers who had come forward since the enactment of the *Loi Mattéi* had met with incomprehension on the part of civil servants.[108]

Prior to the adoption of Royal's proposal, *Loi n° 78-753* of 17 July 1978[109] formed the most important French law dealing with access to various administrative documents, including birth certificates. Its Article 6 lists exceptions to the general rule that information gathered by public authorities should be communicated to the concerned individual.[110] For the *pupilles de l'État* such an exception

---

104 Loi n.° 96-604 du 5 juillet 1996, Official Journal 1996, p. 10208.
105 DEKEUWER-DÉFOSSEZ (1999), p. 42.
106 DEKEUWER-DÉFOSSEZ (1999), p. 43.
107 See Chapter IV.
108 BOURSICOT (2002), p. 7.
109 *Loi n.° 78-753 du 17 Juillet 1978 portand diverses mesures d'amélioration des relations entre l'administration et le public et diverses dispositions d'ordre administratif, social et fiscal,* Official Journal 18 July 1978.
110 As amended by *Ordonnance n. ° 2005-650 du 6 juin 2005 art. 2, art. 3, art. 7,* Official Journal 7 June 2005.

has been made.[111] Before 2002, they fell within the broad category of exceptional 'secrets protected by law in a general way'.

In 2002, however, the *Loi Royal* supplemented this system with a centralised, national council with a view to both facilitating and mainstreaming access to information on 'personal' origins.[112] The relevant provisions of the bill have been inserted into a new chapter of the *Code de l'Action Sociale et des Familles.*[113] A primary function of the CNAOP is to centralise information requests from all départements, overseas territories and relevant organisations and to facilitate access to information concerning one's origins.[114] The composition of the CNAOP reflects concern for striking a fair balance between the various 'interest groups'. Thus, public administration lawyers, medical and social scientists alongside spokespersons of feminist, adoptive parents' and right-to-know organisations are all represented. Even so, an organisation representing the interests of those born under X for partiality has demanded the resignation of the President of the CNAOP, Marie-Christine Le Boursicot, accusing her of downright partiality with regard to the privacy interests of mothers.[115]

In the pursuance of centralising information, the CNAOP has been attributed broad investigatory competences and functions as an intermediary between children and their birthparents. The institution claims a remarkable success rate of over 90% in tracing and establishing contact between birthmothers and their children.[116] In the fulfilment of its aims, public and private hospitals, social security institutions and adoption agencies are all under an obligation to provide whatever relevant information, both identifying and non-identifying, they have concerning the birthparents to the CNAOP.[117]

5.8. ENFORCEMENT OF THE RIGHT TO KNOW ONE'S ORIGINS BEFORE THE CNAOP

The *Loi Royal* requires that all birthmothers be informed of the legal consequences of their decision and of the 'importance for each person to know their origins

111 DUBOSC & VERDIER (2000), 67.

112 *Loi n.° 2002-93 du 22 janvier 2002 relative à l'accès aux origines des personnes adoptées et pupilles de l'Etat*, Official Journal 19, 23 January 2002, 1519.

113 Abbreviated in what follows as: CASF.

114 CASF L.147-1.

115 Www.gopetition.com/petitions/cnaop-la-coupe-est-pleine/sign.html.

116 BOURSICOT (2006), p. 37.

117 CASF L.147-8.

and history'. The women should accordingly be expressly 'invited' to leave as much identifying information as possible in a sealed envelope concerning their name, their and the father's medical information, the child's (geographical) origins and a description of the personal circumstances at birth. The provision of this information is not mandatory, however. The sealed envelope lists the name given to the child, its sex, birthplace and the day and hour of birth. The mothers should also be told that they may choose to make their identity known at any later stage which they deem appropriate. Yet the mother ultimately decides whether her anonymity should be waived. Ultimately, the mother may decide how much (or little) information, either of an identifying or a non-identifying nature, to divulge.

Although the birthmother and the biological father may enquire whether an application has been made, the children and their legal representatives are the only persons who may send a written request for information to the CNAOP or to the President of the *département* of birth. During minority children must either be represented by their (adoptive) parents or have written evidence of their consent.[118] As soon as the mother has been successfully traced by the CNAOP and a written declaration of non-opposition has been obtained that she is no longer opposed to the disclosure of her identity, the identifying information shall be communicated. The disclosure of information does not affect the legal status of either the birthmother or the applicant.[119] Furthermore, no DNA test is taken in principle.

In the absence of the mother's declaration the applicant will, quite simply, have to make do without the information. If the birthmother has already died when the application is submitted to the CNAOP, the information will be provided unless it can be established that the mother had expressed opposition to disclosure during her lifetime. As a basic rule, though, the child will enjoy the benefit of doubt as to the mother's supposed willingness to reveal her identity.

5.9. ANONYMOUS BIRTH IN CONTEMPORARY GERMANY

In Hamburg, in the prevention of infanticide, abortion and child abandonment, around the year 2000 a number of projects were set up by charitable religious foundations and public hospitals. The abandoned children handed over to these private organisations, sometimes doubling as adoption intermediaries, soon

---

118 CASF L.147-2.

119 CASF L.147-7.

became known as *Babyklappen* ('baby-hatches'). By 2001 their number had mushroomed to around sixty nationwide.[120]

Although the number of children born by medically-assisted anonymous birth and in *Babyklappen* is believed to be very low, statistical research is seriously hampered by the covert nature of the phenomenon.[121] Establishing reliable empirical data on the backgrounds of these women is hampered further by the fact that the carers also often know very little, if anything, about their identities and personal circumstances, the guarantee of anonymity being, after all, the very raison d'être of these institutions.

5.10. ANONYMOUS BIRTH IN THE NETHERLANDS AND IN PORTUGAL

Unlike in **France** and contemporary **Germany**, in present-day **Portugal** and **the Netherlands** anonymous (and discreet) births are all but unknown. In **the Netherlands**, the question was also raised in Parliament whether a baby-hatch system should be set up. The **Dutch** State Secretary for Health, Welfare and Sports, Clémence Ross, denounced this idea on the ground of its 'unlawfulness'.[122] Ross suggested that it would be difficult to reconcile with the child's right to know and, moreover, it would be more effective to invest in social aid programmes for mothers in distress. The Child Protection Board and the Ministry of Justice have also reaffirmed that the baby-hatch and anonymous birth are not an 'acceptable solution'.[123]

As for **Portugal**, officially there are no hospitals or other institutions where mothers may give birth anonymously in the country. On this issue, legal scholar Vale e Reis affirms that the '**Portuguese** legal system is opposed to whatever possibility to conceal a mother's identity and does not admit any solution that is similar to *accouchement sous X*, whether inside or outside marriage.'[124] The general public obligation to register births is applicable. Nonetheless, it is hardly a well-kept public secret that a Lisbon birth clinic has a separate section for 'risk pregnancies' where mothers 'comply with' the obligation to register by giving

[120] Www.babyklappe.info.

[121] In Northern Hesse, the total number was 1 to 2 women per annum, according to a spokeswoman for a Babyklappe in Fulda. In the author's interview with her she suggested that this number was not significantly higher in other **German** regions. See also: www.skf.de.

[122] *Kamerstukken II*, 2002/03, nr. 1759.

[123] *Informatieblad vondelingen*, Raad voor de Kinderbescherming 2003 (PDF).

[124] VALE E REIS (2007), p. 266.

apparently false indications as to their names and residence. Between 2001 and 2006 there were allegedly 18 such false declarations of birth.[125]

6. ANONYMOUS BIRTH: MULTIDISCIPLINARY ASPECTS

In the *Odièvre* case, the ECtHR attached preponderant weight to the historical aspect of anonymous birth as a legal tradition and further justified **France**'s margin of appreciation with reference to a set of public health aims. A critical, but careful contextualisation of these aspects therefore seems appropriate before addressing the problem from a comparative law perspective.

6.1. REPRODUCTIVE HEALTH DATA

It is safe to assume that a mother's choice for anonymous birth will typically follow an unwanted or stressful pregnancy. On the basis of the *UN World Fertility Report 2003* it can be concluded that the total number of births per thousand women of child-bearing age in all four countries, or rather the 'fertility rate', is broadly similar in all countries, albeit with slightly higher figures for **the Netherlands**. This report suggests that the use of contraception among 'women in union or in marriage' in the four selected countries is comparably high.[126] Crucially for more transient sexual relations, however, figures concerning the number of unwanted pregnancies involves a dark number.

As for the number of extra-marital births, figures are comparatively high in **France**. Debatably, this suggests that the social stigma attached to illegitimacy is generally less pervasive in **French** society. This would contradict the supposition that anonymous birth forms a 'safe haven' for those burdened by feelings of shame over illegitimacy. But clearly this may be different for a number of **French** women, for example, from ethnic minorities.

The number of unwanted pregnancies can be assessed on the basis of data on lawful abortions in medically licensed clinics too. However, this may reveal little about clandestine abortions which inherently involve a 'dark number'. Even so, it may be assumed that their incidence will be lower to the extent that a country

---

125 *Abandono de bebés nas maternidades disfarçado por falsas identidades*, 12 March 2006, RTP Notícias. Source: www.rtp.pt.

126 Http://www.un.org/esa/population/publications/worldfertility/Definitions_Sources.pdf.

has both a liberal legal regime on abortion and that access to abortion clinics is easy. In such a liberal regime most of the expenses of the procedure will be covered by the state, especially those of economically under-privileged single pregnant women, and the voluntary termination of pregnancy will be permissible up to a comparatively late stage.

Globally, **France** was among the pioneering countries in permitting voluntary termination of pregnancy in 1975. Nonetheless, the time-limit for women to abort a pregnancy now appears to be relatively short in comparison to other European countries. **French** law sets a time-limit of ten weeks for a lawful abortion, which must also be subject to the informed consent of the woman and take place in a certified medical clinic. In spite of the availability of the 'alternative' of anonymous birth, the incidence of abortion in **France** is slightly higher than in most other European countries.[127]

In **Germany**, when *Babyklappen* first appeared, the percentage of aborted pregnancies has remained stable, estimated at around 18% of all known pregnancies, which is a level comparable to other European countries.[128]

The abortion law, which had been passed by the **Dutch** Parliament in 1980 and subsequently entered into force on 17 May 1984 (Wet afbreking zwangerschap (Termination of Pregnancy Act)), drew on clinical practice of the late seventies. By law women have since then been able to voluntarily terminate a pregnancy in a medically licensed clinic up to the 24th week and all expenses are fully incurred by the state. Contrary to what may be expected, abortion levels are amongst the lowest in the world.[129] The low incidence of lawful abortions does not appear to occasion higher levels of child exposure or abandonment in public places (or of clandestine abortions). In 2004 there were no registered cases of child abandonment in **the Netherlands** and in 2005 'just' one.

In **Portugal**, where anonymous birth is outlawed, on 11 February 2007 there was a national referendum on the decriminalization of abortion up to the tenth week of pregnancy. Although 56% of the electorate abstained, a slight majority of 59% voted in favour of a more permissive legislation. Under **Portuguese** law as it

---

127 Loi du 17 janvier 1975 relative à l'interruption volontaire de grossesse ('Loi Veil'), Art.L 162-1. According to statistics of the Ministry of Social Cohesion, in 2004 the number of abortions under this law totalled 210,700. This amounts to some 18.7% of all known pregnancies.

128 Source: http://www.destatis.de/basis/d/gesu/gesutab16.php.

129 From the age of sixteen women are not required to obtain the consent of their parents or guardians.

stood, abortion was only permissible during the first twelve weeks of pregnancy and under restrictive preconditions. Medical evidence had to be put forward suggesting a serious risk for the health of the woman or that of the foetus. Otherwise, abortion was only lawful in the case of rape.[130] Under this restrictive legal regime, a staggering 20,000 clandestine abortions were reported on an annual basis.[131]

6.2. ANONYMOUS BIRTH AS A PUBLIC POLICY INSTRUMENT TO PROTECT REPRODUCTIVE HEALTH

To sum up some key observations, the total fertility rate and the use of modern contraception techniques reveals comparable levels in the four countries. The situation as far as the number of abortions and the legal rules concerning abortion is also largely comparable, with the exception of **Portugal** where a stricter regime currently still applies and clandestine abortions, though necessarily a 'dark number', appear to be frequent. **The Netherlands** provides an example of how liberal abortion laws do not necessarily involve higher abortion rates, one daresay, quite the opposite. Although it goes beyond the scope of this book to analyse the relevance of such data, the foregoing general overview suggests that generally the availability of anonymous birth is not regarded in **France** or in **Germany** as a viable alternative for women who are pregnant against their will.

Nonetheless, caution is warranted in discussing the relevance of reproductive health data and abortion statistics. As such, women who choose a lawful abortion will have to come to their decision at an early stage during pregnancy. This suggests that these women are able to face up to the reality of pregnancy. Since these women do not remain in denial concerning their pregnancy, their personality structure may generally also be quite different from those who bring a pregnancy to term and 'choose' anonymous birth. Thus, in a study of maternal neo-naticide, the **Dutch** criminologist Koenraadt concludes that the psychology of women who undergo an abortion differs markedly from those who abandon the child upon birth or who perpetrate neo-naticide.[132] Accordingly, if their personality structure is typically different, targeting candidates for anonymous birth by further liberalising abortion legislation may not be viable.

---

130 Arts. 140 and 141 of the **Portuguese** Criminal Code.

131 Www.womenonwaves.org. According to this **Dutch** pro-choice organisation, among European countries only **Malta**, **Poland** and **Ireland** have similarly restrictive legal regimes.

132 KOENRAADT (2008), p. 210.

6.3. CRIMINOLOGICAL AND PSYCHOLOGICAL ASPECTS

In **France**, births registered under X totalled approximately 550 in 2002,[133] and in 2004 they allegedly numbered around 600.[134] In **Germany**, only half of the *Babyklappen* responded to an unpublished research from 2003 conducted by the sociologist Swientek and the psychologist Bott, who, incidentally, are both well-known critics of the phenomenon. This study made a rough estimate, however, that ninety children had been handed over during a two-year period from the autumn of 2002.[135] These figures suggest a drastically diminished wish on the part of women to resort to anonymity. These numbers nonetheless still beg questions regarding the primary motives of these women to 'choose' to cut ties with the newborn rigorously.

In 1999 the **French** Department of Women's Rights conducted a social science study into the age, socio-economic and ethnic background of women giving birth anonymously.[136] This study revealed that three-thirds (three-thirds is iedereen! Is dit de bedoeling?) of the women who had given birth under X were between eighteen and thirty-five years of age. Three quarters of this cohort were either unemployed or financially dependent on their own parents. This suggests that 'poverty' continues to be an important motive, even if the report revealed that those financially dependent on their parents did not necessarily come from socio-economically underprivileged backgrounds. Remarkably, a substantial minority of the women came from foreign families (around 40%), of whom nearly half originated in the Maghreb countries. Even so, most of the women descended from native **French** parents.

In the *Mattéi report* attention was drawn to the fact that the women who gave birth under X had very diffuse motives. In some particularly dramatic cases the women had been raped or the pregnancy had resulted from a blood-relative. Others had felt overwhelmed by an 'unthinkable' pregnancy. To some women abortion had from the outset never appeared an ethical alternative or had simply not entered their minds as they had been in denial of the fact that they were pregnant and overdue for undergoing a lawful abortion. This involved psycholo-

---

133 BOURSICOT (2002), p. 8.

134 LEFAUCHEUR (2004), p. 318.

135 As quoted by WIEMANN (2003), http://www.irmelawiemann.de/dl/dl.pdfa?download=Baby klappe_Wiemann.pdf.

136 NYKIEL, *Accouchement sous X et secret des origines, comprendre et accompagner les situations en présence : Étude du service des droits des femmes et de l'égalité, Ministère de l'Emploi et de la solidarité*, Paris 1999.

gical denial throughout or until very late in the pregnancy, even up to the moment of birth.[137] A common feature of most of the women was a pattern of psychological problems connected with sexual abuse within the family or repression by their own parents of their sexual identity.

In **Germany**, the total number of neo-naticides and instances of child abandonment does not appear to have dropped since the foundation of the first *Babyklappen*.[138] The aforementioned Bott and Swientek study suggests that the incidence of neonaticide and child abandonment had not dropped over a two-year period since the autumn of 2000. Moreover, of the ten abandoned newborns that had been found dead between January 2001 and May 2003 in the country, seven had been found in cities with an operating *Babyklappe*.[139] The figures of a study conducted by Terre des Hommes over the period from 1999 until mid-2006 also indicate that the incidence of child abandonment and neo-naticide has not dwindled since 1999, but, quite the opposite, peaked in 2003 at 12 and 31 respectively.[140]

Maternal neo-naticide necessarily involves a 'dark number', especially as perpetrators generally do their utmost to try to conceal the pregnancy, subsequently the birth and, ultimately, the crime.[141] A further obstacle to conducting sound criminological research is presented by the fact that the births have not yet been registered. Moreover, the boundaries between natural and unnatural causes of death may sometimes be blurred, especially when the baby's corpse is found much later. As a result, the instances of maternal neo-naticide that are documented may therefore very well be revealing above all in relation to those 'less deceitful' mothers who fail to elude the criminal law system.

Koenraadt claims that the motives, the social background and the personality structure of women who abandon their children and those who perpetrate neo-naticide are broadly similar. There are indications that women who perpetrate neo naticide are also generally young, unmarried and suffer from psychological problems, although they are rarely also delusional.[142] In contradistinction to

---

137 BONNET (1990), p. 82-97.

138 Again, data sources are scarcely available. According to a study by Hanover University, the total known national number of newborns that were given over to adoption or killed after birth has numbered around 30 from 1999. Source: FRANK & HELMS (2001), p. 1341.

139 As quoted by I. WIEMANN, Babyklappe und anonyme Geburt: Hintergründe – Kritik – Alternativen, at: http://www.irmelawiemann.de/dl/ dl.pdfa?download=Babyklappe_Wiemann.pdf.

140 Http://www.tdh.de/content/themen/weitere/babyklappe/studie_toetung.htm.

141 KOENRAADT (2008), p. 159-161.

142 WARREN, FITCH, DIETZ, ROSENFELD (1991), p. 63-69. SPINELLI (2001), p. 811-813.

women who choose abortion, the perpetrators are typically passive. They are often in denial of the fact that they are pregnant, sometimes even after having been tested medically. This is clearly a characteristic shared with women who give birth anonymously.

Other social science studies about perpetrators of neo-naticide also reveal very diffuse personal backgrounds and motives, which originate in shame about an unwanted or illegitimate child,[143] difficult relationships with parents,[144] emotional immaturity[145] and even a culture that promotes self-destructive impulses.[146]

6.4. CONTEMPORARY RELEVANCE OF THE HISTORICAL TRADITION

As may be deduced from the foregoing, anonymous birth is not an exclusively **French** legal phenomenon. It evolved from a charitable Catholic tradition of southern Europe into a secular legal institution. Notwithstanding this historical evolvement, it has recently made an appearance in countries where it had never previously been accepted, such as **Germany**. This raises questions about the contemporary relevance of legal culture. In that same vein, Lefaucheur claims that since 1990 the **French** general public has become increasingly aware of 'the problem' in view of its heavy mediatisation and politicisation which has led to increased popular sympathy for those searching for their genetic origins.[147]

In contemporary **France,** the supporters of anonymous birth and secrecy are found amongst an unnatural alliance of the conservative and religious right, medics and some feminists. But whereas the conservatives advocate secrecy to 'save children' and prevent infanticide, feminists regard *accouchement sous X* as a further means of escaping maternity, 'to control their own bodies', especially whenever abortion is no longer medically or legally possible. In the view of some feminists, *accouchement sous X* compensates for perceived shortcomings in legislation, in particular the comparatively short period to terminate pregnancy lawfully.

The conceptualisation of maternity as a 'free choice' by feminists interconnects with what Lefaucheur considers a 'highly dominant dogma' among the **French**

143 GREEN, & MANOHAR (1990), p. 121-123.
144 SADOFF (1995), p. 601-605.
145 GREEN & MANOHAR (1990), p. 121-123.
146 LESTER (1991), p. 83-85.
147 LEFAUCHEUR (2004), p. 328; likewise, WENNER (2003), p. 798.

intellectual scene since the **French** Revolution. In a nutshell, this follows the idea that 'whatever is rooted in biology must be bad, whatever is socially constructed is good.'[148] Clearly, though, such a socio-cultural claim will be inherently difficult to either prove or disprove.

However, it is arguably telling that the **French** rejection of 'blood' as a determinant of socio-legal bonds is also reflected to some extent in that other cornerstone of identity, nationality law. This area of the law has traditionally been based on the *droit du sol* as opposed to the *droit du sang*. Thus, a person in principle becomes a **French** citizen either because he or she was born on **French** soil or chooses to share the universal values of the Revolution. In **German** nationality law, the reverse principle of the *droit du sang* has traditionally been dominant. In the establishment of paternity, suffice it to recall that in the original Code Civil paternity claims were prohibited.

In her account of anonymous birth, Lefaucheur also suggests that in **France** the debate is overshadowed by associations with eugenics and Nazi ideology and retrograde ways of thinking.[149] A legal interest in the biological truth thereby becomes associable with an exaltation of its significance to the detriment of social elements of personal identity. Although advocating greater acceptance of the informational interests of those born under X, the psychoanalyst Delaisi de Parseval considers it preferable in this light to refer to 'a right to know one's history' rather than 'the right to know one's origins,' which would bring to mind overtly biologistic and even racist conceptions of humanity.[150]

The all too facile 'ignorance is bliss' argument also resurfaces in this discourse. As such, it has also been suggested that all too often one would be better off not knowing who one's birth parents are, as these may be 'low-lives not really worth knowing in the first place': incestuous, alcoholics, drug addicts, psychiatric patients, the homeless, prostitutes and the otherwise socially stigmatised. [151]According to Dovy, such caricaturised representations of the genetic parents only serve to undermine the recognition of the right to know one's genetic origins in **France**.[152]

---

148 LEFAUCHEUR (2004), p. 332.
149 LEFAUCHEUR (2004), p. 333.
150 DELAISI DE PARSEVAL (2002), p. 208.
151 LEFAUCHEUR (2004), p. 333.
152 DOVY (2002), p. 385.

7. ANONYMOUS BIRTH: THE LEGAL PERSPECTIVE

7.1. INTRODUCTION TO A LEGAL COMPARISON

By now, it has become clear that further social science research is necessary to determine the effectiveness of anonymous birth in pursuing its public aims. For our purposes, it seems safe to say that its effectiveness is limited. The incidence of clandestine abortions, neo-naticide and child exposure does not seem to be contingent upon the availability of anonymous birth. At the same time, from our truth-oriented legal perspective, it is clear that anonymous birth may be difficult to reconcile with the children's right to know their origins. In what follows, the issue shall be framed in a comparative legal analysis, even if it is only sanctioned by law in **France** and tolerated in **Germany**.[153]

7.2. IMPLICATIONS FOR BIRTH REGISTRATION

In **France**, on the problem of registration, the 1999 Dekeuwer-Défossez report did mention (but did not elaborate upon) a greater risk of circumvention of consent requirements in adoption and even for surrogate maternity contracts to escape the public eye.[154] Given the legal grey zone in which anonymous birth operates in **Germany**, there are, from a strictly legal perspective, 'officially' no problems of birth registration either in that country.

Under **German** law the birthmother, whether known or unknown to the child, for all intents and purposes remains the legal mother, as the *mater semper certa* rule retains applicability.[155] Accordingly, births should be registered by the civil registrar within one week.[156] The name of the mother will then in principle be mentioned.[157] In an alternate order the Civil Status Act also lists which persons are under an obligation to register the birth.[158] However, that obligation is drafted in ambiguous language. Thus, the father with parental authority, the custodian, the obstetrician, or 'any person(s) having knowledge of the birth' and, lastly, the mother are required to register the birth. The obligation arguably only

---

153 In **Austria, Belgium, Brazil, the Czech Republic, Hungary, Pakistan, the Philippines** and **South Africa** anonymous birth also operates in a legal grey zone. Source: *NRC Next*, 2 May 2007, p. 21.

154 DEKEUWER-DÉFOSSEZ (1999), p. 60.

155 §1591 BGB. RAUSCHER/STAUDINGER (2004), BGB, §1589, No. 110, 43.

156 §16 PstG.

157 §21 I PstG.

158 §17 I No. 1-5 PstG.

has a subsidiary character inasmuch as it may be read as only being binding if either of the persons mentioned in that consecutive order had not been absent or prevented from registering. In concealing the birth from the other persons, the mother could therefore arguably simply prevent others from taking on this obligation. The bottom-line remains, though, that the birth clinic's board will be under an obligation to declare the birth.

Even so, a somewhat concocted legal basis for a right of the mother not to register the child's birth has been unearthed on the basis of the Pregnancy Conflict Act.[159] Read closely, this provision only guarantees pregnant women a measure of anonymity in dealing with the medical professionals working at a pregnancy care organisation. Whether this measure of anonymity may also be interpreted extensively in relation to others, not least the mother's child, and for an indeterminate period, is circumspect. Given that doubtful legal basis, the mother's duty to register, as determined by the Law on Civil Status, would not appear to be restricted by the Pregnancy Conflict Act.

In seeking to decriminalise anonymous birth and *Babyklappen*, the Christian CDU/CSU coalition[160] proposed to prolong the period of registry from one to ten weeks in 2000.[161] Allegedly, this would have the advantage of giving mothers in distress a period of reflection during which social care institutions could provide intensive counselling to the mother concerned.[162] Even so, the name of the mother would have to be disclosed upon the expiry of this period.

This first proposal met with sharp criticism for its 'reductionism', in its narrow focus on the problem of birth registration.[163] Soon after, a parliamentary commission composed of the SPD,[164] CDU and the *Bündnis 90/Grünen* (Greens) drafted a more comprehensive law proposal.[165] Its primary focus was also on the Civil Status Act.[166] Due to the political circumstances following the terrorist attacks

---

159 Scheiwe (2001), p. 368. §6 II Schwangerschaftskonfliktsgesetz (SchKG) = Pregnancy Conflict Act.

160 Federal Christian-Democrat Party.

161 *BT-Drucks.* 14/4425, 1. Referred to as the 'first proposal' from now in section 2.

162 Hepting (2001), p. 574, who in that connection facetiously refers to seven weeks of '*Seelenmassage*'. Badenberg (2006), p. 148, also favours a period of reflection during which the mother could revoke her anonymity.

163 Wolf (2003), p. 114.

164 Federal Social-Democratic Party

165 *BT-Drucks.* 14/8856, 5.

166 Referred to as the 'second proposal' from now on. For the other issues dealt with see below.

on the Twin Towers on 11 September 2001, the second proposal was remitted to the next parliamentary year, but has in fact hitherto not been readdressed.

The second proposal detracted from the obligation incumbent on mothers and fathers to register births in the case of anonymous birth, for which purpose the scope of the Civil Status Act would have to be widened. It was proposed that the public authorities be notified of the birth within one day by the care-providing institution. The proposal insisted upon strict adherence to *mater semper certa*.[167] However, the child welfare authorities would determine the child's name and take measures towards the child's placement in a foster family.[168] Meanwhile, the mother would enjoy a 'period of reflection' of eight weeks allowing her to review her initial decision.[169] The mother's identity would be disclosed eventually upon the child reaching the age of sixteen. In the aftermath of the 9/11 attacks, none of these proposals were taken further. To date, no further attempts at legislation have been undertaken.

7.3. IMPLICATIONS FOR FATHERS' RIGHTS AND ADOPTION LAW

A father's wish to establish a legal relationship with the child may be precluded by anonymous birth. Thus, practical problems may arise, whenever he had been kept unaware of the pregnancy or could not be present during the moment of birth. He may then be destined to remain ignorant of the child's whereabouts and the circumstances at birth.[170]

In justification of this fundamental weakness of the father's legal position, it has been said – remarkably enough, indeed, by the current President of the CNAOP – that such legal objections can be cast aside. In her view, 'fathers' have, indeed 'for centuries', 'exploited' the facts of human reproduction to their own advantage while 'keeping mothers suppressed in a non-decisional situation'.[171]

---

167 The proposal was remarkably silent on fathers' rights. For unclear reasons the obligation to register births for all the other referred persons would be unaffected in the second proposal.

168 *BT-Drucks.* 14/8856, 7.

169 This was also proposed in a regional Baden-Württemberg Law Proposal, which essentially foresaw in the same set of measures as the second federal proposal: BR-DR 506/02.

170 In **Germany,** the father's rights to claim or challenge paternity are in principle not precluded by anonymous birth from a strictly legal perspective as anonymous birth is formally not legally sanctioned. The chapters concerning the establishment of paternity are therefore relevant here.

171 BOURSICOT (2006), p. 37.

In attempting to mitigate legal objections, quantitative arguments have also been used. Thus, the President of the CNAOP holds that since the foundation of the CNAOP in **France**, only two fathers have sought to establish contact with their children.[172] While reinforcing popular social stereotypes of the aloof father, this quantitative argument clearly disregards the fact that the father may not have been informed of the mother's pregnancy in the first place or that communication between him and the birthmother may be experienced subjectively as an obstacle.

Even so, two judicial decisions have not failed to lay bare the principled objections against this fundamental disequilibrium between mothers and fathers. Thus, in December 1997, the Riom Court of Appeal determined that the recognition by a father of a child born under X had been void, as the mother had never 'existed' pursuant to the legal fiction enshrined in the civil law provision.[173] In the year 2000 another case arose in which the father's rights were directly at issue. The mother had given birth anonymously to a child, Benjamin, in May 2000. Benjamin accordingly became eligible for the state adoption procedure. The father had, however, recognised Benjamin before birth. The father lodged proceedings at the Nancy High Court of Appeal demanding that the child be brought back into his care. Backed by the adoptive parents' association, *Enfance et familles d'adoption* (EFA), the prospective adoptive parents insisted upon the inadmissibility of the claim. They invoked Article 352-1 Code Civil which precludes, from the commencement of the state-run adoption procedure, a restoration of a child to his birth parents.[174] The Nancy Court affirmed that, if the child were to be adopted lawfully, no legal parent-child relationship should have been established previously, while the genetic father would have had to have demonstrated indifference or consented to his child's adoption.

The Cour de Cassation subsequently reaffirmed that in a situation of anonymous birth, a man's prenatal recognition takes effect from the date of birth if he is identified as the genetic father and that his consent is required if identification occurs before consent to adoption has been given by the state.[175]

Implicit in the reasoning of the Nancy Appeal Court had been a combination of biological and volitional notions of parenthood, in affirming that 'the child's interest was to know his father, who had always clearly and unequivocally

172 BOURSICOT (2006), p. 37.

173 CA Riom, 16 December 1997, *JCP* éd. G 1998, 10147.

174 TGI Nancy, 16 May 2003, 01/04002.

175 Cass. I. civ., 7 April 2006, n.° 05-11.285, *Droit de la famille JurisClasseur*, June 2006, 24.

expressed a will to bring up his son'. On balance, the risk that the child would be severely traumatised resultant from the separation from the prospective adoptive parents, with whom Benjamin had meanwhile lived for two years, was considered less serious than his imminent discovery that his biological father had merely been prevented from taking care of him because the authorities had not granted him the prerequisite parental responsibilities order.

The aforementioned cases had concerned prenatal recognitions of paternity by unmarried men. They are therefore also to be distinguished from the situation in which the child born under X is recognised after birth. In that latter situation, **French** law still precludes the biological father from making a recognition once the adoption procedure has begun.[176]

Debatably, this disequilibrium between the father and the mother in **French** law may be considered to be flawed at a fundamental level. While permitting a choice by the mother not to have her name mentioned on the birth certificate, **French** law does not conceive of a similar opt-out to parenthood for the male who has conceived a child through natural reproduction. Rather, an (unmarried) father '*malgré soi*' necessarily risks a paternity suit.[177] Admittedly, though, this equality argument is unduly oblivious not only to the sociological context, but also to the different roles of the sexes in procreation.

There are further legal objections against anonymous birth. In drawing attention to the risk of circumventing adoption requirements under **German** law, Swientek, for example, has made the bold statement that it not only fails to effectively alleviate pregnant women in distress, but rather that it serves to create a new source of adoptable children.[178] In her view, it is not the child and the mother who stand to gain from anonymous birth, but adoption organisations and, no less cynically, irresponsible men and the mother's relatives who do not want the birth to blacken the name of the family. All these parties would pressurise these vulnerable women to 'choose' anonymity.

In exploring that argument, there can be little doubt that the consent of both biological parents is in principle always required under **German** law.[179] If paternity had not been established at the time of birth, the unmarried, putative father

176 CA Grenoble, 11 February 2004, n. 04/00012, *Revue Juridique Personnes & Famille* 2004, No. 7-8, p. 24.
177 Art. 327 **French** Code Civil.
178 Http://www.lux-forum-adoptierter.de/babyklappe.htm.
179 §1747(1) BGB.

must submit evidence that he had a sexual relationship with the mother at the time of conception. There are no grounds to believe that the general requirement of dual consent would not in principle apply in the case of anonymous birth. Nonetheless, if a parent claims to be in a state of incapacity or if a parent cannot be found, this consent requirement in respect of both parents may be dispensed with.[180] Typically in an anonymous birth case, the guardianship court[181] may decide that the child be placed with a foster family. For the child to be adopted subsequently, the ordinary requirements for adoption will then apply.[182] As long as no objections have been (or could be) expressed by the parents, placement with a foster family can in principle occur within six weeks after the child was first handed over to the *Babyklappe*.[183] Pending those first six weeks the child will, however, irremediably linger in a state of legal limbo.

Thus, the adoptive organisation may during that time try to trace the mother and the father, but is under no clear obligation to do so. Cynics might indeed add that little is to be expected from *Babyklappen* either, as many of them will double as adoption agencies. Echoing such sceptical views, it has been suggested that under the veneer of pro-life rhetoric, the Church would have a hidden agenda for lending support to *Babyklappen* as a safe haven for some of these women. Thus, this would help restore the image of the Church in a secular society that is sympathetic to the charitable aims of *Babyklappen*.[184]

7.4. COMPARISON AND EVALUATION

In an abstract sense, it cannot be denied that the right to life of the birthmother and the newborn represent a hierarchically higher-ranking moral value than the right to know. To hold otherwise could lead to the grotesque claim that a 'life without knowing' is not really worth living.

In that connection, in a Concurring Opinion in *Odièvre*, Judge Ress viewed the basic conflict between the child's and the mother's interest in no less dramatic terms. Thus, he suggested that 'persons who seek disclosure at any price, even against the express will of their natural mother, must ask themselves whether they would have been born had it not been for the right to give birth anony-

180 §1747(4) BGB.
181 Vormundschaftsgericht.
182 §§1747 and 1741-1772 BGB.
183 §1745 BGB.
184 Www.babyklappe-nein-danke.info.

mously'.[185] In this assertion the misguided idea resounds that the manifestation of an interest in knowing one's genetic origins at the constitutional level is indicative of overtly individualistic, egotistical urges in contemporary Western societies. In the same vein, it makes a moral appeal to persons who do not know their origins that they should show a humble gratitude to the birthmother to whom they owe their existence.

Accordingly, the right to life of the mother and the newborn cannot be held to be in grave danger for long after birth. For such reasons it is questionable whether the 'sword of Damocles' argument, mentioned in the *Mattéi* report, should be given much importance. Although the birthmother who chooses not to disclose her name may (subjectively) experience a future disclosure as a further drama, this fear surely cannot lead to the conclusion that the child's right to know needs to be prejudged forever. This fails to meet legal requirements of proportionality.

Gone are the days when anonymous birth was legitimised in view of pro-natalist concerns over sustainable demographic growth. Even so, there is some evidence which suggests that hidden agendas in guaranteeing the number of adoptable children may sometimes be implicit. The veto power which the mother still has in withholding identifying information is clearly difficult to reconcile with an idea of procreational responsibility.[186] Furthermore, the current **French** legislation also interferes with the child's decisional privacy to a considerable extent.

In contrast, the maximisation of the mother's decisional privacy is precisely a concern that **French** feminist discourse has raised. Accordingly, anonymous birth is defended on 'pro-choice' rather than 'pro-life' grounds. On that view, the legitimacy of the **French** legal institution is perceived as compensation for the shortcomings in abortion legislation. The Revolutionary conceptualisation of parentage as a social construct, based ultimately upon free will rather than biological fact, would therefore not necessarily come to an end at a child's birth. Such arguments are oblivious to the fact that approximately half of these children will be girls.

Anonymous birth may, however, complicate requirements in adoption law pertaining to the verification of the informed consent of the birthparents. This applies especially in the case of the biological father who in **French** law may find

---

185 See Chapter III.
186 See Chapter V.

himself effectively sidelined if he failed to make a prenatal recognition of paternity and the state has opened up the adoption procedure. In a nutshell, then, there is a wide range of real legal concerns which plead rather strongly against permitting anonymous birth. The enforcement of the child's right to know is but one such important legal concern.

CHAPTER VII
THE IDENTIFICATION OF THE FATHER

1. OUTLINE

From a legal viewpoint, the establishment of paternity still incorporates more complicated legal issues than maternity. Following a long legal tradition, family law codes continue to rely on legal presumptions to determine paternity. Paternity testing based on DNA may, however, have exposed the fictional character of legal presumptions upon which paternity is based for a considerable time.[1] This bio-medical development continues to raise questions in both substantive and procedural law. In this Chapter, substantive parentage law shall be compared and evaluated from a truth-oriented perspective. In Chapter VIII, the procedural aspects of paternity proceedings shall be dealt with.

2. FATHERHOOD AND SUBSTANTIVE PARENTAGE LAW

2.1. ESTABLISHMENT OF PATERNITY ON THE BASIS OF THE MOTHER'S MARRIAGE

2.1.1. The marital presumption rule

The presumption that the husband of the child's mother is the child's father provides one of the most commonly found rules of family law across the world.[2] Known as the marital presumption rule, this paternity presumption is commonly believed to have originated in Roman law.[3] As a way to confer parental status on

---

1 'Paternity' shall be used as a term denoting the legal parentage of a male, whereas 'fatherhood' shall be used exclusively with reference to a man's factual, biological link to his progeny.

2 SCHWENZER (2007), p. 5.

3 Paulus, *Digest* 2, 4, 5. *Pater est quem nuptiae demonstrant.* The father is he whom marriage shows.

men, the rule has always incorporated more than a presumption of biological truth. As such, this marital presumption rule has fulfilled a historical function of extending legitimate status to children conceived before the conclusion of marriage.[4] Even in situations in which the biological link was manifestly improbable, such as a fiancé's prolonged absence or reduced fertility, the presumption could, for example, be a source of legitimisation in 17th and 18th Century **France**.[5]

In the DNA age, however, a 'mere' presumption requires greater justification. Furthermore, it may warrant an explanation from an equality perspective to continue to establish paternity on the basis of a mother's marriage to a man than previously. Thus, given the increased number of children born outside marriage and the ECtHR's sustained efforts to delete all discriminatory national provisions against extramarital children, it may appear less obvious why non-marital children should not be able to benefit from having two legal parents from the moment of birth.

In particular, in respect of other formalised relationships comparable to marriage, such as registered partnerships, it may, for example, be difficult to justify the fact that a presumption of paternity that functions by operation of law is not extended to that situation.[6] From a strictly truth-oriented perspective, an increase in the number of children born under a mere presumption arguably may be perceived as an unwelcome development. Yet from this equality perspective the possibility for non-marital children to benefit from an extension of a legal presumption of paternity in case of a registered partnership could be a sound legislative choice. In brief, then, a truth-oriented perspective and an equality perspective may sometimes diverge.

While devising a fairer parentage law system is not our primary concern, this example does show the tension that may exist between children's interest in knowing the biological truth and the equal status of children from the moment of birth. Suffice it therefore for our truth-oriented approach to note that the absence of a clear typology of non-formalised relationships and the realisation of full status equality from the moment of birth between marital and non-marital children may justify this difference in treatment in the attribution of parental status.[7]

---

4 SCHWENZER (1987), p. 229.
5 LEFEBVRE-TEILLARD (1996), p. 302.
6 SCHRAMA (2008), p. 86-94.
7 SCHRAMA (2008), p. 86-94.

2.1.2. *The scope of the marital presumption outside marriage*

In **France**, the 2005 parentage law reform reaffirmed that the mother's husband is the father.[8] According to contemporary **French** doctrinal views, the primary justification of the presumption rule nowadays relates to the factual probability that it will reflect the man's genetic link to the child.[9]

Even so, in determining the normative force of the presumption, a socio-legal criterion known as *possession d'état* (civil status) is still taken into account.[10] As a legal institution, civil status has been a recurrent feature of **French** parentage law from the 18th Century.[11] Initially, civil status incorporated a means for Protestant children to prove legitimate status by referring to social indications of parental treatment, since they could not claim legitimate status on the basis of their birth documentation following the enactment of the 1685 Edict of Nantes. Traditionally, civil status has since then comprised three defining features: *nomen, tractatus et fama.*[12] The concept has undergone some important changes throughout the last few centuries.[13] It could exceptionally serve as evidence of legitimate status after the codification of the Code Napoléon. It

8 Art. 312 **French** Code Civil. '*L'enfant conçu ou né pendant le mariage a pour père le mari de la mère*'; TERRÉ & FENOUILLET (2006), p. 605.

9 GRIMALDI (1986), p. 1; CARBONNIER (1999), p. 251; TERRÉ & FENOUILLET (2005), p. 577, VASSAUX (2005), p. 1458.

10 In **Portugal** a person's civil status (*posse de estado*) will become relevant if a cessation of a marital presumption had ceased previously pursuant to Art. 1832(2) in conjunction with Art. 1833 PCC but if it does not exist this does not mean that the number of third parties that may challenge paternity will increase. In **the Netherlands**, civil status also occurs in parentage law and is known as *bezit van staat.* Nonetheless, it has remained an underdeveloped legal concept in **Dutch** law. Initially, it could be important to prove legitimate status. Furthermore, the concept functions as a means to prevent third parties from contesting the child's civil status. From Art. 1:209 DCC it can still be inferred that third parties cannot challenge a person's parentage as it appears on his or her birth certificate if such a person does not have a legal status according to such a certificate. Art. 211 DCC now determines that only the child and the heirs of the child, when the child has died during minority or within three years thereafter, may lodge an application to find the existence of a civil status relationship well founded. Nonetheless, Art. 1:210 DCC provides that an application to declare the claim of a legitimate status well founded is not subject to prescription. This ambiguity has given rise to inconsistent case law. See: Hoge Raad, 7 November 2003, *NJ* 2004, p. 98, LJN: AI0360 and Gerechtshof Arnhem, 14 June 2005, LJN:AT8852. In the latter case the procedure was abused as a *de facto* denial of paternity by a third party, namely a half-sibling. On the contemporary relevance of civil status in **Dutch** parentage law and a discussion of relevant case law, see in particular the leading recent contribution on the subject-matter by: SAARLOOS (2006), p. 123-129.

11 LAUTOUR (1973); MORGAND-CANTEGRIT (1993).

12 Name, treatment and reputation; TERRÉ & FENOUILLET (2005), p. 139.

13 LÉVY & CASTALDO (2002), p. 35; MORGAND-CANTEGRIT (1993), p. 31.

escaped legal definition in the Civil Code until the latest 2005 reform. Nowadays, Article 311-1 of the **French** Code Civil has clarified definitional issues surrounding *possession d'état* considerably, by stating that it 'is established through a satisfactory combination of facts which demonstrate the parentage relationship between a person and the family to which he or she is said to belong.'

Drawing on a tradition of centuries-old case law, the most practically relevant of such sociologically relevant legal facts have now been enumerated in Article 311-1. This provision states that in order to have civil status the person must have been treated as a parent by those to whom he or she is said to belong (1); that they have taken care of her or his education, care or accommodation (2); that the person has been recognised as their child in society or within the family (3); that he or she has been treated as such by the public authority (4); and, last but not least, that he or she bears the family surname (5). As a more general criterion, a person's civil status must be 'continuous, undisturbed, public and unequivocal' in accordance with Article 311-2 **French** Code Civil.[14] It is therefore tantamount to a socio-legal rather than a biological reality, even though both may overlap.

Civil status may, for example, become relevant in the case of a divorce. By operation of law, the presumption will not apply if the child had been born within 300 days after the judicial dissolution of the marriage or within 300 days after the conclusion of the contract settling the consequences of the divorce. Furthermore, the presumption will not apply if the child had been born fewer than 180 days after the rejection of the divorce application or the factual reconciliation of the spouses.[15] If the child has a civil status relationship with the husband, the presumption will nonetheless apply if the paternity of a man other than the husband has not yet been established.[16]

Conversely, the presumption does not apply in case the birth certificate does not make mention of the husband's paternity while the child does not have a civil status in respect of the mother's husband.[17] If the mother lived in separation from her husband during the conception period, the presumption may not apply either by operation of law.[18] Nonetheless, if the presumption is not corroborated by the child's civil status, both spouses may seek to have the presumption re-

14 Art. 311-1 **French** Code Civil: '*continue, paisible, publique et non-équivoque*'.
15 Art. 313 **French** Code Civil.
16 Art. 313 **French** Code Civil.
17 Art. 314 **French** Code Civil.
18 Art. 314 **French** Code Civil; VASSAUX (2005), p. 1458.

established. During the child's minority the parents must then put forward indications which suggest that the husband is indeed the child's father.[19] Children may not lodge proceedings involving a re-establishment of the marital presumption until reaching adult age and thereafter subject to a time-limit of ten years.[20]

Since the latest parentage law reform, any means of proof in parentage disputes may in principle be used.[21] Even so, it is conceivable that in a situation in which the husband could not have conceived the child because he had a certified fertility problem but nonetheless has had a durable civil status relationship with the child, he could have a stronger claim to paternity than the actual biological father who had made a recognition.[22] Accordingly, French courts may be willing to deny the biological father the right to challenge the marital presumption on account of the fact that the husband has a civil status relationship with the child.[23]

As in **France**, in **Germany** the husband of the mother is also considered to be the father.[24] Prior to the latest parentage law reform, children born within 302 days after the end or dissolution of marriage were presumed to have been fathered by the former husband. This extension of the marital presumption to the period before and subsequent to the conclusion of the actual marriage came under a critical light for two reasons.[25] Firstly, concerns over the child's legitimate status lost relevance. Secondly, it was predicted that the number of paternity suits would drop since the mother's impregnation by another man often constituted a principal reason for divorce.[26]

In contrast, the situation in which the husband's death ended the marriage was considered to be fundamentally different.[27] As it was believed that in the vast majority of such situations the husband would have fathered the child, the

---

19 Art. 315 in conjunction with Art. 329 **French** Code Civil.
20 Art. 315 in conjunction with Art. 329 **French** Code Civil.
21 Art. 310-3 **French** Code Civil,
22 Cass.Ire civ., 14 February 2006, n. 03-16.101.
23 Cass.Ire civ., 14 March 2006, n. 05-13.825.
24 §1592 I BGB.
25 *BT-Drucks.* 13/4899, p. 83.
26 *BT-Drucks.* 13/4899, p. 52. Sceptical concerning this predicted drop in the number of paternity proceedings: §1592, BGB, MÜNCHENER KOMMENTAR/SEIDL, (2008), BGB, §1593, Rdnr. 2-6.
27 MÜNCHENER KOMMENTAR/SEIDL, BGB(2008), §1593, Rdnr. 2-6; STAUDINGER/RAUSCHER, BGB (2004), §1592, Rdnr. 28.

extended scope of the marital presumption rule would be justified.[28] Thus, under current **German** law, in its extended version, the rule applies only if the child was born later than 300 days after the husband's death. Nonetheless, **German** law allows for exceptions in case of medical evidence that the child had been conceived previously.[29] The medical practitioner will be asked to put forward medical evidence of the moment of conception in that situation.

The Roman adage is also echoed, albeit in plain modern **Dutch**, in Article 1:199 under 1(a) of the DCC. Since the 1998 reform of **Dutch** parentage law, the husband will only be presumed to be the child's father, however, if the marriage had come to an end within 306 days prior to the child's birth because of the husband's death, even if the mother had remarried within this period.[30] Prior to the reform, the widow was required to 'mourn' for a year before being permitted to remarry in the interest of preventing 'blood' or 'offspring confusion'. Again, improvements in scientific testing have exposed the obsoleteness of this argumentation.

Like its **German** counterpart, the **Dutch** legislator also predicted that the number of paternity proceedings would decrease if the marital presumption rule subsequent to divorce ceased to apply, since infidelity was believed to form a primary reason for the marriage breakdown.[31] As in **Germany**, too, it was believed that, in contrast, the likelihood that the deceased husband fathered the child would be high.[32] Even so, if the child had in fact been fathered by a man other than her deceased husband, the mother may also evade judicial proceedings by simply declaring the father's identity before the civil status registrar. If she remarries in the aftermath of the divorce, her new husband will also be presumed to be the father by operation of law.[33] As such, in both of these latter situations, the **Dutch** legislator has great confidence in a mother's willingness 'to speak nothing but the biological truth.' Moreover, the presumption in that case encapsulates the basic idea that the mother's (future) husband should not go back on his word.

---

28 MÜNCHENER KOMMENTAR/SEIDL, (2008), §1593, Rdnr. 2-6.

29 §1593 BGB.

30 Art. 1:199(1) under (b) DCC.

31 *Kamerstukken* 1995/96, 24 649, nr. 3, 7.

32 ASSER-DE BOER (1998), p.402. Noteworthy in this context is also that in determining the length of the period over which the presumption is extended, the point of reference is the moment of the child's birth rather than the moment of conception. It was the latter moment that was deemed decisive in Old **Dutch** law.

33 Art. 1:199(b) DCC.

Since the family law reforms of 1977, the **Portuguese** legislator has come to refer to a 'presumption of paternity' as opposed to the traditional 'presumption of legitimacy'.[34] Article 1826-1 PCC currently holds that 'it is presumed that the child born or conceived in the constancy of the mother's marriage has the husband as his father'.

A simple declaration before the civil status registrar made by one of the two spouses to the effect that the husband is not the father will suffice to render the presumption inapplicable if the child was born within 180 days after the conclusion of the marriage.[35] No scientific test is required in principle. If paternity is denied in this way, the legislator speaks of a 'cessation' of the presumption rather than of a denial of paternity.[36] When the presumption 'ceases', it will pre-empt paternity proceedings since rectification before the civil status registrar will suffice.

This will also occur if the child was born within 300 days after the day of separation. In order to define 'separation', a number of situations are listed in which the possibility of the husband's physical access is remote, including not only divorce but also physical disappearance. Conversely, the presumption will become stronger if evidence of physical access to the mother is put forward. Clearly, this should not to be taken too literally, as it will be assumed if both declare before the civil status registrar that there has been a recent reconciliation.[37]

If the mother remarries before a prior dissolution of her previous marriage, or if the child is born within 300 days after the judicial dissolution of the marriage, the marital presumption will in principle 'cease' as well by giving way to the presumption that the new husband has fathered the child.[38] From the moment that paternity proceedings have been instituted, however, the onus will be, at least nominally, on the mother's new husband to provide evidence that he had fathered the child. Barring the availability of scientific tests, the marital presumption may again revert in favour of the former husband if he has a civil status relationship with the child.[39]

---

34 *A presunção de legitimidade* vs. *a presunção de paternidade.*

35 Art. 1828 PCC.

36 *A cessação da presunção de paternidade.*

37 Art. 1830 PCC.

38 Art. 1834 PCC.

39 Art. 1831 PCC. *Posse de estado.*

Finally, the 1977 reforms also introduced a possibility for the married mother to simply declare before the civil status registrar within 60 days after the delivery of the birth certificate that her own husband is not the father.[40] It was considered that the mother would then feel less inclined to refrain from declaring that she is the mother.[41] Thus, it was not unheard of that mothers did not have the birth registered in order to avert the attribution of paternity to their husband.

2.1.3. Comparison

While the marital presumption rule is known in all four countries, it has been revealed that its scope and nature display some nuanced distinctions. If the child is born during the mother's marriage, the presumption will apply. Nonetheless, in **France**, if the husband has not been mentioned on the birth certificate and the child lacks a civil status, the presumption may not apply by operation of law. In its extended form, the presumption applies in the four jurisdictions if a child is born within roughly ten months after the mother's marriage has come to an end through the husband's death. In **France**, as in **Germany** and **the Netherlands**, the presumption is no longer applicable, however, by operation of law upon divorce.

In **France**, the concept of civil status may sometimes entail that the marital presumption of paternity will apply in respect of the former husband. On the other hand, in **France** a biological father may deny the husband's paternity in the absence of civil status, all the more so if the presumption did not apply in the first place by operation of law. Only in **Portugal** does the presumption still apply in the conception period subsequent to the mother's divorce. However, **Portuguese** law excludes the presumption in some factual scenarios in which sexual relations between the mother and the husband were unlikely. It is open to debate whether this is a token of the preponderant interest that the biological truth may assume in the determination of paternity. As such, this restriction may also suggest that an 'absent' husband[42] irrespective of his genetic link to the child is unlikely to participate together with the mother in the upbringing of the child.

---

40 Art. 1832-1 and Art. 1832-3 PCC. Pursuant to Art. 1833 PCC and Art. 331 of the **Portuguese** Code of Civil Registration (*Código de Registo Civil*) the court has to make a separate declaration of the non-existence of civil status in such cases.

41 See Chapter VI.

42 Compare ECtHR *Kroon and others v. The Netherlands*, Appl. No. 18535/91, 27 October 1994. See Chapter III.

Figure VII.1. The marital presumption of paternity

Paternity of the husband	Marriage to the mother	Upon divorce	After death
Germany	Yes	No	Yes
The Netherlands	Yes	No	Yes
France	Yes	No	Yes
Portugal	Yes	Yes	Yes

2.1.4 Evaluation

From a strictly truth-oriented perspective, legal presumptions of paternity are inherently deficient. Because of the availability of modern DNA testing and the obsolete nature of legitimacy as a legal value, Schwenzer has therefore proposed to lift the *pater est* rule altogether.[43] From a parentage law perspective, which incorporates interests other than biology, the marital presumption rule is quite justifiable for a number of reasons, however. In particular, the marital presumption will reflect the man's intention to bring up the child together with the mother and may thereby ensure the child's interests in being brought up by two parents. Moreover, whatever the statistics, in the vast majority of cases the rule will reflect biological truth since generally the husband will be the mother's only or, at least the most frequent,[44] sexual partner. Added to these advantages, an established 'false' paternity may often also be denied.

For such reasons, it appears excessive to delete a rule that generally functions well. All the same, if the child's informational interest is to be taken seriously as a right to decisional privacy, its effectuation cannot be made completely contingent either upon the question whether a rule of parentage law is functional or socially efficacious.

Given our truth-oriented focus, the conceptual question must therefore be rather what level of accuracy may be required. An initiative that relies on the investigatory attitude of adults may be considered sufficient. However, for minors the situation seems more precarious because they may not be in a factual position to enquire. If a minor does enquire, it seems safe to assume in line with **German** constitutional law that the mother should not withhold from the child available

43 SCHWENZER (2006), p. 96.
44 HENRICH (2007), p. 399.

information to her or him because it could prejudge the child's decisional privacy.[45]

Once the child wishes to have greater certainty, it could arguably be said that the value of accuracy rather than sincerity will matter because the reliability of the parent's information has been called into question.[46] On parentage issues, such accurate information will generally only be obtainable through DNA testing.[47]

2.2. ESTABLISHMENT OF PATERNITY IN RESPECT OF MEN WHO ARE NOT MARRIED TO THE MOTHER

2.2.1. Recognition

In order to establish non-marital paternity, most continental systems have developed the legal institution of (voluntary) recognition.[48] From a parentage law perspective, this institution presents low public cost advantages and minimal state intervention. In addition, just like the marital presumption rule, a recognition lacks any a priori guarantee of biological truthfulness. **France** has a legal tradition of free recognition by social fathers.[49] These recognitions, for which the mother's consent was not required, could be manifestly 'false', serving primarily as a legal instrument to bestow legitimate status on adulterine children. These 'false' recognitions, referred to as *reconnaissances de complaisance*, are still believed to be common.[50]

Following the 2005 reform, it has been reaffirmed that in the absence of the (marital) presumption, paternity may be established by recognition.[51] The recognition may be mentioned on the child's birth certificate, in a (written) declaration drafted by the civil status registrar or an affidavit drafted by a public notary. The recognition may be made before and after birth.[52] It has further been specified that the recognition 'only binds whoever authored it';[53] this means that the recognition establishes a child's legal parentage but may not give rise to legal

45 See Chapter I.

46 See Chapter I on Bernard Williams' *Truth and truthfulness* (2002).

47 See Chapter VIII.

48 SCHWENZER (2007), p. 7.

49 MEULDERS KLEIN (1996), p. 497.

50 MASSIP, annotation of Cass., 6 December 1988, 1989, p. 317; HELMS (1999), p. 67-68.

51 Art. 316 **French** Code Civil.

52 A prenatal recognition accordingly serves the father's interests if the mother chooses to give birth anonymously. VASSAUX (2005), p. 1458.

53 Art. 316 **French** Code Civil. *La reconnaissance n'établit la filiation qu'à l'égard de son auteur.*

consequences beyond the establishment of paternity. Remarkably, under **French** law, the consent of the mother and the child may in principle be dispensed with.[54] A married man may also make a recognition of a child conceived outside his own marriage.[55]

If the paternity of a married man, quite regardless of the fact whether he is or is not the biological father, is not corroborated by a corresponding civil status, nothing stands in the way of another man making a recognition. Moreover, if the marital presumption did not already apply by operation of law, the husband may make a recognition.[56]

If a child is 'born under X' because the mother's identity had been kept secret, the omission of the mother's name on the birth certificate will not be an obstacle for the father in making a recognition. Again, the mother's consent is not expressly required. As such, in April 2006, in the *Benjamin* case, the Cour de Cassation decided in favour of the paternity claim of the biological father who had recognised a child born under X after the birthmother had consented to an adoption order.[57]

In **Germany**, recognition[58] incorporates first and foremost a *Willenserklärung* (declaration of will).[59] It is generally believed, however, to reflect a declaration of the man's 'intention' or will rather than a declaration of (prior) knowledge as to the biological truth.[60] The recognition may be made before and after birth. The legal institution's highly personal nature becomes apparent in considering that no other man will thereafter be able to make a supplementary recognition.[61]

A recognition will always be void if the child already has another father.[62] A recognition may be made before the child's actual birth.[63] Even so, prior to the

---

54 Yet the notion of civil status will mean that a legal father-child relationship may only be possible if the mother allows sociological ties to develop between the man and the child.

55 Terré & Fenouillet (2006), p. 642.

56 Arts. 313, 314 in conjunction with art. 329 **French** Code Civil.

57 Cass.civ. I, 7 April 2006, D.2006.IR. 1 065. See Chapter VI.

58 Die Anerkennung der Vaterschaft.

59 Münchener Komm/Wellenhofer (2008), BGB, §1594, Rdnr. 4.

60 Münchener Komm/Wellenhofer-Klein(2008), BGB, §1594, Rdnr. 4; Gernhuber/Coester-Waltjen (2006), §52 II.

61 §1594 II BGB. Should another man's paternity exist, the recognition will have no effect. It will, however, not be void: Palandt/Diederichsen (2006), BGB, §1594, Rdnr. 7.

62 §1594 III BGB.

63 1594 III BGB.

1998 reform, children's consent, as provided by their legal representative, the Child Welfare Authority, was formally always required after birth, even though the mother acted as the minor's legal representative. Nowadays, only the mother's consent will in principle be required.[64] It is believed that the mother has an autonomous competence qua mother to give consent to the man rather than from her usual quality as a legal representative of the minor.[65] Exceptionally, the obtainment of the child's consent may be required if the mother lacks parental authority.[66] During the child's minority, her or his legal representative will then have to provide consent as well. Legally incapacitated men may also make a recognition, provided they obtain consent from a legal representative appointed by the guardianship court.[67] As another salient feature, there is no formal prohibition in **German** law in respect of a married man to recognise a child born outside his marriage.

In **the Netherlands**, a recognition[68] is not conceived of as a legal instrument that necessarily reflects the biological truth.[69] It is considered to be a legal act, an acceptance of paternity, that gives rise to family law relations between the child and the man who makes the recognition.[70] In that connection, it is interesting that De Boer suggests that a **Dutch** recognition may in fact be an alternative form of adoption whenever the biological father is unknown or not prepared to care for the child.[71] There would therefore be a public interest in 'false' recognitions in such cases. As for formal requirements, a recognition may either be drawn up in an instrument of recognition prepared by a Registrar of Births, Deaths, Marriages and Registered Partnerships or in a notarial instrument.[72] The recognition lacks retroactive force. It is commonly accepted, too, that a recognition can be made lawfully before the child's birth.

A recognition may be null and void in **Dutch** law on a number of grounds. A basic prerequisite is that the child should not already have two legal parents.[73]

---

64 §1595 I BGB.

65 PALANDT/DIEDERICHSEN (2006), BGB, §1595, No. 3, 1852.

66 §1595 II BGB.

67 §1596 I BGB. Third sentence.

68 *Erkenning.*

69 REINHARTZ (2000), p. 72, suggests that a civil status registrar is under an obligation to refuse to draw up a recognition if it is manifestly false.

70 ASSER-DE BOER (2006), p. 574.

71 ASSER-DE BOER (2006), p. 576.

72 Art. 1:203 DCC.

73 Art. 1:204(1)(f) DCC.

The recognition of incestuous children is also formally prohibited.[74] Furthermore, those under the age of sixteen may not recognise a child. Van Raak-Kuiper has argued that this age requirement should be deleted since a family law relationship also exists from birth with the mother regardless of her being a minor.[75] If the child that is recognised is under the age of sixteen, prior written consent must first be obtained from the mother. If the child is older than twelve years of age, her or his prior written consent must further be obtained. Both of these forms of prior written consent may be provided on the occasion of the preparation of the instrument of recognition. Finally, whenever a curator has been appointed on the ground that the man suffers from a mental disorder, the prior consent of the sub-district court will be necessary.[76]

Married men are in principle barred from recognising children conceived or born outside their own marriage. Yet this prohibition is very far from being absolute.[77] Thus, a married man may make a recognition if it is established that he and the mother have or have had a relationship closely resembling marriage closely. Furthermore, a married man may also claim that a close personal relationship exists between him and the child.[78]

Van Raak-Kuiper holds that this latter requirement should be deleted on account of the fact that a close personal relationship between the man and the child is dispensed with in the judicial determination of paternity.[79] Whereas in the latter case the men usually do not want a family law relationship with the child, some married men in this situation may desire this but may find themselves prevented from developing a close relationship with the child. Indeed, for such reasons, this requirement of a 'close personal relationship' appears superfluous. This is all the more so since the mother may still withhold her consent, something which she could also do in respect of unmarried men.[80]

Thus, in respect of both unmarried and married men, **Dutch** case law has expanded on the issue when substitutive replacement by a court of the mother's consent may be obtained. Prior to the reform, the mother's refusal to consent had to involve an 'abuse of circumstances', a legal institution derived from **Dutch**

---

74 Art. 1:41(2) DCC.

75 Raak-Kuiper (2007), p. 110-111.

76 Art.1:204(4) DCC.

77 Hoge Raad, 10 November 1989, *NJ* 1990, p. 450.

78 Art. 1:204(3) DCC.

79 Raak-Kuiper (2007), p. 113.

80 Art. 1:204(3) DCC.

contract law rather than family law. In basing this analogy on contract law, a distinction was made between two situations. If the mother had parental authority, such abuse could only be assumed if the man could prove that the mother lacked an interest worthy of legal protection in withholding consent.[81] In the event that the father had contributed significantly to the child's care and upbringing, the abuse of circumstances on the part of the mother would only be accepted by the courts if the mother could not be considered to have reasonably concluded that consent should be withheld.[82] Furthermore, any recognition by another man with the mother's written consent in order to deprive the begetter of his possibility to recognise 'his' child was also considered null and void.[83]

At present, it is therefore an accepted jurisprudential rule that the mother may effectively only accord a 'provisional' form of consent to a man other than the begetter in that latter situation.[84] That said, the begetter who had at first shown indifference, while the mother had given written consent to another man, may sometimes find himself 'estopped' from thereafter contesting the validity of the other man's recognition.[85] If the man has had regular contact with the child but had threatened and used violence against the mother in the period subsequent to the birth, for example, the biological father ('begetter') may not challenge the recognition by another man.[86]

As far the written consent of the mother is concerned, the basic rule is that her consent is always required unless the child has reached the age of sixteen. In addition to the mother's consent, minors older than twelve should give their own consent. Subject to two conditions, the mother's consent may be replaced by the consent of the district court.[87] First, judicial consent will only be given if the court is satisfied that the interests of the mother in an undisturbed relationship with the child or – in a more general sense, the interests of the child – will not be prejudged. Furthermore, only the man who has begotten the child in a natural way[88] may petition for substitutive judicial consent.[89] Given the distinc-

---

81 Hoge Raad, 18 May 1990, *NJ* 1991, p. 374.
82 Hoge Raad, 8 April 1988, *NJ* 1989, p. 170; Hoge Raad, 20 December 1991, *NJ* 1992, p. 598, Hoge Raad, 28 October 1994, *NJ* 1995, p. 261.
83 Hoge Raad, 22 February 1991, *NJ* 1991, p. 376.
84 Hoge Raad, 31 May 2002, *NJ* 2002, p. 470.
85 Hoge Raad, 12 November 2004, *RvdW* 2004, 125; see also: Nuytinck (2005), *Ars Aequi* 2005, p. 733-738.
86 Hoge Raad, 21 March 2008, LJN: BC4496.
87 Art. 1:204(3) DCC.
88 *De verwekker* = begetter.
89 *De verwekker.*

tion in **Dutch** legal terminology between the generic term 'biological father'[90] and the specific term 'begetter', a sperm donor and life companion of the mother who is known not to have conceived the child in the natural way, will not be able to request substitutive judicial consent. In the legal literature, this exclusion of the life companion of the mother, whose sperm had been used to conceive in an unnatural way, that has justifiably received criticism.[91]

Even though the man had not begotten the child in the natural way, in a case involving a known sperm donor and a female same-sex couple, the **Dutch** Supreme Court acknowledged that there was no compelling reason to consider the man's claim inadmissible, having regard to the existence of a biological link and the existence of 'family life' under Article 8 ECHR between him and the child. Nonetheless, the court concluded that the (birth)mother had a legal interest in denying him her consent.[92]

In **Portugal**, recognition[93] has, as in many civilistic traditions, been defined as 'a personal and free act.'[94] It follows that a priori evidence of the biological truth may be dispensed with. Even so, De Oliveira considers that the fullest possible knowledge of the relevant circumstances is necessary, thereby requiring the man to be convinced in his own mind that he is the (biological) father.[95] Recognitions may be made by means of a declaration before the civil status registrar, or in the form of a testament, an affidavit or court order.[96] It is expressly stated that a recognition may be made at any time, before or after the birth of the child or after her or his death.[97] Nonetheless, the recognition of a nasciturus is only considered lawful subsequent to the moment of conception.[98] Whereas 'free' may in the past have also meant 'optional', as it was left to the man's discretion whether he wished to assume parental responsibilities or not, paternity is nowadays less of a 'free choice', given the greater scientific precision and the greater considera-

90 *De biologische vader.*

91 PUNSELIE (2002), p. 245; EVERS (2004), p. 11; RAAK-KUIPER (2007), p. 116-117.

92 Hoge Raad, 24 January 2003, *NJ* 2003, p. 386.

93 *A perfilhação.*

94 Art. 1849 PCC.

95 OLIVEIRA (1979), p. 110.

96 Art. 1853 PCC (...) *a) declaração prestada perante o funcionário público do registo civil; b) por testamento; c) por escritura pública; d) por termo lavrado em juízo.*

97 Art. 1854 PCC. Pursuant to art. 1854(4) PCC this consent may be petitioned by any interested party. This consent is assumed if the adult child or his/her descendants have not objected within a period of thirty days.

98 Art. 1855 PCC.

tion which is given to the child's interests.[99] It is required that the person be older than sixteen years of age and not mentally incapacitated at the time of making the recognition.[100] In the absence of clear rules, the marital status of the man does not prevent him from making a lawful recognition. In line with the tradition of the **French** Code Civil, there is no requirement in **Portugal** to obtain the mother's consent in order to make a recognition.[101] However, the recognition of persons older than eighteen years of age is subject to their authenticated written consent.[102]

2.2.2. Comparison and evaluation

In all four jurisdictions, recognition constitutes a legal instrument that establishes a family law relationship between a child born outside marriage and a legal father. In all four jurisdictions recognition denotes a personal and voluntary character. It is moreover also subject to certain requirements as regards its form. Crucially, nowhere does biology operate as a precondition for making a lawful recognition. As such, Romanistic systems have been characterized in particular by their lack of any 'check whatsoever on truthfulness'.[103] In **France**, far from incorporating only a presumption of biological truth, the recognition has historically been an expression of will and intention, an act of benevolence bestowed by the man on the illegitimate child.[104] Still, also in **Germany, the Netherlands** and **Portugal**, a recognition may suggest, but does not necessarily require any prior knowledge of the biological truth on the part of the parents. In **the Netherlands**, a recognition may serve under certain circumstances as an alternative to adoption when the person making the recognition is evidently not the child's biological father.

In **France**, the absence of a corresponding civil status in respect of the husband, may mean that a recognition may still be made by another man. As far as the recognition of minors is concerned, the consent of the mother is required in both **the Netherlands** and in **Germany**, but not in **France** or **Portugal.** In **the Netherlands** this consent can generally be replaced, however, by a court if the mother

99 OLIVEIRA (1979), p. 110.

100 Art. 1850 PCC.

101 See also MEULDERS-KLEIN (1996) on this tradition in the Romanistic systems.

102 Art. 1857 PCC.

103 FRANK (1997), p. 93.

104 FRANK (1993), p. 639. '*La reconnaissance de paternité, en droit français, a davantage la signification d'une volonté de "reconnaître son enfant pour le sien" ("je veux être le père"), plutôt que la déclaration du fait véritablement connu ("je suis le père").*'

refuses. In **the Netherlands**, **Germany** and **Portugal**, as the child attains legal majority, the consent of the child will be required. In **France**, the consent of parties other than the man bears no direct legal relevance but recognition may carry less weight in the absence of a civil status relationship.

Figure VII.2. Consent requirements for recognition

	Consent of the mother	Substitutive judicial consent	Consent of the child
Germany	Yes, > 18	No	No
The Netherlands	Yes, > 16	Yes	12 >
France	No	No	No
Portugal	No	No	No, 18 >

2.3. THE JUDICIAL DETERMINATION OF PATERNITY

2.3.1. Relevant substantive law

It is debatable whether in individual cases it will be in the child's interests that courts determine the paternity of the (presumed) biological father when the man in question is manifestly unwilling to assume parental responsibilities or to establish a meaningful and affective relationship with the child.[105] If paternity cannot be established on the basis of a legal presumption or recognition, however, the law may *ab initio* have to identify the biological father with a greater level of certainty in order to establish paternity. Again, the state could conceivably choose to waive its discretionary power. That it does not do so is not necessarily because the states attaches weight to the fact that children should be brought up by both of their genetic parents. Rather, child support and legal benefits reflect a public interest, which is connected to the child having a second legal parent and receiving child maintenance and other ancillary rights.[106]

In **France**, only the child formally has standing in proceedings involving an *action en recherche de paternité* even if, in fact, during the child's minority the

105 DWYER (2006), p. 34. See also Chapter 1.

106 VONK (2007), p. 10. Since the establishment of paternity and not the consequences of status form the subject-matter here, a comparison of the legal consequences of status in each jurisdiction will, however, be well beyond the scope of this book. It will suffice to take note of the fact that these appreciable legal consequences will derive from a judicial determination of paternity in each jurisdiction.

mother will be the child's legal representative.[107] If the mother is not known, legally incapacitated or has died during the child's minority, a guardian will act as a legal representative subsequent to authorization by a family council.[108] Upon having become an adult, only the child may in principle lodge proceedings unless he or she has died and his or her successors act as legal representatives.[109] The period within which paternity should be determined is considerably long in comparison to the time-limit of two years after birth or the end of cohabitation with the putative father or his last payment of child support which applied prior to the reform. This short time-limit was justified in view of the risk that evidence would become less certain with the passage of time.[110] Whereas the validity of this argument has become eroded in view of the availability of DNA testing, it was considered that legal certainty could still indicate that time-limits need to be imposed.

If paternity has not been established by virtue of the mother's marriage to the father or a recognition by him, the **German** legislator suggests that 'paternity is to be determined'.[111] This use of the gerund form suggests that the law finds that the judicial determination of paternity should not be avoided and that it has an obligatory character.[112] Formally, an additional paternity presumption must apply in respect of the man in this situation. The father can clearly not be 'any' man. Accordingly, only the paternity of a man who had sexual relations[113] with the mother during the conception period may be sought.[114] Even so, an indefinite number of men, as long as they had sexual intercourse with the mother during the conception period, may have to be determined.[115] But the presumption cannot apply in case serious doubts already exist prior to testing as regards the man's fatherhood.

---

107 Art. 327 in conjunction with Art. 328(1) **French** Code Civil. GOUTTENOIRE (2006), p. 21.

108 Art. 328(2) **French** Code Civil.

109 Art. 322 **French** Code Civil.

110 MASSIP (2006), p. 54-55.

111 §1600d(1) BGB.

112 MÜNCHENER KOMM/SEIDEL (2008), BGB, §1600d, Rdnr. 1 and 2.

113 The legal term *beiwohnen*, while literally meaning 'to attend' or 'to lie with', is generally understood to suggest sexual intercourse and/or copulation.

114 Pursuant to §1600d III BGB, this conception period is determined at 300 to 181 days before the birth of the child. If it is known that the child was conceived outside this period, this divergent conception period will apply (second sentence of that same provision).

115 §640 II ZPO. KIRCHMEIER (2002), p. 373.

Before the latest reform, the termination of automatic guardianship outside marriage by the Child Welfare Authorities[116] was made contingent upon the willingness of the mother to disclose the name of the man who had fathered the child. If the mother refused or was unable to disclose the name, the Child Welfare Authorities assumed its competence to lodge proceedings to represent the child against a putative father. The reform meant the end of automatic guardianship and created an additional, independent right of the mother to lodge paternity proceedings. During her or his minority the child is now generally represented by her or his legal representative, typically the mother, as long as she has not been divested of her parental authority.

The judicial determination of paternity may be lodged at any time by both the child and the mother.[117] This being so, the mother may in principle lodge proceedings well into the child's adulthood. As Helms suggests, this position is not easily reconciled with the restrictive regime that applies as regards the mother's right to challenge an established paternity.[118] In that latter situation, the mother may only lodge proceedings within the two years subsequent to the child's birth. This short time-limit is to be understood on account of the fact that she will generally know who fathered the child. Following that rationale, it would be unclear why she should be given the opportunity to seek the establishment of paternity when the child may have already become an adult who is opposed to it.[119]

In **the Netherlands**, it was not until the latest 1998 reform that it became possible for a child and her or his mother to lodge proceedings involving a judicial determination of paternity.[120] Even so, it had already been recognised by the **Dutch** Supreme Court that this apparent legislative lacuna could be in breach of Article 8 in conjunction with 14 of the ECHR.[121] Nonetheless, the mother and child could since 1909, without formally establishing the man's paternity,

---

116 *Das Jugendamt.*

117 §640e(2) ZPO. BORTH/MUSIELAK (2007), ZPO, §640e, Rdnr. 5.

118 HELMS (1999), p. 83.

119 HELMS (1999), p. 83.

120 However, in 1992 the **Dutch** Supreme Court determined that the omission of a recognition of paternity could under certain circumstances violate a social duty of care with respect to the child and the mother. It could, for example, be unlawful not to proceed to a recognition if there were good grounds to believe that this recognition would be made. Hoge Raad, 3 April 1992, *NJ* 1993, p. 286. A father cannot lodge proceedings involving a judicial determination of his own paternity. Gerechshof 's Hertogenbosch, 9 September 2003, LJN: AM7857.

121 *Kamerstukken II*, 1995/96, 24 649, No. 3, p. 8.

already lodge proceedings against a begetter to obtain child support.[122] This latter option still co-exists with the judicial determination, and as such, provides an alternative procedural mechanism to obtain child support whenever no family law relationship between the child and the begetter had been contemplated. In **Dutch** case law it has become accepted that there may be cases in which it would become contrary to notions of equity, implicit in tort law, if a man had created expectations that he would recognise paternity, but had refrained to live up to these expectations.[123] Such legitimate expectations could, for example, have been fostered in particular when the mother and putative father had been cohabiting for a prolonged period before the child was born.

The 1998 parentage law reforms ended this discussion and admitted a judicial determination of paternity in respect of 'the begetter or the man who, as a life companion of the mother, has consented to an act that is capable of having caused the begetting of the child'.[124] This definition thereby excludes the establishment of the donor's paternity.

Under **Dutch** law, only the mother and child have legal standing.[125] The right of the mother comes to an end when the child reaches the age of sixteen. The proceedings must be lodged by the mother within five years after the child's birth or, if the identity of the presumptive begetter is unknown or if she does not know his whereabouts, within five years after the day that the identity and whereabouts have become known. For the child, no time-limit applies; he or she may lodge proceedings, even well after the putative father's death. It was deemed necessary to offer the child such leeway in view of the 'last resort' character of the procedure.[126] If the putative father has outlived the (adult) child, a descendant of the child in the first degree may institute the proceedings. In the event that the child has died, the application must be filed within one year from the date of the child's death or within a year after the applicant has become aware of the child's death.[127]

---

122 Art. 1:394 DCC. See also Chapter IV.

123 Hoge Raad, 3 April 1992, *NJ* 1993, p. 286; see also: Von Brucken Fock (2006).

124 Art. 1:207(1) DCC. The procedure is known in Dutch as *de gerechtelijke vaststelling van het vaderschap.*

125 Art. 1:207(1) under (a) and (b) DCC.

126 *Kamerstukken II*, 1996/97, 24 649, No. 3, p. 21.

127 Art. 1:207(4) DCC.

Proceedings may only be lodged if the child does not already have two legal parents.[128] Moreover, if the mother and the putative father are within the prohibited degrees of consanguinity, paternity may not be established.[129] Finally, it has also been said that paternity should not be able to be established in case the putative father is a minor under the age of sixteen.[130] However, it was realised that situations could arise in which paternity could for that reason never be able to be established even after the father became an adult. Paternity may therefore be established if the 'begetter' or 'life companion' died before having reached the age of sixteen.[131]

It is worth pointing out that initially, with respect to the mother, it had been proposed that either a time-limit of five years after the child's birth should apply or five years after the identity and the whereabouts of the begetter became known to the mother. For the child a three-year time-limit to be cast into a dies a quo form was initially proposed.[132] Following a comparative legal overview of neighbouring jurisdictions, these restrictions were, however, lifted.[133]

It was considered that the man, who as the life companion of the mother had agreed to an act which could have resulted in the begetting of the child, should not be in a position to elude paternity proceedings. Notably, this inclusion of the life companion as a potential respondent in a paternity suit has offered scope for claims in respect of men who, as 'life partners', had given their consent to the mother prostituting herself.[134]

Dutch case law adheres to the formula that it is both a 'necessary and sufficient' condition that the respondent may be the child's 'begetter' or the mother's 'life companion'.[135] This formula means that not only is the man's intention irrelevant, but also that in general there will be no balancing of interests.[136] It follows

---

128 Art. 1:207(2) under (a) DCC.

129 Art. 1:207(2) under (b) in conjunction with article 1:41 DCC. See also Chapter I.

130 Otherwise, this would lead to the circumvention of the prohibition for males under sixteen years of age to make a recognition. *Kamerstukken II*, 1995/96, 24 469, No. 3, p. 22.

131 Art. 1:207(2) under (c) DCC.

132 *Kamerstukken II*, 1996/97, 24 649, No. 3, p. 21.

133 *Kamerstukken II*, 1996/97, 24 469, No. 6, p. 41.

134 Hoge Raad, 7 February 2003, AF0044.

135 Hoge Raad, 22 September 2000, *NJ* 647, p. 4993; Hoge Raad, 25 March 2005, *NJ* 2005, p. 313; Rechtbank Haarlem 18 March 2008,LJN:BC999.

136 Asser-De Boer (2006), p. 591. See also Chapter III on ECtHR *Remmerswaal v. The Netherlands*, Appl. No. 3441/05, 9 September 2008. The ECtHR found that it was not its task to assess *in abstracto* the legal theory underlying this piece of legislation in respect of the impact on the father's interests and those of other relatives.

that it is not required that family life exists or has existed between the man and the child.[137]

More remarkably, if focus is put on the biological truth, the provision does not unambiguously require the man to be the biological father. As a result of the fact that the proceedings form the 'last procedural resort' for establishing paternity, but they do not insist upon DNA evidence,[138] the child may sometimes end up with having the mother's consenting life companion or a man other than the biological father as his or her legal father. This paternity can thereafter not be denied, even if it is 'false'. As a further side-effect, it is conceivable that a mother may sometimes choose to have the paternity of either her consenting life companion or the man with whom she had sexual relations established. For such reasons, the current legal definition has justifiably received some criticism.[139]

In **Portugal**, civil status registrars are under a statutory obligation to send an extract of the child's birth certificate to the court if paternity has not been established.[140] Thereafter, proceedings are lodged. These proceedings involve a 'public verification' of paternity, in which the mother is heard.[141] The civil status registrar may not assume this competence if it is known that the putative father and the mother are within prohibited degrees of consanguinity or if two years have already passed since the child's birth.[142]

The Public Prosecutor assesses the validity of the reasons behind the paternity claim. If the Public Prosecutor considers it plausible that the man indicated is indeed the biological father, court proceedings involving a determination of paternity may (or may not) ensue.[143] Alongside this right of the public authorities, however, the child and the mother also have an independent right to institute proceedings directly. If the mother is a minor, she will be represented by a special guardian, for whose appointment her parents' consent may be dispensed with.[144]

---

137 Hoge Raad, 25 March 2005, *NJ* 2005, p. 313.

138 See Chapter VIII.

139 EVERS (2004), p. 14; RAAK-KUIPER (2007), p. 184.

140 Art. 1864 PCC.

141 *A averiguação oficiosa da paternidade.*

142 Art. 1866 PCC.

143 Art. 1869 PCC. *A investigação da paternidade.*

144 Art. 1870 PCC. The time-limits have been reviewed by the Constitutional Court, see Chapter IV.

The burden of proof in principle lies upon the child and/or the mother.[145] All the same, the onus may shift and be and the putative father may be required to show that one of four legal presumptions of paternity does not apply. Drafted at a time when access to scientific evidence was still cumbersome, these presumptions, seemingly obsolete, have so far not been deleted.

Firstly, if the putative father is locally reputed to be the child's father, he may be required to show that he is not. Secondly, he also bears the burden of proof to disprove his fatherhood if a written document exists that indicates that he is indeed the father. Thirdly, if the mother and the man are known to have shared relations in conditions resembling a marriage or to have cohabited over an extended period his fatherhood will be presumed. Fourthly, there is a presumption of paternity in cases involving 'seduction'.[146] The putative father may be required to dispel the claim if there is evidence that he had promised to marry the mother. In case of serious doubts concerning the putative father's paternity, however, none of these presumptions will apply. This therefore means that the general rule applies that the onus will lie on the mother or the child.[147]

2.3.2. Comparison

The judicial determination of paternity can be found in all four legal systems, but it was only introduced in 1998 in **the Netherlands**. It offers the child and, to a more limited extent, the mother a subsidiary means to establish a family law relationship between the father and the child.[148] It follows from the binary conception of legal parentage that a non-biological paternity based on marriage or recognition will first have to be denied before the paternity of the biological father may be judicially determined. This 'last resort' character goes some way in explaining why, time-wise, the restrictions on the child's right tend to be less rigorous than in those proceedings which involve a denial of paternity. With regard to that point, it is recalled that in the *Phinikaridou* case the ECtHR affirmed, that, in Europe, 'a comparative examination of actions for judicial recognition of paternity reveals that there is no uniform approach in this field',

[145] Art. 1869 PCC. The mother's right to lodge proceedings can be deduced indirectly from 1870 PCC. See Chapter IV.

[146] Art. 1871-1 under (d) PCC.

[147] Art. 1871-2 PCC.

[148] This binary conception of parenthood may, pursuant to Art. 1:207 DCC, also extend to same-sex families in **the Netherlands** as mention is made of 'another parent' rather than 'an established paternity'. This distinction does not, however, mitigate the fact that a binary conception of legal parentage also prevails in **the Netherlands**.

but acknowledged that a 'significant number of states do not set limitation periods for children'.[149]

Accordingly, in **Germany** and in **the Netherlands** a legally fatherless child is not bound to any time restraints, even if the child only becomes legally fatherless subsequent to denial proceedings. In contrast, in **Portugal** the judicial determination of paternity had until very recently remained subject to time constraints until these were deemed unconstitutional.[150] Even so, after the last parentage law reform in **France**, the child's right remains restricted in view of a public interest in legal certainty and, possibly, the privacy interest of the father. It is recalled that the ECtHR has also recently acknowledged that it may be legitimate for a state to set time-limits in paternity proceedings so as 'to protect the interests of presumed fathers from stale claims and prevent possible injustice if courts were required to make findings of fact that went back many years'.[151]

Recently, some **Dutch** doctrinal views have also expressed some criticism because of the lack of any procedural time-limits in respect of the child's right, irrespective of that child's age.[152] These authors do not only justifiably suggest that this may go much further than the Strasbourg court requires, but would have little to do with an identity-related interest in cases in which an adult child, quite convinced who his biological father is, only denies a 'false' paternity after the death of the biological father in order to pursue an inheritance claim.[153] This involves a discussion of *post mortem* judicial determination of paternity.

Figure VII.3. The judicial determination of paternity

	Mother	Child	State
France	No, but 'represents' minor	Yes, until 10 years upon becoming an adult	No
Germany	Yes	Yes	No
The Netherlands	Yes, child > 16 y.o.	Yes	No
Portugal	Yes	Yes	Yes

149 ECtHR *Phinikaridou v. Cyprus*, Appl. No. 23890/02, 20 December 2007, para. 58.
150 See Chapter IV.
151 ECtHR *Shofman v. Russia*, No. 74826/01, 39, 24 November 2005, para. 39; ECtHR *Mizzi v. Malta*, Appl. No. 26111/02, 88, 12 January 2006, para. 83; ECtHR *Phinikaridou v. Cyprus*, Appl. No. 23890/02, 20 December 2007, paras. 51 and 53.
152 Heida & Ter Haar (2008), p. 288.
153 Heida & Ter Haar (2008), p. 288.

2.3.3. Evaluation

The judicial determination of the paternity of a living putative father should be viewed as a last resort to establish a legal relationship between the father and the child. Since the genetic link will in this case be the immediate focus of attention, the assumption must be that a judicial determination ensures a greater level of protection of the child's right to information than marriage-based paternity or a recognition.[154] In particular, the institution makes the principle of procreational responsibility visible because the determination of paternity will generally be unavoidable if DNA testing has been conducted but also in case the putative father refuses to go along with testing. However, the **Dutch** legal definition leaves some scope for a definite determination of paternity in which the biological truth may not always be the outcome.

From a truth-oriented perspective it could be problematic when a non-biological paternity can no longer be denied. The child's decisional privacy to access the truth in other ways may then not only be seriously compromised, but the child may also be unable to modify status accordingly.

In addition, it may be considered advantageous that a child may at least be one step closer to the biological truth following a denial of paternity. But this will clearly not always be the outcome if there is no other man who may be suspected of being the biological father.

From a parentage law perspective there may be reasons connected with legal certainty for imposing more restrictive statutory time-limits, especially if the child had previously successfully denied a long-standing socio-legal paternity. Nonetheless, as the *Jäggi* case has suggested, the conclusion must be that an interest in knowing the truth does not decrease with age, but rather as the ECtHR suggests, 'on the contrary.'[155]

2.3.4. Digging up the past: the 'post mortem' judicial determination of paternity

A judicial determination of paternity may be indicated not only whenever a man is unwilling to make a recognition. Court intervention may also be required when, for one reason or another, paternity could not be established while the biological father was still living. From a parentage law perspective, this will

[154] Compare ECtHR *Paulik v. Slovakia*, Appl. No. 10699/05, 10 October 2006 (see Chapter III).
[155] See Chapter III.

generally be important in case of an inheritance claim. From a truth-oriented perspective, it may be important for a descendant to have greater certainty to acquiesce lingering doubts. Given the inherent sensitivity of a *post mortem* determination of paternity, a legal discussion warrants a distinct legal analysis even if the substantive legal provisions may correspond with those governing an 'ordinary' judicial determination of paternity in vivo.

In **France**, the 1997 landmark paternity case involving the exhumation of the renowned singer and entertainer Yves Montand has since then had a profound impact on legislation.[156] It was known that the singer had always objected to recognition while he was alive and following an exhumation the paternity claim proved to be false. A few years after the Montand case, the Orléans Court of Appeal still decided in favour of an exhumation that had been petitioned by a woman who at the beginning of the proceedings was still pregnant. The court decided that the deceased's right to physical integrity had to give way to the mother's claim as it had been proved that the man had been inclined to recognise the child.[157] As an outcome of the media attention that the Yves Montand case had provoked, an Act was passed requiring that written proof of express consent be made in vivo if an exhumation is to proceed.[158] As may be expected, the effect of this rule all but amounts to an effective prohibition, as the number of men (perhaps, incidentally, morbid enough) who have made such a declaration will be negligible. Indeed, it has been reaffirmed that otherwise a refusal by the descendants of the deceased to consent to exhumation constitutes a viable reason to deny the claim.[159]

In **Germany**, the death of the putative father will not in principle preclude proceedings involving a judicial determination of paternity. Such proceedings do not fall within the category of an ordinary civil procedure within the jurisdiction of a family law court, but will be regarded as non-contentious proceedings in view of the problems resulting from the absence of a respondent.[160]

---

156 Court of Appeal of Paris, 6 November 1997, D.1998, 122.

157 Tribunal de Grande Instance of Orléans, 18 October 1999, D.2000.

158 '*Sauf accord exprès de la personne manifesté de son vivant, aucune identification par empreintes génétiques ne peut être réalisé*', pursuant to Art. 16-11(2) **French** Code Civil following the adoption of bill 2004-800 of 6 August 2004.

159 Cass.Ire civ., 25 October 2005, No. 03-14.101, P+ B, rejet, CA Douai, 24 February 2003, *Revue Juridique Personnes & Famille*, p. 26.

160 §1600 e II BGB in conjunction with §621a I **German** Civil Procedure Code (Zivilprozessordnung); GERNHUBER/COESTER-WALTJEN (2006), p. 604.

Cases involving *post mortem* exhumations of a putative father's corpse have, to the author's knowledge, hitherto been far and few between. Still, in one *post mortem* paternity case, the Bavarian Regional Court of Appeal drew inferences rather than ordering an exhumation, stating that it was sufficient that the possibility of paternity was not remote.[161] In another case, the Saarland Regional Court of Appeal suggested that exhumation should only be considered as a subsidiary procedural means to establish paternity when paternity could not be established on the basis of other factual indications.[162] In yet another case involving a *post mortem* denial of paternity, however, the examination by a coroner of a putative father's corpse was accepted.[163]

Doctrinal views are divided on the question whether a deceased person still enjoys a personality right, in particular whether he or she can be considered to have a personality right after death.[164] In drawing analogies with the law governing the transplantations of human organs after death, it has been suggested that persons who are entitled to take care of the grave should have exclusive decisional authority as regards any re-excavation of the grave, especially if the deceased person had during his lifetime made a declaration to that end.[165] It has also been maintained that the ordinary statutory obligation to undergo physical compulsion in parentage testing will not apply if the person has already died.[166]

In **the Netherlands**, even if the putative biological father has died, it will remain a 'necessary and sufficient condition that on the basis of the facts and circumstances of the case it is probable that the concerned person may have fathered the child'.[167] Accordingly, it is not deemed relevant whether or not proceedings have been primarily inspired by an – arguably less benign – exclusively patrimonial motive. As such, a case has been reported where a person was living on social security benefits until successfully lodging proceedings against his deceased putative father, who proved to have been a multi-millionaire who had run

161 Regional Court of Appeal = Oberlandesgericht (OLG) Munich, 14 September 2000, *FamRZ* 2001, 126 = NJW-RR 2000, p. 1603.

162 Regional Court of Appeal = Oberlandesgericht (OLG) Saarbrücken, OLGR 2005, 297.

163 Regional Court of Appeal = Oberlandesgericht (OLG) Hamm, 19 October 2004, *FamRZ* 2005, 1192 = *NJW-RR* 2005, p. 231.

164 HUBMANN (1967), p. 347, MÜLLER (1996), p. 249.

165 LAKKIS (2006), p. 457-458. The authors refer to Federal Constitutional Court = BVerfGE, 28 January 1999, *FamRZ* 1999, 777= *NJW* 1999, p. 3403.

166 LAKKIS (2006), p. 458.

167 Hoge Raad, 22 September 2000, *RvdW* 2000, 1299.

a profitable company with its seat in **Liechtenstein**.[168] Whether or not during his life the putative father had expressed a wish to establish a family law relationship with the claimant was also considered irrelevant.[169]As far as requirements of piety and respect for the interests of close relatives go, a court has gone as far as to state that a post mortem determination of paternity does not infringe upon the family life of such third parties, including siblings.[170]

If the child has not denied the 'false' paternity within the statutory time-limits and, upon the death of the biological father, lodges proceedings involving a judicial determination, a uniform approach is absent. While the Amsterdam district court cast the expiry of the time-limit aside, the Court of Appeal of The Hague admitted it.[171] In that connection, it has been suggested that legal certainty and strict adherence to time-limits require that the claim should be denied, even if the child will remain deprived of a father.[172] On the basis of the *Kroon* formula,[173] the authors consider that if the facts 'clash' with reality and 'go against the wishes of the parties', in particular those of the legal descendants of the deceased, a court should be able to constrain the child's right.[174]

It has been suggested that the objections of close relatives of the deceased require some consideration, even if they do not really carry any legal weight.[175] In **Dutch** legal practice, exhumation is a subsidiary means to acquire evidence in post mortem cases. Full judicial discretion with respect to the ordering of tests will mean that a post mortem examination will only be ordered by the courts in situations where the child is legally fatherless within the ambit of proceedings involving a judicial determination of paternity.[176]

---

168 Gerechtshof Amsterdam, 20 November 2003, LJN: AO8653; Rechtbank Leeuwarden, 10 November 2004, LJN: AR5884.

169 Gerechtshof Amsterdam, 8 July 2004, LJN: AQ0621.

170 Gerechtshof Amsterdam, 8 July 2004, LJN: AQ0621; Hoge Raad, 25 March 2005, LJN: AT0412.

171 Rechtbank Amsterdam 27 August 2007, No. 360518; Gerechtshof 's-Gravenhage, 30 August 2006, LJN: AY7454.

172 HEIDA & TER HAAR (2008), p. 292.

173 ECtHR *Kroon v. The Netherlands*, Appl. No. 18353/91 27 October 1994, para. 40. See Chapter III.

174 HEIDA & TER HAAR (2008), p. 292.

175 PUTTEN (1993), p. 140-154. Compare: Gerechtshof Amsterdam, 8 July 2004, LJN: AQ0621; Hoge Raad, 25 March 2005, LJN: AT0412.

176 Art. 1:207 DCC.

If other traces of DNA can be found, for instance on envelopes,[177] the use of these specimens of genetic material will be indicated. It has also been suggested that when the putative father's descendants refuse to give consent to a post mortem DNA test, the judge should be in a position to draw adverse inferences from their refusal, just like he would be able to do in a 'normal' judicial determination.[178] Paternity could therefore still be established, while the arguably more morbid possibility of exhumation, while providing greater scientific certainty, could be dispensed with. At the same time, it must be recognised that the reasons for a refusal may be different than in an in vivo case, thereby making the case for inferences more controversial.

The fact that *post mortem* cases have remained controversial is underscored by a 2005 case, which involved two sisters in their 40s who had been abandoned at birth and brought up as foster children.[179] For years on end, they had sought to trace the identity of their father and to ask their mother for an answer. Allegedly, not only their mother but a whole small community in the east of **the Netherlands**, Borne, had been fully aware who the sisters' biological father was, but in a community-wide 'conspiracy of silence' they had refused to be open. As the whole village already knew, apart from the two siblings, that the father was the village baker and had died shortly after their birth in 1966. More than forty years later, the Arnhem district court ordered the exhumation of the village baker and it was proved beyond scientific doubt that he had fathered the two sisters.

Finally, in **Portugal**, there are no legal obstacles to a judicial determination of paternity after the presumptive father has died. There is no rule which prohibits a court from ordering the exhumation of a corpse to determine his paternity.[180] Although private parties may, subject to the consent requirements of the parties involved, petition an (extrajudicial) scientific test at the Institute for Legal Medicine while the putative father is alive, for post mortem paternity testing a prior court order is required. So far, however, not a single post mortem case has been reported in **Portugal**.

177 Gerechtshof Amsterdam, 20 November 2003, LJN: AO8653; Gerechtshof Amsterdam, 8 July 2004, LJN: AQ0621.

178 HEIDA (2003), p. 180.

179 Extract from a decision submitted to the author by the Rechtbank Arnhem, December 2005 (the date and names have not been publicly disclosed).

180 Responses of the **Portuguese** government to the *Questionnaire on Access to Genetic Information not related to Health*, CDCJ 2005 [cdcj/docs 2005/cdcj (2005) 9 bil].

In a Separate Opinion, the Public Prosecution Service has voiced the opinion that post mortem genetic testing is not genuinely distinct from testing live persons as both will fall within the ambit of human dignity. This right is enshrined in Article 1 of the **Portuguese** Constitution. As has been stated in Chapter IV, the personality right has been derived from that provision in conjunction with Article 26.-1 of the Constitution, which protects personal identity and the development of one's own personality.[181] A bill has been recently placed before Parliament, however, which foresees a time-limit of three years for applications after the internment of the putative father.[182] Following the expiry of that time-limit, an exhumation would not be permitted. Nonetheless, it has been stated that if a court were faced with a case concerning a post mortem establishment of paternity, the Institute for Legal Medicine would anyhow first seek to avoid an exhumation by testing other relatives who are still alive.[183]

2.3.5. Comparison

A *post mortem* judicial determination of paternity is admitted in the four jurisdictions. Exhumation generally seems to be regarded as a subsidiary means to ascertain paternity in **Dutch** case law. In **Germany** and **Portugal** case law has hitherto remained very much under-developed. In **France**, the requirement of express consent to DNA testing given by the father while he was still alive, in practice will more often than not mean that paternity will have to be based on the basis of presumptions or that it cannot be established at all.

2.3.6. Evaluation

In view of its invasiveness and inherently controversial nature, a different regime will be warranted than in the case of a judicial determination in vivo. It would appear, therefore, that an exhumation should only be used as a subsidiary means to ascertain paternity. If paternity can be established on the basis of DNA found on envelopes or the property of the deceased, for example, this would clearly be less disturbing for third parties such as the father's other descendants. All the same, the child could generally still achieve a reasonable level of certainty about his or her genetic descent. If this is not possible, then a further scrutinisation of the applicant's motives may be necessary, unlike the more abstract

181 Parecer da Procuradoria Geral da Repúbli ca, 1 September 2005, www.dgsi.pt.

182 Law Proposal No. 411/98 of 30 December 2005.

183 Responses of the **Portuguese** Government to the *Questionnaire on Access to Genetic Information not related to Health*, CDCJ (2005) [cdcj/docs 2005/cdcj (2005) 9 bil].

prioritisation of the child's informational interests that may be possible if the father is still living.

In that respect, it is recalled that in *Phinikaridou* the ECtHR drew a distinction 'between cases in which an applicant has no opportunity to obtain knowledge of the facts and, cases where an applicant knows with certainty or has grounds for assuming who his or her father is but for reasons unconnected with the law takes no steps to institute proceedings within the statutory time-limit'.[184] This suggests that if the child remains procedurally inert for a protracted period but has for a long time had more than an inkling of the deceased man's genetic link, but nonetheless refrains from undertaking any procedural action, he or she should not be in a position for too long after the man's death to reap the benefits of inheritance rights. In contrast, a perfectly meritorious claim would involve an expiry of time-limits beyond the child's objective control; a more flexible interpretation of time-limits would then be appropriate. This also seems to have been in the minds of the judges in deciding on the case of *Jäggi*. On the other hand, it may be difficult to establish to what extent a person's ideological interest is genuine. Conceivably, both inheritance-related interests and ideological interests could sometimes conflate in many post mortem paternity claims.

3. THE DENIAL OF PATERNITY

3.1. DENIAL PROCEEDINGS

The 2005 **French** parentage law reform has reaffirmed the principle that the number of parties capable of reviewing legal parentage relations will depend on the level of congruence between the child's civil status and the information contained in the birth certificate (the *titre*). The child, the mother and the legal father as well as the putative biological father may deny paternity if the child's civil status and birth certificate match.[185] Such proceedings may be instituted within five years after the civil status relationship has come to an end, unless the child's civil status and *titre* had been in accordance with each other for longer than five years after birth. In that latter case paternity can no longer be challenged.[186]

[184] ECtHR *Phinikaridou v. Cyprus*, Appl. No. 23890/02, 20 December 2007, para. 63. See Chapter III.

[185] Art. 333 **French** Code Civil.

[186] Cass.Civ.Ire, 19 September 2007, No. 06-21.061, *Juris-Data*, No. 040373.

However, if paternity had been established only on the basis of the civil status recorded in an affidavit, it may be contested by any person who has an interest therein by adducing contrary evidence, within a period of five years from the issuing of the instrument.[187] The claimant will then, in fact, be challenging the child's status, as documented in the affidavit, rather than his genetic link to the child. This means that in principle no DNA test will be required. Even so, just like any other party capable of claiming a sufficient legal interest, the putative biological father may lodge such proceedings.[188]

Moreover, if the legal relationship between the father and child, as attested in the birth certificate, has not been corroborated by the child's civil status, any interested party may challenge paternity.[189] In this case paternity rather than civil status is being contested. These claims become time-barred after ten years as from the day when the person was deprived of the status that he claims, or began to enjoy the status that is contested against him. With respect to the child, that period is suspended during his minority.[190] Controversially, in a 2007 case, a mother successfully challenged a man's recognition of the paternity of her fifteen year-old son who had not had a civil status relationship with that father but had not doubted the man's genetic link to him.[191]

Finally, the **French** state also assumes competence to challenge a 'false' paternity.[192] A lawfully established parentage may be contested by the Public Ministry where circumstantial evidence drawn from the instruments themselves renders it unlikely or in the case of fraud. This state competence now extends to any fictitious form of legal parentage, including (international) surrogacy cases. In case of an effective denial, the court may, however, for the welfare of the child, fix the details of the relations between the latter and the person who had been raising the child.[193]

In striving towards greater equality, the latest **German** parentage law reforms reduced the two distinct procedures for marital and non-marital children to a

---

187 Art. 335 **French** Code Civil. Affidavit = *acte de notoriété.*

188 Granet-Lambrechts & Hauser (2006), p. 23.

189 Art. 334 **French** Code Civil.

190 Art. 321 **French** Code Civil.

191 TGI Lyon, 5 July 2007, D.2007, note A. Gouttenoire.

192 Art. 336 **French** Code Civil.

193 Art. 337 **French** Code Civil.

single procedure.[194] At present, the only ground for denying paternity is 'objective falsity'.[195] The number of persons entitled to challenge paternity under the current legal regime has been circumscribed.[196] They are: 1) the man whose paternity is established on the basis of his marriage to the mother or by virtue of recognition;[197] 2) the man who on oath has declared that he had sexual intercourse[198] with the mother during the period of conception; 3) the mother; 4) the child; and 5) the public authorities. As for the last-mentioned party, since June 2008 the state has assumed competence primarily because of 'fictitious' recognitions by **German** men of foreign mothers with whom no family ties had existed. The attribution of **German** nationality may in this way be avoided.[199]

Originally, the mother's right to challenge paternity had been made subject to the condition that it served the minor's interests.[200] If she denies paternity in her quality as the child's legal representative, however, the clause concerning the minor's interests remains applicable.[201] Now paternity may therefore be denied if it is 'objectively false'. Thus, even if the man is fully aware that he is not the father, he may subsequently deny paternity.[202]

Procedural time-limits were considered necessary for reasons of legal certainty.[203] The current legal regime sets a time-limit of two years. This period starts to run from the moment that the person becomes aware of circumstances which may point against paternity.[204] It can, however, not begin before or during pregnancy. Accordingly, for the mother the period usually starts after she has given birth. For the father, given his informationally asymmetrical relationship with the mother, the time-limit may start considerably later. As a *dies a quo* time-limit, its commencement is contingent upon factors which may be outside the

194 *Die Vaterschaftsanfechtung.* Previously the legitimate status could be challenged (*Die Ehelichkeitsanfechtung*) and recognitions of children born outside marriage could be challenged (*Die Anfechtung der Vaterschaftsanerkennung*).
195 *BT-Drucks.* V/2370, p. 31; MÜNCHENER KOMM/WELLENHOFER-KLEIN (2008), BGB, §1600, Rdnr. 1.
196 §1600 BGB.
197 §1592(1) and (2) and §1593 BGB.
198 *Beiwohnen.*
199 *BT-Drucks.* 624/06, 1 September 2006. Adopted by the Bundestag on 13 March 2008; MÜNCHENER KOMM/WELLENHOFER-KLEIN (2008), §1600, Rdnr. 16.
200 §1600 2 I BGB-E. *BT-Drucks.* 180/96, 22 March 1996.
201 §1600a 4 BGB; WANITZEK (2002), p. 391.
202 MÜNCHENER KOMM/WELLENHOFER-KLEIN (2008), BGB, §1600, Rdnr. 2.
203 *BT-Drucks.* 180/96, 1997.
204 §1600b 2 BGB.

direct control of the person. In other words, he must first become aware of circumstances which may point against his genetic link to the child.

If the legal representative of the minor child has refrained from denying paternity within the aforementioned time-limits, the child can exercise this right on becoming an adult, but again only from the moment that he or she becomes aware of circumstances which may point against paternity.[205]

Only the legal representatives of the child, usually the parents, will have competence as long as the child is legally incapacitated.[206] If the mother is not married to the father and has exclusive parental authority, she may therefore represent the child. If she is married to him, a guardian must be appointed as both parents will in principle have parental authority and a conflict of interests is presumed.[207] For children with restricted legal capacity or for those (fully) legally incapacitated, the consent of their legal representatives will be required.[208] These rules may become relevant for mentally impaired adults, while minors will *ipso iure* be considered legally incapacitated. The court must always make an assessment of whether the denial by a legal representative is in the child's interests.[209]

In contrast, there are two formally distinct regimes for denying paternity in **the Netherlands** depending on whether paternity is based on marriage or on recognition. If the mother is married to the legal father, he and the mother, alongside the child, can rebut the marital presumption.[210] The only ground on which marriage-based paternity can be denied is that the man 'is not the biological father'.[211] As a particular feature of **Dutch** law, the father or the mother cannot deny paternity if the man already knew that the mother was pregnant before marrying her. Even so, paternity may still be challenged on the grounds that the mother had deceived him as regards the person who had fathered the child.[212] Furthermore, the father or the mother also cannot challenge the marital presumption when he had agreed to an act which may have resulted in the begetting of the child. This latter exception will especially have relevance for the

205 §1600b 3 BGB.
206 §1600a 1 BGB. PALANDT/DIEDERICHSEN (2002), §1600a, Rdnr. 2.
207 §1626a II in conjunction with §1629 II and §1795 BGB. WANITZEK (2002), p. 392.
208 §1600a(3) BGB.
209 §1600a(4) BGB.
210 Art. 1:200(1) under (a) and (b) DCC.
211 Art. 1:200(1) DCC.
212 Art. 1:200(2) DCC in conjunction with article 1:200(4) DCC. Note that this does not preclude the child's right to deny the husband's paternity.

husband who had agreed to his wife's prostitution or if she had inseminated herself with the sperm of another man.

Requirements of legal certainty were deemed to carry sufficient weight during the 1998 **Dutch** reform to justify the denial of the husband's paternity to be made contingent upon procedural time constraints. The mother and the father have one year to challenge paternity. For the mother, the time starts to run from a year after the birth. For the father, this time-limit will not begin until the moment that he has become aware of the fact that he was presumed to be the biological father.[213] The child can in principle challenge the husband's paternity within three years of becoming aware of the fact that the man was presumed not to be his or her biological father. However, if, during his or her minority, the child already had become aware of this fact, the application may be lodged within three years after the child has reached the age of majority.[214] As a result, after having reached the age of 21, a child will no longer be able to challenge the husband's paternity if he or she had already been aware of the fact that the mother's husband was probably not her or his biological father.[215] After the court order declaring that a denial of paternity by reason of marriage is well founded has become final and binding, the paternity stemming from the marriage shall be deemed never to have had effect.[216]

If the person who made the recognition is not the child's biological father the recognition may be nullified.[217] The man, as well as the mother[218] and the child,

213 Art. 1:200(5) DCC. Pursuant to Art. 201(1) DCC, when the father dies prior to the expiry of this period, a descendant of the spouses in the first degree, or in the absence of a descendant, a parent of such a spouse may apply to the district court to declare the denial of paternity well founded. This application must be made within a year after the date of death or after the applicant had become aware of the death.

214 Art. 1:200(6) DCC. Pursuant to Art. 1:201(2) DCC, however, when the child dies prior to the expiry of this period, a descendant of the child in the first degree may apply to the district court to declare the denial of paternity well-founded. When the child has reached the age of majority at the time of death, the application shall be made within one year from the date of death or within one year after the applicant became aware of the death. Where the child died during its minority, the application must be made within one year after the child, had it been alive, could have independently made the application or if the applicant became aware of the death at a later time, within one year after his or her having become so aware.

215 Nonetheless, in the case law a posterior denial is sometimes admitted with reference to Art. 8 ECHR. Gerechtshof Amsterdam, 3 November 2005, LJN: AV0711.

216 Art. 1:202(1) DCC.

217 Art. 1:205 DCC.

218 In admitting the legal father's right to deny paternity, the court can insist upon a prior disclosure of the biological father's name to the child by the mother. Gerechtshof 's-Gravenhage, 22 November 2006, LJN: AZ4493.

have standing. The claim of the man and the mother will, however, only be admissible if the recognition had been made due to a threat, mistake, deceit, or, during his minority, duress.[219] The rationale for this rule derives not only from the assumption that the man should in principle have taken responsibility for the possibility that he may not have fathered the child, but also in the child's interests in growing up in a stable family environment.[220] An application may be made within a year after such duress has ceased to operate. In the case of deceit or mistake, the application has to be made within one year after the discovery of the deceit or mistake.

For the child seeking a nullification of recognition, dies a quo time-limits of the same length apply as with regard to the denial of paternity by reason of marriage.[221] If the time-limit has expired due to circumstances which appear to have been beyond the control of the adult 'child', the courts may exceptionally, pursuant to Article 8 ECHR, still permit a denial, while attaching weight to the existence (or the absence) of family life between that applicant and her or his biological father, especially when the person who recognised the child had already died.[222] In case the child dies prior to the expiry of this period, the same regime applies mutatis mutandis as for children born within marriage.[223]

The **Dutch** Public Prosecutor also has an independent right to nullify a recognition of paternity.[224] A paramount consideration for giving the state competence to challenge paternity outside marriage is provided by the curtailment of 'fictitious' recognitions of paternity geared towards merely obtaining **Dutch** nationality.[225] Three years of continued support in the child's care and upbringing are required to obtain **Dutch** nationality after the person has recognised his paternity. The recognition must not only constitute a breach of **Dutch** public policy but the person who made the recognition must also lack a genetic link to the child. There is no time-limit, as the Public Prosecution Service may seek a denial of such a 'fictitious' recognition whenever this is deemed fit.

---

219 Art. 1:205(1) DCC.
220 Hoge Raad, 27 January 2006, LJN: AU5283.
221 Art. 1:205(3) DCC.
222 Hoge Raad, 15 November 2002, *NJ* 2003, p. 228; Rechtbank Dordrecht, 31 August 2005, LJN: AU2843.
223 Art. 1:205(5) DCC.
224 Art. 1:205(2) DCC.
225 The **Dutch** state also has competence to challenge 'fictitious' marriages. Children are therefore presumed to have been born in a lawful marriage.

Although the nullification has retroactive force, its consequences are not quite as onerous as may be presumed.[226] Thus, rights acquired by third parties in good faith shall be respected.[227] In particular, it is worth adding that the nullification does not give rise to any claims involving a reimbursement of child care and support.[228]

In June 2008, **Dutch** nationality law underwent further legislative changes in the public interest in preventing 'fictitious' recognitions, an issue generally connected to the recognition of adolescents and older minors.[229] As a result, **Dutch** nationality is currently attributed automatically to minors under the age of seven in case of a postnatal recognition.[230] In contrast, minors who are recognised or legitimized by the father after having reached the age of seven will only be able to acquire **Dutch** nationality when the father can demonstrate that he is the biological father by undergoing a DNA test.[231] Accordingly, this new norm in nationality law deviates from the evidential rules in parentage proceedings.[232] Furthermore, the insistence upon DNA evidence is remarkable because no a priori evidence is required in order to make a lawful recognition under **Dutch** law.

In **Portugal**, the paternity of the mother's husband can be denied in the absence of his biological link to the child by the husband, the mother, the child and, more remarkably, the biological father through the intervention of the Public Prosecutor.[233] A procedural time-limit of two years applies with regard to the mother from the moment of birth.[234] With respect to the husband, the same time-limit applies but it has a dies a quo character: it does not start until the day that he became aware of circumstances which may point against his paternity.[235] In 2007, the **Portuguese** Constitutional Court declared that the provision which prevents a child from challenging the paternity of the mother's husband up to one year after having become an adult or within a year after having become aware, as an adult, of circumstances pointing against paternity is unconstitutio-

---

226 *Staatsblad* 2008, p. 270. See also: KOK (2008), p. 237.
227 Art. 1:206(2) DCC.
228 Art. 1:206(3) DCC.
229 KOK (2008), p. 237.
230 Art. 4(2) and (3) Netherlands Nationality Act (Rijkswet op het Nederlanderschap).
231 Art. 4(4) Netherlands Nationality Act (Rijkswet op het Nederlanderschap). Besluit DNA – onderzoek vaderschap 20 October 2008, *Staatblad* 2008, 417.
232 See Chapter VIII.
233 Art. 1839-1 PCC.
234 Art. 1842-1(b) PCC.
235 Art. 1842-1(a) PCC.

nal.[236] Following a comparative analysis regarding various legal systems and in considering the case law of the ECtHR and an earlier case involving the legality of a time-limit incumbent on the child with respect to a judicial determination of paternity,[237] the court concluded that procedural time-limits in parentage proceedings must serve the interests of legal certainty and those of the child.

A recognition can also be nullified after the child's death if it had not reflected the biological truth.[238] Furthermore, denial proceedings may be instituted before the court if the recognition had been made under the influence of an error or duress, but only within a year after such circumstances have drawn to an end.[239] A comparison with the regime for marriage-based paternity reveals some appreciable differences. Thus, time-wise considerably more leeway is offered in denying non-marriage-based paternity. This is evident in the unlimited number of claimants[240] and the absence of procedural time-limits in situations other than duress. In that connection, it has been suggested that the Romanistic legal concept of civil status could be a viable legal criterion as this criterion may allow for a better appraisal of the relevance of socio-affective ties and the child's interest in a stable family environment.[241]

3.2. COMPARISON

The ground on which paternity can be denied is that the legal father is not the biological father in paternity proceedings or its 'falsity'. Yet in **France** the lack of a civil status leaves room for denying paternity irrespective of the genetic link in some situations. In all jurisdictions *dies a quo* time-limits apply with respect to the child and the father, although the child also has a right to challenge paternity only after finding out after having reached the age of majority. The mother, the legal father and the child are the main parties.[242] In order to prevent fictitious recognitions geared towards conferring nationality on the child, the state has also assumed competence in **France**, **Germany** and **the Netherlands**. The four jurisdictions all implicitly assume that the mother is aware, or should at least have been aware, of who had fathered her child. For that reason, in respect

236 Art. 1842-1(c) PCC; Tribunal Constitucional, Appl. No. 563/07, 11 December 2007. See Chapter IV.

237 Tribunal Constitucional, Appl. No. 486/2004, 7 July 2004.

238 Art. 1859(1) PCC.

239 Art. 1860 PCC.

240 Art. 1859(2) PCC.

241 Oliveira (1979), p. 134.

242 In **Slovenia** the socio-legal father who has successfully denied paternity may subsequently seek the establishment of the paternity of the presumptive biological father. Novak (2007), p. 267.

of the mother, the time-limit for instituting denial proceedings already starts running from the moment of birth.

Figure VII.4. The denial of paternity

	Marriage-based	Recognition
Germany	Dies a quo?	Dies a quo?
Mother	No, 2 years after birth	No, 2 years after birth
Socio-legal father	Yes, 2 years (unless remarried)	Yes, 2 years
Child	No, 2 years after having become an adult	No, 2 years after having become an adult
The Netherlands	Dies a quo?	Dies a quo?
Mother	No, 1 year after birth	No, 1 year after birth
Socio-legal father	Yes, 1 year, unless married to the mother during pregnancy	Yes, 1 year after the end of duress, etc.
Child	No, 3 years after having become an adult	No, 3 years after having become an adult
France	Dies a quo?	Dies a quo?
Mother	In case of corresponding civil status five years after birth; ten years if no corresponding civil status	In case of corresponding civil status five years after birth; ten years if no corresponding civil status
Socio-legal father	In case of civil status five years after birth; ten years if no corresponding civil status	In case of civil status five years after birth; ten years if no corresponding civil status
Child	ten years after having become an adult in case of an uncorroborated civil status; otherwise, five years after birth	ten years after having become an adult in case of an uncorroborated civil status; otherwise, five years after birth
Portugal	Dies a quo?	Dies a quo?
Mother	No, 2 years	No, 1 year in case of duress; otherwise no time-limit
Socio-legal father	Yes, 2 years	Yes, 1 year in case of duress; otherwise no time-limit
Child	No, 1 year after having become an adult (now unconstitutional)	Yes,1 year after having become an adult; otherwise no time-limit

3.3. EVALUATION

From a truth-oriented perspective, denial proceedings are important in providing a procedural remedy which allows the claimant to expose the 'falsity' of paternity. This may, however, only be a first procedural step in establishing the truth and have profound repercussions for the child's well-being.

In order to protect the child's interests in a stable family environment, it makes legal sense to set time-limits for denying paternity. In that connection, the **French** legal notion of civil status, or *possession d'état*, ensures that important sociological and affective dimensions of parenthood may duly be taken into account. For these reasons, the mother and the father should in principle only be given a short period to deny paternity. If the man knew perfectly well that he was not the biological father at the time of making the recognition and was not under any duress or coercion, it is circumspect whether he should really be permitted to subsequently deny paternity at all from a parentage law perspective.

In the light of the *Phinikaridou* case, a child should, upon having become an adult, be given at least one real procedural opportunity to challenge a 'mis-attributed' paternity. Generally, in the interest of legal certainty in legal child-parent relationships, a relatively short time-limit after the (adult) child has become aware of circumstances indicating a 'false' paternity may be sufficient. If a review of parental status is not at stake, but the procedural interest is connected to an ideological interest, the *Jäggi* case indicates that there will be less reason to withhold the information from an adult.[243]

4. THE LEGAL POSITION OF THE BIOLOGICAL FATHER WITHOUT PARENTAL STATUS

4.1. INTRODUCTION

The biological father who had conceived a child in the natural way may find himself prevented from fulfilling his wish to have his paternity established if a child already has two legal parents. Especially when the child has already bonded with the legal father, the paternity claim of the biological father could under certain circumstances be perceived as a disruptive rather than a constructive procedure. While this has been a reason to deny the biological father a right

---

[243] See the discussion of ECtHR *Jäggi*, in Chapters III and V.

to pursue his paternity claim, in recent years his rights in that respect have been reinforced in a number of jurisdictions.[244]

4.2. THE RIGHTS OF THE BIOLOGICAL FATHER WHOSE PATERNITY HAS NOT BEEN ESTABLISHED

In **France**, the 2005 parentage law reform reinforced the position of the biological father as he now has a limited right to challenge paternity.[245] Thus, the biological father may challenge paternity up to five years after the child has ceased to enjoy the corresponding civil status.[246] It is irrelevant whether paternity is based on marriage or recognition; what is crucial, rather, is the absence of such sociological ties. If this is the case, the biological father, like any other party capable of claiming a sufficient legal interest, may challenge the child's status within the general period of ten years that applies with respect to parentage procedures.[247]

In **Germany**, the position of the biological father without status was strengthened following a decision by the Federal Constitutional Court which turned him almost overnight from a 'legal nobody'[248] into a person with rights with regard to the child.[249] In the 2003 decision, the Federal Constitutional Court gave the legislator thirteen months to enact legislation to strengthen his position. This resulted in legislative changes the following year.[250] In order to forego cavalier claims by those seeking paternity 'out of the blue'[251] a provision was added which requires the biological father to make a declaration under oath[252] that he had

244 In **Russia** and in **Norway** the biological father also has a strong right to challenge an already established paternity (see FRANK 2005 and LØDRUP 2003). In **Norway**, all time restrictions for the biological father to challenge an established paternity, whether based on marriage or on recognition, have even been annulled.

245 Art. 333 **French** Code Civil.

246 Before the reform the parentage of a non-marital child could be challenged during ten years pursuant to Art. 339(3) of the **French** Code Civil (*old*). The parentage of a marital child could not be challenged if her or his parentage was corroborated by civil status as evinced by the information on the birth certificate. There were few exceptions to this rule pursuant to Arts. 316 and 318 **French** Code Civil (*old*).

247 Art. 334 **French** Code Civil: *A défaut de possession d'état conforme au titre, l'action en contestation peut être engagé par toute personne qui y a intérêt dans le délai prévu à l'article 321.*

248 SCHWENZER (1985), p. 8.

249 Federal Constitunial Court = BVerfGE, 9 April.2003 = *NJW* 2003, p. 2151.

250 *Bundesgesetzblatt* 2004, vol. 18, 598, 23 April 2004.

251 *Ins Blaue hinein.*

252 §1600(1) II BGB: '... *der Mann, der an Eides statt versichert'...*

sexual relations[253] with the mother during the conception period. A false oath may entail criminal prosecution.[254] Nevertheless, no preliminary evidence of the man's genetic link to the child is required in this case. As another point of contention, it has been considered that this possibility would induce many a 'rogue' biological father to abuse his procedural rights in order to reside in the country.[255]

The biological father should in principle not be able to challenge the paternity of the mother's husband. This distinction with regard to unmarried fathers was justified on the assumption that whereas a socio-familiar relationship between the child and the father may not be 'taken for granted' outside marriage, it may be assumed when the mother is married to the legal father.[256] This distinction has, however, been dismissed for being obsolete and short-sighted.[257] In the case of 'fictitious' marriages or if the husband's relationship with the mother only exists formally, the biological father would be able to challenge paternity.[258]

Although perhaps not completely certain either, the biological father has to make a declaration under oath as to his paternity while no 'socio-familiar relationship' must exist between the legal father and the child or has existed at the time of the death of the legal father.[259] The criterion 'socio-familiar relationship' is defined in terms of the biological father having a 'factual responsibility' with respect to the child.[260] Even if this factual responsibility had already come to an end, it may still prevent the biological father from challenging paternity, as the two year-limit of §1600b(1) BGB remains applicable.[261]

In 2008, the Federal Constitutional Court reaffirmed that the presumptive biological father did not have a right to challenge an established paternity of a man who had married the mother.[262] In particular, his interest would have to

---

253 *Beiwohnen.* See above. The inclusion of this term may also prevent a donor from challenging paternity. See: SPICKHOFF (2005), p. 942.

254 §§156. 163 **German** Criminal Code (StGB = *Strafgesetzbuch*).

255 BÜTTNER (2005), p. 744, casting (unsubstantiated) doubts about the benevolent intentions of the average biological father, who may often have a hidden agenda, pursuing an interest in obtaining a title for residence, for example, or be motivated primarily by spite with respect to the mother.

256 MÜNCHENER KOMM/WELLENHOFER (2008), §1600, Rdnr. 10.

257 ROTH (2003), p. 3152-3160.

258 Art. 6 II GG. FRANK (2003), p. 133; MÜNCHENER KOMM/WELLENHOFER (2008), §1600, Rdnr. 10.

259 *Eine sozial-familiäre Beziehung.*

260 §1600 III BGB. *Tatsächliche Verantwortung.*

261 ECKEBRECHT (2005), p. 209.

262 BVerfGE, 1 BvR 1548/03, 13 October 2008.

give way to the interests of the mother and the child in a stable legal relationship. Interestingly, it was also said that this presumptive biological father does not have an independent right to have his genetic link verified before the courts as long as he is not willing to assume legal responsibility.[263]

In **the Netherlands**, there is no specific legislation which acknowledges a right of the biological father to challenge an established paternity. Like any other party who is deemed capable of claiming a sufficiently personal interest, he may, however, petition a contact order unless the child is older than twelve years and has opposed contact.[264] Furthermore, the biological father may under certain circumstances be able to challenge the mother's consent to recognition by another man. This may be the case if the mother has 'abused' her discretion only to give her consent to another man, logically often her new partner, rather than the biological father.[265] The mother can, however, only give 'provisional' consent to her new partner in such cases. If the biological father was unaware of the child's birth or existence or is reticent to undertake action within a reasonable period after the recognition by another man, his claim will effectively be 'estopped', however. If no abuse has been made of the mother's discretion to give consent, it may very well remain all but impossible for the biological father to become the legal father thereafter.

If the mother is married to the legal father, the biological father does not have rights with regard to the child. The position of the biological father seems considerably weaker when the mother is married to a legal father, who may very well be unwilling to deny paternity. It remains to be seen whether a claim under Article 8 ECHR, which may be raised directly before the **Dutch** courts, could be successful. He would then at least have to substantiate that he has family life with the child. The genetic link in itself will not be sufficient.[266]

Although the biological father had sought a contact order rather than status, a recent case heard by The Hague Court of Appeal is relevant for our discussion in that respect.[267] In this case the biological father had conceived his child during an extramarital affair with the mother. Following the breakdown of the relationship the mother had returned to her husband shortly before the child's birth. As the child was born during the marriage and the husband did not wish to deny

---

263 §1598a BGB.
264 Art. 1:377a(1) in conjunction with Art. 1:377f(1) DCC.
265 Hoge Raad, 12 November 2004, *NJ* 2005, p. 248.
266 See Chapter III and in particular ECtHR *Keegan v. Ireland*, Appl. No. 16969/90, 26 May 1994.
267 Gerechtshof 's-Gravenhage 10 May 2006, LJN: AY6451. See also: VONK (2007), p. 197.

paternity, the child became the legal child of both spouses, who had, incidentally, also made it clear during the proceedings that they would not ever inform the child of her origins. For its part, the court made it clear, however, that it did not consider this attitude to be indicative of good parenting. 'It may be expected of parents, putting the interest of the child first that they will tell the child who her or his biological father is and enable him or her to have contact with him in one way or another, the more so since the biological father has indicated that he does not mean to interfere with the parenting of the child'.[268]

In **Portugal**, the (presumptive) biological father has been able to lodge paternity proceedings, albeit only through the intervention of the Public Prosecutor, since 1966.[269] As such, prior to the 1974 Carnation Revolution, the ultra right-wing state had not yet been willing to attribute the mother and the child an independent right to challenge the husband's paternity. At the same time, it acknowledged a public interest in the prevalence of the genetic truth in matters of affiliation. As a result, only the biological father was given a conditioned right to challenge the husband's 'false' paternity. After the Carnation Revolution the position of the mother's and the child's position were strengthened,[270] but the biological father's right was preserved. The biological father can only challenge the husband's paternity through the intervention of the state. Thus, the Public Prosecutor assesses the importance of the biological truth in connection with the child's interests before the claim goes to court. In assessing the child's interests, the Public Prosecutor will also hear the mother and the husband.[271]

The time-limit within which the biological father must file his petition is unreasonably rigorous: there is no suitable dies a quo time-limit, but rather a mere sixty-day time-limit following the registration of the husband as the child's father.[272] In marked contrast, if the biological father is capable of substantiating his interest, he will be able to challenge paternity based on a recognition by an unmarried legal father at any time.[273]

---

268 Gerechtshof 's-Gravenhage 10 May 2006, LJN: AY6451. See also: VONK (2007), p. 197.

269 Art. 1839 PCC.

270 The institution has come under the critical scrutiny of the Supremo Tribunal on two occasions. Supremo Tribunal de Justiça, *Boletim do Ministério da Justiça*, 297 (1980), p. 233; Supremo Tribunal de Justiça, *Boletim do Ministério da Justiça*, 316 (1982), p. 133.

271 Art. 1841(3) PCC.

272 Art. 1841(2) PCC.

273 Art. 1859(2) PCC.

4.3. COMPARISON

In **France**, the biological father will become barred from enforcing his claim to paternity if there are indications that the child has civil status with respect to the legal father. Conversely, however, he may challenge paternity with considerable ease when in the absence of such a corresponding civil status relationship, even if the mother is (at least formally) married to the legal father.

In **Germany**, the position of the biological father in establishing paternity has been strengthened in recent years. Indicative of this is the recent recognition of a constitutional right to know one's progeny.[274] This right is nonetheless considered hierarchically inferior to the minor's right to informational self-determination, especially because the latter would also encompass a right not to know.

Since both the mother's husband and the man who recognised the child will more often than not have or have had 'factual responsibility' with respect to the child, his position will however often remain weak. The declaration under oath may be perceived as nothing more than a formal hurdle.

The **Dutch** courts have also come round to recognising that the biological father may exceptionally have a legitimate claim to challenge paternity, but, as in **Germany**, their approach has been more cautious when the mother is married to the legal father. Accordingly, this jurisdiction seems to depart from the idea that the mother's and the child's interests should be protected and cannot be seen in isolation from each other, while the right of the biological father may coincide. Thus, it has been found that the mother may under certain circumstances only give 'provisional' consent to a man other than the biological father to make a recognition. In **Portugal**, the biological father has for decades had a right to challenge an established paternity even if the mother is married, but this is not subject to short time-limits. Challenging the paternity of the unmarried socio-legal father is not bound by any time-limit or preliminary check by the state.

274 See Chapter IV.

Figure VII.5. The biological father's rights in challenging a socio-legally constructed paternity

	Husband's paternity	Unmarried parents
France	Yes, if no corresponding civil status	Yes, if no corresponding civil status
Germany	Not or very exceptionally	Yes, in the absence of a socio-familiar relationship for two years
The Netherlands	No, but possibly under Article 8 ECHR	Yes, in case of 'provisional' consent. Short, indefinite time-limit.
Portugal	Yes, by public intervention, within 60 days	Yes, as an interested party at any time

4.4. EVALUATION

From a parentage law perspective, it will often have to be determined on a case-to-case basis whether the biological father should be able to institute paternity proceedings. In any event, the principle of equality probably does not require a similar level of protection as the birthmother, given the different procreative roles. Furthermore, tokens of family life may have to be taken into account, both in respect of the mother's partner and the biological father himself. Yet the very problem for the biological father will often be that the mother and her partner may actively seek to exclude him from fulfilling any meaningful parental role.

On this difficult issue, the **German** legal scholar Rainer Frank has suggested that **English** law could be superior to the continental legal systems precisely because it is more flexible in allowing the biological father to interfere whenever the child's best interests so dictate in the individual case.[275] There are no time-limits as in most continental systems. Even so, it would appear that the imposition of a short time-limit following the child's birth may be preferable for the sake of the child's secure family environment. The preliminary assessment of the merits of the claim by the Public Ministry, as in **Portugal**, seems interesting but may create unnecessary obstacles for the biological father, when an independent court should also be able to settle the matter.

[275] FRANK (1999), p. 89.

The recognition of a father's ideological interest in establishing the truth at the German constitutional level is remarkable. In any event, that recognition goes well beyond what the ECtHR was willing to offer to the biological father in the *Nylund* case. It may be remembered that the applicant in that case also suggested that he was only interested in knowing whether he had fathered the child rather than seeking parental status and that his interests were essentially the same as the child's in that respect.[276]

It would appear that a 'doubting father's' prolonged state of uncertainty may cause some unrest and turmoil in his life. On the other hand, it may be seriously questioned whether that interest should have gained constitutional recognition in the first place. Could it, for example, also extend to an anonymous donor or to a rapist? Clearly the constitutional right would not have to be conceived of in such an absolute way, but even in respect of the 'meritorious' biological father some questions could be raised. For one thing, it appears that the father's own quest 'for the sake of being able to acquiesce in knowing the truth' is essentially different from the child's. Perhaps crucially, a parent may have a procreational responsibility to inform the child, but in the reverse this cannot be reasonably held.

Therefore, it would seem that the father will have much less of an interest in establishing the biological truth in filling important gaps in his own individual narrative identity than a child. If their rights are considered to be on an equal footing to the child's right, it may become all too easy for the father to claim that his interests in establishing the truth essentially coincide with the child's interests. It may accordingly not be excessive to state that a biological parent would then be put in a position to 'hijack' the child's constitutional right to decisional privacy from which the right to know derives.[277]

---

276 ECtHR *Nylund v. Finland*, Appl. No. 27110/95, 29 June 1999. See Chapter III.

277 See also Chapter V.

CHAPTER VIII
PROCEDURAL ISSUES IN PARENTAGE PROCEEDINGS

1. OUTLINE

In this Chapter a few procedural aspects of paternity proceedings shall be dealt with. Firstly, the breadth of judicial discretion in examining evidence shall be examined. With regard to issues concerning procedural evidence, we shall look into the question to which extent DNA testing may be ordered and the use of compulsion is permitted. In particular, it may be asked whether, in ordering testing, an infringement of a genetic parent's right to physical integrity and privacy is considered proportional. Clearly, this is an important legal question in discussing the enforcement of the child's right to know.

The imposition of compulsory testing perceptibly will not always meet individual informational needs, but a greater level of certainty may nonetheless have been contemplated. Accordingly, a court could, for example, on the basis of a refusal to co-operate also draw inferences against a man on the 'balance of probabilities' that he has fathered the child. Rather than extracting human tissue or DNA directly from the body, it may sometimes be taken from goods that the putative parent has taken hold of. In some other countries, compliance with a judicial order is sought through a system of (cumulative) fines.[1]

As far as ECHR law is concerned, in order to be effective, paternity proceedings will have to meet certain standards. The principle of proportionality requires that an independent authority be enabled to determine the paternity claim speedily.'[2] It is recalled that in *Jäggi*, although a *post mortem* case, the Strasbourg court affirmed that (DNA) testing was relatively unintrusive.[3] DNA testing is therefore clearly not only a permissible but also an effective way for states to

---

1 Compliance with a test through a system of cumulative fines is *inter alia* sought in **Italy** and **Austria**. FRANK (1997), p. 93-97.

2 ECtHR *Mikulic v. Croatia*, Appl. No. 53176/99, 7 February 2002, para. 64.

3 ECtHR *Jäggi v. Switzerland*, Appl. No. 58757/00, 13 July 2006, para. 41. See Chapter III.

meet their obligations under Article 8 ECHR. At the regional level, however, testing will not be the only way through which states may fulfil their obligations under the Convention in ensuring individuals have greater certainty on genetic origins.

In this Chapter, apart from these questions regarding the use of scientific evidence in parentage procedures, it will be examined to which extent preliminary evidence for instituting paternity proceedings is necessary. In **Germany**, the case law has insisted that preliminary evidence may be necessary notwithstanding sharp doctrinal criticism, but in **France** all such preliminary indications were deleted during the 2005 parentage law reform.

Specific attention shall subsequently be drawn to the procedural position of minors in parentage proceedings. In this sub-section, the use of scientific tests in respect of legally incapacitated persons, notably minors but also adults who are not fully able to comprehend or oversee the consequences of their actions, shall also be addressed.

Thereafter, the regulation of extra-judicial ways of obtaining evidence shall be discussed. Some European jurisdictions, in particular **Germany**, have in recent years become exposed to private paternity testing that foregoes direct judicial control. Internet publicity started to offer do-it-yourself kits at a fraction of the costs of a paternity test conducted on the basis of a court order since the beginning of the present century. From a legal viewpoint, it is not only significant that these tests escape direct judicial control. They warrant attention in particular because they enable parties to circumvent legal consent requirements, something which may be done, for example, by gathering hair or saliva from family members secretly. For such reasons, extra-judicial paternity tests have been considered a serious threat to the stability of the family unit. In particular, it has been considered that circumvention of consent requirements presents a threat to the minor's right to informational self-determination, which has been said to encompass not only a right to know, but also a right *not* to know.[4]

In order to provide a judicial alternative to these forms of testing, a new, 'isolated' procedure in **Germany** was created in April 2008. This procedure gives the claimant an enforceable court order to have the genetic link verified at a private laboratory. As a more general aim, this procedural possibility was opened up to promote the effectiveness of both the child's right to know and the (parental)

---

[4] ZUCK (2005), p. 119.

right to know one's progeny.[5] It therefore draws a distinction between the informational needs of family members on the one hand, and their legal relationships, on the other. As a result, distinct informational and 'ordinary' status procedures now co-exist in **Germany**.

2. EVIDENCE

2.1. OVERVIEW

In **France**, a court will in principle only examine, in accordance with general principles of civil procedure, whatever the parties have on their own initiative submitted for judicial enquiry.[6] **French** courts may now already order a parentage test at the preliminary stage of proceedings so as to ascertain the viability of the claim.[7] The Cour de Cassation has considered that insisting upon the use of scientific tests in paternity proceedings is indeed lawful, even though it is of the opinion that the co-operation of parties may not be enforced against their will.[8] Remarkably, however, in 2007 it ruled in a case involving a denial of a husband's paternity that a court order to that effect was obligatory and that the court, not being able to avail itself of a discretion to draw inferences, should therefore have insisted upon a DNA test.[9] Recently, the Cour de Cassation has also affirmed that a court order should in principle be used unless (an otherwise unspecified) legitimate reason is advanced to the contrary.[10]

This latter case drew on the 2005 parentage law reform, which lifted the requirement of 'serious' preliminary indications of non-paternity in proceedings in-

---

5 *Das Recht auf Kenntnis der eigenen Vaterschaft* = the right to know one's own (biological) fatherhood. In a conceptually potentially more bracing view, also referred to as *Das Recht auf Kenntnis des eigenen Nachwuchses* = the right to know one's own *progeny*, offspring or children. This constitutional right has been based on §1686 BGB (parental right with respect to the other parent concerning information on the child) and Art. 2 I in conjunction with Art. 1 I Federal Constitution = Grundgesetz (GG). Federal Constitutional Court = Bundesverfassungsgericht (BVerfG), 13 February 2007, *FamRZ* 2007, p. 441.

6 Art. 7(1) New **French** Civil Procedure Code.

7 Art. 145 New **French** Civil Procedure Code; Cass.civ. 1st Chamber, 4 May 1994, Bull.civ.I, n. 159, 117.

8 Cass. civ. 1, D.2000, 731, annotated by Th. Garé.

9 Cass. civ. Ire., 6 March 2007, *RTD* 2007, p. 762, obs. J. Hauser.

10 Cass. ass. plén., 23 November 2007, No. 05-17.975, Juris-Data No. 041612.

volving a denial.[11] Procedural constraints have therefore become less strict as proceedings have further opened up possibilities to use DNA testing.

Since 1994, the study of the genetic characteristics of a person for purposes other than medical or scientific reasons, or without having obtained the person's prior consent pursuant to the conditions set out under Articles 16-10 of the **French** Code Civil, has been made liable to one year's imprisonment and fines, which may currently be as high as €15, 000.[12] The same criminal law penalties may be imposed for the identification of a person through her or his genetic features for medical or scientific research purposes when the person's prior consent has not been previously obtained pursuant to the conditions of Article 16-11 of the **French** Code Civil.[13] Furthermore, the identification of a (civilian) person on the basis of his DNA profile for purposes which are neither medical nor scientific, or other than in an inquiry or investigation made in the course of judicial proceedings, may also be punished by one year's imprisonment and a fine of €15,000.[14] Accordingly, both a court order and the informed consent of the persons are therefore required for testing.

In **Germany**, the discretion of the courts in deciding which evidence submitted by parties they wish to admit or discard is unlimited.[15] Once paternity has been successfully denied, the court may only take into account facts that have been subsequently submitted by parties if they speak against the denial.[16]

In proceedings geared towards the disclosure of the biological father's name,[17] the children may in principle compel their mother to disclose the father's name before the court.[18] A mother may also in principle be forced to disclose the name of the biological father to the man who has successfully denied paternity in order to enable him to reclaim damages and child support.[19] The **German** court may make a final decision on the basis of the results of the scientific test.[20] In

11 So-called *'indices graves'*.

12 Art. 226-25 **French** Criminal Law Code.

13 Art. 226-27 **French** Criminal Law Code.

14 Art. 226-28 **French** Criminal Law Code.

15 *Kindschaftsache.*

16 §640d ZPO; BORTH/MUSIELAK, §640d **German** Civil Procedure Code, Rdnr.1; Federal Supreme Court = Bundesgerichtshof (BGH), 7 April 1998, *FamRZ* 1998, p. 955.

17 See Chapter IV.

18 See Chapter IV.

19 See Chapter IV.

20 HELMS (1999), 21. BGH, *FamRZ* 1987, p. 583-584; HUMMEL & MUTSCHLER (1991), p. 2929-2930.

denial proceedings, a court may require that the father substantiate his 'preliminary suspicion' that the genetic link is missing.[21] Predictably, this requirement has proven to be a considerable procedural hurdle for some men: mere physical dissimilarity to the child[22] and even scientific proof of infertility have, for example, not been accepted.[23]

There is a general duty under **German** law to undergo physical examinations in parentage proceedings except in the case of health risks.[24] Accordingly, even the risk of disclosing consanguineous or incestuous blood links will in principle not detract from the force of this obligation.[25] The use of compulsory testing is not uncontroversial in view of its legislative history which originates in the national-socialist period.[26] Ever since, the obligatory character of testing has extended to situations in which a person's parentage may only be indirectly at issue, for example, in respect of an inheritance or a child maintenance claim.[27] In principle an unlimited number of (third) persons may fall under the obligation to undergo a physical examination.[28] But only if a person has refused to undergo testing, will physical compulsion be used to promote compliance.[29]

That said, the admission of physical compulsion is believed to have imbued **German** civil procedural law with a certain rigour which sets it apart from many other European legal systems. In that regard, compulsory testing is seen as a key indication that the **German** legislator is prepared to go to great lengths in order to establish the biological truth.[30] It means that **German** law is apparently willing, if required, to sacrifice the right to physical integrity to the right to know.[31]

---

21 ROTH-STIELOW (1988), p. 358; KIRCHMEIER (2002), p. 372.

22 Bundesgerichtshof (BGH), *FamRZ* 2005, p. 342-343.

23 OLG Celle, 29 October 2003, *NJW* 2004, 449= *FamRZ* 2004, p. 481.

24 §372a II ZPO (*Duldungspflicht*).

25 HELMS (1999), p. 207-208; Regional Court of Appeal of North Rhine-Westphalia = Oberlandesgericht (OLG) Hamm, 19 August 1992, *FamRZ* 1993, p. 76-77.

26 FRANK (1995), p. 977.

27 DAMRAU/MÜNCHENER KOMM (2000), BGB, Rdnr. 108.

28 Thus, in a renowned case from Münster four putative fathers had to undergo testing because the mother could not name the father to the child, a duty inferred from §1618a BGB ('mutual care between parents and children') as interpreted on the basis of the constitutional personality right. Regional Court (Landsgericht) of Münster, 21 February 1990, *FamRZ* 1990, p. 1031. See Chapter IV.

29 WANITZEK (2002), p. 398.

30 HELMS (1999), p. 198.

31 Art. 2 Federal Constitutional Constitution = Grundgesetz (GG).

For the procedure involving a denial of paternity, some preliminary factual indications of non-paternity will be required.[32] In that connection, the Federal Supreme Court has held that indications must be present which, viewed as objective facts, give rise to doubts as to the person's biological descent.[33] This insistence upon an 'preliminary suspicion'[34] has been considered indispensable in order to prevent cavalier or vindictive claims by third parties. Furthermore, this 'preliminary suspicion' of non-paternity has been justified on the basis of the personality right and the corporal integrity of the respondent or third party (i.e. mother or child).[35] Such insistence on preliminary indications is virtually unknown elsewhere in Europe.[36]

In **the Netherlands**, it is a general principle of civil procedural law that the court has unlimited discretion to assess the evidence as submitted by the parties.[37] For that reason, the **Dutch** law of civil procedure offers discretion to the courts to order DNA-based parentage tests, which fall within the category of 'scientific tests' and may be ordered in civil procedure as evidence.[38]

The **Dutch** courts are, however, not under an obligation to order that scientific tests be conducted in paternity proceedings. Courts may also waive their discretion to order a DNA test. There is, accordingly, no specific provision on the basis of which the putative father may be forced to undergo testing. Confronted with a man's refusal to co-operate, a **Dutch** court will be able to rely on the possibility to draw adverse inferences against him and establish his paternity.[39]

---

32 '*Tatsächliche, hinreichende Anhaltspunkte*', BGH, 22 April 1998, *FamRZ* 1998, p. 955.

33 Federal Supreme Court = Bundesgerichtshof, BGH 22 April 1998, *FamRZ* 1998, p. 955. However, it is not required that parties specify the circumstances which render the illegitimate status of the child probable.

34 *Anfangsverdacht.*

35 JACOBI (2005), p. 74. He holds, however, that this argument cannot prevail as the putative father will generally find himself in a predicament in finding preliminary factual indications and departing from a position of informational deficiency with regard to the mother.

36 At the 8th Regensburg Conference for European Family Law entitled '*Der Streit um die Abstammung*' ('The struggle over parentage') on 12-14 October 2006, not one of the legal experts from the twelve represented jurisdictions could mention a comparable legal institution in paternity proceedings. SPICKHOFF, SCHWAB, HENRICH, GOTTWALD (2007).

37 Art. 182 in conjunction with Art. 221 of the **Dutch** Civil Procedure Code.

38 Art. 150 in conjunction with Art. 194(1) DCC: *deskundigenberichten.* See also: Hoge Raad, 12 June 1953, *NJ* 1954, p. 61.

39 Hoge Raad, 22 September 2000, *NJ* 2001, p. 647; Hoge Raad, 22 December 2006, LJN: AZ 4163.

It has been held that a refusal to co-operate incurs civil liability under **Dutch** tort law.[40] Not co-operating with a court order would in that view be a violation of a right and an act or omission breaching a duty imposed by law or a rule of unwritten law pertaining to proper social conduct.[41] In 2007, the Leeuwarden Court of Appeal denied a daughter such a civil damages claim in a case involving a refusal by a legal father, who denied that he was the daughter's biological father, to undergo a DNA test.[42] It was held by the court that the child would then have to adduce concrete facts and circumstances that the man could have conceived the child.

De Boer suggests that a system of fines or physical compulsion could be used, especially if a child is first and foremost concerned with obtaining scientific certainty as to the father's identity.[43] Speculating that **Dutch** tort law may be relevant on this point, Voorhoeve drew an analogy with a case heard by the **Dutch** Supreme Court in 1993 in which the court conceded that the refusal of a rapist's consent to an HIV test had breached tort law.[44] Although the **Dutch** Supreme Court had been aware that the violation of corporal integrity[45] implicated in HIV testing would not altogether exclude the possibility that the woman would be infected, the court nonetheless ordered a blood sample from the rapist. In view of the fact that paternity testing based on DNA generally does provide certainty while requiring a much less invasive interference with the presumptive parent's physical integrity than an HIV blood test, Voorhoeve holds that tort should apply by analogy in respect of a man refusing to undergo testing. Van Raak-Kuiper also considers the minimal physical interference involved in DNA testing to be proportional in the light of the weight that the child's right to information carries.[46] But in her view the evidence would have to be used in a subsidiary way: if DNA can be obtained from the man without interfering directly with his physical integrity, this path would be preferable.[47] Not without a sense for bizarre court spectacles, Voorhoeve suggests that the saliva found on the coffee cup from which a man had drunk during the court session can then

40 VOORHOEVE (2008), p. 50-51.
41 Art. 3:296 in conjunction with Art. 6:162 DCC.
42 Gerechtshof Leeuwarden, 20 June 2007, LJN:BA 7894.
43 ASSER-DE BOER (2006), No. 738, p. 591.
44 Hoge Raad, 12 June 1993, *NJ* 1994, p. 347.
45 Art. 11 **Dutch** Constitution.
46 RAAK-KUIPER (2007), p. 193.
47 RAAK-KUIPER (2007). p. 193.

be used as a sample.[48] In this way, principled respect for the man's right to physical integrity would be ensured.

In **Portugal,** too, family courts in principle enjoy unlimited discretion in deciding on the admissibility of evidence that has been submitted by parties in conformity with the general principle of civil procedure.[49] In parentage disputes, there is an express legal basis permitting, but not prescribing, the use of blood samples and 'other' scientific methods, including DNA tests, in parentage proceedings.[50]

The **Portuguese** National Institute of Legal Medicine[51] has at its disposal a scientific committee of experts in bio-technology that carry out genetic tests if there is a basis in court orders in affiliation and criminal matters. On the basis of her remarkable longitudinal research of paternity suits in a court over several decades in the Minho region, the legal sociologist Ferreira Machado concludes that there remains considerable reticence among the judiciary to avail themselves of scientific methods, whatever their accuracy. Rather, as an alternative, it would still not be uncommon for women to be asked probing questions about their sexual history. Moreover, the ordering of tests would be guided by the socio-economic status of both applicants and respondents in judicial determinations of paternity. Even so, as from the mid-1990s, however, the use of scientific methods in DNA testing has steadily increased and become more generalized in the Minho region, which is known for being more conservative than other **Portuguese** regions.[52]

No doctrinal consensus exists in **Portugal** as to whether a person is under a statutory obligation to undergo testing. It is generally assumed that in principle persons can be required to co-operate as much as possible in civil procedure in order to facilitate the establishment of truth.[53] Nonetheless, in the absence of affirmative evidence in the case law, it is rather more circumspect whether a man who persistently refuses to comply should be coerced to undergo testing in view of the implications for his constitutional right to corporal integrity.[54] This latter right, deduced from Article 32 of the **Portuguese** Constitution, generally

---

48 VOORHOEVE (2008), p. 54. Although she recognises that it may then still be factually possible for the man to say that the DNA found on the coffee cup was not actually his.

49 Art. 163 **Portuguese** Civil Procedural Code.

50 Art. 1801 PCC.

51 Instituto de Medicina Legal.

52 FERREIRA MACHADO (2003), p. 378.

53 Art. 519(1) **Portuguese** Civil Procedure Code.

54 Responses of the **Portuguese** Government to the *Questionnaire on Access to Genetic Information not related to Health.*

prohibits any compulsion and a violation of the person's moral and physical integrity.

Nonetheless, in **Portugal** a refusal to comply with a test order need not delay proceedings either. Thus, a putative father's 'right' to refuse to undergo testing will also allow the court to establish paternity on the basis of inferences drawn against him.[55] Moreover, if he does not co-operate or fails to appear in court, the burden of proof will be on him to prove that he is not the biological father.[56] In this way, compliance is also sought.

2.2. COMPARISON

In respect of paternity suits none of the four jurisdictions derogate from the general principle of civil procedure that courts should be free to assess the evidence submitted by parties and to decide accordingly in paternity proceedings. In all jurisdictions, DNA testing is admitted with a view to establishing paternity. As has become clear, courts are nonetheless prepared to assume 'guessing competence' in **France, the Netherlands** and **Portugal**. A court's conviction is therefore considered an efficacious and adequate alternative to a scientist's DNA examination.

Clearly, the child will in this way generally have a sufficiently good reason to believe who her or his biological father is on the basis of such a refusal. At the same time, it is manifest that this will fall short of providing a scientifically accurate and conclusive answer.

In **Germany** the courts do compel parties to undergo parentage testing against their will. Moreover, it has been established that a mother may also be held under a duty to disclose the biological father's name by both the child and the former legal father. Only **German** law insists upon preliminary evidence tantamount to constituting an 'preliminary suspicion' with a view to testing.

---

55 Art. 519(2) **Portuguese** Civil Procedural Code.

56 Art. 344(2) **Portuguese** Civil Procedural Code. See also: Acórdão do Tribunal da Relação do Porto, Acórdão 0631059, 27 April 2006.

Figure VIII.1. Key procedural aspects of paternity proceedings

Paternity testing on presumptive fathers *in vivo*	Must there be preliminary indications of non-paternity to deny paternity?	Is the court under a duty to order scientific methods to establish paternity?	May the putative father be forced to undergo testing upon refusal?	If the putative father refuses to undergo testing, may his paternity still be established?
France	No	No	No	Yes
Germany	Yes	Yes	Yes	Yes
The Netherlands	No	No	No	Yes
Portugal	No	No	No	Yes

2.3. EVALUATION

Scientifically reliable methods, such as DNA tests, will generally provide a proportional measure to establish the genetic parent-child relationship. If scientific accuracy is taken as the supreme legal value, a statutory obligation to undergo DNA testing with a view to a judicial determination of paternity appears indicated. If paternity is only being denied, DNA testing may generally also be indicated, but the protection of the established legal parent-child relationship may then involve a different assessment. This could mean that a court order can only make use of the test within the statutory time-limits with a view to absolving the father from his parental responsibilities.[57] That said, however, outside these time-limits for status proceedings, an ideological interest in verifying the genetic link of the legal father may still very well be present.

If the viewpoint is accepted that truth finding in parentage proceedings requires scientific accuracy, DNA testing will be preferable to drawing inferences on the 'balance of probabilities'.[58] Given the minimal interference with the right to physical integrity, it may be considered proportional to the child's right to information. The right to corporal integrity of the putative parent may, more-

---

57 See Chapter VII.

58 The 'balance of probabilities' is, for example, the standard civil test for ascertaining paternity under **English** law. See; *Re H (Minors) (Sexual Abuse: Standard of Proof)* [1996] AC 563. According to Lord Reid in *S v S, W v. Official Solicitor* (or W) [1972] AC 24 at 41 this means that even weak evidence must prevail if there is no other evidence to counterbalance it. See also: LOWE (2007), in: SPICKHOFF, SCHWAB, HENRICH, GOTTWALD (eds.) (2007), p. 331.

over, be inherently subordinate to the right to know if the principle of procreational responsibility is taken as a rather absolute value. If this is accepted, then, biological parents should generally be required to tolerate a minimal interference with their right to corporal integrity and their right to privacy. This right to privacy they may have partly forfeited, because they have an enduring responsibility for having (pro)created the child.

It is conceivable that in a solely informational procedure there could be fewer objections to testing. In that respect, it may be questioned whether inferences are a sufficient procedural remedy since the object of such a procedure would be to establish the 'truth' about a person's genetic descent. If genetic descent cannot be established in this way anyway, because the exercise of compulsion is impossible, there may be little reason to have such a separate procedure, even though it is open to debate whether absolute DNA certainty is required in meeting the informational needs of individuals. Having said that, it is precisely because status determination will not be as imminent, that the putative parent may generally also feel much less inclined not to abide with a test order because in principle he will not subsequently be considered the legal parent if the proceedings are lodged outside the statutory time-limits for legal parentage proceedings.

As a matter of fact, status proceedings in ordinary parentage law will continue to provide the main legal avenue through which genetic descent will have be verified in the vast majority of jurisdictions. It is unlikely that many jurisdictions will consider adopting an exclusively informational procedure.

Because parentage law is not exclusively concerned with the biological truth, however, there may also be less incentive for legislators to insist rigorously on a scientifically accurate outcome. It is remembered that a presumption already suffices, for example, when the mother is married to the father in most jurisdictions.[59] Arguably, therefore, inferences drawn against the presumptive father will also typically ensure a satisfactory level of certainty. Against a litigious background, the level of certainty may often go well beyond that which most persons, who have not found any reason to call into question the veracity of their genetic parentage, generally have, i.e. a strong probability. Conversely, a persistent refusal of a man to undergo testing will generally be a sufficient indication that the man is almost certainly the genetic father in a judicial determination of paternity. The general conclusion must be that a father will typically have little to fear from testing, especially if parental status determination is not

59 SCHWENZER (2007), p. 7. See Chapter VII.

at stake. Exceptionally, though, a man will not only wish to avoid status determination by refusing to undergo testing, but could also have some ethical or religious objections to testing. In such cases, the child may have to be content with a diminished degree of certainty.

As an alternative to drawing inferences and compulsory testing, a system of cumulative fines for refusing to co-operate may also ensure greater compliance. On the other hand, the imposition of an essentially punitive measure, such as a fine, while respecting a person's right to physical integrity or, exceptionally, religious objections to testing may be seen as inconsistent.

Since countervailing interests may not be ruled out altogether, adherence to a principle of subsidiarity in respect of DNA testing may still be preferable to rigorous insistence upon compulsion. If scientific evidence can, for example, be obtained on the basis of saliva found on a letter or a hair taken from a comb without requiring direct extraction from the human body, this path may be preferable. The right to physical integrity cannot really be said to have been infringed if DNA had already been separated from the body. Consequently, in this scenario the 'inner core' of a countervailing human right to physical integrity will be left 'untouched', while the right to information will generally be possible to effectuate. Even without any direct interference with a person's body, however, the use of DNA may be said to engage the presumptive parent's right to privacy. In the author's view the restriction of the parent's privacy would generally have to be considered acceptable in view of the parent's procreational responsibility, however.

3. MINORS AND LEGALLY INCAPACITATED ADULTS

3.1. RELEVANT LAW

In **France,** only minors formally have standing in a judicial determination of paternity, even though during minority the mother will be the child's legal representative.[60] If the (birth) mother has died or had given birth anonymously, a guardian especially appointed by the court may represent the minor. In view of its highly personal character, the general view is that, in accordance with the basic rules on genetic testing on individuals, consent to testing must always have

[60] Art. 328(1) **French** Code Civil.

been given by the person involved. This also applies in respect of all minors and legally incapacitated adults, unless they suffer from a certified mental incapacity and are unable for this reason to provide informed consent.[61]

In **Germany**, paternity proceedings fall within the category of child-parent status and parental authority procedures.'[62] This category does not only incorporate judicial decisions on parental authority, but also on the (non-) existence of a child-parent relationship. In procedures involving a denial of paternity, all parties, regardless of their legal capacity, have standing before the court.[63] If the person is legally incapacitated, such as a minor, for example, a legal representative will pursue her or his procedural interests and decide on consent.[64] If a child lodges proceedings against the father or *vice versa* the mother must always be summoned to appear before the court as well, whether she exercises parental authority or not.[65] If she also has parental authority over the concerned minor, she will become a party to the proceedings *qua* the legal representative of the minor, too. In case the mother or the child dies prior to the end of the proceedings, the surviving party may continue the proceedings.[66] For minors, the mother, having parental authority, must give consent to testing, even though compulsion may eventually be used against the minor. Notably, compulsory testing may, in accordance with the general rule, also be used against a legally incapacitated person.[67]

---

61 Art. 16-11 **French** Code Civil. Responses of the **French** Government to the *Questionnaire on Access to Genetic Information not related to Health*, CDCJ 2005 [cdcj/docs 2005/cdcj (2005) 9 bil].

62 *Kindschaftsachen.* §640(2) Zivilprozessordnung (ZPO) = **German** Civil Procedural Code.

63 §640b(1) **German** Civil Procedural Code, BORTH/MUSIELAK (2007), §640b ZPO, Rdnr. 3.

64 §640b(2) **German** Civil Procedural Code.

65 §640e in conjunction with §53a **German** Civil Procedural Code; WIESER(1998), p. 2023-2024; WANITZEK (2002), p. 400.

66 §640g **German** Civil Procedural Code = Zivilprozessordnung (ZPO).

67 §372a **German** Civil Procedural Code = Zivilprozessordnung (ZPO). Regional Court of Appeal = Oberlandesgericht (OLG) Hamm.22 March 1991, *FamRZ* 1991, p. 229 On behalf of a four-year old minor the Jugendamt had lodged proceedings under §1618a BGB against a mother, a worker at a psychiatric hospital, to compel her to disclose the identity of the father. The court found three reasons to deny the claim. First, it was considered that the child protection authority (Jugendamt) lacked standing in view of the highly personal nature of the child's right to know. Furthermore, it was deemed more appropriate if the child enforced this right once it would achieve a certain emotional maturity. Third, it was found that the mother exceptionally had a legitimate reason to withhold the information because of her profession as a nurse in a psychiatric hospital, as she believed the father was a patient with whom she had had sexual relations.

In **the Netherlands**, since 1998, an independent special guardian is appointed by the court in parentage proceedings to represent the interests of the minor.[68] The fact that this person will generally be a family lawyer or a representative of the Child Protection Board has been criticised as it would not contribute significantly to creating an independent procedure.[69] In response to this criticism it has been suggested that the minor should him/herself be able to request the appointment of the special guardian in parentage proceedings.[70] For minors under the age of twelve, only the consent of the adults with parental authority will be required.[71] The minor under the age of twelve should, however, in principle always be informed of the treatment.[72] For minors between the age of twelve and sixteen, in addition, the minor's own consent will be required.[73] A legally incapable person will have to be represented by a guardian in court.[74] It has also been suggested, however, that in view of the eminently personal nature of DNA testing, only he should be capable of giving consent.[75]

In **Portugal,** the legal representatives of the minor, also in parentage disputes, are the adult(s) who has or have parental authority over him or her.[76] In case of a serious conflict between both parents, the court may limit their capacity to represent the minor and instead appoint a guardian.[77] The consent to a paternity test should be obtained from the minor him/herself from the age of fourteen. If such consent was not obtained, this will constitute a criminal offence by the medical practitioner or laboratory.[78] The consent of a legally incapacitated parent to have a test conducted must be obtained from his legal representative.[79]

---

68 Art. 1:212 DCC.

69 Steketee, Lunneman, & Overgaag (2004), p. 181.

70 Vlaardingerbroek (2001), p. 101-107.

71 Art. 7:446 DCC. Heida (2003), p. 176-177.

72 Art. 7:448 DCC. Heida (2003), p. 178, suggests that the non-disclosure of the results of the paternity test may therefore 'sometimes be the right way to proceed'. To the author, it would appear that this information should at least not be withheld from the persons with parental authority subsequent to testing.

73 Art. 7:447 DCC. Heida (2003), p. 176-177.

74 Responses of the **Dutch** Government to the *Questionnaire on Access to Genetic Information not related to Health.*

75 Heida (2003), p. 180.

76 Art. 1905 in conjunction with Art. 1906 PCC.

77 Art. 1900 in conjunction with Art. 1901 PCC.

78 Art. 156 **Portuguese** Penal Code.

79 Responses of the **Portuguese** Government to the *Questionnaire on Access to Genetic Information not related to Health.*

3.2. COMPARISON AND EVALUATION

The jurisdictions display broadly similar features, notwithstanding minor differences in the representation of minors and with regard to the age from which their consent to testing must be obtained. Only in **Germany** will minors and legally incapacitated adults, in principle just like any other person, also be forced to undergo parentage testing. Whatever the real extent of their capacity to oversee the consequences of their behaviour and decisions, the consent of both minors and legally incapacitated adults is otherwise sought inasmuch as this is possible. This essentially means that a level of legal protection is sought commensurate with their level of autonomy, within the meaning of decisional privacy.

4. ENFORCEMENT OUTSIDE THE COURTS

4.1 EXTRAJUDICIAL PARENTAGE TESTS

It is recalled that in **France** all forms of genetic testing on individuals are subject to consent requirements of those involved. Without consent, genetic testing is subject to criminal sanctions.[80] Accordingly, this regime leaves little room for the admissibility of extrajudicial evidence in which consent had not been obtained previously by all of the parties concerned. Notwithstanding this prohibitive regime, Internet searches will reveal that a considerable number of private laboratories offer extrajudicial tests, some of which will conduct testing without evidence of consent. Since these laboratories appear to be able to pursue their commercial activities outside the public eye, there appears to be a considerable gap between the *law in the books* and the *law in action* here.

In **Germany**, private laboratories and pharmacies started offering expedient and cheap alternatives to judicial paternity tests from around the year 2000.[81] Offering their services primarily on the Internet, these companies 'callously' started commercial campaigns in places as prosaic and mundane as the Berlin and Cologne underground and supermarkets, thereby provoking widespread media coverage.[82]

---

80 See above. Art. 226-25 **French** Criminal Law Code.

81 In 2005, around 15,000 men made use of these tests in **Germany**. Source: JACOBI (2005), p. 86. RITTNER & RITTNER (2005), p. 187, who estimate that 50,000 extrajudicial paternity tests are conducted per annum.

82 For example, KAHLWEIT, '*Das Recht der Kuckuckskinder*', *SZ*, 19 and 20 July 2003, p. 4.

In 2003, the first significant case arose before the regional Bavarian court, although it was primarily concerned with the ethics of the publicity campaign.[83] The claimant was an advertising company that had lodged proceedings against a private laboratory on the ground of breach of contract consisting of a violation of unwritten moral codes of good commercial practice.[84] The Bavarian court framed the legal issues in another way, however, by stating that the disruptive effect on the family or the harm to the child's interests would typically be less serious than in a court setting; rather, the court suggested that if genetic descent could be ascertained outside court, this could often be a serene solution.[85]

In response to the considerable media outcry that followed over the Bavarian decision, the Federal Minister of Justice Zypries announced that all extrajudicial forms of testing would have to be prohibited and (presumably, male) perpetrators would be sentenced to terms of imprisonment for up to four years.[86] In an interview with *Der Spiegel*, Zypries argued on the basis of the supposed data protection and privacy rights of the mother rather than on the basis of the personality right of the child.[87] As a side-effect, the debate became further charged with genderised ideas.

In 2003, two factually similar cases arose before the Regional Courts of Appeal of Thuringia[88] and Lower Saxony.[89] Whereas in the former case the man had not lodged paternity proceedings, in the latter case resort had been had to an extra-judicial test only after his first denial of paternity had been deemed inadmissible because the 'initial suspicion' of non-paternity was considered insufficiently persuasive. Both courts affirmed that, in overstepping the minor's consent (through the mother), the evidence had been gathered illicitly. Even though the tests had unequivocally excluded that they were genetically linked, the evidence was not admitted as it had been obtained unlawfully.[90]

83 Regional Court of Munich = Landesgericht (LG) München, 22 May 2003, *FamRZ* 2003, p. 1580.
84 §1 of the **German** Act Against Unfair Competition = Gesetz gegen den unlauteren Wettbewerb (UWG).
85 SPICKHOFF & DEUTSCH (2003), p. 1581-1582, who also subscribe to the view that extrajudicial testing should not be criminalised or prohibited but that it should be permissible under the same conditions as tests ordered by courts (time-limits; admissibility grounds; consent).
86 Radio interview by DLF with Ms Brigitte Zypries, 19 January 2004, www.dradio.de/dlf/227888.
87 *Der Spiegel* 2/2005, p. 58.
88 Thuringia Regional Court of Appeal (Jena), 6 March 2003, *FPR* 2003, p. 375-376.
89 Lower Saxony Regional Court of Appeal (Celle), 29 October 2003, *NJW* 2004, 449 = *FamRZ* 2004, p. 481.
90 Thuringia Regional Court of Appeal (Jena), 6 March 2003, *FPR* 2003, p. 375-376.

Subsequently, these two cases were reviewed by the Federal Supreme Court.[91] The court drew particular attention to the minor's right to informational self-determination, this being a derivative of her or his constitutional personality right.[92] Thus, it was considered that a refusal by the mother – *qua* the legal representative of the minor – did not give rise to an obligation to disclose against the will of the minor. The court denounced the men's argument that their right coincided with the minor's constitutional right. At the same time, the court followed the men's argument that a mother's refusal to be open about the child's genetic descent could mean that sexual infidelity could be rewarded with the mother remaining comfortably in a position to pursue her (allegedly) 'exceedingly selfish' interests in receiving child maintenance.[93] Even though this might have been an objection, the court considered that the men had failed to appreciate that the child's right to know also encompassed a right *not* to know.[94] In obtaining the DNA evidence without having obtained consent from the mother, it was argued that the men had infringed the minor's constitutional rights.

Perhaps partly out of sympathy, the court acknowledged that 'fathers' could also have an informational need, while having regard to the child's right *not* to know, it could not be considered to represent a higher constitutional value.[95] For the court, the subordinate character of the father's right in relation to the child's could be appreciated on the basis of the fact that the father's right to deny paternity was subject to shorter time-limits.[96] Even though the child's right to *deny* paternity was also subject to a *dies a quo* time-limit, there was, in contrast, no time bar for lodging proceedings involving a judicial determination.[97] On the basis of this analysis of the relevant time-limits, the court therefore considered the child's right not only to be different, but also to essentially outrank that of the father.

---

91 Federal Supreme Court = Bundesgerichtshof (BGB), 12 January 2005, XII ZR 227/03 (referred by the Regional Court of Appeal of Celle), *NJW* 2005, 497; Federal Supreme Court = Bundesgerichtshof (BGH), 12 January 2005, XII ZR 60/03 (referred by the Thuringia Regional Court of Appeal in Jena).

92 Although the court based this right also on Art. 5 of the UNESCO Universal Declaration of the Human Genome and Human Rights, Art. II-68 of the European Constitution, Art. 8 ECHR and on Arts. 8 I and 16 of the UNCRC.

93 *Höchst egoistische Eigeninteressen der Mutter.*

94 BOHNERT (2002), p. 389.

95 Federal Supreme Court = Bundesgerichtshof (BGH), 20 January 1999, *NJW* 1999, 1632 = *FamRZ* 1999, p. 716.

96 §1600b BGB.

97 RITTNER & RITTNER (2002), p. 1745-1749.

The court framed the cases as a clash between individual constitutional rights. In so doing, it did not mention a possible interest in the stability of family life, even though this interest had received express recognition in its 1989 landmark decision, though already then not to the point of prevailing over the adult child's informational right.[98] This omission was subsequently criticised, notably in view of concerns over the constitutional interpretation of civil law and the risk that one right would be given too much absolute weight.[99] For other reasons, too, the decisions of the Federal Supreme Court on extrajudicial tests received criticism from legal scholars. This mostly concerned the perceived tension between the imposition of short procedural time-limits to institute proceedings in respect of the father, while requiring him to substantiate an 'initial suspicion' of non-paternity before being able to commence proceedings.[100]

Nonetheless, the general view has accepted that 'motherless' evidence should not be accepted in a subsequent paternity procedure.[101] On this issue, Mutschler has stated that the withdrawal of the mother's consent to an extrajudicial test should be seen as a sufficiently persuasive 'preliminary suspicion' if the man had already given her reassurances that he is willing to pay for the test.[102] The mother would then at least not have a financial reason not to go along with testing. Further, Rauscher holds that if a man had first told the mother about his intentions with regard to testing, he should be able, upon her refusal, to simply proceed without having gotten her consent.[103]

As a final point on **German** law on the issue, the relevance of data protection law for the issue is considered marginal. Thus, the scope of the Federal Data Protection Act extends *ratione materiae* to the processing of personal – such as

98 Art. 6(1) Federal Constitution = Grundgesetz (GG). Federal Constitutional Court = Bundesverfassungsgericht (BVerfG), 31 January 1989, *JZ* 1989, p. 335-336.

99 SPICKHOFF (2007), p. 42, in: SPICKHOFF, SCHWAB, HENRICH, GOTTWALD (eds.) (2007).

100 WELLENHOFER (2005), p. 665; KNOCHE (2005), p. 348; WOLF (2005), p. 2417-2418; MUSCHELER (2005), p. 185.

101 RITTNER & RITTNER (2002), p. 1747-1751; WOLF (2005), p. 2419; see also the *Richtlinien der Bundesärztekammer und des Robert Koch-Instituts für die Erstattung von Abstammungsgutachten, Deutsches Ärzteblatt* 2002, 541 (Guidelines of the Federal Chamber of the Medical Profession), which do not expressly denounce extrajudicial forms of testing as such, but emphasise that the need for informed consent of all the persons concerned should not be detracted from.

102 MUTSCHLER (2003), p. 96.

103 RAUSCHER/STAUDINGER (2004), BGB, Intro. §1589, No. 143b, 46.

genetic – information through not only public, but also private bodies.[104] However, federal data protection law permits the use of personal information by private bodies 'for exclusively personal or family activities'.[105]

In **the Netherlands**, for the little doctrinal debate that there has been on the issue, most of it has revolved around the question whether tests, in general, fall within the ambit of **Dutch** medical legislation.[106] The dominant view is that for minors under 12 years of age the consent of those exercising parental authority (usually either both parents or one of them[107]) will be required.[108] In the absence of distinct rules, this regime is no different in the case of an extrajudicial test.

The **Dutch** Data Protection Act from 2001 is brought into connection with the issue of gathering evidence in a 'motherless' paternity test.[109] The **Dutch** personal data protection authority[110] considers that information on genetic fatherhood as gathered by DNA tests cannot be defined as personal data worthy of legal protection within the ambit of the **Dutch** Civil Code. Even so, the **Dutch** personal data protection authority has advised that commercial laboratories should provide adequate information to the parties concerned and to require the informed consent of all parties beforehand, therefore clearly including also that of the mother.

Furthermore, the **Dutch** personal data protection authority holds that any non-consensual processing of personal data will violate requirements of due and adequate notification of the parties that a paternity test will be conducted.[111] In principle one parent may give consent on behalf of the minor if the other parent has not expressed objections.[112] For the purpose of determining parentage through an extrajudicial test, however, it has been said that the consent of the other parent may not simply be presumed to have been given tacitly.[113]

---

104 Bundesdatenschutzgesetz (BDSG) = Federal Data Protection Act 1990, *BGBl.* I, 2594, modified 14 January 2003 (*BGBl.* I, 66), and on the 5 September 2005, *BGBl.* I, 722. The current legislation has been enacted in the implementation of EU Directive 95/46/EC (OJ L 281, 31).

105 Federal Data Protection Act 1990 = Bundesdatenschutzgestez (BDSG) §1 (III).

106 HEIDA (2003), p. 174-180.

107 Arts 1:251, 253b and 253aa DCC.

108 Art. 7:446 DCC. See above. For minors between 12 and 16 their consent will also be required. Over the age of 16, persons may decide for themselves on any medical treatment.

109 Wet Bescherming Persoonsgegevens (WBP) = **Dutch** Data Protection Act.

110 College Bescherming Persoonsgegevens.

111 HOOGHIEMSTRA (2002), p. 61. Www.cbpweb.nl/downloads_av/AV26.pdf.

112 Art. 1:253i DCC.

113 HOOGHIEMSTRA (2002), p. 61. Www.cbpweb.nl/downloads_av/AV26.pdf.

As a principle, the requirement of the consent of the mother, father and the child has also been reaffirmed in the case law where the results of a 'motherless' test conducted in the **United States** were discarded by a **Dutch** court.[114] If a person's informed consent has been dispensed with, no prosecution under criminal law will be made.[115] Nonetheless, the legal representative of the child might be able to seek (civil) damages in tort law for the violation of unwritten norms of civil law.[116] In a case from **the Netherlands Antilles**, however, a mother also sought to obtain a court order for private testing, but the father had already shown himself to be willing to make a recognition. It was therefore decided that there was no real reason to first have the genetic link established because this would only serve informational purposes.[117]

Dutch Internet laboratories distinguish between tests for legal purposes, which require the prior consent of all concerned parties, and other tests aimed at 'acquiescing' lingering feelings of doubts.[118] It is unclear whether laboratories sometimes accept genetic samples taken by the father from the mother or the child without having first obtained their consent for the sake of verifying genetic descent for a man's private interest in dispelling his lingering doubts.

In **Portugal**, a small number of private laboratories operate on the paternity market at competitive prices. There is no regulation as of yet on such extrajudicial tests. The ordinary requirements concerning the obtainment of consent to testing therefore presumably apply by analogy. Thus, for minors the consent of the adult(s) with parental authority will therefore be required beforehand. It has been recognised, moreover, that 'covert' paternity tests may violate important aspects of the personality right enshrined in Article 26 of the **Portuguese** Constitution.[119]

---

114 Rechtbank Maastricht, 14 July 2004, 85868 /FA RK 03-1042.

115 This answer was obtained by the author from the Public Information Department of the Minisitry of Justice.

116 Pursuant to Art. 6:162 DCC.

117 Gemeenschappelijk Hof van Justitie Nederlandse Antillen en Aruba, 14 October 2008, LJN: BG3510.

118 See, notably, www.bsure.nl and www.verilabs.nl.

119 Responses of the **Portuguese** Government to the *Questionnaire on Access to Genetic Information not related to Health*, CDCJ (2005) [cdcj/docs 2005/cdcj (2005) 9 bil].

4.2. COMPARISON

Extrajudicial paternity tests have spurred impassioned legal debates in **Germany**. Elsewhere in Europe the phenomenon has only received scant attention.[120] This contrast may doubtlessly be ascribed to some extent to the restrictive procedural regime for those wishing to deny paternity in **Germany**. Short time-limits, coupled with a rigid judicial insistence on preliminary procedural indications of non-paternity, will hardly induce doubting fathers to first discuss their doubts openly.[121] Quite the opposite, such a regime will presumably encourage doubting fathers to operate in a secretive manner and potentially also further undermine trust. Whereas in **the Netherlands** and **Portugal** extrajudicial paternity tests very much seem to operate in a legal grey zone, in **France** the legal regime is emphatically prohibitive. Obtaining consent from the persons whose genetic samples are taken is nonetheless required in all jurisdictions.

4.3 EVALUATION

If a child's individual informational needs can be met within the family, it may be preferable to choose such a consensual, non-litigious settlement. Covert DNA tests may for such reasons be seen as less intrusive . In this way it may be true that they can acquiesce doubts in a more serene way than court proceedings could ever hope to achieve.[122]

Non-consensual testing in an extrajudicial setting is inherently much more problematic. Still, strife within families could in one view be lessened, for example, if a mother were given the opportunity to have her own doubts as to her partner's fatherhood settled quietly without having to reveal possibly embarrassing details about her private life.[123] After all, the child may have been conceived during a short-lived affair in an otherwise monogamous relationship. Following that rationale, court proceedings would do more harm than good, especially since the paternity of the mother's partner would be confirmed in most cases. If her partner's paternity were not confirmed, the child's interests would sometimes still be said be better served by secrecy. This view is therefore

---

120 SPICKHOFF, SCHWAB, HENRICH, GOTTWALD (2007), in particular in that volume: HENRICH (2007), p. 407-408.

121 SPICKHOFF, SCHWAB, HENRICH, GOTTWALD (2007), in particular in that volume: HENRICH (2007), p. 407-408.

122 BOHNERT (2002), p. 386.

123 BOHNERT (2002), p. 386.

clearly not particularly alarmed by the disruptive influence of secrets on family relationships.[124]

As the Internet offers ample scope for ordering do-it-yourself (DIY) paternity kits from abroad, the ambitions of national legislation may have to be modest. Some national control may, however, be possible. If a court is not satisfied that the evidence had been gathered on the basis of the joint consent of the parties, or a minor's legal representative, the court may award damages for the violation of (unwritten) civil law norms of morality. If it is not satisfied that the test is sufficiently accurate, it may insist upon a new test by a reputable private or public laboratory. Moreover, as has been suggested, some level of judicial monitoring at the national level through the creation of a 'purely informational' procedure might also be achieved. To a discussion of this procedural solution we shall now turn.

5. THE INFORMATIONAL PROCEDURE IN GERMANY

5.1. BACKGROUND

In its 1989 landmark decision, the Federal Constitutional Court had already called on the federal legislature to investigate how the child's right to information could be best enforced. Soon afterwards, the appeal of the Federal Constitutional Court on the legislature reignited the debate on the feasibility of a so-called 'isolated' procedure[125], in which certainty regarding the biological ties would be achieved without thereby modifying status. In another case around the same time, a child also sought the identification of his biological father.[126] The child maintained that he did not wish to see a breakdown of the family law relationship with his legal father. Nonetheless, his claim was found inadmissible as the relevant statutory time-limits for instituting proceedings had expired.[127]

---

124 WISMEIJER (2007), p. 383-389.

125 See Chapter IV, known in **German** as 'isolierte Abstammungsfeststellungsklage'. MÜNCHENER/WELLENHOFER (2008), BGB, §1598a, Rdnr.1.

126 High Regional Court = Oberlandesgericht (OLG) Oldenburg, 17 July 1990, *FamRZ* 1991, p. 351-352.

127 In 1998, the High Regional Court of Hamm reached a similar conclusion in a case which involved a child's 'purely informational' interest. North Rhine-Westphalia Regional Court of Appeal (Hamm), 7 August 1998, *FamRZ* 1998, p. 1365.

A number of **German** scholars soon warmed to this idea of creating a 'solely informational' procedure.[128] They drew attention to adoption, a situation in which the registration of data concerning the biological parents would already serve children's informational needs without calling into question the legal status of the adoptive parents.[129] This analogy was also dismissed, however, in view of the fact that adoption is geared *ab initio* to the creation of a family law relationship with non-biological parents.[130]

In particular, it was feared that, as a 'third parent', the position of the biological father without status would remain ambiguous since the procedure would lead to two sets of parents. As such, it was considered that socio-legal paternity, once the legal façade of biological truth had been removed, his parenthood would become 'downgradable' to a *Zahlvaterschaft*.[131]

Following the 2007 decision of the Federal Constitutional Court the question was again raised in earnest and now at the legislative level.[132] In the relevant decision, the court called directly on the federal legislature to foresee the creation of a legal procedure by 31 March 2008, in principle in order to better protect the father's newly found constitutional 'right to know his own progeny.'[133]

To that end, in October 2007, the federal government drafted a law proposal.[134] Its Preamble formulated a more ambitious aim than had initially been envisaged, namely to promote 'dialogue within the family and society, to protect the family as a social institution and to prevent the intervention of courts as much as possible.'[135] Clearly, the use of the word 'dialogue' was not taken seriously, but

---

128 MUTSCHLER (1994), p. 65-70; SCHUBERT (1997), p. 232-233; more sceptical: GERNHUBER/COESTER-WALTJEN (2006), p. 587-588.

129 COESTER-WALTJEN (1992), p. 369.

130 RAUSCHER/STAUDINGER (2004), BGB, §1592, No. 4, p. 227-228.

131 Zahlvaterschaft = 'fatherhood based on the handing out of money to the child'. Compare the issue of 'duped dads' in the **United States**, see Chapter I.

132 Federal Constitutional Court = Bundesverfassungsgericht (BVerfGE), 13 February 2007, *FamRZ* 2007, p. 441.

133 Art. 2 1 in conjunction with Art. 1 1 Federal Constitution = Grundgesetz (GG). *Recht des rechtlichen Vaters auf Kenntnis seiner Nachkommenschaft (Nachwuchses)*. See Chapter IV.

134 *Entwurf eines Gesetzes zur Klärung der Vaterschaft unabhänging vom Anfechtungsverfahren*, 4 October 2007, *BT-Drucks.* BAMBERGER/ROTH (2008), BGB, §1598a, Rndr. 1.

135 '*Die hier vorgeschlagene Regelung ... soll den Dialog in der Familie und der Gesellschaft fördern, die Familie in ihrem sozialen Besand schützen und die Einschaltung von Gerichten möglichst vermeiden*'. *BT-Drucks.* 16/6561, 10. The use of the word 'dialogue', which suggests ongoing communication and deliberation, in the disclosure of the biological truth and its legal

it provoked a whimsical and sharp critique.[136] Nonetheless, on 1 April 2008 the new procedure entered into force.

5.2. CRITICAL APPRAISAL

It has been said that the co-existence of informational and status procedures could cause 'serious frictions' in parentage law.[137] To begin with, it has been considered problematic that in status procedures a 'preliminary suspicion' remains a prerequisite whereas in the informational procedure it is not. However, this such a preliminary procedural hurdle is lacking in the informational procedure. Once a court order for testing has been obtained, testing will become compulsory in the informational procedure.[138] The results can thereafter still be used for status proceedings provided they are lodged within time.

Moreover, it has been said that tension between both procedures could arise if the evidence gathered in the informational procedure were able to be used in subsequent status proceedings involving a denial of paternity.[139] Who would then still first want to first make amends for making a 'preliminary suspicion'? The time-limit which is currently applicable in the ordinary status procedure has therefore been deferred for two years after the informational procedure had come to verify that there was no genetic link.[140]

Even under those conditions, however, it is possible that situations arise in which testing has to take place no fewer than three times. Thus, testing may first have been refused in a status procedure first because the 'preliminary suspicion' was considered insufficient. The legal father could then still, of course, recur to the informational procedure, which would from that moment then give him another comfortable two-year period within which an attempt could be made to lodge the status procedure yet again. The results may then again have to be submitted to the court as a sufficient 'preliminary suspicion' with a view to denying paternity in the status procedure. If the court is not satisfied, however, that the privately taken test actually meets certain quality requirements, it could still ask for another test. Since even after three (costly) subsequent tests the

---

repercussions was perceived as particularly inept in the mercilessly humorous commentary on this law proposal written by SCHWAB (2008), p. 23.

136 FRANK & HELMS (2008), p. 1277-1281; SCHWAB (2008), p. 23-27.

137 FRANK & HELMS (2008), p. 1278.

138 §1598a(2) BGB.

139 FRANK & HELMS (2008), p. 1278.

140 §1598a(1) in conjunction with §1600b(5) BGB.

biological father's identity may not even have become definite, the dual regime may neither be in the budgetary interest of the regional administration nor in the child's interests.[141] Nonetheless, it must be said that this scenario would probably be quite exceptional, especially so since it remains to be seen whether much use will be made in the first place of this informational procedure.

Furthermore, the perceived friction may also be exaggerated because a family lawyer could advise the informational procedure to be lodged first. Problems seem to derive, above all, primarily from the all too rigid insistence upon preliminary evidence in the status procedure. Since this is an essentially **German** particularity of the parentage law system, it does not mean that the basic idea behind the law is flawed. Rather, it could be said that it provides an appropriate procedural answer to a constitutional development in family law that now already spans two decades.

In addition, some of the tension must surely have been taken away through the insertion of the child's interests clause in the informational procedure. This clause requires an assessment of the child's concrete interests in each individual case. Exceptionally, in case of an emotionally vulnerable adolescent suffers from an eating disorder, for example, disclosure would according to the memorandum have to be postponed. That said, however, some suggest that because compulsory disclosure is the norm rather than the exception, the child's interest could still be jeopardised.[142] But this may be essentially a problem of lack of faith in the judiciary applying a flexible norm in a reasonable way.

A more significant drawback relates to the fact that the biological father is not a party to the new procedure, however. His exclusion is remarkable, if only because his so-called 'right to know his progeny' has received some constitutional recognition.[143] Moreover, as Helms and Frank point out, the very *raison d'être* of the law departed from the idea that biological parentage relationships should be verifiable before the courts, quite regardless of the implications for existing legal parent-child relations.[144] As a matter of fact, however, the informa-

141 MÜNCHENER/SEIDL (2008), BGB, §1598a, Rdnr. 12.

142 §1598a a(3) BGB. FRANK & HELMS (2007), p. 1278, who also suggest that the Federal Constitutional Court should have taken into account the singularity of the creation of an isolated procedure from a comparative law perspective and the fact that **Germany** was already a frontrunner in the national-socialist period of a procedure to ascertain genetic descent, albeit for racist purposes.

143 BVerfGE 816, 9 April 2004, *FamRZ* 2003, p. 816. See Chapter IV and VII.

144 FRANK & HELMS (2008), p. 1279.

tional procedure and a status procedure now co-exist. Still, this may not always further the effectuation of neither the father's informational 'right' nor the child's.

The omission to reinforce the biological father's procedural position was considered a 'necessary evil' for a number of reasons. Thus, it was suggested, that unacceptable situations could arise in which a third party could have his genetic link to the child affirmed while leaving all parental responsibilities to a socio-legal father once the latter is no longer in a position to deny paternity.[145] The biological father would raise doubts in otherwise well-functioning families.[146]

As a result, the biological father's right to challenge paternity remains firmly tied to the status procedure and subject to a *dies a quo* two-year time-limit and the non-existence of a factual 'socio-legal relationship' between the child and the legal father.[147] Justifiably, it has been considered that there would be no valid reason to deny the biological father access to the informational procedure, under such circumstances, i.e. if there are no genuine social ties between the social father and the child. Effectively, then, the biological father currently still has to rely on (unlawful) extrajudicial tests, the prevention of which provided an important reason to create this new procedure.[148]

Furthermore, since the courts leave the choice of a private laboratory to the parties, the results may not always meet scientific standards. As long as the test is 'adequate', it will be accepted by the courts. It can then provide a sufficient 'preliminary suspicion' in the subsequent status procedure.[149]

As a more general observation, it may also be seriously wondered whether a private test will be 'openly' sought through the intervention of the courts. Perhaps especially in cases in which no review of the legal relationship has been contemplated, parties will be more inclined to settle whatever perceived informational needs quietly, and therefore also perhaps, outside the eyes of the court. For the sake of the stability of the family unit, Wellenhofer has considered that an extra-judicial settlement will be a more serene alternative to a judicial solution in case doubts are not very strong.[150] It has been suggested that the problem

145 *BT-Drucks.* 16/6561, p. 12 and 19.
146 MÜNCHENER/WELLENHOFER (2008), BGB, §1598a, Rdnr. 6.
147 FRANK & HELMS (2008), p. 1281.
148 MÜNCHENER/WELLENHOFER (2008), BGB, §1598a, Rdnr. 6.
149 WELLENHOFER (2008), p. 1187.
150 WELLENHOFER (2008), p. 1187-1188.

of covert, extrajudicial tests will therefore remain and that the new procedure will at best acquiesce the concerns of constitutional rights lawyers.[151]

Whatever the practical use of the informational procedure, then, it would be hard to disagree that the new German law has both emblematic and conceptual value. It aligns constitutional developments with those at the procedural level. As such, the informational procedure at least gives both parents and child a lawful opportunity to establish the biological truth 'openly', without this necessarily resulting in a loss of a well-established, legal child-parent relationship. It would have been more consistent to give the child a right to identify the biological father, too, however. Even though a biological father's right to information may be less strong, it would also have been consistent if he could be engaged in the procedure by the child (and, perhaps, the mother) and also lodge proceedings himself if this reflects the child's interests clause.

151 WELLENHOFER (2008), p. 1188.

CHAPTER IX
THE IDENTIFICATION OF THE BIRTHPARENTS IN ADOPTION

1. OUTLINE

Adoption involves the creation of a child-parent relationship between individuals who are not genetically related. As such, adoption may represent a challenge to identity rights because its very purpose has been to terminate a person's link with one family and replace it with another.[1] It was known in Antiquity, in the Code of Hamurrabi and in Roman law as *adoptio* and *adrogatio*. Thereafter, it reappeared in **France** in 1792 and through the Code Civil it spread to other European jurisdictions.[2] Given the wealth of family law and social science literature on adoption, it is considered sufficient for our purposes to compare the consequences of adoption for children's right to access their origins in the four jurisdictions against the backdrop of Chapter V.[3] Accordingly, only a rudimentary overview is provided of the history of the institution in each selected jurisdiction and only the most basic legal requirements in respect of adoptive parents shall be discussed.

The 1993 Hague Convention on Protection of Children and Co-Operation in respect of Intercountry Adoption lists a few relevant but ambiguous criteria.[4] If the Central Authority of the State of origin is satisfied that the child is adoptable, it should prepare a report including information about his or her identity, adoptability, background, social environment, family history, medical history including that of the child's family, and any special needs of the child.[5]

---

1 BAINHAM (2005), p. 301.

2 MEIJDAM-SLAPPENDEL (1996), p. 26.

3 See *inter alia* BRODZINSKY & SCHECHTER (1990); HOKSBERGEN & WALENKAMP (1983); MEIJENDAM-SLAPPENDEL (1996); SANTS (1964); SCHMIDT (1996); TEXTOR (1990); TRISELIOTIS (1973).

4 **France** ratified this Convention on 1 October 1998, **Germany** on 1 March 2002, **the Netherlands** on 1 October 1998 and **Portugal** on 1 July 2004.

5 Art. 16(1) a Hague Convention on Intercountry Adoption.

Moreover, the Contracting State has to ensure that information held by them concerning the child's origin, in particular information concerning the identity of his or her parents, as well as the medical history, is preserved and that the child has access to that information 'under appropriate guidance.'[6] All the same, much of the urgency of these obligations is detracted. Thus, children's access is only required 'in so far as is permitted by the law of that state'. Furthermore, although proof of the necessary consent of the (first legal) parents must have been obtained as well as of the reasons for the placement, states also have to take care not to reveal the identity of the mother and the father if, in the state of origin, these identities may not be disclosed.[7]

2. FRANCE

2.1. HISTORICAL NOTE

In the aftermath of the **French** Revolution, adoption was introduced in order to give parents 'the freedom to choose parentage'.[8] Modern adoption was therefore introduced in **France** in January 1792. Adoption was instantly considered a social policy instrument aiming at a more equal distribution of wealth and as a way of finding children for childless couples.[9]

The original Code Civil of 1804 only recognised adoption in respect of adults and aimed to provide an heir for a childless person as a way of continuing the family line, with a view to passing on property. After the First World War, in order to alleviate the problem of child abandonment, adoption was opened up to persons under the age of 21.

2.2. BASIC LEGAL CRITERIA

Two forms of adoption are known.[10] A **French** court may order both an ordinary adoption (*adoption simple*) and a plenary adoption (*adoption plénière*). For both forms of adoption, single-parent adoption and adoption by married couples is

6 Art. 30(2) Hague Convention on Intercountry Adoption.
7 Art. 16(2) Hague Convention on Intercountry Adoption.
8 Renaut (2003), p. 56.
9 Renaut (2003), p. 57.
10 On adoption law in **France**, see generally, Carbonnier (1999), p. 337-350; Terré & Fenouillet (2006), p. 821-860.

permitted.[11] A married couple must have been married for two years unless both spouses are over twenty-eight years old. This minimum age limit also applies in single-parent adoption unless the child has another parent who is the partner of the single adoptive parent (step-parent adoption).[12] The consent of both legal parents will in principle be required unless one of them is legally incapacitated or deceased. If the parentage of a child is established only with regard to one of his parents, that parent has to give consent to adoption.[13]If the father and mother of the child are dead, unable to express their intention or have been deprived of their rights of parental authority, consent shall be given by the family council, after the advice of the person who actually takes care of the child.[14]

Article 347 of the **French** Code Civil lists three categories of adoptable children:

1. Children to the adoption of whom the father and mother or the family council have validly consented;
2. Wards of the State (*pupilles de l'état*);
3. Children who have been declared abandoned.

Ordinary adoption preserves the connection which the adoptee has with her or his birth family, but creates a legal relationship with the adoptive parents. The adoptive parents have parental authority. There is no age limit with respect to the adoptee.[15] As such, this form of adoption generally extends to older children and takes place within the family of the birthparents. The consent of the adoptee will be required from the age of thirteen in ordinary adoption.[16]

In contrast, in plenary adoption the legal relationship with the birthparents is broken and replaced with a relationship with the adoptive parents. As another distinctive feature, only children up to fifteen years may be adopted in plenary adoption.[17] As in ordinary adoption, children over thirteen years of age must consent to this form of adoption.[18]

---

11 Art. 343 **French** Code Civil.
12 Art. 343-2 **French** Code Civil.
13 Art. 348-1 **French** Code Civil.
14 Art. 348-2 **French** Code Civil.
15 Art. 360 **French** Code Civil.
16 Art. 345-3 **French** Code Civil.
17 Art. 345-1 **French** Code Civil.
18 Art. 360 **French** Code Civil.

In case of compelling reasons the adoption will become revocable, at the request of the adopter or the adoptee, or, where the latter is a minor, on behalf of the Government procurator's office.[19] However, if the child is older than fifteen and had been received before having reached that age by persons who did not fulfil the statutory requirements for adopting or if the child had already been the subject of an ordinary adoption before reaching that age, plenary adoption may in principle be applied for during the minority of the child and within two years thereafter.[20] A plenary adoption is irrevocable, even though it has been recognised that this restriction may not always be in the child's interests.[21]

In contrast, an ordinary adoption may be revoked in the case of serious reasons at the request of the adopter or the adoptee, or, where the latter is a minor, of the Government procurator's office.[22] This request for revocation made by the adopter is admissible only where the adoptee is over fifteen.[23]If the adoptee is a minor, the father and mother by blood or, failing them, a member of the family of origin up to the degree of cousins may also request the revocation. The revocation causes the effects of adoption to cease for the future, but lacks retrospective force.[24]

2.3. ACCESS TO INFORMATION

The possibilities for those born under an *accouchement sous X* to access their origins have already been examined in Chapter VI. Only in the case of a plenary adoption is a new birth act drawn up in the registers of civil status, or, in the case of a foreign adoption, in the central service of civil status of the Ministry of Foreign Affairs.[25] The registration states the day, hour and place of birth, the sex of the child as well as his family name and first names as they result from the adoption order, as well as the first names, names, date and place of birth, occupation and domicile of the adopter(s). The new birth act may not contain any indication as to the actual parentage of the child.[26] The aim of this secretive regime is first and foremost to prevent intrusion by the birthparents in the

[19] Art. 370-1 **French** Code Civil.
[20] Art. 345 **French** Code Civil.
[21] Art. 359 **French** Code Civil; TERRÉ & FENOUILLET (2006), p. 853.
[22] Art. 370 **French** Code Civil. The reasons must be stated in the order pursuant to Art. 370-1 **French** Code Civil; TERRÉ & FENOUILLET (2006), p. 857-859.
[23] Art. 370 **French** Code Civil.
[24] Art. 370-2 **French** Code Civil.
[25] Art. 354 **French** Code Civil.
[26] Art. 354 **French** Code Civil.

adoptee's family.[27] In that light, the legal regime concerning plenary adoption will make it impossible to access their origins through the birth certificate. They will depend on whatever information is contained in the adoption files kept on them by the adoption bureau or intermediary.

3. GERMANY

3.1. HISTORICAL NOTE

Some of the **German** states had adoption laws during the 18th and 19th Century.[28] A uniform parentage law was created in the original Bundesgesetzbuch of 1900. The institution was known as *Annahme an Kindes Statt* but its consequences were minimal.[29] This form of adoption was largely restricted to adults. Moreover, in order to be able to adopt, parents were required not to have any legitimate children, although they could adopt several persons.[30] In 1950 this requirement was lifted and age requirements in respect of adoptive parents were lowered.[31]

The last major reform took place in 1976 when the plenary adoption of children was introduced and became subject to a court order and the prior consent of the biological parents.[32] Nowadays, the most common form of adoption is the so-called *Inkognitoadoption* ('closed adoption') of children. The adoption of adults is also known but has become subject to stricter requirements.[33]

3.2. BASIC LEGAL CRITERIA

Both ordinary and plenary forms of adoption are known.[34] A set of cumulative criteria in respect of all adoptive parents is found in §1741 BGB. Basic requirements for adoption are that the adoption will be in the child's interests and that a 'parent-child relationship' will develop between the adoptive parents and the child. Adoption by one parent is in principle permitted irrespective of that

27 TERRÉ & FENOUILLET (2005), p. 849.
28 MUSCHELER (2007), p. 17.
29 BOSCH (1984), p. 830-834. *Annahme* is still the term which is used in the BGB.
30 MUSCHELER (2007), p. 18.
31 MUSCHELER (2007), p. 26-27.
32 GERNHUBER/COESTER-WALLTJEN (2006), p. 1096-1097.
33 §1766 BGB and further. This form of adoption is known as *Volljährigenadoption.*
34 See generally on current **German** adoption law, PAULITZ (2006); MAURER/MÜNCHENER KOMM (2008), BGB, §1741-1772.

person's civil status.[35] Married couples may only adopt jointly in principle.[36] Adoption by one of the spouses is only possible in case of step-parent adoption, if the age requirement of 21 years has not been reached or in the event of a legal incapacity of one of the spouses.[37]

An indefinite trial period is required before a court order concerning the adoption is given.[38] A child must consent to adoption. The Youth Care Bureau (*Jugendamt*) has a duty to establish whether the adoptive parents are capable of assuming their parental responsibilities.[39] If the child is under fourteen years of age, the birthparents will give substitutive consent.[40] The consent of both birthparents will also generally be required.[41] However, if a birthparent is (fully) legally incapacitated, her or his consent may be dispensed with. Furthermore, if the parent is traceless, consent may be dispensed with. The child may then in principle become adoptable if the parents are unknown for a protracted period.[42]

An adoption may be revoked but only when consent requirements had not been obtained lawfully or during the child's minority when this is in the child's interests and the child can be adopted by other adoptive parents or taken into care by one or both biological parents.[43] Subsequent to a revocation the legal ties with the former legal parents will revive.[44] It has been reported that the revocation of adoption is quite rare in **Germany**.[45]

3.3. ACCESS TO INFORMATION

Information regarding the adoption that requires secrecy may not be disclosed by anyone except by the adoptive parents and the adopted child unless there is a public interest in disclosure.[46] In connection with that general rule, the birth-

---

35 §1741 BGB; ENDERS/BAMBERGER-ROTH (2008), BGB, No. 35.

36 §1741(1) BGB.

37 1741 in conjunction with §1743 BGB; ENDERS/BAMBERGER-ROTH (2008), BGB, No. 36.

38 §1744 BGB. In principle federal guidelines on adoption recommend a trial period of one year. MAURER/MÜNCHENER KOMMENTAR (2008), BGB, No. 9.

39 §1744 BGB.

40 §1746 BGB.

41 §1747 BGB.

42 §1747(2) BGB. It is assumed that a foundling in a *babyklappe* will, for example, become adoptable within six months. MÜNCHENER KOMM/MAURER (2008), BGB, No. 23.

43 §1759 in conjunction with §1760 and §1763 BGB.

44 §1763(3) BGB.

45 ENDERS/BAMBERGER/ROTH (2008), BGB, §1759, Rndr. 1. Ten to twenty-three revocations were reported on an annual basis between 1999 and 2003.

46 §1758 BGB.

parents will not be able to require information about the welfare of the child.[47] Nonetheless, adopted children have a right to petition information concerning their adoptive status in respect of their adoptive parents.[48] It has been argued that after the end of parental authority when the adopted child becomes an adult, he or she will have an independent right to access information, since it may be assumed that the adopted person, like any other person, will then be able to substantiate a legitimate interest in accessing her or his birth certificate.[49] In this birth certificate, the names of the birthmother and possibly the father will generally be found.[50]

Doctrinal views recognise that closed adoption is not irreconcilable with children's right to know their origins, but that it creates tension with this constitutional right.[51] Adopted children can access their birth record from the age of sixteen.[52] However, the disclosure of adoptive status at an earlier stage has been recommended by some authors.[53] The birth record will list the name and the address of the birthparents at the time of adoption. The adopted child will in principle only be given additional information on the nationality, religious background, socio-economic situation and family relations of the birthparents.[54]

On the basis of the constitutional personality right and the equality principle as well as a civil duty of care,[55] it has been held that the adopted child should be able to compel the mother to disclose the name of the biological father.[56] The principle of equality is engaged because the mother has a duty not to withhold information concerning the biological father in respect of other children.[57] Once his name has been disclosed, the (presumptive) biological father cannot be compelled to undergo DNA testing pursuant to the new informational procedure because he is not the legal father.[58] The genetic link of the former legal mother

---

47 §1758 BGB; ENDERS/BAMBERGER ROTH (2008), BGB, §1758 BGB.
48 §1741 in conjunction with §1758 BGB; MAURER/MÜNCHENER KOMMENTAR (2008), BGB, No. 9.
49 §34(1) and (2) Freiwillige Gerichtbarkeit-gesetz (FGG); HELMS (1999), p. 172-173.
50 HELMS (1999), p. 171; MUSCHELER (2008), p. 496.
51 SETHE (1995), p. 44-47; ENDERS/BAMBERGER-ROTH (2008), BGB, No. 23.
52 §61(2) **German** Civil Status Act = Personenstandsgsetz (PstG). See further: HAHN/BAMBERGER-ROTH (2008), BGB, No. 21.
53 KLEINEKE (1976), p. 264-268; TEXTOR (1990), p. 10-11; HELMS (1999), p. 174-175.
54 MUSCHELER (2008), p. 496.
55 Art. 2 1 and 3 I Grundgesetz (GG) = Federal **German** Constitution in conjunction with §242 BGB.
56 MUSCHELER (2008), p .498.
57 MUSCHELER (2008), p. 498.
58 MUSCHELER (2008), p. 498. See Chapter VIII.

may, however, be verified, subsequent to a revocation although this will not modify the establishment of (legal) maternity.[59]

4. THE NETHERLANDS

4.1. HISTORICAL NOTE

The first **Dutch** Civil Code did not preserve the **French** institution of adoption, introduced in 1810, because the codifiers considered that the institution did not reflect **Dutch** customs. Thus, according to Hugo de Groot, only in the province of Friesland was adoption known prior to the introduction of the Napoleonic Civil Code.[60] Modern adoption therefore came late in the Netherlands, not until November 1956.[61] Both the institution itself and the disclosure of identifying information remained a social taboo in those early years.[62] Nonetheless, in the parliamentary debates the need for early disclosure was already acknowledged.[63] Adoption was introduced as a child protection measure rather than as a legal avenue for helping childless parents to find children. As a side-effect of prevalent social taboos, the vast majority of children that were adopted in those early decades had an unmarried **Dutch** mother.[64] Considerable pressure was put on unmarried mothers to sign away parental rights in which they promised never to establish contact with their child after birth.[65]

In January 1957 the Centrale Adoptieraad (CAR)[66] was set up as an advisory organ to the Youth and Childcare Board on each application for adoption and on disclosure issues.[67] The policy of the CAR concerning disclosure conveyed the view that children should be told in full honesty by their parents, unless indicated otherwise by therapists in respect of the specific needs of some children.[68]

---

59 §1591 in conjunction with §1598a BGB.

60 GROTIUS (1631), *Inleidinge tot de Hollandsche Rechtsgeleerdheid* I-6-1.

61 Act of the 26 January 1956, *Staatsblad* 1956, p. 42. NOTA (1969), p. 23.

62 RAAK-KUIPER (2007), p. 39.

63 RAAK-KUIPER (2007), p. 39.

64 DOEK (1982), p. 56.

65 In 1994 the foundation 'Stichting afsandsmoeders' was set up to fulfil an intermediary role between these mothers and their children allowing them to enter into contact with each other and to foster greater solidarity in respect of mothers, both within the country, and abroad. www.afstandsmoeders.nl.

66 'Central Adoption Council'.

67 Act of 26 January 1956, *Staatsblad* 1956, p. 42.

68 NOTA (1969), p. 40.

Courts generally heeded the advice given by the CAR, but sometimes the advice was ignored when parents had indicated that they had no intention to inform the child.[69] In February 1974 the CAR was abolished after having given advice on adoption on innumerable occasions.[70] In 2001 **Dutch** adoption law underwent major changes as a result of the deletion of the requirement that adoptive couples should be married. At the same time, single-parent adoption was permitted.

Since the 1970s, the number of adoptable children of **Dutch** origin had greatly diminished as result of the sharp drop in unwanted pregnancies. At present, there are around 50,000 adoptees in **the Netherlands**, of whom 20,000 are of **Dutch** origin.[71] Because with respect to foreign adoptees the **Dutch** adoption act in respect of foreign children[72] applies, the direct application of **Dutch** adoption law is largely confined to single-parent adoption by the partner of a heterosexual partner and single-parent adoption by the lesbian birthmother's partner, the 'co-mother'.

Since the introduction of single-parent adoption in 1998, the parent is no longer required to adopt the child together with the new parent. Moreover, in 2001 it became possible for same-sex couples to adopt each other's children irrespective of their relationship status.[73] In 2008 an expert commission, the *Commissie Kalsbeck*, set up by the **Dutch** Ministry of Justice, published a report in which certain policy changes regarding inter-country adoption were advocated.[74] Following a public outcry over the *Baby Donna* case and an **Indian** case in which the birthparents claimed not to have consented to adoption, the commission proposed to prevent prospective parents finding adoptive children themselves without the support of a licensed **Dutch** adoption bureau after having obtained permission to adopt. The commission further holds that with regard to the partner of the prospective adoptive parent a strict age-limit of forty-eight years

69 Rechtbank Rotterdam, 25 April 1958, *NJ* 1958, p. 412; Rechtbank Amsterdam, 30 June 1960, *NJ* 1960, p. 507.

70 Centrale adoptieraad, *Slotakkoord*, 1974.

71 Www.adoptiedriehoek.nl.

72 Wet opneming buitenlandse kinderen ter adoptie. This law shall not be discussed here.

73 Wet van 8 maart 2001 tot aanpassing van wetgeving in verband met de openstelling van het huwelijk en de invoering van adoptie door personen van hetzelfde geslacht, *Staatsblad* 2001, No. 128, p. 1.

74 Kalsbeek report, *Rapport Interlandelijke adoptie. Alles van waarde is weerloos*, **Dutch** Ministry of Justice 29 May 2008.

should apply. Both of these proposals have been criticised on the basis of comparative legal research.[75]

4.2. BASIC LEGAL CRITERIA

Only full adoption is known.[76] Title 12 of Book 1 of the **Dutch** Civil Code lists several legal criteria for adoption.[77] Thus, the adoption must be in the manifest interests of the child and the couple must have lived together three years prior to the adoption application.[78] In establishing whether adoption is in the child's manifest interests, the court will also have to take into account the position that the child will lose.

As a general requirement, therefore, the court will have to ascertain that the child has 'nothing further to expect' from the birthparents in their capacity as parents now and in the future.[79]

In addition, for the adoption to take effect, the couple must have taken care of the child for one year, unless the mother's partner is of the same sex.[80] In single-parent adoption, the prospective adoptive parent must have taken care of the child for three years.[81] Only minors may be adopted and they can veto their adoption from the age of twelve.[82] Furthermore, there must be an age difference of eighteen years between the adoptive parent and the child.[83] There is no longer a maximum age for prospective adoptive parents, though the court may decide that adoption by an elderly person or couple is not in the child's interests.[84]

Moreover, the child's parents must not have expressed their opposition to the adoption.[85] Exceptionally, parental consent may be dispensed with.[86] The fact

---

75 Curry Sumner & Vonk (2008), p. 264-272.

76 For a more detailed overview of the current **Dutch** adoption law, see: Mourik & Nuytinck (2002), p. 176-187.

77 Art. 1:227-1:232 DCC.

78 Art. 1:227(1) and Art. 1:227(3) DCC.

79 *Kamerstukken II* 1999/2000, 26 673, No. 3, p. 7.

80 Art. 1:228(1)(f) DCC.

81 Art. 1:228(1)(f) DCC.

82 Art. 1:228(1)(a) and (b) DCC.

83 Art. 1:228(1)(c) DCC.

84 *Kamerstukken II* 1995/96 24 469, No. 3, p. 14. See further: Vonk (2007), p. 103.

85 Art. 1:228(1)(e) DCC.

86 Art. 1:228(2) DCC: if the parents did not live or hardly ever lived together as a family, if the parent has abused his parental responsibility or has grossly neglected the care and upbringing

that a parent has not established legal ties with the child will be a firm indication that the adoption is not in the child's interests. In 2003, the **Dutch** Supreme Court ruled that a biological father who has family life may object to an adoption by the mother's lesbian partner, the co-mother.[87] If the consent of the birth-parents cannot be obtained because their identity cannot be established, this will not in itself form an obstacle to adoption.

The adoption may be revoked by a decision of the district court upon an application by the adopted child.[88] The application is only granted if the revocation is 'manifestly' in the interests of the adopted child and if the court is convinced, in all conscience, that such a revocation is reasonable and the application is lodged two years or more, but no later than five years from the date on which the adopted child reaches the age of majority.[89] Upon revocation legal familial ties cease to exist between the adopted child and his or her children and the adoptive parent(s) and his or her blood relatives, while the legal familial ties that had ceased to exist revive as a result of the revocation.[90] The revocation of adoption is rare.[91]

In drawing an analogy with the possibility for minors to deny paternity, Van Raak-Kuiper has submitted that the possibility to lodge revocation proceedings should also be extended to minors, especially in the case of child abuse by the adoptive parents.[92] In view of the adoptee's adult age, she considers it unnecessary that the familial ties with the child's former legal parents should revive because this is not the direct result of a denial of paternity either. However, this dismisses the fact that the child may sometimes still have an inheritance-related interest. Furthermore, it should be considered that the analogy with denial proceedings is rather relative: at one point in his/her life, the adopted child had two legal parents, usually the birthparents, and a revocation empowers the adoptee to realign his parentage with this past. This cannot be said of denial proceedings. In fact, the requirements are more straightforward and less plurifocal, since the fact that the man is not the biological father forms the sole ground on which paternity may be denied.[93]

---

of the child of if the parent has irrevocably been convicted of certain serious criminal offences against the minor.

87 Hoge Raad, 24 January 2003, *NJ* 2003, p. 386. See further VONK (2007), p. 173.

88 Art. 1:231 DCC.

89 Art. 1:231(2) DCC.

90 Art. 1:232(1) and (2) DCC.

91 LINDEN (2006), p. 53-55.

92 RAAK-KUIPER (2006), p. 167.

93 Art. 1:200(1) and 1:205(1) DCC. See Chapter VII.

4.3. ACCESS TO INFORMATION

One important condition for adoption is that the child has nothing to expect from his parents and that adoption is in the 'manifest interests' of the child.[94] In case of an intercountry adoption, in practice by far the most common form of adoption, immigration law requirements must also have been met.[95]

The 'manifest interests' requirement is generally interpreted as requiring that the child be informed of her or his adoptive status. In addition, the 'expectations' requirement has been held to imply that the family ties between adoptive children and their biological parents should be left intact by way of principle.[96]

In view of the fact that most children adopted in **the Netherlands** are of foreign origin, obtaining information concerning the birthparents is often far from straightforward. Many of these adopted children were foundlings or left at hospitals after birth.

In respect of such older inter-country adoptions, the organisation International Social Services provides legal assistance in helping adopted children to trace their birthparents abroad. Furthermore, some of the adopted children looking for their birthparents seek assistance through the intervention of the television programme *Spoorloos*, which has greatly increased the familiarity of the general public with the issue of unknown origins.

Currently licensed adoption bureaux, in preventing international kidnapping and international child trafficking, require that the personal files of adoptable children are documented as completely as possible.[97] As a corollary, the files must document the reasons behind adoption and, if possible, provide for background information on the children, including their parents. If the birthparents are unknown, this does not mean, however, that the inter-country adoption cannot take place.[98]

---

94 Art. 1:227 in conjunction with Article 1:228(3) DCC.

95 Art. 2 Wet opneming buitenlandse kinderen voor adoptie (Wobka).

96 RAAK-KUIPER (2007), p. 42.

97 Art. 17(b) in conjunction with Art. 17(d) to 17(g) Wobka. Notwithstanding these requirements, in 2007 an international kidnapping scandal involving a child of Indian origin was associated with a licensed **Dutch** adoption bureau.

98 *Memorie van Toelichting* op 24 810 (R1577), No. 3, p. 16.

Discounting inter-country adoption, the vast majority of adoptions in **the Netherlands** occur by virtue of step-parent adoption, also known as partner adoption. Introduced in 1979, this form of adoption creates a family law relationship between the child and the partner of one of the child's (legal) parents. As such, it has been criticised for not genuinely constituting a child protection measure, while breaking the family law relationship with the child's other parent, usually the child's biological father.

In that connection, it has been said that step-parent adoption could be abused as a means to deny the child's past and encourage parents to deceive their children about their genetic origins.[99] Upon divorce, some parents would be inclined to attempt to erase the other parent not only from their own memory, but also from that of the child. However, the indisposition of a mother to inform a child about her origins has induced a court not to consent in a step-parent order.[100] In view of such objections, a less radical solution is therefore often sought in a joint parental authority order between the legal parent and the new partner.[101] As a consequence, the family law relationship between the child and the other parent will remain intact.

If a child has been adopted within **the Netherlands**, this information can be accessed on the basis of the birth act.[102] The person must have a sufficient personal interest, which may be assumed if it concerns the adoptee.[103] This information will make the (birth)mother identifiable[104] and list the legal father's name as well, provided paternity had been established at the time. Access to the birth act will accordingly provide important clues, but it may not give definite answers as to the identity of the child's biological parentage.

Adoption files were kept for thirty years and then destroyed until 1991, but are now stored for an indefinite period by the Child Protection Board. The foundation FIOM acts as an intermediary between adoptive parents and children and provides counselling services.[105] As for the adopted child of foreign norigin, the

---

99 SCHMIDT (1996), p. 190.
100 Rechtbank Leeuwarden, 10 May 2000, LJN AA 5749.
101 Art. 1:253t DCC.
102 Art. 1:17 in conjunction with Art. 1:23b DCC.
103 *Normen 2000, beleidsregels met betrekking tot de werkwijze van de Raad voor de Kinderbescherming.*
104 Art. 1:198 DCC. In a surrogacy case, she may not be the biological mother, however.
105 Www.fiom.nl.

files should be kept for at least thirty years after the child first lawfully entered **the Netherlands**.[106]

5. PORTUGAL

5.1. HISTORICAL NOTE

The nineteenth Century codification of **Portuguese** civil law, known as the *Código de Seabra* (1867), was firmly opposed to adoption. The institution remained unknown during the first half of the twentieth Century.[107] In fact, **Portugal** alongside **the Netherlands** were the last modern Western European jurisdictions to introduce adoption, as late as 1966.[108] In the early years, the institution was geared primarily towards finding suitable parents for **Portuguese** children who had been abandoned or foundlings. Both ordinary adoption (*adopção restrita*) and plenary adoption (*adopção plena*) were introduced. In the first two decades the latter form of adoption was used primarily in respect of abandoned children and children whose parents had died. Prior to the 1977 reform, simple adoption was much more common, according to Sottomayor. This meant that the problem of unknown biological parentage is said to have been much less common than it is today in **Portugal** amongst adopted children.[109]

The 1977 reforms of adoption law established a rather different legal regime which allowed for the full adoption of children whose biological parents were known while making their identification more difficult.[110] In 2003 another major legislative reform was introduced, which included a lowering of the maximum age requirements for adoptive parents to fifty years, an obstruction of the possibility to separate siblings and the codification of the principle that the adoption should be in the 'manifest interests' of the child.[111]

---

106 Art. 17b in conjunction with Art. 17d-g Wobka.
107 Vale e Reis (2007), p. 268-269.
108 Coelho (1987), p. 625.
109 Sottomayor (2002), p. 218.
110 Vale e Reis (2007), p. 271.
111 Lei No. 31/2003, 22 August 2003.

5.2. BASIC LEGAL CRITERIA

Currently, both plenary and simple adoption are known.[112] A court may give an adoption order only if it brings 'real benefits' for the child, does not entail an unjust sacrifice for the other children that the adoptive parent may already have and if it is reasonable to suppose that a relationship that is 'comparable to affiliation/parentage' (*filiacão*) will develop.[113] Though the term that has been used is ambiguous, it may be assumed that an analogy with natural rather than legal affiliation is sought. After a 'sufficient period' compliance with the adoption criteria is evaluated by the public social welfare authorities.[114] In terms of age requirements, adoptive parents must be over twenty five years of age and younger than fifty years to be eligible for both simple and full adoption.[115] In an ordinary adoption the child will keep the surname of the birthparents and all other legal ties are preserved.[116]

Ordinary adoption may be revoked if the parent does not comply with the legal requirements for exercising parental authority or if the adoption otherwise becomes inconvenient for the child's interests or education.[117] In contrast, a plenary adoption is irrevocable.[118] Even so, the court decision involving full adoption may be reviewed in case the consent of the biological parents had not been obtained or obtained through duress or moral coercion.[119] Six weeks must have passed since the moment of birth for a mother to be able to give her lawful consent to the child's full adoption, whether full or simple.[120] All legal ties between the birthparents and the child are broken subsequent to a court order involving plenary adoption.[121] An ordinary adoption may be converted into a full adoption if the legal criteria for this form of adoption have been satisfied.[122] Plenary adoption is irrevocable, even if the adoptive parents and child have consented to revocation.[123]

---

112 For an overview of contemporary **Portuguese** adoption law, see: SOTTOMAYOR (2004), p. 241-258; VALE E REIS (2008), p. 269-278; OLIVEIRA (2006), p. 262-311.

113 Art. 1973 in conjunction with A. 1974-1 PCC.

114 Art. 1974-2 PCC.

115 Art. 1992 PCC. If one of the spouses is younger than fifty years of age, simple adoption is also permitted.

116 Art. 1994 in conjunction with Art. 1996 PCC.

117 Art. 2002-C PCC.

118 Art. 1989 PCC.

119 Art. 1990 PCC.

120 Art. 1982-3 PCC.

121 Art. 1986-1 PCC.

122 Art. 1977 PCC.

123 Art. 1989 PCC. DE OLIVEIRA (2006), p. 301-302.

In ordinary adoption a revocation by the former legal parents, the child and the Public Ministry is exceptionally possible where there are occurrences which make certain statutory heirs unworthy of inheriting,[124] if there has been gross negligence with regard to parental responsibilities[125] or there is evidence of harm to the adopted child's upbringing.[126] The proceedings must then be framed in the context of adoption proceedings while the revocation will not have retrospective effect.[127]

5.3. ACCESS TO INFORMATION

In full adoption, the identity of the adoptive parents will not be disclosed to the birthparents, unless the adoptive parent expressly declares that he or she is not opposed to this form of disclosure.[128] This protection was initially only offered to the adoptive parents of abandoned children who had, prior to their adoption, been taken into healthcare. The norm aims to shield the interests of the adoptive parents in raising their child and to support a public policy geared towards ensuring a sustainable number of adoptive parents.[129] In protecting the adoptive family, in full adoption a re-establishment of the status relationship between the adopted child and the birthparents has also been expressly ruled out.[130]

Furthermore, the birthparents may resist any disclosure of their own identity to the adopted child.[131] The 2003 legislative reform, however, codified the practice for persons who can substantiate a legitimate interest in accessing their adoption files after the Public Ministry has been informed of the child's request.[132]

The current regime has been interpreted as containing a prohibition as far as access to the original birth certificate, on which the identity of the birthparents may be listed, is concerned.[133] Nonetheless, this view has been contested on the

---

124 Art. 2002-B PCC.

125 Art. 2002-C under (a) PCC.

126 Art. 2002-C under (b) PCC.

127 Art. 2002-D PCC. De Oliveira (2006), p. 309-310.

128 Art. 1985-1 PCC.

129 Sottomayor (2002), p. 294.

130 Art. 1987 PCC; Duarte (2003), p. 46; Vale e Reis (2008), p. 316.

131 Art. 1985-2 PCC.

132 Art. 173-1 *Organização da Tutela de Menores* (OTM) = **Portuguese** Act on the Organisation of Youthcare.

133 Sottomayor (2002), p. 222. She insists that the birthmothers may sometimes have a stronger right to privacy especially in societies in which they risk becoming ostracised by their social environment. A case-by-case analysis would therefore be better. In contast, Vale e Reis (2008),

basis of the increased constitutional recognition of the right to know in the **Portuguese** legal order. In that connection, it is telling that the Civil Registry Code also allows adopted persons to access their birth certificate.[134]

6. COMPARISON

In all jurisdictions, in plenary adoption, access to the original birth certificates is restricted during minority thereby allowing adopted children to integrate within the family of the adoptive parents and restricting exposure to the birth-parents in the adopted child's life. Furthermore, all jurisdictions except **the Netherlands** have conceived of a form of 'ordinary adoption.'[135] However, in **the Netherlands**, as in **Germany**, an adult adopted child may sometimes revoke the adoption. In **France** and **Portugal** this only exists exceptionally in simple adoption.

In plenary adoption, the legal effectuation of the child's informational interests are believed to hav been ensured through access to adoption files and legal documentation rather than by means of scientific parentage tests. In **France**, and to a lesser extent in **Portugal**, access to birthparent-identifying information is restricted, however. Still, the possibility to access the birth certificate in **Portugal**, as well as in **the Netherlands** and **Germany,** may lead to the identification of the first legal parent(s) the child had. Although these parents will generally be the birthparents, this may not always be the case. In view of the *mater semper certa* rule it is more likely that the legal mother will, as a rule, be the biological mother. In none of the jurisdictions are the birthparents required to undergo DNA testing. Exceptionally, in **Germany** the birthmother – but not the presumptive biological father – could be required to undergo testing in the new informational procedure subsequent to a prior revocation.[136]

---

p. 299-300 finds that children's right to know their birthparents should in principle be favoured.

134 Art. 213 in conjunction with Art. 214 Código do Registo Civil = **Portuguese** Civil Registration Code. There is a legislative lacuna with regard to the applicant's age. VALE E REIS (2008), p. 304, considers that adoptees who have reached the age of sixteen should be able to access their birth certificate, this also being the age that a person can lawfully marry.

135 'Ordinary adoption' may also be defined as 'weak' or 'simple adoption' in **English**.

136 §1598a BGB in conjunction with §1759 BGB.

7. EVALUATION

From a truth-oriented perspective, it is obvious that ordinary adoption carries within it certain advantages over full adoption. Apart from the intrusiveness of plenary adoption in the family life of the birthparents, this is one reason why its introduction has been advocated by **Dutch** legal scholars.[137] Van Raak-Kuiper even goes as far as to suggest, for example, that plenary adoption should be reduced to cases in which the birthparents are unknown or missing.[138]

Even if the identity of the child's first legal parents is known or documented, however, it can be doubted whether the child will always be in a position to access the prerequisite information. Thus, even if the name and address of the birthparents have been documented in the birth certificate, they may no longer be accurate. In that light, the determination of the veracity of the information contained in the birth certificates may sometimes be problematic.[139]

The informational needs of adoptive children may differ, for example, from those of donor-conceived persons because adoptees may also want to know the reasons why their birthparents had surrendered parental rights.[140]Accordingly, a mere identification of the birthparents is not always straightforward. This identification may, however, be a first prerequisite if the reasons behind adoption are not documented in the child's adoption file. It is circumspect if different legal consequences should be attached to the fact that the informational need of adoptees may be different from other children.

The *responsibility* for disclosing the fact of adoption is primarily incumbent on the adoptive parents, but this has not been specified in any legislation.[141] Although the state plays an active role in selecting adoptive parents through legislation and in deciding on the documentation relating to the identity of the first legal parents, the state does not assume an active role in disclosing information on the birthparents in any jurisdiction, as the adoptee may choose whether he or she wishes to access information. Such access is made contingent upon the child's age.

---

137 SCHMIDT (1996), MEIJDAM-SLAPPENDEL(1996), p. 310-312; PUNSELIE (2006), p. 14.

138 RAAK-KUIPER (2006), p. 187.

139 BUEREN (1995), p. 41.

140 O'DONOVAN (1988), p. 42.

141 Even if, as has been verified, it has been consistent policy in **the Netherlands** to ascertain in the adoption procedure whether the prospective adoptive parents are prepared to observe openness towards the child about adoption.

In plenary adoption, only if the child has achieved a certain maturity will he or she be able to establish details on the parent's identity, of course, inasmuch as these have been documented. Although this may mean that more adults rather than minors will be able to find out about the circumstances surrounding their adoption, this difference in treatment on the basis of age may to some extent be justifiable. After all, the principle of decisional privacy requires that the adoptee must also have a right *not* to choose to search for her or his birthparents. All the same, in order to be able to make this decision and to exert choice, the fact of adoption must at least be known. This will often be less problematic than in respect of donor conceived persons or in case of 'misattributed' paternity. Thus, it is recalled that in view of physical dissimilarities between the child and the adoptive parents, an awareness of the underlying disparity between status and biological parentage will factually be more probable. As a result, the adopted person may have a more genuine choice to decide to pursue identification further. However, the use of birth certificates and the fact that one must often rely on a foreign documentation and registration system, means that the chances of full and certain identification may sometimes be slighter than in other contexts.

CHAPTER X
THE RIGHT TO INFORMATION IN THE CONTEXTS OF ARTIFICIAL REPRODUCTIVE TECHNOLOGIES AND SURROGATE MOTHERHOOD

1. OUTLINE

Over the past few decades, developments in bio-medicine and reproductive technology have further increased possibilities to overcome fertility problems and to procreate without requiring sexual intercourse. This has opened up possibilities for both single parenting and same-sex parenting. Furthermore, Artificial Reproductive Technologies (ART) have become more generally accessible to the public.

In order to better understand the child's right to know his or her biological parents in the ART context, a concise historical overview and description of the various treatments shall first be provided in this Chapter. Attention shall also be given to the legislative history in each jurisdiction. Four situations will then be identified in which the provision of information may become especially pertinent. Firstly, surrogacy arrangements shall be compared. Secondly, a comparison shall be made of the way paternity is attributed to the partner of the woman undergoing fertility treatment. Thirdly, a comparative discussion of the conflict between donor anonymity and the child's right to know shall be made. In particular, this sub-section shall explore various ways to facilitate access to donor-identifying information. Fourthly, a comparison shall be made of post-mortal insemination. In this latter situation, the enforcement of the informational right may be considered to have been prejudged simply because *ab origine* the death of the biological parent clearly sets limits to the child's possibilities to enforce the child's rights beyond establishing the parent's basic legal identity, or to form an impression of the person on the basis of the accounts of others or photographs. Finally, some concluding and evaluative remarks shall be made against the analytical backdrop that Chapter V provides.

2. FORMS OF TREATMENT

2.1. SURROGACY

Broadly speaking, two forms of surrogacy may be distinguished. In low-technological or 'traditional' forms of surrogacy a woman uses self-insemination or a man impregnates her on behalf of another woman, whose intention is to become the child's mother. Examples of this type of surrogacy are found, for example, in the Old Testament.[1] Thus, Sarah asked Abraham to impregnate her maid instead since 'the Lord had restrained her from bearing', which is viewed as a precursor of modern surrogate motherhood contracts.

In contrast, high-technological or modern surrogacy did not take place until the late twentieth Century.[2] In this form of surrogacy, an embryo is created *in vitro* using the sperm and egg of the commissioning couple which is then transferred to inside the surrogate mother's uterus.[3] This form of surrogacy may be indicated when the genetic mother's eggs are viable, but she cannot carry the pregnancy to term. Donor gametes may sometimes also be used when the commissioning mother is unable to produce viable eggs and/or her partner is infertile. It is possible for a couple to use an egg donor, for example, whose ovum upon fertilisation with the commissioning father's sperm is subsequently placed in the surrogate. If the woman providing the ovum does not intend to become the child's legal parent, 'egg donation' may be an alternate way to refer to this type of modern surrogacy. This involves an invasive medical treatment and a synchronisation of the menstrual cycles of both women involved.

In modern forms of surrogacy in particular, the use of the word 'biology' can become problematic in particular: a biological mother could either be the 'gestational mother', since she gives birth to the child, or the 'genetic mother' who provides the gametes through her ovum. For such reasons, Vonk has distinguished four types of mothers.[4] In this Chapter, this choice of terminology shall also be applied inasmuch as it is deemed necessary to avoid confusion.

---

1 Genesis 16:2 and Genesis 30:3.

2 JACKSON (2001), p. 261.

3 JACKSON (2001), p. 261,

4 VONK (2008), p. 120. 1) Biological mother and genetic mother = woman who supplies the ovum and gives birth to the child. 2) Genetic mother = woman who supplies the ovum, but does not give birth to the child. 3) Gestational mother = woman who gives birth to the child, but does not supply the ovum. 4) Non-biological mother = woman who raises the child but is neither genetically related nor has given birth to the child.

In a full surrogacy arrangement, in which both an egg donor and a sperm donor provide their gametes and the commissioning couple do not provide their genetic material, a child could involve no fewer than five adults: the non-biological mother and the commissioning father, the genetic mother, the sperm donor and the gestational mother. In most high-technological surrogacy arrangements, the number of potential parents will however be limited to four persons: the gestational mother, her husband or partner, and the commissioning genetic father and genetic mother.[5]

In our discussion, we shall be primarily concerned with the enforcement of the child's right to information and the transfer of parental rights to the genetic parents. That this involves a problem may already be appreciated considering that a gestational mother could very well assert parental rights during the pregnancy or even after birth. Nonetheless, there may be more legal problems. In fact, surrogacy may give rise to multiple other legal complications.[6] It will be sufficient here to briefly mention some aspects. Thus, the financial compensation sometimes involved in surrogacy may be seen as contentious because it would 'commodify' women and conflict with principles of bodily integrity, in particular if women are in a vulnerable financial position.[7] That said, a degree of financial compensation has also been seen as an appropriate remuneration for the gestational mother, who depending on her character and her socio-economic situation could be regarded as an autonomous person who voluntarily enters into a contract.[8] The enforcement of the contract may also be fraught with complications, however, when the commissioning parents decide to withdraw from the contract, for example because it has emerged that the child has certain birth defects. It may also become difficult for the commissioning parents to seek compliance by the surrogate of a number of seemingly ordinary certain common health standards, such as refraining from smoking or drinking alcohol during pregnancy.

2.2. ARTIFICIAL REPRODUCTIVE TECHNOLOGIES

In homologous artificial insemination (AI) the sperm of the husband or the partner of the woman undergoing fertility treatment is used. The first successful attempt at homologous AI in humans was recorded in **Britain** in 1793 by the physician John Hunter. The first medical description of a successful homologous

5 JACKSON (2001), p. 266.
6 For an overview, see, for example, KINDREGAN & MCBRIEN (2006), p. 134-138.
7 ANDREWS (1995), p. 2345.
8 EPSTEIN (1995), p. 2326.

AI was however published in **France** in 1793.[9] The first AI by the use of sperm of a man other than the woman's husband is believed to have occurred in the **United States** in 1884.[10] Furthermore, in **Britain** and **France** some isolated cases were reported around the First World War. Nevertheless, it was not until the 1940s that the use of AI became more common. As the lowest technological form of ART, artificial insemination (AI) involves the injection of sperm from the husband or male partner or donor into the woman's uterus in order to provoke the fertilization of the gametes. If the sperm of a known or anonymous donor as a stranger to the woman's relationship is used, reference is made to heterologous AI.[11]

The vast majority of living persons born through AI are believed to have been born between the 1950s and 1990s. In the course of the 1990s, other fertility techniques such as *in vitro* fertilisation (IVF) and intracytoplasmatic sperm injection (ICSI) became more common. Nonetheless, it is expected that the demand for the use of AI will in future remain stable in some countries, in particular as a result of the increased demand from lesbian couples.[12]

In 1978 the first ever so-called test-tube baby, Louise Brown, was born in Kershaw's Cottage Hospital in Lancashire, **England**, through IVF. Although IVF can be both emotionally and physically taxing on couples and is a very expensive medical procedure, the technique became a common fertility treatment in the 1980s throughout Europe. IVF involves the removal of the woman's eggs and their fertilisation outside the woman's uterus and may entail three possibilities which may or may not lead to disparities between socio-legal and genetic parentage. First, the sperm and eggs may come from the couple undergoing treatment. Second, sperm or egg may come from an (anonymous) donor. Third, both gametes may stem from an (anonymous) sperm donor or an (anonymous) egg donor. The woman gestating the embryo may or may not be the biological mother. Fertilisation of the gametes takes place in a device made of glass (popularly known as a 'test-tube', although in reality it is a form of Perti dish)) which is subsequently placed in the woman's uterus.

---

9 LEVIE (1975).

10 LEVIE (1975).

11 Since the case of homologous artificial insemination is not directly relevant for our purposes, the abbreviation AI shall henceforth be used to refer exclusively to heterologous forms of artificial insemination unless specified.

12 EVERS & TE VELDE (2001).

From the mid-80s, cryo-preservation of eggs and from the 1990s of supernumerary embryos, resultant from IVF treatments, became medically available. As a result, it became possible for women well beyond their natural gestational age to give birth to a healthy genetically-related child. This has prompted discussions, in particular regarding the risk of social stigmatisation of the child and the importance of the shorter life-span of the woman as a parent. It has been suggested that this conveys a gender bias since nature allows fertile men to father children at an elderly age; moreover, the life expectancy of women in the West is longer than that of men.[13]

The last couple of decades have also witnessed the development of additional fertility treatments which have increased chances for infertile couples to conceive a genetically-related child. Thus, Gamete Intra Fallopian Transfer (GIFT) involves fertilisation through the puncturing of eggs by sperm cells in the woman's egg tube. Intra-Uterine Insemination involves the hormonal stimulation of eggs. At the moment of ovulation, a huge number of spermatozoids from the mother's partner (or a donor) are injected into the woman's body in order to achieve fertilisation. By contrast, in ICSI one sperm cell is singled out prior to its injection into the woman's egg with the aim of provoking a fertilisation outside the woman's body. Once they have fertilised, the gametes are then placed in the woman's uterus.

3. LEGISLATIVE HISTORY

In **France**, *Loi 94-654* and *Loi 95-654*, both adopted on 29 July 1994, provide a comprehensive regulatory framework.[14] This framework draws on the prevalent bio-ethical practice and doctrine developed from the 1970s onwards mainly by the *Centres d'Etudes et de Conservation des Oeufs et du Sperme* (CECOS) and a bio-ethical committee, the *Comité consultatif national d'éthique* (CCNE).[15] In the practice of the CECOS, anonymity was represented as an absolute ethical necessity by medical physicians in accordance with their general duty to observe secrecy. In the criminal law code, disclosure of donor identity became liable to two years' imprisonment.[16] This policy is reflected in the present regulatory

13 Fasouliotis & Schenker (1996), p. 756.

14 Loi n.° 94-654 du 29 juillet relative au don et à l'utilisation des éléments et produits du corps humain, à l'assistance médicale à la procréation et au diagnostic prénatal; Loi n.° 94-653 du 29 juillet 1994 relative au respect du corps humain, *Journal Officiel*, 30 July 1994.

15 Rubellin-Devichi (1996), p. 400.

16 Art. 511-10 **French** Criminal Law Code (Code Pénal).

framework which preserves donor anonymity.[17] The medical professional must, however, document the medical history of the anonymous donor in the prevention of hereditary diseases.[18]

In **Germany**, the use of ART was discouraged by the federal government because of historical associations with a dark eugenic past.[19] Thus, for reasons of public morality, criminal sanctions in tax law for couples and medical practitioners who engaged in heterologous insemination were even proposed in the 1960s. In the mid-80s parliamentary discussions ensued which led to the enactment of the Embryo Protection Act (Embryonenschutzgesetz = EschG) in 1991, which prohibits egg donation.

Even so, there is nowadays broad consensus that ART are not inherently unconstitutional. They do not violate the constitutional notion of human dignity.[20] In the aftermath of the 1989 landmark case by the Federal Constitutional Court, a debate ensued as to whether anonymous sperm donation should not be considered unconstitutional in view of the recognition in that case of a child's constitutional right to information.[21] This thesis has been defended by Rauscher, who argues that anonymous donations involve a transgression of the medical professional duty to document the identity of donors appropriately, a duty he also derives from the child's right to information.[22] This duty to at least document the identity of donors has also been corroborated by other doctrinal views.[23]

To date, the fact remains, though, that no comprehensive regulatory framework exists. Rather, the Embryo Protection Act lists a set of prohibitions.[24] Furthermore, there are soft law instruments which include professional medical guidelines of the Federal Medical Chamber[25] on IVF and embryo transfers. These guidelines, annually adapted, have largely been accepted by the Regional Chambers of the Medical Profession. The Federal Medical Chamber has drafted elaborate guidelines on a wide variety of ART-related aspects such as the screen-

---

17 Art. 16-8 **French** Code Civil in conjunction with Art. L 165-14 of the **French** Public Health Code (Code de la Santé Publique).

18 FURKEL (1996), p. 772-774.

19 COESTER-WALTJEN (1989), p. 520.

20 HELMS (1999), p. 114.

21 COESTER-WALTJEN, *Jura* 1989, p. 520, 523; GIESEN, *JZ* 1989, 368; STARCK, *JZ* 1989, p. 339.

22 RAUSCHER/STAUDINGER (2004), BGB, §1592, Rdnr. 15.

23 RAUSCHER/STAUDINGER (2004), BGB, §1592, Rdnr. 15; MUTSCHELER (1994) 65, 70; STARCK (1989), p. 38.

24 Embryoschutzgesetz (EschG).

25 *Bundesärtztekammer* = Federal Medical Chamber.

ing of recipients and informed consent requirements.[26] Notably, these latter guidelines recommend that in principle only heterosexual married couples should be able to benefit from ART while leaving open the possibility for a woman to undergo treatment as long as she has a sufficiently stable relationship with her male partner comparable to marriage. If the couple are not married, the medical practitioner makes an assessment of the man's willingness to recognise paternity.[27] The Annex to the Federal Medical Chamber Guidelines specifies that sperm donation should only be considered if the donor has given his consent to the child being able to identify his name upon request.

In 1957 the **Dutch** Parliament first addressed ART.[28] Christian political parties drew attention to the child's 'right' to know.[29] Generally, ART was still not considered to be morally acceptable.[30] The National Health Council[31] still concluded in 1960 that AI was far too uncommon and the reliable scientific information far too scarce to require regulation.[32]

Nonetheless, the year 1965 witnessed the publication of a parliamentary, multi-party commission report on ART.[33] In this report it was speculated that AI would expose both families and children to a great amount of emotional tension as children would have a 'natural desire' to know their biological father.[34] By then, the traditional stigma attached to (male) infertility had, however, lessened.[35] Moreover, non-biological parenthood required less justification from the social environment as biological influences on child development were called into question.[36] Even so, the interests of the child were implicitly considered to be less compelling, than those of couples with fertility problems who now relied on sympathy rather than stigmatization.[37]

---

26 (Muster)richtlinie zur Durchführung der assistierten Reproduktion, *Deutsches Ärtzteblatt*, vol. 103, issue 20, 19 May 2006, A1398.

27 By implication no such right to undergo treatment for (foreign) married same-sex couples or single lesbian women appears to have been envisaged. It will be remembered that the child may be recognised before birth pursuant to §1594 IV BGB.

28 *Handelingen* 1956-1957, p. 2659-2683.

29 ZIPPER (1985), p. 43-44.

30 TAKES (2006), p. 41.

31 Gezondheidsraad.

32 ZIPPER (1985), p. 38.

33 *Advies kunstmatige inseminatie bij de mens*, 1965, p, 3.

34 *Advies kunstmatige inseminatie bij de mens*, 1965, p. 11.

35 HOKSBERGEN (1995), p. 34.

36 HOKSBERGEN (1995), p. 34.

37 HOKSBERGEN (1995), p. 35.

By the 1980s, the **Dutch** debate became more oriented towards children's informational needs. Opposition came in particular from the medical profession. Thus, the gynecologist Kremer[38] held that anonymity should be preserved on the basis of a research among 153 couples, whose treatment had resulted in the birth of a child. He considered that the risk of an onset of hereditary diseases among AI children would be so slight as not to warrant any policy change. Moreover, he suspected that the number of donors would decrease dramatically if anonymity were waived. Quite regardless of the possibility for hereditary diseases to develop in the child, however, medical practitioners are reported to have destroyed all information on donors in the course of the 1980s.[39]

In 1987, at the Biomedical Department of the Catholic Study Centre of the Nijmegen Radboud University a few bio-ethicists published another study, which concluded that the individual interest of the child should not be deduced *a priori* from ethical premises, but rather, from empirically measurable facts on the basis of the true experiences of AI children. In spite of this argument, the Nijmegen researchers agreed that truth finding constituted an important ethical public policy consideration.[40] The following year, the Council for Youth Policy of the **Dutch** Ministry of Education also presented its views on the place of the traditional family in contemporary society in general and in particular on the ongoing influences of bio-medical developments. In this report, an AI child's sense of feeling 'unwanted' was believed to be much less common than in adoption in view of the fact that unintentionally childless couples had gone to great lengths to fulfil their wish. Hence, the need to know would also be less ingrained.[41]

The Scientific Bureau of the Christian Democrats suggested, however, that 'AI with the assistance of a sperm donor should not a priori be reduced to a clinical-technical affair and be deprived of its human dimension'.[42] It proposed a legal regime envisaging a phased, ongoing disclosure of identifying information. In response, a physician from Nijmegen, Bierkens, suggested there was no evidence that AI children suffered from the fact that they did not know their origins. In the absence of compelling empirical findings documenting the informational need among donor conceived persons, he considered this increased attention for

---

38 KREMER, FRIJLING & NASS (1981), *Medisch Contact*, p. 44.

39 HOKSBERGEN (1995), p. 41.

40 *Ingrijpen in de menselijke voortplanting* (1987), p. 98. Furthermore: TAKES (2006), p. 73.

41 *Ouderschap zonder onderscheid* (1988), **Dutch** Council of Youth Policy, p. 72.

42 *Zinvol leven* (1988), p. 80.

the child's needs to be misguided. Rather, he mounted an argument for greater societal sympathy for the 'plight' of couples with fertility problems.[43]

Meanwhile, a **Dutch-Belgian** Foundation of physicians for Artificial Insemination[44] was founded which made several bio-ethical recommendations, suggesting the creation of a donor passport listing several social and physical characteristics of the donor. Furthermore, a double-track policy programme was developed which allowed the commissioning parents to either choose for an anonymous donor or a donor whose identifying information would be disclosed at the age of sixteen.[45]

In 1989, the Ministry of Justice authorised a team of child psychiatrists from the Rotterdam Erasmus University to conduct research on the psychological effects of donor anonymity on children. The psychiatrists found it morally objectionable that they should approach parents who, certainly at the time that they had made their reproductive choices, had thought that they could 'rest assured'. Furthermore, a longitudinal research among donor-conceived children who had found out would not yet be practicable. The research was therefore not carried out.[46]

Throughout the 1990s, the Council for Youth Policy advocated openness on account of the increased societal awareness of the (supposed) importance of knowing one's genetic parentage with reference to the experiences of adoptees.[47] In contrast, the Royal **Dutch** Medical Society objected to disclosure, again referring to the sheer lack of empirical data and the lack of ethical consensus.[48] In the second half of the 1990s it was hypothesized, too, that it would be single mothers and lesbian couples who stood to bare the brunt of the imminent drop in available donors in case disclosure was admitted.[49]

Nonetheless, in 1993, a bill was first submitted, albeit unsuccessfully, to Parliament.[50] It conceived of a system of centralized documentation, wherein information would be divided into two broad categories: both 'identifying' and 'non-

---

43 BIERKENS (1992), p. 61.

44 Nederlands-Belgische Vereniging voor Kunstmatige Inseminatie, www.nbvki.nl.

45 TAKES (2006), p. 81.

46 SLIJPER & VERHULST (1991), p. 12-15.

47 *De naam van de ooievaar* (1992), p. 6.

48 *Commentaar op het voortontwerp van wet 'Donorgegevens Kunstmatige Inseminatie'* (1992).

49 WOLFHAGEN (1996), *Nemesis*, p. 96-102.

50 *Kamerstukken II* 1992/93, 23 207 Nos. 1-2.

identifying'. It was suggested that all children should at least have access to the non-identifying information from the age of twelve. In response, it was held that a waiver of anonymity would discourage parents from disclosing any information at all.[51] Moreover, the difficulty of achieving societal consensus would also indicate that government should steer clear of regulation.[52]

Towards the end of the 1980s state regulation had, however, gained broad sympathy from scholars and politicians alike.[53] Favouring state intervention, the bio-ethicist De Ruiter advanced four arguments.[54] This was not only because the state had condoned ART as a permissible alternative means of human reproduction. Rather, the child's informational rights would also be bereft of any real meaning. In that connection, De Ruiter held that disclosure could not really be entrusted to the child's parents since their impartiality would hardly be unambiguous. Moreover, it would be unfair to have medical professionals bear the burden of disclosing the information. For these reasons, state regulation would be the right alternative. In spite of this, in the *Valkenhorst II* case, the **Dutch** Supreme Court still saw in donor anonymity a possible exception to a general right to know.[55] This readiness of the judiciary to treat ART differently may most probably be attributed to the fact that the legislature had just chosen to look further into the issue of donor anonymity, however.

By the turn of the millennium, the liberal democrats and all of the left-wing parties also started to take an interest in what had previously been a favourite ethical issue of the Christian democrats. For both the liberals and the left, the 'child's informational self-determination', expressed in the UNCRC, rather than the dissociation between biology and socio-legal ties was the main concern.[56]

By 2002 the **Dutch** Embryos Act[57] had also entered into force, which imposed limitations on the use of gametes and embryos by listing a set of prohibitions and setting conditions with respect to certain procedures. In drafting this act the legislator had sought to strike a balance between respect for the dignity of the human person, human life and other values, such as not only the care of the sick

51 LEENEN (1993), p. 1101.
52 LEENEN (1993), p. 1101-1106.
53 RUITER (1993), p. 57-62. See also: DOEK (1995), p. 151.
54 RUITER (1993), p. 57-62.
55 See Chapter IV. Hoge Raad, 17 September 1993, *NJ* 1994, p. 272.
56 *Handelingen* 2000-2001, TK, No. 41, 3263.
57 Wet van 20 juni 2002, houdende regels inzake handelingen met geslachtcellen en embryo's ('Embryowet').

and the promotion of their health, but also the well-being of infertile couples and the future child.[58] It also confirmed that the provision of gametes and embryos could no longer be remunerable.

In spite of increased political and societal support for a waiver of anonymity on ethical grounds, the fear that the number of donors would drop almost overnight still provided an incentive for the **Dutch** Government to fund an empirical research.[59] This prompted the Green Left politician Halsema to hold that it was self-contradictory for the government to see a need for empirical research if that same government had already come round to acknowledging that the child had a principled and constitutionally recognised right to know.[60]

This study concluded that approximately half of the available and prospective donors would refrain from sperm donation if anonymity were waived by law.[61] These findings were, however, largely brushed aside by parliamentarians from the various political strata, given that only donors from the 'old school' had been enquired; (stereo)typically, these men had donated as 'penniless' university students for a small fee, whereas the new donor would generally be older, financially independent, more altruistically inclined, ideologically motivated and more emotionally mature.[62]

In **Portugal**, legislation on ART has long been scant. Until 2006 it was restricted to consent requirements in the Civil Code establishing the paternity of the socio-legal father and to a set of prohibitive rules in the Criminal Law Code.[63] A few law proposals and non-binding bio-ethical guidelines had, however, already been drafted prior to the enactment of the 2006 law. Thus, a law proposal[64] required that access to treatment be restricted to medically-attested infertile heterosexual couples over the age of eighteen. Furthermore, all beneficiaries would have to be either married or at least live in conditions analogous to marriage and have the mental capacity allowing them to provide informed consent.

58 OLTSHOORN-HEIM (2006), p. 17.
59 TROMMELEN (1999), p. 43.
60 *Kamerstukken II* 1999/2000, 23 207, No. 14, 5.
61 This estimation indeed did not prove to have been very far off the mark. JANSSENS (2005), p. 1415. According to this study the number of B-donors (accorded provisional anonymity under the Act) showed a significant increase rising from 16 to 78, but was nonetheless insufficient to compensate the sharp drop in the number of donors altogether.
62 *Kamerstukken II* 1999/2000, 23 207, No. 14, 4-5.
63 Decreto-Lei N.° 32/2006, 26 July 2006. Lei da Procriação Medicamente Assistida (LPMA).
64 Decreto-Lei N.° 319/86, 25 September 1986.

This early proposal insisted *inter alia* on strict medical supervision, and permitted the use of homologous artificial insemination and intra-tubary IVF.

In the course of the 1990s, the National Ethics and Life Sciences Council[65] (CNECV) proposed a set of authoritative recommendations, which dealt with donor anonymity among a number of other issues. It considered that the practice of ART in itself should not be considered unethical simply because of the inevitable dissociation between the affective aspects of the sexual act and the process of human reproduction. Still, ART would have to be considered a *subsidiary* and *not an alternative* means of procreation. This would imply that there would have to be evidence that the couple's genuine desire for a child could not be realized through natural reproduction. Further, it meant that same-sex couples and single women would not be eligible.

In 1999, a law proposal was drafted[66] which conceived of a regime of strict donor anonymity and ART as a subsidiary form of human reproduction, as had been suggested by the CNECV. Only the left-wing parties voted in favour. The negative response reflected the opinions of the CNECV which had issued further ethical recommendations in July 1997.[67]

In 2004 the CNECV issued further recommendations following two legislative proposals by the moderate centre-left *Partido Socialista* (PS)[68] and the leftist *Bloco de Esquerda*.[69] Both of these proposals criticised the legislative inertia of the right. Whereas the BE proposed a liberalised regime, the PS proposal argued that in principle only married heterosexual couples should be able to benefit from ART. Both these proposals adhered to donor anonymity making the disclosure of information by third parties liable to prison sentences of up to two years. The moderate left proposal conceded, though, that 'on medically ascertained grounds' AI children should obtain 'any type of information concerning them, including identification of the donor' subsequent to a decision by a family court in the area where he or she had habitual residence.

65 *Conselho Nacional de Ética para as Ciências da Vida.*
66 Decreto-Lei N.° 415/VIII, 30 July 1999.
67 *Relatório – Parecer sobre o Projecto de Lei relativamente à Procriação Assistida*, Conselho Nacional da Ética para as Ciências da Vida, 1997.
68 *Partido Socialista* Projecto de Lei N.° 90/IX.
69 *Bloco de Esquerda* Projecto de Lei N.° 317/IX.

The CNECV turned against both of these proposals.[70] It now held that the child should be allowed to petition identifying information concerning the donor, as long as it could be ensured that an establishment of the donor's paternity could be excluded.

However, this bit of advice was not followed in the present regulatory framework law, which seeks to regulate a whole spectrum of issues involving ART. It foresaw the creation of a new National Council on ART.[71] It has a variety of informational tasks with regard to the general public and enjoys standard-setting competences with regard to the quality of services offered by clinics. It also registers all relevant information concerning the donor, children born through ART and applicants centrally. It is composed of nine eminent persons with recognised expertise in ethical, scientific, social and legal areas. The members are appointed by the government and by Parliament for five years and must report to Parliament and the Ministry of Health annually on its activities.

Both egg and sperm donation are permitted as a subsidiary means of human reproduction. As such, sufficient medical evidence of a fertility problem must first be put forward.[72] Alongside married couples who are not factually living separately only 'different-sex' couples who have cohabited for a minimum of two years in 'conditions analogous to marriage' may undergo treatment.[73]After having been informed in writing of the ethical, social and legal implications, applicants must provide written consent to the medical practitioner. Both parties to the agreement may withdraw their consent freely until the beginning of treatment.

4. SURROGACY

4.1. RELEVANT LAW

During the 1980s **French** legal doctrine and courts were deeply divided over the status of surrogacy contracts. Even so, the homologation of adoption orders by commissioning parents occurred in some instances during that period, sometimes without any further critical enquiry beyond what was perceived to be in the

---

70 *Relatório – Parecer N.º 44 do Conselho Nacional de Ética para as Ciências da Vida sobre a Procriação Medicamente Assistida,* 44/CNECV/4, July 2004.

71 *Conselho Nacional de Procriação Medicamente Assistida.*

72 Art. 4-1 LPMA.

73 Art. 6-1 LPMA.

'interests of the child'. In order to achieve greater legal certainty, the Cour de Cassation ruled in 1991 that surrogacy contracts are null and void on account of the principle of the non-commodification of the human body.[74] Still, surrogacy was not expressly prohibited in the law on artificial reproductive technologies of 29 July 1994.

Since the June 2005 reform of parentage law, the establishment of maternity derives from designation in the birth act of the name of the woman who has given birth, regardless of whether the child is born within or outside marriage.[75] If the surrogate has been designated as the mother, her husband will be the legal father in accordance with the marital presumption rule in AI.[76]

In view of the prohibitive regime that marks the national legislation, it is understandable that **French** case law on surrogacy bears an international imprint. In 2002, for example, a **French** couple entered into an agreement with a surrogate mother from **California,** who then gave birth to twins. The **French** couple had provided their fertilized gametes to the **Californian** surrogate.[77] As in a number of other North American jurisdictions, pursuant to the law of **California** the biological mother is the legal mother.[78] Upon the couple's return to **France**, the commissioning mother made a recognition before the **French** Consulate-General. Suspecting that the birth had resulted from surrogacy, the Consulate-General notified the Nantes Regional Court. Proceedings were lodged by the Public Ministry. Following a successful denial of maternity, the couple were allowed to adopt the child. It follows that subsequent adoption after an international surrogacy agreement may sometimes confer parental status on the commissioning parents in **France**. This jurisprudential leeway was also verifiable in another recent surrogacy case involving an **American** gestational mother. The transfer of parental status was considered to be in the child's interests.[79] Nonetheless, in another case from 2007 a Lille Court denied a **French** commissioning couple a civil status relationship because the surrogacy contract was considered null and void.[80]

---

74 Cass., II, 31 May 1991, *JCP*, 1991, 21.752, 381.

75 Art. 311-25 **French** Code Civil. See Chapter VI.

76 Art. 1:199 (a) DCC.

77 Cour d'Appel de Rennes, 4 July 2002, *Recueil Dalloz* 2002, 2902.

78 The leading **American** surrogacy cases remain *Johnson v. Calvert*. 1993. 30 *Cal. Rptr.* 2d 893 (Cal.Ct.App.) and *Re Marriage of Buzzanca*. 1998. 72 *Cal. Rptr.* 2d 280 (Cal.Ct.App.).

79 TGI Paris, Ire. Ch.C, 25 October 2007, n° 06-00507.

80 TGI Lille, 22nd March 2007, D.2007, *Droit de Famille*, comm. n° 122, note P. Murat.

Recently, however, changes have been proposed by a parliamentary commission appointed by the **French** Senate (*Sénat*). An incentive for reform was provided by a case in which the Court of Appeal in Paris allowed the **French** commissioning parents of twins to be registered as the legal parents, even though a **Californian** surrogate had given birth to them.[81] The commission proposes lifting the ban on surrogacy, allowing for a system in which both the courts and the Bureau for biomedicine would play a preponderant role.[82] In the proposal only non-commercial **French** surrogates may be conscripted by the commissioning parents, although some form of remuneration of healthcare for the costs of carrying the pregnancy to term is permitted. Before placing the embryo in the gestational mother's womb, consent must be obtained from the Bureau for biomedicine and the court. The gestational mother can decide to keep the child within three days after birth; the commissioning parents, who should not be of the same sex and one of whom must have a genetic link to the child, cannot revoke their consent to the surrogacy agreement after having obtained judicial approval. Their names will be entered on the child's birth certificate as the legal parents.

In **Germany**, both the provision of conciliation services[83] and the supply of medical assistance to surrogacy have been prohibited.[84] The prohibition has been derived in a linear way from the right of children to know their origins.[85] In accordance with the *mater semper certa* rule the surrogate or gestational mother will be the child's mother.[86] If the surrogate is married, this means that her husband will be the child's father by operation of law.[87]

In the **German** Mediation in Adoption Act[88] a legal definition of surrogate motherhood may be found.[89] Herein both the provision of conciliation or mediation services have also been prohibited.[90] The person who benefits financially from a surrogacy contract risks imprisonment for two years.[91] If no such profit

81 Cour d'Appel de Paris, Ire Chambre, sect.C., 25 October 2007, *JCP G* 2007, act 547.
82 BRAAT (2008), p. 289-294; MIRKOVIC (2008), p. 9-13.
83 §§13c, 13d Adoptionsvermitlungsgesetz (AdVermG).
84 §1 Nos 1, 2, 6, 7 Embryonenschutzgesetz (EschG) 1990.
85 *BT-Drucks.* 11/5460, 7.
86 §1591 BGB.
87 §1592 (1) BGB.
88 **German** Mediation in Adoption Act = Adoptionvermittlungsgesetz (AdVermG).
89 §13a AdVermG.
90 §13b c and d AdVermG.
91 §14b (1) AdVermG.

has been made, the maximum sentence is one year.[92] The gestational mother and the commissioning parents are exempt from criminal prosecution.[93]

Given this prohibitive regime, it may come as no surprise that the first heterological surrogacy and/or egg donation case before a **German** court is still awaited.[94] Moreover, the *mater semper certa* rule means that the gestational mother will be the child's legal mother.[95] It has even been suggested that a primary reason behind the codification of *mater semper certa* stemmed from the perceived urgency of discouraging couples with fertility problems to enter into 'risky' surrogacy contracts.[96] Even so, it has been suggested that the mother who has provided the gametes should sometimes be able to adopt.[97] If the adoption were to cause harm to the child's interests or if it can be demonstrated that consent requirements with respect to the gestational mother have not been met, the adoption may be annulled, however.[98]

With a view to identifying the biological mother, it is remarkable that the new informational procedure of April 2008 leaves room for the legal father and the child to compel the mother to undergo parentage testing.[99] This means that in surrogacy arrangements, the absence of the gestational mother's biological link can be established before the court. However, in principle the biological mother would not – as a third person – fall under such a duty.

In **the Netherlands**, only commercial surrogacy, whether only consisting of conciliation or medical services, has been expressly prohibited, pursuant to a 1993 reform of the **Dutch** Criminal Law Code.[100] As far as non-commercial forms of surrogacy are concerned, the parties may draw up an agreement. Currently, there are a few **Dutch** clinics that in theory will not deny medical services if a

---

92 §14b (2) AdVermG.

93 §14b (3) AdVermG.

94 COESTER-WALTJEN (1992).

95 §1591 BGB. See Chapter VI. On surrogacy and the establishment of maternity, see PALANDT/DIEDERICHSEN (2006), BGB, Titel 2, Intro, 1854.

96 *BT-Drucks.* 13/4899, 51.

97 QUANTIUS (1998), p. 1151. Under § 1742 II 2 BGB (jointly with her husband) or step-parent pursuant to § 1741 II 3 BGB if her partner's paternity were already established.

98 QUANTIUS (1998), p. 1151. §§ 1759, 1760 I BGB (annulment) and 1746 BGB (child's consent to adoption).

99 Pursuant to §1598a BGB. *BT-Drucks. 16/6561*, p.15. See also: SCHWAB (2008), p. 24-25. See Chapter VIII.

100 Introduction of Arts. 151b and 151c, Neth. Cr. C., *Staatsblad*, 1993, No. 486.

non-commercial agreement has been entered into.[101] Still, these clinics will not be able to help find a surrogate for the commissioning parents.

Dutch law has no specific procedure geared towards transferring parental rights and duties from the surrogate mother (and her husband) to the commissioning parents.[102] The gestational mother is considered to be the mother even where, in surrogacy contracts, the genetic material was not taken from her.[103] The position of the Dutch government is that a transfer from one set of parents to another set of parents should require the voluntary divestment of parental responsibility by one set of parents, after which the intended parents can be vested with parental responsibilities and may eventually adopt the child.[104] The surrogate is under no obligation to hand over the child and the commissioning parents are under no obligation to accept the child.[105]

If the surrogate mother is married, her husband will be the legal father by operation of law.[106] If she is unmarried, a male may recognise the child. In view of the *mater semper certa* rule, for same-sex male parents surrogacy will, however, not be an option in the pursuit of their child wish. A transfer of parental rights in surrogacy may only take effect through: 1) the divestment of parental responsibility followed by adoption in case the surrogate mother is married, 2) recognition by the commissioning father followed by divestment of parental responsibility and partner adoption or 3) recognition followed by the transfer of sole parental responsibility from the surrogate mother to the commissioning father followed by partner adoption in case the surrogate does not have a formalized relationship.[107]

Scholarly literature is divided on the question whether the transfer of parental rights to the commissioning parents should become easier. There is consensus on the general clause that the main clause in a surrogacy contract, namely that a

101 Since 2006 there have been clinics that offer IVF-surrogacy services to married couples in such cases. Www.vumc.nl/afdelingen/patientenfolders-brochures/zoeken-alfabet/D/hoog_technologisch_draagmoe1.pdf.

102 BOELE & ODERKERK (1999), p. 25-44.

103 Art. 1:198 DCC. See Chapter VI.

104 *Kamerstukken II* 1996/97, 25 000-XVI, No. 62, p. 13.

105 However, the guidelines of the Dutch Society for Obstetrics and Gynaecology require that clinics draw up a protocol. One of the conditions is that the gestational mother should have given birth before without complications and should consider her own family to be complete. See VONK (2007), p. 138-139 and www.nvog.nl.

106 Art. 1:199(1)(a) and (b) DCC. See Chapter VII.

107 VONK (2007), p. 140.

surrogate should surrender the child to the commissioning parents after birth, is null and void.[108] For some **Dutch** authors, the 'intention' of the commissioning parents should be the decisive factor in conferring parentage in the surrogacy context.[109] Moltmaker even advocates the creation of specific parentage proceedings for modern forms of surrogacy.[110] In other words, the commissioning mother's stronger child wish at the beginning of the contract should be decisive.

The gynecologist Dermout has expressly advocated the genetic link of the commissioning mother as the preferred determinant of maternity in most high technology surrogacy contracts.[111] Along with legal scholar Hammerstein-Schoonderwoerd Dermout goes as far as to label the genetic mother, for all intents and purposes, 'the real mother'.[112] In order to attribute maternity to her, Dermout proposes a specific procedure in which the gestational mother could deny maternity. In her proposition the genetic mother would lodge concomitant proceedings geared towards the establishment of her maternity through adoption. More recently, an easier procedural route to adoption in the case of high technology surrogacy contracts, following the **English** example, has also been advocated by a number of other authors.[113]

As an alternative, Broekhuijsen-Molenaar has proposed that the attribution of parentage to the commissioning parents in surrogacy should be made subject to a prior, written judicial decree concerning the terms of the contract.[114] This would help to avoid subsequent problems concerning the establishment of legal parentage and parental authority. For the courts, the biological link would then have to be an important, though not necessarily decisive, criterion in conferring the status of legal parent. Whenever sufficiently clear preliminary arrangements have not been made, Broekhuijsen-Molenaar suggests that the ordinary adoption procedure may be followed.[115] This would provide a further incentive for parties to make prior arrangements and deter people from entering into surrogacy contracts without pondering the risks involved.

108 VONK (2008), p. 128.
109 MOLTMAKER (1989), p. 1497-1498.
110 MOLTMAKER (1989), p. 1497-1498
111 DERMOUT (2001), p. 176.
112 HAMMERSTEIN-SCHOONDERWOERD (1988), p. 3.
113 ARKEL (2004), p. 193; SUTORIUS & KERSEN (1997), p. 1116-1120; RAAK-KUIPER (2007), p. 100. In **Greece**, the genetic mother may challenge the gestational mother's claim to maternity. See: KOUTSOURADIS (2007), p. 246.
114 BROEKHUIJSEN-MOLENAAR in BOELE-WOELKI (1999), p. 39.
115 BROEKHUIJSEN-MOLENAAR in BOELE-WOELKI (1999), p. 39.

In 2005, such risks were highlighted in the media coverage of the *Baby Donna* case.[116] The baby was born in February 2005 to a gestational mother who had unilaterally suspended a surrogacy contract with the commissioning **Belgian** couple when, as it turned out, a higher price had been offered. This **Belgian** couple had contacted the gestational mother through an advertisement on the internet in view of the wish of the commissioning mother to have a child with her new partner. A sample of the **Belgian** male's sperm was sent to the gestational mother. The gestational mother made it known to the commissioning parents that she had changed her mind and intended to keep the child, claiming that the child's begetter was her own husband and that the commissioning parent's sperm had not been used. Three days after her birth, Donna was brought to **the Netherlands** and handed over to the care of the **Dutch** couple. In the month leading up to the birth, the Child Care and Protection Board had notified the **Dutch** couple that it would refrain from undertaking any action before the child's birth. The **Dutch** couple openly applied for guardianship to the Haarlem Child Care and Protection Board, to whom they confirmed they wished to adopt the child within one year.

The **Dutch** parents had, however, not provided information on the international character of the underlying transaction: it was not known to the **Dutch** authorities that the child was born in **Belgium** and had **Belgian** nationality. In this way the couple had circumvented the **Dutch** procedure for intercountry adoption.[117] Subsequently, the **Dutch** Child Care Council advised that the newborn be brought into the care of the Youth Care Agency in Utrecht. Apparently not insensitive to the ongoing media coverage, a **Belgian** judge from Oudenaarde then decided to intervene and made an application to the Utrecht juvenile court judge to refer the case to him. Although the Utrecht juvenile court judge consented, the Ghent Appeal Court claimed that **Belgian** courts could not be seised and suspended the lower court's decision to bring the child into the care of a **Belgian** childcare institution accordingly. Thereafter, the case was again referred to the Utrecht Court.

The **Dutch** couple next came with a number of interrelated claims. Firstly, they applied for guardianship concomitant with a suspension of the care of the Youth Care Agency. They also argued that the child could not be kept away from them pending any irrevocable decision to that end. They also requested the Utrecht Court to determine that, while Donna resided with them, they were able to

116 Rechtbank Utrecht, 25 October 2005, LJN: AU4934.

117 VONK (2008), p. 14.

apply for a discharge of the parental authority of the **Belgian** (gestational) parents[118] which would be irrevocable. Pending any decision by the Utrecht court, they requested that Donna remain in their care. The Child Care Council underlined that the **Dutch** couple should have been aware that they could not simply circumvent the legal requirements for adoption. This came along with the assertion that the interests of the child required that Donna be brought back to **Belgium** without any further delay. Furthermore, the Council denied that the **Dutch** couple had any legal competence to apply for a discharge of parental authority. Similarly, the Youth Care Agency and the Public Prosecutor also emphasised that the adoption requirements had not been fulfilled while arguing that the child should be brought back to **Belgium**. The judge concurred with the Public Prosecutor and the Child Care Council that the international and national requirements for adoption had not been complied with. Thus, at least formally, the guardianship of the Youth Care Agency was preserved. Crucially, however, it was found that 'family life' within the meaning of Article 8 ECHR had developed between Donna and the **Dutch** couple over the course of the eight months that she had been residing with them.

The **Dutch** Minister of Justice Donner was asked parliamentary questions on the case by fellow Christian-Democrat De Pater-van de Meer on two occasions.[119] Meanwhile, the **Belgian** commissioning father had obtained scientific proof of his genetic link to Donna. Nonetheless, as family life exists in respect of the **Dutch** foster parents, it was decided in 2008 that Donna should remain in **the Netherlands**. Recently, however, the Amsterdam Court of Appeal has confirmed that the biological father had a family life with the child, making specific reference to certain factual circumstances such as the e-mail correspondence between him and the **Dutch** parents and his presence during medical consultations of the gestational mother with a gynaecologist.[120]

In another recent case, a **Dutch** commissioning couple had contracted an **English** gestational mother who underwent IVF surrogacy treatment.[121] In the adoption decision weight was attached to the genetic link of both **Dutch** commissioning parents to the child and the clear waiver of parental rights of the gestational mother in the contract. For those reasons, the rules for international adoption were considered not to be applicable because from the outset it had been clear

118 Art. 1:267(2) DCC.
119 5357682/05/DJJ 25 May 2005, www.justitie.nl; 5384278/05/DJJ, 31 October 2005, www.justitie.nl.
120 Gerechtshof Amsterdam, 25 November 2008, LJN: BG5157.
121 Rechtbank Rotterdam, 11 December 2007, LJN BB9844.

that the child would grow up with the **Dutch** parents. Interestingly, the court interpreted Article 7 UNCRC so as though it would require that the child knows and be raised by the commissioning (genetic) parents. The same provision was also successfully relied upon in another **Dutch** surrogacy case in which the genetic parents successfully reclaimed a child from the commissioning parents.[122] This differs somewhat from the more bracing doctrinal view which holds that Article 7-1 UNCRC requires that a child should be able to identify *both* the gestational and the genetic mother.[123]

In **Portugal**, the *mater semper certa* rule also applies when a surrogacy arrangement has been made.[124] Thus, the gestational mother will become the mother and, if she is married, her husband will become the father by operation of law.[125] Nonetheless, the Public Ministry may deny a woman's maternity if it is not 'true.'[126] It has been suggested that the state could therefore deny the gestational mother's maternity. Subsequently, the maternity of the genetic mother could be established.[127] Doctrinal views support the idea that the child should be informed of both the identity of the gestational mother and the genetic mother.[128]

The recently enacted **Portuguese** law on medically-assisted procreation aims to further reduce surrogacy arrangements, even though these have not yet been registered. Surrogacy has been defined as 'any situation in which a woman makes her will known to undergo a pregnancy on behalf of someone else and to hand over the child after giving birth, renouncing all competences and obligations pertaining to maternity'.[129] This law has affirmed that both commercial and non-commercial forms of surrogacy are null and void.[130] Parties to a surrogacy contract or who 'promote' such a contract, 'in whatever way', including 'advertisements', may even be sentenced to a custodial sentence of up to two years.[131]

122 Hof Leeuwarden, 6 October 2004, LJN AR3391.
123 RAAK-KUIPER (2007), p. 92.
124 Incidentally, no surrogacy case has yet been registered in **Portugal**.
125 Art. 1826-1 PCC.
126 Art. 1807 PCC.
127 VALE E REIS (2008), p. 485.
128 MARTINHO DA SILVA (1986), p. 76; VALE E REIS (2008), p. 483-484.
129 Art. 8.°-2 Lei n.° 32/2006, de 26 de Julho, relativa à procriação medicamente assistida.
130 Art. 8.°-1 Lei n.° 32/2006.
131 Art. 39.°-1 and 2, Lei n.° 32/2006.

4.2. COMPARISON

All four countries take a prohibitive stance towards surrogacy arrangements, even though non-commercial forms are condoned in **the Netherlands.** Only **Germany** also expressly prohibits egg donation. In that regard, the child's right to know is considered important. In **France**, surrogacy is prohibited because it is considered to violate an underlying principle of non-commodification. At the time of writing, however, significant changes to this regime have been proposed.

In all jurisdictions the surrogate or gestational mother will in principle become the child's legal mother, without the possibility of disestablishment or divestment. This will also lead to the establishment of her husband's paternity by operation of law. This means that the gestational mother will be the child's legal mother. In **Portugal** maternity may be denied by the state, whereas in **the Netherlands a** divestment of parental authority followed by adoption may sometimes allow for a transfer of status.

4.3. EVALUATION

The ECtHR has not yet ruled upon surrogacy. It is clear, however, that surrogacy contracts could create considerable tension with the right to know one's origins as protected under Article 8 of the Convention. The *mater semper certa* rule may discourage some couples from entering into a surrogacy contract. The mother who carries a pregnancy to term will typically not only be the child's legal mother, but also have the intention to be the child's legal parent. From that perspective, the creation of an alternative solution for surrogacy may not be desirable. Yet an exceptional regime for establishing maternity could be desirable. In a surrogacy arrangement, the child only exists because of the intention of the commissioning parents. 'To ignore the centrality of their intention and instead ascribe *prima facie* parenthood to a couple that never intended to keep the child may not promote the child's welfare'[132] One of the main risks is, however, that the intentions of both parties may change in the course of pregnancy and thereafter.

As the case of the **Dutch** couple that contracted an **English** surrogate shows, prohibitive rules may also provide an incentive for procreational tourism.[133] It

132 JACKSON (2001), p. 275.

133 Likewise, some foreign women may choose to give birth anonymously in countries such as **France**. Reproductive tourism motivated by a mother's unwillingness to assume the maternal socio-legal role is not restricted to surrogacy.

is speculative whether this can be prevented, but there are good reasons to assume that this is far from being an isolated phenomenon. A look beyond national frontiers is in part motivated by comparative cost-economic concerns which have become more transparent through the internet. The root cause of reproductive tourism will, however, be found in restrictive legislation in the home country. As Guido Pennings has pointed out, this phenomenon may, however, not necessarily be conceived of as ethically objectionable. This is not only because an infertile couple's desire to have a child may be perfectly legitimate. Rather, Pennings contends that 'the purpose of national regulation should not be to prevent those who disagree to perform certain acts or to make use of certain services or services. Prohibitive laws can only determine which services are available on the territory. As such, the law expresses the moral values of the majority within a community; nothing more, nothing less. Tolerance towards movement by minority members to other countries shows a healthy degree of relativism'. Rather, 'each country constitutes a 'natural experiment' on a limited scale from which the others may collect useful information for their own legislation'.[134] On that view, European harmonisation in a sensitive bio-ethical field like surrogacy would accordingly need to be based on persuasion rather than on coercion and generally have to respect regulatory diversity.

If a prohibitive approach is taken on surrogacy, this could prompt contracting parties to conceal the mode of conception and pregnancy from the public authorities even more. It may therefore be better for a legal system to accommodate surrogacy arrangements to a limited extent. In that connection, a prior written judicial assessment of the terms of a non-commercial arrangement contract could, for example, sometimes help prevent the onset of long-standing parentage disputes, which can surely not be in the child's interests. By creating more openness through judicial documentation, the transfer of parental rights cannot only be achieved. For our specific purposes, it is more significant that this could help to ensure that the child may know how he or she was conceived. At the same time, the child will retain a measure of choice regarding the decision whether identifying information concerning the gestational mother and the genetic mother should be sought. For one thing, it must also be borne in mind that the fact of pregnancy may not only have emotional significance for the mother but also for the child. Thus, the gestational mother can therefore not simply be obliterated from the child's earliest history. In that connection, it may be presumed that if children were to discover perchance how they had been conceived, the emotional impact could be greater and more enduringly harm-

---

[134] PENNINGS (2005), p. 10.

ful.[135] An early disclosure to the child, in principle by the (legal) parents, of the way the person had been conceived would therefore appear indicated. The child's right to information would therefore also involve identification of the gestational mother.

5. HETEROLOGOUS ASSISTED CONCEPTION

5.1. THE STATUS OF THE SOCIO-LEGAL FATHER IN HETEROLOGOUS ART

In **France**, since 1994, the possibility to establish the paternity of the donor has been excluded by law.[136] Previously, there was no rule to prevent the husband from being able to withdraw his consent to treatment after it had begun.[137] Spouses or unmarried male partners of the mother first have their consent confirmed by a court or a public notary (*notaire*).[138] It follows that either party may freely withdraw his or her consent at any stage up to the moment of the implantation of the embryo into the woman; this is expressly provided for in the legislation. Thereafter, paternity can no longer be denied. However, if (somehow) medical evidence can be adduced that the child had been conceived by someone other than a third party donor, paternity can in principle be challenged. This possibility will, however, be largely conjectural since donors remain anonymous while all non-consensual forms of parentage testing have been outlawed.[139]

The consent forms will not be taken into account in the case of the premature death of one of the parties to the treatment, if divorce has been petitioned or in the case of a judicial separation or of a discontinuance of community life, as long as treatment has not begun.[140] Furthermore, consent is deprived of effect if either party revokes it in writing before treatment.[141] If the mother's partner is not married to her and refrains from making a recognition, he may become liable

---

135 See Chapter I.

136 Art. 311-19 **French** Code Civil: 'In case of a medically assisted procreation with a third party donor, no parental bonds may be established between the donor and the child born of the procreation. No claim in tort may lie against a donor'.

137 Cass., 10 July 1990, D.1990, 517.

138 Art. 311-20 **French** Code Civil.

139 See Chapter VIII.

140 Art. 311-20 **French** Code Civil.

141 Art. 311-20 **French** Code Civil.

in civil law in respect of the mother and child.[142] In addition, his paternity may be judicially determined.[143]

In **Germany**, in the absence of regulation, it was for a long time possible for the husband who had given his consent to AI to subsequently deny paternity because there was no genetic link between him and the child. This legal regime came under some critical scrutiny, not least because of the manifestly anomalous position of **German** law from a global comparative law perspective on this particular issue.[144] At first, it was held that such denials of paternity were tantamount to a breach of 'equity' principles[145] or that they could be linked to the implicit civil law principle of *venire contra factum proprium.*[146] In spite of this, proposals by the *Deutsche Juristentag* to make a withdrawal of consent impossible withstood enactment.[147] While this legislative inaction has been ascribed to cumbersome political decision-making,[148] the Federal Constitutional Court hardly promoted legislative change by finding, on no fewer than three occasions, that such denial proceedings by men who had got 'second thoughts' following heterologous AI treatment were indeed constitutional.[149]

It was not until 2002 that greater legal certainty came within reach through the **German** Children's Rights Improvement Act.[150] A new civil law clause was adopted to the effect that a denial of paternity became impossible if there was evidence that the child had been begotten on the basis of the joint consent of the man and the mother to heterologous AI.[151] Even so, the Act did not go as far as to state that the (written) consent in itself should establish the mother's partner's

---

142 Art. 311-20 **French** Code Civil.

143 Art. 311-20 **French** Code Civil.

144 For example, DEUTSCH (1985), p. 177, 180; SPICKHOFF (1997), p. 197.

145 §242 BGB. *Treu und Glaube.*

146 HOLZHAUER (1986), p. 1162-1164; SCHWAB/MÜNCH KOMM (2002), BGB, §1592, No. 35, 68; ROTH (1996), p. 769; GERNHUBER/COESTER-WALTJEN (2006), p. 123, who draws analogies with (prenatal) adoption where unilateral revocation by one future adoptive parent is also precluded.

147 Decision of the 1986 Berlin *Deutsche Juristentag* III.10, 236; *BT-Drucks.* 11/1856, 23 February 1988; Decision of the Hanover *Deutsche Juristentag* B.III.1, 250; *BT-Drucks.* 13/4899 of 13 June 1996, p. 148.

148 GERNHUBER/COESTER-WALTJEN (2006), p. 122.

149 BGHZ 87, 169 = *FamRZ* 1983, p. 686; BGHZ, 3 May 1995= *FamRZ* 1995, p. 861; BGH, 5 October 1994, *FamRZ* 1995, p. 1272.

150 Kindesverbesserungsgesetz = Children's Rights Improvement Act (KindRVBerbG), 9 April 2002, BGBl 2002, effective since 12 April 2002.

151 §1600 V BGB.

paternity.[152] Furthermore, the donor-conceived child can successfully challenge the socio-legal father's paternity.[153] Once the mother's partner's paternity has been denied by the child, a judicial determination of the paternity of the donor will become a possibility, albeit a somewhat conjectural one for he would have to be found first.

As a corollary of the fact that paternity is not based upon the consent form, the woman's unmarried male partner will also have to make a recognition just as he would have to do in the case of natural reproduction.[154] Moreover, if the mother's male partner does not make a recognition, the donor may, by virtue of his biological tie to the child, run the risk that his paternity will be judicially determined if he is identified.[155] Men can therefore still elude the establishment of their paternity if no recognition has been made or if the married father had divorced the mother in the period between conception and the birth.[156]

In **the Netherlands**, following the 1998 parentage law reform, the socio-legal father and the mother will not be able to deny the husband's paternity if the man had 'consented to an act which could have resulted in the begetting of the child'.[157] It is also required that donated sperm is destroyed if the consent has been revoked or if the period during which the sperm may be used for reproductive purposes has expired.[158] Outside marriage, the consenting male partner of the woman undergoing treatment must make a recognition to become the legal father.[159] If he refrains from making a recognition, the mother and child may have his paternity established before the courts on the ground that he, being the mother's 'life-companion', had consented to an act that could have resulted in the begetting of the child.[160] Accordingly, the child may deny the (married) socio-legal father's paternity simply because he bears no genetic link to the claimant.[161] In order to subsequently lodge proceedings involving a judicial determination of paternity, however, in this situation it must be assumed that

152 WANITZEK (2003), p. 733.
153 WANITZEK (2003), p. 733.
154 §1592 II BGB. See the section on fatherhood.
155 §1592 III in conjunction with §1600d I BGB. See the section on fatherhood.
156 GERNHUBER/COESTER-WALTJEN (2006), p. 628.
157 Art. 1:200(3) DCC.
158 Art.6(2) in conjunction with Art. 7 Embryowet = **Dutch** Embryo Act.
159 Art. 1:203 DCC.
160 Art. 1:207(1) DCC. See Chapter VII.
161 Art. 1:200(1) in conjunction with Art. 1:200(6) DCC. Within a three-year dies a quo period or within three years after becoming an adult if the child had become aware of circumstances pointing against paternity during his minority. See Chapter VII.

another man is present, namely the man who had consented to insemination and who was the woman's 'life-partner'. The **Dutch** Supreme Court has clarified that this 'life-partner' of the mother must be a man. Therefore, if a female partner changes her mind after the impregnation of her partner and refuses to adopt the child after she had consented to AI, unlike a man, she will not be able to be 'forced into' having the status of legal parent. In particular, child maintenance may also not be claimed in respect of the mother's female partner if consent had been withdrawn.[162]

Same-sex marriages unlike different-sex marriages do not give rise to legal child-parent relationships in **the Netherlands** by operation of law. In order to achieve greater equality, however, the **Dutch** Minister of Justice and the Minister of Youth and the Family set up a commission which conducted preparatory research to investigate how the attribution of legal parentage to the birthmother's female partner could be improved.[163] This 'Kalsbeek' Commission held that the female partner should be permitted to recognise the donor-conceived child as an alternative to adoption for which the consent of the biological father is required.[164] At the same time, the commission acknowledged the interests that the biological father, in practise often a known donor or male friend of the couple, may have. In practise use is also made by lesbian couples of a donor contract which seeks to regulate his relationship with the child, but the legal status of these contracts is debatable.[165] Once family life is considered to have developed between the (known) donor and the child, **Dutch** courts have been found to be willing to issue a contact order for him.[166] Still, the legal position of the biological father in this situation has so far not been defined further. In a controversial case, the **Dutch** Supreme Court even considered that family life existed between a child and the homosexual biological father who had donated sperm to a lesbian birthmother, even though he had only seen the child once and he had 'waived' all rights in a donor contract.[167] In striking a balance, **Dutch** Supreme Court contrued a pre-existent 'family life' on the basis of a long-standing friendship between the man and the birthmother. This friendship had broken when the man changed his intentions, developing 'fatherly feelings,' with regard to the child during the pregnancy.

---

162 Hoge Raad, 10 August 2001, *NJ* 2002, p. 278.

163 Commissie lesbisch ouderschap en interlandelijke adoptie, Rapport Lesbisch Ouderschap, Dutch Ministry of Justice 2008.

164 See also HENSTRA (2002), p. 181.

165 VONK (2008), p. 132.

166 Art. 1:377(f) DCC.; RAAK-KUIPER (2008), p. 240-243.

167 Hoge Raad, 30 November 2007, LJN BB9094; NUYTINCK (2008), p. 133.

Notably, the *Kalsbeek* Commission also discussed the issue of access to one's origins. Rather than availing itself of the opportunity to review implementation mechanisms to promote the enforcement of the right, it considered that an enforceable duty to disclose the conception method should not be imposed on lesbian mothers 'because it was debatable whether this was desirable'. This was based on an equality argument: after all, were different-sex couples obliged to take the child's right to information to such an extent? No! Accordingly because such an implementation mechanism was also lacking in respect of different-sex parents in the **Dutch** Artificial Insemination (donor information) Act, it would be going too far to require lesbian parents to disclose how the child was conceived. At the time of writing, further developments are awaited.

In **Portugal,** the paternity of the husband of the woman undergoing treatment is directly based on the consent that he had given to treatment. This rule was already drafted in 1977 at a time when AI was still quite uncommon in **Portugal.**[168] The spouses cannot deny the possibility to subsequently challenge paternity.[169] This legislative choice has been reaffirmed in the 2006 law in respect of the husband and extended to the unmarried male partner cohabiting in conditions analogous to marriage with the woman undergoing treatment.[170] However, paternity can be challenged by the male partner if he can prove that he had not given consent to treatment or that the child was not born through AI.[171] The choice is left to the child whether he or she wishes to deny the socio-legal father's paternity. Vale e Reis even considers this right of the child to challenge the 'false' paternity of the socio-legal father to be a dimension of the child's right to know, all the more so since the child, unlike the social parents, had no choice in respect of the conception method.[172] However, the possibility to deny paternity would not entail a right to establish the paternity of the donor. This is also reflected in the 2006 law which establishes that the 'sperm donor cannot be established as the father of the child that will be born and that parental responsibilities or duties will not apply in respect of him.[173]

168 Martinho da Silva (1986), p. 85.
169 Art. 1839-3 PCC.
170 Art. 20-1 LPMA.
171 Art. 20-4 LPMA.
172 Vale e Reis (2008), p. 228.
173 Art. 21 LPMA.

5.2. COMPARISON

In **France** and **Portugal,** the spouses and cohabitants who have been given access to such treatment will not be able to deny paternity after treatment may be said to have begun. This option is left open to the child, however. In **Germany** and **the Netherlands** the child can also deny paternity in this situation. Paternity cannot be denied subsequently either by spouses in **the Netherlands**. In **Germany**, the unmarried man cannot be put in the position that his paternity could be established once he has chosen to withdraw his consent. This may therefore, at least in theoretically, leave the possibility open for the 'knock on the donor's door' and subsequent establishment of his paternity on the 'mere' basis of his biological link. In both **France** and **the Netherlands**, if the male partner withdraws his consent, the child and the mother may lodge proceedings involving a judicial determination of paternity. In **France**, damages may also be claimed in respect of the man who had withdrawn his consent after the implantation.

5.3. EVALUATION

It is recalled that in *Evans*, the ECtHR held that, in determining the scope of the right to private life under Article 8 ECHR, the moment of the withdrawal of consent to a fertility treatment fell within the margin of appreciation of states.[174] The Strasbourg court permitted the **British** 'bright-line' policy on this issue. It follows that it is only consistent with the Convention that the male be unable to withdraw after a certain, pivotal moment during the fertility treatment, such as the moment of fertilisation of the gametes or the placement of the embryo in the mother's womb. Whether more flexible rules could also fall within the margin of appreciation is circumspect because this conceivably creates tension with a principle of legal certainty in what remains a sensitive bio-ethical area for legislators.

In establishing the paternity of the male partner of the woman undergoing treatment, in **France** and **Portugal** the civil law notion of *venire contra factum proprium* applies. Furthermore, a principle of procreational responsibility could also require that the parents should not be able to withdraw their consent to treatment after a definite moment. Accordingly, the recognition by the unmarried male partner should not be challengeable by the parents, because this form

174 See Chapter III.

of parenthood is inherently intentional.[175] This promotes legal certainty and ensures the interests of the donor-conceived child in having two parents. Even so, donor offspring may, however, have an interest in denying the socio-legal father's paternity to the extent that this right has also been recognised in parentage law in cases of 'misattributed paternity'.[176]

Subsequent to a successful denial of paternity by a donor offspring, parental status should never become attributable to an anonymous donor. It is one thing, from a truth-oriented perspective, for a child to be able to establish details concerning his identity. Clearly, it is quite another, from a parentage law perspective, however, to then have his paternity established. Requiring the him to be identifiable is an essentially different matter.

The donor has a legal interest in being shielded from parental obligations, inheritance claims and, possibly, unwanted contact.[177] Ideally, donations of gametes are made with a view to helping the involuntarily childless. A donor from a semen bank should accordingly be screened as to whether he has an interest in parental rights. If a donor has such an interest, it may have been better not to select him as a donor.[178] In the case of donors familiar to the commissioning parents, the risk that the attitude towards parental rights will change is greater. From a parentage law perspective, the risk is. in other words. significant. From a truth-oriented perspective, chances are, however, that the child will have greater possibilities to know the circumstances surrounding her or his conception and to gain an understanding of who the donor is when told at an early age. That said, if donor anonymity can be waived gradually, it may be possible to lay down legal conditions for a more managed process of disclosure when the child feels prepared to get to know this 'third parent.' In the next section, the issue of donor anonymity, and its removal in some jurisdictions, is examined further.

---

175 This debate is essentially about the nature of the legal institution of recognition. Because a recognition by the mother's partner is always 'false' in AI anyway, a recognition by the female partner of the mother is debatably not objectionable. In the AI context, recognition is based on intention rather than a presumption of biological truth in respect of the mother's partner, irrespective of that partner's sex. On the other hand, Van Raak-Kuiper holds that this possibility should be excluded since a presumption of biological motherhood can never be assumed in the case of a recognition by a mother. In this way, she argues, **Dutch** parentage law would drift even further away from the biological truth. RAAK-KUIPER (2007), p. 102-103.

176 It may be consistent, too, for that reason if children can also deny the status of the female partner of the mother if recognition by the female partner were to be admitted.

177 JACKSON (2001), p. 212.

178 RAAK-KUIPER (2007), p. 81.

6. DONOR ANONYMITY

6.1. SECRECY AND HETEROLOGOUS DONOR INSEMINATION

Various reasons have been advanced in support of both secrecy and donor anonymity. In AI, the secrecy surrounding the donor may be said to serve at least four distinct groups of persons who may have interlocking spheres of interest: the commissioning parents, the donor, the medical professional and the donor-conceived child.[179] Clearly only the latter group cannot be said to have been in a position to articulate their own interest in secrecy and donor anonymity, at least during their minority.[180] Even so, the other groups of persons may find that disclosure about the conception method does more harm than it does good for donor offspring. In particular, the commissioning parents may be opposed to disclosure because the AI child could be bullied at school.[181] With regard to donor offspring, it has been suggested that a waiver will not be indicated in respect of earlier donations since the donor may not be able to be traced anyway after the conception method has been disclosed. Thus, in order to preserve secrecy, many Western countries' donor files used to be routinely destroyed when the use of DI first became commonly used. If these 'older' donor offspring learnt how they had been conceived, they would only be likely to experience feelings of frustration and depression as their searches would lead nowhere.[182]

For parents, secrecy may be considered vital since their social environment could ostracise them because of their fertility problem or disapprove of AI.[183] In particular, in some non-Western cultures that are characterised by patrilineal family systems, recourse to donor conception risks ostracism in respect of both parents and child within the family and community.[184] Parents may also be reluctant to disclose because they may find it more difficult than in adoption to find appropriate 'scripts' to tell their children in an appropriate way how they were conceived, because their reproductive choice may not be as easy to explain in terms of a benevolent act towards the child's birthparents as in adoption.[185] Even so, a recent **Swedish** study shows that counselling may help some couples

179 DANIELS & TAYLOR (1993), p. 157-158.
180 DANIELS & TAYLOR (1993), p. 157.
181 SNOWDEN (1983), p. 102, 106.
182 ROWLAND (1985), p. 396.
183 ROWLAND (1985), p. 393.
184 BLYTH (2006).
185 ROWLAND (1985), p. 393; MCWHINNIE (1996).

to find 'scripts' with a view to carefully informing children how about their conception, for example, by referring to the donor as a 'kind man' who was willing to help them overcome their problems.[186]

Within the family, another perceived justification for secrecy stems from the fear that the child could reject his father for not being his 'real' father, in particular during adolescence.[187] Accordingly, secrecy would help preserve certain perceived standards of morality and normality within the family.[188] In connection with that argument, the privacy and the stability of the family life would generally be ensured. It could be that an identifiable donor would intrude into the private and family life of donor-conceived children and their parents. Conversely, a donor offspring might intrude into the donor's private and family life and one day 'knock on the door.' Thus, while the donor may have been a single student at the time of donation, he may have a family of his own when a donor offspring attempts to trace him.[189]

Furthermore, in the absence of legislation which sets limits on the number of donations, anonymity may be perceived by the donor as a more adequate guarantee in warding off emotional or financial claims from parents and donor offspring, quite regardless of whether a legal system already firmly excludes such claims. Secrecy therefore shields the donor in a number of ways. Firstly, it may be perceived as a reassurance for the donor that his legal paternity will not be able to be established. Even if this fear of the potential donor may be considered irrational from a legal perspective, it may still be experienced as sufficiently real not to decide to donate. Secondly, secrecy has also been said to protect donors from possibly disruptive effects on their own marriage or family life. Thirdly, disclosure will reveal the act of masturbation which is considered a mortal sin in some religious circles or at least a topic of jokes across social circles.[190]

A common utilitarian assumption behind preserving donor anonymity is that its abolition would seriously undermine donor supply and thereby threaten the viability of donor conception services.[191] As a side-effect, the lifting of donor anonymity would also induce procreative tourism at clinics abroad, where donor

186 LALOS (2007).
187 LALOS (2007).
188 O'DONOVAN (1989), p. 106.
189 DANIELS & TAYLOR (1993), p. 158.
190 BLYTH (2006), p. 4-13.
191 KREMER & LEENEN (1991), p. 1476-1478.

offspring's right to know has not yet been acknowledged and both ethical and medical standards would not be as high.[192]

Furthermore, as service providers to the general public, medical professionals would have an interest in professional respectability with which a waiver of anonymity would be difficult to reconcile.[193] Therefore professional secrecy would generally be necessary in providing medical services.

6.2. PROMOTING OPENNESS

The principal reasons adduced in support of greater openness may be brought into connection with the more general moral justifications as discussed in Chapter I.[194] Furthermore, it has been suggested that donor-conceived children in particular should be told about their origins because they are likely to feel these family tensions and sense their differences or be told by someone else with potentially disruptive and traumatising effects.[195] Moreover, it has also been argued that openness is ultimately also in the interest of the parents themselves, whether they recognise this or not. Thus, the alternative for parents would be to be burdened by a 'lifetime of deceit' generating a great amount of emotional tension within the family.[196] For the child, this 'conspiracy of silence' within the family may be considered to imply a loss of autonomy and informational self-determination.[197] From an ethical viewpoint it could therefore be said to be objectionable. But there is also increasing psychological evidence that secrets in family life can prove damaging for family members.[198]

In justifying the donor conceived child's right on the basis of respect for the child's right to informational self-determination, Baroness Mary Warnock who in 1984 chaired the Committee of Inquiry into Human Fertilisation and Embryology in the United Kingdom, has stated that '*the child is being used as a means to the parents' ends, namely to have, or seem to have, a 'normal' family', and I*

---

192 An increase in **Swedish** couples seeking fertility treatment to **Finland** was reported after donor anonymity had been waived. See; WENNERGREN (1989), p. 389 and STOLL (2008), p. 16. There has also been an increase in **Dutch** couples seeking fertility treatment in **Belgium** following the entry into force of the **Dutch** Artificial Insemination (donor information) Act. See: PENNINGS (2005), p. 2689-2694.

193 DANIELS & TAYLOR (1993), p. 158.

194 See Chapter I.

195 GIBSON (1992), p. 13.

196 DANIELS & TAYLOR (1993), p. 160.

197 O'DONOVAN (1988), p. 38-39.

198 TRISELIOTIS (1993); IMBER-BLACK (1998); WISMEIJER (2007).

do not think that using one person as a means to another's ends can ever be right, unless the person has consented to be so used ... I cannot argue that children who are told their origins, if they are [DI] children are necessarily happier, or better of in any way that can be estimated. But I do believe that if they are not told, they are being wrongly treated'.[199]

Cultural reasons have also been advanced against donor anonymity. Thus, in a rather general way, in the course of the 1990s donor anonymity for some has come to be associated with the widely discarded, unenlightened ideas of yesteryear regarding gender roles in human production.[200] Essentially, a system in which the donor could donate under the understanding of lifelong anonymity would mask the real intentions of some donors who in some cases would be more concerned about passing on their genes to the next generation without assuming the normal responsibility associated with parenthood. As such, doubts are raised about the altruistic motives of donors. Less scepticism exists with regard to the motives of egg donors, whose intentions have been more consistently viewed as essentially benign, all the more so because egg donation is an emotionally and physically taxing measure. Still precisely because of that, anonymity will also often be less of a problem because the egg donor will often be a close friend or relative of the commissioning couple.[201] In other words, the egg donor is believed to be generally known to at least the medical practitioner and often also the recipient.[202] Even so, empirical studies also underscore some attitudinal differences between egg donors and sperm donors since some research shows that anonymous egg donors are significantly less opposed to disclosure than sperm donors are.[203] Such differences have further genderised the debate to the extent that they now cast a more critical light on the perceived need for sperm donors to rely on separate treatment if they insist that their identity will not be revealed.

It has been under the influence of the greater weight attached to the right to information, however, that a fair number of jurisdictions has now waived donor anonymity. In that respect, **Sweden** pioneered in March 1985. In making this globally unprecedented policy choice the **Swedish** legislator had not found the differences between AI children and adoptees sufficiently compelling to justify

199 WARNOCK (1987), p. 141-155; DANIELS & TAYLOR (1993), p. 159-160.
200 BLYTH & FARRAND (2004), p. 90.
201 JACKSON (2001), p. 212.
202 HAIMES (1993), p. 91.
203 BRAVERMAN (1993), p. 1216-1220. BLYTH & CRADSHAW(2004), p. 2617-2626.

a difference in treatment.[204] Apart from **Sweden**, however, **Austria**, **Finland, the Netherlands, New Zealand, Norway**, **Switzerland,** the **United Kingdom** and the Australian state of **Western Australia** now also have laws foreseeing the disclosure of a gamete donor's identity.[205] It has been predicted that this trend will continue to extend to more countries, partly because research has shown that traditional justifications of secrecy have lost much of their value.[206]

In both **Sweden** and in the **United Kingdom**, it has been debated whether information concerning the donor should be entered on the birth certificate. At least from a technical viewpoint, this would greatly increase chances for donor offspring to find out how they had been conceived. Moreover, it would be a cost-effective public policy choice.[207] This policy choice could signify an important first step in tracing the child's genetic parent. The information could be entered in a relatively discreet way so that it would only be seen when a full extract of the register is ordered, for example, by marking the letter 'D' of donor discreetly in the act. Nonetheless, in **Sweden** this possibility was rejected for being too invasive. Furthermore, it has been said that this would serve no real function, since the donor lacks any status close to ever having been the child's legal parent.[208] In that respect, the situation of donor-conceived children would be distinguishable from adopted children. While the latter could infer from their birth certificate that their birthparents are not their legal parents, for adoptees their birthparents had, at one point, been their legal parents.

In the **United Kingdom**, this measure was also rejected out of concern over both the parents' and the child's privacy. It was however recognized that this could create an incentive for parents to tell the child of the fact of donor conception and would go some way to addressing the value of knowledge for medical purposes.[209] Another reason to include the information in the birth certificate would be that ART involved the public authorities. Thus, as the state sanctions ART by licencing clinics to provide fertility treatment, so the state should also be concerned about not colluding in the deception of children in any way.

Yet it is clear that this measure could also be viewed as a source of embarrassment and an unwanted form of 'labelling' by some donor conceived persons who

---

204 Report of the **Dutch** Insemination Committee 1983, p. 2.
205 Lalos (2007).
206 Frith (2001), p. 823.
207 Stoll (2008), p. 119.
208 Stoll (2008), p. 116.
209 Http://www.publications.parliament.uk/pa/jt200607/jtselect/jtembryos/169/169.pdf.

could feel that they have been singled out. To some extent, this possible disadvantage of public exposure could be removed if the public authorities notified an adult donor-conceived person more discreetly, for example, by sending a letter about the fact of donor conception.[210] This idea could be supported by the view that the parents had not fulfilled their *duty* to be open about disclosure. But such a duty would then first have to be recognized more expressly. In the **Dutch** Artificial Insemination (Donor Information) Act no mention is made of such a duty, even though a child's right to know clearly lies at the basis of this law.

Furthermore, to find out at a late age about donor conception through a letter could still be experienced as disturbing. Especially if the donor-conceived person is not subsequently given an opportunity to benefit from commensurate publicly-funded forms of counselling, state interference could be perceived as 'politically correct' way but callous way of informing donor conceived persons about their origins.

If publicly-funded counselling could be a helpful measure to provide assistance to donor-conceived persons, so it could perhaps also be beneficial if parents were more carefully monitored regarding their attitudes towards disclosure before treatment begins as they are in adoption. In this way they could get the 'scripts' they may need in order to tell the donor conceived child. However, the attitudes of prospective parents may be quite different than after the child has been born. Once bonding with the donor-conceived child has begun, disclosure is more likely to be experienced as a difficult task to undertake. To alleviate this concern of parents, after the child has been born, counselling services would therefore also be offered.[211] Parents could be contacted every few years by the public authorities or by the clinic during the donor offspring's childhood and adolescence and questioned on the steps they have taken towards greater openness. Furthermore, a potentially less invasive measure would engage the distribution of leaflets on the possible importance for the child of finding out about her or his origins or a publicity campaign.[212]

As yet another *informal* implementation mechanism, the use of voluntary contact registers could be more openly promoted and subsidized. Such registers have been set up in the **United Kingdom** and in the **Australian** state of **Victoria**. In **Victoria**, donor offspring, descendants, donors, recipient couples and other

210 Stoll (2008), p. 121.

211 Stoll (2008), p. 106.

212 This policy has been undertaken by the Health Department of the Government of **Victoria**, **Australia**.

relatives have been able to request the Infertility Treatment Authority since 1995 to enter their names and addresses and ask for identifying information while having their own information released upon a related person's request. In 2003, the **United Kingdom** Department of Health also launched and funded such a register with a view to facilitating contact between adults affected by donor insemination before record-keeping became required after 1991.[213] All involved adults may, in fact, have a DNA test taken and verify whether they are genetically related on the basis of their voluntary consent. As an additional advantage, the register therefore also extends to half and full siblings who had been conceived by a single donor.

6.3. DOUBLE-TRACK SYSTEMS: A COMPROMISE SOLUTION?

As a compromise solution, a double-track system could also be considered. In this system some donors choose to donate anonymously while the anonymity of other, identity-registered donors could eventually be waived upon the request of a donor offspring. Notably, the **Belgian** ethicist Guido Pennings has defended such a solution, since it would strike a fairer balance between the competing interests of donors, parents and children.[214] This would have the added advantage that more men would still be willing to donate, thereby ensuring fertility treatment to couples. In that sense, it may be a more serene solution. However, such a solution disregards the fact that two sets of children will then be born in a single jurisdiction: some who can access information and others who will not be able to do so. This 'solution' would therefore appear to seriously undermine the constitutional principle of equality as discussed in Chapter V.

6.4. EMPIRICAL STUDIES

On the basis of studies in adoption, researchers and counsellors tend to advise parents that the best time to tell their children is when they are at a very young age.[215] Empirical research exists in support of that view.[216] Adolescents from the general population have also been found in a recent **Australian** study to have views largely consistent with those of donor-conceived adults.[217] Thus, they identify the social father as the parent but also acknowledge the importance of

213 Www.ukdonorlink.org.uk.
214 PENNINGS (1997), p. 2834-2839; PENNINGS (2001), p. 621-622.
215 KIRKMAN (2005), p. 153-169.
216 SCHEIB (2005), p. 239-252.
217 KIRKMAN (2003), p. 1-7.

genetic information about the donor. They also took the view that the (legal) parents should be responsible for telling.

Some early studies on parental disclosure patterns have, however, attested to considerable parental reluctance to be open, especially in the case of sperm donation. Thus, in an early **British** study, Snowden suggested that while verbal expressions of concerns by parents were often vocal about protecting vulnerable children, the overall impression was that behind such concerns parents sheltered their own interests, especially to avoid stigmatization because of the socio-legal father's infertility.[218] In another **British** study on egg donors, it was revealed that ninety per cent of recipients were strongly against the donor contacting the child later in life but fifty four per cent had no objection to the child contacting them, while less than half of the recipients were in favour of telling their child that the child had a different genetic mother.[219] Remarkably, eighty-six per cent of recipients and fifty-six per cent of donors felt that if they had been born from a donated oocyte, they would not want to know.

On the basis of an **Anglo-American** study, some of the major problems for non-disclosure have been identified: acknowledgement of the father's fertility problem and uncertainty about the best time and the best method ('script') for telling the child.[220] Further, in a **German** study, it was found that among a cohort of 40 couples, 10 were reluctant to disclose the conception method to the child.[221]

In 2000, Gottlieb found that 89 per cent of a cohort of **Swedish** parents had not informed their children about donor conception.[222] Nonetheless, this high percentage may be ascribed to the fact that the average age of the children was around 3½ years at the time the study was conducted.[223] In a follow-up study, it was revealed that 61 per cent of the respondents (legal parents) were willing to tell their children as to how they had been conceived.[224] This higher incidence may be accounted for to some extent because the average age of the children at that time was seven years. On the other hand, the cohort was slightly smaller

218 SNOWDEN (1983), p. 106-107.
219 KIRKLAND (1992), p. 355-357.
220 COOK (1995), p. 556.
221 SCHILLING (1995), p. 16-17.
222 GOTTLIEB (2000), p. 2052.
223 STOLL (2008), p. 76.
224 LALOS (2007), p. 1761.

than in the initial study while the information was gathered through telephone conversations.[225]

The reasons parents gave for telling were the avoidance of an accidental discovery, a general desire for openness and a person's fundamental right to know.[226] A vast majority of both women and men stated that the children had not asked follow-up questions, but had instead responded with relative indifference or taken it as a pleasant surprise, like '*aha?!* and '*so what*?!' Still, parents who did not intend to tell considered AI a private matter and tended to be more afraid of other people's attitudes.[227] A great majority of those who had been encouraged by medical staff to tell their children had already done so, but when disclosure had not been consistently encouraged during and after treatment the willingness to inform the child/ren was found to be lower.[228] In a **Swedish** study from 2006, it was found on the basis of personal interviews that 75 per cent of parents had disclosed or intended to disclose.[229] Even though this percentage may therefore be considered high, the fact that the cohort only numbered twenty couples has been considered a weakness.[230]

In **the Netherlands**, a study was undertaken in 2003 on lesbian and heterosexual recipient parents who, in line with the **Dutch** double-track policy as it stood, had the option of choosing between an identity-registered donor and an anonymous donor. The study revealed that 98 per cent of lesbian couples and 63 per cent of heterosexual couples selected an identity-registered donor.[231] Among the parents who had selected an identity-registered donor, 93 per cent had said that they would tell their child about donor conception.[232] However, only 17 per cent of couples who had selected an anonymous donor in the **Dutch** study intended to tell about the conception method.[233] Although a similar research has not been undertaken since this double-track policy was abolished, Brewaeys concludes that a compulsory choice for an identifiable donor will not change individual motives and may even instill in some parents a more secretive attitude.[234] Interestingly, in an earlier study, Brewaeys found that 26 per cent of parents had

225 STOLL (2004), p. 79.
226 LALOS (2007).
227 LALOS (2007).
228 LALOS (2007).
229 LEEB-LUNDBERG (2006), p. 80.
230 STOLL (2008), p. 80.
231 BREWAEYS (2005), p. 820.
232 BREWAEYS (2005), p. 823.
233 BREWAEYS (2005), p. 823.
234 BREWAEYS (2005), p. 823.

been open about donor conception to close friends and family members, even though they were not willing to disclose information to the child.[235] Accordingly, there could be a greater risk that a child first finds out about donor conception perchance through someone other than the parents.

In a **British** study from 2000, it was revealed that 40 per cent among a cohort of 83 individuals had told their child about donor conception.[236] The average age of the children was 3½ years. In an **Australian** study, in which 53 women were questioned, the intended disclosure rate of single women and lesbian women was considered to be significantly higher than among women in heterosexual relationships.[237] In the light of available empirical research, Blyth concludes that, generally, it may be assumed that the number of parents who have used donor conception who will not be inclined to tell their children about their conception is likely to be large.[238] This conclusion has also recently been reached by Stoll.[239]

6.5. ANALOGIES WITH ADOPTION

As a shared feature of both adoption and AI, family ties are given to children who otherwise might not have had them.[240] In both situations, moreover, there will be at least one genetic parent who lacks the intention to become the child's legal parent. The public dimension may be more apparent than in natural reproduction because the state operates as an intermediary in licensing both adoption bureaus and fertility clinics. Furthermore, the state could screen prospective legal parents.[241] Thus, if a state recognises the right to know one's origins at the constitutional level and provides such licences in both situations, it may be expected from the state that it also takes steps in creating implementation mechanisms that facilitate access to information.

That said, the fact that parents may had to choose between adoption or AI to fulfil theur wish to have a child means that the state must be careful to respect their privacy interest and their right to family life just like it should with regard to those parents who had been able to reproduce in the natural way. Disclosure

---

235 BREWAEYS (1997), p. 1593-1594.
236 HUNTER (2000), p. 157-163.
237 GODMAN (2006), p. 3022-3023. See STOLL (2008), p. 88-89.
238 BLYTH (2006), p. 14.
239 STOLL (20080, p. 96.
240 HAIMES (1988), p. 47.
241 Clearly, it may also have a role in screening donors. In adoption this will not be relevant since the genetic parents already exist. It would be more invasive to set limits to the liberty to procreate in other situations.

might be perceived to a greater extent as a *shared* public and private responsibility of respectively the state and the parents in adoption and AI, however, because, unlike natural reproduction, these situations require a greater measure of public intervention.[242] In contrast, in a case of 'misattributed paternity' it will be much more difficult for the state to encroach on the parents' private and family life.

Among adoption and AI, however, there are appreciable differences which are arguably not easily dismissed.[243] Whereas adoption involves children born into pre-existing families, AI is directed towards creating a child in order to create a family.[244] Moreover, adopted children may sometimes have a vivid memory of their birthparents or early childhood, while this sort of notion of a narrative identity is absent in donor-conceived children.[245] If some adopted children have to deal with the fact that they have been abandoned, the donor-conceived child is often the outcome of a long-standing wish of the commissioning couple to have a child.[246] Furthermore, whereas in adoption both parents will not be genetically related to the child, in heterologous egg or sperm donation one parent will be. At least for heterosexual couples it will therefore often be easier to pass off the family as genetically related. In particular, the genetic parents in AI do not share any joint history, unlike in adoption or even a fleeting sexual encounter. For such reasons, it has been said by some that the interests of donor-conceived children in knowing should generally not be considered to be as compelling as those of the adoptee.[247] In this way, then, a notion of 'procreational responsibility' in respect of the donor is not assumed, perhaps because of the perceived 'altruistic' nature of DI. Furthermore, in their interpretation of the 'principle of equality', as discussed in Chapter V, the different circumstances under which a person is conceived or born are apparently so great that the need to find out would also be different. It is concluded then that a difference in treatment would in this view also be justifiable.

To the author, whether the differences between AI and adoption really justify a difference in treatment – by having regard to the principles of decisional privacy, procreational responsibility and equality – is doubtful, however. Even

---

242 O'Donovan (1988), p. 39; Ruiter (1993), p. 57-60; Bueren (1995), p. 41.

243 However, context-specific arguments may be considered largely irrelevant in acknowledging a right to know 'in the abstract', if the discussion is framed primarily on the basis of the child's basic innocence versus the procreational responsibility of the earlier generation. See Chapter V.

244 Haimes (1988), p. 48.

245 Humphrey & Humphrey (1986), p. 138-140.

246 O'Donovan (1988), p. 41.

247 Haimes (1988), p. 48.

though it cannot be excluded that further empirical research would be able to demonstrate that the wish to find out about their birthparents is generally stronger among adopted children than among donor conceived persons, a case for difference in treatment will be difficult to justify if the ethical viewpoint is accepted that the donor, as a biological parent, in principle has a (procreational) responsibility to be identifiable and that children have a principled right to choose whether they wish to identify him.

It is remarkable that the informational needs of donor conceived persons have only come to be recognised so much later than those of adopted children. A full answer to this question may be difficult to provide. As a matter of fact, though, the professions most closely engaged in the two procedures are essentially different. It has been suggested, for example, that whatever is decided by the medical profession as being appropriate to their procedures will be perceived as carrying much more societal weight than that what social workers could hope to achieve in adoption.[248] This medical opposition would help explain why secrecy has been ingrained in AI for much longer than in adoption.[249]

6.6. RELEVANT LAW

The continued adherence in **France** to donor anonymity has not been considered objectionable by **French** scholars on two basic grounds. Firstly, secrecy would be preferable because of the 'classical' utilitarian argument that the number of donors would drop,[250] promoting reproductive tourism, and secondly because it is linked to a 'sliding-scale' risk of eugenic pre-selection of gametes on the basis of the quality of the donor's hereditary characteristics.[251] If donors were known, the commissioning parents would demand certain qualities. The commissioning couple may not 'choose' a donor from whom they wish to receive gametes with a view to fertilization.[252] However, the physician must document the identity of the donor in the prevention of hereditary diseases.[253] Meanwhile, 'whoever' discloses the identity of a donor registered in **France** is in principle liable to criminal prosecution.[254]

---

248 HAIMES (1988), p. 48.
249 BLYTH (2006).
250 BAUDOUIN & LABRUSSE-RIOU (1987), p. 53.
251 CADOU in LABRUSSE-RIOU (1996),p. 25; Critical: DELAISI DE PARSEVAL (1998), p. 30.
252 Art. L 673-7 **French** Public Health Code (Code de la Santé Publique).
253 FURKEL (1996), p. 772-774.
254 Art. 511-10 **French** Criminal Code (Code Pénal).

Recipient couples must be married. Alternatively, though, they may also be an unmarried different-sex couple with a durable relationship. Moreover, they must have medically certified fertility problems and still be of childbearing age, as DI is considered to be a subsidiary rather than an alternative to natural reproduction.[255] However, since 1999 couples prone to a greater risk of incurable hereditary diseases of a particular gravity have also been permitted access to ART. Donors may not gain financial profits from their donations. Anonymity is bidirectional, i.e. the donor may not come out in the open and the child may not seek his identification either. Deviations from this general rule are only permitted for medical ('therapeutic') reasons.[256]

In **Germany**, donor anonymity has so far escaped legal regulation.[257] This is remarkable given the strongly biological imprint of **German** parentage law and the recognition of a constitutional right to know.[258] It is believed that it is unlawful for the parents to withhold disclosure of the fact of donation.[259] Formally, the child may require the medical professional to disclose the identity of the donor.[260] Muscheler and Bloch have claimed that the child's right to information prevails over donor anonymity as well as the medical professional duty to observe confidentiality.[261] It has been proposed by scholars that a duty to document the identity of donors should exist.[262] A law foreseeing in a disclosure of the donor's identity would in that view also be necessary and consistent with constitutional developments.[263]

The **Dutch** Artificial Insemination (donor information) Act was enacted on 25 April 2002.[264] The Act made it impossible to donate anonymously after 1 June 2004. It follows that the Act lacks retroactive force in respect of earlier donations. Its entry into force marked the end of the 'go-between' double-track policy of the 1990s. At present, donors may no longer rely on an absolute guarantee of anonymity. Even so, the double-track policy has not been abandoned

---

255 Art. L 152-2 **French** Public Health Code (Code de la Santé Publique).
256 Art. L 1211-5 Code de la Santé Publique = **French** Public Health Code. Art. 15-2 LPMA.
257 WEYRAUCH (2003), p. 109.
258 MANSEES (1988), p. 2984; MUSCHELER & BLOCH (2002), p. 345; MÜNCH KOMM/SEIDL (2000), BGB, §1589f, Rdnr. 77.
259 GIESEN (1989), p. 364-367; COESTER-WALTJEN (1992), p. 371.
260 Art. 2 I i. V. mit Art. 1 I GG in conjunction with §810 BGB. MUSCHELER & BLOCH (2002), p. 345.
261 MUSCHELER & BLOCH (2002), p. 345.
262 WEYRAUCH (2003), p. 134.
263 HELMS (1999), p. 188.
264 *Staatsblad* No. 240, 28 May 2002.

completely. Thus, it is still possible to register anonymously, but only on a provisional basis. Disclosure can no longer be excluded if the donor offspring seeks identification. Such a request will, however, be contingent upon the condition that the child has become aware of the circumstances of conception in the first place. It follows that in some cases the donor can still remain anonymous.

The Act vests responsibility for storing, maintaining and disclosing information in a central public authority. This is a foundation established under **Dutch** law.[265] The Executive Board of the Foundation consists of a president and six members who shall be appointed – and dismissed – by the **Dutch** Ministry of Health. Although selection criteria for the professional background of the president have remarkably enough not been specified, at least three of the six members must be professionally engaged in artificial reproduction.[266] One of the three members must be an expert in the implicated psychological-social aspects, while three other members must have a relevant medical background. Of the remaining three members there must be one with a legal background, one with an ethical and one with a pedagogical background.[267]

As a further salient feature, the Foundation is under a statutory obligation to store information regarding the donor carefully for a minimum period of eighty years.[268] **Dutch** municipalities are required to provide the Foundation with copies and extracts upon request in order for the Foundation to fulfil its functions.[269] The finances for the Foundation's activities are covered by practising medical professionals and by hospitals that offer fertility treatments. Costs may not, in any event, exceed those that are incurred in the fulfilment of the Foundation's statutory functions.[270]

Information concerning the donor falls into three broad categories: medical, physical and personal. In contrast to 'personal information', the need for medical information concerning the donor apparently defies any notion of time. Thus, 'medical information that can be of relevance for the healthy development of the child' may be disclosed at any age if the child's physician takes the view that there is a corresponding medical need.[271] The medical condition must be conside-

---

265 Art. 4(1) Artificial Insemination (donor information) Act.

266 Art. 5(1) and 5(2) Artificial Insemination (donor information) Act.

267 Art. 5(2) Artificial Insemination (donor insemination) Act.

268 Art. 8 Artificial Insemination (donor insemination) Act.

269 Art. 9 Artificial Insemination (donor insemination) Act.

270 Art. 7 Artificial Insemination (donor insemination) Act.

271 Art. 3(1) under (a) Artificial Insemination (donor insemination) Act.

red to be sufficiently serious to prompt a disclosure of the donor's medical record. In accordance with secondary legislation, sufficiently compelling conditions include such diseases as cardiovascular ailments and diabetes.[272]

Physical information in respect of the donor is also subject to further, possibly evolving definitions in secondary legislation.[273] Physical information should not 'separately or in combination make it possible that the individual donor can be traced'.[274] This will allow the child to already form an image of the donor. These include the donor's hair colour, complexion, weight, eye colour and height at the time of donation. Finally, the remaining category, 'personal information', has not been further defined either. It is telling, however, that 'the surname, date of birth and domicile' have been considered sufficiently important in the right's overall enforcement so as to be cast into a separate, single provision.[275] Physical information must be provided at the request of the person who knows or presumes that he or she has been born through AI from the age of twelve.[276] Before the child reaches this age this information must also be provided to the child's parents upon their request. It is not clear whether the socio-legal parents, once they have been given a physical description of the donor, can subsequently lawfully withhold 'physical information' from the child. In view of the aims and the spirit of the Act, this would certainly seem unlikely.

The category 'personal information' includes the donor's name, surname, date of birth and domicile.[277] The provision specifies that 'information identifying the person' shall be provided to the person who, having reached the age of sixteen, knowing or presuming that he or she was conceived through AI makes an application to that end to the Foundation, which will then seek the written consent of the donor.[278] As for 'personal information', it may be safely assumed that this relates – at least – to the same data as those referred to in Article 3(2) of the Act, i.e. the donor's surname, date of birth and domicile. Here it is specified that 'information identifying the person' shall be provided to the person who, having reached the age of sixteen, knowing or presuming that he or she

272 Art. 2 Besluit donorgegevens kunstmatige bevruchting, 11 August 2003, p. 4.

273 Art. 3(1) under (b) Artificial Insemination (donor insemination) Act.

274 Art. 3(2) Artificial Insemination (donor insemination) act; *Kamerstukken* 1997/98, 23 207, No. 9, p. 2.

275 Art. 3(1) under (c) Artificial Insemination (donor insemination) Act.

276 Art. 2(1) under (b) in conjunction with Art. 3(1) under (b) Articial Insemination (donor insemination) Act.

277 Art. 2(1) under (c) Artificial Insemination (donor insemination) Act.

278 Art. 3(3) Artificial Insemination (donor insemination) Act.

was conceived through AI makes an application to that end to the Foundation, which will then seek the written consent of the donor.[279]

'Personal information' must be communicated not only to the child, but also to both or one of the parents if they express a request to that end.[280] Throughout this process of disclosure, the Foundation is under the legal obligation to provide services of professional counselling, which will extend not only to the child but also to the legal parents.[281]

A request for personal information in respect of the donor emanating from a child younger than sixteen years must be communicated by the Foundation to the parents, who may also receive the information.[282] Throughout this process of phased disclosure, the Foundation is under the legal obligation to provide services of professional counseling, extending perhaps not only to the child but also to the legal parents.[283]

It remains to be seen what could happen if the donor refuses to give his written consent to the disclosure of his 'personal information'. In any event, the donor will be given a period of thirty days subsequent to the day that the notification had been sent by the foundation to express his objections to disclosure. The requested information is not provided to the petitioner until the Foundation has made an irrevocable decision on the issue.[284]

Exceptionally, the information will not be provided in case of 'appreciable interests' of the donor. The open-endedness of this norm leaves the Foundation with some discretion to weigh the competing interests. It may very turn out to be elusive for the Foundation to make a realistic assessment of the (psychological) impact non-disclosure could have for the petitioner. Moreover, it may be so that the mention of the donor's interests will only involve nominal respect. In view of the overall tone and spirit of the Act it may be said that there is a strong presumption in favour of the child's right to information.

A donor may at present no longer rely on the fact that he can remain anonymous, after all, even if he has meanwhile formed a family of his own and wishes

279 Art. 3(3) Artificial Insemination (donor insemination) Act.
280 Art. 3(6) Artificial Insemination (donor insemination) Act.
281 Art. 3(7) Artificial Insemination (donor insemination) Act.
282 Art. 3(6) Artificial Insemination (donor insemination) Act.
283 Art. 3(7) Artificial Insemination (donor insemination) Act.
284 Art. 3(4) Artificial Insemination (donor insemination) Act.

to avoid possibly unpleasant confrontations. It may therefore be unlikely that the Foundation would consider the donor's interest to be sufficiently cogent.

If a donor has subsequently died or cannot be traced, he will be presumed to have refused to give his consent to the disclosure of his personal identity.[285] In those situations, the spouse, registered partner or life-partner of the donor will be approached by the Foundation, or if one of these persons is missing, a blood-relative in the first or second degree. These persons close to the donor will be asked to give their written consent. If they refuse, they will be given an opportunity to adduce reasons why the donor's identity should not be disclosed.[286]

It is worth adding, too, that it was considered too politically sensitive to allow for a form of compulsory DNA testing with a view to the identification of the donor.[287] Even so, the donor's blood group shall be documented. The law assumes that an examination of the sperm donor's blood group in combination with the medically documented hour of donation will generally provide sufficient evidence that a genetic link exists between the donor and the child. Only if the donor consents, may a paternity test be conducted. This squares well with the idea that consent to DNA testing is in principle required in parentage testing under **Dutch** law.

When AI first came to be used with some regularity in **Portugal** around the 1980s, the legal literature tended to advocate a strict preservation of donor anonymity.[288] In this debate familiar arguments connected with the donor's right to privacy and the availability of donors resounded. Following the adoption of the 2006 framework law, a rather strict regime of donor anonymity has been chosen. Violations of this legal regime involve criminal liability in the form of custodial sentences of up to one year or imprisonment of 240 days. The birth act may not specify that the child was born through AI. Keeping the identity of the donor secret as well as the practice of ART in itself has been conceived of as a duty that is not only incumbent on the medical practitioner and the commissioning parents, but also on anyone who knows about the donor and the fact of donation. Nonetheless, both the child and the practising clinics may petition genetic information on the donor for medical reasons. This may however not lead to the fully-fledged identification of the donor. The service provider and the child, as well as the National Council on ART, may also petition non-identifying

285 Art. 3(3) Artificial Insemination (donor insemination) Act.
286 Art. 3(3) Artificial Insemination (donor insemination) Act.
287 Explanatory Note to the Besluit donorgegevens kunstmatige bevruchting, p. 7.
288 See LOPES CARDOSO (1991), p. 23; RAMALHO DA SILVA GONÇALVES (1995), p. 33.

information concerning the donor in the event of the possible existence of a marriage within the prohibited degrees of consanguinity. It has been recognised that the donor may then choose to reveal his identity. Identifying information may also be disclosed whenever weighty reasons for disclosure have been recognised in a court decision. In effect, then, the possibilities to know the identity of the donor are likely to be remote. They will depend on the willingness of the parents to be open in revealing the fact of donation. Subsequently the child would need to advance weighty reasons before a court to obtain identifying information.

In **Portugal,** secrecy may impact a great number of parties, including parents and potentially also third parties who 'find out'. Thus, whoever finds out about the fact of donation is under an obligation to keep their identity a secret as well as their use of ART subject to a custodial sentence of one year.[289] Nonetheless, **Portuguese** law may leave some leeway for more extensive interpretations permitting some access to personal information concerning the donor, but not his identification. Thus, 'persons born through medically assisted conception by the use of gamete donation or embryo donation, may, like the competent health service providers, obtain information of a genetic nature, that concerns them, excluding the identification of the donor'.[290] Moreover, persons born through gamete donation may, next to the National Council on ART,[291] seek information as to whether there exists a legal obstacle to marriage, namely relationships within the prohibited degrees of consanguinity.[292] The anonymity of the donor will then be preserved, unless the donor expressly allows himself to be identified.[293]

It must be added, however, that a clause technically leaves some room for jurisprudential developments in future that could acknowledge a right to full identification of the donor. As such, identifying information may be petitioned, presumably by the donor-conceived person and the parents, by submitting a request to the court.[294] It has been suggested by Vale e Reis that this rule should be modified. He considers that some sort of balance could be struck between the competing interests by allowing donor-conceived persons to have access to a court and request the identification of the donor.[295] The donor would then have

---

289 Art. 15-1 in conjunction with Art. 43 LPMA.

290 Art. 15-2 LPMA.

291 *Conselho nacional sobre a procriação medicamente assistida.*

292 Art. 15-3 LPMA.

293 Art. 15-3 LPMA.

294 Art. 5-4 LPMA.

295 Vale e Reis (2008), p. 478-479.

to be given a chance to be heard and to object, through the intervention of a Public Prosecutor, within a period of fifteen to thirty days to the disclosure of his identity. If no objection is made, he could become identifiable.

6.7. COMPARISON

Currently, among the four selected systems, only **the Netherlands** has enacted legislation foreseeing a (gradual) waiver of donor anonymity. It is significant for the delineation of the conceptual scope of the right to know that disclosure is contingent upon the child's age and that a categorisation of information has been made as to whether the information is identifying or non-identifying. In case the donor has died or cannot be traced, the basic presumption underlying the law reverses, however, in the sense that the donor's personal identity should in principle then not be disclosed. But this does not appear to be a hard rule and the Foundation will probably in such a situation still attempt to reassure the donor's family by notifying them about the importance of the child's right. The Foundation could also inform the family in those situations that disclosure will have no legal consequences for the family's rights to the donor's inheritance and that it does not affect child maintenance claims either. As such, a disclosure of the deceased donor's personal information need not encroach much into their family life, conceivably much less than if the donor were still living. Conceivably, too, if counseling services were offered with public funds their initial shock and discomfort could be reduced considerably; if such reassurances can be provided, disclosure of the identifying information to the child need not taint the memories they may have of the man who may, indeed, never have told his family that at one point in his life he had been a donor.

In **Germany**, **France** and **Portugal**, donor anonymity still holds sway. Whereas **Germany** lacks relevant legislation or regulation, **France** and **Portugal** foresee, however, a restricted possibility of disclosure in case the child is exposed to genetic diseases. In **Portugal**, recent legislation leaves the door open for case-law developments that may go into the direction of a much more generalized right to identify the donor when medical reasons are absent. It must further be concluded that the medical rationale for providing information concerning the donor has been acknowledged in at least three of the four jurisdictions.

6.8 EVALUATION

The **Dutch** Donor Insemination (artificial insemination) Act has established a central registry system. The enforcement of the donor offspring's right to information has been made entirely contingent upon the willingness of parents to disclose how the child had been conceived. The parents therefore retain primary responsibility in disclosing information. This raises the question of what other implementation mechanisms could help to maximize a donor offspring's choice in accessing donor identifying information.

Enforcing a donor-conceived child's right to know involves at least two steps. In order to identify the donor, the donor offspring must already have become aware how he or she had been conceived. This is an important distinction. It is conceivable, for example, that some donor offspring will not wish to establish the identity of the donor, but still want to find out about the way they had been conceived. Since a donor-conceived child may have a right *not* to be informed about conception by persons other than the primary carers, it will generally be commendable to vest primary responsibility for disclosure in the child's parents. The state should have a subsidiary role in facilitating disclosure and should avoid being complicit in an institutionalised form of deception, but at the same time, it should also be careful not to take overtly invasive measures. These may be perceived as discriminatory with regard to the recipient couples. An ongoing commitment to offering professional guidance to parents and the child in facilitating disclosure during minority may therefore be preferable to imposing a publicly enforceable duty on parents to tell. This might even instill in some parents a more secretive attitude, which will hardly be in children's interest in respect for their decisional privacy.

Must the state then content itself with drafting emblematic laws foreseeing a waiver of donor anonymity? For one thing, in the eyes of the **Dutch** legislator, making a principled choice for the child's right to know was openly acknowledged as a sufficient reason to make an end to the guarantee of anonymity. This principled choice has not been taken to extremes, however, or become absolute. The law still leaves some room for donor anonymity. This point may not only be appreciated on account of the fact that primary responsibility to disclose is still left to the parents.

In case the donor has died or cannot be traced, the basic legal presumption, that automatically assumes an interest on the part of the child in identifying the donor without requiring the donor conceived person to adduce further evidence of her or his 'psychological motives', seems to be absent. Or at least it is less strong, for the Foundation may still try to persuade the relatives to give written consent and if they refuse to do so, it is they who must carry the onus of proving why they are opposed to disclosure. The same onus is put on the living donor if he refuses and refuses to consent. This makes sense: any prospective donor should, following a waiver of anonymity, be aware of the fact that his identity may one day be revealed. Yet the donor should still have a right to be heard if his personal circumstances change as to why he opposes disclosure. The donor like any other person, has a right to private life.

The basic presumption must, however, be that the donor has a procreational responsibility to become identifiable once his anonymity has been waived. Clearly, this is a different sort of responsibility than a duty to become a legal parent for this should be firmly excluded. Still, the principle of procreational responsibility means that the onus should be on him or, after his death, on his family in opposing disclosure for personal reasons. In contrast, the child's interest in knowing may generally be assumed on the basis of the principles of equality and decisional privacy.

As another strong point of the **Dutch** law, reference should be made to the nuanced distinction between identifying and non-identifying information that the phased disclosure scheme proposes, generally may be said to reflect an original and careful consideration of the donor offspring's growing informational interests. More could be done by the state, however, without imposing measures that could be considered as overtly invasive.

In examining more invasive measures, an advantage of entering information on the birth certificate would admittedly be that more donor offspring could find out how they have been conceived. However, it may be questioned if this does not create tension with the 'inner core' of other rights, such as the recipient couple's interest in the child's upbringing, which may be considered to be an aspect of their right to private life. Since some empirical studies suggest that disclosure rates among parents may already be on the increase, entering the fact of donor conception on the birth certificate could be considered a disproportionate measure. But the possibility of introducing a 'triggering text' on every birth certificate to alert that birth certificates are not necessarily a guarantee of biological parentage should be worth considering.

According to Bainham, the proposed text could involve a general warning on every single birth certificate – not merely those of donor conceived persons – along the lines that:

'This certificate records legal parentage and is not to be relied upon as a guaran tee of biological parentage'.[296]

This would also have the advantage of not singling out donor conceived persons and thereby avoiding possible stigmatisation. It is not likely, moreover, that this measure would entail high public costs. But it is probably realistic to say that at present most states will not yet be ready to take such a measure, perhaps because they misguidedly believe that the birth certificate cannot be used to that end or that this would somehow discriminate against socio-legal forms of parentage. If entering this 'triggering text' is considered too , then a publicity campaign that draws attention to this point could, however, perhaps be feasible to promote greater awareness of the potential importance for children to find out.

Other less invasive solutions than entering the fact of donation on the birth certificate could also make it easier for persons to find out how they had been conceived. In **New Zealand**, for example, there had been a proposal by that country's Law Commission to the effect that donor conceived persons would get two birth certificates instead of one. There would be a full certificate stating the child's genetic parentage on the 'donor conception certificate' which would have a long and a short version. The short version, that would only record the child's legal parentage, would be used for registration and schools and other purposes. The long version would, however, state the parents' legal names and nobody else but mention the fact of donation. This would be used in passports, for example, thereby encouraging parents to tell the child at a young age. Ultimately, this proposal was not accepted because it was feared that this would involve an overtly bureaucratic system to operate. As further objections, it was believed that this measure would compromise the parents' decision when to tell as well as the donor's privacy.[297]

As a general conclusion, it may be said, however, that laws that waive donor anonymity signify an important step forward. They will in most societies at least instill a greater awareness of the legal problem of unknown origins. Complementary state measures will be required, however, if such laws are not destined to remain emblematic. Less invasive public (and private) measures could often provide more appropriate and effective ways of facilitating the right to know. Public funding of a voluntary contact register could set a good example that the state is not willing to be complicit in deception. Furthermore, for those born

---

296 Bainham (2008), p. 473.

297 New Zealand Law Commission R88, New Issues in Legal Parenthood: Family, p. 117-118.

prior to the waiver of donor anonymity this could help some donor conceived persons to identify the donor. But such a system cannot dispense with respect for the donor's interests for these men donated at a time when anonymity was often sanctioned under the law. As such, they must still be able to rely on the fact that his identity will not be revealed against his will.

7. POST-MORTAL ARTIFICIAL INSEMINATION AND EMBRYO TRANSFER

7.1. THE BLOOD CASE

In its decision in *Diane Blood,* the **English** Court of Appeal relied on the free movement of goods in European Community (EC) law in its argumentation that the Human Fertilization and Embryology Authority had acted unlawfully in refusing to allow Ms Blood to export to **Belgium** sperm which had been taken from her dying husband without his written consent (in fact while he was unconscious and on a life-support machine).[298] The *Diane Blood* case raised the issue of the extent to which EC law is an appropriate legal avenue for regulating human reproduction in the Member states as well as questions about reproductive tourism.[299] Furthermore, it raised questions regarding the scope of the right to know one's origins given that the child will only be able to obtain information about the father on the basis of the accounts of others, thereby prejudging the child's decisional privacy. In spite of this significant objection, public support for Ms Blood extended beyond compassion for a young widow to include support for her decision to pursue a desire to have a child.[300]

7.2. RELEVANT LAW

In **France**, all forms of post-mortal insemination and embryo transfer were expressly prohibited in the 1994 Act.[301] It follows that persons who had donated their gametes must in principle be living when the gametes are used for treat-

298 Court of Appeal (*R v. Human Fertilisation and Embryology Authority, ex parte Blood* [1997] 2 All ER 687).

299 HERVEY (1998), p. 207-234; DEECH (2003), p. 425-432; PENNINGS (2005), p. 2689-2694; SPAR (2005), p. 231-233.

300 JACKSON (2001), p. 209-211.

301 Art. 2141-2(3) Code de la Santé Publique = **French** Public Health Code.

ment. Supernumerary embryos may either be destroyed or used for scientific research, but not used for pregnancies.[302]

In **Germany**, sperm donation in homologous AI after the death of the male partner of the woman undergoing fertility treatment has not been formally prohibited. In such a situation the ordinary rules governing the determination of paternity must therefore be presumed to be fully applicable.[303] This means that if the child is born within 300 days after the husband's death, he shall be considered to be the father under the law.[304]

If the child has been recognised before birth by an unmarried male partner who dies before the child's birth, the deceased will be the father.[305] Paternity would then not be challengeable posthumously by the mother.[306] Nonetheless, there would be no legal obstacle for the child to deny paternity and subsequently trace the identity of the donor in order to have the latter's paternity established. In the absence of regulation heterologous *post-mortem* AI and *post-mortem* embryo transfer have not been formally prohibited either.

In **the Netherlands**, the Embryos Act specifies that gametes should be destroyed after it has become known to the (legal) person storing them that the gamete provider has died.[307] However, if the man had expressly given his written consent to their use while he was still living, they may in principle still be used with a view to fertilisation. Whether the sperm of the deceased will actually be used for procreative purposes is contingent upon the physician's assessment, however.[308] The physician will in every single case have to determine the interests of both the unborn child and of the woman in question. It is circumspect whether this assessment would extend to an enquiry into the child's (prospective) interests in 'knowing' his father in the broad sense. For the gametes to be used for procreative purposes, the hospital must, in addition, already dispose of a protocol that sets forth its policy on *post-mortem* insemination.[309] As such, there are five hospitals in **the Netherlands** that are known to engage in *post-mortem* forms of AI.[310]

---

302 Art. 2141-1 and 2141-6 Code de la Santé Publique = **French** Public Health Code.
303 RAUSCHER/STAUDINGER (2004), BGB, §1592, No. 9, 229.
304 §1593 BGB.
305 §1594 IV BGB.
306 §1600 V BGB.
307 Art. 7 **Dutch** Embryos Act.
308 BREEMHAAR (2007), p. 167.
309 *Kamerstukken II* 2000/01, 27 423, No. 3, 18-19.
310 *Evaluatie Embryowet*, p. 66.

Embryos created outside the woman's body may in principle not be preserved but need to be destroyed after the death of the woman's male partner.[311] If this deceased male had given written consent to their use, a hospital may decide to use them for a pregnancy while taking into account the future child's and woman's interests and its own Protocol. So far only one **Dutch** hospital has permitted *post-mortem* embryo transfer following its argument that human life should already be assumed to exist.[312]

In **Portugal**, the 2006 LPMA Act expressly banned all forms of *post-mortem* AI, indeed even with the existence of proof of the man's consent *in vivo* to the use of his semen.[313] If the man dies during the course of the woman's fertility treatment, the frozen semen will need to be destroyed.[314] The regime on *post-mortem* embryo transfer differs in the sense that it has been permitted under the strict conditions that express written consent had been given prior to the man's death and that a period of reflection considered appropriate for the mother to make the decision has been observed.[315] The deceased will then be the resultant child's legal father. If, in violation of the prohibition of *post-mortem* AI, a child is born, the deceased man will also be considered the child's legal father.[316] If the deceased man had been married to the mother or had cohabited with her for over two years, the consent to the act of (heterologous) insemination will in such cases be regarded as the legal basis of the man's paternity.[317] What this effectively boils down to, is a legal impossibility for anyone except the child to subsequently deny the paternity of the deceased. This legal regime also applies *mutatis mutandis* to *post-mortem* egg or sperm donation followed by IVF treatment.[318]

7.3. COMPARISON

Prohibitive legislation exists in **France** and **Portugal** regarding the use of post-mortal AI. In **the Netherlands** the use is only exceptionally permitted if the father was living during the donation and consented to the use of his sperm after

---

311 Art. 8 **Dutch** Embryos Act.

312 *Evaluatie Embryowet*, p. 66.

313 Art. 22-1 Lei 32/2006 sobre a procriação medicamente assistida (LPMA) = **Portuguese** law on medically-assisted procreation.

314 Art. 22-2 Lei 32/2006 sobre a procriação medicamente assistida (LPMA) = **Portuguese** law on medically-assisted procreation

315 Art. 22-3 LPMA.

316 Art. 23-1 LPMA.

317 Art. 23-2 LPMA in conjunction with Art. 1839-3 PCC.

318 Art. 26 Lei 32/2006 sobre a procriação medicamente assistida (LPMA) = **Portuguese** law on medically-assisted procreation.

his death. Under this condition in **the Netherlands** the physician will sometimes be able to proceed with treatment. In **Germany** there is a legislative lacuna on this issue.

7.4. EVALUATION

It is in the wider context of the mobility of knowledge and people that the *Blood* case occurred, It laid bare some of the serious ethical and public policy issues which governments may face in seeking to find national solutions.[319] Given the reality of procreational tourism, the effect of national prohibitions will therefore sometimes be limited. But national laws may still seek to set an example.

Apart from these problems associated with reproductive tourism, the media attention surrounding the *Blood* case also raised questions as to whether courts are susceptible to the strength of popular sympathy for involuntarily childless people. This is hard to either prove or disprove. For our discussion, it is more directly relevant to note that post-mortal AI will deprive the child, above all, from the moment of birth of the possibility to (get to) know the father. Sure enough, the legal identity of the deceased may still be documented and communicated to the child. In that sense, the child's right not to information may not be considered to have been prejudged through the use of post-mortal AI. Yet clearly it will not be in the child's informational interests to be able to know the father through second-hand information passed on by the mothers and others alone. It will be a 'false comfort' to then say that this will at least be much more than most donor-conceived children from anonymous donors may be able to achieve. Furthermore, post-mortal insemination will also be objectionable from a parentage law perspective on the child's interests. Thus, it must be borne in mind that the child of a single woman following post-mortal insemination is not only deprived of his or her biological father from the moment of birth, but also of having a second legal parent.[320]

319 DEECH (2003), p. 427-428.
320 WATT (2002), p. 103.

PART V
CLOSING REFLECTIONS

CHAPTER XI
CONCLUDING REMARKS

1. OUTLINE

In the previous chapters a thematic comparison has been provided of the most common situations in which the right to know one's genetic origins may be at issue. This analysis has made visible the differences and similarities between the selected jurisdictions. A central aim of this research has been to establish whether the current legal structures should be considered to be capable of effectively meeting the informational interests children may (or may not) have in establishing the identity of their biological parents. In connection with that aim, the question has been raised to what extent national legal interpretations of the right to know one's genetic origins are consistent with the relevant international and regional constitutional legal structures.

In this Chapter the main evaluative points that have already been made on the basis of this comparison shall be integrated. Accordingly, the question shall be raised how the right to know could be best accommodated while having regard to the legal principles that were formulated in Chapter V. It shall also be explored to which extent the law may be considered a suitable vehicle to help implement children's right to information. In that respect, some evaluative points shall be made with regard to the question of where the outer limits of state involvement in promoting greater openness concerning biological parentage may lie.

2. PRINCIPLES

In Chapter V three main legal principles have been derived from the analysis of the constitutional legal order. Because these principles have been found to guide constitutional legal discourse at various levels, their normative force across various factual contexts has been examined. On the basis of the comparative analysis in the preceding chapters it therefore seems appropriate to assess the validity of each of the principles and their interconnectedness in the following sections.

3. DECISIONAL PRIVACY

A principle of decisional privacy concerning important personal issues underlies the right to private life. The right to private life is protected under Article 8 ECHR. Likewise, the personality right, which incorporates a right to informational self-determination, is found in the **Dutch**, **German** and **Portuguese** national constitutional legal orders and forms the primary constitutional basis of the right to know one's origins in these jurisdictions. **French** constitutional doctrine, however, does not conceive of any personality right and has not derived a right to know one's biological origins from the national constitution. Even so, the permeation of European and international legal standards and scholarly discourses have also induced this jurisdiction to review its legislation on anonymous birth and to accommodate children's informational interests to a greater extent than previously.

As has been established in Chapter I, biological parentage should be considered to be an aspect of a person's *fixed identity*. As an ontological and immutable quality, fixed identity is also closely connected with the notion of *numerical identity*. Because of this fixed character, a 'principle of decisional privacy' has been considered to be a more appropriate term than the term 'informational self-determination'. The notion of decisional privacy more clearly transmits the idea that people should in principle have a free *choice* in interpreting their fixed identity. Even so, it has also been found that the right to know also connects with a more fluid and dynamic concept of identity which has been called *narrative identity*.

Having a measure of a decisional privacy to access one's fixed identity is a prerequisite for a person to shape and interpret one's own evolving, narrative identity. Legal recognition of the fact that persons should be given a measure of decisional privacy in interpreting their own narrative identity does not in itself involve an excessive valorisation of the biological truth to the detriment of notions of social parentage. Rather, as a fluid concept closely associated with the passage of time, narrative identity may also involve the interpretation of alterable, sociological notions of parentage. As David Gollancz, a donor conceived person born in 1952, has argued:

'It is important to say that this is an argument not based on evidence about individual emotional welfare; there is not enough evidence available. It is based on the proposition that no-one has the right to decide on the other person's behalf whether that other person should or should not be able to know about their own history.'[1]

Would social parentage not require the same sort of protection as an identity right? Does recognition of the right to know not exalt the importance of the biological ties at the detriment of socio-legal forms of parentage? These arguments cannot be sustained because socio-legally constructed parentage cannot be said to concern a person's fixed identity to the same extent as biological parentage does, whatever the cultural bias towards the latter. Precisely because the identity of the socio-legal parents will usually have been documented somewhere during a period after birth or already have become familiar during childhood, the interest in a separate constitutional recognition of this aspect of one's narrative identity will generally be less compelling. In contrast, biological parents may have been unknown from the moment of birth, It follows that the child's decisional privacy may become more seriously prejudged in case the child does not know who his biological parents are.

In Chapter I, it has been conceded, however, that the informational need must be considered to be partially socially constructed. Furthermore, it has been established in Chapter I, too, that the informational right has become more pressing as a result of the adoption movement and bio-medical developments. Even so, acknowledging this does not mean that the upsurge of interest in a right to know is only a contemporary phenomenon. Viewed as representing a moral interest *not to be deceived* by one's parents it defies such historicist interpretations.

3.1. DECISIONAL PRIVACY, DECEPTION AND THE RIGHT NOT TO KNOW IN RESPECT OF ADULTS

In Chapter V it was established that decisional privacy constitutes a key principle in delineating the strength of the right to information. Furthermore, it has been held that this notion of decisional privacy must also protect, to some extent, a right *not* to know. This is a notion that is also implicit in the term 'right to informational self-determination'. It has not yet been discussed, however, what

1 Human Tissue and Embryos (Draft) Bill, Volume II, Evidence, HL Paper 169-II, HC Paper 630-II, EV 44. See also BAINHAM (2008), p. 464-465.

this right *not* to know involves. A clear counter-argument against the existence of such a right could be that most people, 'in fact', know who their parents are. Therefore, a constitutional right *not* to know that should apply to all cannot really exist or would be a legal folly. The fallacy of this counter-argument is, however, exposed by the fact that what most people know about their parents is, in fact, a sincere belief. If it is true that one must have at least some prior knowledge to have a right *not* to know, then in the case of unknown parentage this knowledge could conceivably be kept at a minimum. Thus, whenever no DNA testing has taken place, our prior 'knowledge' is in fact a belief. Indeed, fortunately for the courts, most people do not pursue their interest (or lack of interest) in accurate information beyond that belief. The docket of cases could perhaps soon become insurmountable. Could it not be then, the pragmatic jurist asks from the viewpoint of judicial economics, that a principle of social efficaciousness is not ultimately more important than the person's right to decisional privacy?

We may leave that question for what it is, since a massive run to the courts of every legal subject for biological certainty is unlikely to happen. For most people, the idea of an uncertain parentage may indeed never have crossed their minds. What may be said, however, is that principled respect for an adult's right *not* to know should entail recognition of the fact that that adult may not wish to act upon the basic awareness that there will almost always be a slight chance that our parents do not share a genetic link to us. This basic awareness, which we may consider to be a form of 'prior knowledge' that is necessary to make a choice, in principle extends to everyone. This means recognition that just as everyone, on the basis of the principle of decisional privacy, should have a principled right to articulate her or his legal interest in obtaining accurate parent-identifying information, so every self-governing individual in principle should also have a right not to pursue this legal aim. That is precisely why the right to know also encompasses a right not to know for children who have become adults ('adult children'). Even so, this right *not* to know, like other rights, cannot be considered to be absolute either: conceivably, there could, for example, be a public health interest in requesting an adult child to go along with parentage testing if this minimises the exposure of the general public to a hereditary disease.

This autonomy-based approach to the right *not* to know has been defended by the **Argentine** bio-ethicist Andorno, who has claimed that, 'the choice of not knowing the results of genetic tests does not fall into a paternalistic attitude because the challenge to medical paternalism is precisely based on the idea that people should be free to make their own choices with respect to information.[2] Therefore, he concludes that the right *not* to know should – at least in principle – be as fully respected as the right to know. He suggests that the right not to know should first be able to become 'activated' as an exception to the general rule that a patient has a 'right to know' while a medical professional has a 'duty to inform.'

Although Andorno is primarily concerned with the right *not* to know in the field of medical genetic tests, it is submitted that his argumentation could also be analogised to genetic testing in parentage issues to some extent. In the present author's understanding of an 'activation' of a right *not* to know, one could conceive of an adult who makes an express choice not to request the person he presumes to be his father to undergo testing, perhaps because this putative father had a troubled relationship with the mother and feels, misguidedly or not, that pursuing identification any further because this would be an insult to the mother. That said, however, it must be said that in most cases most of us will clearly not make or be able to make such an expressly activated choice *not* to know.

Thus, especially in those cases in which no explicit choice has been made, it may be difficult to argue that one has 'actively' or consciously chosen not to enforce one's right to information. Only when substantial doubts have already arisen, is certainty over parentage likely to become an issue for most. On the right not to know in medical genetic testing, **Scottish** bio-ethicist Laurie holds that this means that there must be a reversal of the burden of proof: the onus of justifying disclosure must generally be firmly on the shoulders of those who seek to justify disclosure.[3] In his academic discussion with Adorno, who had previously insisted that a right not to know must in some way always first be 'activated', Laurie takes the view that we cannot assume anything about what (autonomous) people want in the absence of actual knowledge about their (possible) wishes. Therefore, Laurie insists that some measure of caution is always necessary. Laurie concedes that withholding information whenever no explicit choice is made involves a paternalistic approach, but that the nature of the dilemma necessarily makes it so.[4]

---

2 ANDORNO (2006), p. 436.
3 LAURIE (2001), p. 259.
4 LAURIE (2004), p. 440.

What could this mean for testing among two generations of adults only for the sake of establishing the existence of a genetic link between them? For Laurie, this form of genetic testing might mean that an adult child should also be required to bear the burden of proof regarding the question whether testing is actually necessary if the parent had expressed a wish not to want to know, because we cannot assume anything about that parent's wishes and both individuals involved are adults. For Andorno, it might mean, however, that the parent's right *not* to know must first also be expressed or 'activated' in one way or another. Conversely, in the opposite case, when it is the adult child that does not wish to be tested but the adult parent does, it may be said that this interferes with the adult child's right *not* to know. For minor children, clearly, the case is even more complicated for children lack full decisional privacy in that regard (see 3.3).

What is more important to note at this point is that neither Andorno's nor Laurie's approach to the right not to know are geared towards providing answers about the right's enforcement. Thus, in this study it has been argued that the principle of decisional privacy cannot be the only principle relevant for our discussion. Decisional privacy cannot account for the (necessary) idea that parents are in principle responsible for accurate information and may, for that reason, also in principle be required to co-operate with DNA testing. Conversely, it has been held that the reverse generally does not hold true: a parent should not be able to compel a child, whatever that child's age, to undergo testing. In order to draw this distinction and to be able to make an argument for co-operation, it has been necessary to refer to another principle: the principle of procreational responsibility.[5] It follows that the autonomy-model of decisional privacy in itself is not sufficient to explain why a parent may have to waive his decisional privacy if this is required for the implementation of the (adult) child's right to information.[6]

3.2. CONTINGENCY

It should be added also that differences in the degrees of (non-)disclosure will, as a matter of fact, often be inevitable. It follows that the principle of decisional privacy, incorporating both a right to know and a right *not* to know, cannot always be respected. This is not only because the extent to which one has certainty means that one cannot at the same time have a right not to have

---

5 See Chapter V and below.

6 See Chapter V, VIII and below.

certainty regarding that particular area where certainty has been achieved. Rather, this conclusion must also be derived in examining some factual and legal differences in context.

Thus, if we conceive of persons, who suspecting that they had been conceived through donor conception, filing for a name and address of the donor from a hospital, for example, it may be said that these persons have clearly waived their right *not* to know completely. Yet some of these persons may not wish to find out more than establishing some details about the donor's medical or social background, but may only petition identifying information in a given legal system. As far as the disclosure of the name and identity are concerned, they may still want to 'actively' exercise their right *not* to know but they may be unable to. Yet it may turn out to be an 'all-or-nothing' affair: non-identification will have become impossible. In this sense, knowing and not knowing will indeed be mutually exclusive. The specific nature of donor insemination will, however, allow for some nuanced distinction between types of information, something which will be difficult to realise in case of a 'misattributed paternity'. Here, once the child is confronted with the proverbial 'milkman' or someone else in one's social environment, it may indeed be impossible to ignore or *not* to know him.

How different is the case of AI? For one thing, it is not without irony that the separation between distinct types of identifying and non-identifying information in the **Dutch** Articial Insemination (Donor Information) Act respects minor children's right *not* to identify the donor to the greatest extent imaginable, while also acknowledging their right to identify him in a principled way. In fact, donor conceived persons may still never find out at all how they were conceived if they do not raise any questions and file an application for information. Assuming that they will inquire, donor-conceived persons have a clear right to obtain certain information but in petitioning identifying information it has been found that the presumption in favour of the child is not quite as strong. If they wish to obtain a description of the donor's physical appearance and social or professional background, they can get this information in a straightforward way. They can then decide for themselves whether or not they want more than this and will generally be able to obtain identifying information also subject to some consent requirements with regard to the donor. Likewise, an adopted child upon having reached a certain age will be able to access the birth certificate and be content with the information contained therein, without pursuing any further contact. In some cases, it may also be possible only to access the adoption file while remaining ignorant about the legal identity of the birthparents.

In brief, then, the extent that the identity of the biological parent has been documented but the parent has been removed from the child's upbringing at an early stage will be important factors in ensuring a child's right not to know and thereby maximising the realisation of the principle of decisional privacy. Conversely, in natural reproduction it may often be next to impossible to distinguish between types of information when the father turns out to be someone in the mother's social environment. Full identification, as well as a family law relationship, will in status proceedings often be the outcome.

In this respect, in **Germany** and **the Netherlands** the possibility to compel some mothers to disclose the father's name has been discussed in doctrine and case law. As such, the procedure will be geared towards disclosure of the father's name, rather than a 'mere' disclosure of information concerning his social background. In brief, what is being requested is the 'whole package'. Likewise, also in a case of a judicial determination of paternity the disclosure of the presumptive biological father's name logically follows, as the procedure is geared towards the creation of a family law relationship between the father and the child. In other words, respect for this child's decisional privacy, especially the right *not* to know, can in this context not be as easily ensured under the law as it can be for adoptees or for donor-conceived children.[7] This is not only because the putative father is more likely to be a familiar person and part of the child's social environment prior to proceedings, but also because the father will not only become responsible for his identification, but also as a legal parent.

3.3. THE SCOPE OF THE RIGHT NOT TO KNOW IN RESPECT OF MINORS

Having established that adults have a right to decisional privacy, questions remain regarding the implications of the principle of decisional privacy for minors. At a minimum, it has been argued that during minority one should not be deceived about the question whether there is a disparity between status and parentage. During minority, the child's right to know would therefore in the author's view have to be considered to generally supersede the minor's right not to know. It is only when minors have become acquainted with the fact that

7 For children born in a surrogacy contract, this may be even more difficult because the child will generally not be informed at all by the commissioning parents about the existence of a genetic mother. This genetic mother will disappear from the child's life after birth, but her identity has not been documented in a way that is comparable to those of adoptees or where donors are registered centrally and without a guarantee of anonymity, as is now the case in **the Netherlands**.

parental status probably does not reflect the biological truth that they may, depending on the context, also be in a position to decide later, perhaps during late adolescence, whether full identification or parentage testing must also follow. Accuracy can only come after Sincerity and Sincerity will only sometimes be questioned. Thus, the minor must have become more than minimally aware, however, of the fact that there may be an underlying disparity between status and the biological truth.

It would therefore seem that the minor's right *not* to know cannot demand the same level of protection as that of adults.[8] Quite simply, some interference with the child's decisional privacy may therefore be necessary if the right to know is to be ensured and it has indeed been our assumption that some degree of parental identification will generally be in the child's interests. The general rule must therefore be that the child has a right to know and exceptionally a right not to know when the minor's informational interest risks becoming subjugated to the parent's own interpretation of the minor's informational interests. This risk may sometimes be great, as has been noted, in the case of extra-judicial paternity testing.[9] This approach, in which a parent may 'usurp' the child's right, has accordingly justifiably received criticism, notably in the case-law of the ECtHR.

A more nuanced approach may be possible in the contexts wherein the disclosure of a parent's identity need not include the 'whole package' of parental rights. If donor-conceived children suspect that they had been conceived through donor conception and request a name and address of the donor from a hospital, for example, this will have the benefit of ensuring a greater measure of true choice. Thus, these children will then in the process have completely waived their right *not* to know. As such, some donor-conceived persons who are of a discerning age may not wish to find out more than establishing some details about the donor's medical or social background. As far as the disclosure of the name and identity of the donor are concerned, they may therefore 'actively' decide not to know.

Broadly speaking, it must be concluded, however, that the extent to which the identity of the biological parent has been documented and the question whether

---

8 ANDORNO (2004), p. 436, argues that 'the situation is probably different in case of minors, in which case genetic tests for adult onset genetic disorders should perhaps simply be banned, particularly when no cure is possible'. As such, perhaps he might also argue that parentage testing should not be permitted on minors, although the consequences for the child's psychological integrity will then usually be less grave than in medical testing.

9 See Chapter VIII.

the parent had been removed from the child's upbringing at an early stage in childhood will be decisive factors in ensuring a minimum level of protection for children's decisional privacy in deciding to access their principled right to accurate information to the fullest.[10]

3.4. INITIATIVE AND INVESTIGATIVE INVESTMENTS

Above all, perhaps, decisional privacy means that 'to know the truth just for the sake of knowing the truth' should in principle be a sufficiently good reason for adults to pursue the identification of a biological parent. Since all adults are in a position to make an *investigative investment*, it could be said that their decisional privacy may to some extent be assumed. Nonetheless, it has also been said that a 'triggering text' on birth certificates that legal parentage need not reflect biological parentage could instill greater awareness of the possibility that one's legal parents are not one's biological parents.

Furthermore, it must be observed that some older adolescents may just like adults also be quite capable of assessing the importance of this information for themselves but their informational needs may still need to be 'activated'. As far as very young minors are concerned, however, an assessment of their individual interests could require a closer critical enquiry especially when the emotional impact of disclosure may not be overseen by the minor. The interest in preserving the minor's psychological integrity will therefore probably always require an assessment that more expressly takes into account the possible benefits or disadvantages of disclosure.

If the child's interests were determined primarily on the basis of their possible beneficence or the presumed lack thereof, it would also be more likely that the informational interests of the minor risk ending up being subjugated entirely to the (legal) parent's possibly paternalistic appraisal of the child's interests.

It could, in fact, be argued that a reading of the clause 'as far as possible' in Article 7-1 UNCRC requires first and foremost an objective assessment of a minor's real potential for making reasonably informed, individual choices. This

---

10 For children born in a surrogacy contract, this may be even more difficult because the child will generally not be informed at all by the commissioning parents about the existence of a genetic mother. This genetic mother will disappear from the child's life after birth, but her identity has not been documented in a way that is comparable to those of adoptees or where donors are registered centrally and without a guarantee of anonymity, as is now the case in **the Netherlands**.

assessment is probably better made by counsellors than by courts. From an autonomy-based perspective as regards the clause 'as far as possible' in the UNCRC, it must be conceded therefore that a recognition of the minor's individuality and specific needs will be necessary, thereby indicating a case-to-case approach.

Finally, it cannot be stressed enough that the principle of decisional privacy should not be seen in isolation from other legally relevant principles. As has been suggested, decisional privacy in itself does not generate the answers as to how legislative choices about exercising one's right to know have to be made. What the principle of decisional privacy does demand from the law, however, is that children, like adults, are given a genuine opportunity to freely choose to articulate their own interest in accessing parent-identifying information before an independent authority, in a way that is commensurate with their own decisional powers and maturity. It follows that decisional privacy cannot be seen as an abstract, ethical value that can be seen in isolation from individual interests, for respect for the person's psychological integrity is the reason why the exercise of such a choice should be protected.[11]

4. RESPONSIBILITY

4.1. CONTINGENCY: PROCREATIONAL RESPONSIBILITY FROM A HISTORICAL PERSPECTIVE

If the right to know one's biological parentage is to be an effective right, some degree of responsibility for disclosure on the part of parents and the state must be assumed.

For John Eekelaar, this notion seems to impose a certain hierarchy of rights in view of the fact that 'the interests that children have in knowing the physical truth are (always) stronger than those of adults, because for children they give rise to claims in justice, whereas for adults they form the basis for attempts at exercising power, sometimes beyond the grave'.[12] It follows that a prioritization

---

11 As ANDORNO (2006), p. 437, holds: 'Autonomy is the immediate source of the right not to know, but what is in the end protected is the psychological integrity of the person.' Conversely, and in the light of our discussion, this interest can also be said to extend to a right to know one's origins, as this protects individual psychological interests in having a narrative identity. See Chapter 1.

12 EEKELAAR, (2006), p. 76.

of children's rights may generally be possible on the basis of this principle. This has, indeed, also been the author's normative assumption in Chapter V.[13]

It must be conceded, though, that such an abstract prioritisation of the child's interests has not become discernible. A corresponding duty of the parent or the state to inform is lacking in the framework of the UNCRC. Given the adherence of the ECtHR to the margin of appreciation doctrine, the imposition of such a duty to disclose incumbent on parents is probably not a realistic expectation either. In *Odièvre*, it was particularly manifest that the court did not reason on the basis of a child's basic innocence and a birthparent's responsibility to remain identifiable.[14] Thus, the Strasbourg court found that the right to information of an adult and the right to privacy of an (adult) birthmother in principle had to be settled on an 'equal footing'. Although this approach has not been verified to a similar extent in some of the more recent case law from the Strasbourg court, it cannot be said that the court now views parents as unequivocally also having a duty to inform simply because the child's right to information appears to have gained greater recognition.

In this study it has also been found, however, that a great focus on parental responsibility for disclosure can be overtly moralising and give rise to radical interpretations that may very well be oblivious to the parent's situation at the time of conception. In this light, it must be conceded, too, that it is only realistic to conceive of a notion of procreational responsibility for disclosure in societies in which reproductive choices may be presumed, or at least for the most part, to derive from informed and consensual choice. As such, access to birth control methods must generally be known and available in a given society. Is it any surprise that the right to know, as a supposedly 'fancy' human right, has been able to gain greater constitutional recognition in Western jurisdictions?

Furthermore, in order to be able to view parents as duty-bearers of children's right to information, it will be important that parents who make reproductive choices outside marriage or who have recourse to assisted conception will not be ostracised by large segments of society. Otherwise, it is submitted, the use of legal terminology that focuses on parental responsibilities for disclosure might do little more than imbuing them with a sense of shame, instead of promoting an attitude of openness.

---

13 In Besson's view, however, this innocence is already sufficiently weighed in the child's interests in knowing. BESSON (2007), p. 159.

14 See Chapter III.

In that connection, it is recalled that in a not too distant past emphasis on a parental duty to disclose would not have been desirable. It is ironic, for example, that in the *Valkenhorst II* case, the **Dutch** Supreme Court in stressing a parent's ongoing responsibility in making her or his identity accessible to the child was quite oblivious to the radically altered medical and societal circumstances that had occurred since the applicant had been conceived. Accordingly, the court showed marked insensitivity and assumed the moral high ground, disregarding the fact that the mother in question had given birth at a time when unmarried mothers were still ostracised by large segments of **Dutch** society.

Nowadays, however, it is ventured that the principle of procreational responsibility will generally hold in most Western societies where the stigma attached to extramarital birth and to infertility has decreased considerably, while access to assisted conception has become more widely available and accepted. It follows that a certain prioritisation of the person's right to information has become not only be seen more generally to be normatively correct but also feasible., while greater emphasis has also been able to be put on the responsibility of parents to make themselves identifiable.

4.2. CONTINGENCY: PROCREATIONAL RESPONSIBILITY IN PARENTAGE LAW

In none of the jurisdictions may a codified obligation incumbent on the parents to disclose the identity of the biological parents be discerned. Nevertheless, the comparative analysis has demonstrated that the principle of procreational responsibility has become an important underlying consideration in ensuring that children have access to parent-identifying information. In Chapter IV it was verified, moreover, that the mother may in **Germany** and **the Netherlands** in principle be held responsible for disclosing the father's name. It has so far remained circumspect in these jurisdictions whether her refusal to mention the father's name could mean that a mother may incur civil law liability under tort law. In the author's view, this procedural remedy should certainly not be excluded a priori, not only because it could induce some parents to be open but also because it will in many cases also entail an appropriate form of civil law retribution. Thus, especially if it turns out in a given case that the wilful deception of a child by a parent has gone on for years on end, this form of deception may in the author's view be said to constitute a violation of unwritten social norms in respect of children.

In substantive parentage law, legal expressions of the principle of procreational responsibility can also be found. Thus, the adherence to the *mater semper certa* rule, known in all selected jurisdictions except **France**, requires that the birth-mother be identifiable to the child.[15] Nonetheless, it has also been found that the *mater semper certa* rule may exceptionally also present an obstacle to the disclosure of the identity of the genetic mother in the case of surrogacy.

As far as paternity is concerned, the principle of procreational responsibility is sometimes operationalised in a much less straightforward way under the law. Thus, the continued existence of presumptions of paternity in all jurisdictions attests to the fact that responsibility for the disclosure of the biological truth is only implicit. Thus, the marital presumption rule and recognition by an unmarried man do not require *a priori* evidence of the biological truth. All the same, presumptions of paternity have been found to be challengeable when it is presumed that they do not reflect the biological truth.[16]

All in all, it cannot be said on the basis of this study that the state assumes a very active role in challenging presumptions on its own initiative. This has the obvious advantage of respecting the privacy and stability of families. Generally, the state only assumes such a competence to challenge paternity when paternity had been attributed with the ulterior aim of conferring nationality on the child. Only exceptionally, as is the case in **Portugal**, the state *does* take an active interest in uncovering the biological truth by enabling the biological father to file an application to the Public Prosecutor to challenge the marital presumption rule.

If paternity is denied in status proceedings, this may signify an important procedural step for a person in coming a bit closer to finding out the biological truth. Even so, it is clear that an imminent loss of parental status in these proceedings will not always be in the child's interests. In that light, it may therefore be said that truth-oriented and parentage law perspectives on the child's interests could sometimes diverge. Thus, if there is no other second legal parent available, the loss of a legal parent because of the absence of a genetic link could be excessive if the child loses child maintenance and other ancillary rights that derive from parental status. More fundamentally, in attempting to establish the biological truth, the child may have found out that his legal father is not the biological

15 See also SCHWENZER (2007).
16 See Chapter VII.

father, but this will not always mean that the biological father will subsequently be identified.

In proceedings involving a judicial determination of paternity, in contrast, the notion of responsibility is made much more explicit. On the basis of the *Mikulić* case, it may be said that fathers can no longer 'dodge' their responsibility. Thus, the invocation of the *exceptio plurium concubentium* has now been relegated to the past throughout Europe. The father is not only required to assume parental responsibilities associated with parental status. As a corollary, his identity will also be revealed once recourse has been taken to DNA testing. In the absence of a strict time-limit for children to lodge such proceedings (except for **France**), an ongoing responsibility on the part of the father to make his identity accessible may be discerned. The possibility of *post-mortem* determination, admitted in all jurisdictions but severely restrained in **France**, attests to the fact that this involves an ongoing responsibility that may indeed literally extend beyond the grave. Nonetheless, in all jurisdictions this procedure may only be instigated when the child does not already have a legal father. Often this possibility will therefore only become available after a 'false' paternity has been denied. If this has not been done within the statutory time-limits, paternity may no longer be judicially determined. Hence, the biological father will also remain unknown.

In all of the examined jurisdictions DNA testing is admitted and used regularly in parentage proceedings. Accordingly, a great level of accuracy will be ensured in proceedings involving a judicial determination of paternity. As such, it is not without a twist of irony that those who have been legally fatherless will often obtain the greatest level of certainty, perhaps more than 'the rest of us who, at the end of the day, may only *think* we know'. Even so, DNA tests are not always used in judicial determination proceedings. Thus, **French**, **Dutch** and **Portuguese** courts will also draw inferences if the father refuses to go along with a paternity test or other circumstances of the case indicate that he is the father. Only in **Germany** will scientific accuracy almost always be attained because use has been made of compulsory testing since the 1930s. In view of this legislative history, the use of compulsion in parentage proceedings is still controversial in that jurisdiction.

4.3. CONTINGENCY: PROCREATIONAL RESPONSIBILITY IN OTHER SITUATIONS

Outside parentage law, the relevance of the principle of procreational responsibility for disclosing the identity of biological parents has also been verified. As far as plenary adoption is concerned, the birthparents – more correctly, the child's first legal parents – may be said to have been held responsible for disclosure to the extent that their identity will be documented. This possibility to access such information is guaranteed to adoptees from late adolescence in all jurisdictions except for **France**.

In the context of assisted donor conception, making donors responsible for an eventual disclosure of their identity has for much longer been considered undesirable. In fact, secrecy has for a long time been ingrained in donor conception treatment, thereby serving the interests of the legal parents, medical professionals and donors. Only over the past few decades have donor-conceived persons' rights to information also been recognised and so far only in a small number of jurisdictions. As far as the position of donors is concerned in the selected jurisdictions, it may be said that they have only been held responsible for an (eventual) disclosure of their identity in **the Netherlands**. A wide range of identifying and non-identifying information is therefore now stored centrally.

The legal parents in **the Netherlands** are only held responsible for disclosing the fact of donation to the child in a very indirect way. In fact, they are not under any formal legal duty to notify the child of the fact of donation, but it is clear from the legislative history that the legislature considered that the parents should be the primary persons responsible for informing the child of the method of conception. In the other jurisdictions, however, the argument cannot really be sustained that the parents, much less the donor, have been held responsible for disclosure through the imposition of a legal duty to disclose.

In **France**, as in **Portugal**, the donor's identity may be documented by the medical professional but disclosure to the child will in principle always be limited to the release of medical information in case of 'compelling reasons' by the clinic. It has been predicted, however, that the **Portuguese** courts will interpret this clause liberally in future so that anonymity will eventually be waived, a tendency verified in some other jurisdictions that have not been studied in-depth in this book.[17] Strikingly for a jurisdiction that has fulfilled such a pioneering role in the recognition of the right to information, however, in **Germany** there has for a long time been a legislative lacuna as regards the issue of donor identification.

---

17 See Chapter X and VALE E REIS (2008).

It has been argued that as long as status-related concerns such as maintenance in respect of donors can be neatly distinguished from an eventual duty to disclose, donors should not be treated differently from other biological fathers. Just like all other 'parents', donors will have to be required to at least have their identity documented and made accessible for donor-conceived persons. Perhaps more than in any other context, this *right to a name* should therefore mark the *outer conceptual limit* of the right to information. Unless the donor and the donor offspring both wish to have contact, a contact order will clearly be undesirable.

4.4. RESPONSIBILITY OF THE STATE IN ITS QUALITY OF AN 'INDEPENDENT AUTHORITY'

In 1989, in the *Gaskin* case, the ECtHR first postulated the requirement that an 'independent authority' be made available to individuals who seek access to information concerning their basic identity. Logically, this case was subsequently analogised with the question of accessing biological origins across Europe. Therefore, *Gaskin* still marks a watershed in the recognition of the right to information at both the regional and national level.[18] In analogising this case with people's access to biological origins, it may be said that an 'independent authority' will also be important in facilitating access to information. This need for a subsidiary independent authority is legitimised largely on the basis of the assumption that parents will not take their responsibility seriously enough.

Incidentally, it has been found that most empirical studies have, for example, demonstrated relatively low disclosure rates among different-sex recipient couples of donor treatment.[19] In order to fulfil such a subsidiary role in facilitating accurate information concerning one's biological parents, the democratic state governed by the rule of law, whether in the quality of the judiciary or the legislature, will be the most obvious candidate because of its principled independence. Even so, it is rather more questionable whether the state also has an active duty to inform children directly, especially because it seems safe to assume that most parents are not actively engaged in deceiving their children.

In all jurisdictions it has been found that the judiciary functions as an 'independent authority' in dealing with identification issues. In paternity proceedings courts have discretion to review whether parental status has been aligned with

---

18 ECtHR *Gaskin v. United Kingdom*, Appl. No. 10454/83, 7 July 1989. See Chapter III.

19 See Chapters I and X.

the biological truth. However, given the wide array of legal consequences attached to legal parentage, it has been held that the stakes may often be high, indeed too high if the 'mere' concern of the procedure is to uncover the biological truth about one's parentage because of reasons connected to one's narrative identity or, perhaps, to assess one's predisposition to certain hereditary medical conditions. From this viewpoint, the loss of ancillary rights and duties associated with parental status may often neither be said to be in the legal parent's nor in the child's interests.

Therefore, the basic argument has been made that the law must now investigate how a separate legal avenue to promote access to the biological truth can be incorporated into the legal system without the realisation of people's informational interests necessarily involving a review of the legal relationship with their socio-legal parents. Indeed, this has also been found to be a sounder solution because it reflects developments at the constitutional level that now already stretch back twenty years.

4.5. SEPARATE INFORMATIONAL PROCEDURES AS A RESPONSE TO CONSTITUTIONAL DEMANDS?

In a sense, separate procedures with solely informational purposes have existed in the adoption context for a considerable time by now as adoptees may in many jurisdictions access birth certificates, containing information about their first legal parent(s) upon a certain age. More recently, **France** set up an informational system to access origins in the specific case of anonymous birth through the enactment of the Loi Royal which led to the foundation of a National Council for Access to One's Origins (CNAOP). Although this law sought to conciliate the interests of all parties, the mother still effectively retains a veto in opposing the disclosure of her identity if she wishes, however.[20]

In contrast, in the **Dutch** Donor Insemination (Artificial Insemination) Act, which like the CNAOP also has a central registry system, full identification will generally be possible upon request. Only in the case of the donor having compelling reasons will identifying information be withheld. It has been held by Van Raak-Kuiper that the competences of the foundation should also be extended to other situations, in which access to information may be at issue.[21] It is far from clear, however, how such a system could be operationalised outside the donor

20 See Chapter VI.

21 See Chapter X. See further: RAAK-KUIPER (2007), p. 190 and 201.

conception context. A public foundation, such as the Donor Data Foundation will, for example, not be a competent authority in deciding on issues affecting access to information concerning a 'misattributed paternity' resultant from the mother having partnered with someone other than the husband or the unmarried legal father. Moreover, it would appear that requiring persons to submit their application to the Foundation first when a family court could also have authority to decide on such a request, would set procedural hurdles.

Courts should therefore generally be believed to be a sufficiently 'independent authority' to decide upon matters regarding access to parent-identifying information for personal identity and medically related purposes. Courts have been designated as the competent authority in the framework of the new informational procedure introduced in **Germany** in April 2008.[22] As has been established in Chapter VIII, this informational procedure in principle allows the child, along with the legal parents, to establish whether they indeed share a genetic link by allowing them to obtain a court order for private testing at any time. In the absence of the genetic link, a loss of parental status is not a necessary legal consequence. As has been observed, this procedure thereby also allows for a verification of the genetic link between the legal mother and the child. Only exceptionally will a court order for testing be withheld when the court finds that disclosure could pose a threat to the minor's welfare. In this way the procedure can be considered sufficiently flexible to accommodate the different sort of individual needs that minors may have. As such, the informational procedure also seeks to make amends for the minor's right *not* to know, in principle whenever a parent takes the initiative for disclosure and this risks jeopardising the child's interests in having a stable family environment. That said, the basic assumption behind the law remains firmly that it will normally be in the child's interests even where parents may not agree on the need to undergo testing.

As a serious flaw of this informational procedure, though, the identification of a third party as one's biological father or mother is not at present possible. Court-sanctioned testing is, after all, only possible within the legal family that consists of the legal mother, the legal father and the child. As a result, the child may often still only be able to establish the identity of the biological father through a subsequent judicial determination of paternity. Although the law aimed at restricting the problem of private paternity tests, this form of testing will effectively remain the only way for both children and the biological father to have the matter clarified without resorting to status proceedings. For such reasons, the

[22] See Chapter VIII.

procedure cannot yet be considered truly effective in meeting the child's informational needs. At present, the biological father, as a thirdy party, may in some cases, however, lodge status proceedings and thereby still become the child's legal father instead of the socio-legal father.[23] Should the socio-legal father have become unable to deny paternity anymore because the procedural time-limit to lodge such proceedings has already expired, it is not clear, however, why the biological father should therefore also no longer be able to be identified before court, apparently because he cannot become the legal parent anymore and therefore pose a threat to the family unit. As has been argued throughout the comparative analysis, a careful distinction should be drawn between *truth-oriented* and a *parentage law* perspectives on parent-child relationships in that regard.

5. EQUALITY

A principle of equality has been found to be an implicit feature of the constitutional recognition that the right to know one's genetic origins has undergone. In the author's view, it is questionable whether the differences between the various situations are sufficiently important in themselves to justify broadly distinct rules at the procedural level. It has been held that the differences between adoption and assisted conception are in principle not significant enough so as to justify a denial of access to information to donor-conceived persons.[24] This is primarily because the principle of procreational responsibility, as conceptualised in this book, must be considered to have a mitigating influence on the significance of such differences. Broadly speaking, the more one is willing to recognise the principle of procreational responsibility generally holds, the less relevant such differences will have to be considered. In other words, differences between the various situations generally will lose their importance because they cannot be imputed to the child, whatever this child's age may be.

A more abstract prioritisation of the child's informational interests has therefore been defended. This means that the child who seeks information, whatever his or her age, should *in principle* not be required to substantiate her or his psychological interest, much less need to have certain problems in order to pursue the parent's identification. The interest in knowing may be assumed and vests foremost in the child's *decisional privacy* and the (procreational) *responsibility*.

---

23 §1600 1) under 2 and 2) and 4) BGB. See Chapter VII.

24 See Chapter V.

Nonetheless, caution is warranted and a case-to-case analysis may sometimes still be appropriate. Thus, an individual motive may, however, exceptionally be a relevant distinguishing factor. Especially when it is manifest that the interest is not ideologically motivated at all *and* the applicant is an adult, attributing less interest to the principle of procreational responsibility may be justified. The onus of proof could then, as in other cases in which the principle of procreational responsibility cannot reasonably be said to hold, reverse to the (adult) child. This position can be problematic too, however. Thus, it has not only been found that requiring the applicant to first substantiate her or his individual psychological need to know would seem excessive on the basis of decisional privacy in most other cases.[25] Rather, it may also be difficult for the person to establish a causal link between the lack of knowledge about one's biological parentage and one's present psychological problems.

In this light, it may be said that at the regional level excessive weight is sometimes attached to the applicant's motive: in *Jäggi*, the fact that the applicant had not suffered any psychological problems as a result of knowing, seems to have been taken into account as a pertinent factor.[26] Moreover, in *Haas* and *Phinikaridou* the motives of the applicant in requiring parent-identifying information seem to have been factors that negatively influenced the outcome of the case.[27] In the light of the circumstances of those cases, however, it has been argued that the ECtHR justifiably attached weight to the applicant's motive. Thus, if an (adult) child remains procedurally inert for a prolonged period and his interest is apparently inspired by financial gain, it may be justifiable to place the onus on the child of proving that his or her interest *also* derives from an identity-related interest.

5.1. THE PRINCIPLE OF EQUALITY AND DIFFERENCES AT THE PROCEDURAL LEVEL

At the procedural level, the possibilities to enforce the right to information have been found to diverge and to be contingent upon context. It may be held that this difference in treatment can to some extent be justified. In view of the state's

[25] See Chapters IV, V and VII.

[26] ECtHR *Jäggi v. Switzerland*, Appl. No. 58757/00, 13 July 2006. See Chapters III and V.

[27] ECtHR *Haas v. the Netherlands*, Appl. No. 36983/97, 13 January 2004; ECtHR *Phinikaridou v. Cyprus*, Appl. No. 23890/02, 20 December 2007. However, the applicants were also considered in both cases to already have had a considerable degree of certainty regarding their parentage. See Chapter III.

immersion in adoption and assisted conception through screening prospective parents, the public interest in making parents responsible for access to information will be greater than in natural reproduction. It follows that the state may also be said to be entitled to a greater extent to articulate its demands in respect of parents in assuming their primary responsibility to inform adopted and donor-conceived children. Conversely, the same would also go for parents who have (commercially) contracted a surrogate where this is sanctioned under criminal law. An emphasis on the child's rights under Article 7-1 UNCRC would then seem most appropriate if the commissioning parents show no intention of being open to the child.

In contrast, it would, for example, probably have to be considered overtly intrusive if the state probed into the mother's private life and urge her to disclose the name of the father through the imposition of cumulative fines. If such a measure were taken, the social efficaciousness that constitutional recognition of the right must have to become an effective right could gradually erode.

Nonetheless, the differences in treatment do not necessarily mean that the state should only assume responsibility in making information more accessible in the context of adoption, donor-assisted conception and surrogacy while keeping a low profile in other situations. As a general point, though, it may be said that the state's positive obligations in enforcing the right to information may be easier to justify in such situations given the regulatory competences of the state in those situations. As the comparative analysis has shown, however, less intrusive measures may also be considered proportionate in implementing the right in other areas. This may have the added advantage from an equality perspective that adoptive and DI parents are not being 'targeted' to a greater extent than parents who had been able to conceive in the natural way.

5.2. CONTINGENCY: GENDER

The scope of children's right to information has self-evidently not been made contingent upon the child's gender as this would be a manifestly unjustifiable violation of the principle of equality. Parentage law itself is, however, maybe the most heavily genderised area of law imaginable. In all of the selected jurisdictions, gender-related differences in treatment are discernible in the possibilities to obtain parental status. Basically, a *mater semper certa* rule co-exists with presumptions of paternity in all jurisdictions. In **France,** the birthmother has a principled choice in status determination, while in the other jurisdictions the mother's desire to have parental status will be irrelevant after having given birth.

Broadly speaking, as far as the establishment of paternity is concerned, however, biology will only become decisive when the veracity of status has been called into question or the child has been or has become legally fatherless. As a result, in each jurisdiction, parentage law still leaves room for forms of purely intentional fatherhood.

Suffice it for our child-oriented perspective to take note of the fact that these informational interests of the child operate at a distinct ideological level that is far removed from a notion of gender politics: essentially, they require first and foremost respect for the child's decisional privacy and require responsibility for making information on one's biological parentage accessible to all children. Although the biological father's own interest in having certainty should not be considered to necessarily conflate with the child's interests, it would also appear unjustifiable to deny him an equitable access to accurate information and to the status of parent. Especially when the child does not have a second legal parent or in case the socio-legal father has not had family life with the child it may often be good to give him the opportunity to claim the status of legal parent.

In any event, the charge that the right to know in itself represents a threat to women's rights seems to be misguided. If the realisation of children's informational needs often means that the father will get access to parental rights, then the roots of this 'problem' should be found in the way parentage law operates rather than in the child's right to information *per se*. Incidentally, however, it must be added that mothers exert a large measure of control regarding fathers' access to parental status through marriage across all jurisdictions, while their consent to recognition by an unmarried man is in principle required in both **Germany** and **the Netherlands**. In contrast, the *mater semper certa* rule accords parental status to the birthmother on the basis of the fact of birth. This does not mean that mothers and parents necessarily would have to be accorded the same parental rights from the moment of the child's birth. However, viewed from this perspective, the argument can surely not be that parentage law tendentiously disfavours mothers in the examined jurisdictions.

5.3. CONTINGENCY: AGE

The comparative analysis has shown that the procedural scope of the right to information will depend on the applicant's age. As far as plenary adoption is concerned, it has been found that access is generally made possible from late adolescence. The CNAOP will only consider requests from living adults born under X or their descendants, unless they are minors who have received consent from those vested with parental authority.[28]

For **Dutch** donor-conceived children, too, only from the age of sixteen will the identification of a donor's name and address be in sight. Even so, the phased disclosure regime makes the disclosure of other non-identifying as well as medical information possible at an earlier age.

In status proceedings, the child will generally have a possibility to deny paternity during minority and during adulthood within a *dies a quo* time-limit. In contrast, the judicial determination of paternity is not bound to any specific time-limit for the child, with the notable exception of **France**.[29] From a parentage law perspective, in denial proceedings these time-limits are justifiable because of the public interest in legal certainty. As has been suggested, this interest could also require the imposition of a time-limit if an adult child institutes proceedings involving a judicial determination of paternity long after denying the paternity of the socio-legal father even though there can be no doubt that this adult child already 'knew' who the biological father was. Whether the privacy interest of this type of father, possibly also his relatives, could also increase as he comes of age, will depend on the way the relationship between the principle of procreational responsibility and the principle of equality is framed. Assuming that the principle of procreational responsibility will generally represent a preponderant and enduring legal value, this question would have to be answered in the negative.

The state has a certain interest in an adequately functioning system of birth registration and the continuity of legal child-parent relationships. This public interest in legal certainty will represent a much less compelling concern, however, if this interest is not related to review of legal status but essentially sets obstacles to the realisation of individual identity-related interests in uncovering the truth about our biological parentage. Accordingly, ECtHR law justifiably requires that the child be at least given 'one real opportunity' to align paternity with the biological truth.[30] Drawing on the assumption that the 'age factor' will be largely irrelevant in determining such an individualised informational need,

---

28 Art. 147-2 Code de l'Action sociale et des familles. See Chapter VI.

29 See Chapter VII.

30 ECtHR *Phinikaridou v. Cyprus*, Appl. No. 23890/02, 20 December 2007. See Chapter VII.

the new **German** informational procedure, for example, in principle allows for proceedings to be instituted at any time during the applicant's life.[31]

6. CONFLICT OF INTERESTS AND RIGHTS

6.1. PRIVACY IN PARENTAGE LAW

As has become clear in the previous Chapters, a number of private interests may run into conflict with a child's right to information. A parent's privacy interest has been expressly recognised at the regional level. At the national level, it has been verified, however, that in all jurisdictions a broad trend has emerged which shows that less weight is currently being attached to the parent's privacy as greater legal emphasis is being put on the child's right to information. A mother's right to privacy in not disclosing the father's name has been expressly recognised in both **the Netherlands** and **Germany**, but not specified further. Given the preponderant weight that the child's right to know has assumed over the last few decades, it may be seriously questioned, however, what remains of this eroded parental privacy interest. It has been found that both in regional and national constitutional law the privacy interest is mentioned, but that courts refrain from defining what this interest could entail.[32] At least in her relation to the state, the unmarried mother may in **Germany** now withhold information about the biological father on the basis of her personality right.[33]

In particular, the previous Chapters have also shown that such privacy interests of fathers either remain rather indefinite or are expressly denied. The need to balance interests between the parent and the child has been expressly denied in the context of a judicial determination of paternity in view of the 'last resort' nature of the proceedings. The possibility to establish a man's paternity against his will over a protracted period, even to the point of exhumation of his corpse after his death, provides a glaring example of the fact that not much weight is attached to his plausible privacy interest. Nonetheless, the child may sometimes be prevented in some jurisdictions from 'haunting' the father with paternity claims.

---

31 See Chapter VIII. As has been verified, in the event that time-limited status proceedings will be lodged, the applicable time-limit for these proceedings will be deferred.

32 See Chapters III and IV.

33 See Chapter IV.

Likewise, the legal basis for a mother's right to privacy is scant where the *mater semper certa* rule is still applicable. Exceptionally, the mother may in some jurisdictions still block an attempt by children to identify her, as has been discussed extensively in Chapter VI. Indeed, this right to privacy also engages that of the father in the case of *accouchement sous X*. In brief, then, it seems safe to conclude that the privacy interest of the parent is in large measure contingent upon the very way the principle procreational responsibility has been weighed in legislation and in the case law.

6.2. OTHER PRIVATE INTERESTS

As an aspect of the parent's privacy, the right to physical integrity is still lent nominal protection in all jurisdictions except for **Germany**, which is the only one of the selected jurisdictions where testing is compulsory in *all* parentage proceedings. In the other jurisdictions respect for the parent's right to physical integrity subsists given the absence of a strict obligation to undergo parentage testing in parentage proceedings. However, in **the Netherlands**, cumulative fines have, for example, been imposed in cases where a man refused to co-operate. Moreover, compulsory testing has recently been introduced in cases where a fictitious recognition of a foreign child has been made by a **Dutch** national.[34]

DNA testing on living parents provides both an effective and proportionate means to achieve accurate information. It is open to debate whether compulsion should be used in case of a refusal. In the author's view, the use of compulsion in testing will generally not need to be considered very objectionable in view of the fact that the interference is minimal while the child's interest in having certainty may generally be prioritised on the basis of a principle of procreational responsibility. Direct interference with the presumptive parent's physical integrity may be avoided when parts of human tissue detached from that person's body are used, but this could create additional problems of identification. Thus, it is inescapable that testing will often interfere to some extent, however minimal, with the parent's decisional privacy. Conceivably, some parents may also have some ethical or religious objections against testing.

Alongside these possible objections, it could also be argued that in status proceedings certainty is not the primary objective as the establishment of the biological truth is only one among several considerations in devising an adequately functioning parentage law system. In that light, inferences could also be said to general-

---

34 See Chapter VII.

ly lead to an acceptable result in case of a refusal by the parent to go along with testing because the probability of genetic descent will generally be very high even though the test is not actually taken.

All the same, such a moderate position could also be said to be only defensible to the extent that an alternative, effective procedural remedy is available to enforce the right to information as such. In a solely informational procedure, the interest in obtaining accurate, rather than reliable, information may after all be more absolute. If the use of compulsion were to be firmly excluded, the procedure could lose much, if not all, of its significance. On the other hand, because under such an informational procedure the parent can rest assured that disclosure will not be as consequential as it may be the status procedure, it may be presumed that more of them would also find that they have a much less compelling interest in refusing to undergo a test and therefore not use their right to physical integrity as a possible pretext to dodge their responsibility. It follows that in the absence of legal effects related to parental status, greater compliance by parents with test orders might also be expected.

With regard to the case where the parent had already died by the time proceedings are instituted, it has been found that the use of testing should be considered only as a subsidiary way of achieving certainty on genetic descent. In the case of a *post-mortem* determination, alongside a public interest in preserving the sanctity of graves, the interests of the family of the deceased father as well as a right to rest in peace will become pertinent legal factors. If the presumptive parent has died, it has been argued on the basis of the comparative analysis that testing should therefore only be considered as a subsidiary way to achieve certainty.

6.3. PRIVACY INTERESTS IN OTHER CONTEXTS

On the basis of the comparative analysis it may be concluded that recognition of the privacy interest of the birthparents in plenary adoption has now been considered to have largely eroded.[35] In commercial surrogacy the privacy of the mother is clearly not sanctioned by law in view of the prohibitive regime that exists in all jurisdictions.[36] In the context of donor-assisted conception, however, the privacy interest is generally still legally protected.[37] Even in **the Netherlands**,

35 See Chapter IX.

36 See Chapter X.

37 See Chapter X.

where donor anonymity has been waived, the donor will often be able to remain anonymous during childhood and in some, if not most, cases could forever remain anonymous to the extent that children may remain unaware of the fact that they had been conceived through gamete donation. It is clear, however, from the foregone analysis in Chapter IX that the aim of the **Dutch** regulation is not to protect the privacy of donors so much as it is to prioritise the informational interests of donor-conceived persons.

In the context of anonymous birth, in **France**, the privacy interests of both the mother and the father are also well protected.[38] It has been observed that this protection of the mother's rights is still rather absolute and may also create tension with the father's interests in establishing a family law relationship with the child. Even assuming that the mother has such a privacy interest subsequent to birth, it would have to be argued that this interest should, time-wise, be restrained. It cannot be argued that this interest will always remain so strong that it can legitimise an impossibility to identify the mother once the distressful situation has passed. As has been established, admitting the possibility of anonymous birth is not a solution for alleviating the plight of mothers in distress. The argument of the imminent 'sword of Damocles' bearing over the mother's head is not convincing. Rather, possible solutions should be sought in counselling programmes during pregnancy and, if necessary, in the temporary divestment of the mother's parental authority subsequent to birth or placement of the child in foster families.

6.4. PUBLIC RIGHTS AND INTERESTS

It may be concluded on the basis of the comparative analysis that the public interests that will restrict access to parent-identifying information cover a wide range of public policy aims. The previous Chapters have demonstrated, for example, that procedural time-limits exist in all jurisdictions to help ensure a public interest in legal certainty. Thus, the state has an interest in not seeing the status of its citizens continually reviewed. It has been concluded, however, that this public interest in status continuity may not be as urgent from a truth-oriented perspective, all the more so because the state does not have a direct interest in restricting the informational interests of persons when a person's legal status is not at issue. As another clear example of a restriction of access by the

[38] See Chapter VI and above.

state, however, the examined legislation on the prohibitive degrees of consanguinity has been considered.[39]

As far as assisted donor conception is concerned, legal certainty will also require that anonymity should not be waived in respect of the older generation of donors who had been given a guarantee that their identity would never be disclosed. Since the identity of these older donors may not have been documented, it could also be considered objectionable, if not downright cruel, to disclose the fact of donation to such donor offspring if it is certain that they will not be able to subsequently identify the donor. Even if some donor-conceived persons could acquiesce in knowing merely how they had been conceived, conceivably for others this could be a shattering revelation, all the more so since their wish for more information will be destined to remain unfulfilled. As has been verified, this is a real risk in case of older donations since medical files on donors used to be routinely destroyed by fertility clinics.

In **France**, in anonymous birth, the state has also relied on a set of public aims, as the legislation seeks to protect the mother's and child's health at the birth and to prevent abortions, in particular illegal abortions, and prevent that children would otherwise be abandoned in public places. In connection to these public aims that will restrict a person's possibilities to access parent-identifying information, the general protection of the right to life was also invoked by the **French** state in the *Odièvre* case.[40] It has been concluded, however, that anonymous birth is neither effective nor a proportionate way of guaranteeing the realisation of these public aims nowadays.

7. FACILITATING ACCESS TO INFORMATION

7.1. INFORMAL IMPLEMENTATION MECHANISMS

As has become clear, informal implementation mechanisms play an important role in facilitating access to information. Thus, in a number of countries a number of private organisations and media programmes fulfil a role as intermediaries in helping people, in particular adopted persons, to trace their biological parents.

---

39 See Chapter I.

40 ECtHR *Odièvre v. France*, Appl. No. 42326/98, 13 February 2003. See Chapter III.

In addition, voluntary contact registers based on the Internet also promote access to information. In **the Netherlands**, such a voluntary contact register also exists in respect of both donor-conceived children who were born before the entry into force of the Artificial Insemination (Donor Insemination) Act and children conceived by a man other than their legal father.[41] DNA tests are used to verify whether a genetic link exists between donors and donor-conceived persons.

In some other countries these voluntary contact registers have been set up with public aid and funding. In the Australian state of **Victoria,** for example, it is possible for donor offspring, descendants of donor offspring, donors, recipient couples and other relatives to ask the Infertility Treatment Authority to enter their names and addresses on voluntary registers along with their wishes in respect of obtaining information.[42] The success of this system, however, is clearly entirely dependent on the consensus and co-operation between parties. Moreover, it might still appear contrary to the nature of donation and to the decisional privacy of donor-conceived persons that the donor has been enabled to come forward and actively seek the identification of his offspring. Thus, it may be said that upon having become adults, the donor-conceived persons themselves should be the only persons who should be entitled to access identifying information.

In the **United Kingdom**, the *Donorlink* programme also provides assistance to donor-conceived persons, their donors and half-siblings to exchange information and where desired to enter into contact with each other.[43] In this programme, DNA testing is also used in view of the fact that there was insufficient or little information available from clinics to establish whether persons were genetically related before the enactment of the 1990 Human Fertilisation and Embryology Act. Given the voluntary character of the programme, it may be said that Donorlink fully respects the legitimate expectations of older donors that their information will only be released if they first come forward. In this way, it respects an important requirement of legal certainty in respect of older donors.

Outside assisted conception and adoption contexts, other informal ways of implementing the right to information may also be found. A Children's Ombudsman could promote awareness and understanding of children's views and interests among all sectors of society, both public and private as well as monitoring and promoting the rights of children. Such a non-governmental, indepen-

41 Www.donorkind.nl and www.verwantschapsvragen.nl.

42 Infertility Treatment Act 1995 (Vic), s 82 in relation to the Post-1988 Voluntary Register and s 92C in relation to the Pre-1988 Voluntary Register. See further: STOLL (2008), p. 125.

43 Www.ukdononorlink.org.uk.

dent institution exists under **French** and **Portuguese** law, for example.[44] In **Norway**, for example, the Children's Ombudsman receives complaints from children who affect their rights under the UNCRC.[45] Though the **Norwegian** Children's Ombudsman has found that parentage law is a suitable legal avenue for realising a child's informational interests under Article 7-1 UNCRC, it has urged the state to take further steps and subsidise a publicity campaign on the importance for children to know their genetic parentage.

As a controversial means of obtaining accurate parent-identifying information, private laboratories that operate on the Internet, and conduct parentage tests based on DIY kits, raise a number of important legal concerns. In the absence of public monitoring mechanisms, there may often be no guarantee that these tests will actually meet the scientific standards of judicial tests. Apart from this issue concerning quality standard-setting, legal problems derive in particular from the fact that consent requirements can easily be circumvented or dispensed with. Faced with this problem, it has been considered that the state should be able to monitor laboratories and streamline quality standards and establish professional guidelines. At the same time, courts should be able to avail themselves of the discretion to discard DNA evidence if no written evidence of prior or subsequent consent can be shown or that the evidence was obtained at a reputable laboratory.[46] As long as such requirements have been met, however, it has been held that extra-judicial evidence may, in fact, be quite acceptable in subsequent status proceedings.

What is more, it has been observed that private tests might actually entail certain advantages in comparison to court-ordered tests. Nonetheless, these advantages may bear the mark of paternalism as some of the concerned parties will be left in the dark. Debatably, this leaves open the question whether 'ignorance may sometimes be bliss.' Conceivably, however, a mother who doubts whether her husband is the biological father could, for example, often settle the issue quietly without needing to be exposed to the stress of court proceedings, all the more so because in many cases the genetic link will probably be confirmed. Ideally, if the

---

44 In **France**, the children's ombudsman is known as the Défenseur des Enfants. See: www.defenseurdesenfants.fr. In **Portugal**, the national ombudsman, the *Provedor de Justiça*, operates a telephone line for children's complaints and information requests about their rights. See: www.provedor-jus.pt. In **Germany** such an institution does not exist. In **the Netherlands** a bill was recently presented to the government by the social-democrat Member of Parliament Arib. See: *Kamerstukken II* 2008/09, 31 381, No. 1, 29 December 2008.

45 Www.barneombudet.no/horingsutt6/2007/felles_ukt/?utskrift=1.

46 See Chapter VIII.

genetic link is disproved, this result would also help the mother to face up to her responsibility to disclose the truth to both the legal father and the child. Outside a courtroom, it is suggested that this could often be less emotionally taxing. In that light, it must be concluded that the conducting of DNA tests in a private setting should not be perceived as a necessarily murky means to find out about one's genetic descent.

7.2. FORMAL IMPLEMENTATION MECHANISMS: THE ROLE OF THE STATE

7.2.1 Non-intrusive state measures

In its case law, the ECtHR typically affirms that the boundaries between positive and negative state obligations in implementing the rights protected under the Convention do not lend themselves to a precise definition. As far as accessing identifying information is concerned, it has been verified that the duty of the States Parties will, in large measure, be contingent upon the context in which the informational need has arisen. Some differences in treatment will be justifiable on the basis of the principle of equality to the extent that the state is involved in screening recipient couples in adoption and assisted conception, for example. Outside these contexts, it may become very difficult to justify intrusive measures if their right to private life and right to family life are also to be protected. Moreover, it is conceivable that the social efficaciousness of the right could eventually be eroded if overtly intrusive measures were taken in an issue on which social consensus may be difficult to achieve. In connection with this argument concerning the right's social efficaciousness, it is also important to state that there is at present insufficient evidence to suggest that parental deception is a particularly widespread phenomenon.[47]

A general conclusion in this respect must therefore be that the state should refrain from imposing overtly intrusive measures in promoting greater openness but only fulfil a subsidiary role in promoting greater openness. If there is evidence that parents are not assuming their own responsibility for disclosure, it would appear that more intrusive measures should only exceptionally be considered. In making apparent that society expects parents to be open, however, the state may first consider a set of non-intrusive measures.

---

[47] See, however, the empirical studies discussed in Chapter I.

Thus, in civil codes, the obligation of legal parents in this regard could be codified as an important aspect in exercising parental authority in general terms to remind them of the fact that society expects them to be open. In this way, a good example may be set for all parents, not only adoptive parents and the recipient couples of fertility treatment. Even so, if this measure were implemented, it would have to be conceded that parents without parental authority would still not be able to be held responsible at all for disclosure.

As has been suggested above, the judiciary could also affirm more emphatically that children's right to information should, as a rule, be prioritised because of this responsibility. As has become clear, in some surrogacy cases, for example, courts justifiably assume their discretion to clarify that the children should be informed about their origins.

All the same, such public measures could still be perceived as overtly emblematic and therefore ineffective. True, some parents will cast aside such admonishments from the public authorities. Nonetheless, it is ventured that emblematic legislation is not without significance in a sensitive area for legislation. It has been found, for example, that the 'soft law' admonishments of the UN Children's Rights Committee have prompted the **French** government to review its legislation on *accouchement sous X*. This is an important indication of the fact that states are, in fact, already assuming to a greater extent than before their responsibility in implementing the right, which surely cannot be discarded as a small achievement.

7.2.2. Intrusive public measures

7.2.2.1. Intrusive public measures in the context of adoption and donor-assisted conception

As has been concluded in Chapter IX, in adoption it will often be possible to find out on the basis of the birth certificate whether one has been adopted if this is not clear from the outset because of physical dissimilarities. In this way, the fact of adoption will generally be known, even though incidentally an adopted person may not have wished to have been informed. This exposure will be justifiable, however, because the adopted child had other legal parents before being adopted.

A reason to document the identity of the donor or other biological parents in the birth certificate may be more difficult to defend when they have never been legal parents. In particular, entering the fact of donation on the birth certificate could raise objections from an equality perspective, all the more so, perhaps, because it would be plainly unthinkable if birth certificates were to state also that a child had a different biological father. Likewise, it could also create tension with the person's privacy if donor-conceived persons were confronted with their particular condition in this way. They could find such a notification stigmatising and the public exposure of their otherness undesirable.

As a further intrusive measure, the screening of recipient couples' willingness to disclose in the context of donor conception could be mentioned. If a duty to inform were strictly imposed, treatment could be withheld if the couple declared that they will not disclose the truth as the child comes of age. Yet few couples are likely to give reliable answers prior to treatment. In fact, it could then instil in them an even greater reticence to be open. As an alternative, Stoll has raised the idea that every few years parents could be questioned by a counsellor as to whether they have undertaken their responsibility to be open.[48] However, she recognises that this measure could also be perceived as stigmatising by the parents.

It could also be wondered whether biological parents, in particular donors, should not come forward and play a more active role in making their identity known. Conceivably, the incidence of parental disclosure of the fact of donation would increase if the donor were encouraged to make his identity known regardless of the legal parents' consent. Clearly, however, this solution has some significant disadvantages, as it may be questioned whether the donor should really be the person to take the initiative and interfere with a child's decisional privacy.

Having said that, however, if it turns out that the **Dutch** Donor Insemination (Artificial Insemination) Act is ineffective because the Foundation receives few requests for identifying information, such a solution that foregoes parental consent could be considered. Thus, the Foundation could then, for example, approach donors while fulfilling the role of an intermediary between the donor and children who have reached the age of sixteen but have not yet requested any information. Clearly, the current **Dutch** legislation would then have to be reviewed, as the Foundation has not yet been given any such interventionist competence.

---

48 STOLL (2008), p. 99.

Finally, as another way of increasing awareness among children about the way they have been conceived, in a centralised donor registry system, a discreet letter could be sent by the central donor registry to the donor-conceived person upon reaching the age from which full identification may be requested. Upon having received this letter, the donor-conceived person could then decide whether he or she also wishes to proceed with a view to the full identification of the donor. Although this solution could also be seen as an intrusive measure, it may meet the requirements of the principle of decisional privacy. After all, the person may still decide not to pursue the identification any further.

7.2.2.2. Intrusive public measures in other contexts

As has been suggested, in respect of the informational needs of persons with a 'false' paternity the best solution could be the creation of a separate informational procedure. In the surrogacy context this procedure may incidentally also lead to an identification of both mothers without, however, transferring parental status from the gestational mother to the genetic mother. If a legal procedure with solely informational purposes is to be realised, however, it must be ensured that the presumptive biological father without status could also be required to undergo DNA testing. Whether his whereabouts will then actually be known will of course be a factual matter. But the state may at least be expected not to obstruct his identification. Rather, it should create a low-key legal avenue through which information can be obtained in a way that will in principle be inconsequential for the child's legal status. Children will accordingly have an effective procedural remedy allowing them to identify the biological father. Admittedly, though, this extension of the informational procedure will not solve all conflicts between the child's legal father and the newly found biological father. The child's legal father may not wish to break legal ties with the child, while some biological fathers, once identified, may wish to have full parental status.

In order to attenuate this legal tension, the biological father should not be enabled to challenge a well-established paternity of the socio-legal father unconditionally. In most cases the biological father may have had a genuine opportunity of establishing a family law relationship with the child, but has failed to make a timely recognition. If this had not been the case, for example because the mother's consent was withheld, he should be able to deny the paternity of the legal father as long as this can reasonably be said to be in the child's interests. A court will only be able to decide whether this is the case on an individual basis, but even so it may generally be assumed that the duration and the nature of the family law relationship between the legal father and the child will be pertinent factors. Again, this question will be more a question of parentage law than a question concerning the implementation of the right to information, however. As such, the child may still have an informational interest in identifying the biological father. Conversely, it has also been established that the informational interests of the biological father should not be considered to necessarily coincide with the informational needs of the child, in particular because the child's decisional privacy will also warrant respect.

8. CLOSING REFLECTIONS

The truth is incontrovertible, malice may attack it,
ignorance may deride it, but in the end: there it is.
Sir Winston Churchill

An attempt has been made in this study to help delineate the conceptual and procedural scope of the right to know one's origins. In the examined jurisdictions the main legal source of the right to know one's origins is provided by the right to private life and the personality right. As such, the right to parent-identifying information has justifiably been considered to be 'rooted' in the child's autonomy and human dignity. Autonomy in the meaning of decisional privacy cannot be seen in isolation from the psychological interests that the constitutional recognition of the right to information ultimately seeks to protect.

With regard to adults possessing discretion and judgement, genuine respect for their decisional privacy will mean that both the positive and negative dimensions of the right will require legal protection. Once children have reached emotional and legal maturity they should be the only ones to decide whether more certainty about their genetic parentage is in their legal interests.

Respect for decisional privacy will remain a more problematic notion in relation to minors. Since a basic awareness of an underlying disparity between the truth and legal fact is required, the minor's positive right may generally be believed to outweigh an interest in not receiving (any) information. If a more absolute respect for the minor's right not to know were sought, the door could be open for sliding-scale interpretations of paternalism and welfarism.

As far as the content of the right is concerned, it should be concluded that the 'inner core' of the right to information involves the identification of the parent's name and possibly other cornerstones of legal identity, such as the parent's domicile. Possibly, this 'inner core' of the right to information, as a legal concept, could also include a legal right of the child to obtain a passport photograph of the parent. Even so, the law must be careful in distinguishing the right to know one's origins from the right to contact with a biological parent. The boundaries between the right to contact and the right to information will in reality often be fluid. The child will, after all, generally also have an interest in establishing contact with the biological parent, if only to attach a face to this possibly unknown though 'familiar' stranger. Generally, the right to contact will have profound legal repercussions that go well beyond the establishment of the parent's legal identity. Presumably, more potential donors could be put off by the prospect that they would be required to have regular contact with the child than if they are merely required to become identifiable as the donor-conceived person matures. Nonetheless, as has been argued, they should at least be required to be identifiable for the children they have helped create.

A further general conclusion must be that the right to information has not yet become an effective right in all situations in any of the selected jurisdictions. Procedural solutions have so far generally been tailor-made and context-specific and not quite as effective as they could perhaps be. Nonetheless, the right's revindication at the constitutional level is too recent to draw general conclusions on the procedural effectiveness of the right.

For now, it must be admitted that substantial gains have been made over the last few decades thereby suggesting a climate of greater openness across all of the jurisdictions examined in this book. The right to know one's origins has now been broadly accepted at the international, regional and national levels. In fulfilling their obligations under the UNCRC and the ECtHR, all of the jurisdictions have made serious attempts to improve the procedural position of children while respecting the interests of others. This heralds a promising legal development.

It has also been found that differences in treatment are not necessarily problematic because a holistic solution is neither feasible nor practicable. To say the least, the right to information is a very multi-faceted right. Even so, this fact should not relieve the state of its obligations in implementing its obligations under the UNCRC. The clause that a child has the right to know 'as far as possible' should not be taken as an escape clause.

In the end, few would contest the fact that the 'degree of importance which knowledge of genetic identity holds for an individual can be judged only by *that* individual'.[49] The (legal) truth in this area seems destined to remain relative. Yet the state should be careful not to interpret the clause 'as far as possible' in Article 7-1 UNCRC as a licence for obscuring facts that will remain of foundational significance, whatever our age or the subjective value we attribute to personal ties, both broken and continuous.

49 EEKELAAR (2006), p. 75.

BIBLIOGRAPHY

AIJMER (1998), G. AIJMER, The triumph of hypothesis: Edward Westermarck and Chinese Almost-Incestuous Marriages, *Current Anthropology*, vol. 39, p. 174.

ALBRECHT & SCHULTHEISS (2004), K. ALBRECHT & D. SCHULTHEISS, 'Proof of paternity: historical reflections', 2004, *Andrologia*, p. 31-37.

ALEXY (2002a), R. ALEXY, *A theory of constitutional rights*, Oxford: Oxford University Press.

ALEXY (2002b), R. ALEXY, *The Argument from Injustice*, Oxford: Oxford University Press.

ALEXY (2003a), R. ALEXY, On Balancing and Subsumption, *Ratio Juris*, vol.16, p. 433-449.

ALEXY (2003b), R. ALEXY, Constitutional rights, balancing and rationality, *Ratio Juris*, vol.16, p.131-140.

ANDERLIK (2003), M.R. ANDERLIK, Assessing the quality of DNA-based parentage testings; findings from a survey of laboratories, *Jurimetrics Journal*, vol. 43, p. 291-314.

ANDORNO (2004), R. ANDORNO, The Right Not To Know: An Autonomy-Based Approach, *Journal of Medical Ethics*, 30, p. 435-440.

ANDRÉOLI (1998), M. ANDRÉOLI, *Heredity and paternity*, in: L. SPAAS, *Paternity and fatherhood: myths and realities*, London: MacMillan Press, p.15-39.

ANDREWS (1995), L. ANDREWS, Beyond doctrinal boundaries: a legal framework for surrogate motherhood, *Virginia Law Journal*, 81, p. 2343-2375.

ANTOKOLSKAIA (2006), M.V. ANTOKOLSKAIA, *Harmonisation of Family Law in Europe: a historical perspective*, Antwerpen-Oxford: Intersentia.

ARISTOTLE, Metaphysics, Oxford: Clarendon Press, 1958, p. 1.

ARKEL (2004), H. VAN ARKEL, J. SCHOOTS & S. DERMOUT, Wetsaanpassing in verband met draagmoederschap?, *FJR*, p. 189-194.

ASSER-DE BOER (1998), J. DE BOER, *Mr. C. Asser's Handleiding tot de beoefening van het Nederlands burgerlijk recht: Personen- en familierecht,* 10th edition commented my Mr. J. de Boer, Deventer: Kluwer.

ASSER-DE BOER (2006), J. DE BOER, *Mr. C. Asser's Handleiding tot de beoefening van het Nederlands burgerlijk recht: Personen- en familierecht*, 17th edition commented by Mr. J. de Boer, Deventer: Kluwer.

AZOUX BACRIE (2003), L. AZOUX BACRIE, Accès à la connaissance des origines personneless et médiation, in: G. TEBOUL, C. DAVID & P-F. RACINE, *Procréation et droits de l'enfant,* Bruxelles: Bruylant.

BADENBERG (2006), F. BADENBERG, *Das Recht des Kindes auf Kenntnis der eigenen Abstammung unter Berücksichtigung der Problematik der anonymen Geburt*, Frankfurt am Main: Peter Lang.

BAINHAM (1999), A. BAINHAM, S. SCLATER & M. RICHARDS, *What is a parent? A socio-legal analysis*, Oxford: Hart Publishing.

BAINHAM (2005), A. BAINHAM, *Children: the Modern Law*, 3rd edition, Bristol: Family Law.

BAINHAM (2008), A. BAINHAM, What is the point of birth registration?, *Child and Family Law Quarterly*, vol. 20, no. 4, p. 449-474.

BAKER & BELLIS (1993), R. BAKER & M. BELLIS, DNA-onderzoek vaderschap in Liverpool (1989-1992, in: RIDLEY (1993), *Sex and the evolution of human nature, The Red Queen*, p.218.

BAMBERGER/ROTH (2008), *Kommentar zum Bürgerlichen Gesetzbuch*, 2nd edition 2008, Munich: Beck Verlag.

BAUDOUIN & LABRUSSE-RIOU (1987), J-L. BAUDOUIN & C. LABRUSSE-RIOU, *Produire l'homme: de quel droit?, Etude juridique et éthique des procréations artificielles*, Paris: Presses Universitaires de France.

BERECZKEI, GYURIS & WEISFELD (2003), T. BEREZCKEI, P. GYURIS & G. WEISFELD, Sexual imprinting in human mate choice, *Proc. R. Soc. Lond.* 271, p. 1129-1134.

BESSON (2007), S. BESSON, Enforcing the child's right to know her origins: contrasting approaches under the Convention on the Rights of the Child and the European Convention on Human Rights, *International Journal of Law, Policy and the Family*, vol. 21, p. 137-159.

BIERKENS (1992), P. BIERKENS, Spermadonorschap en geheimhouding, *De psycholoog*, p. 57-61.

BLAUWHOFF (2008), R.J. BLAUWHOFF, Tracing down the historical development of the legal concept of the right to know one's origins: has 'to know' or 'not to know' ever been the legal question?, *Utrecht Law Review*, vol. 4. p. 99-116.

BLYTH (2006), E. BLYTH, Donor anonymity and secrecy versus openness concerning the genetic origins of the offspring: international perspectives, *Jewish Medical Ethics*, 2, p. 4-13.

BLYTH & CRAWSHAW (2004), E. BLYTH & M. CRAWSHAW, Policy formation in gamete donation and egg sharing in the UK – a critical appraisal, *Social Science and Medicine*, vol. 59, p. 2617-2626.

BLYTH & FARRAND (2004), E. BLYTH & A. FARRAND, Anonymity in donor-assisted conception and the UN Convention on the Rights of the Child, *The international journal of Children's Rights*, vol. 12, p. 89-104.

BOELE-WOELKI & DE HONDT (1998), K. BOELE-WOELKI, W. DE HONDT, W. SCHRAMA, G. STEENHOFF & A. STILLE, De aansprakelijkheid van de verwekker in historisch en rechtsvergelijkend perspectief, in: J. VAN BUREN-DEE, F. GROSHEIDE, P. KOTTENHAGEN-EDZES & M. KROEZE (eds.), *Tussen de polen van bescherming en vrijheid: aspecten van aansprakelijkheid*, Antwerp-Groningen: Intersentia, p. 27-54.

BOER (1998), J. DE BOER, Verjaring van de vaderschapsactie is discriminatoir geworden, *NJB* 1998, vol. 3, p. 1075.

BOHNERT (2002), C. BOHNERT, Zur Zulässigkeit privater Vaterschaftstests, *FPR*, p. 383-389.

BOLUSSET (1998), P. BOLUSSET, Père and Mère: Unequals in Language, in: *Paternity and fatherhood: myths and realities*, London: MacMillan Press, p. 74-82.

BONNET (1990), C. BONNET, *Geste d'amour: l'accouchement sous X*, Editions Odile Jacob.

BONNET (1993), C. BONNET, *Geste d'amour: l'accouchement sous X*, Paris: Odile Jacob.

BONNET (1993), C. BONNET, Adoption at birth: prevention against abandonment or neonaticide, *Child Abuse & Neglect: the international journal*, p. 501-514.

BORTH/MUSIELAK (2007), *Kommentar zur Zivilprozessordnung*, ZPO, 5th edition, Munich: Beck Verlag.

BOSWELL (1988), J. BOSWELL, *The Kindness of Strangers: the abandonment of children in Western Europe from late Antiquity to the Renaissance*, New York: Pantheon Books.

BOSZORMENYI-NAGY & G. SPARK (1973), I. BOSZORMENYI-NAGY, *Invisible loyalties: reciprocity in intergenerational family therapy*, New York City: Brunner Mazel.

BOURSICOT (2006), C. LE BOURISCOT, La volonté de symétrie entre filiation paternelle et maternelle remet-elle en cause la filiation par adoption?, *Revue Lamy Droit Civil*, p. 35.

BRAAT (2008), B. BRAAT, Buitenrechterlijke echtscheiding en draagmoederschap. Is Frankrijk er klaar voor?, *FJR*, vol.12, p. 289-294.

BRAVERMAN (1993), A. BRAVERMAN, Survey results on the current practice of ovum donation, *Fertility and Sterility* 59, p. 1216-1220.

BREEMHAAR (2007), W. BREEMHAAR, Streit um die Abstammung im niederländischen Recht, in: A. SPICKHOFF, D. SCHWAB, D. HENRICH, P. GOTTWALD (eds.) (2007), *Streit um die Abstammung: ein europäischer Vergleich, Beiträge zum europäischen Familienrecht*, Bielefeld: Gieseking.

BREWAEYS (1997), A. BREWAEYS, *Donor insemination: family relationships and child development in lesbian and heterosexual families*, diss. Leiden University, Katwijk: All In.

BREWAEYS (2005), A. BREWAEYS, J. DE BRUYN, L. LOUWE & F. HELMERHORST, Anonymous or identity-registered sperm donors? A study of Dutch recipients, *Human Reproduction*, 20, p. 820-824.

BRINK (2006), M. VAN DEN BRINK, *Moeders in de mainstream: een genderanalyse van het werk van het VN-Kinderrechtencomité*, PhD thesis Utrecht University, Nijmegen: Wolf Publishers.

BRODZINSKY (1992), D. BRODZINSKY, M.D. SCHECHTER, R.M. HENIG, *Geadopteerd, een leven lang op zoek naar jezelf*, Amsterdam: Anthos/Ambo 1992.

BRODZINSKY & SCHECHTER (1990), D. BRODZINSKY & M. SCHECHTER, *The psychology of adoption*, New York & Oxford: Oxford University Press.

BRUCKEN FOCK (1996), E. VON BRUCKEN FOCK, De Hoge Raad laat Jeroen in de kou staan – de biologische vader wil geen omgang met Jeroen, *FJR*, vol. 18, p. 62-64.

BUEREN (1995), G. VAN BUEREN, Children's access to adoption records – state discretion or an enforceable legal right?, *Modern Law Review*, vol. 58, p. 37-53.

BUEREN (1998), G. VAN BUEREN, *The international law on the rights of the child*, Dordrecht: Nijhoff.

BUREN-DEE, GROSHEIDE, KOTTENHAGEN-EDZES & KROEZE (1998), J. VAN BUREN-DEE, F. GROSHEIDE, P. KOTTENHAGEN-EDZES & M. KROEZE (eds.), *Tussen de polen van bescherming en vrijheid: aspecten van aansprakelijkheid*, Antwerp-Groningen: Intersentia.

BUXTON (2004), R. BUXTON, *The Complete World of Greek Mythology*, London: Thames & Hudson.

CADOU (1996), E. CADOU, La 'biologisation' du droit de la filiation, in: C. LABRUSSE-RIOU, *Le droit saisi par la biologie : des juristes au laboratoire*, Paris: LGDJ.

CALLUS (2004), T. CALLUS, Tempered hope? A qualified right to know one's genetic origin: Odièvre v. France, *Modern Law Review*, vol. 67, p. 658-669.

CANOTILHO & MOREIRA (2007), *Constituição da República Anotada*, 4th revised edition, Coimbra: Coimbra Editora.

CARBONNIER (1999), J. CARBONNIER, *Droit Civil: Introduction*, 26th edition, Paris: Thémis Droit Privé.

CARBONNIER (1995), J. CARBONNIER, *Droit Civil, vol. 2, La famille, les incapacités*, 17th edition, Paris.

CATALA (1997), P. CATALA, La jeune fille et le mort : du droit de connaître ses origines et des moyens de l'obtenir, *Droit de la famille*, p. 4-7.

COESTER-WALTJEN (1989), D. COESTER-WALTJEN, Zum Recht auf Kenntnis der eigenen Abstammung, *Jura*, p. 520-523.

COESTER-WALTJEN (1992), D. COESTER-WALTJEN, Künstliche Fortpflanzung und Zivilrecht, vol. 4, *FamRZ*, p. 369-373.

COESTER-WALTJEN/GERNHUBER (2006), D. COESTER-WALTJEN & J. GERNHUBER, *Familienrecht*, 5th fully revised edition, Munich: Beck Verlag.

COLLIER & SHELDON (2008), R. COLLIER & S. SHELDON, *Fragmenting Fatherhood: A Socio-Legal Study*, Oxford & Portland, Oregon: Hart Publishing.

COOK (1995), R. COOK, S. GOLOMBOK, A. BISH & C. MURRAY, Disclosure of donor insemination: parental attitudes, *American Journal of Orthopsychiatry*, vol. 65, p. 549-559.

CROMBRUGGE (1991), H. VAN CROMBRUGGE, Uw kinderen zijn uw kinderen wel. Argumenten voor het toewijzen van de pedagogische verantwoordelijkheid aan de biologische ouders, *Comenius*, vol. 50, p. 237-253.

CURRY-SUMNER (2005), I. CURRY-SUMNER, *All's well that ends registered? The Substantive and Private International Law Aspects of Non-Marital Registered Relationships in Europe*, Ph.D thesis Utrecht University, Antwerp-Oxford: Intersentia.

CURRY-SUMNER & VONK (2008), I. CURRY-SUMNER & M. VONK, Ontwikkelingen op het gebied van internationale adoptie, *FJR*, vol. 12, p. 264-272.

DANIELS & TAYLOR (1993), K.R. DANIELS & K. TAYLOR, Secrecy and openness in donor insemination, *Politics and Life Sciences*, p. 155-170.

DEECH (2003), R. DEECH, Reproductive tourism in Europe: Infertility and Human Rights, *Global Governance*, vol. 9, p. 425-432.

DEGRAZIA (2005), D. DEGRAZIA, *Human identity and bio-ethics*, Cambridge: Cambridge University Press.

DEICHFUß (1988), H. DEICHFUß, Recht des Kindes auf Kenntnis seiner blutsmäßigen (genetischen) Abstammung? Zur Diskussion um die Zulässigkeit der heterologen Insemination, *NJW* 1988, p. 113-117.

DEKEUWER-DEFOSSEZ (1999), F. DEKEUWER-DEFOSSEZ, *Rénover le droit de la famille : propositions pour un droit adapté aux réalités et aux aspirations de notre temps, rapport au Garde des Sceaux, Ministre de la Justice*, Paris: La Documentation Française.

DELAISI DE PARSEVAL & VERDIER (1994), G. DELAISI DE PARSEVAL & P. VERDIER, *Enfant de personne*, Paris: Odile Jacob.

DELAISI DE PARSEVAL (1998), G. DELAISI DE PARSEVAL, Secret et anonymat dans l'assistance médicale à la procréation, *Médecine et Droit*, vol. 30, p. 23-27.

DELAISI DE PARSEVAL (2002), G. DELAISI DE PARSEVAL, *Le roman familial d'Isadora D.*, Paris: Odile Jacob.

DELAISI DE PARSEVAL (2003), G. DELAISI DE PARSEVAL, *Origines ou histoire ? Plutôt tenter de se construire une identité narrative*, AJ Famille, vol. 3, p. 94.

DERMOUT (2001), S. DERMOUT, *De eerste logeerpartij, hoogtechnologisch draagmoederschap in Nederland*, diss. Groningen University, Zaandam.

DETRICK (1999), S. DETRICK, A commentary on the United Nations Law on the Rights of the Child, PhD thesis, The Hague: Nijhoff.

DEUTSCH (1985), E. DEUTSCH, Artifizielle Wege menschlicher Reproduktion: Rechtsgrundsätze – Konservierung von Sperma, Eiern und Embryonen: künstliche Information und außerkörperliche Fertilisation, *MDR*, p. 177.

DEWAR (2000), J. DEWAR, Family law and its discontents, *International Journal of Law, Policy and the Family*, vol. 14 (1), p. 59-85.

DOEK & DELFOS (1982), J. DOEK & G. DELFOS, *Vaderschap, afstamming en adoptie*, Zwolle: W.E.J. Tjeenk Willink.

DOEK (1995), J. DOEK, Kunstmatige voortplanting en genetische manipulatie: enige juridische kanttekeningen, in R. HOKSBERGEN (1995), *Hoe vergaan we? Moderne voortplanting in feitelijk en ethisch perspectief*, Baarn: Ambo, p. 142-159.

DOVY (2002), M. DOVY, *L'enfant et le droit de savoir : l'accès à ses origines familiales*, diss. Lyon Jean Moulin Lyon 3, 2002.

DUBOSC & VERDIER (2000), M. DUBOSC & P. VERDIER, *Face au secret des origines*, Paris: Dunod.

DWORKIN (1977), R. DWORKIN, *Taking rights seriously*, London: Duckworth (1991 reprint).

DWORKIN (1993), R. DWORKIN, *Life's dominion*, New York: Haper Collins.

DWORKIN (2001), R. DWORKIN, *Sovereign virtue*, Cambridge, Massachusetts: Harvard University Press.

DWYER (2006), J. DWYER, *The Relationship Rights of Children*, Cambridge: Cambridge University Press.

ECKEBRECHT (2005), M. ECKEBRECHT, Neuere Gesetze zur Stärkung der Vaterrechte, *FPR*, p. 205-209.

EDENFELD (1996), S. EDENFELD, Das neue Abstammungsrecht der Bundesrepublik Deutschland im nationalen und internationalen Vergleich, *FuR*, p. 190-196.

EEKELAAR & ŠARČEVIČ (1993), J. EEKELAAR & P. ŠARČEVIČ, *Parenthood in modern society: legal and social issues for the twenty-first century*, Dordrecht: Nijhoff.

EEKELAAR (2006), J. EEKELAAR, *Family law and personal life*, Oxford: Oxford University Press.

EIDENMÜLLER (1998), H. EIDENMÜLLER, Benennung des leiblichen Vaters, *JuS*, p. 789-795.

ELLENBOGEN (2008), K. ELLENBOGEN, Strafbarkeit des Beischlafs zwischen Verwandten: ein Relikt aus der Vergangenheit, *ZRP*, p. 190-192.

ENDERS/BAMBERGER-ROTH (2008), *Kommentar zum Bürgerlichen Gesetzbuch*, 2nd edition 2008, Munich: Beck Verlag.

ENNECCURUS & NIPPERDEY (1959), L. ENNECCURUS & H. NIPPERDEY, *Allgemeiner Teil des Bürgerlichen Rechts*, 15. Auflage, Tübingen 1959.

EPSTEIN (1995), R. EPSTEIN, Surrogacy: the case for full contractual enforcement, *Virginia Law Journal*, p. 2307-2339.

EVERS (2004) J. EVERS, De gerechtelijke vaststelling van het vaderschap en de zwakke positie van de vader, *FJR*, 3, p. 10-16.

EVERS & TE VELDE (2001), J. EVERS & E. TE VELDE, Vruchtbaarheidsstoornissen: in: M. HEINEMAN (ed.), *Obstetrie en gynaecologie, de voortplanting van de mens*, Maarssen: Elseviers Gezondheidszorg.

FASOULIOTIS & SCHENKER (1996), S. FASOULIOTIS & J. SCHENKER, Cryopreservation of embryos: medical, ethical, and legal issues. Journal of assisted reproduction and genetics, *Assist Reprod Genetics*, 13, p. 763-768.

FERRAND (2007), F. FERRAND, Streit um die Abstammung in Frankreich, in: A. SPICKHOFF, D. SCHWAB, D. HENRICH, P. GOTTWALD (eds.), *Streit um die Abstammung: ein europäischer Vergleich, Beiträge zum europäischen Familienrecht*, Bielefeld: Gieseking, p. 93-118.

FERREIRA MACHADO (2003), H. FERREIRA MACHADO, *Tribunais, género, ciência e cidadania: uma abordagem sociológica da investigação judicial de paternidade*, diss. Universidade do Minho.

FISCHER (1936), P. FISCHER, Die Feststellung der blutmässigen Abstammung, *JW* 1936, p. 237-238.

FONTE (2005), T. FONTE, *No limiar da honra e da pobreza: a infância desvalida e abandonada no Alto Minho (1698-1924)*, Vila Praia de Âncora: NEPS Universidade do Minho.

FORDER (1995), C.J. FORDER, *The legal establishment of the parent-child relationship: constitutional principles*, PhD thesis Maastricht University, Maastricht.

FORDER (1997), C. FORDER, Article 8 ECHR: the utter limits of 'family life' and the law of parenthood, *Maastricht Journal of European and Comparative Law*, vol. 4, p. 125-142.

FORDER (1998), C. FORDER, Het recht op afstammingsgegevens: 'wilde' speculations?, *Ars Aequi*, vol. 47, p. 87-90.

FOTTRELL (2000), D. FOTTRELL, One step forward or two steps sideways? Assessing the first decade of the Children's Rights Convention on the Rights of the Child, in: D. FOTTRELL (ed.), *Revisiting children's rights; 10 years of the*

United Nations Convention on the Rights of the Child, 2000, The Hague, London, Boston: Kluwer.

FRANK (1993), R. FRANK, La signification différente attachée à la filiation par le sang en droit allemand et français de la famille, *Revue Internationale de Droit Comparé*, vol. 45, p. 635-658.

FRANK (1995), R. FRANK, Die zwangsweise körperliche Untersuchung zur Feststellung der Abstammung, *FamRZ*, p. 975-981.

FRANK (1997), R. FRANK, German parentage law reformed, *International Survey of Family Law*, p. 167-175.

FRANK (1999), R. FRANK, The establishment and the consequences of maternal and paternal affiliation, *Legal problems relating to parentage: proceedings. XXVIIth Colloquy on European Law Foundation for International Studies*, Valletta: 1999, p. 83-104.

FRANK (2005), R. FRANK, Observations comparatives sur la contestation de la paternité, *Revue Internationale de Droit Comparé*, vol. 1, p. 85-102.

FRANK & HELMS (2008), R. FRANK & T. HELMS, Entwurf eines Gesetzes zur Klärung der Vaterschaft unabhängig vom Anfechtungsverfahren, *FamRZ*, p. 7-9.

FREEMAN (1996), M. FREEMAN, The new birth right? Identity and the child of the reproductive revolution, 4 *International Journal of Children's Rights*, vol. 3, p. 273-297.

FRITH (2001), L. FRITH, Gamete donation and anonymity: the ethical and legal debate, *Human Reproduction*, vol. 16, No. 5, p. 818-824.

FURKEL (1996), F. FURKEL, Die französischen Gesetze über Bioethik vom 29. Juli 1994 und Ihr Einfluß auf das Kindschaftsrecht, *FamRZ*, p. 772-777.

GARAUD & SZRAMKIEWICZ (1978), M. GARAUD & R. SZRAMKIEWICZ, *La revolution française et la famille*, Paris.

GARÉ (2003), T. GARÉ, L'accouchement sous X n'efface pas les droits du père par le sang, *Revue Juridique Personnes & Famille*, p. 20-21.

GAUL (1997), H. GAUL, Neuregelung des Abstammungsrechts, *FamRZ*, p. 1441-1465.

GERARDS (2002), J.H. GERARDS, *Rechterlijke toetsing aan het gelijkheidsbeginsel: een rechtsvergelijkend onderzoek naar een algemeen toetsingsmodel*, PhD thesis Maastricht University, The Hague: Sdu uitgevers.

GESERICK (2002), G. GESERICK, Richtlinien für die Erstattung von Abstammungsgutachten, *FPR*, 8, p. 380-383.

GIBSON (1992), E. GIBSON, Artificial insemination by donor: information, communication and regulation, *Journal of Family Law of the University of Louisville School of Law*, vol. 30, p. 1-43.

GIESEN (1989), D. GIESEN, Genetische Abstammung und Recht, *JZ*, p. 364-277.

GODMAN (2006), K. GODMAN, K. SANDERS, M. ROSENBERG & P. BURTON, 'Potential sperm donors', 'recipients' and their partners' opinions towards the release of identifying information in Western Australia, *Human Reproduction*, 21, p. 3022-3026.

GOOR (1988), S. VAN DE GOOR, *Recht op afstammingsvoorlichting, moderne voortplantingstechnieken en het belang van het kind*, The Hague: Nederlandse Gezinsraad Instituut voor Primaire Levensvormen.

GOTTLIEB (2000), C. GOTTLIEB, O. LALOS & F. LINDBLAD, 'Disclosure of donor insemination to the child: The impact of Swedish legislation on couples' attitudes', *Human Reproduction*, 15, p. 2052-2056.

GRAAF, MAK & VAN WIJK (2008), J. DE GRAAF, C. MAK & F. VAN WIJK, *Rechten van het kind en ouderlijke verantwoordelijkheid*, Nijmegen: Ars Aequi Libri.

GRANET-LAMBRECHTS (2006), F. GRANET-LAMBRECHTS, La présomption de paternité, *Droit de la famille*, p. 11-13.

GRANET-LAMBRECHTS & HAUSER (2006), F. GRANET-LAMBRECHTS & J. HAUSER, Le nouveau droit de la filiation, *Recueil Dalloz*, p. 17-23.

GRANET-LAMBRECHTS & HAUSER (2006), F. GRANET-LAMBRECHTS & J. HAUSER, Le *nouveau droit de la filiation*, Recueil Dalloz, p. 17-28.

GREEN & MANOHAR (1990), C.M. GREEN & S.V. MANOHAR, Neonaticide and hysterical denial of pregnancy, *British Journal of Psychiatry* 1990, p. 121-123.

GREENBERG & LITTLEWOOD (1995), M. GREENBERG & R. LITTLEWOOD, Post-adoption incest and phenotypic matching: experience, personal meanings and biosocial implications, *British Journal of Medical Psychology*, 3, p. 29-44.

GRIMALDI, La contestation de la paternité légitime après l'interprétation a contrario de l'article 322 du code civil, *Gazette du Palais*, p. 1.

DE GROOT & TRATNIK (2002), G.R. DE GROOT & M. TRATNIK, *Nederlands nationaliteitsrecht*, Deventer: Kluwer.

GROSSBERG (1985), M. GROSSBERG, *Governing the hearth: law and the family in nineteenth Century America*, Chapel Hill: University of North Carolina Press.

GROTIUS (1631), H. FISCHER & E.M. MEIJERS (eds.), Hugo de Groot, *Inleidinge tot de Hollandsche Rechtsgeleerdheid*, Leiden: Universitaire Pers, 1952.

GRUNDERBEECK (2003), D. VAN GRUNDERBEECK, *Beginselen van personen- en familierecht: een mensenrechtelijke benadering*, PhD thesis, Intersentia: Antwerp-Groningen-Oxford.

GUGGUMOS (1947), M. GUGGUMOS, Die Abstammungsklage des unehelichen Kindes, *NJW* 1947-1948, p. 59.

GUIMARÃES SÁ (2000), I. DOS GUIMARÃES SÁ, Circulation of children in eighteenth Century Portugal, in: C. PANTER-BRICK & M. SMITH, *Abandoned children*, Cambridge: Cambridge University Press. p. 27-41.

HAAS & WALDENMAIER (2004), H. HAAS & C. WALDENMAIER, *Der Kuckucksfactor: raffinierte Frauen? Verheimlichte Kinder? Zweifelnde Väter?,* Prien: Gennethos Verlag.

HABERMAS (1996), J. HABERMAS, *Between facts and norms*, Cambridge, Massachusetts: Harvard University Press.

HADERKA (1997), J. HADERKA, Affiliation and bioethics, in: *Legal problems relating to parentage: proceedings*. XXVIIth Colloquy of the European Law Foundation for International Studies, Valletta.

HAFEN & HAFEN (1996), B. HAFEN & J. HAFEN, Abandoning children to their autonomy: the United Nations Convention on the Rights of the Child, *Harvard International Law Journal*, vol. 137, p. 449-491.

HAHN in: BAMBERGER-ROTH (2008), *Kommentar zum Bürgerlichen Gesetzbuch*, 2nd edition, Munich: Beck Verlag.

HAIMES (1988), E. HAIMES, 'Secrecy': What Can Artificial Reproduction Learn from Adoption?, *International Journal of Law and the Family*, 2, p. 46-61.

HAIMES & TIMMS (1985), E. HAIMES & N. TIMMS, *Adoption, identity and social policy: the search for distant relatives*, Gower: Aldershot.

HAJAL & ROSENBERG (1991) F. HAJAL & E. ROSENBERG, The family cycle in adoptive families, 1991, *American Journal of Orthopsychiatry*, p. 78.

HAMMERSTEIN-SCHOONDERWOERD (1988), W. HAMMERSTEIN-SCHOONDERWOERD, *Ouderschap anders geregeld*, Zwolle: W.E.J. Tjeenk Willink.

HART (1994), *The Concept of Law*, 2nd edition, Oxford: Oxford University Press.

HART (1998), H.L. HART, Kelsen's doctrine of the unity of law, in: PAULSON, *Normativity and norms*, Oxford Clarendon Press.

HASSENSTEIN (1988), B. HASSENSTEIN, Der Wert der Kenntnis der eigenen genetischen Abstammung, *FamRZ* 1988, p. 120-123.

HAUSER (2006), J. HAUSER, La Réforme de la filiation et ses principes fondamentaux, *Droit de la Famille*, p. 6-9.

HEIDA (2002), A. HEIDA, Vaderschapsprocedures en DNA-onderzoek, *FJR*, p. 122-129.

HEIDA (2003), A. HEIDA, DNA-onderzoek bij vaderschapsacties, *FJR*, p. 174-180.

HEIDA & TER HAAR (2008), A. HEIDA & J. TER HAAR, Grenzen aan de vaststelling van de gerechtelijke vaststelling van het vaderschap, *WPNR*, vol. 139, p. 288-293.

HEINEMAN (2001), M. HEINEMAN (ed.), *Obstetrie en gynaecologie, de voortplanting van de mens*, Maarssen: Elseviers Gezondheidszorg.

HELMS (1999), T. HELMS, *Die Feststellung der biologischen Abstammung: eine rechtsvergleichende Untersuchung zum deutschen und französischen Recht, Schriften zum Internationalen Recht*, Band 112, diss. Universität Freiburg, Berlin: Ducker & Humblot.

HENRICH (2006), D. HENRICH, *Deutsches, ausländisches und internationales Familien- und Erbrecht: ausgewählte Beiträge*, Bielefeld: Gieseking.

HENSTRA (2002), A. HENSTRA, *Van afstammingsrecht naar ouderschapsrecht. Een beschouwing over de positie van sociale en biologische ouders in het familierecht*, PhD thesis Utrecht University, The Hague: Boom Juridische Uitgevers.

HEPTING (2001), R. HEPTING, 'Babyklappe' und 'anonyme Geburt', *FamRZ*, vol. 23, p. 1573-1585.

HERINGA (2005), A. HERINGA, International and national legal instruments, in: J. GERARDS, A. HERINGA & H. JANSSEN, *Genetic discrimination and genetic privacy in a comparative perspective*, Antwerp-Oxford-New York: Intersentia.

HERVEY (1998), T. HERVEY, Buy Baby: The European Union and Regulation of Human Reproduction, *Oxford Legal Studies*, vol. 18, 1, p. 207-234.

HODGKIN & NEWELL (2002), R. HODGKIN & P. NEWELL, Implementation handbook for the Convention on the Rights of the Child, New York: UNICEF.

HODGSON (1993), D. HODGSON, The international protection of the child's right to a legal identity and the problem of statelessness, *International Journal of Law, Policy and the Family*, vol. 7, p. 255-270.

HOKSBERGEN & WALENKAMP (1983), R. HOKSBERGEN & A. WALENKAMP, *Adoptie uit de kinderschoenen*, Boom Uitgevers 1983.

HOKSBERGEN (1995), R. HOKSBERGEN, *Hoe ver gaan we? Moderne voortplanting in feitelijk en ethisch perspectief*, Baarn: Ambo.

HOLMES & SUNSTEIN (2000), S. HOLMES & C. SUNSTEIN, *The cost of rights: why liberty depends on taxes*, New York: WW Norton & Co.

HOLTRUST (1993), N. HOLTRUST, *Aan moeders knie: de juridische afstammingsrelatie tussen moeder en kind*, Nijmegen: Ars Aequi Libri.

HOLZHAUER (1996), H. HOLZHAUER, *Gentechnik und Künstliche Fortfplanzung: zu den für den 56. Deutschen Juristentag erstatteten Gutachten*, p. 1162-1166.

HOOGHIEMSTRA (2002), T. HOOGHIEMSTRA, *Privacy bij ICT in de zorg: bescherming van persoonsgegevens in de informatie-infrastructuur voor de gezondheidszorg*, The Hague: Dutch Data Protection Authority.

HÖRNLE (2008), T. HÖRNLE, Das Verbot des Geschwisterinzests – Verfassungsgerichtliche Bestätigung und verfassungsrechtliche Kritik, *NJW*, p. 2085-2088.

HUMMEL & MUTSCHLER (1991), K. HUMMEL & D. MUTSCHLER, Zum Umfang der Beweisaufnahme bei gerichtlicher Vaterschaftsfeststellung, *NJW* 1991, p. 2929-2932.

HUMPHREY & HUMPHREY (1986), M. HUMPHREY & H. HUMPHREY, A fresh look at 'genealogical bewilderment', *British Journal of Medical Psychology*, 59, p. 133-140.

HUNTER (2000), M. HUNTER, N. SALTE-KING & L. GLOVER, Donor insemination: telling children about their origins, *Child Psychology and Psychiatry Review*, vol. 5, p. 157-163.

HUSA (2004), J. HUSA, Classification of legal families today – Is it time for a memorial hymn?, *Revue Internationale de Droit Comparé*, vol. 56, p. 11-38.

IMBER-BLACK (1998), E. IMBER-BLACK, *Secrets in families and family therapy*, New York: Norton.

JACOBI (2005), J. JACOBI, *Der Unterhaltsregreß des Scheinvaters*, Hamburg: Verlag Dr. Kovač.

JACKSON (2001), E. JACKSON, *Regulating reproduction: law, technology and autonomy*, Oxford-Portland, Oregon: Hart Publishing.

JANSSENS (2005), P. JANSSENS, G. DUNSELMAN, A. SIMONS & M. KLOOSTERMAN, *Wet Donorgegevens Kunstmatige Bevruchting: inhoud en gevolgen, Nederlands Tijdschrift voor Geneeskunde*, 149, p. 1412-1416.

JONES & KIRKMAN (eds.), Sperm *Wars: The Rights and Wrongs of Reproduction*, Sydney: ABC Book 2005.

KAMPEN (1990), L. VAN KAMPEN, W. KNOOPS, M. MEERUM TERWORGT & C. REIJNDERS, Onbekendheid met de biologische vader als een belemmerende factor in de identiteitsontwikkeling: een empirische exploratie, *Nederlands Tijdschrift voor de Psychologie*, 1990, nr. 45, p. 283-288.

KANT (1785), I. KANT, 'Groundwork of the Metaphysics of Morals' in: *Practical Philosophy*, Cambridge Edition of the Works of Immanuel Kant in Translation, 1997, p. 80.

KELSEN (1991), H. KELSEN, General Theory of Norms, Oxford: Clarendon Press.

KILKELLY (2000), U. KILKELLY, The impact of the convention on the case-law of the European Court of Human Rights, in: D. FOTTRELL, *Revisiting children's rights; 10 years of the United Nations Convention on the Rights of the Child*, The Hague, London, Boston: Kluwer.

KILKELLY (2004), U. KILKELLY, *Annual review of international family law*, in: International Survey of Family Law, Bristol: International Society of Family Law, p. 1-20.

KINDREGAN & MCBRIEN (2006), C. KINDREGAN & M. MCBRIEN, *Assisted Reproductive Technology: A Lawyer's Guide to Emerging Law and Science*, Chicago: American Bar Association.

KIRCHMEIER (2002), K. KIRCHMEIER, Einführung in das Vaterschaftsfeststellungsverfahren, *FPR*, p. 370-376.

KIRKLAND (1992), A. KIRKLAND, M. POWER, G. BURTON, R. BABER, J. STUDD & H. ABDALLA, Comparison of attitudes of donors and recipients to occyte donation, vol. 7, 3, Human *Reproduction*, p. 355-357.

KIRKMAN (2005), M. KIRKMAN, Going home and forgetting about it: donor insemination and the secrecy debate: in: JONES & KIRKMAN (eds.), Sperm *Wars: The Rights and Wrongs of Reproduction*, Sydney: ABC Books, p. 153-169.

KIRKMAN (2007), M. KIRKMAN, D. ROSENTHAL & L. JOHNSON, Families working it out: adolescents' views on communicating about donor-assisted conception, *Human Reproduction*, 1, p. 1-7.

KLEINEKE (1976), W. KLEINEKE, *Das Recht auf Kenntnis der Eigenen Abstammung*, Diss. Göttingen 1976.

KNOCHE (2005), J. KNOCHE, Chancen einer erfolgreichen Vaterschaftsanfechtung nach den BGH – Entscheidungen zu heimlichen DNA-Tests, *Familie und Recht 2005*, p. 348-355.

KOCH (1990), E. KOCH, Der Anspruch der Deszendenten auf Klärung der genetischen Abstammung – ein Paradigmawechsel im Abstammungsrecht, *FamRZ* 1990, p. 569-574.

KOENRAADT (2008), F. KOENRAADT, Moordouders: kinderdoding in Nederland, *MGV*, vol. 63, p. 159-161.

KOK (2008), J. KOK, Vereisten vaderschapsonderzoek, *FJR*, vol. 20, p. 237.

KOKKINI-IATRIDOU (1988), D. KOKKINI-IATRIDOU, *Een inleiding tot het rechtsvergelijkende onderzoek*, Deventer: Kluwer.

KORSGAARD (1986), C. KORSGAARD, The right to lie: Kant on dealing with evil, *Philosophy and public affairs*, vol. 4, p. 325-349.

KOUTSOURADIS (2007), A. KOUTSOURADIS, Zum aktuellen Stand des griechischen Abstammungsrechts, in: SPICKHOFF, SCHWAB, HENRICH, GOTTWALD (2007): A. SPICKHOFF, D. SCHWAB, D. HENRICH, P. GOTTWALD (eds.), *Streit um die Abstammung: ein europäischer Vergleich, Beiträge zum europäischen Familienrecht*, Bielefeld: Gieseking, p. 205-258.

KREMER, FRIJLING & NASS (1981), J. KREMER, B. FRIJLING & J. NASS, Donorinseminatie en privacy, *Medisch Contact*, 2, p. 41-44.

KREMER & LEENEN (1991), J. KREMER & H. LEENEN, De anonimiteit van de donor bij kunstmatige inseminatie met donorsperma in historisch perspectief, *Nederlands Tijdschrift voor Geneeskunde*, 33, p. 1476-1478.

KRÜGER (1960), H. KRÜGER, *Die Rechtsstellung des unehelichen Kindes nach dem Grundgesetz*, Berlin 1960.

KÜTHE & TURVEY (2007), M. KÜTHE & M. TURVEY, Rechtspraak: Raad van Europa – EHRM 10 april 2007; Evans tegen het Verenigd Koninkrijk – wie weegt wat?, *NCJM-Bulletin*, p. 872-886.

LABRUSSE-RIOU (1996), C. LABRUSSE-RIOU, *Le droit saisi par la biologie: des juristes au laboratoire*, Paris: LGDJ.

LABRUSSE-RIOU & GUIDEC (1996), C. LABRUSSE-RIOU & R. LE GUIDEC, *Filiation légitime, Encyclopédie Dalloz, Répertoire de droit civil*, Paris: Dalloz.

LAKKIS (2006), P. LAKKIS, Die Exhumierung zur postmortalen Vaterschafts-feststellung- und anfechtung, *FamRZ*, p. 454-462.

LALOS (2007), A. LALOS, C. GOTTLIEB & O. LALOS, Legislated right for donor-insemination children to know their genetic orgins: a study of parental thinking, 22, *Human Reproduction*, p. 1759-1768.

LARSON & CHASTAIN (1990), D.G. LARSON & R.L. CHASTAIN, Self-concealment: conceptualization, measurement and health implications, *Journal of Social and Clinical Psychology*, 9, p. 439-455.

LAURIE (2001), G. LAURIE, *Genetic Privacy: A Challenge to Medico-Legal Norms*. Cambridge: Cambridge University Press.

LAURIE (2004), G. LAURIE, The Right Not To Know: An Autonomy Based Approach – A Response to Adorno, *Journal of Medical Ethics*, 30, p. 439-440.

LAWRENCE HILL (1991), J. LAWRENCE HILL, What does it mean to be a 'parent'?: the claims of biology as the basis for parental rights, *New York University Law Review*, p. 353-420.

LEEB-LUNDBERG (2006), S. LEEB-LUNDBERG, S. KJELLBERG & G. SYDSJÖ, Helping parents to tell their children about the use of donor insemination (DI) and determining their opinions about open-identity donors, 85, *Acta obstetriciana et Gynecologica*, p. 78-81.

LEENEN (1993), H. LEENEN, Het recht op kennisname van de identiteit van de gametendonor en diens anonimiteit, *NJ*, vol. 68, 31, p. 1101-1106.

LEENEN (1999), C. LEENEN, Het recht van het kind op informatie over ouders, broers en zussen, *FJR*, vol. 21, p. 58-61.

LEFAUCHEUR (2004), N. LEFAUCHEUR, The French tradition of anonymous birth: the lines of argument, *International Journal of Law, Policy and the Family*, vol. 18, p. 319-342.

LEFEBVRE-TEILLARD (1996), A. LEFEBVRE-TEILLARD, *Introduction historique au droit des personnes et de la famille*, Paris: Presses Universitaires de France.

LESTER (1991), D. LESTER, Murdering babies: a cross-national study, *Social Psychiatry & Epidemiology* 1991, 26, p. 83-85.

LEVIE (1975), L. LEVIE, *Kunstmatige inseminatie bij de mens*, 2nd edition, Leiden: Stafleu.

LÉVY & CASTALDO (2002), J.-P. LÉVY & A. CASTALDO, Histoire du droit civil, Paris: Dalloz.

LINDEN (2006), A. VAN DER LINDEN, *Adoptierecht*, Monografieën Familie, Jeugd en recht, deel 3, The Hague: Sdu.

LØDRUP (2003), P. LØDRUP, Challenges to an established paternity – radical changes in Norwegian law, *International Society of Family Law*, p. 353-362.

LÖHNIG (2001), M. LÖHNIG, *Das Recht des Kindes nicht verheirateter Eltern: Abstammungsrecht –Sorgerecht –Umgangsrecht – Namenrecht – Unterhalt*, Berlin: Erich Schmidt.

LOPES CARDOSO (1991), A. LOPES CARDOSO, Procriação humana assistida – alguns aspectos jurídicos, *Revista da Ordem dos Advogados*, 51, p. 5-27.

MADLENER (1969), K. MADLENER, *Das französische Unehelichenrecht*, Bielefeld.

MALAURIE-AYNÈS (1996), P. MALAURIE-AYNÈS, *Cours de Droit Civil, La famille*, 5th edition, Paris: Cujas 1996.

MALLET-BRICOUT (2003), B. MALLET-BRICOUT, Droit d'accès aux origines personnelles: l'embarras de la Cour européenne des droits de l'homme, *La Semaine Juridique*, p. 1240-1245.

MANSEES (1988), N. MANSEES, Jeder Mensch hat Recht auf Kenntnis seiner genetischen Herkunft!, *NJW*, 47, p. 2984-2987.

MARTINHO DA SILVA (1986), P. MARTINHO DA SILVA, *A procriação artificial: aspectos jurídicos*, Lisboa: Moraes Editores.

MASSIP (2006), J. MASSIP, *Le nouveau droit de la filiation*, Paris: Defrénois.

MCGEE, VAUGHAN-BRAKMAN & GURMARKIN (2001), G. MCGEE, S. VAUGHAN-BRAKMAN & A. GURMARKIN, Debate: Disclosure to Children Conceived With Donor Gametes. *Human Reproduction* 2001, vol. 10, p. 2033-6.

MCGEE, VAUGHAN-BAKMAN & GURMANKIN (2001), G. MCGEE, S. VAUGHAN-BAKMAN, A. GURMANKIN, Gamete reproduction and anonymity, *Human Reproduction*, vol.16, p. 2033-2038.

MCWHINNIE (1996), A. MCWINNIE, *Families following assisted conception: what do we tell our child?*, Dundee: Department of Social Work: University of Dundee.

MEERUM TERWORGT (1989), M. MEERUM TERWORGT, C. REIJNDERS, L. VAN KAMPEN, *Identiteitsproblematiek bij donorkinderen, Tijdschrift voor ontwikkelingspsychologie*, vol. 4, p. 209-216.

MEIJDAM-SLAPPENDEL (1996), M. MEIJDAM-SLAPPENDEL, *De adoptie in Nederland*, diss. Leiden University.

MEULDERS-KEIN (1996), M.-T. MEULDERS-KLEIN, The status of the father in European legislation, *American Journal of Comparative Law*, vol. 44, p. 487-520.

MEUWESE, MORELLI & WOLTHUIS (2000), S. MEUWESE, C. MORELLI & A. WOLTHUIS, Gezinshereniging in het Nederlandse vreemdelingenrecht getoetst aan het VN-Verdrag inzake de rechten van het kind, *Migrantenrecht*, vol. 15, p. 188-194.

MICHIELS & OVERKLEEFT-VERBURG (2000), F. MICHIELS & G. OVERKLEEFT-VERBURG, Hoofdzaken van het bestuursrecht, *Rechtsgeleerd Magazijn Themis* (2000), vol. 7, p. 270.

MIRKOVIC (2008), A. MIRKOVIC, À propos de la maternité pour autrui, *Droit de la Famille*, p. 9-13.

MOLENGRAAFF (1896), W. MOLENGRAAFF, Onderzoek naar het vaderschap, *De Gids*, p. 93-121.

MOLTMAKER & HOEVEN-OUD (1989), J. MOLTMAKER & J. VAN DER HOEVEN-OUD, *Tijdschrift voor Privaatrecht*, vol. 26, p. 1491-1537.

MORGAND-CANTEGRIT (1993), V. MORGAND-CANTEGRIT, *La possession d'état*, diss. Lille II.

MOSSMAN (1998), C. MOSSMAN, DNA and the stakes of embodying paternity, in: L. SPAAS, *Paternity and fatherhood: myths and realities*, London; MacMillan Press, p. 40-48.

MOURIK & NUYTINCK (2002), M. VAN MOURIK & A. NUYTINCK, *Personen- en familierecht, huwelijks-, vermogens- en erfrecht*, 2nd edition, Deventer: Kluwer.

MULLIEZ (1989), J. MULLIEZ, *Pater is est ..., la source juridique de la puissance paternelle du droit révolutionnaire au Code Civil*, in: THERY & BIET (eds.), *La famille, la loi, l'état – de la Révolution au Code Civil*, Paris 1989, p. 491.

MÜNCH KOMM/SEIDEL (2000), *Kommentar zum Bürgerlichen Gesetzbuch*, 4th edition, Munich: Beck Verlag.

MÜNCHENER KOMM/WELLENHOFER-KLEIN(2002), Kommentar zum Bürgerlichen Gesetzbuch, 4th edition, Munich: Beck Verlag.

MÜNCHENER KOMM/WELLENHOFER-KLEIN (2008). Kommentar zum Bürgerlichen Gesetzbuch, 5th edition, Munich: Beck-Verlag.

MURAT (2006), P. MURAT, L'action de l'ordonnance du 4 juillet 2005 sur la possession d'état, *Droit de la famille*, p. 17-22.

MURRAY (2005), T. MURRAY, Three meanings of parenthood, in M. ROTHSTEIN, T. MURRAY, G. KAEBNICK, M. MAJUMDER, *Genetic ties and the family: the impact of paternity testing on parents and children*, John Hopkins University Press, Baltimore 2005, p. 18-33.

MUSCHELER (2005), K. MUSCHELER, Das Recht des Vaters auf Kenntnis seiner Vaterschaft, *FPR*, p. 185-188.

MUSCHELER (2007), K. MUSCHELER, *Seminar: Deutsche Rechtsgeschichte 'Geschichte des Familien- und Erbrechts', Seminarthema: Geschichte der Adoption, vorgelegt von stud.iur. Kirsten Pardey*, Dortmund.

MUSCHELER (2008), K. MUSCHELER, Die elterliche Sorge des nichtehelichen Vaters, in: Festschrift für Rainer Frank zum 70. Geburtstag am 14. Juli 2008, Lebendiges Familienrecht, Herausgeber: Tobias Helms und Jens Martin Zeppernick, Frankfurt am Main 2008.

MUSCHELER & BEISENHERTZ (1999), K. MUSCHELER & T. BEISENHERZ, Das neue Abstammungsrecht, *JR*, p. 356-361.

MUSCHELER & BLOCH (2002), Das Recht auf Kenntnis der genetischen Abstammung und der Anspruch des Kindes gegen die Mutter auf Nennung des leiblichen Vaters, *FPR*, 8, p. 339-353.

MUTSCHLER (1994), D. MUTSCHLER, Emanzipation und Verantwortung – Zur Neuordnung des Abstammungsrechts, *FamRZ* 1994, p. 65-70.

NEHMELMAN (2002), R. NEHMELMAN, Het algemeen persoonlijkheidsrecht: een rechtsvergelijkende studie naat het algemeen persoonlijkheidsrecht in Duitsland en Nederland, Deventer: Kluwer.

NELKIN (2005), D. NELKIN, Paternity palaver in the media: selling identity tests, M. ROTHSTEIN, T. MURRAY, G. KAEBNICK, M. MAJUMDER, *Genetic ties and the family: the impact of paternity testing on parents and children*, John Hopkins University Press, Baltimore 2005, p. 3-18.

NEUMANN (1995), *Findelkinder, Waisenhäuser, Kindsmord: unversorgte Kinder in der frühneuzeitlichen Gesellschaft,* München: Oldenbourg.

NEUMANN-DUESBERG (1950), H. NEUMANN-DUESBERG, Die Abstammungs-Feststellungsklage, *NJW* 1950, p. 14.

NEYRINCK (2006), C. NEYRINCK, La maternité, *Droit de la Famille*, p. 9-11.

NOTA (1969), J. NOTA, *De adoptie, rechtsinstituut in ontwikkeling*, Deventer: Kluwer.

NOVAK (2007), B. NOVAK, Das Abstammungsrecht in Slowenien, in: SPICKHOFF, SCHWAB, HENRICH, GOTTWALD (2007): A. SPICKHOFF, D. SCHWAB, D. HENRICH, P. GOTTWALD (eds.), Streit um die Abstammung: ein europäischer Vergleich, Beiträge zum europäischen Familienrecht, Bielefeld: Gieseking, p. 259-279.

NOWAK (2005), M. NOWAK, *UN Covenant on Civil and Political Rights: CCPR Commentary*, Kehl, Strasbourg & Arlington: N.P. Engel.

NUYTINCK (2008), A. NUYTINCK, Het omgangsrecht van de spermadonor op grond van diens nauwe persoonlijke betrekking met het kind, *Ars Aequi*, vol. 57, 2, p. 133-138.

NYKIEL (1999) F. NYKIEL, *Accouchement sous X et secret des origines, comprendre et accompagner les situations en présence: Étude du service des droits des femmes et de l'égalité, Ministère de l'Emploi et de la solidarité*, Paris 1999.

OBERLOSKAMP (1991), H. OBERLOSKAMP, Recht auf Kenntnis der eigenen Abstammung, *FuR* 1991, p. 263.

ODERKERK (1999), A. ODERKERK, *De preliminaire fase van het rechtsvergelijkend onderzoek*, Nijmegen: Ars Aequi Libri.

O'DONOVAN (1988), K. O'DONOVAN, A right to know one's parentage?, *International Journal of Law, Policy and the Family*, vol. 2, p. 27-45.

O'DONOVAN (2000), K. O'DONOVAN, Interpretation of children's identity rights, in: D. FOTTRELL (ed.), *Revisiting children's rights: 10 years of the United*

Nations Convention on the Rights of the Child, The Hague, London, Boston: Kluwer.

OKIN (1989), S. OKIN, *Justice, gender and the family*, New York: Basic Books.

OLIVEIRA (1979), G. DE OLIVEIRA, *Estabelecimento da filiação*, Coimbra: Almedina, 7th edition 2003.

OLIVEIRA (2003), G. DE OLIVEIRA, *Critério jurídico da paternidade*, Coimbra: Almedina.

OLIVEIRA (2004), G. DE OLIVEIRA, *Caducidade das acções de investigação, Revista Lex Familiae, Revista Portuguesa de Direito da Família*, p. 7-13.

OLIVEIRA (2006), G. DE OLIVEIRA, *Curso de direito da família, vol.II: direito da filiação, tomo I, estabelecimento da filiação, adopção*, Coimbra: Coimbra Editora.

OLTSHOORN-HEIM(2006), E. OLTSHOORN-HEIM, G. DE WERT & G. DE WINTER, *Evaluatie Embryowet*, The Hague: ZonMW.

ÖRÜCÜ (2004), E. ÖRÜCÜ, *The enigma of comparative law*, Leiden-Boston: Martinus Nijhoff Publishers.

ÖRÜCÜ (2007), E. ÖRÜCÜ, *Methodological aspects of comparative law, European Journal of law reform*, vol.VIII, no. 1, p. 29-42.

PALANDT/DIEDERICHSEN (2006), *Kommentar zum BGB*, 65th edition, Munich: Beck Verlag.

PANTER-BRICK & SMITH (2000), C. PANTER-BRICK & M. SMITH, Abandoned children, Cambridge: Cambridge University Press.

PARKER (1992), S. PARKER, Rights and utility in Anglo-Australian Family Law, Modern *Law Review*, vol. 55, p. 311-330.

PASQUALE, MASTROIANNI & MASTROIANNI (2001), P. PASQUALE, A. MASTROIANNI & L. MASTROIANNI, Disclosure to children conceived with donor material should be optional, *Human Reproduction*, vol. 16, p. 2036-2038.

PAULSON (1998), S. PAULSON, *Normativity and norms*, Oxford: Oxford Clarendon Press.

PENNINGS (2001), G. PENNINGS, The right to privacy and access to information about one's genetic origins, *Medicine and Law*, vol. 20, p. 1-15.

PENNINGS (2005), G. PENNINGS, Legal harmonization and reproductive tourism in Europe, *Human Reproduction*, 2004, 19, p. 2689-2694.

POUSSON-PETIT (2003), J. POUSSON-PETIT, *L'identité de la personne humaine: étude de droit français et de droit comparé*, Bruxelles: Bruylant.

PUNSELIE (2002), E. PUNSELIE, Erkenning door verwekker zonder family life, *FJR*, p. 245.

PUNSELIE (2006), E. PUNSELIE, *Voor een pleegkind met recht een toekomst. Een studie naar de (rechts)positie van (pleeg)ouders en (pleeg)kinderen in geval van langdurige uithuisplaatsing*, Deventer: Kluwer.

PUTTEN (1993), W. VAN DER PUTTEN, *Handboek Wet op de lijkbezorging*, Lelystad: Koninklijke Vermande.

QUANTIUS (1998), Die Elternschaftsanfechtung durch das künstlich gezeugte Kind, *FamRZ*, p. 1145-1152.

RAAK-KUIPER (2007), J. VAN RAAK-KUIPER, *Koekoeksinderen en het recht op afstammingsinformatie*, diss. Tilburg, Nijmegen: WLP.

RAAK-KUIPER (2008), J. VAN RAAK-KUIPER, De donor en zijn vaderrol, een roze wolk?, *FJR*, vol.11, p. 240-245.

RAMALHO DA SILVA GONÇALVES (1995), M.-J. RAMALHO DA SILVA GONÇALVES, *Os Novos Aspectos da Biomedicina e o Estabelecimento da Filiação*, diss. Coimbra University, Coimbra.

RAMM (1989), T. RAMM, Ehelichkeitsanfechtung und Bundesverfassungsgericht, *NJW* 1989, p. 220.

RAUSCHER (2002), T. RAUSCHER, Vaterschaft auf Grund Anerkennung, *FPR*, p. 359-369.

RAWLS (1971), J. RAWLS, *A theory of justice*, Harvard: Harvard University Press.

REINHARTZ (2000), B. REINHARTZ, *De familie geregeld*, Lelystad: Koninklijke Vermande.

RENAUT (2003), M.-T. RENAUT, *Histoire du droit de la famille*, Paris: Ellipses.

RENIERS (2001), J. RENIERS, The post-migration survival of traditional marriage-patterns: consanguineous marriages among Turks and Moroccans in Belgium, *Journal of Comparative Family Studies*, vol. 32, p. 21-25.

RITTNER & RITTNER (2002), C. RITTNER & M. RITTNER, Unerlaubte DNA-Gutachten zur Feststellung der Abstammung – eine Grauzone, *NJW*, p. 1745-1753.

RITTNER & RITTNER (2005), C. RITTNER & M. RITTNER, Rechtsdogma und Rechtswirklichkeit am Beispiel so genannter heimlicher Vaterschaftstests, *NJW*, p. 945-948.

ROQUETTE (1935), H. ROQUETTE, Ist §644 ZPO heute noch anwendbar?, *JW* 1935, p. 2476.

ROTH (1996), A. ROTH, Die Zustimmung eines Mannes zur heterologen Insemination bei seiner Ehefrau, *FamRZ*, 13, p. 769-772.

ROTH (2003), A. ROTH, Vaterschaftsanfechtung durch den biologischen Vater, *NJW*, p. 3153-3161.

ROTHSTEIN (2005), M. ROTHSTEIN, Translating values and interests into the law of parentage determination, in: M. ROTHSTEIN, T. MURRAY, G. KAEBNICK, M. MAJUMDER, *Genetic ties and the family: the impact of paternity testing on parents and children*, John Hopkins University Press, Baltimore 2005, p. 213-237.

ROWLAND (1985), R. ROWLAND, The social and psychological consequences of secrecy in DI by donor programmes, *Soc.Sci.Med.*, 4, p. 391-396.
RUBELLIN-DEVICHI (1993), J. RUBELLIN-DEVICHI, Une importante réforme en droit de la famille: la loi no. 93-22 du 8 janvier 1993, *JCP*, I, p. 3569.
RUBELLIN-DEVICHI (1996), J. RUBELLIN-DEVICHI, *Droit de la famille*, Paris: Dalloz.
RUITENBERG (2003), G. RUITENBERG, *Het VN-Kinderrechtenverdrag in de Nederlandse rechtspraak*, Amsterdam: SWP.
RUITER & SUTORIUS (1993), M. DE RUITER & E. SUTORIUS, Manipuleren met leven, Handelingen Nederlandse Juristenvereniging, jaargang 123, deel 1993-1, Zwolle: W.E.J. Tjeenk Willink.
SAARLOOS (2006), K. SAARLOOS, 'Bezit van staat' of het wormvormig aanhangsel van het Nederlandse afstammingsrecht?, *WPNR*, vol. 137, p. 123-129.
SADOFF (1995), R. SADOFF, Mothers who kill their children. *Psychiatry Ann.* 1995, p. 601-605.
SANTS (1964), H.J. SANTS, *Genealogical bewilderment in children with substitute parents, British Journal of medical psychology*, vol. 37, p. 133-41.
SCHAPIRO (2006), T. SCHAPIRO, Kantian rigorism and mitigating circumstances, *Ethics*, vol. 117, p. 32-57.
SCHECHTER & BERTOCCI (1990), M. SCHECHTER & D. BERTOCCI, The meaning of the search. In: D. BRODZINSKY & M. SCHECHTER, *The psychology of adoption*, Oxford University Press, New York, p. 62-90.
SCHEIB (2005), J. SCHEIB, M. RIORDAN & S. RUBIN, Adolescents with open-identity sperm donors: reports from 12-17 year olds, *Human Reproduction*, 20, p. 239-252.
SCHEIWE (2001), K. SCHEIWE, Babyklappe und anonyme Geburt, – wohin mit Mütterrechten, Väterrechten, Kinderrechten? *Zeitschrift für Rechtspolitik*, p. 368-373.
SCHILLING (1995), G. SCHILLING, Zur Problematik familiärer Geheimnisse am Beispiel der heterologen Insemination, *Psychotherapie, Psychosomatik, Medizinische Psychologie*, 45, p. 16-23.
SCHMIDT (1996), G. SCHMIDT, *Sterke en zwakke adoptie: een rechtsvergelijkend onderzoek*, diss. University of Amsterdam, The Hague: T.M.C.Asser Instituut.
SCHMIDT-HIDDING (1967), W. SCHMIDT-HIDDING, *Die Stellung der Feststellung der Unehelichkeit in den romanischen Rechtsordnungen Europas*, Bielefeld.
SCHRAMA (2008), W. SCHRAMA, *Family function over family form in the law of parentage? The legal position of children born in informal relationships*, International Journal of Law, Policy and the Family, vol. 22, p. 311-332.
SCHUBERT (1977), W. SCHUBERT, *Französisches Recht in Deutschland zu begin des 19. Jahrhunderts*, Cologne.
SCHWAB (2005), D. SCHWAB, *Familienrecht*, 13th edition, München: Beck Verlag.

SCHWAB (2008), D. SCHWAB, 'Abstammungserklärung leicht gemacht; Neuer Dialog in der Familie', 2008 *Zeitschrift für das gesamte Familienrecht (FamRZ)*, p. 23-26.

SCHWAB & MÜNCH KOMM (2002), *Kommentar zum Bürgerlichen Gesetzbuch*, 4th edition, Munich: Beck Verlag.

SCHWENZER (1987), I. SCHWENZER, Vom status zur Realbeziehung: Familienrecht im Wandel, Habilitationsschrift Freiburg, Baden-Baden.

SCHWENZER (2007), I. SCHWENZER, *Tensions between legal, biological and social conceptions of parentage*, Antwerp-Oxford: Intersentia.

SETHE (1995), H. VON SETHE, *Die Durchsetzbarkeit des Rechts auf Kenntis der eigenen Abstammung aus der Sicht des Kindes*, Diss. Münster 1995.

SHAW (2001), A. SHAW, Kinship, cultural preference and immigration: consanguineous marriage among British Pakistanis, *Journal of the Royal Anthropological Institute*, vol. 7, p. 315-320.

SIMITIS (1970), S. SIMITIS, *Personen- und personenstandsrechtliche Grundfragen des neuen Nichtehelichenrechts*, StAZ, p. 255-256.

SLIJPER & VERHULST (1991), F. SLIJPER & F. VERHULST, *Rapport betreffende de onderzoekbaarheid van psychische gevolgen voor KID-kinderen om geen toegang tot hun afstammingsgegevens te hebben*, Rotterdam: Sophia Kinderziekenhuis.

SMITS (1997), V. SMITS, Waar komen de kinderen straks vandaan? Het nieuwe afstammings- en adoptierecht, *Nemesis: tijdschrift over vrouwen en recht*, p. 27-31.

SNOWDEN (1983), R. SNOWDEN, G. MITCHELL & E. SNOWDEN, Artificial reproduction: A social investigation, London: George Allen & Unwin.

SOTTOMAYOR (2002), M.C. SOTTOMAYOR, Quem são os verdadeiros pais? Adopção plena de menor e oposição dos pais biológicos, *Direito e Justiça*, Vol. XVI, 2002, p. 191-241.

SOULÉ & NOEL (1986), M. SOULÉ & J. NOEL, *Aspects psychologiques des notions de filiation et d'identité et le secret des origines*, in: VERDIER/SOULÉ, *Le secret sur les origines*, Paris 1986, p. 64.

SPAAS (1998), L. SPAAS, Paternity and fatherhood: myths and realities, London & New York, MacMillan.

SPAR (2005), D. SPAR, Reproductive tourism and the regulatory map, *New England Journal of Medicine*, vol. 352, 6, p. 531-533.

SPICKHOFF (1997), A. SPICKHOFF, Vaterschaft und konsentierte Fremdinsemination, *AcP*, 197, p. 398.

SPICKHOFF (2005), A. SPICKHOFF, *Vaterschaft und Fortpflanzungsmedizin. Die Einwilligung zur künstlichen Befruchtung mittels Samenspende eines Drit-*

ten, in: Festschrift für Dieter Schwab zum 70. Geburtstag, (Hrsg.: Sibylle Hofer, Diethelm Klippel, Ute Walter), Bielefeld: Gieseking.

SPICKHOFF, SCHWAB, HENRICH, GOTTWALD (2007), A. SPICKHOFF, D. SCHWAB, D. HENRICH, P. GOTTWALD (eds.), *Streit um die Abstammung: ein europäischer Vergleich, Beiträge zum europäischen Familienrecht*, Bielefeld: Gieseking.

SPINELLI (2001), M. SPINELLI, A systematic investigation of 16 cases of neonaticide, *American Journal of Psychiatry* 2001, 158, p. 811-813.

STARCK (1989), C. STARCK, Anmerkung BVerfG vom 31.1.1989, *JZ* 1989, p. 338.

STAUDINGER & RAUSCHER (2004), *J. von Staudingers Kommentar zum Bürgerlichen Gesetzbuch*, 13th edition, Munich: Beck Verlag.

STEKETEE, LÜNNEMAN & OVERGAAG (2004), M. STEKETEE, K. LÜNNEMAN, A. OVERGAAG, Met een bijzondere curator zelf naar de rechter?, *FJR*, p. 176-182.

STEWART (1992), G. STEWART, Interpreting the child's right to identity in the UN Convention on the Rights of the Child, *Family Law Quarterly,* vol. 26, p. 221-233

STOLL (2008), J. STOLL, *Swedish donor offspring and their legal right to information*, Licenciate thesis Uppsala University, Uppsala: Universitetstryckeriet.

SUTORIUS & KERSTEN (1997), E. SUTORIUS & H. KERSTEN, Het gezag van draagmoeders, *NJB* 1997, vol. 25, p. 1116-1120.

SZRAMKIEWICZ (1995), R. SZRAMKIEWICZ, *Histoire du droit français de la famille*, Paris 1995.

TAKES (2006), F. TAKES, *Het recht te weten: 'het belang van het kind' in het debat over gametendonatie*, Wageningen, Ponsen & Looijen, diss. Nijmegen.

TEBOUL, DAVID & RACINE (2003), G. TEBOUL, C. DAVID & P-F. RACINE, *Procréation et droits de l'enfant,* Bruxelles: Bruylant.

TERRÉ & FENOUILLET (2006), F. TERRÉ & D. FENOUILLET, *Droit Civil: les personnes, la famille, les incapacités*, 7th edition, Paris: Dalloz.

TEXTOR (1990), M. TEXTOR, Die unbekannten Eltern: Adoptierte auf der Suche nach ihren Wurzeln, *ZfJ*, p. 10-14.

THERY & BIET (1989), I. THERY & C. BIET (eds.), *La famille, la loi, l'état – de la Révolution au Code Civil*, Paris: Centre Georges Pompidou.

TRISELIOTIS (1973), J. TRISELIOTIS, *In search of origins, the experience of adopted people*, London: Routledge 1973.

TROMMELEN (1999), M. TROMMELEN, M. DEN OTTER & G. VAN DER VEEN, *Bereidheid tot donatie van sperma bij opheffing van de anonimiteitswaarborg*, Swoka: Instituut voor strategisch consumentenonderzoek 1999.

TURNER & COYLE (2000), A. TURNER & A. COYLE, What does it mean to be a donor offspring? The identity experiences of adults conceived by donor insemination and the implications for counselling and therapy, *Human Reproduction*, 15, p. 2041-2051.

VALE E REIS (2008), R. VALE E REIS, *O direito ao conhecimento das origens genéticas*, PhD thesis, Universidade de Coimbra, Coimbra: Coimbra Editora.
VANDENHOLE (2004), W. VANDENHOLE, *The procedures before the UN Human Rights Treaty bodies: convergence or divergence?*, Antwerp: Intersentia.
VANGELISTI (1994), A.L. VANGELISTI, *Family secrets: forms, functions and correlates, Journal of Social and Personal Relationships*, 11, p. 113-135.
VASSAUX (2005), J. VASSAUX, Premières vues sur la réforme du droit de la filiation Ordonnance n 2005-759, 4 juill. 2005, *La semaine juridique*, p. 1911.
VERLOO (1997), M. VERLOO, Een valse start: de EER en het wetsvoorstel afstammingsrecht, *Nemesis: tijdschrift over vrouwen en recht*, vol. 13, p. 166-171.
VIAZZO, BORTOLOTTO & ZANOTTO (2000), P. VIAZZO, M. BORTOLOTTO & A. ZANOTTO, Five centuries of foundling history in Florence: changing patterns of abandonment, care and mortality, in: C. PANTER-BRICK & M. SMITH, Abandoned children, Cambridge: Cambridge University Press, p. 70-92.
VIDAL (1978), J. VIDAL, *La place de la vérité dans le droit de la filiation*, Toulouse: Mélanges Marty.
VLAARDINGERBROEK (2004), P. VLAARDINGERBROEK,NAAR een qua termijn ongelimiteerde ontkenning van het vaderschap, *FJR*, p. 137.
VLAARDINGERBROEK & BLANKMAN (2004), P. VLAARDINGERBROEK, K. BLANKMAN, A. HEIDA, A. VAN DER LINDEN, E. PUNSELIE & J. VAN RAAK-KUIPER, *Het hedendaagse personen- en familierecht*, 4th edition, Deventer: Kluwer.
VONK (2007), M. VONK, *Children and their parents: a comparative study of the legal position of children with regard to their intentional and biological parents in English and Dutch law*, PhD thesis Utrecht University, Antwerp-Oxford: Intersentia.
VOORHOEVE (2008), M. VOORHOEVE, Waarheid bij de gerechtelijke vaststelling van het vaderschap van de verwekker, in: J. DE GRAAF, C. MAK & F. VAN WIJK (2008), *Rechten van het kind en ouderlijke verantwoordelijkheid*, Nijmegen: Ars Aequi Libri, p. 43-58.
WALLBANK (2004), J. WALLBANK, The role of rights and utility in instituting a child's right to know her genetic history, *Social and legal studies*, vol. 13, p. 246-264.
WANITZEK (2002), U. WANITZEK, Vaterschaftsanfechtung, *FPR*, p. 390-401.
WANITZEK (2003), U. WANITZEK, *Ergänzungen des Abstammungsrechts durch das Kinderrechteverbesserungsgesetz, FamRZ*, p. 730-736.
WARNOCK (1987), M. WARNOCK, The Good of the Child, *Bio-ethics*, 2, p. 141-155.
WARREN, FITCH, DIETZ & ROSENFELD (1991), J. WARREN, W. FITCH, L. DIETZ & P. ROSENFELD, Criminal offense, psychiatric diagnosis, and psycholegal opinion:

an analysis of 894 pretrial referrals. *Bulletin of the American Academy of Psychiatry and the Law* 1991, p. 63-69.

WATT (2002), H. WATT, The Diane Blood Case, *Linacre Centre of Healthcare Ethics*, p. 1-3.

WELLENHOFER (2005), M. WELLENHOFER, Die prozessuale Verwertbarkeit privater Abstammungsgutachten, *FamRZ*, p. 665-688.

WENNER (2003), E. WENNER, Allemagne: le droit aux origines face à l'émergence de l'anonymat, in: J. POUSSON-PETIT (2003), *L'identité de la personne humaine: étude de droit français et de droit comparé*, Bruxelles: Bruylant.

WENNER (2003), E. WENNER, Allemagne: le droit aux origines face à l'émergence de l'anonymat (à propos des <<casiers à bébé>>), in: J. POUSSON-PETIT, *L'identité de la personne humaine: étude de droit français et de droit comparé*, Bruxelles: Bruylant, p. 787-810.

WERT & EVERS (1993), G. DE WERT & J. EVERS, Eiceldonatie: de schaarste voorbij? Ethische overwegingen, arts en samenleving, *Nederlands Tijdschrift voor Geneeskunde*, 1993, p. 2155-2158.

WEYRAUCH (2003), V. WEYRAUCH, *Zulässigkeitsfragen und abstammungsrechtliche Folgeprobleme bei künstlicher Fortpflanzung im deutschen und US-amerikanischen Recht, Jurawelt*, diss. Düsseldorf, Juristische Reihe Tenea.

WIEMANN (2003), I. WIEMANN, Babyklappe und anonyme Geburt: Hintergründe – Kritik – Alternativen, p. 1-13. PDF document, accessible through www.imelawiemann.de.

WIGLEVEN (1997), M. WIGLEVEN, Personen- en familierecht 1997, The Hague: SDU Uitgevers Juridisch & Fiscaal.

WILLENBACHER (2004), B. WILLENBACHER, Legal transfer of French traditions? German and Austrian initiatives to introduce anonymous birth, *International Journal of Law, Policy and the Family*, p. 343-354.

WILLIAMS (2002), B. WILLIAMS, *Truth and truthfulness*, Princeton: Princeton University Press.

WILSON (1997), S. WILSON, Identity, genealogy and the social family: the case of donor insemination, *International Journal of Law, Policy and the Family*, vol. 11, p. 270-297.

WESTEN (1982), P. WESTEN, The empty idea of equality, *Harvard Law Review*, vol. 95, p. 537.

WISMEIJER (2007), A. WISMEIJER & A. VINGERHOETS, De emotionele belasting van geheimen: gevolgen voor de somatische gezondheid en implicaties voor de hulpverlening, *Tijdschrift voor Psychiatrie*, 6, p. 383-389.

WOLF (2003) A. WOLF, Über Konsequenzen aus den gescheiterten Versuchen, Babyklappen und 'anonyme' Geburten durch Gesetz zu legalisieren, *FPR*, p. 112-119.

WOLF (2005), A. WOLF, Biologische Abstammung und rechtliche Zuordnung, *NJW*, p. 2417-2421.
WOLFHAGEN (1996), D. WOLFHAGEN, Wat niet weet, wat niet deert, *Nemesis: Tijdschrift over Vrouwen en Recht*, vol. 7, p. 98-103.
ZIPPER (1985), J. ZIPPER, *Het zaad der twijfel: politieke debatten over kunstmatige inseminatie in de jaren '50-'65: verslag van een deelonderzoek in het kader van het onderzoek Vrouwen, Staat en Familierecht*, Amsterdam: Universiteit van Amsterdam, Afdeling Studiezaken.
ZUCK (2005), R. ZUCK, Der (heimliche) Vaterschaftstest: Was kann der Gesetzgeber tun?, *Zeitschrift für Rechtspolitik*, p. 117-119.
ZUCCA (2007), L. ZUCCA, Constitutional dilemmas: conflicts of fundamental legal rights in Europe and the USA, PhD thesis European University Institute, Florence, Oxford: Oxford University Press.
ZWEIGERT & KÖTZ (1995), K. ZWEIGERT & H. KÖTZ, An introduction to comparative law, Oxford: Clarington Press.

COUNCIL OF EUROPE

Legal problems relating to parentage: proceedings. XXVIIth Colloquy on European Law Foundation for International Studies, Valletta 1997
Explanatory Report to the Convention on Biomedicine
[CJFA/docs2001/cj-fa (2001) 16 Rev] PDF.Doc
Responses of the Portuguese government to the *Questionnaire of Access on Access to Genetic Information not related to Health*, CDCJ 2005 [cdcj/docs 2005/cdcj (2005) 9 bil]

EUROPEAN UNION

EC Directive 95/46/EC, Official Journal No. L 281/14

UNITED NATIONS

ICJ Reports (1955), p. 23
UN Doc. CCPR/C/72/D/930/2000
UN Doc. CCPR/C/53/D/514/1992
UN Doc. E/CN.4/L.1366/Rev.1
UN Docs. E/CN.4/L.1542, para. 37 (1980); E/CN.4/1989/WG.1/CRP.1/Add.1, p. 4; E/CN.4/1989/48, para. 106
UN Doc. UNCRC/C/58, 13-14, paras. 48, 53 (1996
UN Doc. A/52/40 (Part I), para. 454

UN Doc. E/Cn.4/1989/48, 18-22
Denmark IRCO, Add. 33, para.11
France IRCO, Add. 20, par.14; Luxembourg IRCO, Add.92, paras.11 and 29
UN Doc. A/48/40 (Part I)

FRANCE

Loi n.° 96-604 du 5 juillet 1996, Official Journal 1996
Ordonnance Nr. 2005-759 of 4 July 2005, *Journal Officiel* of 6 July 2005, p. 11159
Circulaire CIV/13/06 de presentation de l'ordonnance n.759-2005 du 4 juillet 2005 portant réforme de la filiation

GERMANY

BT-Drucks. III/530, 7 August 1958, 2, 14
BT-Drucks. 11/1856, 23 February 1988
BT-Drucks. 13/4899, 13 June 1996, p. 148
BT-Drucks. V/2370, 7 December 1967, p. 37
BT-Drucks. 180/96, 1997
BT-Drucks. 13/4899,
BT-Drucks. 13/4899, p. 56
BT-Drucks. 14/8856
BT-Drucks. 14/4425
Der Spiegel 2/2005, p. 58
(Muster)richtlinie zur Durchführung der assistierten Reproduktion, Deutsches Ärtzteblatt, vol. 103, issue 20, 19 May 2006
BT-Drucks.8/2788, p. 36-43

THE NETHERLANDS

Act of 26 January 1956, *Staatsblad* 1956, p. 42
Handelingen 1956/57
Advies kunstmatige inseminatie bij de mens, 1965
Ingrijpen in de menselijke voortplanting: Kunstmatige inseminatie Donor (5). Katholiek Studiecentrum, werkgroep biowetenschappen, Nijmegen 1987
Kamerstukken II 1992/93, 23 207
Staatsblad, 1993, No. 486
NRC Handelsblad, Saturday 17 June 1995, p. 1
Kamerstukken II 1996/97, 24 649

Kamerstukken II, 1996/97, 24 649
Kamerstukken II 1997/98, 23 207
NVOG Richtlijn 1999
Normen 2000, beleidsregels met betrekking tot de werkwijze van de Raad voor de Kinderbescherming
Kamerstukken II, 2000/01, 27 423
Handelingen 2000/01, TK, nr. 41, 3263
Wet van 8 maart 2001 tot aanpassing van wetgeving in verband met de openstelling van het huwelijk en de invoering van adoptie door personen van hetzelfde geslacht, *Staatsblad* 2001, nr. 128
Memorie van Toelichting op 24 810 (R1577), nr. 3
Commissie lesbisch ouderschap en interlandelijke adoptie, *Rapport Lesbisch Ouderschap*, Ministerie van Justitie 2007
NRC Next, 2 May 2007, p. 21
Sunday Times, 5 October 2008, p. 10
Kalsbeek report, *Rapport Interlandelijke adoptie. Alles van waarde is weerloos*, Dutch Ministry of Justice 29 May 2008
Ouderschap zonder onderscheid
De raam van de ooievaar

PORTUGAL

Decreto-Lei N.º 319/86, 25 September 1986
Relatório – Parecer sobre o Projecto de Lei relativamente à Procriação Assistida, Conselho Nacional da Ética para as Ciências da Vida, 1997
Decreto-Lei N.º 415/VIII, 30 July 1999
Lei no. 31/2003, 22 August 2003
Relatório – Parecer N.º 44 do Conselho Nacional de Ética para as Ciências da Vida sobre a Procriação Medicamente Assistida, 44/CNECV/4, July 2004
Lei Proposta N.º 411/98, 30 December 2005
Parecer da Procuradoria Geral da República, 1 September 2005
Decreto-Lei N.º 32/2006, 26 July 2006. Lei da Procriação Medicamente Assistida
Partido Socialista Projecto de Lei N.º 90/IX

TABLE OF CASES

EUROPEAN COURT OF HUMAN RIGHTS

ECtHR *Marckx v. Belgium*, Appl.No.6833/74, 13 June 1979
ECtHR *Silver and Others v. the United Kingdom*, Appl. No. 5747/22, 24 October 1983.
ECtHR *Rasmussen v. Denmark*, Appl. No. 8777/79, 28 November 1984
ECtHR *Gaskin v. United Kingdom*, Appl. No. 10454/83, 7 July 1989
ECtHR *Niemitz v. Germany*, Appl. No. 13710/88, 16 December 1992
ECtHR *J.R.M. v. the Netherlands*, Appl. No. 16944/90, 8 February 1993
ECtHR *M.B. v. United Kingdom*, Appl. No. 22920/93, 6 April 1994
ECtHR *Keegan v. Ireland*, Appl. No.16969/90, 26 May 1994
ECtHR *Kroon v. The Netherlands*, Appl. No.18353/91 27 October 1994
ECtHR *X, Y and Z v. the United Kingdom*, Appl. No. 21830/93, 22 April 1997
ECtHR *Tiziana Pipoli v. Italy*, Appl.No.27145/95, 30 March 1999
ECtHR *Nylund v. Finland*, Appl. No. 27110/95, 29 June 1999
ECtHR *Ibrahim Yildirim v. Austria*, Appl. No. 34308/96, 19 October 1999
ECtHR *Camp and Bourimi v. The Netherlands*, Appl. No. 28369/95, 3 October 2000
ECtHR *Bánošová v. Slovakia*, Appl. No. 38798/97, 19 April 2001
ECtHR *Pretty v. United Kingdom*, Appl. No. 2346/02, 29 April 2002
ECtHR *Mikulić v. Croatia*, Appl. No. 53176/99, 7 February 2002
ECtHR *Szarapo v. Poland*, Appl. No. 40835/98, 23 May 2002
ECtHR *Mikulić v. Croatia*, Appl. No. 53176/99, 7 February 2002
ECtHR *Odièvre v. France*, Appl. No. 42326/98, 13 February 2003
ECtHR *Haas v. the Netherlands*, Appl. No. 36983/97, 13 January 2004
ECtHR *Vo v. France*, Appl. No. 53924/00, 8 July 2004
ECtHR, *Shofman v. Russia*, Appl. No. 74826/01, 24 November 2005
ECtHR *Mizzi v. Malta*, Appl. No. 26111/02, 12 January 2006
ECtHR *Evans v. the United Kingdom*, Appl. No. 6339/05, 7 March 2006
ECtHR *Dickson v. the United Kingdom*, Appl. No. 44362/04, 18 April 2006
ECtHR *Różański v. Poland*, Appl. No. 55339/00, 18 May 2006
ECtHR *Ebrü v. Turkey*, Appl. No. 60176/00, 30 May 2006
ECtHR *Jäggi v. Switzerland*, Appl. No. 58757/00, 13 July 2006

ECtHR *Dickson v. the United Kingdom*, Appl. No. 44362/04, 4 December 2007
ECtHR *Phinikaridou v. Cyprus*, Appl. No. 23890/02, 20 December 2007
ECtHR *Kearns v. France*, Appl. No. 35991/04, 10 January 2008
ECtHR *Remmerswaal v. the Netherlands*, Appl. No. 34441/05, 9 September 2008

FRANCE

TGI Paris, 19 June 1979, D.1980, obs. Huet-Weiller
TGI Paris, 21 September 1982, D.1983, IR obs. Huet-Weiller
Cass., 10 July 1990, D.1990, 517
Cass., II, 31 May 1991, JCP, 1991, 21.752, 381
CA Paris 13 March 1992, D.1993, Somm. 43
TGI Paris, 1 March 1994, *RTD civ.*1994, p. 577
Cass. Ire civ., 5 October 1994, *JurisData* 1994-003006
CA Riom, 16 December 1997, *JCP* éd. G 1998, 10147
CA Paris, 6 November 1997, D.1998, 122
TGI Orléans, 18 October 1999, D.2000
CA Riom, 23 February 1999, D.2000, sommaire 158, obs. Granet
CA Rennes, 4 July 2002, *Droit de la Famille*, comm. 142, note P. Murat, *Recueil Dalloz*, p. 2902
TGI Nancy, 16 May 2003, 01/04002
CA Grenoble, 11 February 2004, no. 04/00012, *Revue Juridique Personnes & Famille* 2004, no. 7-8, 24
Cass. Ire civ., 14 February 2006, no. 03-16.101
Cass. Ire civ., 14 March 2006, no. 05-13.825
Cass. Ire. civ., 7 April 2006, no. 05-11.285, *Droit de la famille,* June 2006, p. 24
Cass. Ire. civ., 19 September 2007, no. 06-21.061, *Juris-Data*, no. 040373
Cass. Ire. civ., 6 March 2007, *RTD* 2007, p. 762, obs. J. Hauser
TGI Lille, 22 March 2007, D.2007, *Droit de Famille*, comm. no. 122, note P. Murat
TGI Lyon, 5 July 2007, D.2007, note A. Gouttenoire
Cass. Ire.civ., 19 September 2007, no. 06-21.061, *Juris-Data*, no. 040373
CA Paris, Ire Chambre, sect.C., 25 October 2007, *JCP G* 2007, act. 547
TGI Paris, 25 October 2007, no. 06-00507, D.2007, obs. F. Luxembourg
Cass.ass.plén., 23 November 2007, no. 05-17.975, *Juris-Data* no. 041612

GERMANY

RG, 14 October 1937, *JW* 1938, p. 245-246
RG, 15 June 1939, *RGZ* 160, p. 293-296
OLG Celle, *JW* 1939, p. 967-968
RGZ 160, 24 May 1941, p. 293-296
BGH 28 April 1952, p. 385-397
OLG Stuttgart, 11 May 1956, *MDR* 1956, p. 621
BGH 20 October 1958, *FamRZ* 1959, p. 16-7
LG Köln, 30 October 1962, *FamRZ* 1963, p. 55
BayOLG, 6 June 1972, *FamRZ* 1972, p. 521-522
BGH, 8 October 1981, BGHZ 82, 173=*NJW* 1982, p. 381
BGH, 11 November 1981, *FamRZ* 1982, p. 159-160
BGHZ 87, 169 = *FamRZ* 1983, p. 686
AG Passau, 15 July 1987, *FamRZ* 1987
LG Passau, 26 November 1987, *NJW* 1988, p. 144
BVerfGE, 18 January 1988, *FamRZ* 1989, p. 147
BVerfGE, 31 January 1989, *FamRZ* 1989, p. 255
LG Münster, 21 January 1990, *FamRZ* 1990
LG Münster, 21 February 1990, *FamRZ* 1990, p. 1031
OLG Hamm, 22 March 1991, *FamRZ* 1991, p. 229
BVerfGE, 26 April 1994, *FamRZ* 1994, p. 881
BGH, 5 October 1994, *FamRZ* 1995, p. 1272
BayObLG *FamRZ* 1995, p. 185
BGHZ, 3 May 1995= *FamRZ* 1995, p. 861
BVerfGE 79, 256, 6 May 1997, *FamRZ* 1997, p. 869-871
BGH 22 April 1998, *FamRZ* 1998, p. 955
BVerfGE, 28 January 1999, *FamRZ* 1999, 777= *NJW* 1999, p. 3403
OLG München, 14 September 2000, *FamRZ* 2001, 126 = NJW-RR 2000, p. 1603
OLG Jena, 6 March 2003, *FPR* 2003, p. 375-376
BVerfGE 816, 9 April 2004, *FamRZ* 2003, p. 816
OLG Celle, 29 October 2003, *FamRZ* 2004, p. 481 = *NJW* 2004, p. 449
OLG Hamm, 19 October 2004, *FamRZ* 2005, p. 1192
BGH, 12 January 2005, XII ZR 60/03
BVerfGE, 13 February 2007, *FamRZ* 2007, p. 441
BVerfGE, 1 BvR 1548/03, 13 October 2008

THE NETHERLANDS

Hoge Raad, 12 June 1953, *NJ* 1954, 61, m.nt. DJV
Hoge Raad, 8 April 1988, *NJ* 1989, 170
Rechtbank Breda, 20 June 1989, *NJ* 1989, 726
Hoge Raad, 10 November 1989, *NJ* 1990, p. 450
Hoge Raad, 18 May 1990, *NJ* 1991, 374
Hoge Raad, 22 February 1991, *NJ* 1991, p. 376
Hoge Raad, 20 December 1991, *NJ* 1992, p. 598
Hoge Raad, 17 September 1993, *NJ* 1994 272, p. 1745
Hoge Raad, 12 June 1993, *NJ* 1994, 347
Hoge Raad, 28 October 1994, *NJ* 1995, p. 261
Hoge Raad, 17 January 1997, *NJ* 1997, p. 483
Rechtbank 's-Hertogenbosch, 27 March 1997, *KG* 1997, nr 147
Gerechtshof 's-Hertogenbosch, 9 September 2003, LJN: AM7857
Hoge Raad, 12 November 2004, *RvdW* 2004, p. 125
Hoge Raad, 22 September 2000, *NJ* 647, p. 4993
Hoge Raad, 10 August 2001, *NJ* 2002, 278
Hoge Raad, 22 September 2000, *RvdW* 2000, p. 1299
Hoge Raad, 24 January 2003, *NJ* 2003, 386.
Hoge Raad, 7 February 2003, AF0044
Hoge Raad, 7 November 2003, *NJ* 2004, 98, LJN: AI0360
Rechtbank Leeuwarden, 10 November 2004, LJN: AR5884
Gerechtshof Amsterdam, 20 November 2003, LJN: AO8653
Gerechtshof Amsterdam, 8 July 2004, LJN: AQ0621
Gerechtshof Leeuwarden, 6 October 2004, LJN AR3391
Hoge Raad, 12 November 2004, *NJ* 2005, No. 248
Hoge Raad, 25 March 2005, *JPFR* 2005
Gerechtshof Arnhem, 14 June 2005, LJN: AT8852
Rechtbank Dordrecht, 31 August 2005, LJN: AU2843
Rechtbank Utrecht, 25 October 2005, LJN: AU4934
Gerechtshof Amsterdam, 3 November 2005, LJN: AV0711
Rechtbank Arnhem, December 2005 (date and names not disclosed)
Gerechtshof 's-Gravenhage, 10 May 2006, LJN: AY6451
Gerechtshof 's-Gravenhage, 22 November 2006, LJN: AZ4493
Hoge Raad, 22 December 2006, LJN: AZ4163
Gerechtshof Leeuwarden, 20 June 2007, LJN: BA7894
Rechtbank Amsterdam, 27 August 2007, nr. 360518
Rechtbank Rotterdam, 11 December 2007, LJN: BB9844
Rechtbank Haarlem, 18 March 2008, LJN: BC999

Hoge Raad, 21 March 2008, LJN:BC4496
Gemeenschappelijk Hof van Justitie Nederlandse Antillen en Aruba, 14 October 2008, LJN: BG3510

PORTUGAL

Supremo Tribunal de Justiça, *Boletim do Ministério da Justiça*, 297 (1980), p. 233
Supremo Tribunal de Justiça, *Boletim do Ministério da Justiça*, 316 (1982), p.133
Tribunal Constitucional, Acórdão N.° 99/88, 22 August 1988
Tribunal Constitucional, 213/89, 31 May 1989
Tribunal Constitucional, 218/89, 21 June 1989; Tribunal Constitucional, Acórdão N.° 371/92, 25 September 1991
Tribunal Constitucional, Acórdão N.° 96/96, 5 December 1995
Tribunal Constitucional, Appl. No. 486/2004, 7 July 2004
Tribunal Constitucional, n. 486/2004, 7 July 2005
Tribunal Constitucional, n. 23/2006/ 10 January 2006
Tribunal Constitucional, n. 563/07, 11 December 2007

OTHER JURISDICTIONS

Cases

Johnson v. Calvert. 1993. 30 Cal. Rptr. 2d 893 (Cal.Ct.App.) (California)
Court of Appeal (*R* v *Human Fertilisation and Embryology Authority, ex parte Blood* [1997] 2 All ER 687). (England)
Re Marriage of Buzzanca. 1998. 72 Cal. Rptr. 2d 280 (Cal.Ct.App.) (California)

Other sources

New York Times, 16 December 1972
Svensk förtfattningssamling (SFS), Swedish Code of Statutes, SFS 1984, p.1140
New Zealand Law Commission: New Issues in Legal Parenthood: Family, NZLC R88 (PDF document available at www.lawcom.govt.nz)

Websites

www.adoptiedriehoek.nl
www.afstandsmoeders.nl

www.babyklappe-nein-danke.info
www.barneombudet.no
www.bsure.nl
www.coe.int
www.donorkind.nl
www.donorsiblingregistry.com
www.dgsi.pt
www.dradio.de/dlf/227888
www.ec-europa.eu/eurostat
www.fiom.nl
www.gopetition.com/petitions/cnaop-la-coupe-est-pleine/sign.html
www.irmelawiemann.de
www.justitie.nl
www.lawcom.govt.nz
www.linacre.org
www.lux-forum-adoptierter.de/babyklappe.htm
www.nvbki.nl
www.ohchr.org/english/bodies/UNUNCRC/index.htm
www.publications.parliament.uk/pa/jt200607/jtselect/jtembryos/169/169.pdf
www.ukdonorlink.org.uk
www.un.org/esa/population/publications/worldfertility/Definitions_Sources.pdf
www.verilabs.nl
www.womenonwaves.org

SAMENVATTING

GRONDFEITEN EN BETREKKELIJKE WAARHEDEN: EEN RECHTSVERGELIJKENDE STUDIE OVER HET RECHT VAN HET KIND OP AFSTAMMINGSVOORLICHTING

Dit boek omvat een rechtsvergelijkend onderzoek naar de reikwijdte van het recht op afstammingsvoorlichting. Hierin worden de meest recente internationale, Europeesrechtelijke ontwikkelingen en de reikwijdte van dit recht binnen een viertal rechtsstelsels besproken. Een dergelijk rechtsvergelijkend onderzoek is niet eerder uitgevoerd.

Sinds de laatste decennia van de vorige eeuw is het belang om de eigen biologische ouders te kennen als een grondrecht erkend in internationale mensenrechtenverdragen, waaronder het Kinderrechtenverdrag van de Verenigde Naties. Daarnaast is sindsdien op grond van artikel 8 van het Europese Verdrag van de Rechten van de Mens (EVRM) een gestage stroom aan jurisprudentie op gang gekomen rondom deze thematiek.

Het doel van dit onderzoek is om te bepalen in hoeverre het recht op afstammingsvoorlichting in een aantal Europese landen nu al met toereikende rechtswaarborgen omkleed is. Om dit te beoordelen zijn in dit onderzoek constitutionele rechtsbeginselen afgeleid uit een kritische analyse van de internationale, Europese en nationale constitutionele regelgeving en grondrechtelijke theorieën. Deze rechtsbeginselen kunnen meer in het algemeen als richtsnoer dienen voor de afweging van het recht op afstammingsvoorlichting ten opzichte van andere rechtsbelangen in het concrete geval.

Voorts behelst dit rechtsvergelijkend onderzoek een inventarisatie van de verscheidene mogelijkheden om het recht op afstammingsvoorlichting beter te effectueren. In dat kader is nagegaan welke nationale regelgeving reeds beantwoordt aan de vigerende internationale en Europese regelgeving.

Hoofdstuk I omvat een algemene inleiding. Het vertrekpunt van de analyse is dat voor de meeste mensen kennis omtrent de biologische afstamming vanaf de vroege jeugd een vanzelfsprekendheid is. Bijgevolg wordt afstamming doorgaans niet ter discussie gesteld binnen het gezin. Pas wanneer er voldoende aanleiding bestaat om de waarheid in twijfel te trekken, zal een behoefte aan (wetenschappelijk) *accurate* informatie omtrent het ouderschap gearticuleerd worden. Dit morele recht op accurate informatie zal zich soms juridisch kunnen laten vertalen in een aanspraak op een verwantschapstest. De theorie van de Britse filosoof Bernard Williams dienen voor wat betreft de discussie over een dieper moreel recht op waarheid belangrijke inzichten voor wat betreft dit onderscheid.

In het inleidende hoofdstuk wordt tevens een aantal basissituaties onderscheiden waarin onzekerheid over de biologische herkomst ontstaat. Behalve voor geadopteerden is afstammingsvoorlichting ook in een aantal andere situaties van belang. Waar het juridische vermoeden omtrent het vaderschap evenmin met de biologische waarheid strookt, kan het kind evenzeer afstammingsvoorlichting wensen. Daarnaast zal kennis omtrent de eigen biologische afstamming vaak ontbreken in geval van kunstmatige donorbevruchting met behulp van een anonieme zaad- of eiceldonor of een draagmoeder. Ten slotte is het in sommige landen, zoals Frankrijk, mogelijk voor de moeder om haar identiteitsgegevens niet prijs te geven na de bevalling.

Hoofdstuk I biedt voorts bij wijze van inleiding een overzicht van de relevante literatuur met betrekking tot de (morele) onderbouwing van de grondrechtelijke status van het recht op afstammingsvoorlichting, ook al is dit geen onderzoeksdoelstelling. Het lijdt nauwelijks twijfel dat de bio-medische wetenschap en met name de DNA-technologie hierop van grote invloed zijn geweest, maar de behoefte aan waarheidsvinding gaat volgens de auteur ook terug op een oudere Westerse filosofische traditie en daarvan niet los kan worden gezien. De DNA-technologie heeft het recht echter wel blootgesteld aan de mogelijkheid van een grotere zekerheid over afstamming en vormt bijgevolg een directe aanleiding voor een aantal afstammingsrechtelijke hervormingen waarin een zo groot mogelijke aansluiting bij de biologische waarheid nagestreefd wordt.

Globaal gezien kan de vraag inzake de rechtvaardiging van een het recht op afstammingsvoorlichting op twee manieren benaderd worden. In een utilistische zienswijze op afstammingsvoorlichting ligt de nadruk op het nut van voorlichting voor het kind. Hierin schuilt het risico dat voorlichting uit zal blijven wanneer een derde, met name de ouders of de staat dit niet in het belang van het (meerderjarige) kind achten. Omdat dit betekent dat het betrokken kind geen eigen keuze heeft kunnen maken om accurate informatie na te streven, staat dit op gespannen voet met de informationele zelfbeschikking van de betrokkene.

In de alternatieve ('rights') benadering van het recht op afstammingsvoorlichting is het uitgangspunt veeleer dat het recht op voorlichting beschouwd dient te worden als een afgeleide van het recht op informationele zelfbeschikking of de autonomie van het kind. De specifieke achtergrond van de behoefte aan zekerheid is in deze benadering daarom ook minder direct van belang. Vanuit een gelijkheidsperspectief zou het van de betrokkenen moeilijk verlangd kunnen worden dat zij hun belang aannemelijk maken, nu het merendeel van de mensen vanaf de geboorte een grote mate van zekerheid over de identiteit van hun biologische ouders heeft.

Een strikt onderscheid tussen beide zienswijzen ('utility' versus 'rights') blijkt bij nader inzien echter toch moeilijk te handhaven. Verdedigd kan immers worden dat óók de bescherming van een recht op informationele zelfbeschikking uiteindelijk ook altijd het psychologische belang (nut) van een vrije ontwikkeling van de persoonlijkheid zal dienen. Ook in een 'rights' -benadering kan keuzevrijheid op zichzelf de grondrechtelijke positie niet legitimeren, zonder een nadere verwijzing naar de belangensferen die deze keuzevrijheid beschermt..

Onderkend dient in beide besproken zienswijzen daarom te worden dat kennis omtrent de biologische afstamming een belang dient. Dit belang verhoudt zich tot de gedachte dat afstammingsvoorlichting een sleutelfunctie voor de identiteitsvorming heeft. Hoewel een psychologisch belang bij een *narratieve identiteit* al geruime tijd onderkend wordt in empirische sociale-wetenschappelijke studies met betrekking tot geadopteerden, zijn er veel minder empirische studies die het belang van afstammingsvoorlichting voor andere groepen kinderen aantonen omdat dit onderzoek nauwelijks heeft plaatsgevonden. Toch is steeds meer bekend over de psychisch schadelijke gevolgen van familiegeheimen voor kinderen, met name voor kinderen die verwekt zijn door een donor. Afgezien van een psychologisch belang stoelt het recht op afstammingsvoorlichting tevens op een medisch belang, bijvoorbeeld bij een verhoogd risico op erfelijke aandoeningen. Voorts kan het in verband met de preventie van incestueuze relaties van belang zijn om openheid over afstamming te betrachten. In de 'rights' benadering zal de nadruk dus echter minder liggen op een zoektocht naar meer bewijs op grond van het nut van voorlichting zoals dat kan blijken op grond van empirische gegevens als wel op grond van ethische argumenten.

Na de verdere afbakening van de onderzoeksvragen- en doelen volgt in hoofdstuk I een uiteenzetting over de gehanteerde rechtsvergelijkende methodologie. Er is gekozen voor een *functionele* methode om hiermee overeenkomsten en verschillen tussen de rechtsstelsels op een gedetailleerd niveau inzichtelijk te maken. In het vooronderzoek ter selectie van de rechtsstelsels, is onder meer rekening gehouden met de mate waarin het recht op afstammingsvoorlichting grondrechtelijk erkend is. Er is gekozen voor een studie van het Duitse, Franse, Nederlandse en Portugese recht.

In hoofdstuk II wordt de reikwijdte van het recht op afstammingsvoorlichting binnen de *internationale* rechtsorde besproken. Het Kinderrechtenverdrag kent een aantal bepalingen die als rechtsbasis kunnen worden aangemerkt. Het meest expliciet is artikel 7 (1) van het IVRK, waarin het recht is vervat om 'voor zover mogelijk' de ouders te kennen en door hen verzorgd te worden. Daarnaast bepaalt artikel 8 IVRK dat kinderen het recht hebben op bescherming van de 'eigen identiteit,' waaronder tevens het behoud van de familierelaties van het kind wordt begrepen.

In hoofdstuk III wordt ingegaan op de rechtsontwikkeling op *Europees* niveau. In dit kader verschaft het hoofdstuk een kritisch overzicht van alle relevante jurisprudentie van het Europese Hof van de Rechten van de Mens (EHRM). In het arrest *Gaskin* bepaalde het EHRM dat staten een 'onafhankelijke autoriteit' in het leven dienen te roepen waar de identiteitsgegevens van de betrokkene in het geding zijn. Sindsdien is de rechtspraak op grond van artikel 8 van het EVRM met betrekking tot afstamming steeds verder ontwikkeld. Hieruit kunnen de juridische randvoorwaarden afgeleid worden die van belang zijn voor de afweging van het recht op afstammingsvoorlichting.

De recentste uitspraken van het EHRM duiden op een zekere kentering ten gunste van een grotere erkenning. Toch geldt het recht van het (meerderjarige) kind op afstammingsvoorlichting zeker niet als een absoluut recht. Het Straatsburgse hof weegt het recht telkens af tegen belangen die zich tegen afstammingszekerheid kunnen verzetten. Zo werd in het *Odièvre* arrest bepaald dat het recht van een Franse moeder die haar kind anoniem ter wereld had gebracht, prevaleerde boven het recht van haar volwassen kind om haar te identificeren. Daarbij speelde de volwassen leeftijd van beide partijen een rol en een openbaar gezondheidsbelang bij de preventie van illegale abortus dat de mogelijkheid van anonieme geboorte zou legitimeren. Zowel de afwezigheid van financiële en erfrechtelijke motieven als de hoge leeftijd van de verzoeker geven met name in de *Jäggi* zaak echter aanleiding tot een ruimere interpretatie door het EHRM.

In hoofdstuk IV wordt stilgestaan bij de rechtsontwikkeling op nationaal constitutioneel niveau in de verschillende landen. Het Duitse Bundesverfassungsgericht heeft sinds zijn arrest van 31 januari 1989 een belangrijke impuls gegeven aan de grondrechtelijke erkenning van het recht op afstammingsvoorlichting op basis van het persoonlijkheidsrecht, dat een recht op informationele zelfbeschikking omvat. Er kan zelfs gesteld worden dat mede onder invloed van deze Duitse persoonlijkheidsrechtsdoctrine het recht op afstammingsvoorlichting in Nederland en Portugal grondrechtelijk is erkend. In Nederland blijven de twee *Valkenhorst*-arresten voor deze erkenning bepalend. Behalve door het vitaal belang van dit recht voor het kind wordt de voorrang van het recht op afstammingsvoorlichting volgens de Hoge Raad gewettigd door de omstandigheid dat de moeder in de regel medeverantwoordelijkheid draagt voor het bestaan van het kind. In Frankrijk is het recht op afstammingsvoorlichting in tegenstelling tot de andere besproken rechtsstelsels tot dusver nog niet grondrechtelijk erkend.

In hoofdstuk V worden met behulp van de grondrechtelijke theorieën van Alexy, Dworkin en Zucca uit de analyse van de internationale, Europese en nationale grondrechtelijke ontwikkelingen enkele constitutionele rechtsbeginselen afgeleid die van belang zijn bij de afweging van grondrechten. In dat verband worden tevens de belangen in kaart gebracht die in kunnen druisen tegen het recht op afstammingsvoorlichting. Daarbij komen onder meer de aard van het recht op privacy van de ouder en het openbare belang bij rechtszekerheid aan bod. Bij wijze van deelconclusie wordt gesteld dat drie rechtsbeginselen richtinggevend dienen te zijn: het beginsel van informationele zelfbeschikking ('beslissingsprivacy'), het beginsel van procreatieve verantwoordelijkheid alsmede het gelijkheidsbeginsel.

Het rechtsbeginsel beslissingsprivacy brengt volgens de auteur met zich mee dat zekerheid over de biologische afstamming primair als een keuzerecht beschouwd moet worden. Dit brengt met zich mee dat het recht niet zondermeer op een utilistische manier benaderd mag worden, maar dat een mate van keuzevrijheid aan de verzoeker gegarandeerd dient te worden. Dit betekent dat een recht om *niet* te weten in beginsel ook gewaarborgd moet worden.

Het beginsel van procreatieve verantwoordelijkheid is een andere onmisbare bouwsteen voor de theorievorming. Dit beginsel houdt in dat de biologische ouder in beginsel identificeerbaar moet zijn voor het kind en dat op de ouders in eerste instantie de plicht dient te rusten om de afstammingsgeschiedenis van het kind toegankelijk te maken. Ook de zaaddonor dient op grond van dit beginsel identificeerbaar (maar bijvoorbeeld niet onderhoudsplichtig) te zijn.

Strikte toepassing van dit beginsel is echter onwenselijk wanneer overduidelijk geen sprake is geweest van consensueel geslachtsverkeer, zoals bij een verkrachting of in geval van incestueuze relaties. Het beginsel dient verder in een sociaalhistorische context begrepen te worden. Een grote mate van procreatieve keuzevrijheid vormt een basisvoorwaarde voor het kunnen aannemen van een dergelijke vorm van principiële verantwoordelijkheid van de ouder. Waar deze anticonceptiemethoden en abortuswetgeving in het geheel niet of nauwelijks voorhanden zijn of waar op buitenechtelijke geboorte een groot sociaal taboe rust, zal het bijvoorbeeld al snel te moraliserend dan wel te dogmatisch zijn om aan deze verantwoordelijkheidsgedachte juridische argument voor een dergelijke identificatieplicht te ontlenen. Daarmee hangt samen dat voor oudere zaaddonoren die vóór opheffing van de anonimiteitswaarborg hadden gedoneerd het onredelijk is om hun een identificatieplicht op te leggen.

Voorts kan ook het gelijkheidsbeginsel richtinggevend zijn. Het kan hierbij enerzijds gaan om de vraag in hoeverre men de verschillen tussen de uiteenlopende situaties, variërend van adoptie tot kunstmatige inseminatie, relevant acht voor de aanspraak op voorlichting. Waar veeleer het beginsel van procreatieve verantwoordelijkheid als uitgangspunt genomen wordt, lijken dergelijke verschillen minder van belang. In de meeste situaties zal dit volgens de auteur het geval zijn: de verantwoordelijkheid van de ouder om identificeerbaar weegt zwaarder dan het onderscheid dat die verantwoordelijkheid zou temperen. Ook het onderscheid naar *leeftijd* zal in zijn algemeenheid geen goede grond vormen om de reikwijdte van het recht op afstammingsvoorlichting te beperken.

Daarnaast kan het recht op afstammingsvoorlichting gevolgen hebben voor de interpretatie van het gelijkheidsbeginsel op *gender*-niveau. Wanneer het juridische vaderschap, bijvoorbeeld door een openbaar ministerie of door het (meerderjarige) kind, tegen de wil van de moeder gerechtelijk vastgesteld wordt op de 'enkele' grond dat de man een biologische band heeft met het kind, wordt deze 'fixatie' op de biologische afstamming door sommigen als een inperking van vrouwenrechten aangemerkt. Ook de wettelijke mogelijkheid voor de moeder om een kind anoniem ter wereld te brengen wordt door sommige Franse feministen verdedigd vanuit de zienswijze dat het (juridische) moederschap primair een keuze dient te zijn en dat de abortuswetgeving ontoereikend is.

De hoofdstukken VI tot en met X omvatten de eigenlijke rechtsvergelijkende analyse van de reikwijdte van het recht op afstammingsvoorlichting in de voornaamste situaties waarin een informatiebehoefte kan ontstaan bij het kind.

In hoofdstuk VI komt de vaststelling van de identiteit van de genetische moeder aan de orde in geval van een natuurlijke verwekking. De fysieke waarneembaarheid van de bevalling en het *mater semper certa*-beginsel uit het Romeinse recht waarborgen reeds een grote mate van bekendheid met de genetische moeder. De mogelijkheid om bij de geboorte de identiteitsgegevens van de moeder achter te houden komt van oudsher bovenal in Zuid-Europa en in Frankrijk voor. Ook in Duitsland is het *de facto* sinds omstreeks het jaar 2000 mogelijk voor moeders om anoniem met behulp van een babyluikje (*Babyklappe*) te bevallen. De auteur acht deze situatie rechtens onhoudbaar, omdat het een te duurzame inperking van de keuzevrijheid van het kind met zich meebrengt. Ook op grond van het beginsel van procreatieve verantwoordelijkheid roept het instituut van de anonieme geboorte soms bezwaren op. Bovendien blijkt uit empirische data dat de abortus- en neo-naticidecijfers niet navenant hoger liggen in landen die geen anonieme geboorte toelaten, waardoor de mogelijkheid om anoniem te bevallen legitimering ontbeert.

In hoofdstuk VII komt het materiële recht inzake de vaststelling van het juridische vaderschap aan de orde. In geen enkel stelsel is bewijs van vaderschap een vereiste voor de echtgenoot van de moeder om juridisch vader te worden. Evenmin stelt de wet in een van de onderzochte rechtsstelsel als vereiste dat de (ongetrouwde) man die het kind wil erkennen reeds bewijs moet leveren van het bestaan van de biologische band behalve wanneer het gaat om een fictieve erkenning door een buitenlander. Zowel het huwelijkse als het erkende vaderschap kan overal ontkend worden. Weigert de man om het kind te erkennen, dan kan in ieder stelsel vaderschapsbewijs met behulp van een verwantschapstest verlangd worden. Het juridische vaderschap kent in alle onderzochte landen ingrijpende rechtsgevolgen op het gebied van het erfrecht, het nationaliteitsrecht en het ouderlijk gezag en het naamrecht. De vraag rijst daarom of een loskoppeling van de rechtsgevolgen van afstamming en het op emotionele en medische gronden ingegeven rechtsbelang bij zekerheid over de afstamming een alternatief is. Wanneer de verzoeker slechts afstammingszekerheid verlangt onder behoud van de bestaande familierechtelijke betrekkingen met de sociaal-juridische vader, lijkt een dergelijke rechtsingang geïndiceerd.

In hoofdstuk VIII worden vervolgens een aantal belangrijke procesrechtelijke aspecten besproken die bij vaderschapsacties komen kijken. Geconstateerd wordt dat in de vaderschapsprocedures in alle onderzochte rechtsstelsels gebruik gemaakt wordt van DNA-verwantschapstests. Dat neemt echter niet weg dat de rechter in alle stelsels, met uitzondering van Duitsland, een discretionaire bevoegdheid behoudt om af te zien van het gelasten van een dergelijk deskundigenbericht. Het recht op fysieke integriteit van de vermeende vader wordt in dit opzicht nog gewaarborgd in Nederland, Frankrijk en Portugal. In Duitsland kunnen meerdere potentiële vaders gedwongen worden om hun lichaamsmateriaal af te staan ten behoeve van een verwantschapstest. Weigert de man een verwantschapstest te ondergaan, dan zal de rechter in de overige stelsels echter meestal de 'conclusie trekken die hij reeds geraden achtte' als gevolg van de weigering van de man. Het juridische vaderschap wordt alsdan, niettegenstaande de afwezigheid van een wetenschappelijk bewijs, tóch vastgesteld.

Bij een postmortale vaststelling van het vaderschap worden vanuit piëteit met de nabestaanden in sommige stelsels andere eisen gesteld aan de effectuering van het recht op afstammingsvoorlichting. Rechtsverwerking van vaderschapsacties zou wellicht soms niet uitgesloten moeten worden wanneer zonneklaar is dat het motief van de verzoeker zich niet richt op afstammingszekerheid, maar louter op het realiseren van een erfrechtelijk gevolg. Dit zou bijvoorbeeld het geval kunnen zijn wanneer er een grote mate van zekerheid over de identiteit van de verwekker reeds bestond bij het meerderjarig kind en het sociaal-juridische vaderschap pas vlak voor dat moment ontkend wordt. Blijkens het *Jäggi* arrest van het EHRM zal bij aanwezigheid van een duidelijk ideologisch motief echter juist niet strikt de hand gehouden moeten worden aan een wettelijke procedurele tijdsbeperking.

Voorts wordt ingegaan op een louter op informatie gerichte afstammingsprocedure die in april 2008 in Duitsland in werking is getreden. Op grond hiervan is het voor de juridische vader, de moeder en het kind mogelijk om een rechtstitel te verkrijgen om een DNA-test buitengerechtelijk af te laten nemen. Blijkt de biologische band nooit te hebben bestaan, dan brengt dit resultaat op zichzelf geen rechtsgevolgen voor de bestaande familierechtelijke betrekkingen en blijven erf- en onderhoudsrechtelijke gevolgen in beginsel uit. Voor een ontkenning van het juridische vaderschap blijft een aan tijdsbeperkingen onderhevige afstammingsrechtelijke procedure vereist waarvoor het vaderschapsbewijs in de informationele procedure meestal aangewend zal kunnen worden.

De Duitse wetgever heeft getracht met de invoering van deze procedure het gebruik van goedkopere buitengerechtelijke vaderschapstests op het Internet, waarbij gemakkelijk voorbijgegaan kan worden aan de instemming van de moeder en de autonome keuze van het kind, tegen te gaan. Betwijfeld dient echter te worden of vaders nu eerder geneigd zullen zijn om van deze mogelijkheid gebruik te maken om zodoende via de rechter DNA- zekerheid te verkrijgen. Vanuit een normatief oogpunt dient deze nieuwe informatief bedoelde rechtsprocedure echter wel te worden beschouwd als een principiële stap die tegemoetkomt aan de rechtsontwikkelingen op constitutioneel niveau die inmiddels reeds twintig jaar teruggaan. Immers, deze wet maakt een scherp onderscheid tussen het (emotionele) belang bij waarheidsvinding en het (juridische) belang bij behoud van bestaande familierechtelijke betrekkingen. Toch schiet de wet echter tekort in haar doelstelling om het recht op afstammingsvoorlichting met betere procedurele waarborgen te omkleden nu het onmogelijk blijft om het biologische vaderschap van de vermeende verwekker vast te stellen zonder daaraan juridische gevolgen te verbinden. Dat de biologische vader zelf de toegang tot deze procedure nog ontzegd wordt, houdt onder meer verband met de veronderstelling dat er een strijd zou kunnen ontstaan tussen hem en de 'betalende' juridische vader (*Zahlvater*). De laatstgenoemde zou zijn vaderschap na het verstrijken van de procedurele termijn immers niet meer zal kunnen ontkennen, maar de biologische vader zou dan nog wel op ideologische gronden een bepaalde rechtsstatus kunnen rekenen maar verder geen ouderlijke verantwoordelijkheden, zoals onderhoudsverplichtingen.

Hoofdstuk IX omvat een rechtsvergelijkende analyse van de toegang tot afstammingsgegevens door geadopteerde kinderen. In het hoofdstuk wordt ingegaan op de manieren waarop geadopteerden de identiteit van hun oorspronkelijke ouders kunnen achterhalen. Niet altijd zal hun identiteit via het adoptiedossier en de in de geboorteakte vermelde gegevens achterhaald kunnen worden. Alle onderzochte stelsels behalve Nederland kennen de zwakke adoptie waarbij de juridische banden met de oorspronkelijke ouders niet verbroken worden. Vanuit een op de biologische waarheid georiënteerd perspectief zijn er goede redenen aan te wijzen om de zwakke adoptie in te voeren nu het kind daarmee gemakkelijker zijn biologische ouders zal kennen en met hen contact kan onderhouden.

In hoofdstuk X komt de reikwijdte van het recht op afstammingsvoorlichting aan bod van kinderen die als gevolg van kunstmatige bevruchting of draagmoederschap zijn verwekt. In alle onderzochte stelsels is het (commerciële) draagmoederschap verboden. Verdedigd wordt dat het recht op afstammingsvoorlichting zich in dit verband in ieder geval betrekking heeft op zowel de genetische moeder (de wensouder) als de draagmoeder.

Van de onderzochte stelsels bestaat slechts op grond van de Nederlandse Wet donorgegevens geen anonimiteitswaarborg voor donoren meer. Zowel niet-identificerende en identificerende informatie van donoren wordt centraal beheerd door de Stichting donorgegevens. De *rights*-benadering komt met name tot uiting in een (impliciete) presumptie ten gunste van het recht van het kind op afstammingsvoorlichting. Deze presumptie blijkt onder meer hieruit dat van het kind niet verwacht wordt dat hij zijn psychologische belang bij het verkrijgen van de informatie aantoont. In dat licht kan gesteld worden dat het recht op afstammingsvoorlichting in de Wet donorgegevens tevens nauw verbonden is met het leidende rechtsbeginsel 'beslissingsprivacy.' In geval van zwaarwegende belangen van de donor kan identificerende informatie en bij vooroverlijden kan de identificerende informatie echter worden achtergehouden.

Voorop gesteld dient te worden dat de Nederlandse wetgever dankzij de invoering van de Wet donorgegevens een belangrijk signaal heeft afgegeven dat kennis van de biologische afstamming van belang is. De wetgeving is echter tot dusver beperkt tot een regulering van de afstammingsgegevens van donorkinderen. Een problematisch aspect van de Wet donorgegevens vormt bovendien de statusvoorlichting. Wanneer voorlichting over de wijze van verwekking geheel aan de juridische ouders wordt achtergelaten, zal dit een praktisch beletsel vormen om nadien de donor te identificeren. Immers, het kind zal zich slechts tot de Stichting donorgegevens wenden wanneer het kind reeds vermoedt of weet hoe hij of zij verwekt is. Sociaal-empirische studies tonen aan dat heteroseksuele paren slechts in beperkte mate bereid zijn om het kind over zijn verwekkingswijze voor te lichten.

Het primaat van de verantwoordelijkheid voor statusvoorlichting blijft in de Wet donorgegevens derhalve vooral bij de ouders liggen. Hoe kan het kind over zijn status voorgelicht worden? Een aantekening in de geboorteakte dient als buitenproportioneel beschouwd te worden. Toch zal een dergelijke inbreuk op de beslissingsprivacy van het minderjarige kind, dat wellicht ook een recht heeft om niet te weten hoe het verwekt is, wellicht gerechtvaardigd zijn wanneer blijkt dat de ouders hun verantwoordelijkheid niet nemen.

Een inbreuk op de beslissingsprivacy van het kind met betrekking tot de statusvoorlichting lijkt dus vereist om de daaropvolgende implementatie van het recht van het kind om de donor ook te kunnen identificeren te waarborgen: het lijkt niet haalbaar om het minderjarige kind voor wat betreft de inlichting hoe het kind verwekt is tevens een recht om *niet* te weten te garanderen. Immers, een minimaal geïnformeerde keuze om niet te weten zal bij de minderjarige nog ontbreken, terwijl er vanuit gegaan mag worden dat het kind er belang bij heeft om tijdens de vroege dan wel late adolescentie nog de donor te identificeren. Met betrekking tot adolescenten en meerderjarigen lijkt iedere inbreuk op het recht niet te weten echter maar moeilijk te rechtvaardigen. De meerderjarige heeft op grond van diens recht op informationele zelfbeschikking een recht om niet te weten dat twee componenten heeft. Hij of zij en niemand anders heeft het recht om ervoor te kiezen niet te weten dat hij of zij door kunstmatige bevruchting is verwekt en (daarenboven) tevens een recht om er ook voor te kiezen om de donor niet te identificeren. Met betrekking tot meerderjarigen voldoet de Wet donorgegevens daarmee aan de eisen die het beginsel van beslissingsprivacy stelt. Met betrekking tot meerderjarigen voldoet de Wet donorgegevens daarmee aan de eisen die het beginsel van beslissingsprivacy stelt

De overheid beschikt over andere middelen om ouders tot grotere openheid te bewegen dan een (gefaseerde) opheffing van de anonimiteitswaarborg middels wetgeving. Het introduceren van een algemene waarschuwing in iedere geboorteakte, die zich niet expliciet tot die kinderen die door donorinseminatie zijn verwekt richt, en die ertoe strekt de betrokkenen ervan bewust te maken dat afstammingsgegevens niet noodzakelijkerwijs een afspiegeling vormen van de biologische waarheid, verdient aanbeveling.

In hoofdstuk X wordt daarnaast het probleem van de postmortale bevruchting met het zaad van de overleden partner van de moeder aangekaart. Zowel vanuit een op de waarheid georiënteerd perspectief op het belang van de biologische band tussen ouders en kinderen als vanuit afstammingsrechtelijk perspectief zou met deze mogelijkheid terughoudend omgegaan moeten worden. Het kind kan immers weliswaar de identiteitsgegevens van zijn overleden vader achterhalen, waarmee wellicht gezegd zou kunnen worden dat het recht *strictu sensu* geëffectueerd kan worden, maar het recht legitimeert daarmee een situatie waarin het kind de biologische vader *ab origine* niet persoonlijk kunnen leren kennen. Ook vanuit een afstammingsrechtelijk perspectief zijn tegen postmortale bevruchting bezwaren in te brengen nu vaststaat dat het kind slechts één levende juridische ouder vanaf de geboorte heeft, terwijl het afstammingsrecht er doorgaans van uitgaat dat het kind belang heeft bij het hebben van twee juridische ouders.

Hoofdstuk XI omvat een synthese van het gehele rechtsvergelijkende gedeelte. In dat verband wordt in dit hoofdstuk ook ingegaan op de vraag of de rechtsstelsels beantwoorden aan de in hoofdstuk V geformuleerde rechtsbeginselen. De vraag rijst of de staat dan wel de ouders hoofdverantwoordelijkheid dienen te dragen bij het toegankelijk maken van afstammingsgegevens voor het kind. Bij adoptie en kunstmatige bevruchting is meer ingrijpende regelgeving gepast omdat de staat deze rechtsinstituten op verschillende wijzen gereguleerd heeft met vergunningen aan adoptiebureaus en middels publieke financiële steun aan kunstmatige bevruchting. In andere situaties lijkt een meer terughoudende rol van de overheid gepast.

Dit betekent niet dat de staat verder geen verantwoordelijkheid heeft met betrekking tot het faciliteren van de toegang tot afstammingsvoorlichting. Gedacht kan bijvoorbeeld worden aan een algemene, afzonderlijke louter informatief bedoelde rechtsingang. Een informele aanpak komt in sommige situaties echter eerder in beeld dan prescriptieve wetgeving. Dankzij een vrijwillig donorregister kunnen sommigen die vóór de inwerkingtreding van de Wet donorgegevens zijn verwekt alsnog de identiteit van de donor kunnen achterhalen, wanneer deze laatste hiermee instemt. In sommige landen kunnen kinderen zich met afstammingsvragen ook tot de Kinderombudsman wenden, die hierin een bemiddelende en onderzoekende rol kan spelen Voorts kan bijvoorbeeld gedacht worden aan gesubsidieerde publiciteitscampagnes.

In alle situaties dient de gekozen effectueringsmethode behalve aan de rechtsbeginselen die in hoofdstuk V zijn omschreven in ieder geval ook aan proportionaliteits- en subsidiariteitsvereisten te voldoen, die contextafhankelijk zijn. Een geïntegreerde, context-onafhankelijke aanpak is dus niet haalbaar. De in de rechtspraak vaak aangehaalde gemeenplaats dat het recht op afstammingsinformatie 'geen absoluut recht is', mag echter geen vrijbrief zijn voor de staat om zijn medeverantwoordelijkheid als gevolg van zijn mensenrechtelijke verplichtingen onder het Kinderrechtenverdrag en artikel 8 EVRM te veronachtzamen, op welke leeftijd of in welke situatie de vraag naar afstammingszekerheid ook maar van belang wordt. Een solide rechtsbasis is thans reeds aanwezig, twintig jaar nadat het Kinderrechtenverdrag is aangenomen, voor een verdere rechtsontwikkeling, hoe betrekkelijk de waarheid voor het individu in het concrete geval ook mag zijn.

ZUSAMMENFASSUNG

TATSACHEN UND RELATIVE WAHRHEITEN: EINE RECHTSVERGLEICHENDE UNTERSUCHUNG DES RECHTS DES KINDES AUF KENNTNIS DER GENETISCHEN ABSTAMMUNG

Die vorliegende Arbeit befasst sich in einer rechtsvergleichenden Studie mit dem Recht des Kindes auf Kenntnis der eigenen Abstammung. In den letzten Dekaden des vergangenen Jahrhunderts ist das Bedürfnis des Kindes, Kenntnis von der Identität der genetischen Eltern zu erlangen, in internationalen Übereinkommen, darunter die Konvention der Vereinten Nationen über die Rechte des Kindes, als grundlegendes Recht anerkannt worden. Daneben findet sich, basierend auf Artikel 8 der Europäischen Konvention der Menschenrechte und Grundfreiheiten (EMRK), der das Recht auf Privat- und Familienleben schützt, eine stetig steigende Zahl von Judikaten zu der Problematik.

Die Untersuchung soll zeigen, in welchem Umfang das Recht auf Kenntnis der eigenen Abstammung bereits in ausreichendem Maße gewährt wird. Um dies beurteilen zu können, werden im Wege kritischer Analyse der internationalen, europäischen und nationalen verfassungsrechtlichen Vorgaben und auf der Basis verfassungsrechtlicher Theorien verfassungsrechtliche Prinzipien ermittelt. Diese Prinzipien dienen als Leitlinie für die Abwägung des Rechts auf Kenntnis der eigenen Abstammung mit anderen, in den betreffenden Fällen berührten Rechten und Interessen .

Darüber hinaus bietet die rechtsvergleichende Arbeit einen Überblick über die verschiedenen Optionen der Durchsetzung des Rechts auf Kenntnis der eigenen Abstammung. Dabei wird untersucht, ob die nationalen Regelungen bereits den internationalen und europäischen Vorgaben entsprechen.

Das erste Kapitel gibt eine allgemeine Einführung in die Thematik. Ausgangspunkt ist die Tatsache, dass für die meisten Menschen die Kenntnis der eigenen Abstammung als Selbstverständlichkeit angesehen wird. Dementsprechend ist die Frage der Abstammung in den meisten Familien auch nicht Gegenstand der

Diskussion. Bestehen allerdings Zweifel an der Richtigkeit der vermeintlichen Abstammung, kann dieser Umstand einen Anspruch nicht nur auf ehrliche, sondern auch auf wahrheitsgemäße Auskunft über die eigene Herkunft begründen. Das moralische Recht auf wahrheitsgemäße Auskunft mag sich dabei verschiedentlich auch in einem rechtlich begründeten Anspruch auf Durchführung eines Abstammungstests manifestieren. Insofern bietet die Theorie des britischen Philosophen Bernard Williams interessante Erkenntnisse über den Unterschied zwischen Sincerity und Accuracy im Kontext des moralischen 'Rechts auf die Wahrheit'.

Die Kenntnis der eigenen Abstammung kann nicht nur für Adoptierte besondere Bedeutung besitzen, sondern auch in anderem Zusammenhang von Relevanz sein. So entsprechen etwa die gesetzlichen Vaterschaftsvermutungen keineswegs immer den biologischen Tatsachen. In Fällen künstlicher Befruchtung kann es bei einer Samen- oder Eispende an Informationen über den Spender fehlen. Auch sehen einige Rechtsordnungen, darunter das französische Recht, die Möglichkeit einer anonymen Entbindung vor.

Das erste Kapitel bietet des Weiteren einen Überblick über das Schrifttum zu dem moralischen Hintergrund des Grundrechts auf Kenntnis der eigenen Abstammung, wenngleich die betreffende Analyse nicht Zielsetzung dieser Arbeit ist. Zwar steht außer Frage, dass die biomedische Wissenschaft, vor allem die Entdeckung der menschlichen DNA, einen erheblichen Einfluss auf die Rechtsentwicklung gehabt hat; nach Auffassung des Verfassers geht das Bedürfnis nach Wahrheitsfindung aber ebenso auf ältere Traditionen in der westlichen Philosophie zurück und kann von diesen nicht abstrahiert werden. Die DNA-Analyse eröffnet allerdings die Möglichkeit, größere Sicherheit über die Abstammung zu erlangen und ist daher verschiedentlich Anlass für abstammungsrechtliche Reformen gewesen, die darauf abzielen, die rechtliche und die biologische Abstammung möglichst in Übereinstimmung zu bringen.

Allgemein ist es möglich, sich der Frage der Rechtfertigung des Rechts auf Kenntnis der eigenen Abstammung auf zweierlei Weise zu nähern. Aus einem utilistischen Blickwinkel geht es in erster Linie um den Nutzen der Informationen für das Kind. Allerdings besteht hier die Gefahr, dass Auskünfte verweigert werden, wenn ein Dritter, etwa die Eltern oder die Behörden, die Kenntnis der Abstammung nicht als für das Kindesinteresse wesentlich erachten. Da das Kind in diesem Fall keine Möglichkeit hat, sein Recht auf wahrheitsgemäße Auskunft selber durchzusetzen, kommt es zu Spannungen mit dem Recht auf informationelle Selbstbestimmung.

Entsprechend ist nach anderer Auffassung (rights approach) davon auszugehen, dass das Recht auf Kenntnis der eigenen Abstammung als Aspekt des Rechts auf informationelle Selbstbestimmung zu betrachten ist.

Eine klare Trennung zwischen den aufgezeigten Perspektiven (*utility* auf der einen, *rights* auf der anderen Seite) lässt sich jedoch bei näherer Betrachtung kaum rechtfertigen. Dies erhellt aus der Tatsache, dass auch die Wahrung des Rechts auf informationelle Selbstbestimmung der Entfaltung der eigenen Persönlichkeit dient und damit einen spezifischen Nutzen hat.

Aus beiden Perspektiven werden daher Interessen geschützt. Die Überlegung stützt sich auf die Erkenntnis, dass Auskünften über die genetische Abstammung eine Schlüsselfunktion für die eigene Identitätsentwicklung zukommt. Obwohl ein psychologisches Interesse an einer narrativen Identität (narrative identity) schon lange aufgrund empirischer sozialwissenschaftlicher Studien in Bezug auf die Erfahrungen von Adoptierten anerkannt wird, gibt es bislang kaum vergleichbare Untersuchungen über das Informationsbedürfnis anderer Gruppen von Kindern. Immerhin dürfte die Erkenntnis als gesichert gelten, dass das Vorenthalten von Informationen generell schädliche Auswirkungen für die betroffenen Kinder haben kann, etwa auch für die Kinder von Samenspendern. Abgesehen von möglichen psychologischen Konsequenzen wird das Recht auf Kenntnis der eigenen Abstammung hier auch auf medizinische Erwägungen gestützt, zum Beispiel das Risiko erblich bedingter Krankheiten. Auch soll der Gefahr inzestuösen Verkehrs begegnet werden.

Im ersten Kapitel finden sich schließlich noch Ausführungen zu der angewandten rechtsvergleichenden Methode. Der Verfasser hat sich für eine funktionelle Methode entschieden. Verglichen werden das deutsche, das französische, das niederländische und das portugiesische Recht.

Im zweiten Kapitel wird die Reichweite des Rechts auf Kenntnis der eigenen Abstammung auf internationaler Ebene behandelt. Das VN-Übereinkommen über Kinderrechte enthält einige Bestimmungen, die als Rechtsgrundlage betrachtet werden können. Die klarste Aussage trifft insofern Artikel 7-1, in dem das Recht des Kindes, 'soweit möglich' seine Eltern zu kennen und von ihnen gepflegt zu werden, statuiert ist. Daneben bestimmt Artikel 8 des Übereinkommens, dass Kinder das Recht auf Schutz der 'eigenen Identität' haben, wozu auch die familiären Verhältnisse des Kindes gezählt werden.

Im dritten Kapitel wird auf die Rechtsentwicklung auf europäischer Ebene eingegangen. Das Kapitel gibt einen kritischen Überblick über die einschlägige Rechtsprechung des Europäischen Gerichtshofs für Menschenrechte. In dem Urteil *Gaskin* legte der Gerichtshof fest, dass die Mitgliedstaaten eine 'unabhängige Behörde' einzurichten haben, wenn persönliche Daten des Bürgers betroffen sind. Seitdem hat sich die Rechtsprechung auf der Grundlage von Artikel 8 der Europäischen Konvention weiter entwickelt. Aus den Judikaten lassen sich Rahmenbedingungen ableiten, denen bei der Frage der Zuerkennung des Rechts auf Kenntnis der Abstammung Bedeutung zukommt.

Die jüngsten Urteile des Europäischen Gerichtshofs für Menschenrechte weisen eine klare Tendenz in Richtung auf eine Befürwortung des Rechts auf Kenntnis der eigenen Abstammung auf. Dennoch gilt das Recht auf Kenntnis der eigenen Abstammung noch immer nicht als absolutes Recht, das sich gegenüber anderen Rechten stets durchzusetzen vermöchte. Das Straßburger Gericht wägt das Recht weiterhin gegenüber sonstigen Belangen ab. Im Urteil *Odièvre* aus dem Jahr 2003 wurde festgestellt, dass das Interesse einer französischen Mutter, anonym zu entbinden, als größer anzusehen ist, als das Recht des mittlerweile volljährigen Kindes auf Kenntnis der eigenen Abstammung. Dabei spielte das Alter der Parteien ebenso eine Rolle wie das öffentliche Interesse, illegale Abtreibungen zu verhindern und damit das Leben der Neugeborenen zu schützen. Auf der anderen Seite spielte das Fehlen finanzieller und erbrechtlicher Motive und, anders als im Fall *Odièvre*, das hohe Alter des Antragstellers in der Entscheidung *Jäggi* eine wichtige Rolle für die Bereitschaft des Gerichts, das Recht auf Kenntnis der Abstammung anzuerkennen.

Im vierten Kapitel wird die Rechtsentwicklung auf der Eben des nationalen Verfassungsrechts in Blick genommen. Das deutsche Bundesverfassungsgericht hat mit seinem Grundsatzurteil vom 31.1.1989 die Rechtsentwicklung maßgeblich beeinflusst. Das Gericht hat das Recht auf Kenntnis der eigenen Abstammung aus dem allgemeinen Persönlichkeitsrecht abgeleitet, das das Recht auf informationelle Selbstbestimmung einschließt. Unter Einfluss der deutschen Judikatur zum Persönlichkeitsrecht wurde schließlich auch in den Niederlanden und in Portugal das Recht auf Kenntnis der eigenen Abstammung in den neunziger Jahren verfassungsrechtlich anerkannt. Soweit die Niederlande betroffen sind, kommt den zwei *Valkenhorst* – Urteilen des Hoge Raad entscheidende Bedeutung zu, da in diesen aus dem im niederländischen Recht bis dahin wenig entwickelten Persönlichkeitsrecht ein Recht auf Kenntnis der Abstammung abgeleitet wurde. In Portugal wird das Recht auf Kenntnis der Abstammung ebenfalls aus dem verfassungsrechtlich geschützten Persönlichkeitsrecht gefolgert. In Frankreich ist das Recht auf Kenntnis der eigenen Abstammung demgegenüber nicht verfassungsrechtlich verankert.

Im fünften Kapitel werden unter Rückgriff auf die Grundrechtstheorien von Alexy, Dworkin und Zucca auf der Grundlage der in den vorstehenden Kapiteln gewonnenen Erkenntnisse Rechtsgrundsätze abgeleitet, die der Verfasser im Rahmen einer Grundrechtsabwägung für maßgeblich erachtet. In diesem Zusammenhang findet auch eine Auseinandersetzung mit den Interessen statt, die dem Recht auf Kenntnis der Abstammung entgegenstehen können. In Betracht kommen hier etwa die gegenläufigen Interessen der Eltern oder das öffentliche Interesse an Rechtssicherheit. Als Zwischenfazit kommt die Arbeit zu dem Schluss, dass drei Grundsätze als entscheidungserheblich anzusehen sind: die informationelle Selbstbestimmung, die Verantwortlichkeit aufgrund Erzeugung und der Gleichheitsgrundsatz.

Informationelle Selbstbestimmung meint nach Auffassung des Verfassers primär, dass die Sicherheit betreffend die genetische Abstammung vor allem als ein Selbstbestimmungsrecht angesehen werden sollte. Das bedeutet, dass man sich dem Recht auf Kenntnis der eigenen Abstammung nicht lediglich in utilistischer Weise nähern kann, sondern dass dem Betroffenen ein bestimmtes Maß an Selbstbestimmung zukommt, das es ihm erlaubt, darüber zu entscheiden, ob er nach informationeller Sicherheit streben möchte. Dies schließt das Recht ein, keine Kenntnis über die eigene Abstammung erlangen zu wollen.

Der Rechtsgrundsatz der Verantwortlichkeit aufgrund Erzeugung zielt darauf, dass genetische Eltern, wenn möglich, für das Kind identifizierbar sein sollten. Die Eltern sind danach grundsätzlich verpflichtet, dem Kind Zugang zu den Informationen betreffend seine Abstammung zu verschaffen. Dies gilt auch für den Samenspender, ohne dass dies zugleich mit einer Unterhaltspflicht zu verbinden wäre.

Ausnahmen sind allerdings zu machen, wenn der Verkehr zwischen den Eltern nicht einverständlich erfolgte, etwa bei einer Vergewaltigung der Mutter oder im Fall inzestuöser Beziehungen. Der Grundsatz muss zudem in einem sozialhistorischen Kontext verstanden werden. Ein bestimmtes Maß tatsächlicher prokreativer Freiheit ist die Grundvoraussetzung dafür, dass von den genetischen Eltern verlangt werden kann, die Verantwortung für die Existenz ihrer Kinder zu übernehmen. Wo es keine Geburtenkontrolle gibt, Abtreibungen unter Strafe gestellt sind oder die außereheliche Geburt gesellschaftlich stigmatisiert wird, erscheint es moralisierend und realitätsfern, den Eltern eine Identifikationspflicht gegenüber ihren Kindern aufzuerlegen. Dies gilt auch für Samenspender, denen im Zeitpunkt der Spende Anonymität zugesichert worden war.

Schließlich kann auch dem Gleichheitsgrundsatz bei einer Abwägung Bedeutung zukommen. Hier stellt sich zunächst die Frage, ob die tatsächlichen Unterschiede zwischen den möglichen Sachverhalten, etwa zwischen Adoption und künstlicher Befruchtung, so groß sind, dass sie eine Einschränkung des Rechts auf Kenntnis der eigenen Abstammung rechtfertigen können. Erachtet man die Verantwortlichkeit der Eltern dem Kind gegenüber als entscheidend, stellen sich die Unterschiede, obgleich objektiv vorhanden, nicht als wesentlich dar. Auch eine Unterscheidung anhand des Alters vermag im Allgemeinen eine Einschränkung des Rechts auf Kenntnis der Abstammung nicht zu rechtfertigen.

Darüber hinaus ist festzustellen, dass das Recht auf Kenntnis der eigenen Abstammung auch Konsequenzen hat für die Interpretation des Gleichheitsgrundsatzes zwischen den Geschlechtern. Wenn die Feststellung der genetischen Vaterschaft gegen den Willen der Mutter erfolgt, zum Beispiel von Behördenseite oder durch Betreiben des (volljährigen) Kindes, kann dies als erhebliche Einschränkung der Rechte der Frau betrachtet werden.

In den Kapiteln VI bis X erfolgt dann die eigentliche rechtsvergleichende Analyse des Rechts auf Kenntnis der eigenen Abstammung.

Kapitel VI behandelt die Feststellung der Identität der genetischen Mutter im Fall natürlicher Erzeugung. Die physische Anschaulichkeit der Entbindung sowie der (römische) mater semper certa – Grundsatz führen im Regelfall dazu, dass dem Kind die Identität der Mutter bekannt ist. Die Möglichkeit, die Identität nicht offen zulegen, besitzt die Mutter traditionell vor allem in Süd-Europa und Frankreich. Auch in Deutschland besteht seit 2000 die Möglichkeit, das Kind anonym in eine Babyklappe zu legen; allerdings handelt es sich hier um eine rechtliche Grauzone. Nach Auffassung des Verfassers stellt dies eine untragbare Lage dar, nicht zuletzt, weil die anonyme Geburt eine dauerhafte Einschränkung der Entscheidungsfreiheit des Kindes mit sich bringt. Auch vor dem Hintergrund der Verantwortlichkeit aufgrund Erzeugung bestehen Bedenken gegen die anonyme Geburt. Im Übrigen belegen empirische sozialwissenschaftliche Studien, dass die Abtreibungs- und Neugeborenenquoten nicht höher sind als in Ländern, in denen die anonyme Geburt verboten ist.

Kapitel VII beschäftigt sich mit der Feststellung der Vaterschaft nach materiellem Recht. In keinem der untersuchten Rechtssysteme ist ein Vaterschaftsnachweis erforderlich, um als Ehemann der Mutter die Stellung eines rechtlichen Vaters ihrer Kinder zu erhalten. Das gleiche gilt, wenn ein nicht mit der Mutter verheirateter Mann das Kind anerkennen möchte: Keine der in die Studie einbezogenen Rechtsordnungen sieht in diesem Fall den Nachweis der genetischen Abstammung vor. Sowohl die Ehe-indizierte Vaterschaft als auch die Vaterschaft durch Anerkennung des Kindes können allerdings innerhalb bestimmter Fristen angefochten werden. Weigert sich der nicht mit der Mutter verheiratete Vater, das Kind anzuerkennen, sehen alle untersuchten Rechtsordnungen die Möglichkeit vor, die Vaterschaft gerichtlich feststellen zu lassen und die genetische Abstammung durch DNA-Gutachten nachzuweisen. Der rechtlichen Vaterschaft kommen in allen untersuchten Rechtsordnungen Rechtsfolgen auf dem Gebiet des Erbrechts, des Staatsangehörigkeitsrechts, der elterlichen Verantwortung und des Namensrechts zu. Vor diesem Hintergrund stellt sich die Frage, ob eine isolierte Feststellungsklage, die solche Rechtsfolgen nicht zeitigt, sondern lediglich das Interesse des Kindes an der Kenntnis der eigenen Abstammung schützt, aus emotionalen oder medizinischen Gründen zu rechtfertigen ist.

Kapitel VIII wendet sich dann den prozessrechtlichen Aspekten des Vaterschaftsfeststellungsverfahrens zu. Hier fällt auf, dass in fast allen Rechtsordnungen die Möglichkeit besteht, DNA-Gutachten einzuholen. Auf der anderen Seite kann der Richter aber auch in allen untersuchten Ländern, ausgenommen Deutschland, von der Einholung eines solchen Gutachtens absehen. Das Recht auf körperliche Unversehrtheit des Putativvaters gewähren insofern noch Frankreich, die Niederlande und Portugal. In Deutschland findet sich Rechtsprechung, in der die Mutter dazu angehalten wurde, die Namen mehrerer möglicher Erzeuger bekannt zu geben; die Betreffenden sollten sämtlich auf ihre genetische Verwandtschaft mit dem Kind untersucht werden. Weigert sich der Mann, an einer entsprechenden Begutachtung mitzuwirken, hindert dies den Richter in den übrigen Ländern grundsätzlich nicht, aus diesem Umstand auf die Vaterschaft zu schließen, sofern im Übrigen ausreichende Anhaltspunkte für die Abstammung vorliegen.

In Kapitel VIII wird auch die im April 2008 in Deutschland eingeführte 'Anfechtungsklage unabhängig vom Statusverfahren' angesprochen. Aufgrund dieser Gesetzesnovelle können der rechtliche Vater, die rechtliche Mutter und das Kind vor Gericht ein außergerichtliches Privatgutachten beantragen, um Sicherheit über ihre genetische Verwandtschaft zu erlangen. Stellt sich heraus, dass kein Verwandtschaftsverhältnis besteht, hat dieser Umstand keinerlei

Rechtsfolgen für den bestehenden familienrechtlichen Status und dessen Konsequenzen, etwa im Hinblick auf das Erb- oder das Unterhaltsrecht.

Der deutsche Gesetzgeber intendierte mit der Einführung dieser Klageoption, die Durchführung heimlicher Vaterschaftstests einzuschränken. Ob dieses Ziel erreicht wurde, ist allerdings zu bezweifeln. Aus normativer Sicht bestehen jedenfalls keine verfassungsrechtlichen Bedenken; die neue Option entspricht (zumindest partiell) den verfassungsrechtlichen Entwicklungen der letzten Jahrzehnte. Das deutsche Gesetz trennt scharf zwischen dem (emotionalen) Interesse an Abstammungssicherheit und der Erhaltung der familienrechtlichen Beziehungen zwischen Kindern und Eltern. Dennoch greift das deutsche Recht noch zu kurz, da es nach wie vor nicht möglich ist, die genetische Vaterschaft festzustellen, ohne damit auch rechtliche Konsequenzen zu verbinden. Insofern bestehen angeblich Bedenken, dass es zu Streitigkeiten kommen könnte zwischen dem rechtlichen 'Zahlvater', der seine Vaterschaft nach Ablauf der Anfechtungsfristen nicht mehr anfechten kann, und dem genetischen Vater, dem aus emotionalen Gründen ein bestimmter Rechtsstatus zukommt, der jedoch keine rechtliche Verantwortlichkeit dem Kind gegenüber trägt, zum Beispiel nicht zu Unterhaltsleistungen verpflichtet ist.

In Kapitel IX folgt eine rechtsvergleichende Auseinandersetzung mit der Frage, ob adoptierte Kinder Zugang zu ihren Abstammungsdaten erhalten sollten. In diesem Kapitel werden die unterschiedlichen Möglichkeiten von Adoptierten diskutiert, Informationen über ihre genetische Abstammung zu erlangen. Nicht immer kann die Identität der Eltern durch entsprechende Daten in der Geburtsurkunde ermittelt werden. In allen untersuchten Rechtsordnungen, ausgenommen die Niederlande, gibt es das Institut der 'schwachen' Adoption; hier werden die rechtlichen Verbindungen zu den ursprünglichen Eltern nicht abgebrochen. Angesichts des Umstandes, dass die Kenntnis der eigenen Abstammung für Adoptierte wesentliche Bedeutung besitzt, bestehen gute Gründe, eine solche Adoption zuzulassen.

In Kapitel X wird auf das Recht auf Kenntnis der eigenen Abstammung im Fall von künstlicher Befruchtung und Leihmutterschaft eingegangen. In allen untersuchten Rechtsordnungen ist die (kommerzielle) Leihmutterschaft verboten.

Lediglich in den Niederlanden existiert zur Zeit ein Gesetz, dem zufolge – seit April 2004 – die Anonymität von Samenspendern nicht länger geschützt wird. Sowohl solche Daten, die nicht zur Identifizierung dienen, also auch jene Daten, die eine Identifizierung des Spenders ermöglichen, werden zentral von einer öffentlichen Stiftung gespeichert. Liegen gewichtige Gründe in der Person des Samenspenders vor, Informationen über seine Identität nicht Preis zu geben, hat die Stiftung allerdings die Möglichkeit, entsprechende Auskünfte zu verweigern.

Nach Auffassung des Verfassers hat der niederländische Gesetzgeber mit dem Gesetz zu den Samenspenderdaten gezeigt, dass er der Kenntnis der eigenen Abstammung erhebliche Bedeutung zuerkennt. Dennoch ist anzumerken, dass sich die Gesetzgebung bislang auf eine Archivierung von Daten beschränkt. Nach wie vor problematisch erscheint, dass das Kind zunächst Kenntnis von den Umständen seiner Erzeugung erlangen muss, damit es den Weg über die Stiftung überhaupt einschlagen kann. Liegt die Verantwortung für die Weitergabe entsprechender Informationen bei den Eltern, kann es mit erheblichen Schwierigkeiten verbunden sein, den Spender tatsächlich zu identifizieren. Sozialwissenschaftliche empirische Forschungen belegen, dass heterosexuelle Paare nur wenig Bereitschaft zeigen, dem Kind Informationen über seine Zeugung zukommen zu lassen.

Damit stellt sich die Frage, wie dem Kind Informationen über die Umstände seiner Zeugung zugänglich gemacht werden können, ohne dass das Kind selber Forschungen anstellen muss. Eine Eintragung in der Geburtsurkunde erscheint zunächst unverhältnismäßig. Sollte sich jedoch zeigen, dass die Eltern auch künftig nur zurückhaltend bereit sind, ihre Kinder über deren Abstammung zu informieren, wäre gegebenenfalls doch über einen derartigen Eingriff in die informationelle Selbstbestimmung des Kindes (das schließlich auch ein Recht darauf hat, *nicht* zu wissen, wer seine genetischen Eltern sind) nachzudenken. Das Recht auf *positive* Kenntnis überwiegt hier das Recht auf Nichtwissen.

Für (ältere) Minderjährige oder Volljährige ist ein derartiger Eingriff allerdings nur schwer zu rechtfertigen. Volljährige haben sowohl das Recht, *nicht* zu erfahren, wie sie gezeugt wurden, als auch, *nicht* zu erfahren, *wer* sie gezeugt hat. In Bezug auf Volljährige entspricht das niederländische Samenspenderdatengesetz daher den Anforderungen, die der Grundsatz der informationellen Selbstbestimmung an das Recht stellt.

In Kapitel X wird schließlich auch das Problem der postmortalen Befruchtung mit dem Samen des verstorbenen Lebenspartners der Mutter angesprochen. Nach Auffassung des Verfassers sollte von dieser medizinischen Möglichkeit nur zurückhaltend Gebrauch gemacht werden. Allerdings kann das Kind ohne weiteres Informationen über die Identität seines verstorbenen Vaters erlangen, so dass das Recht auf Kenntnis der Abstammung nicht verletzt ist. Auf der anderen Seite toleriert der Gesetzgeber, dass das Kind Zeit seines Lebens seinen genetischen Vater nicht kennen lernen wird. Auch stößt die postmortale Befruchtung insofern auf Bedenken, als das Kind von Geburt an nur einen statt zwei rechtliche Elternteile besitzt.

Kapitel XI beinhaltet eine Synthese des rechtsvergleichenden Teils der Arbeit. In diesem Zusammenhang wird auch die Frage aufgeworfen, ob die untersuchten Rechtssysteme den in Kapitel V formulierten Grundsätzen genügen. Insbesondere stellt sich die Frage, ob die staatlichen Behörden oder die Eltern die Hauptverantwortlichkeit dafür tragen sollten, dass die Abstammungsdaten dem Kind zugänglich gemacht werden. Bei der Adoption und der künstlichen Befruchtung im Wege der Samen- oder Eispende erscheint es dem Verfasser angemessen, die Behörden mit entsprechenden Kompetenzen auszustatten. In anderen Fällen, in denen sich die Frage der genetischen Abstammung stellen kann, erscheint es dagegen vorzugswürdig, den Behörden eine eher zurückhaltende Rolle zuzuerkennen.

In allen Konstellationen, in denen sich die Frage der Abstammung stellen kann, sollte der Weg, auf dem das Recht auf Kenntnis der eigenen Abstammung durchgesetzt wird, auch den Verhältnismäßigkeits- und Subsidiaritätsanforderungen genügen. Die Feststellung, dass das Recht auf Kenntnis der eigenen Abstammung 'kein absolutes Recht' ist, darf kein Freibrief dafür sein, dass der Staat seiner auf menschenrechtlichen Verpflichtungen beruhende Mitverantwortung für die Durchsetzung des Rechts nicht nachkommt. Ein tragfähiger Rechtsgrund existierte bereits vor zwanzig Jahren, als das VN-Übereinkommen über Kinderrechte gezeichnet wurde – nicht zu reden von dem unschätzbaren Wert, den die Kenntnis der Wahrheit für den einzelnen Menschen haben kann.

CURRICULUM VITAE

Richard John Blauwhoff was born in Leiden, the Netherlands, on 26 March 1977. He is the son of a Northern Irish mother and a Dutch father. After having finished grammar school in Hilversum, he studied Spanish in Granada, Spain. In September 1996 he began his law studies at Utrecht University and soon specialised in International and European Law. Richard wrote his Master's thesis on the co-operation among the European Union, the Council of Europe and the OSCE in protecting linguistic minority rights. At Utrecht University, he also studied Portuguese Linguistics and Literature, specialising in the history of international relations. In his Master thesis he compared the literary representation of Asians in 16th and 17th Century Portuguese and Dutch travel literature on Southern India and Ceylon. He finished both his law and language studies in the Spring of 2003.

Having worked briefly as a translator after his graduation, Richard moved to Brussels where he started to work as a trainee at the Legal Service of the European Commission in 2004. Following his return to the Netherlands, Richard began working at Utrecht University's Molengraaff Institute for Private Law as a PhD researcher in December 2004. Though based in Utrecht, Richard spent a substantial part of his comparative research abroad. He went to the University of Coimbra (Portugal) first and thereafter spent a research period at the Philipps-Universität in Marburg (Germany) and finally spent a few months at the Université Jean Moulin of Lyon 3 at Lyons (France) in 2007. Richard Blauwhoff has published in the field of family law and human rights. At present he works as a senior court administrator at the family law sector of the Hague Court of Appeal.

European Family Law Series

1. *Legal Recognition of Same-Sex Couples in Europe*, K. Boele-Woelki and A. Fuchs (eds.)
2. *European Family Law in Action Volume I: Grounds for divorce*, K. Boele-Woelki, B. Braat and I. Sumner (eds.)
3. *European Family Law in Action Volume II: Maintenance Between Former Spouses*, K. Boele-Woelki, B. Braat and I. Sumner (eds.)
4. *Perspectives for the Unification and Harmonisation of Family Law in Europe*, K. Boele-Woelki (ed.)
5. *Family Law Legislation of the Netherlands*, I. Sumner and H. Warendorf
6. *Indépendance et interdépendance patrimoniales des époux dans le régime matrimonial légal des droits néerlandais, français et suisse*, B. Braat
7. *Principles of European Family Law Regarding Divorce and Maintenance Between Former Spouses*, K. Boele-Woelki, F. Ferrand, C. González Beilfuss, M. Jänterä-Jareborg, N. Lowe, D. Martiny and W. Pintens
8. *Inheritance Law Legislation of the Netherlands*, I. Sumner and H. Warendorf
9. *European Family Law in Action Volume III: Parental Responsibilities*, K. Boele-Woelki, B. Braat and I. Curry-Sumner (eds.)
10. *Common Core and Better Law in European Family Law*, K. Boele-Woelki (ed.)
11. *All's well that ends registered?*, I. Curry-Sumner (ed.)
12. *Model Family Code – From a global perspective*, I. Schwenzer and M. Dimsey
13. *Harmonisation of Family Law in Europe. A Historical Perspective*, M. Antokolskaia
14. *Brussels II bis: Its Impact and Application in the Member States*, Katharina Boele-Woelki and Cristina González Beilfuss (eds.)
15. *Tensions between Legal, Biological and Social Conceptions of Parentage*, I. Schwenzer (ed.)
16. *Principles of European Family Law Regarding Parental Responsibilities*, K. Boele-Woelki, F. Ferrand, C. González Beilfuss, M. Jänterä-Jareborg, N. Lowe, D. Martiny and W. Pintens (eds.)
17. *Juxtaposing Legal Systems and the Principles of European Family Law on Divorce and Maintenance*, E. Örücü and J. Mair (eds.)
18. *Convergence and Divergence of Family Law in Europe*, M. Antokolskaia (ed.)
19. *European Challenges in Contemporary Family Law*, K. Sverdrup (eds.)
20. *Children and their parents*, M. Vonk
21. *La capacité de l'enfant dans les droits français, anglais et écossais*, L. Francoz-Terminal
22. *Joint Parental Authority*, C.G. Jeppesen de Boer
23. *Debates in Family Law around the Globe at the Dawn of the 21st Century*, K. Boele-Woelki (ed.)
24. *European Family Law in Action Volume IV: Property Relations between Spouses*, K. Boele-Woelki, B. Braat and I. Curry-Sumner (eds.)
25. *Foundational Facts, Relative Truths. A Comparative Law Study on Children's Right to Know Their Genetic Origins*, Richard J. Blauwhoff

www.ingramcontent.com/pod-product-compliance
Ingram Content Group UK Ltd.
Pitfield, Milton Keynes, MK11 3LW, UK
UKHW051925100926
8556IPUK00022B/1369

9 789050 959131